The Art Direction Handbook for Film & Television

SECOND EDITION

The Art Direction Handbook for Film & Television

SECOND EDITION

Michael Rizzo

Focal Press
Taylor & Francis Group

NEW YORK AND LONDON

First published 2015
by Focal Press
70 Blanchard Road, Suite 402, Burlington, MA 01803

and by Focal Press
2 Park Square, Milton Park, Abingdon, Oxon OX14 4RN

Focal Press is an imprint of the Taylor & Francis Group, an informa business

Notices

Knowledge and best practice in this field are constantly changing. As new research and experience broaden our understanding, changes in research methods, professional practices, or medical treatment may become necessary.

Practitioners and researchers must always rely on their own experience and knowledge in evaluating and using any information, methods, compounds, or experiments described herein. In using such information or methods they should be mindful of their own safety and the safety of others, including

parties for whom they have a professional responsibility.

Product or corporate names may be trademarks or registered trademarks, and are used only for identification and explanation without intent to infringe.

Library of Congress Cataloging in Publication Data

Rizzo, Michael.
   The art direction handbook for film & television / Michael Rizzo.
      pages cm
  1. Motion pictures—Art direction—Handbooks, manuals, etc. 2. Television—
Art direction—Handbooks, manuals, etc. I. Title.
   PN1995.9.A74R583 2014
   791.4302′5—dc23
   2013049140

ISBN: 978-0-415-84279-2 (pbk)
ISBN: 978-1-315-77087-1 (ebk)

Typeset in TrumpMediaeval
By Apex CoVantage, LLC

Printed and bound in India by Replika Press Pvt. Ltd.

For my Father

Contents

Acknowledgments

The task of writing a definitive guide on a subject as specialized as art direction is daunting. In order to include as much information as necessary to complete such a comprehensive undertaking, I relied on personal wisdom gleaned from working in the collaborative art of filmmaking, which has taught me to trust the collective experience and knowledge of my peers.

Colleagues I have worked with or met in the context of preparing this book whose effort, conversation, or willingness to contribute images and interview text, must be acknowledged: Steve Arnold, Penny Bergman, Lark Bernini, Michelle Collier, Chad Frey, Darren Gilford, Jim Hewitt, Rob Johnson, Andrew Leitch, Jeff Markwith, Barbara Mesney, David Negron, Greg Papalia, Chris Ross, Joaquin Sedillo, David Utley, Randy Wilkins, Ed Verreaux. These individuals and others like them can always be counted on to run interference and support me as an art director. Along with the satisfaction of another film in the can comes the knowledge of what creative interchange and true collaboration can produce. It is the most precious gift to take away from a project, not a baseball cap or jacket.

Lillian Michelson was particularly supportive in my image search. As always, Lillian is welcoming and willing to share her individual experience, friends, stories, wisdom, and time.

Carlin Bowers, my editor at Focal Press, has been everything an editor should be. Her effort and dedication have shaped this book.

Allan White is another key player who requires special thanks. He is not a filmmaker. Without his towering presence, this book would not exist.

Preface

An updated version of an art direction handbook for film and television is long overdue. In the past, an aspiring art director could study architecture or theater, learn construction theory or stagecraft, discuss a bit of design theory in film class, and emerge from a four-year program feeling fairly confident with a modicum of hands-on experience. The advent of 3D animation for video games and a related explosion of visual effects for digital cinematography—in short, a new demand for computer-assisted moviemaking and its inherent speed—has redefined how we do our jobs, given the demands of that technology. Otherwise, nothing has fundamentally changed. The historical filmmaking techniques with which some readers are already familiar have been updated and recycled into a more exciting, more believable cinematic product. Not only will this handbook demonstrate that evolution in terms of how an art director's job has been impacted, but it will also establish a comfort level with state-of-the-art technologies now used in media.

As a straightforward manual of how to become or perform the job functions of an art director, this book is perfect for the newcomer. In addition to the fundamental information it provides, the second edition of *The Art Direction Handbook for Film & Television* has been written to meet the needs of newly graduated students and other aspiring filmmakers eager for some first job experience. This new edition expands the scope of the book from film to include television as well. A concise history of the mechanical development of both media demonstrates how function follows form—TV, as an outgrowth of science, and cinema, an extension of photography—with all media operating and interacting alone or together. The twenty-first-century art director is now challenged to navigate all aspects of the mediosphere effortlessly.

Networking within the low-budget and indie filmmaking realm is presented from first-hand experience of art directors established in successful careers by providing various entry-level viewpoints and how-to scenarios. This information derived from direct experience is delivered regularly throughout the book and is invaluable. Sometimes offered as a helpful anecdote or directly as advice, the newcomer can easily put the pieces together and navigate the beginning of their new career.

This handbook also exposes the primary function of the Art Director as design manager. It begins by clearly and finally drawing the distinction between the terms "production designer" and "art director" and then explains how the innate creative and aesthetic qualities of who an art director is must be combined with the practical and business aspects of what an art director is expected to do. Four levels of responsibility—to the Production Designer, the art department, the Director, and the studio—are detailed in terms of relationships and political expectations. Hands-on aspects of how an art director functions during the three phases of film production—pre-production, production, and post-production—serve as technical, straight-ahead extensions of day-to-day scenarios on any film project experience that might be encountered. This guide concludes with a comprehensive appendix of reference and source lists, contracts and forms, list of figures, expanded glossary, and index.

My intention, by writing this guide, is not to make the job of art directing any more complicated or important than it really is. As a matter of fact, the job of the Art Director is as straightforward as any creative manager. The workday is long, and the work intensity reflects the rigors of this demanding position. And now, the quickly evolving layers of technology offer additional challenges. But what differentiates this creative/managerial job from those in the civilian population is its cache of privilege and entitlement. Moreover, the thrust of this handbook strives to contemporize what the Art Director does within the context of the twenty-first century.

SECTION I

Pre-Production Process

CHAPTER 1

Introduction

Art directing is somewhat like snowboarding or skydiving—the essence of the activity is in the doing. In that way, an art director is by nature an action figure. The definitive art director is also a unique amalgam of contradictions. On one hand, creativity reigns with few boundaries; on the other hand, practicality takes primary focus. Balancing pairs of opposites, like art and commerce, make the job of art directing unique and challenging. Getting right down to it, an art director is best described as a design manager.

How can this be? Doesn't the job description of art direction include phrases like "seminal creative force" or "visionary?" It certainly does, but indirectly so. As a design manager, the Art Director on a film project operates as a department manager in form but as an artist in substance. In other words, business decisions for the art department are made on a daily basis, enabling the physical side of creative film production to happen according to schedule, while creativity provides the foundation for those decisions. Before we venture too far, perhaps it's best to establish a fundamental difference between the "Production Designer" and the "Art Director."

CLARIFICATION

Talent and title are important aspects of filmmaking, generally referred to as **billing.** When we examine the art department hierarchy, the Production Designer is found at the top with the Art Director close at hand (see Figure 1.1). As a side-by-side relationship, the production designer and art director complement one another. Although the terms "production designer" and "art director" are constantly used in substitution for one another, they are not interchangeable or synonymous. Why? Sharing the same hierarchy level of the film pyramid with the Director and Cinematographer, the Production Designer delivers the visual concept of a film through the design and construction of physical scenery. In this sense, the designer *is* the seminal, creative force of the art department. Referring back to the image of the action figure, an art director *drives* the process of design from sketch to actual physical scenery. The Art Director, or design manager, heads and runs

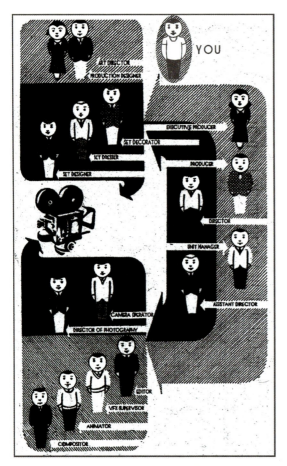

Figure 1.1   Film Hierarchy, Simplified.

the art department, interfaces with all other departments, supports the art department arm of the shooting crew, oversees scenery fabrication, and controls all aspects of the department expense and scenery budgets. Although an art director's creative input is essential to support the initial creative ideas of the designer, the totality of the design in terms of conception and responsibility belongs solely to the designer. This idea of symbiotic, creative support is echoed in a recent interview with art director Linda Berger (*Angelmaker, Forrest Gump, Death Becomes Her*):

Interview with Linda Berger

● *Why are you an art director?*
I have been thinking about the silent film designers most of my adult life. In the past ten years [1994–2004], especially through my work with the Art Directors Guild Film Society, I have begun to look at them within the whole context of art direction. As a professional in the field of moviemaking who started out in the theater, my earliest adventure in the networking process was to go to New York City right out of design school at the Goodman and the Art Institute of Chicago—with no connections, no anything except my education, a handful of very close friends, and two seasons of professional summer stock in Pennsylvania and upstate New York. When I arrived in New York City, I did everything I could to find my way and continue to learn. I was an Off-Broadway lighting electrician, a lighting designer's assistant at the Brooklyn Academy of Music for the ballet and modern dance, and worked in costume shops at Lincoln Center and in the individual shops of costume designers. I worked props and painted scenery. I also worked in television as an animation assistant and did lots of commercials. Eventually, I became an Off-Broadway theatrical designer. The first time I saw my name on the marquee from across the street, I almost fainted. Regardless, I challenged myself to meet people and explore the possibilities. It thrilled me to walk around the city and actually stand in the places where great designers stood. Now, many years later, I continue to do exactly that when I work with a production designer. And, to have eventually met some of them, I allow myself to climb within their skins so I can see from their angle of vision in order to fully understand how to contribute to their vision. That's how I view art direction.

I can't speak for everyone, but I think most people look at art direction from the outside in. There's nothing wrong with that. I tend to do it from the inside out; it's my instinct to do it that way. Expressing myself as an art director in this way allows me to leapfrog through time and enter the mind and spirit of any great artist or designer. Oftentimes, certain art directors have such a difficult time doing their jobs because they are in competition with the designer. Most importantly, they're missing a great opportunity. In its own way, projecting myself into the designer's mind that way is very gratifying because I learn so much about myself in the process. It's thrilling to make another person's vision a reality.

● *Art directors share a great creative component with the designer, but do you also see yourself as a creative manager, for the most part?*
I'm not fully doing my job if I'm just nuts-and-bolts managing the art department. The daily process is a creative process in how I deal with people, how I process instructions from above, how I convey ideas to those who need answers from me, and how I think on my feet when I'm on set. Understanding my designer's tastes and aesthetic responses supports how I supply what is needed at any given moment. How I fulfill my job changes slightly as I work with different designers, given the differences in perspective. In the same way, the designer has to think the way the director thinks in order to do his or her job properly.

There's a line of thought and function that connects everything in a collaborative environment like a movie. Storytelling drives what we do. Two questions are always asked. What is the story we want to tell, and how are we going to tell it? The biggest part of my job, then, is storytelling through the interpretation of the production designer and director's vision.[1]

Together, both the designer and the creative manager strategize about the functioning of the art department and scenery output, but the Art Director alone spearheads design management on a tactical level by delegating responsibility and guiding each task to completion. With the creative integrity of art directing kept in mind, this book will deconstruct this creative department head more as a marketing and operations manager rather than a seminal creative force. In the end, the reader will view the Art Director not only as a peerless, organizing force for the art department but also as a powerful shaper of policy and systems management for the larger film or television project.

THE FIRST ART DIRECTOR: WILFRED BUCKLAND

All production designers are art directors, and formerly, there were no production designers at all—there were *only* art directors. In earliest American film memory, the first creative moviemaker to be given the title of "Art Director" was Wilfred Buckland (Figure 1.2) who is widely credited as one of the most important influences "on the *look* of Hollywood cinema."[2]

Previously, he had designed Broadway theatrical productions, and later for the fledgling movie business developed a form of minimalist, Caravaggio-like lighting that engulfed the characters in darkness except for a single source of side illumination. This dramatic theatrical effect quickly became a silent film trademark known as "Lasky lighting," after the production

Figure 1.2 Wilfred Buckland, the first Hollywood Art Director.

company that made *The Cheat* (1915), his most successful film (see Figure 1.3). It was also one of Cecil B. DeMille's masterpieces, shot in Standard 35mm spherical 1.37:1 format, combining all the ingredients typical of the infamous DeMille style "a mixture of sex, sadism, and sacrifice, washed down with lurid melodrama."[3] Buckland's lighting contributions were groundbreaking. Two signature scenes in the film—the branding of the heroine by her wealthy Japanese paramour and the subsequent shooting scene—are lit with such theatrical richness and integrity that our attention is just as adroitly manipulated today as it was during its initial release.

This early maverick's scenic designs created an equally powerful tour de force for filmgoing audiences in the early 1920s. Towering 40 feet above Santa Monica Boulevard and La Brea Avenue, King Richard's castle, the centerpiece for Douglas Fairbank's *Robin Hood* (1922), is arguably the largest set ever constructed in Hollywood history. It took 500 workmen three solid months to build. Considering Los Angeles was more of a wide spot in the road then, the silhouette of the completed castle set could be seen for miles. It exemplified Buckland's penchant for creating extravagant, naturalistic sets, and it attests to his flair and flexibility as an early art director. Allan Dwan, director and trained engineer, recalled:

We worked out a couple of interesting engineering stunts for the big sets. On the interiors, the walls meshed together with a matrix, which we designed and built, so they could be put together rapidly in sections. The interior of the castle was very vast—too big to light with ordinary arcs. We didn't have enough. It was an open set, and certain sections were blacked out to give the right atmosphere. So to light them we constructed huge tin reflectors, about twenty feet across, which picked up the sun and shot the light back onto the arches inside. Then we could make effects.[4]

This set was larger than life in all ways—from the completion of the steel-frame, reinforced, working drawbridge, signifying the end of set construction, to the fact that the shooting of the film on its massive sets was a big tourist attraction (see Figure 1.4). And the magic of the Dream Factory continues to stir our imaginations.

Figure 1.3

A) Production still from *The Cheat*,

B) An example of a "Lasky Lighting" effect for the same scene, designed by Wilfred Buckland.

A

B

A

B

C

Figure 1.4

A) Perspective aerial close-up of Robin Hood castle,

B) High aerial shot of Robin Hood castle,

C) Production shot of the Robin Hood castle: The glass painted matte above the existing set suggests additional architecture within or beyond,

Figure 1.4

D) Interior: Great Hall with the Robin Hood castle,

E) Interior: A battle scene is fought just inside the main courtyard entrance of the castle set,

F) Holding court just outside the Robin Hood castle walls.

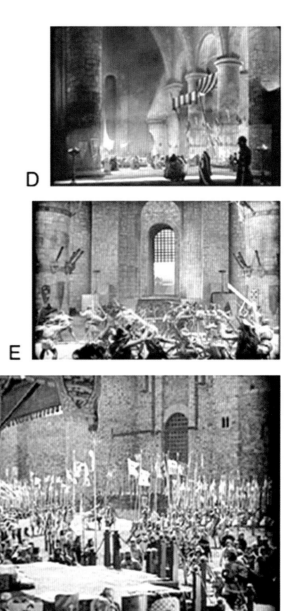

Under the steady but tumultuous employ of Cecil B. De Mille, Buckland was a prolific film designer—more than 80 films listed on www.imdb.com—spanning the years 1914 to 1927 (see Appendix A, Buckland Filmography), rivaling the overlapping accomplishments of a younger upstart, William Cameron Menzies. Incidentally, as the Supervising Art Director, Buckland ran the art department for *Robin Hood*, overseeing Anton Grot and William Cameron Menzies, not credited as assistant art directors. The practical vision of Buckland, the Hollywood Art Director and initiator of the use of controlled lighting within studio environments, set a standard in the first decades of the twentieth century that has become as commonplace as shooting film sequences in Hollywood sound stages today. He stands as an art-directing giant; his creative ingenuity ennobles the craft of film design even now.

The stills shown in Figures 1.3 and 1.4 illustrate the enormous sense of theatricality belying his earlier, formative years in New York City. His exuberance for designing these impressive, interior castle shots for *Robin Hood* matches that of the swashbuckling star and sole producer of the film, Douglas Fairbanks.

PAST CHANGES

The function and title of art direction continued into the next decades before the landscape of the art department was changed forever. Since Buckland's inauguration, Hollywood's creative visual managers were simply called art directors. Each of the existing studios including 20th Century Fox, Columbia Pictures, Paramount Pictures, Metro-Goldwyn-Mayer, and Warner Brothers contained stables of art directors overseen by a supervising art department head. The paradigm shift began in 1939 during the Golden Age of the American Studio System. William Cameron Menzies, having grown up under Buckland's tutelage, set a new standard for visual excellence by mapping the film epic, *Gone With the Wind*, with detailed concept sketches and storyboards, and adamantly insisting on using them as guides for shooting the film. David O. Selznick, the film's producer, rewarded Menzies' efforts of managing every detailed aspect of *GWTW* from a visual standpoint by crediting him with the title of "production designer." By the way, *GWTW* was art directed by Lyle Wheeler and set decorated by Edward G. Boyle.

This distinction continues to the present. Regardless, the titles continue to be blurred. Why is that? The television industry has consistently maintained the original label for the designer as "art director." Despite the confusion of terms between industries, one fact remains: two different titles refer to two separate job descriptions—plain and simple. When in Hollywood, speak specifically.

PRESENT CHANGES

Several years ago, the Art Directors Guild in Los Angeles was in a minor uproar when the title of our union, Local 876, had come up for review and subsequent vote by the membership. As we have just seen, the battle of who's who had gone on intermittently in an informal way during the many years since Hollywood's Golden Age. A handful of committed members called for a formal discussion and vote to resolve the squabbling for a truly descriptive title for the Guild, once and for all. After a lengthy debate, the name of the art directors' union was changed from Society of Motion Picture and Television Art Directors to Local 800 Art Directors Guild and Scenic, Title and Graphic Artists or, Local 800, informally.[5] Holding title in a designing capacity or not, art directors continue to occupy a vital place within the context of cinema's creative operatives. Formally being called an "art director" now more than ever personally connects us to our glorious past and reminds us of our historic roots without pretension.

One would think that after all this, the issue would be resolved. Friend and fellow art director Phil Dagort (*Six Feet Under, X-Files, The Stupids*) reminded me of the following small piece of information.

Interview with Phil Dagort

● *In your understanding of it, Phil, is there a distinct difference between a production designer and an art director?*

That's an interesting point. A producer is not required to hire both a production designer and an art director in terms of fulfilling the needs of a typical project. Officially, the studio considers the designer as the art direction lead on a film project and "designer" is the given title. For your book, you might want to consider this in defining the terms.[6]

For the purpose of this book, I will continue to refer to the production designer as the titular visionary guiding the course of the entire physical, visual look of a film. Art directors make the vision real. We are the art cops, the watchdogs who preserve the vision and ensure its delivery.

TYPECASTING: A FULLER PICTURE

Basic personality traits define the working style of every art director. Despite the marker traits that make an art director unique, there are other indications that are universal to all. As described briefly in the introduction, the basic personality of an art director is creatively practical; without it, this person is most likely a production designer. I'm not inferring here that production designers are impractical, but without a highly developed sense of practicality, an art director is ineffective. This hybrid marker trait also compels some art directors to question just how creative they should be. When in doubt, leave the realm of full creativity to the production designer and concentrate on the practical aspects of film design work: scheduling, drafting and building of scenery, its placement onstage, or retrofitting it into a location.

If you are a list-maker, you undoubtedly have an art director gene lurking somewhere in your chromosomal patterns. Not organized? No inclination for insisting on detail, and controlling every aspect of a project with anal-retentive fervor? Then keep your day job and stop the daydreaming. My point is that you cannot do this job correctly without a sharp sense of priority when strategizing a process. Unless that sensibility is firmly in place, there is no way you will be able to shoot from the hip in your daily participation in the game "The Quick and the Dead." A strong ability to make an effective priority list enables improvisation and the exercising of sharp reflexes. Consider this scenario: the Production Designer and shooting crew have flown off to the next location on the schedule leaving you and the **second unit** behind to get some pick-up shots of a new Lexus crashing into a plate glass window in a downtown Baltimore storefront. Two hours before **call time** you learn from the assistant **transpo** captain that the car delivery will not happen according to schedule. Most importantly, it has to be a Lexus because of what has been established in the previous day's **dailies.** The camera crew is beginning to set up the three-camera shot. What do you do? You meet with the **second unit director** and based on your knowledge of the **shooting schedule,** determine if you can wait an extra day to shoot with the proper car in Baltimore, or **wrap** it and figure out if you can replicate the scene in one of the other subsequent cities on the shooting schedule. A quick call is made to the Unit Production Manager for decision approval and an announcement is made to the attending crew. This decision could not have happened without the ability to be flexible and inflexible simultaneously. Like it or not, you're also a tightrope walker.

The film business attracts extroverts, and this includes art directors, being part and parcel of such a collaborative medium. What's more, the willingness to be a solid team player with a high level of energy, is another prerequisite. This charming caricature in Figure 1.5 of the art director is a relic of the Hollywood studio system. Some qualities omitted from this chart are currently found in the digital art department. Phil Dagort provides additional commentary:

Interview with Phil Dagort continued . . .

The art department is still built on job descriptions and breakdowns created in the studio system of the 1930s. In terms of the digital art department now, it's still surprisingly antiquated. What's significant about the digital art department is that job descriptions are beginning to run together, creating a more flexible and maybe even more creative overall experience. The old breakdown won't withstand the pressures of the visual effects department as an integral part of the current art department in terms of pre-visualization. The old system can't last—it has to give way to the new.

● *How do you structure your art department in terms of management?*
There is always a danger of overmanaging or undermanaging—I've made mistakes both ways. Achieving a balance and gauging your response is the challenge. The beauty of our job is the fact that on every project we get to choose who we work with by preference. Being hired and in a position to hire comes down to the fact that this business is very personality-oriented. It makes our jobs very political but also very pleasant as well. I understand that my hiring an art department crew is driven by the personality of the project. I do a lot of homework before I make calls to set up interviews because we all operate on references. Some people who might be on one person's No-No list will work surprisingly well with a different person. So, that's an important thing to remember.

𝒯𝒽𝑒 MOTION PICTURE ART DIRECTOR

•HIS RESPONSIBILITIES, FUNCTIONS, AND ACCOMPLISHMENTS•

The Society of Motion Picture Art Directors, Local 876 - IATSE

7715 Sunset Boulevard   Hollywood, California 90046

ART DIRECTOR IS ASSIGNED TO STORY BY THE PRODUCER.

SET CONFERENCE WITH THE PRODUCER AND THE DIRECTOR.

THOROUGH STUDY & RESEARCH FOR PURPOSE OF AUTHENTICITY.

ART DIRECTOR GIVES GRAPHIC FORM TO HIS CONCEPT OF SETTINGS.

COMPLETE ARCHITECTURAL DRAWINGS MADE BY SET DESIGNERS.

SKETCH ARTISTS SHOW, IN SKETCHES, HOW SETS WILL LOOK ON SCREEN

SCALE MODELS OF ALL SETS ARE BUILT BY MODEL ARTISTS.

PROPOSED SCHEMES FOR SETS APPROVED BY PRODUCER & DIRECTOR.

ESTIMATED SET COSTS ARE BUDGETED BY THE ART DIRECTOR.

ART DIRECTOR'S PLANS ARE APPROVED BY PRODUCTION MANAGER.

ART DIRECTOR AIDS IN "LOCATION" SELECTION OUTSIDE OF STUDIO.

PROGRESS OF SETTING CONSTRUCTION CHECKED IN WOODWORKING MILL.

SET CONSTRUCTION SUPERVISED BY ART DIRECTOR ON STAGES

MECHANICAL UNITS DEVELOPED FROM WORKING DRAWINGS.

ART DIRECTOR SELECTS PAINTS, WALL PAPERS, & SURFACE TEXTURES.

DIRECTION OF STYLE AND PLACEMENT OF SIGNS & LETTERING.

SCENIC ARTISTS PAINT BACK DROPS FROM DETAILED DRAWINGS.

PLASTIC ORNAMENT AND SCULPTURED UNITS REQUIRE DIRECTION.

SELECTION OF TREES AND SHRUBBERY FOR LANDSCAPING.

ART DIRECTOR SELECTS PLUMBING FIXTURES & DIRECTS INSTALLATION.

CARRIAGES, BOATS AND "PROPS" BUILT FROM DETAILED DRAWINGS.

ART DIRECTOR SELECTS FABRICS AND SPECIAL DRAPERY MATERIALS.

LIGHTING FIXTURES OF PROPER PERIOD DESIGNED & SELECTED

INTERIOR DECORATIVE FURNISHINGS SELECTED AND APPROVED.

ART DIRECTOR DETERMINES PROPER PLACEMENT OF BACK DROPS.

CONFERENCE WITH DIRECTOR REGARDING MONTAGE SEQUENCES

PROCESS AND "TRICK" SHOTS REFLECT TECHNICAL TRAINING & EXPERIENCE

CAMERAMAN AND ART DIRECTOR CO-OPERATE IN ILLUMINATION.

THE SET IS READY, AND PHOTOGRAPHY OF THE PLAY BEGINS.

PICTORIAL PERFECTION OF THE SETTING AIDS IN TELLING EVERY STORY.

R. D. WILKINS

Figure 1.5 The Motion Picture Art Director: Responsibilities, functions and accomplishments. Used by permission of ADG—Local 800 IATSE.

● *Phil, what is your basic approach to art directing?*

My approach to art direction is in the question, "What are we forgetting now?" or "Why am I sitting still; what should I be doing?" I have to be constantly in motion. I admire people who can be smooth and a lot more laid-back about it. I really envy them. Not worrying is a skill to be developed. In our end of the business it's 20% art and the rest is organizing how it happens, although on some projects I could never get it to add up to 100% and on other projects it was a clear 50-50 spread. I've been fortunate in having worked with people who have allowed me to do my job by delegating responsibility and the work at hand. Having developed that experience and the people skills necessary to do my job has been really important in order to answer my question "What am I forgetting?"

The scope of the activities of an art director is dependent on the designer's comfort level. To be effective, the designer/art director relationship has to be close and really tight—a best brothers (or sisters) kind of thing. I ask each production designer I work with to tell me everything: what has been communicated to the set decorator and construction coordinator, what has been discussed with the director, and what the up-to-the-minute details are. We have to be in sync because when I'm out there on the floor, the crew is going to ask me the same questions they've asked the designer to see if they get the same answers. They only do that to know that they are on track. There has to be a basic trust or there could be terrible problems if the designer is not constantly downloading that information. Again, it's not really about an art director setting the ground rules for the relationship, but more about how the Production Designer is calling the shots. Insisting on open communication is what the art director can contribute.[7]

Most importantly, an art director also has to be a generally effective, hands-on communicator—by this I am specifically referring to one-on-one interpersonal skills. Smart-phones and digital networking have simplified our lives and freed us but have also diminished our physical interactive abilities. In order to be effective team players, our communication must be direct and clean, delivered in a way that is inclusive and supportive. Instructors who have reviewed the first edition of this book have unanimously agreed that their students, by and large, lack this critical ability. I agree. Communication is a critical skill to develop.

TWO PATHS

There is no better way to learn how the art department operates than by working for a time as an art director. For some, a solid supporting role as design manager is exciting and appeals to a more detail-oriented, hands-on personality. For others, the seductiveness of a more visible and politically dynamic role in the spotlight as a production designer offers a more feasible career direction. Both positions are equally prestigious, containing respective pros and cons, and both will be discussed briefly here.

Design Manager: The Lifers

Some art directors are career professionals—they choose not to **production design** or necessarily aspire to it. Instead, they are delegators of responsibility both within the art department and other departments of a film. They are judges of quality of work, arbiters of visual sensibility, and transmitters of information. As communicators and efficiency experts, they ensure that whatever needs to be in front of the camera gets there through relentless attention to detail and data cross-checking. In addition to their managerial responsibilities, the Lifers also assume the role of co-creator. It is very gratifying to experience this level of art directing. It evolves as a result of a long-term and mutually satisfying relationship with a production designer. Having worked with several designers, the most notable relationship that effortlessly comes to mind was with Roy Forge Smith (*Monty Python and the Holy Grail, Mrs. Soffel, Robin Hood: Men in Tights, Bill & Ted's Excellent Adventure*). From Roy's perspective, his designer/art director relationship is ultimately founded on trust, not micromanagement. A contemporary of both Henry Bumstead and Robert Boyle, Roy is a secure designer, accepting of his art director's visual intelligence and unique creative process. In addition to his quiet generosity, he is patient and very creative. Embracing that kind of camaraderie in this business is rare. Other designers who do not possess the poise of Roy's experience and professionalism tend to be histrionic; these designers only add to the length of an already challenging day. Engaging in and nurturing a relationship with a designer like Roy Smith signifies the hallmark of a well-rounded film career.

Production Designer-in-Embryo

The chasm separating art direction from production design is deceptive. It seems easy to be a production designer, but that assumption can be an illusion. For some aspiring production designers, it is a matter of finding the narrowest section of the stream and simply stepping over the singing water; for others, there is no boat in sight to help cross the vast expanse of the raging currents. Why? Time and place have a lot to do with it. And so does perseverance. Those art directors who successfully use their current position as a catapult from the art department guild system find that it is only a matter of time before they are hired by a director to design a first film. Again, there is no easy journey, regardless of how effortless some people make it look. The resolve to do whatever it takes is often met with other conditions that must be relinquished in order to achieve the goal. For instance, it may be necessary to make the difficult choice between having a personal life, a relationship, and a family in lieu of developing a solid career as a designer. There are many trade-offs to make along the way, and it is ultimately a highly personal affair. In any case, it is this initial, compelling dream that lures so many hopefuls into the art department in the first place. When Steve Saklad (*Spider-Man 2, Red Dragon, The Mambo Kings*) was asked why he was an art director, he responded as follows.

Interview with Steve Saklad

- *What do you or don't you enjoy about art directing?*
  Like most art directors out there, I'm also inclined to want to production design. The larger projects like *Spider-Man 2* are projects that I can also contribute a lot of design ideas to, even as art director. Designers like Neil Spisak, Kristi Zea, and Stuart Wurtzel want their art directors to

bring a lot to the party in terms of architectural expertise, a sense of theatricality and detailing, and inspired solutions to design problems. I enjoy the application of choosing molding details for interiors, and similarly these designers appreciate my participation down to that level. Each of those people doesn't usually sketch like professional illustrators can. My ability to rough sketch or doodle quickly what I interpret as their idea is not only invaluable to them but a pleasure for me.

● *Did you stand out as a young art director because of those abilities or was it because of your organizational and management skills?*
The easy answer is that it is always about the creative. There have been times that I've had to apologize for having to catch up on the management aspects, although each of those designers has been happy with my organizational skills. I hate to say it in this day and age, but the computer is not my friend; I use it only when absolutely necessary.

● *Would you talk a little about the challenges you faced on Spider-Man 2?*
On *Spider-Man 2* there were five art directors: Scott Murphy, who dealt with all the New York locations; Jeff Knipp, who dealt exclusively with Doc Ock, his tentacles, and related equipment; Tom Wilkins and myself primarily split the Sony stage sets in LA as well as the LA locations; and Tom Valentine, who had previous experience with Sony Imageworks, and dealt with everything that overlapped between the **CGI** world and physical scenery.

In effect, three of us were creative, but in totally different ways. Tom Wilkins supervised four of the biggest sets in the movie, including Otto's lab, the planetarium, the *Bugle* office, and the massive pier set, plus a handful of smaller sets, and he managed the budget and memo paperwork as well. Tom Valentine had his hands full with all the photo-driven backings, all **bluescreen** work, the clock tower set, the two built miniatures: one 1/6 scale model of the interior pier set, and another miniature of the entire exterior pier and dock. Some of these sets at Sony, for example, held an array of bluescreens angled above and around, engulfing the sets. In addition, large mirrors were butted against the edges of the set walls, reflecting bluescreens below for digitizing. Yet, he still found time to create timeline flowcharts indicating due dates for designing, building, dressing, shooting, and striking each set.

I was responsible for a long list of mid-scale sets that were meant to show a real sense of New York City: Peter's apartment, an East Village deli, a burning tenement building, the Off-Broadway theater world, a mid-town hospital operating room, Harry's East Side mansion, as well as action-filled street scenes not shot in Manhattan but on the Universal backlot or in downtown LA. I was also the only one of the three art directors to get a chance to sketch some of the set ideas the old-fashioned way, in the form of ink-and-marker drawings on large sheets of **onionskin.**

We all played well together but would all agree that there existed a friendly sibling rivalry in terms of currying favor to get good sets. I was on the movie for 15 months, Wilkins for 18, and Valentine for 21. When we all started, there wasn't a finished script and consequently no known set list to divvy up beforehand. Neil Spisak, Production Designer, and I had a special relationship we garnered from our mutual work in the theater, decades before. But everyone was playing on a much more expensive field here. Things ultimately seemed to work to each person's strong suit. And the final product each of the three art directors helped to create was, I think, pretty extraordinary.[8]

Throughout this book, many points of view are presented to enrich the experience of the reader. It is deliberately done because the activity of art directing is, in the final analysis, more subjective than following a list of procedures or clutching to a fistful of rules. Via the process of interviewing several art directors and art department creatives, our combined perceptions have drawn a more dynamic picture of our filmmaking process.

NOTES

1   Linda Berger interview, August 16, 2004, North Hollywood, CA.

2   Mann, William J., 2002. *Behind the Screen: How Gays and Lesbians Shaped Hollywood, 1910–1969.* New York: Viking Press, page 32.

3   Brownlow, Kevin, 1968. *The Parade's Gone By.* Berkeley, CA: University of California Press, page 180.

4   Ibid., page 250.

5   Since the Art Directors Guild adopted its new name, it has merged since 2003 with two other IATSE guilds: Scenic Artists, and Title and Graphic Artists, all collectively known as IA Local 800.

6   Phil Dagort interview, June 6, 2004, Toluca Lake, CA.

7   Ibid.

8   Steve Saklad interview, August 17, 2004, Silverlake, CA.

CHAPTER 2
The Responsibilities, the Relationships, and the Setup

HIERARCHY OF RESPONSIBILITIES

First Responsibilities

An art director's initial relationship to the production designer is as intense and short-lived as most film project relationships. Anyone who experienced summer camp as a child understands this dynamic. First encounters on a new film project are driven by the personal need to establish a sense of belonging to a special group, your department, and a political need to define one's place in the psychological hierarchy of the film. The bond between the prime art department figureheads—the Production Designer and the Art Director—is forged by these human forces and compels the Art Director to fulfill first responsibilities.

How does an art director repay the favor of being hired by a designer? The Art Director begins by acting as a credible emissary for the partnership. By being responsible to your designer, you are also being responsible to yourself. As codependent as this might sound, it remains as a key factor contributing to the effectiveness of the position. First, your production designer relies on your support as an ally. Most situations will demand this. For example, you are on location in Europe, and you are presented with conflicting information regarding the exact placement of an exterior, wooded escarpment for shooting a series of important script shots. This specific location had been decided on after a full day's worth of **scouting** similar locations several weeks before. Even the location manager's photos look very much alike; the truth is, no one remembers or is really sure. Essentially, this quickly escalating argument is between the designer and the director. You are in the middle, and it is time for you to speak. What do you do? You do what is expected. You take the side of your designer. And you do this diplomatically and with logic. You refer back to your **scout** notes, you present quick plan sketches you made during the original scouting of the location in question, you recall specific conversation at the time of the decision, and you smile. Politically, you cannot afford to offend anyone. Morally, your duty is to your designer. Bonding through these kinds of experiences on a film crew is legendary. In the process, first responsibilities are fulfilled and lifelong working relationships are assured.

Second, the art department budget demands this. The set budget, linked to the visual shopping list of the script, is an outline of how the funds to realize the visual concept will be spent. A good art director defends a production designer's vision by managing the budget with the indispensable help of the Construction Coordinator by strategizing how the funds are dispersed over the set list (see "The Relationships," this chapter). The unit production manager (**UPM**), the producer, and the head accountant are also an integral part of this process. They are given copies of the set list and budget, and they are constantly kept within the loop of set changes and developments via a daily cost report. The ultimate goal here is to preserve the visual concept as much as possible, without going over budget or relinquishing the designer's original ideas in the process. (See Chapter 8, "Art Department Tactical Strategy: Minding the Budget," for a more detailed discussion.)

Third, being an effective art director demands that you are always ready. The brief scenario described previously illustrates this. Always carry something to sketch on (an iPad) and learn how to scribble or enter data while you are talking. You are always relied upon to have exactly the right information at hand for precise decision-making. Readiness also includes knowing every aspect of the script extremely well, reading every page of script changes and memorizing the most recent revision, staying close to the events in the production office and on set, and having set expense data always at your fingertips. The Production Designer is doing the same thing, but expects you to close the gaps whenever necessary. This is the only way to market yourselves as the "dynamic duo" you truly are.

Christa Munro, art director (*Jack Reacher, Mission: Impossible—Ghost Protocol, Good Night and Good Luck, Erin Brockovich*), and Gae Buckley, art director (*The Book of Eli, The Sisterhood of the Traveling Pants, Coyote Ugly, What Women Want*), share similar thoughts.

Interviews with Christa Munro and Gae Buckley

● *Christa, in order to make your relationship with your production designer work well, is communication the core?*
A dialogue based on trust, a mutual acknowledgement of strengths and weaknesses and things we mutually like/don't like to do. That way you can really help one another out. It should be kind of fun.

● *What quality separates a great art director from a good art director?*
Someone who can create a really strong partnership with the Production Designer is most effective. Of course, it depends on your designer wanting the same type of relationship.[1]

● *Gae, what separates a great art director from a good art director?*
I think of a great art director as a clear conduit of information both within the art department and with all other related departments. Ideally, it is someone who possesses an extensive background in art, architecture, design, theater, and film. Aside from talent, skill, and experience, an even-keeled and respectful personality enables you to get people to do their best work for you. It's extremely important, especially in Hollywood. Regarding the expression of personality, it's also necessary to sublimate your personality and taste to some degree to get into the head and vision of the designer. Ultimately, you're facilitating someone else's vision. Realistically, I would have to say that a great art director must be able to graciously defer to the designer while still managing the art and craft of the film.[2]

Second Responsibilities

The art department is home away from home: 12 to 18 hours a day, six days a week, for the duration of anywhere from three to six months to a year. The art department people become your primary family while your actual primary family often takes on a secondary, surrogate role to your professional life. So, responsibility to the art department is another fundamental concern. As formal head of the department, the art director is its leader-protector. As such, exercising the power to hire only the best crewmembers available reinforces core competencies for the art department. The art department coordinator (see "Art Department Setup," this chapter) is the art director's inter- and intra-organizational interface and most valuable player. Both of you work diligently to keep the machine well-oiled and running smoothly. Comfortable working conditions, excellent office equipment, and connection to a Cloud-based server make daily life an effortlessly shared experience via smartphone technology. At this point in time, a secured server is typical on most productions—it's a rare project where your tenacity will be necessary to convince the UPM to install an art department server to assist the archivist's task in organizing thousands of digital images for a larger show. Of course, this kind of equipment requires full time IT care, but will benefit *everyone* on the production. It is only your persuasiveness that will make the difference for the success of your department. External online servers are an indispensable and affordable option. Once again, Christa Munro shares her observations.

Interview with Christa Munro continued . . .

● *How can the art department operate more smoothly?*
My primary thought about that right now is about expanding my staff with an assistant art director and possibly two. Part of that completes the archiving question, and the other part addresses the fact that the "paperless office" isn't a reality. We generate a much larger paper trail now with our technology than we ever have, and it needs constant attention. Something you said to me a long time ago comes to mind—you were actually describing what an art director really is in six words or less—"a glorified, middle management executive secretary." The funny thing is we need secretarial backup more now because we need that support just to stay on top of it through

the entire show. With that established, I'm more readily available to make changes and also it makes wrap a lot easier.

- *Are you a hands-on art department manager, or do you tend to delegate tasks?*
  I'm a delegator. In order to do that well, you have to read the person as well as the situation. Personally, I like to get someone directed and then let them take it and build on it. You see very quickly if they'll rise to the occasion or not. You know, some people are lost without some direction–they need clearly defined parameters. Lately, I find myself double-checking my delegating decisions and re-evaluating midstream as required. The fact is, people get tired after four months on a film going full speed, day in and day out. The evaluation check allows me to see how everyone's holding up and where s/he might need to go in order that the project can easily complete itself.

- *How wired is your art department?*
  It's totally wired. The art department is continually uploading stuff to an online server. They were very helpful, had good tech support, and it was pretty easy for all of us to learn how to use. On projects which have many different locations, combining all of the location photos in the same place with the production info and schedules is a beautiful thing. Although we generally hire great art department coordinators, I can see the need for an archivist in an ideal world. That person would solely handle the images and perhaps also manage clearances but mainly trafficking the images. The documentation aspect of it alone is a huge amount of work. The server issue we've already discussed, and the computer rental issues, i.e., jurisdictional conflicts regarding large format printers, are two small tasks I continually reinvestigate so I can fully address them on future projects.

- *I suppose your smartphone and/or iPad is always on hand, then?*
  They have become indispensable. For instance, on a former project we had to break apart an ambulance and re-create it as a stage set. We could rapidly document every detail required– quick shots of the perfect door pull–snap the items, send them, and then leave a message at the office, "When the boss comes in, let him know he's got some images on email."[3]

Third Responsibilities

The director is an art director's other boss, wielding the primary vision for the look of the film. Reading the director correctly is just as important as an art director's regard for the vision of the production designer. For example, most directors are purely verbal, translating the words of a screenplay, and in most cases, the rewriting of the script. Most likely labeled "an actor's director," they entrust the visual responsibility of the script to the design team. Other directors are exceedingly visual, spending a vast amount of time in the art department during the pre-production phase of moviemaking; they speak the same visual language as the artists creating the imagery. As a result, the visual information plastering the walls of the art department and production designer's office is welcomed and easily digested by visual directors. Concept sketches or ideas scribbled on napkins at mealtimes become an overriding form of this shorthand communication. Drawn plans, elevations, and details with supporting white models and computer pre-visualization presentations easily exist as understandable, workable tools for further debate and change in the process of nailing the look of the film. We in the art department like this breed of director because they make our lives easier. One favorite champion of the art department was John Gray (*Helter Skelter, Martin and Lewis, The Seventh Stream, The Hunley*). Early in the process, he entered the workspace with a palpable enthusiasm that never diminished and left us with a clear visual concept. During the prep for *The Day Lincoln Was Shot* (1998), he simply said he was going against the expectations of a sepia-toned vision of the past by shooting the film in blues and gray tonalities as a premonition of the Civil War. Holding fast to that notion throughout, such a salient visual metaphor became our design beacon, inspiring countless choices and clearly answering many questions that would inevitably arise.

Amalgamating the visions of a director and production designer is the obvious challenge. Just because the visual concept for a film project arises out of similar conversations does not translate into unanimous agreement. A third-party interpretation (yours) on top of those of each of your bosses can easily become a Gordian knot. Care must be taken to maintain a keen sense of neutrality and objectivity, in addition to a well-honed ability for **active listening.** In most cases, although your input might be brilliant, your goal is to steadfastly translate and maintain the unity of both "primary" visions at all costs. Again, the art director is an enabler of other wishes, points-of-view, and demands—a servant to many masters.

Fourth Responsibilities

The final reporting relationship discussed here is with the studio, its representative—the UPM, and the film project in general. It tends to be a more straightforward relationship because it is a business relationship; the superimposed layers of creativity and artifice do not as easily compound the business of making art, as the previously discussed responsibilities. The UPM and the Studio are interested in film as product; here, the focus is on the "business" aspect of "show business." Film production, as a commodity, is about getting the best quality for the least amount of money spent. Taking this a step further, it is about **economies of scale,** a basic financial concept that states that the average unit cost of a good or service can be reduced by increasing its output rate.[4] Although we are not producing donuts or widgets, this formula works especially well in terms of the ratio of added crew numbers and the production of finished sets per week on a heavy film schedule or episodic musical television schedule, like *Glee.* On this level, an art director is operating for the company, or studio, in an efficiency capacity of most operations managers in the business world. Avoiding bottlenecks within the art department, as well as how it effectively functions with all other departments, is the goal. Optimizing division of labor and corresponding labor costs directly relates to economies of scale. On a union film, supervising the management of the construction crew, for example, to work efficiently and by steering away from working on sixth and seventh days, unless absolutely necessary—i.e., a crisis schedule—would automatically boost production level but keep down inflated labor costs, correctly supporting economies of scale. On a low-budget film, achieving economies of scale, especially in terms of increasing output rate, becomes a challenge considering the smaller size of the labor pool and how thinly everyone's efforts are already stretched. All of this directly relates to the pragmatic management of the art department budget.

The UPM demands the fiscal loyalty of each department head by requiring strict adherence to the allocated budget figures. Inevitably, changes on both sides of the equation demand a constant adjustment to the numbers. Sometime during the mid-point of the production phase, the once rigid budget brick more closely resembles an overworked wad of Silly Putty. Again, an art director's ability to roll with the punches acts as a release valve for the pressures of handling someone else's money.

A last consideration as a major footnote is an art director's responsibility to the Art Directors Guild and other sister unions also collaborating on a film. All deal memos, contracts, and paperwork must be in order to satisfy union quotas and requirements. By default, the Art Director is the union watchdog also responsible to the vigilant union reps waiting like referees at a sporting event to spot a foul. If a union-related grievance call is made and is in turn ignored by production, the union can—and often will—shut down the film. This happened in the early 1990s in New Mexico on the Morgan Creek production *White Sands,* early on in the pre-production process. When the lead actors of the film stood in solidarity with the rest of us on strike, the slowdown was more quickly resolved than if they had not given their support, and production resumed as if nothing had happened. On non-union films, allegiance to the art department crew tends to be fierce and solidarity more unshakable because of the lack of union support and intervention. Typically, events like this catapult non-union people into the various guilds and film craft unions, thereby bestowing union status. My title changed to union art director during that summer. It was an experience where I also learned invaluable lessons on being a union activist before I had legitimate union membership (see Chapter 10).

The constant "push-me-pull-you" allegiance to the financial, political, and creative forces playing on the Art Director is extreme in both union and non-union scenarios. Successfully working in a highly collaborative industry like the movie business reinforces fast thinking, self-confidence, action, creativity, and negotiating large egos. It is not for the thin-skinned or weak-minded. It prods at your resiliency, as well as your pragmatism and determination. By relentlessly testing your social skills as well as your inner strengths, art directing presents a range of challenges in the professional film arena bar none.

THE RELATIONSHIPS

Developing relationships in Hollywood translates to cowboy work. From the first moment a tenderfoot steps out of the creaky stagecoach onto the dusty dude ranch dirt, that neophyte is looking for a leg up. Throughout the process of mucking stalls, splitting rails to put up and tear down corrals, learning how to chew tobacco and win spitting contests, tying a proper lariat knot or choking on round-up dust, getting a hand with the hard work and patting other cowpokes on the back, the journey continues from cattle drive to cattle drive. What could be more classically American western film plot? Learning the ropes by giving a hand and getting a hand—shorthand for basic film etiquette—is just as critical as understanding the motion capture process. Remember, filmmaking is a collaborative endeavor. One person with a Mac and Final Cut Pro just cannot do it in a vacuum. This next section will explore fundamental relationships and their reciprocal implications.

Art Department

Historically, the art department is seen as the imagery hub of film production (See Figure 2.1). More than this, it also exists as the central department providing a strategic guide for all crewmembers in their respective departments. As keeper of the visual concept, the art department has creatively inspired and monitored all related activities for decades.

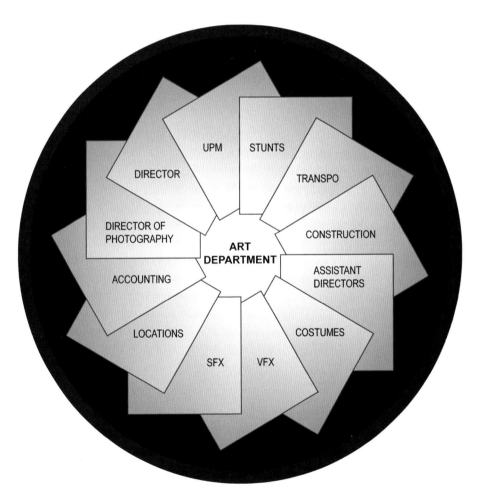

Figure 2.1   Wheel of art department influence.

Relationship marketing is transacted in the art department—more specifically, an exchange process of services, support, ideas, options, and value for energy expended. The buzzword is show business—emphasis on the word "business." The aim of this creative relationship marketing is to build long-term, mutually satisfying interactions between players, suppliers, and even vendors outside the film circle, in order to develop and retain lifelong preference and business acumen. Life and work continue beyond any particular film project, so shortsightedness will not do if a productive network of business relations would exist in the future. Whether you are working on a studio picture or just getting started as an art director on a low-budget **indie,** promising and delivering high-quality service and product at reasonable prices to your immediate customers—the director, UPM, and producers—are your main goals especially in non-union projects. The relationships established with other department heads and vendors on a current project had better be extendable into the next project, or you're just spinning your wheels. Why not develop proper etiquette and business form from the onset of your career? It's certainly the best way to give *yourself* a leg up.

Interdepartmental PR

Head Accountant and Staff

Before I begin my first day of work on a film, usually on the same day I interview with the UPM to set up my deal memo and corresponding perk package, I make a beeline to the head accountant's office. This is a vital PR stop more than anything else. Making friends with the head accountant beforehand positively ensures that payroll will happen effortlessly—that vendor checks might be assured to happen within a 24-hour turnaround and that a healthy communication channel is established. Nurturing this relationship is the key to money flow. Once in the Schiphol International Airport, Amsterdam, I boarded a crowded terminal-to-plane shuttle and freely offered my seat to a weary, raven-haired woman who quietly said, "Thank you" in an unmistakably Midwestern American accent. Our first paragraph of conversation revealed that we were both headed for the same 16-seater jet to Luxembourg City to begin work on a TV film. She was our head accountant, Dana Reaves Bolla (*Immortals, With or Without You, The Naked Man, The Lost Battalion*). Being the first of a handful of arrivals to set up our respective departments, we became fast friends, exploring the local restaurants for dinner and creating a unilateral offensive to the many challenges we would encounter during the course of the film. In this case, it is important to mention that having her as a solid ally was a significant plus in getting anything and everything done with the parent studio being 5,318 miles away. On this same film, the UPM and Dana were old war buddies and were determined to deliver the studio's financial and contractual agenda to the local film company. Befriending the head accountant and UPM extended my own political invincibility and helped ease the demands of my daily tactical tasks.

Locations Manager and Staff

Another early arrival in the pre-production phase is the locations manager. Logistics is what cements your relationship: the locations finally chosen to satisfy the design concept, the schedule of in-and-out movement at a location, access and parking, and strict adherence to what can and cannot be physically done are some of the issues you will face together. Much like an art director, the locations manager is the first to arrive and the last to leave any and all locations. An emissary for the production itself, the locations manager is the ultimate PR agent for the film company. Together, as external marketing managers, your combined efforts need to be direct and credible to people or companies in the community where you happen to be shooting, in Los Angeles or elsewhere. Although the actual location deals and contracts are the responsibility of a locations manager, an art director's presence and support is fully expected.

This relationship is unique in terms of interdepartmental PR, but it is more client-oriented outside of the film project. In this situation, you are actively working to combine the brand images of the art department, the locations department, and the larger film. On the Warner Bros. film *My Fellow Americans* (1996), I was the North Carolina art director and Ned Shapiro (*The Kids Are All Right, W., Intolerable Cruelty, Identity, Legally Blonde, Bulworth, Apollo 13*) was the location manager for the entire film, both in LA and Asheville. Our biggest challenges were to convince the Biltmore Estate to allow us to build the south façade of the White House on their pristine grounds for the course of two months; to land a Sikorsky helicopter in a mountain glen and then explode it on takeoff; and also, to stage a Gay Pride parade in downtown Asheville. Literally the first two people to arrive in the on-location production office, Ned and I carefully established solid, trusting community relationships by laying pre-film crew groundwork. Without a well-conceived strategy, our efforts could not have been as persuasive. This combined with the right amounts of goodwill and location rental cash will always get the job done.

UPM, Production Supervisor, and Production Office Staff

The bulk of your interdepartmental marketing efforts are exercised with the production office, the other nerve center of film production. All final decisions are made in this office. Your goal as an effective art department manager with the UPM, production supervisor, and production office coordinator is to provide good offensive support. For instance, pretend you are working on a marine movie like *Titanic*. In addition to the normal requirements, such as building many variations of the ship and completing the sets, there are special considerations that demand specific attention, like building the entire studio: soundstages, office buildings, facilities for art department, construction, props, wardrobe, dressing rooms, etc. At the last minute, production receives its **green light** for this film in June and is expected to be ready for shooting **hero** sets in September. Simple issues like arranging the paperwork, regulations, and permit processes, as well as getting the materials and supplies for scenery building, become somewhat challenging in Rosarito Beach, Mexico because of tariff and tactical considerations. Forcing an elephant of expectation through this keyhole of reality within such a narrow window of time demands flawless strategy and coordination. Without proper art department PR, willingness to cooperate, and a great deal of experience and common sense, the odds of success are minimized.

It would be impractical for the art director to get in the way of such a challenging process as noted in the *Titanic* scenario. Instead, establishing and telegraphing the benefits of cooperation, flexibility, and anticipation to the production office serve the art department in the long run. Staying in front of paperwork, scheduling, and being ready for every obstacle that will arise, positively projects reliability and instills mutual respect. Admittedly, the *Titanic* scenario is exceptional and true. Nevertheless, the same concept applies to an Indie. Budgetary and staff restraints on a low-budget feature can just as seriously undermine the reliability of strategy and scheduling as much as tariff and border restrictions on an international blockbuster. The key to overcoming obstacles like this is to consider a coin: be flexible enough to compromise on one hand, but be uncompromising about letting go of your initial strategy on the other hand. Playing win-win politics in typical issues like this can mean the difference between good managing tactics and lousy PR. In the wise words of Greg Papalia, (*GI Joe: The Rise of Cobra, The Italian Job, The Patriot, Legends of the Fall*):

> *My philosophy as a supervising art director is you never bring your problem to the producer–you always bring their problem to them, with solutions.*[5]

Indie work is most challenging in a similar way. When I designed *Notes from Underground* (1995), an adaptation of the Fyodor Dostoevsky novel set in downtown Los Angeles, I was already an art director with a considerable track record. The budgetary restrictions for our small art department were not an obstacle as much as maintaining a steadfast commitment to what I wanted to see on the screen. Director Gary Walkow (*Crashing, The Trouble with Dick, Beat*) and I discussed our joint effort to maintain realism and faithfulness to the original text. For the kind of control the typical low-budget location work doesn't allow, we opted to design six small sets into 9,000 square feet of the smallest of the Delfino Studios stages in Sylmar, California. By figuring the costs of **retrofitting** available **flattage** and other pre-existing scenery, repainting, and dressing against the costs of location rentals and lack of noise and traffic control, our decision to set up and work in that small soundstage not only benefited the producers but ensured my visual control needs. Plus, we came in under budget at $14,600 with benefits far outweighing costs.

First Assistant Director and Staff

The influence of a good art director should be felt everywhere at once. Unfortunately, the shooting crew and its activity on a **hot set** are not an art director's legitimate domain; the first assistant director, the second assistant director, and the second-second assistant director will continuously remind you of that fact. Regardless, you need to do your job despite any restrictions; acknowledging that the domain status of the First Assistant Director (1st AD) is key to working within those restrictions.

What is the job of an art director on set during shooting? Members of the extended art department: the on-set dresser, the on-set prop person, on-set carpenter, and on-set scenic artist require supervision, especially when key scenes in hero sets are being shot. Daily visits to the set just before **call time** allow enough time to chat and clarify what is put in front of the camera for a certain shot, or for an art director to provide moral and political support at a specified time. Suppose there is some confusion about whether a foldable, cloth battle map for a WWI film—requested at the last minute—is right for a close-up shot in a pivotal scene scheduled for shooting later in the day. Ideally, a hero prop's importance demands attention days before it will actually be used in a scene. Having gotten the information about the hand prop in question at **wrap time** at the end of the previous day, there is now little time to act. Did I mention you are also on location in Luxembourg? Organizing a brief fact-finding meeting at call time with the First AD, Director and On-set Prop Person might determine that the map, quickly crafted in the art department from 6:00 pm to 6:00 am that morning, is too large, too rectangular (needs to be square), looks too new, and must easily fit into the character's upper coat pocket. That's a lot of new information to receive, demanding fast work that needs to be done back at the art department, and be ready for shooting in six hours. Because the prop person must remain on set, the art director is obliged to make this directorial request his/her prime task until it is completed exactly to specification. Handing the task off to someone else will not insure exactness or speed, but supervising the task yourself will. Also, updating the First AD as you progress is just as important. Necessary calls are made to reschedule other morning and afternoon meetings, as well as contacting the wardrobe department for the size of the coat pocket and whoever else must be involved in the current emergency. When the task is completed, it is rushed to the set before lunch. Another brief meeting with the First AD and Director informs you of additional changes to the prop, but more importantly that the scene has been cut from the day's shooting schedule and will be added to other **insert shots** to be gotten later in the schedule that week.

This scenario is typical. Enrolling the power of the First AD in any shooting crew or scheduling decision is a smart move. Working respectfully with Him/Her is like working with an on-set version of yourself. Drew Rosenberg (*Helter Skelter, Stealing Harvard, Along Came Polly*), 1st AD for *The Hunley,* comes to mind as one who exerted her influence consistently and judiciously. Fighting natural disasters, changing weather conditions, and temperamental actors in order to keep production on schedule, she strove to make my challenges with her all win-win experiences within reason, or the dictates of any given situation. Realistically, this could not have happened without my strength as an equal management agent providing alliance, mutual respect, and support.

Pre-visualization Supervisor and Staff

The advent of 3D animation and how it has affected the design landscape has forced film designers to rethink the process of matching human and animation film elements seamlessly into the visual fabric of cinematography. A healthy respect now governs this young relationship between the art department and **visual effects** (or VFX) folks. It cannot properly function as an adversarial one because our perpetually advancing technology demands a paradigm shift. The marriage of minds to create a singular vision has arrived and with it, a rethinking of boundaries.

The relationship between the art department and the visual effects department is obliged to merge as hands connected to arms belonging to the same creative body. Fulltime cooperation has already begun to happen out of necessity. The art department has doubled its size by embracing digital sub-departments and creating 3D templates modeled in Form-Z and Rhino by digital set designers for 3D animators in the visual effects department. The process of pre-visualization (or pre-vis) before any scenery is built is an ongoing expectation of the Director. All digital images are currently catalogued and transmitted to other department computer screens via the art department server and maintained by an archivist. No longer a question of when but to what degree is now the challenge. Again, Greg Papalia shares some insight.

Interview with Greg Papalia

● *Over the past couple of decades, VFX has contributed more to the design of a film. In one way or another, this has increasingly impacted the concept design of the art department. Greg, in your experience, have these early issues gotten resolved over time?*

These issues remain—if anything, they're bigger. The reason is that historically, an art director is serving two masters: the director and the film (or script). Now, visual effects has become a third master requiring digital models for pre-vis presentations. The problem is that their needs are oftentimes out of step with construction's needs. The visual effects department is no longer considered as just a post-production process. Their budget is large and extends over the entire filming timeline. They are also under a tremendous amount of pressure to produce numbers to satisfy the business end of their work. As a result, they lean on the art department for pre-vis assistance. This reinforces our ability to keep a control on our design but, at the same time, it complicates the efficiency of the art department workflow.

● *Could the solution to this issue simply be to combine both departments?*

Yes, at the very least. Classically, you have two pretty big egos as the heads of those departments. In VFX, some people just want to get the shots done and some want to design. This fact is where the problem lies. Also realize that pre-vis is now governed by the visual effects department. Pre-vis is created and organized by them, and they only come to the production designer for material. Historically, all sequencing was conceived by storyboard artists and production designers in the art department. These days production designers have been glad to give that up for two reasons: 1) many don't understand storyboarding and blocking of action sequences; and 2) the design job has become so complicated that taking on the directing of the sequencing by spending time with set modelers and pre-vis people is really more than one person can handle. I do feel that this can be managed by the supervising art director if the pre-vis department were a formal part of the ever-expanding art department. Currently, it's not because of budget costs. VFX uses small pre-vis sketches, if you will, to get prices from visual effects houses as they are compiling their larger film budget. So, once again, the pre-vis process is stuck somewhere between the two departments mostly because the costs as seen through pre-vis are more key to the VFX budget and less to the art department budget. The reality of action, superhero films is the desire to enlarge the scope even more–that added pressure ripples through the visual departments, leaving little time to resolve the issues we're discussing here. It isn't a bad thing, necessarily, but just becomes a more complicated endeavor.[6]

In the final analysis, the Art Director as marketing manager currently has the task to promote the new and improved brand of the digital art department. Within this constantly evolving relationship, the focus has shifted from interdepartmental to intradepartmental, mixed media to merged media. Effectively marrying two peripherally related departments must be accomplished much like the merger of two corporate cultures. The Art Director at this point must wear yet another hat as "the human relations director" to effectively assist the smooth transition of both worlds.

ART DEPARTMENT SETUP

An art director contributes to the physical and creative setup of the art department by interviewing and hiring an art department coordinator, archivist, digital modelers, set designers, model makers, concept illustrators, storyboard artists and a graphic designer, as well as supervising extended art department personnel: prop master, set decorator and set dressers, set buyers, on-set decorators, prop makers, a mechanical effects coordinator, carpenters, welders, plasterers, foam sculptors, set painters and scenic artists, aircraft pilots, marine coordinator, and art department PAs.

When I worked on low-budget films, I got to do the jobs of 65% of all those people and be paid the salary of one. It was certainly worth the effort of all the sleep-deprived weeks as I gathered the firsthand knowledge of my new experiences as a department head in the art department. While navigating the world of Indies or rappelling the canyons of Hollywood, we hire our friends and tap into our carefully constructed networks. Pre-production is a time to carefully create the comfort zone by surrounding ourselves with the best creative team possible, which will enable us to easily outperform ourselves.

Even on the smallest staffed films, the art department tends to be the most densely populated working area of a movie. The creative team requires ample space to spread out to adequately perform our daily tasks. Square footage often comes at a premium; it is a benefit that this creative department has first dibs on workspace early in the pre-production process. During the first weeks of setup time, various department heads drop in on one another and the Art Director for regular, informally scheduled daily meetings. The Art Director is the managing director of this intradepartmental event (see Figure 2.2).

Art Department Coordinator

An art department coordinator is an indispensible, logistical angel. The position is represented by Local 871, now known as IA Local 871, Script Supervisors/Continuity,

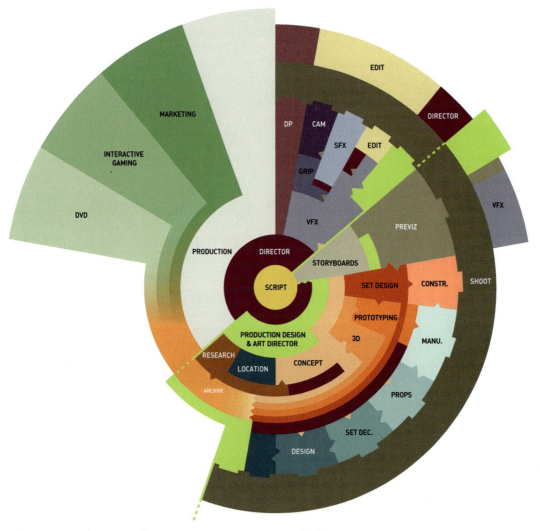

Figure 2.2a   The Revised Art Department. Courtesy of Alex McDowell © 2002.

Coordinators, Accountants and Allied Production Specialists Guild. This job title is short-hand for an efficiency expert who establishes the tone of the department through common sense, organizational skills, and friendly coercion.

First duties include the mutual planning of the physical space, defined by a section of an office suite in any of the Hollywood studios, or the dispersal of trailers-on-wheels or warehouse space at base camp on location. Given the limits of the existing space, the art department takes physical form. Art director and production designer ideally occupy adjoining rooms or share an office with a door and a bulletproof window. The bullpen is

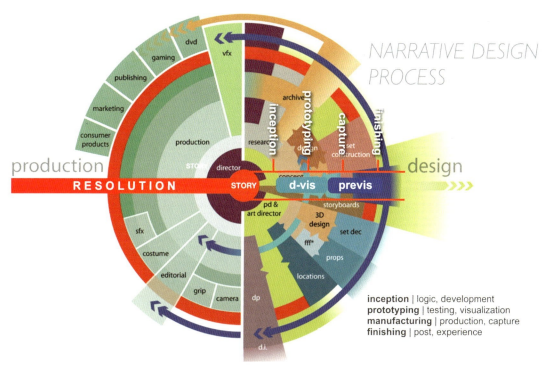

Figure 2.2b This overlay of the "Narrative Design Process" indicates how the basic story of a film/TV production exists as the foundation for the d-vis and previs processes, driving the "inception, prototyping, capture and finishing" of everything from scenery to props to marketing.

supervised by the coordinator and contains various production assistants or PAs. It is the nerve center of the department containing two critical machines: 1) A color printer work-center with email, Internet fax, network scanning, scan to PC, scan to mailbox, and send from mailbox capabilities; and 2) A 36″ color plotter with print, scan, and copy capabilities. Accept no less. Before settling in with furniture, Ethernet and wireless Internet connectivity on top of a normal phone extension and routing system is mandatory. (This is particularly important for the archivist's basic needs.) Believe it or not, lighting requirements can also enhance creative performance. A quick purchase of a dozen clip-on lamps that can be directed to a wall or the ceiling easily combat the flicker of ubiquitous fluorescent lighting, visually competing with PC screens. Indirect, subdued lighting psychologically establishes a calmer, more inviting environment.

Beyond providing the physical comforts for the art department crew, functional and political skills are also necessary. A coordinator should be computer literate and equally comfortable with the functioning and interfacing of PCs and Macs to ensure the quick creation of word processing or image-making tasks. No doubt many of the folks in the art department will be creating Mac files to be shared with people both inside and outside of the art department. In that case, it is necessary to be well versed in negotiating both platforms.

In addition to basic organizational ability, a coordinator's most hirable skill is the ability to research anything—quickly. Even a contemporary, non-period film will require Web research for specific visual information and also mining hard-to-find data. When I was working in Luxembourg as my own coordinator, reliable Web connectivity provided most of the visual data on WWI research for France, Belgium, and the surrounding area despite the fact that the data was extracted from the University of Kansas historical archives. Once within the site, I simply typed in search words for specific images I needed, and the server's search engine did the rest. Without it, even the small library of reference material we amassed before leaving for Europe would not have given us the depth and range of visual and text data the project required.

A coordinator's most vital job is dealing with clearances. Michelle Collier (*Water for Elephants*, *Iron Man 2*), art department coordinator for *Glee* eloquently describes her position.

Interview with Michelle Collier

- *Would you draw a comparison between film and episodic TV art coordination?*
  In film, the coordinator tracks clearance but we don't actually pursue the clearance, whereas in television, the clearance people are so overwhelmed by the sheer number of shows to service, that their response to needing to clear a photo of Barbra Streisand, for example, is: "Great. Here is her agent's phone number." Both clearance and product placement coordinators are hired onto a film as separate department heads; television requires coordinators to wear several hats.

- *In your working experience, how does archival work figure into the mix?*
  Technology has simplified our jobs but also has complicated them as the advancements continue. Now, job duties have been divided into specialized people. For example, the digital asset manager is now a part of the art director's union and is hired as an assistant art director. When I was working on large features before *Glee,* our digital asset manager was an advanced PA. Tracking the daily activity on the server is the basic job description. It includes digital files from set designers, concept renderings from off-site illustrators, transferring data and keeping an eye on all current updates. During my most recent films, this person was hired by production, specifically as a highly paid PA assistant to the production designer. I think the trick is to find a person who is art department savvy but also has deep enough IT skills to really run the servers. And, because the trend is to have people work from home, appointing a digital wrangler to remind people at the end of the day to download into their dropboxes is very important.

- *So, what we're now discussing is the physical shrinking of the in-office art department.*
  Where the computer screen actually sits is becoming a non-issue. It saves production money because they don't have to buy a big bullpen for ten set designers and five concept illustrators. There are pros and cons to this argument. And it's discussed on every show I've worked on recently. I think the answer to this is subjective and it is finally about what works best for the designer and the film.

●	*Back to your responsibilities: please talk a bit about clearances for film and Glee on TV.*
In terms of how a group of studio lawyers will interpret a clearance question, it's probably harder on a film because you actually have to get the item cleared. On a TV show, due to time restraints, it's all about risk management. If something is seen as a high-risk clearance issue then I will be told to clear it. The exceptions to this are: background set dressing or incidental prop usage not specifically called out in dialogue. Back to film: saying something has not cleared is not an option. Transitioning onto episodic television, the actual possibility of clearance is determined by the amount of time you have. I think it's safe to say that it's more about gambling on a show like *Glee*—simply because scripts will sometimes arrive the night before shooting—in which case, there is no way to clear something in that timeframe. Back in the day, they let just about anything go unless a prop was specifically called out in a script. Then sometime in the 1990s manufacturers realized they could sue film companies who had not gotten permission to use a specific product. This scared the studios into the current process of paying for use of artwork and graphics. The trend I've recently noticed on *Glee* is an interpretation, led by the HBO model: if an artwork created by an artist like a book cover is being used as intended, in a non-derogatory way, it's used without any real worries. *Glee*'s current concern is less about product usage and more about re-creating previously created work; for example the re-creation of the original choreography for *Rocky Horror Picture Show* proved to be problematic after the fact. Again, *Glee* remains a special case in terms of these **grand rights** issues that arise as we showcase each homage in many of our episodes. If you've paid for the grand rights to the play *West Side Story,* then you are permitted to reproduce it in its entirety as it was written. Changing choreography or satirizing it would put you in violation of the grand rights agreement because you have, in a sense, degraded the original product. Many times on *Glee* we're uncertain while prepping an episode whether or not purchasing grand rights is necessary or not. This continues to particularly be the case with our musical numbers. So, if you decide not to pay for grand rights then you are forced to change everything, or be sued for copyright infringement. These are questions and answers that need to be resolved before we begin the design process. Consequently, life on an episodic show like *Glee* is particularly challenging.

●	*And, finally, product placement lands outside of your jurisdiction.*
Yes, a good percentage of product placement is covered by the set dressing department (e.g., furniture, cleaning supplies, or musical instruments)—the rest is the responsibility of the property department. Product placement by props is very dependent upon what is called for in the script. What originally started as featuring specific products has now become all about blended brand integration. A smartphone is seamlessly worked into the action of a script, highlighted subtly as an everyday object—the scene is shot with the advertising for the product embedded into it. Regardless, a clearance form still needs to be signed; usually promo houses connected to companies whose products are being repped will sign the forms because they are doing the placement work. Intent is still a key issue. Here is a typical scenario: a shot begins with a close-up on a Toshiba keyboard piano logo and tilts up to the featured player. Network came back after viewing this scene and said: avoid this usage. Even though it had been properly promo-ed, the network maintained it could present possible legal problems, most likely due to advertising

conflicts. So, it would seem that it might be easier to secure placement of product into a show, the fact is: it is just as surprising a challenge as any clearance issue.[7]

Archivist

Archiving is a new concept borne out of technological necessity. The paradigm shift from traditional to digital filmmaking combined with the ubiquitous use of laptops in the workplace has reinforced our daily reliance on digital media tools. In fact, the movie business is populated with first adopters of new technology gadgets. The collecting and cataloguing of imagery is a specific skill necessitating a fulltime position in order to satisfy the needs of the digital art department. So the digital station of the **digital asset manager** was born. (The abbreviation DAM also refers to "digital asset management.")

Created as a practical job to handle the load of thousands of images created and shared, the need quickly arose in other related departments on larger, well-funded films—now every size film can use the skills of an archivist. This digital station requires a computer server to be maintained either by the archivist, preferably with some IT training, either in the same room or via an online service or both. A highly skilled PA would normally be employed as an assistant to the archivist and savvy computer techie for the art department. If a server is a budgetary impossibility, then an online service with high-speed capability could handle the upload/download volumes and size of documents relayed during the course of a busy day.

It's much more cost-effective to email images than physically messenger them. In most cases, an archivist's box rental might include a top-of-the-line oversize scanner and inkjet color printer in addition to the typical list of required gear: laptop and digital camera. If not, the production should consider these technical purchases for communal use in the art department. This team member needs to have impeccable imaging and technical skills, as the art coordinator needs similar troubleshooting familiarity with the copy and fax machines. Without an archivist, the speed of visual exchange is extremely hampered.

From a recent interview, J. André Chaintreuil, digital set designer (*Spider-Man 2, The Terminal, Superman Returns*), recalls his experience on *Minority Report* (2002):

Interview with J. André Chaintreuil

Alex McDowell, production designer of *Minority Report,* understands the computer and how to take advantage of it in the modern art department. He did an incredible setup for the production, one I'd only seen at that level in his art departments. He had a server set up for the show that everyone could access with his/her own dropbox on the server and there was a full-time archivist/ IT person to maintain the system. Our PA, Sam Page, now a digital Senior Set Designer, had those incredible skills. We were encouraged to use the server to archive, share key images, drop and pick up files from one another, and collaborate on designs within the department. It was also great for passing jokes and mp3 files. Another fabulous aspect of the server was watching the progress of the construction as it unfolded through digital set photographs. Other departments were tying into the server with databases, making everyone's process with the art department a lot smoother. Basically, Alex was imitating a modern architectural office by setting up an infrastructure that allowed all involved to share access to top-of-the-line color laser printers, plotters, and of course, file sharing. The server helped the flow of information in the department a great deal.

- *How do you casually give someone a file if you're not using the server?*
  Sneakernet [Big laugh]. Burning a CD and walking it to the next person, or by using email, instant messaging, or a USB thumb drive, especially if there is no local server available.[8]

Digital Artists

It's no longer enough for an art director to solely be an arbiter of good taste. Lack of digital skills or at least a surface understanding of basic digital concepts will disqualify potential art directors from the running, especially on an animated flick. An intermediate skillset helps determine what is technically feasible with specific software packages, and enables easy expression of ideas between an art director and the digital staff. Consequently, this current prerequisite demands the advanced skills of your digital set designers, using Adobe Photoshop to tweak 2D and 3D imagery for **key frame** shots, or enhancing images modeled in Rhino and Vectorworks for digital drafting of scenery. From the perspective of digital artist and set designer, Luke Freeborn (*Lemony Snicket's A Series of Unfortunate Events, The Terminal, The Chronicles of Riddick, Van Helsing*):

> *Now, getting ideas out quickly is very important because you have much less time to do more work. As a tool, the computer only assists the workload. It will not magically make a bad designer a good designer, but it could make a good designer a faster designer.[9]*

On the TNT movie-of-the-week *The Hunley*, the Civil War submarine of the same name was drafted by our set designers in Charleston, South Carolina and transferred to the visual effects group, Station X Studios, in Santa Monica, California. They animated its submersion and underwater travel. Our draftsmen's skills combined with the animation skills of the visual effects department created three- to five-second sequences of uncompromising reality. Ability to speak the languages of Lightwave and TurboCAD made my presence more credible to the digital artists in both locations.

Set Designers

Digital or traditional patience is a virtue, evident especially in set designers. Draftsmen constantly redraw whatever they have already drawn. With the assistance of the archivist, every Rhino and CAD document fragment, or drafted scrap of tracing paper, or napkin scribble can be scanned and saved to help ensure that erasures and revisions can happen a lot easier. Draftsmen who are manually <u>and</u> digitally adept are very desirable—this double indemnity insures performance whether the power is on or off (see Chapter 4 for additional information).

Set Decorator

The set decorator is the most valuable player in the art department. The production designer and art director create the structure for a film by defining its concept parameters. The set decorator provides context, subtext, and texture. In a 2004 Film Society tribute to Bob Boyle (*It Came from Outer Space, Saboteur, Cape Fear, The Shootist, The Birds*)—then a Universal Studios design legend at 94, he sadly passed away at the age of 100 in 2010—he clearly defined the camera as a stand-in for the audience, in terms of point of view. Taking this concept he learned from Alfred Hitchcock a step further, he suggested that subtext, "the underlying personality of a dramatic character as implied by a script or text and interpreted by an actor in performance"[10] can be implied in scenic terms and interpreted by the set decorator. Bob Boyle also reminded us that, "Visual narrative supports the storytelling. A jail cell can telegraph volumes of information; it can be blatant or whisper in subtle undertones. Without this vital information present to visually guide us, the most well-articulated design spaces remain as impressive but empty icons." Cloudia Rebar (*Vanilla Sky, Without Limits, Mr. Wrong*) sees set decorating like skydiving:

> *Working in film is like jumping out of an airplane 12 hours a day–striving to get it right and constantly realizing you've just pulled off another miracle is exhilarating. Being on that edge and riding that adrenaline rush keeps my attention sharp, keeps me going.[11]*

Leadman

A leadman (as opposed to lead man) is an art director's on-the-ground man.

As a set decorator—like a production designer—live in a conceptual world, someone has to make practical sense of the set dressing. The most practical guy on the set and liaison between construction, paint, lighting, **SFX** and rigging grips, your leadman and his band of merry, can-do guys otherwise known as the swing gang, assemble chandeliers, install window treatments and hotel parquet floors or, load five-ton trucks regularly. These are Union men and women guaranteed 60 hours a week, or five 12-hour days to fetch the decorative crust for this Beef Wellington we're preparing.

He and I show up for early morning work at the same time, to troubleshoot. Keeping one another on pointe—we check and double check questionable script points against each others interpretations of the concept meeting. We also spread gossip in order to get to the bottom of what we're shooting tomorrow; not having a clear idea what you're preparing for from one day to the next is expected in episodic television. Our problem is we need to be several days ahead of the shooting crew because we present the initial creative vision after the Director's. Once we're headed off the set, then the finishing touches of the grip and lighting crews can happen with enough time for all departments to have "last looks", before the camera rolls.

Greensman

A Decorator's domain extends beyond the interior confines of built scenery *onstage* to the great outdoors. A greensman and crew exist as an extension of the set-dressing department. The scope of a film determines just how involved an art director is in the process of greens dressing, especially if the location is a sensitive one in terms of contract stipulations. Otherwise, the set decorator will supervise the detailing of landscaped exterior sets according to the specifications of the script and a designer or director. The greensman is available to the Set Decorator and Art Director as an expert botanist and landscape architect.

Prop Master

This is the realm of cinematic detail both literally and figuratively. In general, the broad strokes of a set decorator are distilled into minutiae in this position. Specifically, whatever an actor touches as a hand prop in the blocking of a scene becomes the focus of a prop master. An ancient coin or a cell phone can be fabricated or real, and is either found on the prop man's truck or procured by the Prop Man. If it's a hero prop, it must be run by the scrutiny of the Art Director before it is used in an extreme close-up (ECU) shot. Mediating the efforts of prop persons and the final decision-making process of the Director illustrates how the Art Director controls the visual concept of the film down to the design of a matchbook.

Construction Coordinator

Before the stateroom of the *Titanic* is painted and dressed, the literal framework of that set contained within the larger boat must have a solid, shootable structure. Every construction coordinator is a practical expert in answering questions of physical and structural problem-solving. For example, is it more efficient to build a three-story shooting platform out of steel tubing or standard wood construction? Given the material, what is the maximum weight, including the camera, that the platform will support? Translating that figure into people, what crew size can easily be supported? Can the same platform be built in modules so it can be reused for other scenes and be durable enough to transport and reassemble? Despite the fact that construction reference guides like *Architectural Graphics Standards* or Sequoia Publisher's *Pocket Ref* can help an art director determine the answers to those questions, it's always best to compare notes before making these decisions.

As an operations manager, the head carpenter's domain includes his immediate staff of foremen and gang bosses, and then scores of prop makers (carpenters), laborers and painters as support crew. A labor force this size requires close daily scrutiny of man-hours worked and materials used. These budget items are the direct responsibility of the Construction Coordinator, although the Art Director is ultimately responsible for potential budget increases and modifications.

It is also important to mention that the detailing work of the Lead Scenic Artist, who operates under the aegis of the Construction Coordinator, conveys subtext for the visual narrative of set dressing. The literal application of paint color, wallpaper, texture, aging, and surface sealing complete whatever "local reality" is necessary to properly finish the look of the set. Contrary to what one might guess, this is the responsibility of the on-set scenic artist and not the Set Decorator regarding the fabrication of mechanical and hand-written signage, for example, used ultimately as on-set dressing. Working with the shooting crew, this specialist's scenic skills provide on-set solutions for on-the-spot signage, scenery touch-up, and aging of vehicles.

Mechanical Special Effects

There is a significant amount of overlap between this sub-department and construction. Generally, the fabrication of any special piece of mechanical scenery used in a scene is the responsibility of the mechanical effects coordinator. The rotating, interior module of a Mars shuttle for the Disney comedy *RocketMan* (1997) is a perfect example of this shared responsibility because there was a safety factor involved in the flawless operation of the **gimbaled,** revolving set. The welded steel construction of this human-size hamster wheel was finished by the carpenters and scenic artists to match the rest of the space shuttle interior set. On the same project, Jeff Jarvis, the Mechanical Effects Coordinator (*Cast Away, Always, Firestarter, Poltergeist*), also supervised the design and functioning of a full-scale centrifuge with a locked-off camera mount, allowing the Director to shoot the effects of g-force at variable speeds. Live action sequences like these support script requirements for most action films and utilize the expertise of such specialty artists. A more common name for the mechanical effects supervisor is the Special Effects Supervisor.

Stunts

Traditionally connected to the mechanical effects department, stuntmen straddle both the **below-the-line** section of the film crew and the directing department, as physical effects consultants and second unit assistant directors. Although not necessarily connected to the art department, their active participation in the mechanical effects department requires close scrutiny of how a certain stunt will impact the look of a film and consequently will need to be art directed.

This sub-sub-department is an exceptional case, requiring the attention given to hero hand props, for instance. In most cases, the lead stuntman will most likely request **breakaway** scenery (shatterable plate glass) or breakaway props (shatterable glassware, furniture, etc.) for action scenes and fight scenes from the art department. An art director's only significant responsibility here is to insure that whatever is requested by the stunt coordinator makes its way to the set for shooting.

Visual Effects and Pre-visualization

This subject has been briefly addressed earlier in this chapter ("The Relationships"). Victor Martinez, a digital set designer and concept modeler for *The Cat in the Hat* (2003), shares some additional observations.

> *Alex McDowell, Production Designer, typically includes the pre-vis department within the art department. He doesn't use pre-vis as a conceptual design tool as much as a device for dealing with more pragmatic issues. A pre-visualization environment will tell him if a camera will be able to fit into a small set, or whether we might consider shrinking the size of a set or enlarging it, depending on the needs of a shot. This aspect of our new technology encourages directors particularly to make those decisions confidently way ahead of time. A production designer like Alex can more easily help inform his director and then inform me, someone who is involved in more conceptual set designing, of my direction. As the boundaries between the art and pre-vis departments get more blurred, our definitions become less clearly defined. On The Cat in the Hat, I routinely exported pre-vis digital models of the sets I was working on, so that they could be used as models in their proprietary 3D modeling environments.*

Transportation

Picture vehicles, or hero cars, are shot in just about every film and this art department related sub-department provides them. In addition to its appropriate historical period, a vehicle might need to be found in triplicate or quadruplicate for work in mechanical effects scenes or simply be dusted down with **movie dirt** by the on-set scenic artist to suggest aging and passage of time. Inevitably, "transpo" deals with every department because it is responsible for parking caravans of talent trailers, five-ton trucks, production trailers, and crew vehicles on all off-studio location sites. This department is directly related to the locations department.

At this point, it should be abundantly clear that the influence of an art director's supervision and management skills extends consistently into many creative areas. Lists and schedules help keep us organized, consistent decision-making skills help keep us focused on the designer and director's visual concept, and hiring the best talent available ensures the best quality of the art department product. One department not yet described in this chapter, the locations department, shares a unique relationship with the art department. It qualifies for being included as an integral part of Chapter 5: The Physical Design because of the extensive role it plays in assisting to establish all locations-as-sets outside of the controlled studio soundstage environment.

NOTES

1 Christa Munro interview, September 11, 2004, Flintridge, CA.

2 Gae Buckley interview, September 11, 2004, Studio City, CA.

3 Christa Munro interview.

4 "There are four principal reasons why this operates: construction costs are reduced, costs of purchased materials are also cut, fixed costs are spread over many units, and process advantages are found by avoiding bottlenecks as much as possible." Krajewski, L., 1999. *Operations Management: Strategy and Analysis,* 5th edition. New York: Addison-Wesley Publishing Company, page 304.

5 Greg Papalia interview, March 5, 2013, phone interview.

6 Ibid.

7 Michelle Collier interview, September 5, 2013, Paramount Studios, Hollywood, CA.

8 J. André Chaintreuil interview, April 28, 2004, North Hollywood, CA.

9 Luke Freeborn Interview, May 6, 2004, West Los Angeles, CA.

10 *Webster's II New College Dictionary.* New York: Houghton-Mifflin Company, 2001, page 1100.

11 Cloudia Rebar interview, October 1, 2000, Studio City, CA.

CHAPTER 3

Visual History

The visual history of film and television can be distilled from what we understand about how we view "apparent" motion of moving pictures. It is generally agreed that the majority of people use vision to navigate through the world by interpreting the visual information they encounter. And, it is equally correct to say that the psychological processing of this visual information is known as visual perception. But here is where scientists and filmmakers have parted ways for more than a century; they disagree about *how* we perceive *what* we perceive. **Persistence of vision** is the myth in question. "It answers our central question of origin: Why, when we look at a succession of still images on the film screen or TV set, are we able to see a continuous moving image? We answer, 'Persistence of Vision.' Persistence of vision is the name given to the miracle by which the still silver halide dust of photography is transformed into palpable, living motion."[1] It is an inaccurate and inadequate explanation of apparent motion found in a moving picture—and it is wrong. Despite this, film scholars and theorists have perpetuated this myth since Peter Mark Roget titled a paper he presented to the Royal Society, "Persistence of Vision with Regard to Moving Objects" in 1824. A critical part of understanding these visual perception phenomena is that the eye *is not a video camera:* there is no "frame rate" or "scan rate" in the eye: instead, the eye/brain system has a combination of motion detectors, detail detectors and pattern detectors, the outputs of all of which are combined to create the visual experience.[2]

Still after almost two centuries, the myth stubbornly persisted until recent clinical evidence in: 1) perception of apparent motion vs. actual motion; 2) patients with akinetopsia: the inability to perceive objects in motion but the ability to see objects at rest; and 3) evidence that two separate physical/functional areas of the brain's visual cortex are each responsible for a) the processing of moving objects and b) the processing of shape, color and texture of objects. This level of experimentation, begun in 1993, has been providing concrete scientific answers—not self-perpetuating, romantic superstition—for people who demand them.

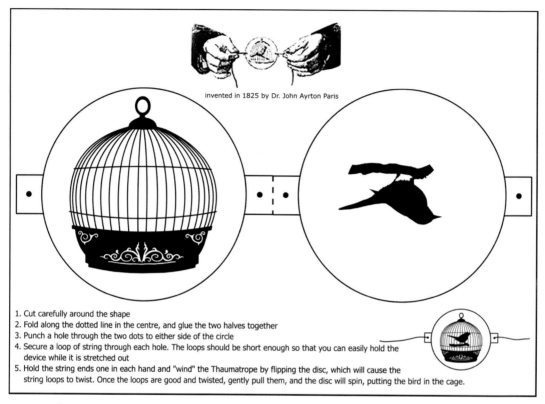

invented in 1825 by Dr. John Ayrton Paris

1. Cut carefully around the shape
2. Fold along the dotted line in the centre, and glue the two halves together
3. Punch a hole through the two dots to either side of the circle
4. Secure a loop of string through each hole. The loops should be short enough so that you can easily hold the device while it is stretched out
5. Hold the string ends one in each hand and "wind" the Thaumatrope by flipping the disc, which will cause the string loops to twist. Once the loops are good and twisted, gently pull them, and the disc will spin, putting the bird in the cage.

Figure 3.1   Thaumatrope: [Greek: "wonder-turn"] A card with different pictures on opposite sides, appearing as if combined when the card is twirled rapidly, illustrating "the persistence of vision". It was invented by John Ayrton Paris in 1825. This simple child's toy, as innocuous as it may seem to a twenty-first-century sensibility, held the dream of imagination, as the nineteenth and twentieth centuries merged.

This is important to address because you will inevitably encounter the notion of persistence of vision as you make your way through the industry, and you will have some facts at your disposal that will undoubtedly make you enemies. Having said this, one question stubbornly remains: why do intelligent film professionals continue to resuscitate this myth? Is it because the persistence of vision explanation has served so well in accounting for the origin of the motion picture? Probably yes. Furthermore, when some sleight-of-hand is pulled off exceptionally well, the spark of a dream is ignited. Just a simple, flickering image like the **thaumatrope** shown in Figure 3.1 feeds a compliant imagination as the rapid alternation of the cage and bird drawings are forged in the brain as a single image. This simple concept, obviously, is the basis for all filmmaking. The sequencing of images is common to media; all video and film images contain these sequences but at different rates. It is here, at the intersection of television and cinema images—**telecine**—where we will begin our comparison of both media styles.

TELECINE

Telecine enables the images of a motion picture, captured originally on film stock, to be viewed with standard video equipment. Playing a movie directly onto tape media in a television camera results in flickering when the film frame changes mid-field in the TV frame. You might recall that film is shot at 24 **frames per second;** this is the case for both physical film and digital film systems. It is important to distinguish between the frame rate and the flicker rate, which are not necessarily the same. In physical film systems, it's necessary to pull down the film frame, and this pulldown needs to be obscured by a shutter to avoid the appearance of blurring, so there needs to be at least one flicker per frame in film. To reduce the appearance of flicker, virtually all modern projector shutters are designed to add additional flicker periods.[3]

For the film's motion to be accurately rendered on the video signal, a telecine must use a technique called the **2:3 pulldown** to convert it from 24 frames/second to 29.97 frames/second. What does this mean? The obvious solution is to add frames to make up for the difference—much experimenting determined that there should optimally be two *frames* of film for every three *fields* of video, which results in a much smoother image display. (See the video at www.institut-lumiere.org/english/lumiere/cinematographe.html.)

This solution, formalized by the National Television System Committee (**NTSC**), although seemingly simple is actually quite complicated. Why attempt to do this in the first place? The answer lies in programming: in the early days of popular broadcast television—post-World War II, from 1946 to 1950—producers realized they needed more than live television programming to fill the airwaves. By turning to film-originated material, they would have access to a treasure trove of movies made for the cinema in addition to recorded television programming already on film that could be aired at different times. Thus, the telecine process was born out of necessity. Currently, to avoid 2:3 pulldown, film shot specifically for NTSC television is often taken at 30 frames per second.[4]

TELEVISION

Television is the triumph of the image over the printed word.
            Moses Znaimer, chairman/executive producer of MZTV Museum of Television

What then is the all-important and pervasive function that television emulates in our brain? Imagination. TV is a technological and collective imagination at work, much more so than film.
            Derrick de Kerckhove, Professor, McLuhan Program, University of Toronto

Telegraph, Telephone, Radio

It seems as though television has always existed in our cultural consciousness.

Television's origins are traced back among the developments of telegraph, telephone and radio over the course of a century, roughly 1837–1947. The nineteenth century particularly was a time of tremendous mechanical and scientific thought, experimentation, and technical development. The inventions of practical visionaries such as Hiraga Gennai, Samuel Morse, Alessandro Volta, Alexander Graham Bell, Nikola Tesla, Guglielmo Marconi, and Thomas Alva Edison signaled the dawning of information and communications technology. Mankind had always imagined connection with other cultures, but at this particular juncture in time, the experiences of

TELE *(far off)* **>< PHONE** *(to hear)*
TELE *(far off)* **>< VISION** *(to see)*

were imminent. At the advent of the nineteenth century, certain natural phenomena, which had previously been considered a mystery, were elucidated; the existence of electricity was a lab tested, tangible fact: Hiraga Gennai constructed the first friction generator in Japan; on the other side of the world, Italian physicist Alessandro Volta invented the battery. Both discoveries, mutually independent, provided a solid foundation for inventions to follow, and signified the naissance of a communications global shift.

An electrical telegraph was independently developed and patented in 1837 by American, Samuel Morse with the help of his assistant, Alfred Vail. They sent the first telegram in the United States in 1838 near Morristown, New Jersey (see Figure 3.2). The Morse/Vail telegraph was quickly adopted in the following two decades; the overland telegraph connected the West Coast of the American continent to the East Coast by late 1861, bringing an end to the Pony Express.

The telegraph and telephone are both wire-based electrical systems. The telegraph had been an established means of communication for three decades when Alexander Graham Bell began experimenting with electrical signals. Although commonly acknowledged as a highly successful system, the telegraph, with its dot-and-dash Morse code, was basically limited to receiving and sending one message at a time. Bell offered his own musical or harmonic approach as a possible practical solution. A "harmonic telegraph" was based on

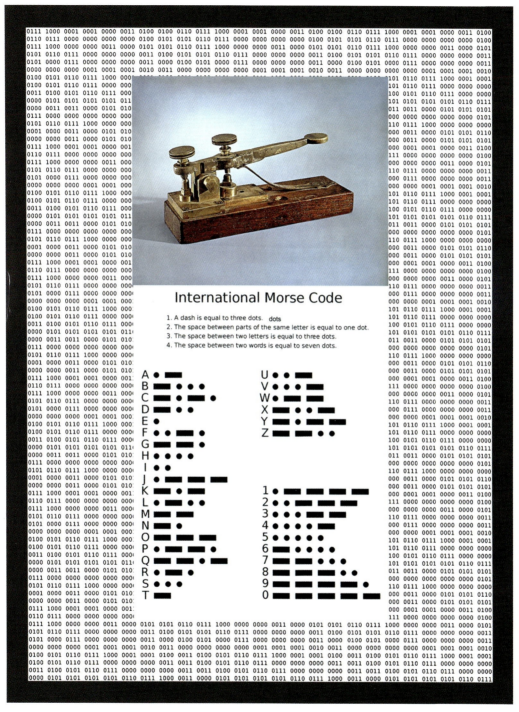

Figure 3.2   Morse Code Telegraph Machine and International Morse Code

the principle that several notes could be sent simultaneously along the same wire if the notes (or signals) differed in pitch. Although the idea of a multiple telegraph had been in existence for some time, Alexander Graham Bell's success with the telephone came as a direct result of his attempts to improve the telegraph.[5]

Videophone

By 1876, the first patenting of Alexander Graham Bell's telephone sparked the world's imagination. Early concepts of videophones and widescreen television hybrids (featured in *Punch's Almanack for 1879*, Figure 3.3a and 3.3b), inspired by European periodicals and

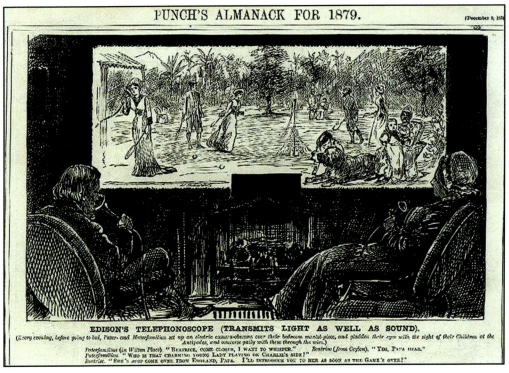

Figure 3.3a George du Maurier's cartoon for Punch's Almanack of 'an electric **camera-obscura**' is often cited as an early prediction of television. It also anticipates the videophone, wide screen formats and flat screens. The screen is approximately 2 meters wide and has an aspect ratio of 2.7:1, the same as Ultra Panavision.

The difficult to read dialogue on the image is printed here:

(Every evening, before going to bed, Pater- and Mater-Familiae set up an electronic camera obscura over their bedroom mantelpiece and gladden their eyes with the sight of their Children at the Antipodes, and converse gaily with them through the wire.)

Pater-Familiae: "Beatrice, come closer, I want to whisper."

Beatrice: "Yes, Papa dear."

Pater-Familiae: "Who is that charming young lady playing on Charles' side?"

Beatrice: "She's just come from England, Papa. I'll introduce you to her as soon as the game's over."

LE JOURNAL TÉLÉPHONOSCOPIQUE

Figure 3.3b Illustration: *"Le Journal Telephonoscopique"* (*The Telephonoscope Newspaper*) (1883). Albert Robida published a series of books in futuristic literature. This drawing describes the story of the telephonoscope, a conveyor of transmitting both sight and sound in real-time, anywhere—a truly visionary concept.

science fiction novels of the day, fed the feverish imaginations of everyday folks who, using the new communications device, boldly imagined that "objects or people anywhere in the world could be seen anywhere by anybody." Albert Robida, a visionary artist and writer, was also very much taken by this awesome invention. In *Le Vingtième Siècle* (*The Twentieth Century*), he depicts a future of fluid motion combined with sound via electronic transmission 24 hours a day, 365 days a year (Figure 3.3b). In his description of his **telephonoscope,** Robida gives us television, video, video-conferencing, and email all rolled into one, including the cable news channels. Robida likely saw a copy of *Punch's Almanack of 1879* while drafting his novel. Although these fantasy devices were falsely ascribed to visionaries like Alexander Graham Bell and Thomas Alva Edison, the simple truth was that popular culture was ready to embrace whatever realities they *could* manifest. Bell's mind was personally open to a similar idea he had been formulating—an electrical

FAR-OFF SPEAKERS SEEN AS WELL AS HEARD HERE IN A TEST OF TELEVISION

LIKE A PHOTO COME TO LIFE

Hoover's Face Plainly Imaged as He Speaks in Washington.

THE FIRST TIME IN HISTORY

Pictures Are Flashed by Wire and Radio Synchronizing With Speaker's Voice.

COMMERCIAL USE IN DOUBT

But A. T. & T. Head Sees a New Step in Conquest of Nature After Years of Research.

Herbert Hoover made a speech in Washington yesterday afternoon. An audience in New York heard him and saw him.

More than 200 miles of space intervening between the speaker and his audience was annihilated by the television apparatus developed by the Bell Laboratories of the American Telephone and Telegraph Company and demonstrated publicly for the first time yesterday.

The apparatus shot images of Mr. Hoover by wire from Washington to New York at the rate of eighteen a second. These were thrown on a screen as motion pictures, while the loudspeaker reproduced the speech. As each syllable was heard, the motion of the speaker's lips and his changes of expression were flashed on the screen in the demonstration room of the Bell Telephone Laboratories at 55 Bethune Street.

When the television pictures were thrown on a screen two by three inches, the likeness was excellent. It was as if a photograph had suddenly come to life and begun to talk, smile, nod its head and look this way and that. When the screen was enlarged to two by three feet, the results were not so good.

The New York Times
Published: April 8, 1927
Copyright © The New York Times

Figure 3.4   NY Times headline and first paragraph.

radiophone—by predicting: "The day would come when the man at the telephone would be able to see the distant person to whom he was speaking."[6] Imagine that! It happened at first, not quite as Bell had envisioned, on April 8, 1927: Secretary Hoover gave a speech that was televised in New York City on a 2″ high by 3″ wide monitor; the fidelity was perfect until the same image was projected at 2′ by 3′, when a lot of detail was lost. Still, the modern television media age was born during a political rally (see Figure 3.4 for the *New York Times* headline and article.)

Robotics and Radio Patents

It was Nikola Tesla's breakthrough discoveries in radio communication and AC power transmission, particularly, that literally sparked the light bulb in 1879. Most, if not all, contemporary inventors in the last three decades of the nineteenth century built upon the accomplishments of each other's work. As early as 1892, Nikola Tesla created a basic design for radio in a startlingly unique way. In 1898, he patented a radio controlled robot-boat and demonstrated its hands-free maneuvering in an exhibition in Madison Square Garden. Tesla's robot-boat operated simply: an antenna transmitted the radio waves; those radio waves were received by a radio-sensitive device called "coherer," which transmitted the radio waves into mechanical movements of the propellers on the boat. Tesla changed the boat's direction with manually operated controls from a command post. This first application of radio waves was a sensation and made front-page news. The father of remote control robotics, AC current, and wireless radio transmission laid a solid foundation for the technological achievements of the twentieth century to follow.

EARLY TELEVISION

Realize that the handful of nineteenth-century scientific breakthroughs that will be discussed in this chapter began as germinations in human collective consciousness many centuries earlier. The impulse to capture and behold the human voice and human image are as old as the song of the Homeric Sirens and the wonder of the camera obscura. And during this century, at every new turn "a significant breakthrough"—people conversing across the oceans, "another surprising discovery"—photosensitive emulsion, or "an improved version"—color rather than monochromatic TV: these developments seem inevitable, now. The 1800s signified a century of new science and engendered electromagnetic energy, transmission of human speech, and the birth of robotics, as well as Morse code and cathode ray tubes. Early television inventors attempted to either build a mechanical television system based on the technology of Paul Nipkow's rotating disks, or they attempted to build an electronic television system using a cathode ray tube developed by A.A. Campbell-Swinton. In the course of the next few pages, we will discover that electronic television systems worked better and eventual replaced mechanical systems.

Mechanical TV

Paul Gottlieb Nipkow

Many nineteenth-century European scientists like Guglielmo Marconi were focused on transmitting audio signals. Unlike most, one stand-out German engineer/inventor, Paul Nipkow, was fascinated by optics and the transmission of visual signals, and his elegantly simple mechanical invention in 1873 addressed this. The Nipkow disk was a rotating mechanism with holes arranged in a spiral around its outer edge (see Figure 3.5). As the disk turned one full rotation, an image of a lit object was scanned by the perforations in the disk, and light from different portions of it passed to a light-sensitive selenium photocell. The number of scanned lines was equal to the number of perforations on the spiral and each rotation of the disk formed a rectangular raster image on a projection screen.[7] Once the image was scanned and received, it could then be sent via radio waves to a receiver and the same rectangular raster image was displayed. These images were crude—mechanical viewers had the serious limitation of resolution and brightness. Also, Nipkow's system couldn't scan and deliver a clear, live-action image. No one is sure if Paul Nipkow actually built a working prototype of his television system; it would take the development of the amplification tube in 1907 before the Nipkow disk could become practical.

Nipkow recounted his first sight of television at a Berlin radio show in 1928:

The televisions stood in dark cells. Hundreds stood and waited patiently for the moment at which they would see television for the first time. I waited among them, growing ever more nervous. Now for the first time I would see what I had devised 45 years ago.[8]

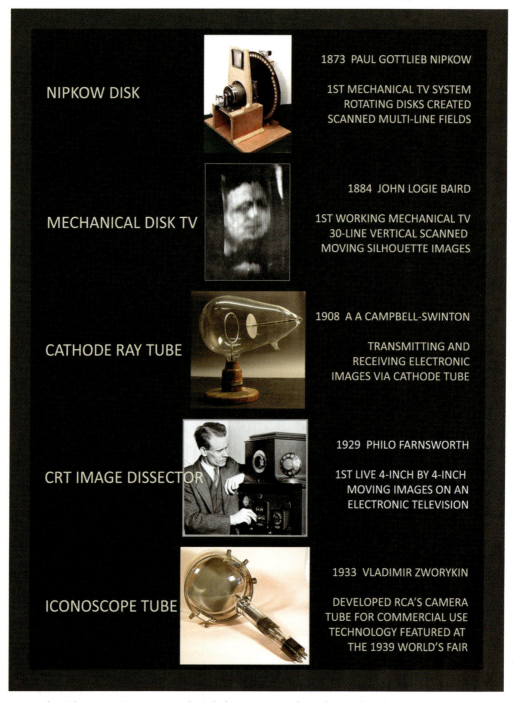

Figure 3.5   Early Television History: Landmark forerunners of mechanical and electronic television development.

Regardless of its shortcomings, this single invention challenged a handful of engineers and inventors to develop improved and marketable mechanical TV systems during the late 1920s.

Most improvements were encouraged by the amateur radio community through shared information, avid involvement and relentless experimentation. "Radiovision" was in its infancy and readily exploited by corporations like the General Electric Company whose three-inch "Octagon" mechanical television was just the beginning of mass production of these home entertainment products in 1928 (See Figure 3.6). That same year in partnership with RCA Radio, GE decided to test its 48-line television system by transmitting the first internationally recognized drama, *The Queen's Messenger,* in Schenectady, New York.[9]

John Logie Baird

The "Televisor," produced by the Plessy Company in 1930, was designed and engineered by John Logie Baird and quickly became Britain's first mass-produced scanning disk television which sold 1,000 units (See Figure 3.6). Lack of a common picture definition standard, inspired Baird to standardize 30-line vertically scanned image quality; by doing this, he demonstrated the commercial possibilities of the Nipkow system by sending the first television picture in October 1925. Using mechanical scanning with electronic amplification at both the transmitter and the receiver, his images were able to be sent by either radio or telephone lines over long distances. A televised demonstration of his mechanical prowess can be viewed at www.bairdtelevision.com/firstdemo.html.

Baird's improved technology preceded his first transatlantic TV signal transmission in 1928. Meanwhile, Baird continued to regularly broadcast public demonstrations. Surprisingly, the largest TV studios in Europe and the most powerful television transmitters in the world were not owned and operated by the BBC in the late 1920s to the mid-1930s. They were situated in the Crystal Palace in South London at the corporate home of Baird Television Limited. The BBC, eager for a stronger foothold in the burgeoning television industry sweeping Europe and America, formed an alliance with the popular Baird Television. With full, on-air service established in March 1930, Baird/BBC tested the entertainment value of its new service by broadcasting an adaptation of a short Pirandello play, *The Man with the Flower in His Mouth,* the second internationally recognized television drama broadcast.[10]

The broadcast was wildly embraced by popular culture. Regardless of this success and other public acknowledgements, Baird was plagued with financial troubles—a visionary first and businessman second, he sold his company to the Gaumont-British Picture Corporation. In 1932, while in England to raise money for his legal battles with RCA, Philo Taylor Farnsworth, an Idaho Mormon, met with Baird; he was seeking to develop electronic television receivers. Farnsworth conceived his television system in 1923, while still in high school (see Figure 3.7). Utilizing a cathode ray tube, his design predated Vladimir Zworykin's Iconoscope by a decade. In 1934, the year he met Baird, he was deeply entangled in patent litigation suits with RCA. By licensing the Image Dissector in Great Britain, he hoped to sidestep RCA and claim a piece of the European market. Baird was present in

1928   BAIRD MODEL "C" (BRITISH)

1928   G.E. OCTAGON (AMERICAN)

1929   SEMIVISOR (FRENCH)

1930   BAIRD TELEVISOR (BRITISH)

1934   PIONEER TM3 (RUSSIAN)

Figure 3.6 Popular Mechanical Televisions of the 1920s and 1930's.

London for Farnsworth's demonstration of the Image Dissector and was stunned by what he saw. The best resolution Baird had achieved was 180 lines per frame: Farnsworth's Image Dissector displayed an astounding 300 lines per frame. Gaumont-British's executives were also duly impressed: they signed an agreement with Farnsworth and gave Baird the task of putting the Image Dissector at the core of a new television system. "Baird and Farnsworth competed with **EMI** for the UK standard television system, but EMI merged with the Marconi Company in 1934, gaining access to the RCA Iconoscope patents. After trials of both systems, the BBC committee chose the Marconi-EMI system, which was by then virtually identical to RCA's system. The Image Dissector scanned well, but had poor light sensitivity compared to the Marconi-EMI Iconoscopes, dubbed 'Emitrons.'"[11]

Electronic TV

All mechanical television systems (See Figure 3.6) were outmoded in 1934 by electronic television systems that hinged on the development of the cathode ray tube or CRT, aka picture tube. CRTs were found in all electronic television sets up until the invention of the less bulky **LCD** screens that we mount on our walls today. Large companies in the 1930s—Westinghouse and Radio Corporation of America (RCA) in the US, and BBC and Gaumont-British in England—were vying for the lion's share of the expanding TV industry. At this time, the collective brilliance of the three Scottish, American, and Russian inventors discussed here, was caught in the crosshairs of market share and profit at the expense of scientific breakthrough.

Science versus Commerce

A race to file the first patent for the "all-electronic camera tube" dominated the lives of Vladimir Zworykin and Philo Farnsworth. In 1929, while employed by Westinghouse, the Russian émigré Zworykin produced both the "Kinescope," a more sophisticated cathode-ray picture tube, and the "Iconoscope," the first all-electronic camera tube. Philo T. Farnsworth, presented a fully functional electronic television to the public in 1927. His device incorporated an "Image Dissector" or electronic TV camera tube, which he filed a patent for in 1930 (See Figure 3.5). An industrious and practical genius, Farnsworth was driven to produce a sellable television and, consequently, founded his company, Farnsworth Radio and Television, as his only solid financial back-up. Zworykin's financial ally was the formidable RCA Company, his employer, for whom he acted as the director of its Electronic Research Laboratory. In 1934, British-Gaumont bought a license from Farnsworth to develop and make electronic television systems based on his designs; in 1939, RCA did the same. Obviously, both companies saw Farnsworth as a main competitor and adversary.

The patent wars had begun and David Sarnoff, vice-president of RCA, was determined that his corporation would control television technology. Having spent $10 million on a major R&D effort, Sarnoff proclaimed the launch of commercial television at the opening of the 1939 New York World's Fair. To ensure the authenticity of this event, President

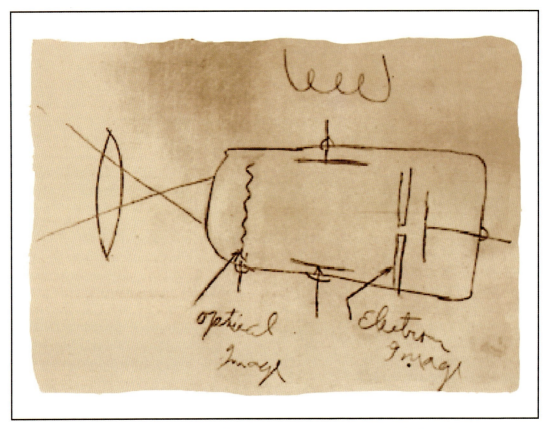

Figure 3.7   Philo T. Farnsworth's Television Design Sketch, done as a 15-year old. This sketch was compelling evidence that helped win a decade-long lawsuit with RCA over the validity of the first all-electronic television tube patent.

Franklin D. Roosevelt was locally telecast ten days later by the newly formed National Broadcasting Company (NBC)—although the camera used for the demonstration at the World's Fair was inadequate and Sarnoff and RCA didn't own a single patent.[12] Farnsworth's 1930 patent for an all-electronic television eventually forced RCA to pay $1 million in licensing fees in the 1940s. What won the patent court case was a sketch the 15-year-old Farnsworth did of an electronic television that his high school teacher presented to the presiding judge (See Figure 3.7). But by that time, Zworykin's system had won the race to the public for RCA.

Television development and marketing slowed during the course of the Second World War (1939–1945):

In 1946, there were only about 7,000 TV sets in American homes. By 1950, however, there were 10,000,000 and most of them, whether manufactured by RCA or others, used the same basic technology as Vladimir Zworykin's 1939 model. Even today, each of the 605 million TV sets in use world-wide gets its picture from what is essentially the "kinescope."[11]

Zworykin's "storage principle" continues to be the basis of modern TV.

TELEVISION PROGRAMMING

The official authorized launch of commercial TV by the FCC approved the NTSC standard of 525 lines at 30 fps on July 1, 1941—this was an American pronouncement not an internationally agreed upon formality. Programming styles differ from country to country, although American formats based on marketing, market share, and ratings provided a powerful benchmark for other nations. A television format describes the overall concept, premise, and branding of a copyrighted television program. The format is licensed by TV networks, so that they can produce a version of the show tailored to their nationality and audience. Formats are a major part of the international television market. Format purchasing is popular with broadcasters, for the following reasons:

- The lower risk and extra revenue potential associated with an already-proven idea.
- The ability to tailor a show for a particular market.
- The preference of national audiences to watch national programming as opposed to broadcasting the original, foreign version of the show.

Format should not be confused with genre. Genres are formed by conventions that change over time. The following list of genres of fiction, non-fiction, education, and entertainment are based on a specific set of stylistic criteria; older genres are archived as new genres are created. Note the multiple genre categories like "infomercial' which combine various conventions:

Action, adult content, adventure, animated cartoon, anthology, art television, children's, daytime television, documentary, docudrama, dramality, courtroom drama, legal drama, medical drama, mockumentary, educational, reality, fantasy, game show, music, news, police procedural, public broadcasting, religious, sci-fi, serial: episodic, soap opera, telenovela, sitcom, stand-up, sports, infomercials, variety show, western, space western.

For simplicity's sake, we will explore the serial genre, specifically the episodic format within this book. Serial genre tells one continuous story; each episode picks up from where the last one left off; the story arc usually shifts with a new season. Soap opera is a subset of serial storytelling, usually on every day of the week instead of once a week; remarkably, some have continued for more than 20 years: *All My Children, Days of our Lives, The Young and the Restless, General Hospital,* and *Coronation Street*—are the most internationally popular. Recall that modern television formatting is modeled on the existing radio broadcasting systems developed in the 1920s—this is especially true in the structure of the serialized story. Currently, a singular example of how a weekly television show based on an episodic, as well as musical format, is the internationally successful *Glee.* The show's cinematographer and colleague, Joaquin Sedillo (*Veronica Mars, Single Ladies, Memento*), shares valuable thoughts about working in television and creatively telling a story through the motion of the lens:

Interview with Joaquin Sedillo

- *Aside from the ability to be at home while working, what attracts you to TV?*
  The main reason for working in TV is the obvious stability for more longtime work that only a few blockbuster films will guarantee; employment for ten continuous months allows me to stay "in the groove" with the same crew, especially if you're lucky enough to work on a show that runs several seasons. Provided that personalities mesh well and as long as everyone does a good job and works hard and with integrity, then being able to go from year to year with the same crew intact is a valuable benefit. The kind of working shorthand that quickly develops with your crew after several seasons on a show such as *Glee* is a remarkable bonus.

- *Learning that shorthand and knowing the drill on such a demanding show as Glee is golden, isn't it? We all learned in a very short period of time to trust each other's skills and to actively watch one another's backs because when you're moving as swiftly as we do, there's no other way to operate. If I've got your back, then ultimately, there's safety for everyone.*
  Some people hate it, saying that's a sure way to lose autonomy, but I love it. Knowing we are going to see and shoot 75% the same sets, having the ability to look back after the 22-episode marathon and ask, "What would've made this easier?" The answer lies in a strong collaborative spirit. Kevin's new eyes on the sets have helped tremendously and his openness to make adjustments where necessary is also vital [Kevin Constant, the new production designer starting at Season 5]. For example, just adding 4' of ceiling along the main wall of the choir room has increased the realism/believability, as well as adding some upper clerestory windows has improved the visual interest to a well-shot, reoccurring main set.

- *Having said all this to support our working style, some detractors might insist that television work is less creative than film. Is there a shred of truth in that statement where laziness might be borne out of boredom and repetition?*
  The tone of every new episode provides opportunities for creativity, especially on a show about kids in high school. I suppose it's easy to throw up your hands in defeat and then shoot it the same way every time but I don't operate that way. Once the broad strokes for shooting two people walking down a hallway are established, flashes of creativity surprises me with splashes of light around the edges of a seemingly familiar shot. People can eat chicken five days a week but

if you've got the basic cooking down, then you can experiment with spices and new ways to prepare and present it. For me, interactive light just outside the edges of the frame invites us to explore the turn at the hallway intersection as the characters move through the space. Also, I'll do mirror reflections on the walls of a set to suggest sun reflection in the day or headlights at night of cars going by, or even a pulse of colored light washing on a wall at night to suggest the changing of a traffic light. Sometimes the light changes are just perceptible enough to add that layer of realistic truth to a set you've seen time and again. Through my creativity, I have a reason to bring the world from the outside into the space with the characters.

On a project I recently directed, if a scene needed to be shot in a small office set, for the sake of time, I would go in and get the meat and potatoes, then I'd get all the coverage through that window in the larger office space, if I could sneak in another camera I'd do another mini-master plate, then to finish in this room I'd place a camera at the back wall and shoot all this stuff on the desk but also include stuff beyond this window plane like partial faces of the actors, and maybe do a slight move or just sit here and let the camera find them. I'm very fond of putting the camera where most people wouldn't think of putting it. Back in this small office, even if the room didn't have a window in it, I'd still place the camera back here and ask the person at the beginning of the scene to open that door and walk out through it, revealing just a bit of the world outside of the room. Similarly, I've done the same thing in a restaurant: asking the actor to open the kitchen door and exit so we get a fleeting sense of the life in the next room. First, it gives me the depth I like to include and, second, it feels somewhat unplanned or impromptu, especially if it's appropriate to the story. It invites the audience to join the scene while discovering what's happening together.

NIELSEN

TV isn't just on the TV anymore, it's everywhere: it's on multiple channels on multiple devices—on your iPad, smartphone, and laptop. There were only a few hundred sets in the world in 1936 when Arthur C. Nielsen, founder of Nielsen Media Research™, invented TV audience measurement and analytics by investing in the first television-metering device. Today, Nielsen measures more than 40% of the world's viewing behavior—hundreds of channels, thousands of programs, millions of viewers—how they watch, surf, and stream.

Originally, companies that sponsored TV shows and networks that created them were contented just to know the most current Nielsen rating. Currently, this is still very much the case. Television, a consumer- and marketing-driven medium, relies on critical demographic models to provide a picture of the audiences of any given show, network, or programming hour. All information gathered reduces down to a comparison of two numbers: a number of the sample audience watching and percentage of TV sets tuned to the program. What does this ratio reveal about a program's content and coding? This powerful indicator measures two important things: ratings points and share, always indicated as "ratings points/share." A single national **ratings point** measures the viewership of a particular television program. For example, if there are 139 million television households in the US, then 1,390,000 is the sample used for the airing of that program. Ratings points are often used for specific demographics rather than just households—to describe *who* is listening rather than just *how many* people are listening. Nielsen re-estimates the number of TV-equipped households each August for the upcoming television season for accurate and timely rating samples.

> **Share** *is the percentage of television sets in use tuned to the program. For example, Nielsen may report a show as receiving a 9.2/15 during its broadcast, meaning that on average 9.2% of all television-equipped households were tuned in to that program at any given moment, while 15% of households watching TV were tuned into that program during this time slot. The difference between rating and share is that a rating reflects the percentage of the total population of televisions tuned to a particular program while share reflects the percentage of televisions actually in use.*[14]

Changing systems of viewing have impacted Nielsen's methods of market research. Understanding the detailed viewing habits of its audience is a powerful determiner of how a network or corporate sponsor sells its product via the chosen device at hand at the time of viewing. Three examples of broadcast reach in terms of "most watched international events," noted below, give a clear indication of how a potential audience is marketed to by companies:[15]

- On July 20, 1969, 530 million people—14% of the total population of the world at the time—watched the first man ever to walk on the surface of the moon.
- The 2008 Summer Olympics is the current record holder for a multi-day broadcast; Nielsen Media Research estimated that up to 4.7 billion individual viewers—70% of the world's population—watched some part of the coverage.
- The 2011 Cricket World Cup semi-final between India and Pakistan is reported to have been watched by about one billion people based on the available data.

Presently, Nielsen Marketing Research measures how consumers engage with media across TV, WebTV, online, and mobile, while continuously exploring emerging technologies. Improved television meters continue to provide a real-time, electronic snapshot of consumer viewing. Internet user panels provide immediate online audience metrics and they are now using on-device meters to record interactions with smartphones and tablets.

WEBTV

> *As consumers watch their favorite TV shows across Internet-connected devices, measurement in this area becomes critical to the long-term health of the entire industry.*
> *Jean-Paul Colaco, senior vice-president for advertising on Hulu*

Table 3.1   UK: Most watched TV programs—1981–2013.

Year	Programme	Date	Millions of Viewers	Network
	UNITED KINGDOM : Most Watched Programs			
1981	Film: Jaws	8 Oct 1981	23.30	ITV
1982	Film: The Spy Who Loved Me	28 March 1982	22.90	ITV
1983	Coronation Street	23 February 1983	18.45	ITV
1984	The Royal Variety Performance 1984	25 November 1984	20.55	BBC One
1985	East Enders	26 December 1985	23.55	BBC One
1986	East Enders	25 December 1986	30.15	BBC One
1987	East Enders	1 January 1987	28.00	BBC One
1988	East Enders	5 February 1988	24.15	BBC One
1989	Film: Crocodile Dundee	25 December 1989	21.77	BBC One
1990	Neighbours	26 January 1990	21.16	BBC One
1991	Coronation Street	25 November 1991	20.45	ITV
1992	Coronation Street	22 January 1992	22.45	ITV
1993	Coronation Street	22 March 1993	20.73	ITV
1994	Torvill and Dean – Olympic Ice Dance Championship	21 February 1994	23.95	BBC One
1995	Panorama Special: Princess Diana	20 November 1995	22.78	BBC One
1996	Only Fools and Horses	29 December 1996	24.35	BBC One
1997	Funeral of Diana, Princess of Wales	6 September 1997	19.29	BBC One
1998	World Cup 98: England v Argentina	30 June 1998	23.78	ITV
1999	Coronation Street	7 March 1999	19.82	ITV
2000	Coronation Street	3 January 2000	18.96	ITV
2001	Only Fools & Horses	25 December 2001	21.35	BBC One
2002	Only Fools & Horses	25 December 2002	17.40	BBC One
2003	Coronation Street	24 February 2003	19.43	ITV
2004	Euro 2004: England v Portugal	24 June 2004	20.66	BBC One
2005	Coronation Street	21 February 2005	14.36	ITV
2006	World Cup 2006: England v Sweden	20 June 2006	18.46	ITV
2007	EastEnders	25 December 2007	14.38	BBC One
2008	Wallace and Gromit: A Matter of Loaf and Death	25 December 2008	16.15	BBC One
2009	Britain's Got Talent Final Result	30 May 2009	18.29	ITV
2010	The X Factor Results	12 December 2010	16.55	ITV
2011	The Royal Wedding	29 April 2011	13.59	BBC One
2012	2012 Summer Olympics Closing Ceremony	12 August 2012	24.46	BBC One
2013	Call the Midwife	3 February 2013	10.85	BBC One

Source: http://en.wikipedia.org/wiki/List_of_most_watched_television_broadcasts.

Everyone reading this book is familiar with how Internet TV works. For our purposes, we will dispense with introductory information and reveal some facts about WebTV's history and its relationship to traditional television programming.

- **1995:** *The Spot* became the first episodic fiction website, and the first Web soap opera. It also received the first Webby Award for "Site of the Year."
- **1996:** The *Wall Street Journal* announced the coming of Web television. "Zenith Electronics is planning a television set that will incorporate a microprocessor and modem, as well as technology developed by Diba Inc. that allows viewers to surf the Web via a remote control device."[16] At that time, much of what computers did on the Internet was exchange text and still pictures because dial-up modems were ineffective for conveying the large packets of information required in sending online video data. To

effectively achieve this, streaming—not yet perfected—was crucial. Microsoft, the visionary software giant, bought WebTV in 1997. This company above all others understood the value of multitasking while watching TV—suddenly, the act of TV-watching would no longer be a passive endeavor. Viewers could check their email, surf the net, watch video, and listen to streaming audio simultaneously. As WebTV equipment evolved, MSN added a hard drive, a wireless keyboard, and broadcast television access; showing dominance in the marketplace, and changing the name of the company from WebTV to MSN TV to MSN TV2.[17] Microsoft opened the Internet TV playing field to many familiar companies, among them AOL, Amazon Prime, Hulu, Yahoo!, Disney, Sony Pictures, and YouTube.

- **2000–2005:** During this five-year period, streaming was perfected as broadband bandwidth increased in speed and availability; delivering high-quality video became ubiquitous. The Internet continued to grow as a marketing tool and outlet for independent creators to display their work. WebTV continued to improve in breadth and flexibility, rivaling network television. Online activity acknowledged the needs/behavior of its users. Creativity flourished and independent producers gained popularity, demonstrating that Web television was a legitimate medium, and that Web series would be more than a passing fad. Web Central TV, YouTube, Vimeo, and DailyMotion launched their services to deliver original video. The major networks and studios took notice of the trend, and began to debut their own original series.

- **2009:** The International Academy of Web Television was established; it is devoted to the advancement of the arts and sciences of Web television production. It initiated the first awards program for the web television industry, called the Streamy Awards.

- **2012:** Company executives report that users spent 50% more time watching YouTube, which now has more than one billion unique users each month and six billion hours of video uploaded monthly. In very raw terms, it's the biggest "television" network in the world.[18]

After some trial-and-error experimentation in the early 2000s, distributing online television is now accomplished by two delivery systems:

- Streaming from a single or multiple websites.
- Downloadable media, in the form of video podcasts.

Web television series are often distributed as video podcasts or **vodcasts.** Used for Web television they are typically short-form, anywhere from two to nine minutes per episode, relying on smartphones, smart TVs, PVRs, and tablets to deliver original shows or series to an audience. Typically vodcasts are used for advertising, video blogs, amateur filming, journalism, and convergence with traditional media. Next-generation WebTV users prefer to keep updated with their favorite episodic Web programming—variously called Web series, webisodes, bitcoms, minicoms, Web television, and cybersoaps—via the small screen. To quote one clever anonymous pundit: "Television isn't a medium, it's a small." This is the newest form of convergence—uniting film, TV and new media. Penny Bergman, first assistant director on the cybersoap *All My Children*, offers some observations about transitioning from a 41-year running traditional TV serial to WebTV:

Interview with Penny Bergman

● *Historically, a similar paradigm shift happened years ago when Guiding Light moved from radio to television. What is the biggest hurdle for your job position now that your original episodic TV format has changed to WebTV?*

When two of Agnes Nixon's soaps, *All My Children* (*AMC*) and *One Life to Live* (*OLTL*), moved from the ABC studios in Manhattan to the Connecticut Film Center in Stanford, our online production team faced a huge learning curve in two areas. The first challenge was the volume of our daily workload. Soap operas regularly shoot 100 pages a day. That's a lot of material and we go very fast. We were forced to develop a system to get our Connecticut crew–used to a feature film/nighttime episodic pace–up to speed in terms of preparation, endurance, and accurate execution. The sheer amount of production work we managed to get "in the can" every day was astounding. The following online interview explains it further, www.youtube.com/watch?v=a8bq0QLkZ2E.

Our second hurdle was to meld the film and daytime cultures together. For example, my DGA title is "stage manager" rather than "first assistant director." Although basically the same job, I assume this is a holdover from the early days of live TV when shows were produced on a television stage rather than in a film studio. Normally in the soap opera world, two stage managers run the studio floor. The crew had to adjust to listening to their stage managers' voices all day long, rather than having our usual non-DGA PA personnel on set relaying and reinforcing the AD's instructions. And we, in turn, adjusted by learning film crew job titles and specific responsibilities, so that we asked the right person to perform a task and got the necessary result.

● *Other changes are in programming: Soap operas were an hour format, now 30 minutes; formerly, the shows aired five days a week, now reduced to two days a week. What are the other significant changes that affect your working schedule?*

Back in the day, we shot a full hour episode in one day, just like a play: Prologue through Act 6, in order. Music and sound effects, opening and closing credits were laid in live. With the complete switch to digital editing, scenes from many episodes are shot, set by set. And rehearsal time has been drastically reduced. Although cost-effective, what has been lost is an intangible: the director's artistic vision for an entire episode. Also, on the network, we were used to working a ten- to 15-hour day, with only a few weeks off a year. For the Internet production, we alternate shooting five weeks of *AMC* with five weeks of *OLTL* production. And we try our best to get it all done in ten hours.

As we are pioneers bringing new *AMC* episodes to online viewers, the distribution model of how many shows per week are released has been fluid. It's really a grand experiment: the phenomenon of binge watching versus tuning in Monday through Friday at one o'clock to see your favorite soap means that online distribution models are being tested and new ones created as we go along. *AMC* really takes on twenty-first-century viewing patterns if people are watching ten shows at a time. Getting those completed shows in the can is our job, no matter what the distribution model. We shot our first 60 episodes for the Internet, and called it Season 1.

- *When we worked on* All My Children, *I remember getting in early, tweaking the dressing on sets while lighting was finishing up, then shooting, then breaking all sets down after the shooting day and resetting new sets in place for the following day's work. Same deal or different?*
  Currently there's a minimal amount of breaking down, resetting and transporting sets in and out of the soundstage. The big shift happens at the five-week mark when *AMC* production switches over to *OLTL*. In my opinion, Tim Goodmanson did a brilliant job of designing a flexible studio with both shows having permanent sets: **limbos,** one-off nightclubs, offices, and secret gardens were added on as needed.

- *Most of the money Prospect Park, the production company, makes will be from ads viewers see when they watch the shows on Hulu, and ads depend on viewership numbers. What do the numbers look like—more like TiVo numbers—as viewers tape then watch? Have the Nielsen ratings changed significantly?*
  Sorry, I can't answer that. All I know is that *All My Children* beat *Downton Abbey* and *Mad Men* in Hulu and iTunes downloads. And as of July 2013, the show is broadcast daily on Oprah Winfrey's OWN cable television network. So it's interesting that these soaps started on network, went to online, and then were picked up for cable.

- *On the Internet, they'll assume everyone watches everything, all the time, so there will be no filler and stories will move faster. On the Internet, you can also explore stories that might seem too risqué for TV, and use language that wouldn't cut it on a network. Is this a "brave new world?"*
  All My Children started on the Internet with language that would have been banished by ABC's Broadcast Standard and Practices—aka, the censors. Ironically now, two months into Season 1, Prospect Park has decided to scale back on the cuss words. So much for risqué.

YouTube's colossal success and the hype surrounding shows like *House of Cards*[19] have spawned an online original programming arms race. *House of Cards,* the original Netflix series, is particularly unique because it was created as a rental item for the Web company that produced it; extraordinary creative freedom permitted filmmakers to write, direct, and produce without undue supervision or second-guessing of a major Hollywood studio. This describes a new paradigm.

Production designer, Steve Arnold, talks about his design experience for *House of Cards:*

Interview with Steve Arnold

- *Did you encounter any new parameters while designing a film for Web release?*
  I wouldn't say that I was aware of very many differences in the process of shooting a series for the Internet. Having had no previous experience shooting a regular TV series, I don't have that much to compare it with. We typically shot two episodes concurrently (cross-boarded) so we could

combine work that shared the same sets. We shot these two episodes in 20 days, during which time we would be scouting and building sets for the next two episodes. Generally, we would get a new director for each two episodes who would arrive a couple of weeks prior to starting the shooting of their episodes. I'm not sure if this is typical in regular TV but I think it's the routine for things like HBO shows.

● *I have no experience with Web work, so I wonder: 1) how the prepping and shooting schedules were affected, if at all; 2) are budgets limited or extravagant at this point; 3) was director David Fincher wanting to be one of the first to explore the medium?*
This was kind of a first for Netflix producing their own content and I think they felt the need to provide adequate budgetary support, so although I would not characterize it as extravagant, the budget was definitely comfortable for TV. Since shooting in Washington, DC, is difficult at best and the storylines many times required very specific recognizable locations, we built a large number of stage sets (and still are for Season 2), many of which are expensive not only from the construction standpoint but also in terms of the set dressing.

David is always experimenting to a degree and is one of those directors who is ahead of the curve in terms of technology. We always had the latest cutting-edge camera and lens equipment. Knowing he would be saddled with many of the limitations of shooting a series (unlike his normal feature work), I think he went into it with a plan that still allowed him to shoot as brilliantly as usual. There was an enormous amount of pre-planning, pre-rigging and pre-lighting whenever possible so he could walk onto a set and shoot with no lost time.

● *On the Internet, they'll assume everyone watches everything, all the time, so there will be no filler and stories will move faster. On the Internet, you can also explore stories that might seem too risqué even for both Film or TV, and use language that wouldn't cut it on a network, for example. Is this a "brave new world?"*
A difference that is actually more of a writing aspect I noticed was that, with no built-in commercial breaks, the scripts tend to read much more like features; they are not broken into acts the way many TV shows are. Since they are made so they can be watched continuously, there is more flow in the stories like you might have in a mini-series or serial type features. I do think the face of TV is changing rapidly, as is the world of film, and when it comes to serious adult drama it seems to be finding a place beyond the glitzy blockbuster tent-poles of cinema and coming back to the somewhat smaller screens that the Web now services.

At the 2007 Encounter Generation conference, Kevin Kelly shared a fun stat: the World Wide Web, as we know it, was only 5,000 days old. So, Kelly asked, how can we predict what's coming in the next 5,000 days? We are constructing "One Machine," a single global source for everything. He suggests that every screen in the world is a portal that is looking into the One Machine. What originally linked page to page will soon link data system to data system or idea to idea, word to word, image to image. Through total personalization we will automatically surrender to and achieve total transparency. The coming Internet experience will be smarter and more ubiquitous; becoming an Internet of things. Finally, *we* become the One.[20]

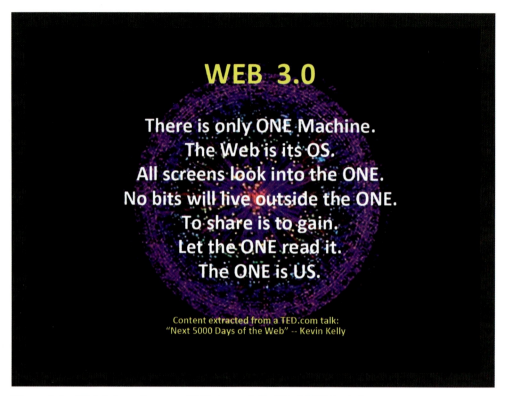

Figure 3.8   Web 3.0, or the next 5000 days of the World Wide Web

POPULAR CULTURE

American-derived popular culture—mass-produced for mass consumption by mass media—defines television and, in turn, how television itself defines the entirety of ideas, perspectives, attitudes, memes, images, and other social phenomena that evolve from within the mainstream of pop culture. It is quixotic and emerges from both the living room and the street. Ironically, folk life is often hidden in full view. From it, folklore arises. Folklore is the secret languages of children, the codenames of CB operators or screen names of bloggers, and the working slang of street-punks and doctors; it endures—from ancient to future—because it is an oral expression of the traditional, unofficial, non-institutional part of common culture.

Television is the forge of pop culture. Basically defined as lowbrow or less than intellectual, cultural pundits have dismissed this as merely a symptom of mass consumerism; a fundamental paradox: the increase in technological and cultural sophistication, combined with an increase in superficiality and dehumanization. Its critics run the gamut from

Gore Vidal[21]—"I never miss a chance to have sex, or appear on television"—to Alfred Hitchcock—"Television has brought murder back into the home, where it belongs"—to Camille Paglia[22]—"Television is actually closer to reality than anything in books. The madness of TV is the madness of human life."

For our purposes, this wide gamut of opinion can be reduced to semiotics: that television as a social **meme**—a unit for carrying cultural ideas, symbols, or practices—can be transmitted from one mind to another through writing, speech, gestures, rituals, or other imitable phenomena. In other words, memes spread by the imitated behaviors that they generate in their hosts. Television—*the* unit of cultural transmission—surpasses even the artistry of filmmaking in its transformative power simply because it is always "on."

Peter Wollens, film historian, supports the onset of this argument in an interview on the British Film Institute website:

> *I wanted to establish, first and foremost, that film was an art and therefore it should be studied for its own sake in the same way as the other arts–literature, painting, music, etc. At that time [1968], film was primarily seen in the context of the mass media, which led to a communications [semiotic] or sociological approach, rather than an aesthetic approach. Of course, viewing the mass media as art was polemical and provocative.[23]*

FILM

The moment there is imagination, there is myth.

Camille Paglia, intellectual feminist writer

Early Film History

Much like the development of early television inventions, film's origins in photography began earnestly in the early decades of the nineteenth century. The timeline in Table 3.2 (Please refer to this table at the end of Chapter 3.) makes it abundantly clear that there were many hands building the foundation of the film industry both in Europe and America. What is not evident is that the driving force from the onset of this process in 1827—the capture of Joseph Nicéphore Niépce's first image, "View from the Window at Le Gras"— was forged from intense competition for profit on both sides of the Atlantic, even then (See Figure 3.9). As with early television, the issue of patents also drove the engines of development, improvement, and delivery to cityfolk craving entertainment. We will examine

View from a Window at Le Gras -- Niepce -- 1827

Figure 3.9 "View from a Window at Le Gras", 1827, Claude Niepce, The Father of Photography. The top image, barely recognizable, is the first recorded photograph. The Sun was the light source that burned the image in eight hours onto a polished pewter plate. What remained after a mixture of lavender oil and white petroleum dissolved the leftover bitumen was a direct positive picture, less than a decade before British inventor William Henry Fox Talbot would produce the first paper negative. The bottom image is a reconstruction of the top image, originally taken almost 200 years ago.

the development of "visual toys"—mechanical animated objects made initially for entertainment—and the application of photographic experimentation and its ensuing processes, as two tributaries of the modern cinematic lexicon.

MECHANICAL DEVICES

Early experiments around 1830 with optical toys, the **phenakistoscope** (Plateau) and the **zoetrope** (Horner) showed that moving pictures could be generated from a series of rotating static images. The former illusion toy was a simple device holding two spinning disks parallel to one another; the images arranged around the outer edges of the back disk were seen as "moving" through the slots arranged around the outer edges of the front disk. The latter illusion toy was a drum perforated with slots placed between successive images on the inside of the revolving cylinder. Although one toy moved by a vertical axis spin as opposed to a horizontal axis spin for the other, the principle is the same: creating the magic of apparent movement. As these tabletop novelties were developed, the method of animating images became more sophisticated. A device patented in 1877, the **praxinoscope** (Reynaud) was an improvement on the zoetrope; spinning on a horizontal axis, the faceted mirrors of an inverted cone-shaped drum reflected the images from a disk below. Instead of using the inside of a rotating drum, it is the outside producing the animation (See Figure 3.10a). Unfortunately, these early machines could only accommodate very small numbers of spectators. Limited viewing was solved by the invention of the first image projector called an **electrostachyscope** (Anschutz). This invention enabled a small audience to gather in a parlor to watch a series of moving images on a clear wall surface or screen. Keep in mind, all of the images presented by these machines are illustrations *as* animations—flights of fancy frozen in a loop of repetitive motion. One of the more compelling, later peepshow devices was a **mutoscope.** Expanding the simple flip-book principle, the mutoscope contained a sequence of photographs arranged around the perimeter of a drum. A simple turn of a handle flipped the image cards on the drum rapidly, creating perceived movement. Viewers willing to have some fun could customize their experience by controlling the speed of the handle to fast-forward or reverse direction. This basic operation was quickly improved by Herman Casler and William Kennedy Dickson. They perfected a camera with a mirror device for the mutoscope (see Figure 3.10b). They called it the **biograph** and it was in operation by early June of 1895 with some of the first films taken by Dickson, an accomplished photographer, and employee of Thomas Edison.[24]

Unlike early television devices invented in the same century but developed out of scientific inquiry, all of these animated devices were demonstrated or sold as amusement novelties. The rise of the industrial wealth of the middle class created more time for leisure activity and the demand for inexpensive entertainment. (See Figure 3.11a and b). At same time, the rapidly developing photographic image was an exercise in mutual,

Figure 3.10a   Early Animation Devices

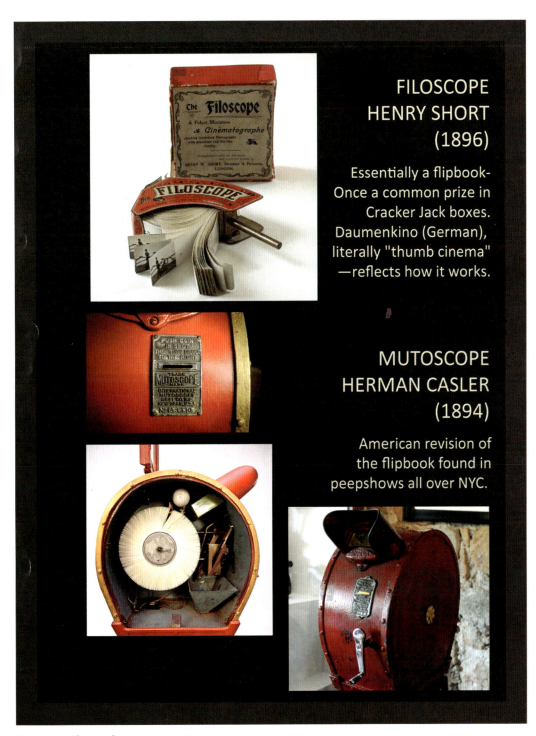

**FILOSCOPE
HENRY SHORT
(1896)**

Essentially a flipbook-
Once a common prize in
Cracker Jack boxes.
Daumenkino (German),
literally "thumb cinema"
—reflects how it works.

**MUTOSCOPE
HERMAN CASLER
(1894)**

American revision of
the flipbook found in
peepshows all over NYC.

Figure 3.10b Early Animation Devices

Figure 3.11a *Fred Ott's Sneeze* (1894)
W. K. Dickson. The first U.S. copyright
for an identifiable motion picture was
given to Edison.

Figure 3.11b *Dickson's
Greeting* (1891), an 18-minute
short experimental film.

competitive inspiration for European and American entrepreneurs. Other photographic
pioneers beyond the work of Niépce will be discussed in detail in the next section, "Photography." In addition, a timeline of early cinema advancements can be found in Table 3.2,
at the end of this chapter.

Thomas Alva Edison

The application of photographic principles and the production of photographic-quality cellu-loid in 1878 inspired Thomas Alva Edison and William Kennedy Dickson to develop their own, improved moving-picture device at the Edison Manufacturing Company. Edison was a practical and enterprising genius: a man of many patents. He made his fortune by taking his knowledge as a telegraph operator and creating the "stock ticker" and also a "sound-recording and reproducing-phonograph" the same year. Edison's laboratory was also responsible for the invention of the **kinetograph** (a motion picture camera) and the **kinetoscope** (a peephole motion picture viewer) both first publicly exhibited on May 20, 1891 (see Figures 3.12a, 3.12b and Figure 3.13) Regarding the kinetograph, Edison said several years earlier: "I am experi-menting upon an instrument which does for the eye what the phonograph does for the ear, which is the recording and reproduction of things in motion."[25] From his lab, he did the electromechanical design while his employee Dickson worked on the photographic and opti-cal development. Once the film was captured on the kinetograph and processed, it needed another device to display it, so the kinetoscope—an "Apparatus for Exhibiting Photographs of Moving Objects"[26]—was installed in penny arcades, where people could watch these sim-ple films. Viewers looked into a peephole in the top of a large wooden cabinet to see pictures moving as short, amusing animations. The Library of Congress, American Memory collec-tion features 341 Edison kinetoscope films, viewable online (see Figure 3.14a and b) at www. youtube.com/watch?v=vfqUjBDIkT8.

It's important to note that the development of the kinetoscope, particularly, was not Edison's alone; much of the credit for these inventions belongs to Dickson. Also, Edison's two-month excursion to Europe and the Exposition Universelle in Paris 1889, impelled him to rethink and improve on the work of Marey, Renaud, and Anschütz, respectively: for flexible film designed to capture sequential images at 12 frames per second; the first motion picture system to employ a perforated image band; and the electric tachyscope, a disc-based projection device is often referred to as an important conceptual source for the development of the kinetoscope. Without the initial groundwork laid by these three Euro-pean scientist/entrepreneurs, Edison would have little with which to return to America. He was a clever opportunist to file a patent for everything he encountered; upon returning from his European business trip, he filed a patent caveat which described a kinetoscope based not just on a flexible filmstrip, but one in which the film was perforated to allow for its engagement by sprockets, making its mechanical conveyance much smoother and more reliable. The Edison manufacturing lab also developed a motor-powered camera. To govern the intermittent movement of the film in the camera, allowing the strip to stop long enough so each frame could be fully revealed and then advancing it quickly to the next frame, the sprocket wheel system that engaged the strip was driven by an escapement disc mechanism (like that found in watches or clocks). The kinetograph was certainly the first practical system for the high-speed stop-and-go film movement that would be the founda-tion for the next century of cinematography.

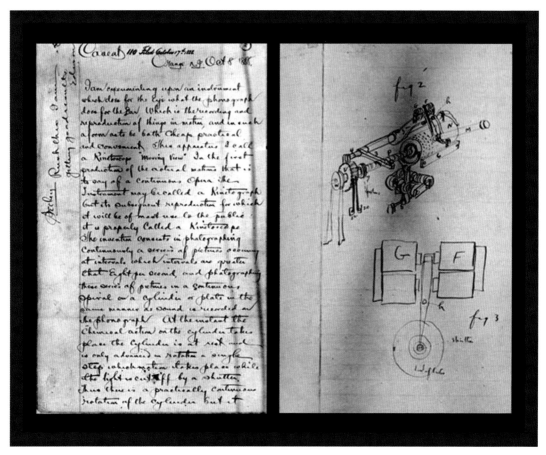

Figure 3.12a   Patent caveat page and Kinetoscope sketch. Patent filed October 8, 1888 by T. A. Edison. The full text reads: *"I am experimenting upon an instrument which does for the Eye what the phonograph does for the Ear, which is the recording and reproduction of things in motion, and in such a form acts to be cheap, practical and convenient. The apparatus I call a Kinetoscope 'moving view' in the first production of the actual motion that is to say of a continuous opera. The instrument may be called a Kinetograph but its subsequent reproduction for which it will be of most use to the public, it is properly called a Kinetoscope. The invention consists in photographing these series of pictures in a continuous spiral on a cylinder or plate in the same manner as sound is recorded on the phonograph. At the instant the chemical action on the cylinder takes place, the cylinder is at rest and is only advanced in rotation a single step which motion takes place while the light is cut off by a shutter."*

Say what you will about Edison, his appetite for generating idea into reality was prodigious. The revenue from the kinetoscope's success funded the next obvious direction for this American entrepreneur: the Black Maria (pronounced: mah-ráh-yah), Edison's movie production studio in West Orange, New Jersey. The first motion pictures made in the Black Maria were deposited for copyright by William Dickson, the company photographer, at the

UNDERWRITERS MODEL, TYPE B,
EDISON PROJECTING KINETOSCOPE
MADE BY
EDISON MANUFACTURING COMPANY, ORANGE, N. J. U.S.A.
MER'S SERIAL No 1645 SPECIAL LICENSE No 87

PATENTED : March 2, 1897

Figure 3.12b   Thomas Edison's Kinetoscope

Library of Congress in August 1893. In early January 1894, *The Edison Kinetoscopic Record of A Sneeze* was one of the first series of short films made by Dickson for the Kinetoscope in Edison's Black Maria studio with fellow assistant Fred Ott. As usual, Edison, the mechanical genius and showman, used *Fred Ott's Sneeze* for publicity purposes, as a series of still photographs to accompany an article in *Harper's Weekly Magazine*. It was the earliest motion picture to be registered for copyright.

But it wasn't the earliest American motion picture to be shot. William Dickson was filmed in an 18-second short of himself in 1891 simply titled *Dickson's Greeting*. It's obviously a clean, easy-to-read repeating image but it is unfortunately not as compelling as the "sneeze," so the boss pushed it aside. Edison completely understood the value of hype.

The Black Maria was covered in black tarpaper and had a huge window in the ceiling that opened up to allow sunlight in for shooting. It was cleverly built on a turntable so the skylight could rotate with the Sun's movement throughout the day, supplying enough natural light for hundreds of Edison movie productions over its eight-year lifespan. Apparently, the building was a cramped and uncomfortable place to work. Dickson and Jonathan

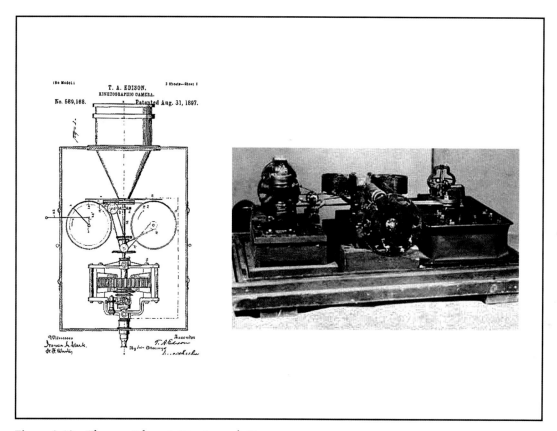

Figure 3.13   Thomas Edison's Kinetograph Camera

Campbell, another Edison employee, coined the name—it reminded them of police Black Marias (police vans or paddy wagons of the time) because they fit the same description. Edison, however, called it "The Doghouse."[27]

The Lumière Brothers

Auguste and Louis Lumière worked beside their father, Antoine, building a successful business manufacturing and supplying photographic equipment outside of Lyons. Louis developed a new "dry plate" process in 1881, at the age of 17, which revolutionized the development process of photography. In a span of three years, the Lumière Company was producing around 15,000,000 plates per year.[28] Antoine, by now a successful and well-known businessman, was invited to a demonstration of Edison's "peephole kinetoscope" in Paris. Edison had not paid the fee for international copyright; Antoine shrewdly challenged his sons to research and develop a superior product of their own. By February 1895, the brothers patented a machine

Figure 3.14b　*St. Anthony, a Woman and a Skull* (1900) William Dickson.

Figure 3.14a　*Butterfly Dance* (ca. 1895) William Dickson. This is a section of a 35 mm filmstrip featuring Annabelle Whitford Moore, in the format that would become standard for both still and motion picture photography around the world. A tinted film-base provides the coloration of this filmstrip.

combining camera with printer and projector and called it the **cinématographe.** Their device was much smaller than Edison's kinetograph, and was lightweight and hand-cranked. The Lumières employed a film speed of 16 frames per second, much slower than Edison's 48 fps—not only was less film used but the clatter and grinding associated with Edison's more cumbersome device was reduced. Most significant was the decision to include an idea that Edison had abandoned: to incorporate the principle of intermittent movement utilizing a device similar to one used in a sewing machine. The brothers quickly registered their patent in London in 1895 and began holding a series of soirées and screenings. Louis, the photographic prodigy, shot his first film, *La Sortie des Usines Lumière* (1895), of workers leaving the Lumière factory at day's end. Louis was prodigious in 1895, making nine additional films in preparation for their first public screening at the Grand Cafe on Paris's Boulevard de Capucines:

- *La Sortie des Usines Lumière* (*Leaving the Lumière Factory*)
- *La Voltige* (*Acrobatics*)
- *La Pêche aux Poissons Rouges* (*Fishing for Goldfish*)

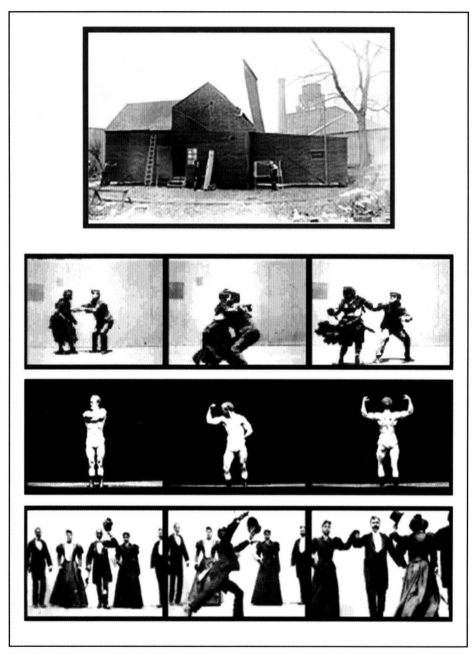

Figure 3.15   TOP IMAGE: Edison's Black Maria Studio. Look closely to see the edge of the turntable on which it rotates. BOTTOM STRIPS: These three images were taken (c. 1894–1899) at the Studio by William Dickerson: *A Tough Dance, Sandow the Strongman, Cake Walk*. Turn-of-the-twentieth-century copyright law provided protection for photographs but not for early motion pictures. Edison, among a number of clever early film producers protected their work by copyrighting paper contact prints of the film's individual frames.

Figure 3.16 Cinématographe (1895) The Lumière Brothers patented a machine combining camera with printer and projector—a major improvement on Edison's kinetograph and kinetoscope.

- *La Débarquement du Congres de Photographie à Lyons (The Landings of the Congress of Photography in Lyons)*
- *Les Forgerons (The Smithies)*
- *L' Arroseur Arrose (The Sprinkler Waters)*
- *Repas de Bébé (Baby's Meal)*
- *Place des Cordeliers à Lyon (Cordeliers Square in Lyons)*
- *La Mer (The Sea)*

By 1903, the catalogue of Lumière brothers films showed more than 2,000 films—prodigious indeed! The Lumière family once again capitalized on their mechanical/creative efforts and opened theaters called "**cinemas**" to present their films in London, Brussels, Belgium, and New York. Brilliant businessmen and showmen themselves, the brothers projected a film on a huge 99' by 79' screen at the Paris Exposition in 1900. Formidable!

PHOTOGRAPHY

Eadweard Muybridge and Étienne-Jules Marey

Two giants of photographic experimentation cross-pollinated in the 1870s and 1880s. Muybridge, an English professional photographer working in America, and Marey, a French scientist, were capturing motion and inspiring one another's work. How was this possible on two separate continents, divided by an ocean in an age without the Internet? News could only travel as fast as the swiftest horse or the fastest sailing ship; at the time, news rarely reached North America from Europe in less than two weeks. America and Europe were connected by telegraph cable by 1866, so it is plausible that the accomplishments of either man could be known within a reasonably short amount of time. It is also likely that exposure in journals specializing in photography—such as *Scientific American* and *La Nature*—chronicled groundbreaking technical developments. My point here is not to validate "who was the first" to prove that all four legs of a galloping horse were in mid-air for a brief moment, for example, but to say that the genius of both men outweighs a "nationalism contest." It might be helpful to look at Table 3.3—a brief timeline of the activities of Marey, Muybridge, and Edison's global movement and planned meetings—to get a sense of how scientific and aesthetic pollination occurred, and within how much time this actually did take.[29] You will also note that many European artists, such as Marcel Duchamp, were exposed to the work of Muybridge during his lectures and demonstrations while in Europe—a more extensive Muybridge timeline can be found at www.stephenherbert.co. uk/tmlin.htm; I leave it to the reader to draw whatever conclusions are required.

Étienne-Jules Marey

To blithely say that Étienne-Jules Marey was an influential pioneer in both photography and cinematography is superficially focusing on the tip of the iceberg of his genius. First and foremost, he was an innovator; he approached every thought, project, interest, and experiment with the focused intent of a scientist searching for the invisible. Via his observational lab work he eventually found it through the young "science" of photography via scientific documentation. Fundamentally, he was fascinated by life's movement—the flight of birds, the locomotion of a horse or microscopic organism, the sinuous circulation of smoke or the observation of the human body—as the fluctuation of curves indicated by graphs and documented by photography. The result of his photographic experimentation is astounding in its volume and image clarity. It's appropriate to say that he was the Leonardo da Vinci of the nineteenth century, for whom the frontiers between art and science ceased to exist.

Marey's innovative and visionary discoveries as well as his influence on the arts reveal him as the creator of the first motion pictures. His process began as early as 1878 when he photographed a galloping horse, noted in a letter to him by E. Muybridge, explaining how his work inspired Governor Stanford to have him shoot the gallop again in California.[30] In 1882 Étienne-Jules Marey designed a photographic rifle to be used for **chronophotography,**

Figure 3.17a Motion-capture photos of a heron and a pelican in flight (c. 1894) Étienne-Jules Marey. The image also shows a profile shot of his chronophotograhic rifle and an insert (bottom left) of Marey holding his camera-rifle.

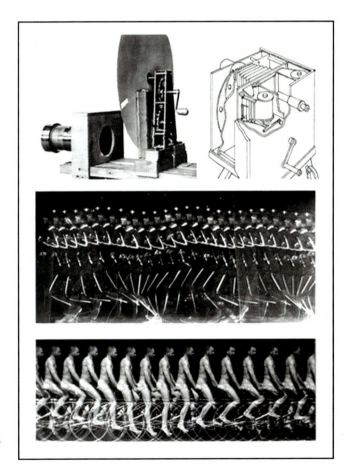

Figure 3.17b Interior mechanism of Marey's chronophotographic box camera (upper left); and various motion capture images. Note: Marey often attached light-reflective strips to the clothes of his subjects to accentuate the movement.

a series of images taken at set time intervals. His chronophotography rifle contained a rotating wheel with slits. When light passed through one of the slits, that portion of the photographic plate was exposed; it was capable of taking 12 consecutive frames a second on its circular, rotating photographic glass plate and disk shutter. This ingenious invention initiated the cinematographic movement and other fundamental techniques of motion pictures. His efforts, followed by the cinematography of the Lumière brothers, formed the basis of modern cinematography. Realize that Muybridge's demonstration of his zoopraxiscope at the home of Marey in September of 1881 must have directly inspired the host of this event to improve on all aspects of the cumbersome box Muybridge was exhibiting. Marey's camera rifle was manual, lightweight, and flexible; it was not stationary and so encouraged spontaneous recording of any event.

The next innovation enabled accurate scientific study and consequently, led to the first modern movie camera. It employed a silver bromide emulsion on a paper ribbon, brought intermittently to rest behind a lens, obscured by a rotating shutter while advancing the next exposure. With the gelatin-based film that George Eastman introduced in 1885, Marey obtained 60 images per second each 9cm × 9cm. These were truly the first modern cinematography films.[31] With this camera, Marey not only recorded a wide variety of animal and human movements but also employed high speed technique to slow down rapid movements, as well as inventing the reverse-technique and time-lapse, to speed up slow movements. Marey freely acknowledged that his innovations were the inevitable extension of the inventions of the nineteenth-century French astronomer Pierre Janssen and of Muybridge to adequately address the split-second accuracy that they sought.

Marey's greatest achievement was his use of photography to study movement. His chronophotographs—multiple exposures on single glass plates and on strips of film that passed automatically through a camera of his own design—had an important influence on both science and the arts, and established a pragmatic foundation of the recording of moving pictures.

Marey invented a chronophotographic fixed plate camera in 1882, equipped with a timed shutter, combining several successive images of a single movement. To facilitate the shooting of motion-capture images in different positions, the camera was placed inside a large wooden cabinet that ran on rails—this essentially, was the first dolly camera. In 1888 Marey again improved his invention by replacing the glass plate with a long strip of sensitized paper. Two years later, Marey replaced the paper strip with a transparent celluloid film 90mm wide; while shooting, a pressure-plate held the film firmly in place and a spring restarted it when the pressure was released.[32] All the cameras developed well into the twentieth century were based on the principle first applied by Marey: the intermittent movement of a sensitive film behind an objective lens.

For those interested, Marey published a comprehensive catalogue of his scientific/photographic legacy, *Le Mouvement* (1894). A tribute to Marey exists at www.greco-casadesus.com/marey-2011/marey-english.html.

Étienne-Jules Marey influenced all the pioneering inventors of the cinema in the 1890s; his works, widely reported in the international press, were a strong inspiration for

Edison, Muybridge and the Lumière brothers, among others. Marey was the founding father of cinematography technique.

Eadweard Muybridge

To adequately answer questions about rapid movement that the unaided human eye is unable to see, Eadweard Muybridge developed a clever system of multiple cameras in a line with very fast shutters. A moving object, like a running horse, would trip a guide wire attached to each of the cameras; in sequence, each took a still photograph within a fraction of a section. A spectacular portfolio of **stop-motion** shots, much like those taken by Marey in France, emerged from those sessions. Muybridge was later able to photograph people and other moving objects with a single camera with a very fast shutter. In the 1880s, Muybridge entered a very productive period at the University of Pennsylvania in Philadelphia, producing more than 100,000 images of animals and humans in motion. In 1887, the photos were published as a massive portfolio, with 781 plates comprising 20,000 of the photographs, in a groundbreaking collection titled *Animal Locomotion: An Electro-Photographic Investigation of Connective Phases of Animal Movements.*[33] Muybridge's work contributed substantially to developments in the science of biomechanics and the mechanics of athletics. (Again, the parallels between Marey and Muybridge are stunningly similar; the only difference lies in approach. Marey always operated as a scientist but the aesthetic aspect of the imagery he produced was secondary to his intent; Muybridge, on the other hand, was trained as a photographer in England so his focus throughout his career in America was aesthetic with the assistance of some basic scientific application.) Consider this: whether or not Eadweard Muybridge was the "Father of Motion Pictures" is debatable. Look closely at his horse galloping and realize that the horse gallops on the spot—as if on a treadmill—giving an illusion of the ground being moved under the horse's feet, as in a zoetrope. What we are viewing is the analysis of motion; without a drama of subjective involvement with the viewer (observed in Marey's short film of a bird's flight shot with his photographic rifle), there is no transformation of motion into action. What cinema celebrates isn't the movement but the *action.*

Muybridge also developed a projection system to playback his photographs as short animations in 1879. Most of the catalogue of photographs he was accumulating was of animals; the device was appropriately named a **zoopraxiscope.** Its main moving part was a glass wheel that contained an array of individual photographic images printed around the outside edge of the disc. As the images on the wheel rotated rapidly past a light source, they projected onto a nearby surface and created the illusion of animation. Essentially, this projector applied the same principles as a flip-book and relied on the concept of persistence of vision (see "Mechanical Devices," this chapter).

Two known liaisons between Muybridge and Edison occurred in 1883 and 1888; the latter, to consider the combining of Muybridge's zoopraxiscope for vision and Edison's phonograph for audio, thereby laying the groundwork of a complete animation-projecting device. Nothing formally developed from these meetings; Edison, in typical fashion,

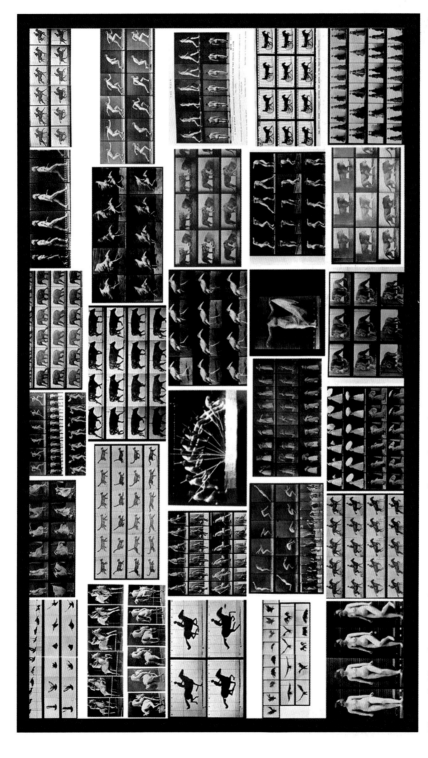

Figure 3.18a   Some motion-capture images by Eadweard Muybridge included in a massive portfolio, with 781 plates comprising 20,000 of the photographs, in a groundbreaking collection titled *Animal Locomotion: an Electro-Photographic Investigation of Connective Phases of Animal Movements*.

Figure 3.18b Although Marcel Duchamps' *Nude Descending a Staircase* (1912) combines elements of Cubist and Futuristic movements, he recognized the influence of Muybridge's stop-motion photography. A good example showing art imitating art.

assimilated any new ideas into the ongoing experiments at his Menlo Park lab and applied for probable patents that might arise in the process. In fact, in 1891 Thomas Edison and William Dickson used the technology of Muybridge's animation projector along with other early projection systems to develop a camera that would record still images *on* film and a projection system that displayed the images *from* the film.

It is debated whether the zoopraxiscope is the first film projector that actually showed motion photography in public; nonetheless, Muybridge was the most significant pioneer in the capture and presentation of stop-motion animated images in North America. As the twentieth century progressed, this zoopraxiscope device was more solidly regarded as an early movie projector, and the process as an intermediate stage toward motion pictures or cinematography.

For more in-depth information, visit these links: www.kingston.gov.uk/info/200246/museum_collections_and_exhibitions/539/eadweard_muybridge; www.stephenherbert.co.uk/muybCOMPLEAT.htm.

THE FIRST DECADE

Georges Méliès

Training as a boy in stage design, stage illusion and puppetry, Méliès' principle contribution to cinema was the fusion of traditional theatrical technique to motion pictures—dozens of illusions he devised while working in London theatre he later used in his filmmaking process. Deeply impressed by the 1895 public demonstration of the Lumière brothers' camera, Méliès built his own and was making films by 1896. Cinema folklore recounts a story about a camera jam during a "take" of a small filming project that later inspired him. From this mishap, he discovered in the editing process that cinema had the potential for manipulating time and space; he quickly devised and expanded a "signature repertoire" of complex special effects. Fantasy films are an integral part of the cinematic lexicon he left for us to enjoy. He pioneered the first double exposure in *La Caverne Maudite* (*The Cursed Cave*), 1898; the first split screen with performers acting opposite themselves in *Un Homme de Tête* (*A Head Man*), 1898; and the first dissolve in *Cendrillon* (*Cinderella*) 1899.[34]

Méliès constructed a studio, Star-Film Company, in 1897, where he was able to stage his fully elaborate productions and perfect his trick work. This illusion work demanded a static camera, meaning the camera had to be **locked-off** or fastened into a frozen position so his multiple exposures, for example, could be seamlessly executed and flawlessly effective. His rich imagination informed the lavishness of costuming and fantastically designed/painted scenery—the achievement of "vues composées" or ***mise en scène***—everything that appears before the camera and its arrangement: composition, sets, props, actors, costumes, sounds, and lighting became his visual signature, especially in his fantasy-inspired films, rather than the **"actualities"** that were the regular subjects of the first filmmakers like the Lumière brothers or Charles Urban and George Albert Smith. Méliès himself took charge of the design and execution of it all to ensure that his vision was exactly realized. In addition, Méliès was a pioneer in assembling a number of "films" or shots to tell a continuous story, a technique analogous to the tableau style of magic lantern narrative rather than to modern notions of film editing; but from 1898 to 1900 it was a significant advance in the quickly maturing craft of cinema. The sheer variety of his body of work was staggering; apart from the trick films based on his stage illusions, his 500 films included historical actualities such as *The Coronation of King Edward VII*, fairytales such as *Le petit Chaperon Rouge* (*Little Red Riding Hood*), topical satires, historical subjects, and adaptations of Shakespeare's *Julius Caesar* and *Hamlet*. His most spectacular and well-known are his comedy/science fiction films in gentle parody of Jules Verne, such as *Voyage dans la Lune* (*Trip to the Moon*) and *Voyage à Travers l'impossible* (*The Impossible Journey*). The cinema he owned, Le Théâtre Robert-Houdin, is where he showed his masterpieces until changes after the First World War swept it away.

Georges Méliès directed hundreds of films including the following—his full filmography can be found at www.imdb.com/name/nm0617588/?ref_=sr_1.

- *Steam Thresher/Batteuse à vapeur* (1896)
- *Baby and Girls/Bébé et fillettes* (1896)
- *The Encampment Le bivouac* (1896)
- *Italian Boulevard des Italiens* (1896)
- *Cleopatra's Tomb* (1899)
- *Cinderella/Cendrillon* (1899)

- *The Dreyfus Affair/L'affaire Dreyfus* (1899)
- *Joan of Arc/Jeanne d'Arc* (1900)
- *A Trip to the Moon/Le Voyage dans la lune* (1902)
- *The Man With The Rubber Head/L'Homme à la tête de caoutchouc* (1902)
- *Gulliver's Travels/Le Voyage de Gulliver à Lilliput et chez les Géants* (1902)
- *The Inn Where No Man Rests/L'Auberge du Bon Repos* (1903)
- *The Mystical Flame/La Flamme merveilleuse* (1903)
- *Faust in Hell* (1903)
- *Kingdom of the Fairies/Le Royaume des fées* (1903)
- *The Impossible Voyage/Voyage à travers l'impossible* (1904)
- *The Adventurous Automobile Trip* (1904)
- *Hilarious Posters/Les Affiches en goguette* (1905)
- *Palace of the Arabian Knights/Le Palais des Mille et une Nuits* (1905)
- *Paris to Monte Carlo/Le Raid Paris-Monte Carlo en deux Heures* (1905)
- *The Mysterious Retort/L'Alchimiste Parafaragamus ou La Cornue infernale* (1906)
- *20,000 Leagues Under the Sea/20.000 Lieues sous les mers* (1907)
- *Humanity Through the Ages* (1908)
- *Conquest of the Pole/A la conquête du pôle* (1912)
- *Baron Munchausen's Dream/Les Hallucinations du baron de Münchausen* (1911)
- *The Ranchman's Debt of Honor* (1911)
- *The Knight of the Snows/Le Chevalier des Neiges* (1912)
- *Cinderella or The Glass Slipper/Cendrillon ou La Pantoufle mystérieuse* (1912)
- *The Ghost of Sulpher Mountain* (1912)
- *The Prisoner's Story* (1912)
- *The Bourrichon Family Trip Le Voyage de la famille Bourrichon* (1913)

During the end of the first decade of the twentieth century, litigation over patents among all the major American filmmaking companies—Pathé, Edison, Biograph, and Vitagraph—continued aggressively until the end of 1908 when they decided to pool their patents and form a "Trust", the Motion Picture Patents Company (MPPC), to control the American film business.[35] The Eastman Kodak Company, the only manufacturer of film stock in the United States, agreed to only supply the members with film stock. The producing companies of the Trust were allocated production quotas in terms of reels to produce per week—two for the biggest ones, one for the smaller companies—which were supposed to be enough to fill the programs of the licensed exhibitors. Star-Film Company, Georges Méliès' company, was one of the smaller companies with satellite offices in America, headed by his impractical brother; most films he offered for the quotas were either damaged or unusable, finally defaulting on their obligations. This as well as a deal Méliès made with the Pathé Frères Company eventually destroyed his career. The unchanging, graphic style of his work rendered his short but astonishingly productive career as a film maverick sadly obsolete by the vision of American pioneers like D. W. Griffith.

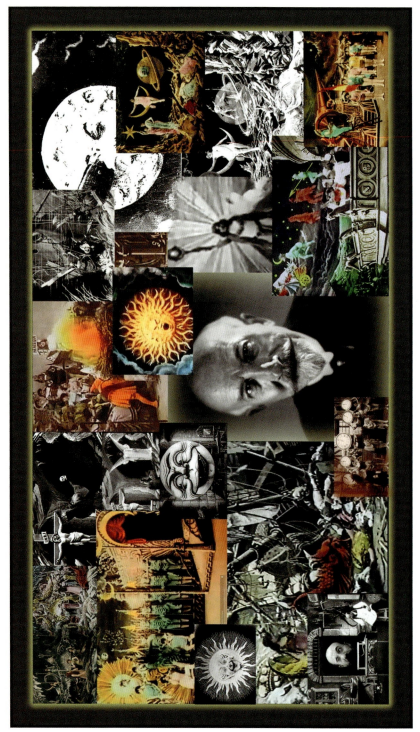

Figure 3.19   The whimsical, theatrical genius of Georges Méliès, an inspirational pioneer of the early twentieth century.

THE TWENTIETH CENTURY

A New Film Business

The films spanning 1895 to 1910 were public events shown in temporary storefront spaces and as acts in vaudeville programs or presented by traveling exhibitors who had bought the films they peddled. A film might run under a minute long, usually presenting a single scene of everyday life, a public or sporting event, or bawdy vaudevillian slapstick. There was little to no cinematic technique: no editing, usually no camera movement, and flat, stagey compositions. But the novelty of moving photographic images was enough for a young motion picture business to explode into an international industry. Cheaply made "movies" were a simpler and faster way of providing popular entertainment to the masses of the late Victorian age. The last 15 years of that era (1886–1901) reveal motion pictures moving from a dime-store novelty to an established large-scale entertainment industry. These early creative experiments represent a movement from films consisting of one shot, completely made by one person with a few assistants, towards substantially longer films consisting of several shots, made by large companies in industrial conditions. Roughly 4,000 small "nickelodeon" cinemas, set up in the established entertainment districts of many cities peppered the landscape in the United States by 1907; there were very few larger cinemas in some of the biggest cities. At first, the majority of films in the 30-minute programs offered were Pathé films—internationally, the largest film production company at the time—shown with the accompaniment of a pianist. The typical reel of film contained one individual film; this became the standard unit of film production and exhibition during this era. The change to nickelodeon exhibition established by Pathé produced a change in commerce: from selling films outright to renting them through film exchanges.

D.W. Griffith

The activity of the MPPC (discussed above) pressed all members to produce their expected quotas. In 1908 Biograph lost their one working director, so they offered the job to D.W. Griffith, an unrecognized actor and playwright, who accepted and found his calling. Alone he made all the Biograph films from 1908 to 1910. This fact is astonishing because it meant that he produced 30 minutes of screen time a week for 156 weeks—the modern equivalent of shooting almost 3.5 seasons of a half-hour television series. According to the Internet Movie Database, he directed 535 films between 1908 and 1931.[36]

Although Griffith did not invent any new film techniques, he was the best film director working up to 1913; he made better dramatic and artistic use of the medium than other directors. A particular focus of his was the structure he gave his films, most often the final scene mirroring the opening scene, as in *The Country Doctor* (1909) or *A Drunkard's Reformation* (1909). He was an actor's director, one of the first to hold extensive rehearsals to help his cast work out important but natural gestures during key scenes, like the jealous husband in *The Voice of the Child* (1911). Griffith's increased use of both cross-cutting between parallel actions and close-up shots, helped him to get at least twice as many shots in his pictures compared to his contemporaries. Motion pictures were classified into genres, established centuries before in stagecraft and theatre, as drama and comedy. The comedy category was subdivided either as slapstick, "burlesque farce," or alternatively "polite comedy." Griffith made a small number of the latter type of film in his first two years at Biograph but had little interest or aptitude for the genre. From 1910 he let Frank Powell, and then Mack Sennett direct the Biograph comedies. Sennett left in 1912 to set up the Keystone Company, where he could give his enthusiasm for the slapstick comedy style derived from the earlier Pathé.[37]

A compelling dramatic plot was also significant for Griffith, who influenced the simplification of film stories. After he had been at Biograph for a year, he made films that had much less story content than any previous one-reel films. This reflected the general American tendency to simplify the plots borrowed from novels and plays so the minimum of titling and the maximum of straightforward narrative continuity could happen. The exception to this was found in European films where plot information that was difficult to film and lacking in strong dramatic interest was assigned a narrative title frame to explain each scene it preceded. Here, a significant difference in approach began between American and European filmmaking and continued to mid-century when at the height of **Neo-Realism** and the **French New Wave,** stylistic differences were most contrasted.

Hollywood Studios Emerge

The years of the First World War were a complex transitional period for the film industry for the following reasons:

- It was the period when the exhibition of films changed from short programs of one-reel films to longer shows of a feature film of four or more reels.
- With a change in feature length, exhibition venues also changed from small nickelodeon cinemas to larger cinemas charging higher prices.
- Nearly all the founding film companies that formed the MPPC went out of business because of their resistance to the changeover to long feature films—the single exception was the Vitagraph Company.
- The bulk of American film production moved towards the West Coast, specifically, Los Angeles. The newly forming Hollywood community saw the rapid grouping of entrant studio production companies organized under Universal Film Manufacturing Company (1912), an umbrella for many of the independent producing companies.

This umbrella organization had to exist to protect the creative integrity, not only of independent companies, but the major studios of the time. Thomas Edison and the Patents Trust put a death grip on the motion picture industry around 1908. The Motion Picture Patents Company's basic premise was that it had the patent on motion picture film and the mechanical movement inside movie cameras that transported the film. No movie could be made without its approval and it didn't approve of movies made by anyone outside "the Trust." It even had enforcers that would go to the set of films in production and destroy the camera then and there. It sued everyone that tried to make an independent film. It also made it so no movie was to be made with screen credits. No credits for actors, directors, or crew—credits were to be for the production companies only.[38]

- **1909:** Carl Laemmle creates Universal Studios out of the dissolution of Thomas Edison's legislation to create a trust, the Motion Picture Patents Company, designed to eliminate independent film producers of which Laemmle was one. Creating Universal and destroying "the Trust" was his great success that year.
- **1912:** Universal Motion Picture Manufacturing Company founded by Carl Laemmle and partners. Mack Sennett sets up the Keystone Company.
- **1913:** Jesse Lasky Feature Play Company and Famous Players known for reproducing stage plays thereby enticing the best actors from the legitimate stage into a **photoplay** for motion pictures.
- **1915:** World Film Company recruited most of the French directors, cameramen, and designers from Pathé.
- **1916:** Jesse Lasky Feature Play Company and Famous Players amalgamated into Famous Players-Lasky with distribution of their films handled by the new Paramount Pictures Corporation. The famous players included celebrities like Mary Pickford, Rudolph Valentino, Gloria Swanson, and Clara Bow. Also in this year, Goldwyn Pictures was founded by Samuel Goldwyn.
- **1915–1917:** Triangle, with Mack Sennett, D. W. Griffith, and Thomas Ince heading its production units, took its films to Paramount for distribution.
- **1918:** Harry, Albert, Sam, and Jack created the Warner Bros. Studio.
- **1919:** United Artists is founded.
- **1924:** Columbia Pictures is founded.

An outstanding success during the war years was D. W. Griffith's *The Birth of a Nation* (1915), a Triangle film production. Griffith's box office success met the social scorn of many critics including the National Association for the Advancement of Colored People (NAACP). Stung by the criticism of his film, Griffith made an even bigger film with an even bigger theme, *Intolerance* (1916). Griffith's success and notoriety are generally undisputed, although according to Martin Scorsese, it was Giovanni Pastrone, the Italian director of *Cabiria* (1914), who invented the epic movie and deserves credit for many of the innovations, such as the first use of the moving camera—usually attributed to the Americans Griffiths and Cecil B. DeMille—that freed narrative film from "static gaze." His work is worth considering and investigating, as is that of many other European filmmakers of the period.

British Studios Emerge

British film history is 118 years old. Internationally it was devastated by both world wars but rebounded several times before reaching its stride in the 1950s and 1960s. The modest list of that follows, indicates highlights of the richness of British creative inventiveness and milestones of steady filmmaking evolution.

- **1895:** Filmmaking was formally launched by Robert W. Paul, England's foremost scientific instrument maker, and Birt Acres, an American cameraman, who together created the Paul-Acres camera, England's first. Paul later used a revised version of his reverse-crank camera to cleverly superimpose images—with this discovery, he filmed *Scrooge, or Marley's Ghost* (1901), the oldest film adaptation of Charles Dickens' story.
- **1888:** Louis Le Prince, a Frenchman working in England, shot the first moving pictures on Eastman paper film using a single-lens camera of *Roundhay Garden Scene* and later *Leeds Bridge.* He was dubbed "The Father of Cinematography," since his work predated that of the Lumière brothers and Edison. Experimentation and revision of the technical aspects of early filming paralleled the number of American entrants into the competition as well as output of film work.
- **1892:** George Albert Smith, inventor and showman, established the Brighton Film Factory and who later became a pioneering filmmaker, developing the grammar of editing and various film techniques. With the expertise of Alfred Darling, Smith patented his own camera and projector system (1897). His showmanship and entrepreneur's spirit was as irrepressible as his creativity as a film artist, mentored by George Méliès, blossomed in 1899, after taking a lease on St. Anne's Well Gardens in Brighton, and constructing a glass conservatory film studio. Experimenting with dream-time and dissolve effects in *Let Me Dream Again* (1900); pioneering use of the close-up in *Spider's Web* (1900) and experimentation with film reversal *The House that Jack Built* are some examples of how his creativity flourished. In many ways, Smith's early film work paralleled that of Edison Lab's William Dickson in the simplicity and immediacy of the subject matter he shot. In 1904, the Laboratory Lodge was founded in Southwick, Sussex where he developed and subsequently improved on the first successful color film process, **kinemacolor.** Marking his outstanding body of work and exhaustive achievements in cinematography, he was awarded the Silver Medal by the Royal Society of Arts in 1909.
- **1898:** The Warwick Trading Company was formed out of the British branch of the American firm Maguire and Baucus. It was the leading film producer in Britain at the turn of the century, eventually producing early color films.
- **1906:** Gaumont Co. Ltd. established in London and Pathé opens London branch.
- **1913:** London Film Company opens Twickenham Studios.
- **1914:** Neptune Film Company builds studio at Borehamwood. Just before WWI, Britain could not compete with advances in technology and methodology being made abroad and so declined; in 1924 the Cinematographer's Trade Bill was enacted by Parliament to guarantee a home market for films despite the public's clamoring for American films. This legislation stimulated the production of many poor quality films.
- **1921:** British National Film League formed for protection and development of British film industry.

- **1926:** J. D. Williams sets up British National Pictures and builds studios in Boreham-wood, Elstree.
- **1929:** First British sound feature *Blackmail* made by director, Alfred Hitchcock.
- **1931:** Work begins on vast studios at Denham, Buckinghamshire.
- **1932:** Shepperton Studios opens.
- **1933:** The advent of sound spurred new growth and the founding of British National by J. Arthur Rank marked two gigantic milestones in the Industry. Pinewood Studios built at Iver, Buckinghamshire.
- **1935:** J. Arthur Rank, partnering with C. M. Woolf, took over the Pinewood Studios and founded the Rank Organization.
- **1935:** Rank Organization expands its reach by acquiring from the Gaumont Company, the Odeon cinema chain, throughout Europe. Rank affected British film by encouraging lots of independent filmmakers; but he is also attributed as the man behind the break-up of the British film industry.
- **1936:** The Trade Bill, with all good intentions, ultimately had a negative effect by over-saturating the market with films that no one wanted; enterprising American companies bought bankrupt British production companies, qualifying under the home market quota, just in time for another down-swing in production during WWII. The UK celebrates an all-time high in film production in this year.
- **1940s:** The British Golden Age of Cinema.
- **WWII:** Documentaries and war movies are produced with great success, despite the tremendous decline and closing of British film theatres due to the war, and the immediacy and popularity of television.
- **1955–1975:** Restrictions on US studios prompted an influx into the UK as a prime production ground and outpost for American film production. At that time, MGM-British, a subsidiary of Metro-Goldwyn-Mayer studios created caliber of films like *2001: A Space Odyssey* (1968). Anglo-American cinema becomes inextricably linked during these two decades.
- **1958:** The *Carry On* series gets underway with *Carry On Sergeant.*
- **1970–1980:** British production turned more to TV development and production, and to fostering blockbuster special effects projects, i.e. *Superman, Star Wars,* and *James Bond* series projects.
- **1980s:** With the cessation of film production by the Rank Organization and a new government regulation prohibiting foreign studios filming in Britain to write off some of their costs, many studios closed down or downsized their operations.
- **2000:** UK Film Council launched to promote British filmmaking.
- **2005:** The first short film, *Me at the Zoo*, is uploaded to a new video upload site, YouTube, by one of the site's co-founders, Jawed Karim.[39]

THE SOUND ERA

Samuel Warner was part owner in a small Hollywood studio with big ambitions; he could not pass up a good deal when it crossed his path. Having recently purchased New York's

Vitagraph studios in 1925, he persuaded his brothers to experiment with their state-of-the-art sound system to ensure they could be the leading studio to produce the first "talkie"—the experiment lasted for a couple of years. Meantime, the "Big Five" studios: Paramount, MGM, Universal, First National, and Producers Distributing Corporation (PDC) signed an agreement in February 1927 to collectively select just one provider for sound conversion. This was a practical decision to support the mixing/editing process and also simplify the installation of speakers throughout their collective system of movie houses. Later that year, in October, Warner Brothers' *The Jazz Singer* premiered as a smash box office success starring Al Jolson. In true irrepressible form, Sam Warner made three sound films right after his big hit. Late in 1928, Paul Terry's first animated cartoon *Dinner Time* was produced and released; immediately after, Walt Disney's *Steamboat Willie* starring Mickey Mouse hit the theatres. Within the three groundbreaking years discussed here, three additional mid-level studios—Fox, Columbia Pictures, and United Artists—joined the rank and file, as sound charged-up movie screens with an evanescence no one had imagined (except maybe for Edison, of course). New technology was now vibrantly alive and ready for its close-up.

EARLY COLOR

All of the first moving pictures displayed the luminosity of the black-and-white image—light, shade, form and movement—but not color. Méliès and the Pathé Frères extensively used various tinting and hand-coloring methods of adding color to the surface of the film strip; consequently, Pathé Color (renamed "pathechrome" in 1929) became the most reliable/accurate stencil coloring system. The first color systems used in filmmaking were additive color systems, as it was understood from the Mid-Nineteenth century that of all natural colors in the light spectrum could be produced with additive combinations of the primaries, and that mixing the primary colors equally will produce white light. Edward R. Turner received an English patent in 1899 for his pioneering three-color filming process. The difference between the filming and final projecting of a rotating set of red, blue, and green filters working on each machine created inaccurate registration problems in the final projection of a film using this process.

A still from *The Tartans of Scotland* (1902) demonstrates just how unmanageable the delivery aspect of the three-color process was (Figure 3.20). Even seven years into experimentation, **fringing** or non-registration happened to moving objects (the children) in the camera view and not to stationary objects (the swingset). Turner applied for and received a two-color patent in 1906; this resolved the fringing problem enough until the demise of Kinemacolor Hollywood in 1913.

Practical, commercially viable color in motion picture technology was introduced in 1906 as kinemacolor by George Albert Smith and promoted by his partner, Charles Urban, one of the greatest film pioneers of the early twentieth century. The kinemacolor process consisted of alternating frames of specially sensitized black-and-white film exposed at 32 frames per second through a rotating filter with alternating red and green areas. The film was then printed and projected through the same alternating red and green filter at the

Figure 3.20 This still from *The Tartans of Scotland* (1902) remains as an early experiment with a three-color additive color process.

Figure 3.21 Screen-grab from *Toll of the Sea* (1922-MGM) starring Anna May Wong.

Figure 3.22 Screen-grab from *Becky Sharp* (1934-RKO), a break-through success for Technicolor Inc. and a new industry standard for Hollywood. Note: Despite what most people think, *The Wizard of Oz* was not the first movie shot in Technicolor.

same speed. The sense of color was achieved through a combination of separate red and green alternating images.

A Visit to the Seaside (1908) was Smith and Urban's first, two-color Kinemacolor movie. It's an eight-minute short film of people on Brighton Beach, directed by George Albert Smith. Because of its color fidelity and clarity it is ranked of high historical importance. *The World, the Flesh and the Devil* was the first full-length kinemacolor movie. It was directed by F. Martin Thornton and photographed also using the additive color kinemacolor process.

Technicolor

Many experimental stages of early Technicolor preceded the final three-strip camera that was used extensively from 1934 to 1955. All the processes that it had tried and failed until 1931 didn't succeed because of lack of ingenuity; shooting footage with more than two colors was simply more difficult and the technology hadn't developed sufficiently to make the considerable extra cost worthwhile. So, Technicolor, Inc., the company that owned the Technicolor process, continued research and development to resolve two major challenges: getting the color registration perfected and improving the color quality to achieve clear, chromatic blues. Before color development, blue-green and red-orange were the only two colors that were achievable. This level of chromatic success is beautifully rendered in *Toll of the Sea* (1922) starring Anna May Wong (see Figure 3.21). It was a first commercial success for Technicolor Inc., founded in 1915 by a group of physicists/MIT grads—hence the "tech" in the name.

It would be another 12 years before a second significant breakthrough in color technology—the interim saw the introduction of an advanced three-color strip system. *Becky Sharp* (1934) produced by Pioneer and released through RKO Radio Pictures, was the singular achievement of this new process. Shooting three-strip Technicolor required very bright lighting because the film speed was extremely low. That issue compounded with the bulk of the cameras and the fact that this new technology required a learning curve for film technicians, made for skepticism in the studio board rooms because its viability had not been proven.

A few short sentences taken from a 1934 article in *Fortune Magazine*, "What? Color in the Movies Again?" offers both tongue-in-cheek and astute observations about the necessity of the new technological upgrade, and gives an idea of the misgivings of the Hollywood community in general:

> *But color is not so pronounced a revolution as sound. Sound gave the pictures an appeal to the ear as well as the eye; it created dialogue; it established a whole new set of dramatic values. Color adds no new sense, but it is one step closer to reality than black and white. Whether color can make black and white pictures as obsolete as sound made silent pictures, is, as suggested, quite another question . . . For although experience has taught us to take a flat, black and white picture and mentally endow it with color and a third dimension, pictures in color will make this transference easier and more convincing.*[40]

Issues or not, Technicolor was ultimately embraced by the hesitant studio heads and continued as the filmmaker's medium for the next two decades. Figure A1.6, an abbreviated version of Figure A1.5a–d, found in Appendix A, enumerates and clarifies the breakthrough technologies in film emulsion and film-formatting covered in this section. Technicolor, the last major advance in modern film technology was improved upon throughout the course of the last century and has neatly delivered us to the advent of

Figure 3.23 *The Adventures of Robin Hood.*
(1938) Licensed by Warner Bros. Entertainment Inc.
All rights reserved.

Figure 3.24 Screen grab from *The Wizard of Oz* (1939-MGM).

Figure 3.25 Technicolor Camera

digital cinema in the twenty-first century, which receives similar professional aesthetic and financial scrutiny. Creating a new paradigm has its inherent risks.

DIGITAL FILM

Interestingly, at the onset of every technological advance in Hollywood over the past century, a consensus of studio heads is required: first, the MPPC in 1908; more currently, the DCI in 2002. Digital Cinema Initiatives is a joint venture of major studios—MGM, Paramount Pictures, Sony Pictures Entertainment, 20th Century Fox, Universal Studios, the Walt Disney Company, and Warner Bros.—formed to establish a standard architecture for digital cinema systems, which ensures a uniformly high level of technical performance, reliability, and quality. Its influence extends to software developers and equipment manufacturers in the digital cinema marketplace, placing everyone on the same digital page.

By 1998, the introduction of professional digital video cameras and HDCAM recorders signaled the onset of digital cinematography. Since then, 2K has been the most continuous format for digitally acquired images; currently, 4K is becoming the more commonly chosen format. Sony, Panasonic, JVC, and Canon offer a variety of choices for shooting high-definition video. Cameras from Sony, Vision Research, Arriflex, Silicon Imaging, Panavision, Grass Valley, and Red offer resolution and dynamic range that exceeds that of traditional video cameras, which are designed for the limited needs of broadcast television.[42]

The reaction to all new paradigms is polarizing; Hollywood's reaction to filmmaking's digital turn is no different. A list of pros and cons provides a compelling argument for ongoing conversation on both sides of the digital divide:

- **Convenience and flexibility:** Photographic film is made with specific, unchangeable characteristics of color temperature and sensitivity, or ISO. Digital film allows adjustment at each shot, manually or automatically. Digital images store conveniently but require tremendous storage capability and energy. Modern film cameras are not power hogs.
- **Cost:** Obsolescence increases cost for new digital software, hardware and all peripherals. Film cameras, especially "used" equipment in excellent condition, are inexpensive to purchase.
- **Film speed:** Digital equipment is superior: capable of much higher speeds or sensitivities, can perform easily in low light situations, and speed adjustments happen at will, while film cameras require changing the film to change the speed.
- **Integrity:** Film produces a self-contained, first generation (raw) image; therefore it lends itself artistically to a more "authentic" expression—this is debatable. Because of this limitation, filming choices require a substantial amount of forethought and planning. Digital capture is more quixotic.
- **Spatial resolution, noise and grain, dynamic range and effects of sensor size:** These parameters are complex and demand a technical skill level and understanding best left

to professional, technical explanation. Regardless, these issues should be addressed. A good place to start is www.motion.kodak.com/motion/uploadedFiles/US_plugins_acrobat_en_motion_education_film_info.pdf.

For every enthusiastic endorsement of shooting digitally, there are counterarguments worth noting—heavy-hitting directors Christopher Nolan and Paul Franklin, have these arguments to preferring film to digital:

> For the last ten years, I've felt increasing pressure to stop shooting film and start shooting video, but I've never understood why. It's cheaper to work on film, it's far better looking, it's the technology that's been known and understood for 100 years, and it's extremely reliable. I think, truthfully, it boils down to the economic interest of manufacturers and [a production] industry that makes more money through change rather than through maintaining the status quo. We save a lot of money shooting on film and projecting film and not doing digital intermediates. In fact, I've never done a digital intermediate. Photo-chemically, you can time film with a good timer in three or four passes, which takes about 12 to 14 hours as opposed to seven or eight weeks in a DI suite. That's the way everyone was doing it ten years ago, and I've just carried on making films in the way that works best and waiting until there's a good reason to change. But I haven't seen that reason yet.[43]

Christopher Nolan

> I believe in an absolute difference between animation and photography. However sophisticated your computer-generated imagery is, if it's been created from no physical elements and you haven't shot anything, it's going to feel like animation. There are usually two different goals in a visual effects movie. One is to fool the audience into seeing something seamless, and that's how I try to use it. The other is to impress the audience with the amount of money spent on the spectacle of the visual effect, and that, I have no interest in. We try to enhance our stunt work and floor effects with extraordinary CGI tools like wire and rig removals. If you put a lot of time and effort into matching your original film elements, the kind of enhancements you can put into the frames can really trick the eye, offering results far beyond what was possible 20 years ago. The problem for me is if you don't first shoot something with the camera on which to base the shot, the visual effect is going to stick out if the film you're making has a realistic style or patina. I prefer films that feel more like real life, so any CGI has to be very carefully handled to fit into that.[44]

Paul Franklin

NOTES

1 Anderson, Joseph and Barbara, 1993. "The Myth of Persistence of Vision Revisited," *Journal of Film and Video*, Vol. 45, No. 1: 3–12.

2 www.wordiq.com/definition/Persistence_of_vision.

3 http://en.wikipedia.org/wiki/National_Television_System_Committee.

4 Ibid.

5 http://memory.loc.gov/ammem/bellhtml/belltelph.html.

6 http://en.wikipedia.org/wiki/Videophone.

7 http://inventors.about.com/od/tstartinventions/a/Television.htm.

8 www.netprolive.com/television.php.

9 www.bairdtelevision.com/1930.html.

10 Ibid.

11 http://scripophily.net/fateracode.html.

12 http://web.mit.edu/invent/iow/zworykin.html.

13 Ibid.

14 http://en.wikipedia.org/wiki/Nielsen_ratings.

15 http://en.wikipedia.org/wiki/List_of_most_watched_television_broadcasts.

16 *Wall Street Journal*, May 10, 1996.

17 www.steves-digicams.com/knowledge-center/how-tos/online-sharing-social-networking/the-history-of-web-television.html.

18 www.buzzfeed.com/charliewarzel/an-exhaustive-list-of-every-new-online-tv-show.

19 www.imdb.com/title/tt1856010/?ref_ = sr_1.

20 www.ted.com/search?cat = ss_all&q = Kevin+Kelly.

21 Best known as a prolific American essayist, historical biographer, and playwright, Vidal was also infamous for frequent talk-show appearances and witty political criticism.

22 An intrepid journalist, intellectual, feminist, novelist and uniquely incisive cultural critic. Paglia's quotes, like Dorothy Parker's, are well-known for their acidity and truth. See www.brainyquote.com/quotes/authors/c/camille_paglia.html.

23 www.bfi.org.uk/news-opinion/news-bfi/interviews/looking-signs-meaning-cinema.

24 www.earlycinema.com/technology/mutoscope.html.

25 http://memory.loc.gov/ammem/edhtml/edmvhm.html.

26 http://en.wikipedia.org/wiki/kinetoscope.

27 http://en.wikipedia.org/wiki/Edison%27s_Black_Maria.

28 www.earlycinema.com/pioneers/lumiere_bio.html.

29 For an insightful treatment of the Edison-Dickson-Muybridge-Marey connection, see Spehr, Paul, 2002. "Edison, Dickson and the Chronophotographers: Creating an Illusion," in François Albera, Marta Braun, and André Gaudreault (eds.) *Stop Motion, Fragmentation of Time.* Lausanne: Payot, pages189–221; also Braun, Marta, 1992. *Picturing Time: The Work of Etienne-Jules Marey (1830–1904)*, Chicago: University of Chicago Press.

30 www.stephenherbert.co.uk/muychron02a.htm#part4.

31 www.ctie.monash.edu.au/hargrave/marey.html.

32 www.victorian-cinema.net/marey.

33 www.precinemahistory.net/1885.htm.

34 www.earlycinema.com/pioneers/melies_bio.html.

35 http://en.wikipedia.org/wiki/History_of_film.

36 http://en.wikipedia.org/wiki/D._W._Griffith_filmography.

37 http://en.wikipedia.org/wiki/History_of_film.

38 Ibid.

39 www.screenonline.org.uk/film/timeline/index.php?t = 1.

40 www.widescreenmuseum.com/oldcolor/fortune-page01.htm.

41 http://en.wikipedia.org/wiki/Digital_cinematography.

42 Ressner, Jeffrey, 2012. "The Traditionalist," *DGA Quarterly,* www.dga.org/Craft/DGAQ/All-Articles/1202-Spring-2012/DGA-Interview-Christopher-Nolan.aspx.

43 Ibid.

44 Russell, Terrence, 2010. "How Inception's Astonishing Visuals Came to Life." *Wired,* www.wired.com/underwire/2010/07/inception-visual-effects.

Table 3.2   Timeline: Early Cinema. Courtesy of Jonathan Walters, webmaster: www.earlycinema.com/timeline/index.html.

EARLY CINEMA TIMELINE

1600s   17th Century Use of Magic Lanterns

1827   First still photograph taken, using a glass plate technique **Claude Niepce**'s photograph the "View from a Window at Le Gras" took nearly eight hours to expose.

1832   **Joseph Plateau** and sons introduce the Phenakistoscope. Like other toys of its kind, the Phenakistoscope was one of the more successful illusion toys. Pictures on one disc viewed through slots in the other, appeared to move when the two were spun and viewed in a mirror.

1834   Another illusion toy - the Zoetrope was introduced by **William George Horner**. The Zoetrope used the same principle as Plateau's Phenakistoscope but instead of discs the pictures and slots are combined in a rotating drum. Zoetrope's were widely sold after 1867.

1839   **Henry Fox Talbot** makes an important advancement in photograph production with the introduction of negatives on paper - as opposed to glass. Also around this time it became possible to print photographic images on glass slides which could be projected using magic lanterns.

1846   Important in the development of motion pictures was the invention of intermittent mechanisms - particularly those used in sewing machines.

1877   **Emile Reynaud** introduces the Praxinoscope. Similar in design to Horner's Zoetrope, the illusion of movement produced by the Praxinoscope was viewed on mirrors in the center of the drum rather than through slots on the outside.

1878   **Eadweard Muybridge** achieves success after five years of experimenting to **capture movement in photography**. Muybridge was asked, in 1873, by the ex-governor of California - Leland Stanford to settle a bet as to whether horses' hooves left the

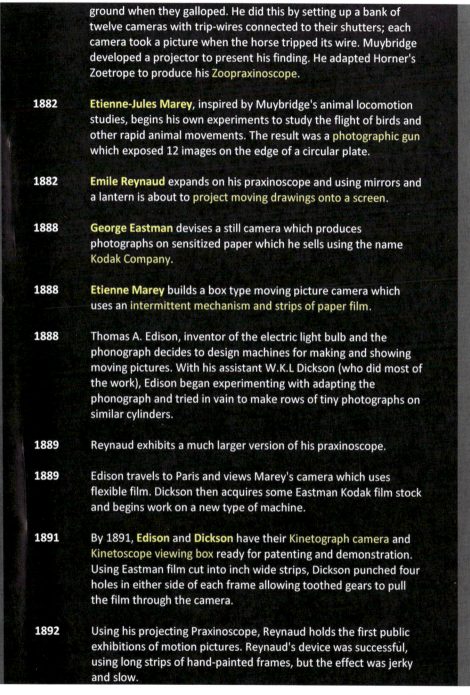

ground when they galloped. He did this by setting up a bank of twelve cameras with trip-wires connected to their shutters; each camera took a picture when the horse tripped its wire. Muybridge developed a projector to present his finding. He adapted Horner's Zoetrope to produce his Zoopraxinoscope.

1882   **Etienne-Jules Marey**, inspired by Muybridge's animal locomotion studies, begins his own experiments to study the flight of birds and other rapid animal movements. The result was a photographic gun which exposed 12 images on the edge of a circular plate.

1882   **Emile Reynaud** expands on his praxinoscope and using mirrors and a lantern is about to project moving drawings onto a screen.

1888   **George Eastman** devises a still camera which produces photographs on sensitized paper which he sells using the name Kodak Company.

1888   **Etienne Marey** builds a box type moving picture camera which uses an intermittent mechanism and strips of paper film.

1888   Thomas A. Edison, inventor of the electric light bulb and the phonograph decides to design machines for making and showing moving pictures. With his assistant W.K.L Dickson (who did most of the work), Edison began experimenting with adapting the phonograph and tried in vain to make rows of tiny photographs on similar cylinders.

1889   Reynaud exhibits a much larger version of his praxinoscope.

1889   Edison travels to Paris and views Marey's camera which uses flexible film. Dickson then acquires some Eastman Kodak film stock and begins work on a new type of machine.

1891   By 1891, **Edison** and **Dickson** have their Kinetograph camera and Kinetoscope viewing box ready for patenting and demonstration. Using Eastman film cut into inch wide strips, Dickson punched four holes in either side of each frame allowing toothed gears to pull the film through the camera.

1892   Using his projecting Praxinoscope, Reynaud holds the first public exhibitions of motion pictures. Reynaud's device was successful, using long strips of hand-painted frames, but the effect was jerky and slow.

(Continued)

Table 3.2   (Continued)

1893	**Edison** and **Dickson** build a studio on the grounds of Edison's laboratories in New Jersey, to produce films for their kinetoscope. The Black Maria studio was ready for film production at the end of January.
1893	The Cinématographe uses flexible film cut into 35mm wide strips and used an intermittent mechanism modeled on the sewing machine. The camera shot films at sixteen frames per second (rather than the forty six which Edison used), this became the standard film rate for nearly 25 years.
1894	During this year **Woodville Latham** and his sons Otway and Gray began working on their own camera and projector.
1894	In October of 1894, Edison's Kinetoscope made its debut in London. The parlour which hosted these machines did remarkably well and its owner approached R.W Paul, a maker of photographic equipment to make some extra machines for it. Incredibly, Edison hadn't patented his kinetoscope outside of the U.S., so Paul was free to sell copies to anyone; however, because Edison would only supply films to exhibitors who leased his machines, Paul had to invent his own camera to make films to go with his duplicate kinetoscopes.
1894	Another peepshow device, similar to the kinetoscope arrived in the Autumn of 1894. The Mutoscope was patented by **Herman Casler**, and worked using a flip-card device to provide the motion picture. Needing a camera he turned to his friend W.K.L Dickson who, unhappy at the Edison Company cooperates and with several others they form the American Mutoscope Company.
1894	**The Lumière Family** is the biggest manufacturer of photographic plates in Europe. A local kinetoscope exhibitor asks brothers Louis and Auguste to make films which are cheaper than the ones sold by Edison.
1895	**Louis** and **Auguste Lumiere** design a camera which serves as both a recording device and a projecting device. They call it the Cinématographe.

| 1895 | One of the **most famous film screenings in history** took place on December 28th, 1895. The venue was the Grand Cafe in Paris and customers paid one Franc for a twenty-five minute program of ten Lumière films. These included: "Feeding the Baby", "The Waterer Watered" and "A View of the Sea". |

The first film shot with the Cinématographe camera is "La Sortie de l'usine Lumière a Lyon" (Workers leaving the Lumière factory at Lyon). Shot in March it is shown in public at a meeting of the Societe d'Encouragement a l'industrie Nationale in Paris that same month.

| 1895 | In March of 1895, **R.W Paul** and his partner **Birt Acres** had a functional camera which was based partly on Marey's 1888 camera. In just half a year they had created a camera and shot 13 films for use with the kinetoscope. The partnership broke up, Paul continuing to improve upon the camera while Acres concentrating on creating a projector. |

| 1895 | **The Lathams** too had succeeded in creating a camera and a projector and on April 21st 1895 they showed one film to reporters. In May they opened a small storefront theatre. Their projector received only a small amount of attention as the image projected was very dim. The Lathams did however contribute greatly to motion picture history. Their projectors employed a system which looped the film making it less susceptible to breaks and tears. The Latham Loop as it was dubbed later is still in use in modern motion picture projectors. |

| 1895 | Atlanta, Georgia was the setting for another partnership. **C. Francis Jenkins** and **Thomas Armat** exhibit their phantoscope projector but like Latham, it attracts a moderate audience due to its dim, unsteady projector and competition from the Kinetoscope parlours. Later that year, Jenkins and Armat split. **Armat** continued to improve upon the projector and renames it the Vitascope, and obtained backing from American entrepreneurs Norman Raff and Frank Gammon. |

| 1896 | Early in 1896, **Herman Casler** and **W.K.L Dickson** had developed their camera to go with Casler's Mutoscope. However the market for peepshow devices was in decline and they decided to concentrate on producing a projection system. The camera and projector they produced were unusual as they used 70mm film which gave very clear images. |

(Continued)

Table 3.2 (Continued)

1896	January 14th saw Birt Acres present a selection of his films to the Royal Photographic Society - these included the famous "Rough Sea at Dover"; soon projected films were shown there regularly.
1896	The Lumière brothers sent a representative from their company to London and started a successful run of Cinématographe films.
1896	R.W. Paul continued to improve his camera and invented a projector which began by showing copies of Acres' films from the previous year. He sold his machines rather than leasing them and, as a result, sped up the spread of the film industry in Britain as well as abroad, supplying filmmakers and exhibitors which included George Méliès.
1896	After agreeing to back Armat's Vitascope, Raff and Gammon approached Edison; Edison agrees to manufacture the Vitascope marketing it as "Edison's Vitascope". April 23rd saw the first public premiere of the Vitascope at Koster and Bial's Music Hall. Six films were shown in all, five of which were orginally shot for kinetoscope, the sixth being Birt Acres' "Rough Sea at Dover".
1897	By 1897 the American Mutoscope Company become the most popular film company in America - both projecting films and with the peephole Mutoscope which was considered more reliable than the kinetoscope.
1899	The American Mutoscope Company changes its name to the American Mutoscope & Biograph Company to include its projection and peepshow devices.
1900	British filmmaker **James Williamson** produces "The Big Swallow" which demonstrated the ingenuity of the Brighton School (of filmmakers), of which he and **George Smith** were principle contributors.
1902	**Georges Méliès** produces his magnificent "Voyage to the Moon", a fifteen minute epic fantasy parodying the writings of Jules Verne and HG Wells. The film used innovative special effect techniques and introduced color to the screen through hand-painting and tinting.
1903	British film maker **George Smith** makes "Mary Jane's Mishap" which was praised for its sophisticated use of editing. The film uses medium close-ups to draw the viewer's attention to the scene,

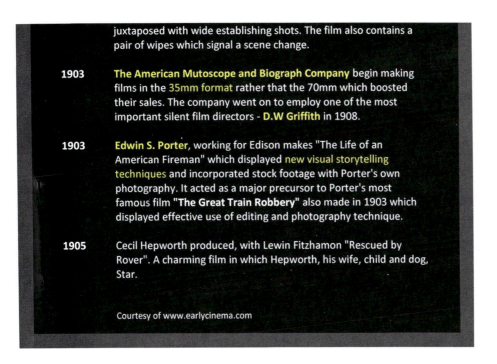

juxtaposed with wide establishing shots. The film also contains a pair of wipes which signal a scene change.

1903   **The American Mutoscope and Biograph Company** begin making films in the 35mm format rather that the 70mm which boosted their sales. The company went on to employ one of the most important silent film directors - **D.W Griffith** in 1908.

1903   **Edwin S. Porter**, working for Edison makes "The Life of an American Fireman" which displayed new visual storytelling techniques and incorporated stock footage with Porter's own photography. It acted as a major precursor to Porter's most famous film **"The Great Train Robbery"** also made in 1903 which displayed effective use of editing and photography technique.

1905   Cecil Hepworth produced, with Lewin Fitzhamon "Rescued by Rover". A charming film in which Hepworth, his wife, child and dog, Star.

Courtesy of www.earlycinema.com

Table 3.3 A timeline connecting Étienne-Jules Marey, Eadweard Muybridge, and Thomas Alva Edison.

TIMELINE: LINKING MAREY-MUYBRIDGE-EDISON

1862	**Muybridge** spends time in Paris.
1872	**Muybridge** takes instantaneous horse photograph at Sacramento racetrack, for Leland Stanford.
1879	**Muybridge:** More series photographs taken at Palo Alto, including athletes.
Sep-Nov1881; 1882	**Muybridge** lectures in London. **Muybridge** lectures in France.
September 26, 1881	**Muybridge** exhibits Zoopraxiscope at home of **Etienne-Jules Marey**, physiologist, in Paris. Photographer Nadar, physicists Helmholtz and Bjerknes, and Emile Duhousset, present.
September 1881	**Muybridge** in **Marey's laboratory** Muybridge worked for the first time with the new very sensitive dry plates.
November 1881	**Muybridge** presentations of Zoopraxiscope at Paris home of Jean Louis Ernest Meissonier, French painter.
November 17, 1881	*Bucks County Gazette* (USA)...'Mr. Muybridge, the eminent San Francisco photographer, has exhibited his photographic marvels to Prof. **E-J Marey** in Paris. He is now able to take photograph in the hundredth part of a second.
November 26, 1881	**Muybridge** presentation of Zoopraxiscope, operated by Alfred Molteni (projection expert) at Paris home of Jean Louis Ernest Meissonier, French painter. 200 guests including famous artists.
1882	**E-J. Marey** builds 'rifle' sequence camera, revolving plate—sets up Physiological Station.
March 7, 1882	Letter, **Muybridge** to Shay: 'I meet a number of RAs this evening at the house of Alma-Tadema to talk the matter over.' (i.e. possible Royal Academy of Arts lecture).
May 30, 1882	**Muybridge** writes to **E-J Marey**, asking for his collaboration.
June 8, 1882	**Muybridge** lectures at home of artist John J Atkinson.
1888	**Muybridge** gave a lecture in E. Orange, N.J. that likely included a demonstration of his zoopraxiscope.
	Muybridge visits **Edison**, discusses joining Zoopraxiscope with phonograph.
1889	**Edison's** two month European business trip, including participation in the Exposition Universelle in Paris.
1889	**Edison** met **Marey** and the Lumieres at a dinner commemorating the 50th anniversary of photography.
1891	**Muybridge** lectures in mainland Europe

CHAPTER 4

The Design Process

THE CONCEPTUAL DESIGN: VISUALIZATION–LANDING A VISUAL CONCEPT

Filmmakers tell stories. The ideas and emotions evoked by **screenplays** must transcend the page to be captured within the rectangle of a phone or movie screen. What is captured and how it is organized and presented defines the telling of the story. The visual translation of the written word is the visualization process.

Words of a newly read screenplay spark images on the mirror of the imagination. It, in turn, reflects the images back to a hand poised on a digital drawing stylus, magic marker, or cell phone video camera button, waiting to record the initial dialogue of visual inspiration. The imagination alone does not necessarily drive this process; the *rhythm* of these two mirrors is the foundation of visualization. A **visual concept,** or the core of this inner/outer messaging, encourages the process to be consistent.

OK, so what *is* a visual concept? It is shorthand for a longer explanation; it abbreviates words into symbols, metaphors, or **tropes;** it is an image that defines the central idea of a movie. Do all films have a central idea? They should and they are presented in **iconic** terms. Why do we do this? A core image provides coherence and continuity for a film. It is the aesthetic glue that optically binds all sections of the movie, and it defines why the production designer, art director, and art department exist in the first place. Thematic manipulation threads the visual concept throughout cinema—an excellent example of it is found later in this chapter. It is the metaphor of an egg used as the basic shape of the interior pre-cog chamber of *Minority Report.* As you read the text and view the images of that particular set, you might consider why an ovoid is a better shape than a pyramid for the "idea" of this interior set within this movie. Similarly, Ken Adam's visual concepts for *Dr. Strangelove or How I Learned to Stop Worrying and Love the Bomb* (1964) or *Barry Lyndon* (1975) are perfect metaphors for their respective film designs.

Finding this key metaphor as the way into the design of a film is essential. It informs and shapes every choice, every decision throughout the art direction process. The approach you choose to take will assist you in finding the core ideas, emotions, concepts and

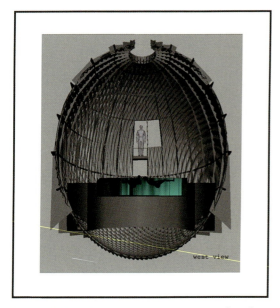

Figure 4.1a *Minority Report*, Pre-cog Chamber (2002). From *Minority Report* © 2002 Twentieth Century Fox.

imagery that can shape the design of a film. Several paths to uncovering a visual concept are listed here:

- Finding the visual arcs within the story.
- Identifying thematic elements.
- Recognizing emotional tones.
- Understanding the subtle differences between underscoring versus contrasting.

Once the visual arc of the film is established, it will reflect, support and enrich the narrative.

Let's take the search for a visual concept further. If we dig deep enough into a well-written script, there is something deeper than just designing going on—there is a primal process operating through our collective genetic information. Neuroscience is unlocking how and why good design moves us. It relates directly to the "golden

Figure 4.1b   Screen grab of the War Room model from *Dr. Strangelove* 1964.

Figure 4.1c   Screen grab at the gambling table from *Barry Lyndon* 1975.

rectangle," a concept taken from simple geometry. In ancient buildings, such as the Parthe-non and Notre Dame, a ratio of 5:8 is consistent throughout the design into the architec-tural details. A common misunderstanding is that the x and y of this ratio represent actual length and height. This is false; they actually represent the *relation* between width and height or in simplest terms, a ratio. Is this just an arbitrary pair of numbers? Apparently not. If you draw a five by eight rectangle and subtract the section of a square from it, you are left with another golden rectangle, and so on. Scientists also know that as our eyes scan the visual field for information, the golden rectangle is easiest and fastest shape to see and read. These shapes are right in front of our eyes. The paragraph rectangles containing the text of what you are reading at this moment are similar tropes to this golden mean, most conducive to "reading" the field you are scanning and retaining for future use. So is a cin-ema screen or iPhone screen. Everything old is new again.

Classic human cultures observed and used this information, and modern technology has continued to observe and reinterpret new data. It has found that human beings have remained remarkably consistent throughout its evolution—that we not only prefer images like these but also tend towards liking the basic 5:8 unit filled with an optimal fractal density[1]—about 1.3 in a range from 1 to 2. This means: the **fractal** patterns we see in nature are universal.

Our eyes, over the millennia, have grown used to this "expectation" in the visual field and feel comfortable if the picture frame or aspect ratio is filled with just enough information

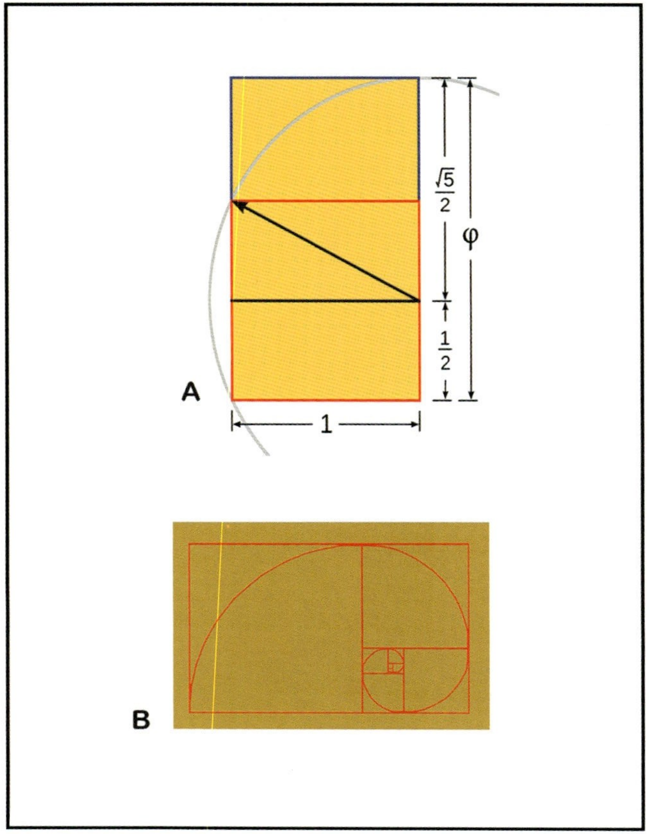

Figure 4.2b A) *Mona Lisa, 1505*. What else does this iconic image reveal? Leonardo da Vinci was determined to reveal truth through painting. B) *Convergence*, 1952. Jackson Pollack was also searching for optimal fractal density in his body of work—distilling images to reveal a balanced ratio of information?

Figure 4.2a A) A method to construct a golden rectangle. The square is outlined in red. The resulting dimensions are in the golden ratio. B) A Fibonacci spiral approximates the golden spiral using quarter circle arcs inscribed in squares of integer Fibonacci-numbers, shown for square sizes 1, 1, 2, 3, 5, 8, 13, 21 and 34.

(see "Designing for the Lens" and "Aspect Ratio," this chapter). Too much visual information contained within the golden rectangle is chaotic, and unfocused; too little creates a deficit in visual field and a craving for an acceptable stasis. The Goldilocks solution of a trope that's "just right" is key to the creation of cinematic images that satisfy.

Keep this in mind as you read through this chapter. From time to time as an aspiring art director, you will find yourself inspiring your colleagues, especially in the visual effects/art departments, to create imagery that has a hook: presented with clarity, brevity, and universality. This concept applies across the range of cinematic media—here we will focus on the disciplines of film and television.

BEGINNING THE DESIGNING PROCESS

Interactive smart media has accelerated the process of visualization. As newer technology tools become available to creative artists, the design process will become redefined as it has within the past decade. The following pages will demonstrate how both traditional and digital aspects of visualization grow out of different expressions of the same creative impulse.

Tablets such as iPads facilitate the meshing of two points of view on the same screen; with any drawing app both you and your designer can scribble with styluses or fingers to clarify conversation into imagery. Once the sketches are drawn and discussed, they can then be saved to Adobe Creative Cloud or any online server—the most practical solution for team shared visual documents. Special offer pricing for teams that hold Adobe Creative Suite edition products can be purchased at a nominal month-to-month or annual subscription fee. An initial discussion with your UPM and digital asset manager to set this up should happen early in pre-production so that each creative artist hired can connect and share effortlessly. Of course you can sketch on a napkin and scan to save but many small extra steps like that will ultimately slow down a typical hectic daily schedule. The beauty of the media devices that are evolving with more advanced intuitive features—such as voice activation and touchscreen interactivity—is that they more closely replicate the natural hand mind eye wiring of our intrinsic creativity.

An art director brings to the creative table his/her own style of uncovering and expressing imagery, which will support the visual concept of the project at hand. You will know within the first week of pre-production whether or not your creative process meshes with that of the designer. Your main goal at this time is to find a way to adjust yours to comply; then establish it as fundamental to the basic language of the collective creative departments. Other departments should come to expect a format size, nomenclature, and comprehensive quality of work from everything that is produced by the art department during the formulation process. Your closest allies to help accomplish this task are, first, your art department coordinator and, second, your archivist/digital asset manager. Setting template parameters for presentation which PAs and assistant art directors can easily replicate is an essential, as well as maintaining the level of quality you demand.

Physical concept boards are a hands-on, old-school way of sharing visual intent. Pushing imagery through the screens of our media devices provides instantaneous delivery of

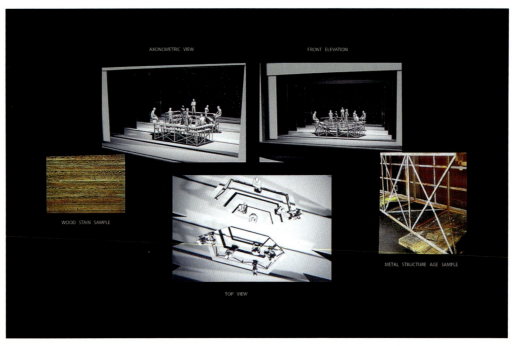

Figure 4.3   Concept Board for musical number, "Say What You Need to Say" for *Glee*. Courtesy of Chad Frey.

image content and design intent. I often find myself composing a digital presentation board of images I have culled from the Web into my iPad. This satisfies the need for mobile image updates my designer is waiting on, while scouting locations across the city. In addition to my Mac laptop and iPad I use in the office, I also work at home on a HP desktop with a touchscreen. The concept board image collage for a *Glee* Season 4 episode was created with an app that comes with the PC software. I keep the formatting to a simple minimum to allow the images to speak for themselves.

DIGITAL ASSETS AND NOMENCLATURE

"IMG_1243.jpg" is not a file name. File names are the key to having our digital assets sorted, searchable, and immediately available for use—immediate is the operative word here. Non-file names like the example at the beginning of this paragraph make "immediate" impossible. For appropriate use in the art department, something more specific to the project that is instantly accessible through search filters is extremely important to establish. The ability to search effortlessly happens through metadata, or information attached to a file which identifies it, such as file size, author, date originated, date modified, permissions, approvals, GPS info, or version tracking. Anyone familiar with Adobe Photoshop, has seen the option to enter this information as an advanced form of saving an image file,

Figure 4.4a Naming Convention #1. Created by Aaron Haye, assistant art director, for *The Curious Case of Benjamin Button.*

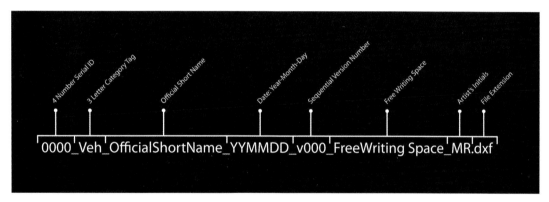

Figure 4.4b Naming Convention #2. Created by Page Buckner for *Ironman 2.*

in addition to giving the file just a name. This basic file metadata is logged automatically by Photoshop. Another way to think of metadata is as tags—the same tags we see in iPhoto or on blogs, Facebook, or Twitter, when we attach images. The real beauty of metadata is that once it is attached to a file, automatically or by the author, the search for it in the server is easy because you are simply allowing the server do the work for you, *provided you have correctly named the file.*

Nomenclature facilitates the self-organizing aspect of our digital assets.

Believe it or not, discussions about file-naming continue as every art department is organized. Why? Every creative artist's work habits are diffuse and personal. Nomenclature serves as an easy way to regiment the fruits of everyone's labor. Otherwise, allowing personal file-naming is like herding cats—virtually impossible! I've provided several examples of nomenclature used on several projects that could easily apply to one's art directing sensibility.

Naming convention #1 presents basic organizing information: category, set number or ID number, set name, description, date, author's initials and file extension. First thing to note is that "category" is a three-letter tag; "ID numbers" for sets are becoming more commonplace as set numbers are changeable throughout the filming process for one reason or another; "set name" is the official short name of a set—once established by the Art Director

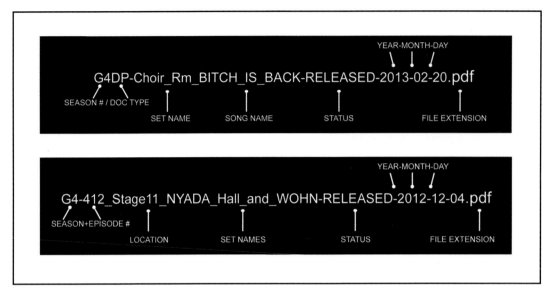

Figure 4.4c Naming Convention #3. Created by Chad Frey, set designer, for *Glee.* Note: Plans for musical numbers and typical Directors Plans are named differently.

it *does not change;* "date" is always a six-digit number written consecutively as year, then month, then day. This is a good naming convention to adopt for its shortness and because it is concise and easily readable.

Naming convention #2 contains more metadata: More metadata is more comprehensive, allowing for more searchable server tag options; some shows, by their very nature, require this level of detail in order to keep very close track of an enormous list of images, especially if there are multiple artists working on the same file.

"Category tags" are three-letter abbreviations and, as you can see, cover a sizable range of items; "free writing space" allows for additional, pertinent information for the artists or supervisors tracking the file. It could include version number information, but these would not be formal. Underscores are allowed here but no spaces; and the area for "artist's initials" allows for one or multiple artists working on the same file—all artists add their initials to keep the document up-to-date and correct. Again, this second naming convention is cumbersome and requires much more attention than most art department employees have the patience to maintain. Still, it is a legitimate option.

Naming convention #3 was designed for the episodic TV show, *Glee.* It is one that I prefer for several pragmatic reasons. Chad Frey created this particular naming sequence so that art department and online server file names mirror those of the physical flat files living in the art department. Figure 4.5 indicates a *Glee* Season 4 director's plan for the Rooftop set. In addition to showing placement of significant set pieces, director's plans are helpful to the choreographer. Art department flat files contain a separate drawer for director's plans in **tabloid format** at 11" × 17". Figure 4.6 indicates a spotting plan for Stage 11 set placement for NYADA

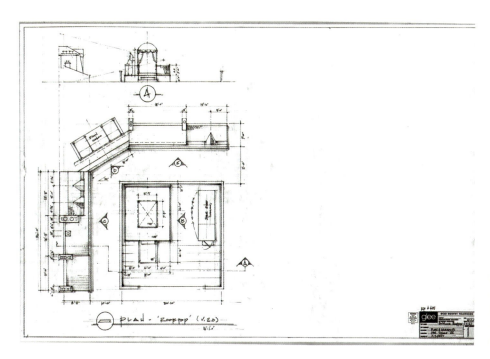

Figure 4.5
Glee Director's
Plan: Rooftop Set.
Courtesy of Chad
Frey.

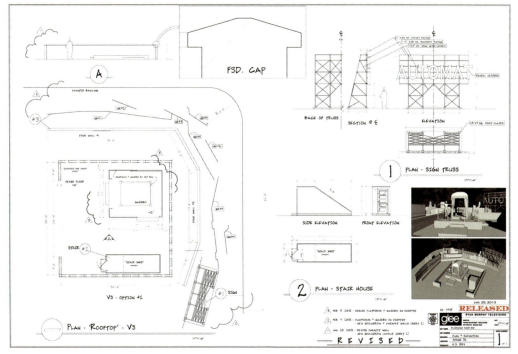

Figure 4.6 Paramount Studios, Stage 11 Spotting Plan: *Glee,* Season 4. NYADA Hallway and WOHN News Sets. Courtesy of Chad Frey.

hallway and the WOHN News set. Basically, this is a director's plan showing multiple sets. Hard, original printed copies of all drafting are printed on Arch D at 24″ × 36″ format.

The samples shown are not the shortest of naming conventions but provide all information necessary for tracking and sharing; completing the convergence of digital and paper worlds.

BUDGETING

Constructing a budget that fits the architecture of your current film is as critical as defining a solid visual metaphor for the film; it establishes a gravitas and reality to the images that will translate into physical scenery. Creating a budget to reflect the strict parameters of the new project happens within an art director's first weeks of pre-production. The purpose of budgeting is to establish certain benchmarks for things you understand—a sense of cost based on previous work experience.

Today there is no such thing as green-lighting a budget but there is a thing called locking the budget. Our initial work on budgets is done to see if the project is actually worth the expense; it's an exercise you perform for your producer. With a director, every sequence has a dollar value and trade value, as well, for all key departments. Trade value is usually for cast members. From there, the horse trading begins, and then ends with scenes or segments of the film traded for actors. Locking your numbers into the first pass of a budget enables the upper management trading game. Understanding that this process is happening behind your budgeting efforts will assist in determining what scenes might be expendable and mutable.

It's a game, that played well, can keep a budget in realistic perspective.

SET LIST AND SCHEDULING

The set list informs the workflow and the labor budget. A set list is created by scanning the script and highlighting headings—listed sets or locations formally called out in the script— and sub-headings—for graphics, significant props and set dressing items to be built by construction, visual effect sets, and vehicles. The sub-headings exist so nothing slips between the cracks. Use it as an active reference tool for scheduling work time for art department employees. Everyone working on a task to produce on item and a corresponding sub-item on the set list will create a more accurate budget assessment.

To begin, you must figure DBD or "drawing, build, and dress" time, seen as a single column on the flowchart (see details in Figure 4.18a–d). This particular process is harder if you haven't drawn as a set designer. When you're estimating drawing time you have to think about the whole process: you consider the personalities of the production designer and director, the information you have (or the lack of it), and, of course, drawing a scenery item just once or twice. There is a direct relationship between your set design time and your construction budget—the average set designer can produce $35,000–40,000 of drawings per week: e.g., living room, dining room, and simple kitchen. So, add up drawing time in terms of weeks. Sometimes, the scenery is easy and inexpensive to draw but expensive to build, e.g., sets for *Star Trek: The Next Generation.* Also, realize that digital drafting takes more time than pencil drawing; computer crashes, printer malfunctions, and plotter document backlogs take a third more time. Multiply total weeks of drawing time by a median number like $37,000 to get a rough idea of the total drawing budget. The set total is the first part of your final presentation to the UPM and should include model-making. The second part of your final presentation is the overall total. Next, after meeting with the designer on materials and "look," sit down with the construction coordinator and production designer to review sketches, photos, and research to arrive at a first budget pass. If your estimate and your coordinator's estimate are far apart, then the drawing time and/or model-making work has been underestimated. Expect to spend one week per concept illustration at best. The concept illustration list examines how many views are needed, impacting weekly work output—another sub-list of the larger set list. The graphics estimated sub-list is more about workflow rather than number of graphics per week. And, finally, schedule in some time and money for art department personnel life changes (having a baby) and other personal (medical) time considerations.

Here are some additional budget notes to consider:

- If location or build are possibilities, then give two budget numbers.
- It is important to know how other department budgets work—set dressing, props, locations, and visual effects—and when the cross-flow is significant for a producer.
- Fill large stages like Sony Studio's Stage 15: 135' × 311' or Stage 27: 134' × 237', and you will spend $1 million.
- Vehicles: everything in a vehicle is a prototype and a close-up, therefore expensive.

LABOR BUDGET AND SCHEDULING

Multiple art directors indicate split shifts, multiple units, staggered work weeks, and location work—less art directors are needed for studio work. An art director's work week is tied to the shooting schedule. Labor budget items you will address are: position name, weekly rate, box allowance, vehicle allowance, start date/finish date, pre-production weeks, shoot weeks, wrap, and total. For box rental line items, insert what is fair and what is right, not the studio's concept of what should be allotted. Wrap weeks are the flexible area on the budget page. This is specific to digital set designers: organizing files—product assets—onto storage media. Reshoots are more a likelihood than a possibility. Certain miniature models will not be charged to construction but to another department. Those work hours are calculated as work time on a set.

Fast Track Software

This software was developed for large construction industry projects. It's a very intuitive program and designing the schedule is a lot like doing a drawing. A Fast Track workflow chart follows the set list and is the most important document to generate. It includes DBD and not strike.

Take note: the first questions a producer asks are: how many stages are needed and what are the size requirements? This schedule will help determine when a producer can rent stage space between scheduled shooting times for the project at hand but it also indicates the basic rental expense for the run of the shooting time. Keep this in the back of your mind as you continue.

As you begin your first pass on the budget, consider the drawing weeks based on the first pass of the shooting schedule, if it exists. Remember, the chart only reflects set design time and subsequent construction. The schedule shown in Figure 4.18a–d represents the efforts of approx. 450 people. It also shows backing deliveries and when they will shoot. This schedule is designed before any drawing has been done. As soon as it is set in motion, it becomes a living, organic drawing. It is a constant juggling act but it is the truth.

If you do this schedule *first*, then you know more about the film than anybody. You know where the shooting crew is headed, when they'll get in trouble and when it will get tough for your department.

Delivering the Message

You can't deliver a message to someone who won't listen. So, what do you do? You will use the Fast Track schedule as a "picture" of the process, much like the overall view of a one-line schedule. As an art director it's your job to keep stoking the fire to fuel the entire effort. Also, referring to the schedule, keeping both eyes on the beginning of each of the colored lines—the commencement of another set, vehicle, set of graphics, or set dressing related built pieces. All of this data allows an art director to budget and speak with authority at large meetings. You have to defend everything you do and every action you put into motion; it's easiest when you have the edge over most on the project with this information.

DIGITAL TOOLS AND WORKFLOW

Previously, we have defined how visual imagery emerges and discussed the basics of how digital assets are named and organized. Now let's explore image creation and the workflow it generates.

The Art Director stands at the nexus of this workflow, delineating the management of a growing digital burden. The digital tools currently at our disposal impact a dozen different areas of pre-vis: research, stage plans, set info, graphics, locations, props and specialties, set construction, CAD/CAM, set decoration, document lists, rented or manufactured backings, and the VFX pipeline. The tool options available to us are numerous, so the question remains: what programs should I learn to function in the art department? The answer I provide here is based on a decade of observation, discussion, comparing notes with colleagues, and a consensus on what serves us best.

Rhino

Rhinoceros (Rhino) is a standalone, NURBS-based 3-D modeling software, originally developed by Robert McNeel & Associates as a plug-in for AutoCAD. The software is well-suited to the entertainment industry because of its common uses in industrial design, architecture, marine design, jewelry design, automotive design, CAD/CAM, rapid prototyping, reverse engineering, and product design, as well as the multimedia and graphic design industries. More than 100 third-party plugins are available, including plugins for CAM and CNC milling. For our use in the art department, Rhino supports the following CAD and image file formats natively without use of external plugins: DWG/DXF (AutoCAD 200x, 14, 13, and 12), uncompressed TIFF, Google SketchUp. Maya, MAX 3.0. At this time (2013), DWF and DWFx file formats from Autodesk products are not supported.[2]

Rhino's increasing popularity is based on its diversity, multidisciplinary functions, low learning-curve, relatively low cost, and its ability to import and export more than 30 file formats, which allows Rhino to act as a "converter" tool between programs in a design workflow. Its paper space allows for non-destructive section cuts to be clearly labeled and dimensioned for working drawings (see www.rhino3d.com/features.htm).

Photoshop

Adobe Photoshop is *the* premier graphics editing program for all aspects of our multidimensional industry. The more robust of its two editions, Adobe Photoshop Extended, contains extra 3D image creation, motion graphics editing, and advanced image analysis features.[3]

The ability to now paint 3D models with three-dimensional brushes and warping tools has made Photoshop an extremely powerful pre-vis tool. Realism in all aspects of texture, aging, and variety of surface quality on any dimensional object can be done effortlessly. Simple text extrusion; an available library of materials for three-dimensional application; and even wrapping two-dimensional images around 3D geometry have made Photoshop a premier art department tool.

A significant 2D feature worth discussing is the "straighten tool," which allows a user to simply draw a line anywhere on an image, parallel to a plane in the image. The canvas will reorient itself so that the line drawn becomes horizontal, and adjusts the media accordingly, reorienting the image to that plane to easier achieve certain perspectives. This has its obvious benefits.

SketchUp

SketchUp is a 3D modeling program for a broad range of applications: architectural, civic, mechanical, and film, as well as video game design—it is available in free as well as professional versions. The program highlights its ease of use, and its online repository of model assemblies (3D Warehouse) enables designers to locate, download, use and contribute free models. The program includes a drawing layout functionality, allows surface rendering in variable "styles," accommodates third-party plug-in programs enabling other capabilities (e.g., near photo realistic rendering) and enables placement of its models within Google Earth.

SketchUp lets you export raster images up to 10,000 pixels square, so generating an image that you can send in an email, publish in a document, or project on a wall is as easy as choosing a few options: .tiff, .jpeg or .png and clicking "Export." The free version of SketchUp can export 3D to .dae and Google Earth's .kmz file format. The pro version extends exporting support to include the .3ds, .dwg, .dxf, .fbx, .obj, .xsi, and .wrl file formats. SketchUp can also save elevations or renderings of a model, called "screenshots," as .bmp, .png, .jpg, .tiff, with the pro version also supporting .pdf, .eps, .epx, .dwg, and .dxf.[4]

Downloading SketchUp-Pro is a prerequisite for professional work in the art department.

- SketchUp-Pro allows you to import and export DXFs and DWGs, giving you an easy way to move plans, sections, elevations, or even your whole model into and out of your favorite CAD program. Imported and exported geometry remains at 1:1 scale, and layers are preserved.
- With the pro version of SketchUp, you can export views of your models in PDF and EPS format, allowing you to continue to work on them in vector editing programs like Illustrator and Freehand—especially for 2D images that need to be resolution-independent.
- You can export your models to a number of useful 3D formats. These exporters allow SketchUp-Pro to join most professional workflows by offering interoperability with 3D modeling applications.
- The paper space in LayOut is very rudimentary; too limited for proper, dimensioned, working drawings. Despite this drawback, SketchUp has quickly become an art department standard and digital game-changer for 3D renderings beyond Photoshop.

As powerful and versatile as SketchUp has become, it is important to stress the fact that it is primarily a tool for pre-visualization; a 3D modeling "sketch" of proposed scenery. It should *not* be thought of as an illustration program, nor should it be used by anyone in the art department as a replacement for the skills of a concept illustrator—this would be in direct violation of current union contracts—and must be vigilantly monitored by the Art Director.

The combined power of these tools we just reviewed allows a smooth workflow to occur within the confines of the art department and the network of the larger creative effort of a TV or film project. Media merge is the goal; if any of the tools take precedence at any time, then focus on the finished product has been lost. The blending of technique, method, and supervision keep the workflow unencumbered. The variables of budget and workflow are directly interlinked; a sure way to keep both intact is to hire excellent personnel who can stay focused and consistently deliver. Keep this in mind as you continue your journey through this chapter.

RESEARCH

Gathering visual research is a powerful way to define the visual concept. Within the first several weeks of pre-production, the walls of the art department quickly become plastered as a repository of photocopied and color printed images: icons, **indexes, symbols,** and

metaphors of the visual concept for the film. We surround ourselves with these images and live within them while we design. The Internet and public libraries are inexpensive ways to accumulate data, and are also more visually comprehensive for research data and imagery than one might guess. Most of the research done for the TV movie *The Lost Battalion* (2001) was downloaded from the World War I archives of the University of Kansas to my PC terminal on location in Luxembourg City.

Rare portraits of Cher Ami, a carrier pigeon and First World War hero, and specific photographic references to his carrying cages, and a typical message tube strapped to his ankle, were pulled from the University of Kansas historical archives website (See Figure 4.7). No book was able to provide this kind of indispensable, arcane information. Most research is found through the normal channels mentioned and can also be bought from private photographic collections, as is the case for Figure 4.8, which shows several images taken in San Francisco in the 1940s.

In Los Angeles, if actual video and DVD rental for hard-to-locate film research is required, Eddie Brandt's Saturday Matinee located in North Hollywood is available for a nominal fee. Its catalogue of films includes animation, film noir, sci-fi, exploitation, documentary, live entertainment, foreign, silents, serials, and black films—titles and genres not available at Netflix. As the front page of its catalogue boasts, "We've acquired three centuries of movies in 33 years!"

Figure 4.7 Cher Ami, pigeon carrier cages and message tube—examples of hard-to-find Internet research images.

A designated research budget can buy 30-minute increments of research time (in 2014, at the time this edition was compiled) at the 20th Century Fox Studios Research Library, the Warner Bros. Research Collection in Burbank, the Lillian Michelson Research Library now located at DreamWorks, and the Margaret Herrick Library at the Motion Picture Academy of Arts and Sciences in Los Angeles. These research facilities tend to be expensive, but they are also extraordinary source centers of rare, well-archived images either custom-burned onto CD or beautifully photocopied at the customer's request. Several of the images used for this book came from those collections.

The Fox Studio Research Library is unique among the studios and popular with art department research teams for the scope of its available material. For example, it provides assistance for all types of projects throughout the production process, features a collection of more than 40,000 non-fiction books on all topics, more than 100 current periodical subscriptions, computer workstations with high-speed Internet access and powerful graphics capabilities including color copier/printer/scanner/CDRW,

Figure 4.8   Typical research images *Murder in the First*, a 1940's period film.

online services including Nexis, *Reader's Guide,* and *New York Times* archives, and supplies art department creatives with 2D and moving picture, visual reference materials. Like most research libraries you can also phone or email your research requests.

During the earliest stages of pre-production, the art department by default becomes the center of visual source materials for the entire production. Gathering research during pre-production is a time to steep your psyche into the era presented within the pages of the script, and it is a time to become as deeply knowledgeable about the historical context of your film to help resolve whatever questions that might arise. In the case of Cher Ami, the World War I hero pigeon, several downloaded photos in-hand were undisputed evidence for which pigeon to cast in the starring role based on the original bird's feather markings. Our relentless drive to produce critical data and visual information makes the art department the premier place to answer these questions. Historical dramas, in particular, demand tremendous detail and scrutiny through research sourcing and data gathering. Linda Berger, assistant art director and key art department researcher for *Forrest Gump* (1994), recalls a landmark experience in her early career.

Interview with Linda Berger

● *Linda, on* Forrest Gump *you were the Assistant Art Director and managed the research for the film. Would you tell us a little bit about that?*

I was one of the first people hired onto pre-production. The vision of Rick Carter, the Production Designer, was very clear and straightforward: the film was a character-driven piece and needed to feel real and human, not like a documentary, although the fictional story clearly had its basis in historical events. It needed to be infused with the humanity of the time we were portraying—meaning, because we were creating history that was relatively recent, we needed to be true not only to that history as it really was, but to History as people who actually experienced it or remembered it in their mind's eye. With that concept in mind, I built the beginnings of a huge research library. It was truly exciting for me. Kacy Magedman, art department coordinator, and assistant coordinator Anna Hayward did a great deal of footwork for us all along the way. And we kept adding to it, and it eventually filled a room with file cabinets and stacks of information. I focused on sources of recent history like prominent newspapers and *Life, Look, Time,* and *Better Homes and Gardens* magazines. *Time* was a great source for Vietnam research, and the others provided a rich diversity of pop-cultural images. And, of course, Lillian Michelson was a tremendous help to me.

In Washington, DC, I also found police newsreels about the 1960s anti-war demonstrations and other rallies that had taken place at the Lincoln Memorial where our staged film rally would take place. Also, at hippie campsites in and around DC and the Jefferson Memorial, where the protestors had stayed overnight, I learned about the kinds of buses that had come from all over the country to bring protesters to the city. Period newsreels were a wealth of information showing signage, buttons, graphics, and banners, as well as style of dress. There was also loads of information to be found about TV trucks and cars, sound and TV equipment, TV cameras' scaffolding and staging, as well as research on police cars and equipment; a lot of it very surprising and sobering. Every image was used as a "true image"—we didn't guess about what we would see–down to creating signs, for example, and we tried to re-create them in their original materials such as cardboard from the backs of cardboard boxes with the folds still attached and poster paints or canvas. Paramount Sign Shop was tremendously helpful. They did the bulk of the work preparing the signage. They reserved a whole crew of sign writers to work on well over 1,700 images including signs, banners, and so on. Robin Miller, our brilliant Prop Master, created armbands, buttons, and many of the bumper stickers—all based on much of the research we did together.

Much additional info in DC came from tech people I talked to at the networks who did on-the-spot reporting at the time. We were also able to track down some of the original photographers who had gone to some of the actual rallies and were able to purchase their personal photos of the events. These were extremely valuable. Other research came from the Library of Congress, which helped us understand the importance of getting it all historically correct. I was able to hire a great researcher in Washington, who culled through all kinds of police reports and records to help me find information that shed light on a lot of historical background information about the Vietnam era as well as Watergate. And Rick Porras and Steven Boyd, working then in Bob Zemeckis' office, spent weeks during pre-production in Washington going through film archives for images that would be seen in the film, such as the images of Kennedy, Johnson, and many others. They brought back many clips that were also of great use to me for research as well.

With all of those wonderful places as a springboard, we began to create an outline marrying our historical and current events timelines with the one emerging for Forrest and Jenny, the two main characters. Their childhood and adulthood events needed to mirror or coincide with cultural history in order to remain true to Rick's visual concept of "real and human." Rick loved collages as a way to find the essence of character and asked me to create a visual timeline for Jenny's character, for example. It took up one entire wall in the art department. It was dedicated to everything that might have been present in her daily life and overall life history, such as magazine ads, book images reflecting the lifestyle of the 1950s through the 1980s, and even her route through her drug use, reflected in her character in terms of the times in which the story was being told. Along the top of her personal historical timeline were the years broken down into months of the year and decades; along the side of the chart, there was a section designed for specifics such as hair, dress, school, entertainment, furnishings, cultural interests, etc. Everyone used the wall containing the story of Jenny's life. Joanna Johnston, Costume Designer, in particular found it very valuable. Once I had collected enough information, I began to make large books, and these were available for everyone to look through and use as research. There was a Washington history Vietnam War Rally research book, the largest and heaviest of all of them, and others ranging from the Southern US, the Vietnam War, to the strip clubs and discos, and the New York City of the 1970s. Art Directors, Jim Teegarden in LA and Leslie McDonald down in Beaufort, South Carolina, and Savannah, Georgia, used these books and added even more research.

I had the great good fortune to go to Washington and supervise the creation of the Lincoln Memorial Rally and campsites and Watergate events with Robin Miller. I'll never forget it. It was such a wonderful and inspiring creative experience. The day we shot the rally at the Lincoln Memorial, Eric Roth, the Screenwriter, remarked to me—and I'll never forget it—that the way it all looked and felt that day was as he had imagined it in his mind's eye. That was a truly gratifying moment for both Rick and me. I'm very proud of what we were all able to accomplish there.[5]

WHO IS DESIGNING?

Storyboarding

Although there is no specific outline available for a designer's visualization process, some are inclined to rely on storyboards as an effective shorthand method of visually communicating with the Director and Cinematographer. What we now refer to as "animatics," has its roots in storyboard sketching. Harold Michelson's boards for *The Ten Commandments* (1956) and *The Cotton Club* (1984), Figure 4.9a and b respectively, are extraordinary examples of pre-visualizing the shooting sequence of a motion picture.

Even though digital tools exist to perform the same tasks as hand-drawn storyboards and concept sketching, both forms of storytelling continue to be used because they are immediate and also explore idea possibilities in a way that **CGI** cannot. Most often, the storyboard artist and concept modeler on computer are working simultaneously on different aspects of the same visual concept. The storyboard artist is drawing two-dimensionally, bound by the rectangular **aspect ratio** of the actual movie screen and filling in the boxes with the continuity of images, while the concept modeler/digital set designer is sculpting digital space to present a different angle of the same ideas presented in the storyboard sketches. Both paths eventually lead to the same place and both descriptions of the journey help to create a richer design.

Animatics

In comparison, the animatics image pages shown in Figure 4.10a–d are fully self-explanatory. Each cell or window of the typical storyboard page sequence is expanded onto its own page. As you can see, each page of the pre-visualized, computer-generated sketch indicates plan, elevation, isometric sketches for specific scenes, set info, camera info, and additional equipment info, e.g., use of a Techno crane as well as camera blocking data.

Timing is essential in cinematic storytelling because it is directly reflected in the budget. So, using animatic formats is not only helpful in linking sound and visual elements in the storytelling process but also in optimizing shooting time. Currently, video game production uses animatic formats, usually linking motion capture data in the mix. (This is an area of entertainment technology not examined in this book; other Focal Press publications will be helpful.)

The terms "animatics" and "Pixel Front Liberation" are synonymous. PLF (*Iron Man, Green Lantern, Rise of the Planet of the Apes, The Matrix Reloaded*) is located in Venice, California and provides CGI and other special effects services for clients in the film, TV, advertising, music videos, and interactive games industries. The company also creates 3D computer animation software that helps movie directors plan film shoots, indicated in the pages for *Panic Room* (2002) show in Figure 4.10a–d. The first section of a recent interview with PLF founder and creative director Colin Green explains the vital contribution of storyboarding on the pre-vis process and how a design resolves itself through animatics.

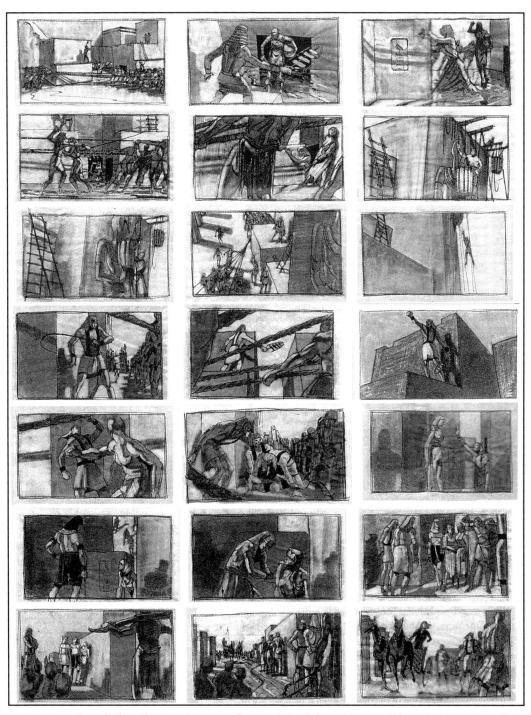

Figure 4.9a   Storyboards for *The Ten Commandments* (1956) drawn by Harold Michelson. These boards read from L to R across the page. Courtesy of of Lillian Michelson and Paramount Studios.

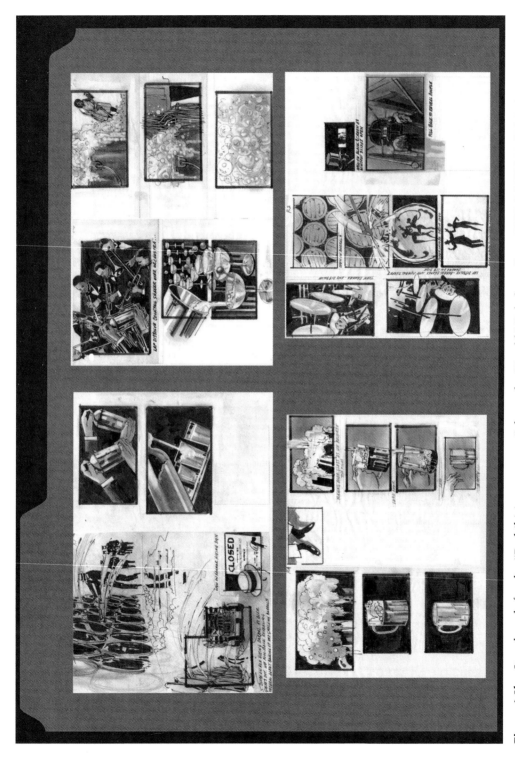

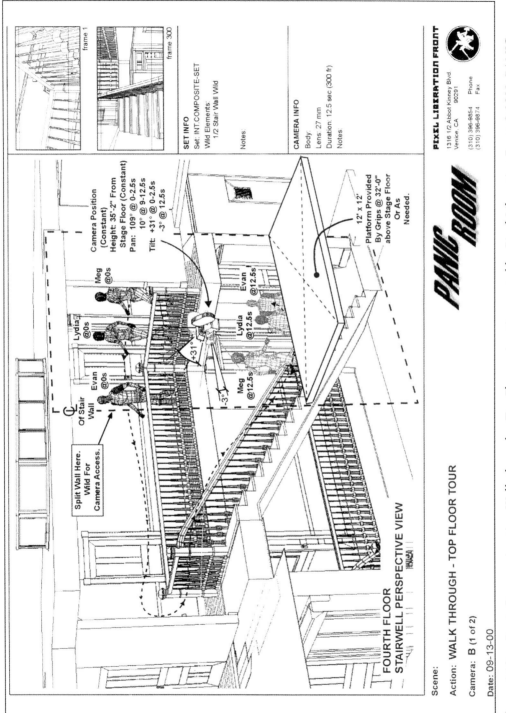

Figure 4.10a *Panic Room* animatics. Walk through—Top Floor animatic, created by Pixel Liberation Front © 2000. PANIC ROOM © Columbia Pictures Industries, Inc. All Rights Reserved—Courtesy of Columbia Pictures.

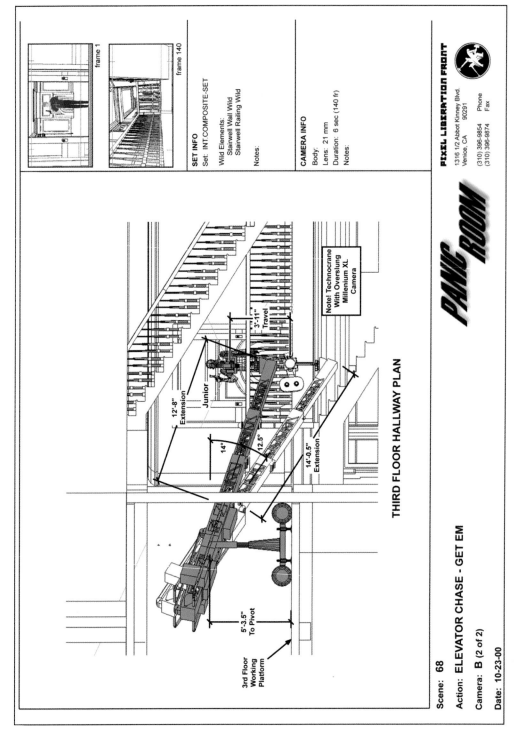

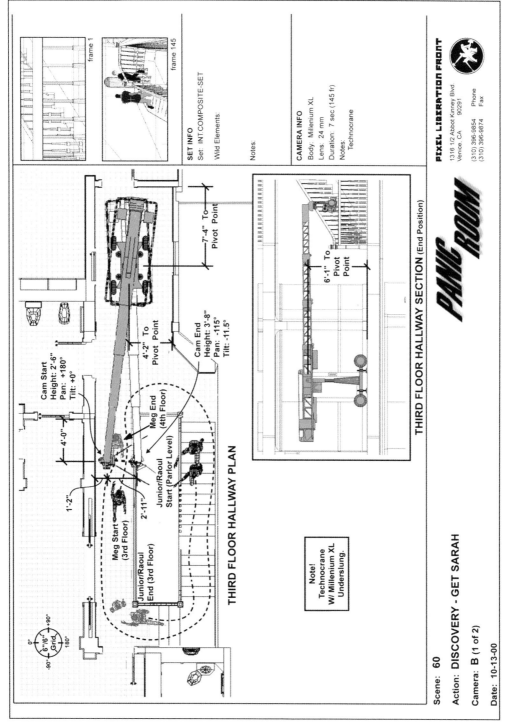

Figure 4.10c Discovery—Get Sarah animatic, created by Pixel Liberation © 2000. PANIC ROOM © Columbia Pictures Industries, Inc. All Rights Reserved—Courtesy of Columbia Pictures.

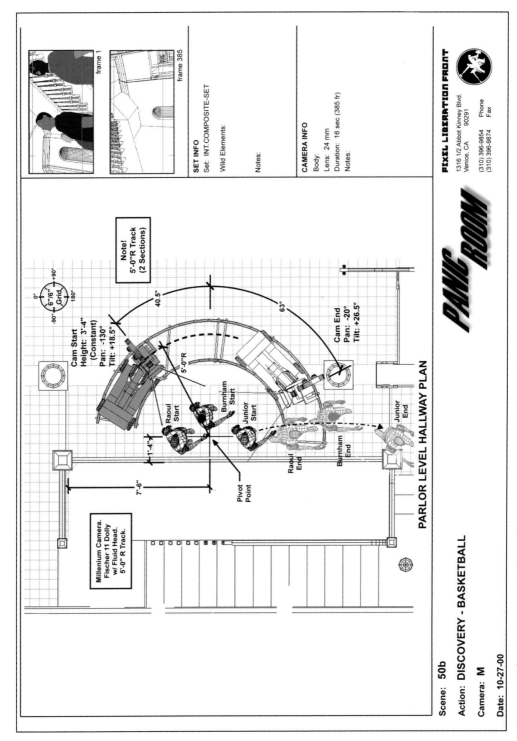

Figure 4.10d Discovery—Basketball animatic, created by Pixel Liberation Front © 2000. PANIC ROOM © Columbia Pictures Industries, Inc. All Rights Reserved—Courtesy of Columbia Pictures.

Interview with Colin Green

● *Did you work alongside a storyboard artist on* Panic Room?

Peter Ramsey was the storyboard artist on our team. He would sit with us and spend a lot of time tweaking and finessing the camera angles and the blocking as a filter on David Fincher's direction. Peter was able to scribble all of his thumbnails down and digest David's stream of director-ese as he quickly and carefully laid out his initial shooting sequence to both of us. Peter was instrumental in getting us oriented; as computer animators, we had had little exposure to that much information, that fast. Our first pass found us compiling our shot list. The secondary pass focused on finessing and refining the composition.

One of the main reasons David wanted us to participate in that film is because of the unique way that set was built, with all four floors of that brownstone built within their proper relationship. All floors were set up in the new Raleigh Studios in Manhattan Beach, California, as they would be in reality. As you know, you would normally split the levels of the house into separate floors onto a sound stage **spotting plan** with the ability to **wild** rooms for shooting easy access. All four walls of all rooms on all four floors were built and set in place, as they would be on a location. So there was a lot of sharing of blueline drawings back and forth. Paul Westcott was the draftsperson liaison for both departments.

We were doing shots with motion control that initially required precise grip participation. David did many takes he wasn't happy about. You can't look at a single shot and say, "That's right or wrong." You have to look at it in sequence. In the film there was the big shot running about four minutes, tracking along the staircase, through a keyhole, and up through the ceiling. That shot was scheduled originally to be a Techno crane shot segment. Because the **gripology** involved in hitting the mark or getting the shot as smooth as David would've preferred was not being accomplished, we collectively decided to build the shot in the computer and then feed that data to the motion control camera where the shot would be executed pixel by pixel. In that way, the camera would do exactly what David had approved in terms of certain speed changes and framing relationships he wanted. The tricky thing was finding that single piece of equipment that was available and could reach all those spots that needed to be reached. Of course, the boom had to be long enough but agile enough not to bump into scenery architecture, and the track needed to fit on the staircase but not be in the shot. The Gazelle camera system is the one that fulfilled all requests.[6]

The balance of the Colin Green interview concludes in Chapter 7 and provides some insight on integrating art department imagery into the animatic process, the intimacy of the director–pre-vis working relationship, and the expectations of pre-visualization.

CONCEPT ILLUSTRATING

The work of James Clyne, concept illustrator (*Lincoln, Cowboys & Aliens, Avatar, Minority Report, Bicentennial Man*), presented in Figure 4.11, underlines the importance of pre-visualization in sketching and drawing. In essence, a concept sketch can be a single frame plucked from a continuity storyboard, or it can represent a visual concept for a set,

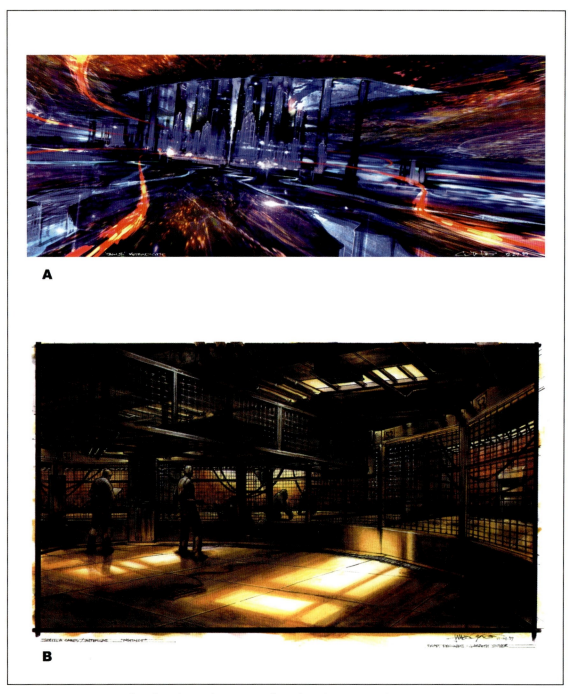

Figure 4.11   Concept sketches drawn by James Clyne for A) *Tron 2* and B) *Instinct* © Disney.

a scene, or an entire film. A concept illustrator, whose skills are often shared between a designer and a director, is a fundamental interpreter of ideas in an ongoing creative dialogue. In many **high concept** films, the development of an illustrator's key visual metaphors must forward the development of a designer's visual concept. Often, the inherent imagery of an illustrator's productivity is a strong factor in the final design concept and realization of physical scenery. James Clyne reinforces this fact.

Interview with James Clyne

● *James, do most directors give you an indication of their vision for a particular sequence, or are you expected to generate conceptual options in order to begin your working relationship?*
It varies from director to director. Everyone has a different style of working. Most directors will come to me with very specific ideas and very few will be able to draw them. After our first meeting, I usually have a pretty good idea of where someone is going and what is necessary to see so we can really begin the process. Every director relies on me to interpret ideas quickly like a storyboard artist. I'm good at thinking on my feet and can come up with something that gets a strong response.

   If an image I create is strong enough, then sometimes a conceptual sketch can define the look of an entire film. One image that quickly comes to mind is a sketch I did for *TRON: Legacy* for Disney (Figure 4.11). We explored a few ways to define the world inside the computer environment. The sketch idea is a powerful example of how the concept of a world we've never seen but only can imagine can exist first on a piece of paper.[7]

COMPUTER MODELING

Architecture has traditionally provided the original source for visualizing a constructed form through the disciplines of drafting and model making. The film industry has quickly adopted its pre-visualization methods by empowering the art department's ability to explore the structural possibilities of sets before they are built. What was once only achievable in post-production, can now happen in real time from the earliest stages of pre-visualization throughout the fullest range of digital and physical scenery production. Currently, no stone remains unturned. In addition to developing a unique pre-vis vocabulary for motion picture design, we are also providing accurate design data to the visual effects department. A sophisticated understanding of digital technology and a networked team of people using digital tools places the designer and art department closer to the center of information generation that will determine and control the look of a film. Evidence of this is showcased in images from *The Terminal* (2004), shown in Figures 4.12–4.14. Except for the photograph of *The Terminal* set shot in Figure 4.12, the remaining five images are digitally derived or enhanced. These images particularly, exemplify commonplace uses of state-of-the-art cinema software. Advances in this technology multiply the possibility of creative cinematic vision and also ensure the delivery of specific storytelling elements of all creative participants.

Figure 4.12   A) CG model of interior newsstand set for *The Terminal*. B) Set shot of interior set for *The Terminal* showing elliptical backing and reflective ceiling. Photograph by Merrick Morton for the motion picture *The Terminal*™ © 2004 DW Studios, LLC. All Rights Reserved.

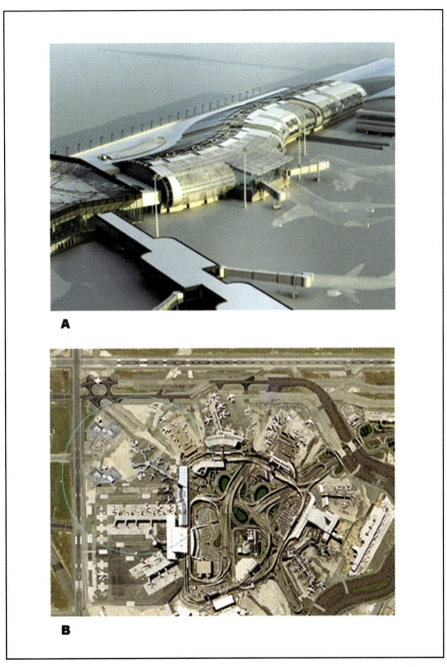

Figure 4.13   A) CG model of the exterior of the terminal set for *The Terminal*. B) Aerial view of JFK Airport showing CG addition (circled) for *The Terminal*. Photograph by Merrick Morton for the motion picture *The Terminal*™ © 2004 DW Studios, LLC. All Rights Reserved.

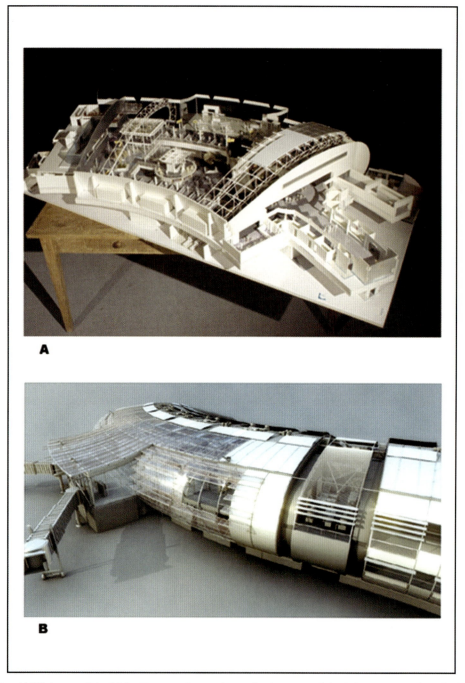

Figure 4.14   A) White model of *The Terminal* set. B) Finished CG model of the exterior detail of *The Terminal* set. Courtesy of Alex McDowell. Photograph by Merrick Morton for the motion picture *The Terminal*™ © 2004 DreamWorks L.L.C., reprinted with permission by DreamWorks L.L.C.

More specific updates in digital modeling are explained by the rapid prototyping process on *Reign of Fire* (2002) in a brief section from a longer interview with concept artist and digital set designer Victor Martinez.

Interview with Victor Martinez

● *Victor, was NURBS (Non-Uniform Rational Bezier Splines) modeling the basis for the rapid prototyping used in Reign of Fire?*

The rapid prototyping done on *Reign of Fire* involved the process called stereolithography requiring .STL files. These files are polygonal not NURBS, and require solid modeling, or totally closed volumes, versus surface modeling. All the modeling had to be done as solids and converted to polygonal objects. There are other types of rapid prototyping techniques that favor NURBS surfaces rather than solid polygonal objects. It all depends on the type of fabrication technique being used.

On that show, I was solely in the VFX department doing rapid prototyping modeling. It's a different ball game from traditional set design modeling in that we were creating pieces that would be grown out of wax. We had manageable, miniature model pieces capable of being casted off and fabricated in multiple. Our main project was a miniature of the House of Parliament in quarter-inch scale that ended up being 20 feet long. It took six to eight weeks to get the modeling and fabricating ready for two to three weeks of painting and detailing. The model shop supervisor mentioned that by utilizing digital modeling and rapid prototyping in the fabrication of the miniature model, we were able to expedite that process, and in the end, save money on the total cost of its production rather than make the model entirely by hand.

● *When you're rapid prototyping aren't you modeling in full scale?*

Yes, I worked in real scale where a foot is a foot. When I exported it out to the fabricators, it was in quarter-inch scale, so it's much like printing a page from 11 × 17 to 8.5 × 11. The wax is "printed" in layers on top of a base sheet as opposed to other types of prototyping where you can do undercuts from full 3D blocks of material. As you might guess, this finished wax model in its many pieces acts as a positive mold for the final model measuring 20 feet in length. An advantage to this was that we had unlimited pieces that could be generated from the original and used for creating other models. It was used as a composite matte shot with live action in the foreground and the miniature in background, essentially like any other miniature matte shot would've been.[8]

WHITE MODELS

Sometimes, it is actually easier to physically build a white model than to take the time to generate a digital concept model on a computer screen. Luke Freeborn, digital set designer and modeler (*Inception, The Terminal, The Chronicles of Riddick, Van Helsing*) supports this:

A major portion of what we do has to be done by pencil and paper or a physical model because it can be faster, given where you are in the process. So, a napkin and a pen can be a stronger tool than anything else.[9]

With its origins in architecture, a white model is not as developed as an architectural model of a building—it acts as a 3D sketch of a scenery volume, representing a set or a full-scale scenic object like the oversized kitchen table in *Eternal Sunshine of the Spotless Mind* (2004). A white model happens quickly. Drafting for interior sets, for instance, is photocopied and then spray mounted onto 3/16″ fomecore. The set walls are cut out of the fomecore as individual pieces, then glued or t-pinned together as rough 1/4″ model sketches. Like computer-generated concept models, white models allow the viewer to analyze the structure and make appropriate changes to the evolving design. This small, easily handled, physical replica of a set or scenic piece then underlines the value of constructing a quick and dirty white model from 1/4″ scale drafting to support the visual understanding of a set for the Director and Cinematographer (See Figure 4.14). Looking into a white model and studying its volumetric relationships can easily determine the need for **wild walls,** for example, where none had originally been indicated. As integral as CG modeling has become in the pre-vis process, there are instances when a physical model is more dynamic in its ability to reveal the potential of built scenery.

SKETCHUP

The future plans for SketchUp were recently discussed at SketchUp Basecamp, a semi-annual event in Boulder, Colorado, that attracts SketchUp users from around the world for a three-day conference. Here's the abbreviated breakdown Trimble has set for the 3D modeler: 1) The program is going to stay simple to use, and it's going to get a lot more complex as well, and 2) The company sees SketchUp as a platform as well as an application. Besides this news from the 2012 conference, these are some additional points that should answer most people's questions about the future of the platform/application:

- There will always be a free version of SketchUp available and the basic program will never be more complicated to learn.
- The Pro version will continue to be developed and you will see a continually greater difference between its abilities and those of the free version.
- They will continue to support third-party developers in creating compatible software and plugins to work within SketchUp. More than 45% of users have and use third-party plugins with SketchUp and they want to continue to support the creation of useful additions that they would never develop in-house, hoping that each industry will take the initiative in creating plugins for specific needs.
- They will continue to support "everyone else" as well. Since the program is used in so many varied industries and vocations, the company wants the software to be truly useful to anyone who uses it to create.
- They plan to continue to make the software run bigger and more complex models as fast as possible by any means they can.
- The company is ramping up their team size and is currently looking for new talent. Trimble is pumping a lot of money into the company, especially in LayOut, their

software for creating construction drawings from Sketch Up models. They plan on continuing to improve the drawing program to equal any CAD package out there.

- Starting in 2013 with the release of the next version, the company will go to annual updates instead of the random release dates we've become used to. Another sign that the software's development is going to proceed at a much faster rate than it did at Google.
- Also, there are plans to overhaul the 3D Warehouse. The Warehouse now contains over two million models with over one thousand new models added each week, many by major manufacturers. They plan to update it to make it easier to use and easier to find content.
- Finally, it was announced that the company has developed an STL importer/exporter for creating model files for use in stereolithography and 3D printing. Now that companies like Makerbot have made desk-top 3D printers available in the $2,000 range, 3D printing may soon become as common as paper printers.

All art directors are now fluent in Sketch Up as a daily working tool. As a matter of fact, it is so ubiquitous that assistant ADs, production assistants and art coordinators have acquired a basic skill level. Like Photoshop, it has become the great democratizer of the art department.

One of the most versatile set designers I know shares observations and experience: Randy Wilkins is a Hollywood veteran (*TRON: Legacy, The Social Network, The Girl with the Dragon Tattoo, The Curious Case of Benjamin Button, Catch Me if You Can*). He discusses the scope of his work as a set designer and how he incorporates SketchUp and various plug-ins into his workflow.

Interview with Randy Wilkins

- *How does Sketch Up relate to what you do?*

  Since LayOut was added to SketchUp Pro, I pretty much do 95% of all my work in SketchUp and LayOut, and I'm always finding new ways to use it. We have to create a lot of our drawings from photographs either to recreate a historic building or furniture piece or to match a location for sets built on stage or on a back lot. With LayOut I can add textures, shading or even paste in my hand drawings into my documents. They just have a lot more life than CAD drawings do. People are now realizing that SketchUp is much more than a modeling program. I still get surprised responses from some people when they see a drawing package I've done in Sketch Up. I did some work for the television series *Glee*. They wanted to recreate the theater they used for their first season, so I surveyed the location and modeled a slightly smaller version in SketchUp and executed the drawings in LayOut. The key grip looked at the prospective sections I included with the drawings and asked about the software I used; he was surprised when I told him it was SketchUp.

  The film *Catch Me If You Can* (2002) opens with a re-creation of a popular television show from the 1970s called *To Tell the Truth*. Production designer Jeannine Oppewall asked me to create construction drawings to build a replica of the original set that was accurate enough to matte-in portions of video from the original show. The original drawings were long gone, and the only reference I had was a still from the video. To accomplish this, I used technique called **back-projection** which basically uses the rules of perspective in reverse, as in Figure 4.15. From a photo we can figure out a scale to create measured drawings as well as determine the size of the original lens, camera height, tilt and so on. I determined it was much easier to do the process in Sketch Up, by creating the plan view to scale, right in the model.

Another Sketch-Up tool I use a lot is Match Photo, which is a nice companion to doing a back-projection. I've been using it to create models of buildings that no longer exist. For a film called *A Question Of Loyalty* which did really well on the festival circuit. It takes place in Germany and deals with the loss of civil liberties in the late 1930s. The story takes place mostly in an apartment of the Reitlinger House, designed by the architect Friedrich Weinbrenner, and destroyed during World War II. I used several period photos and Weinbrenner's original plan to reconstruct a SketchUp model to determine how much of the building needed to be a physical set and how much could be digital (Figure 4.16).

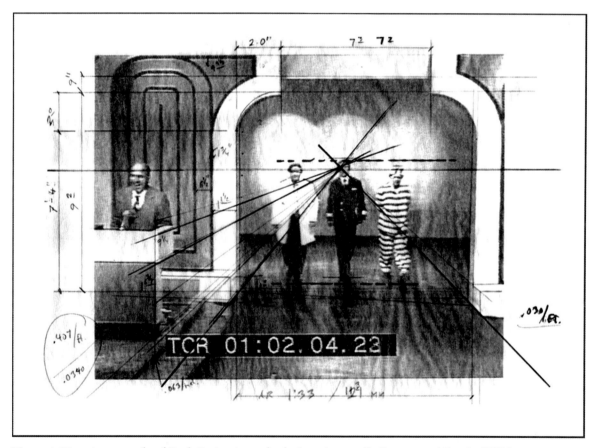

Figure 4.15a   An example of Back Projection calculations in pencil. Courtesy of Randy Wilkins.

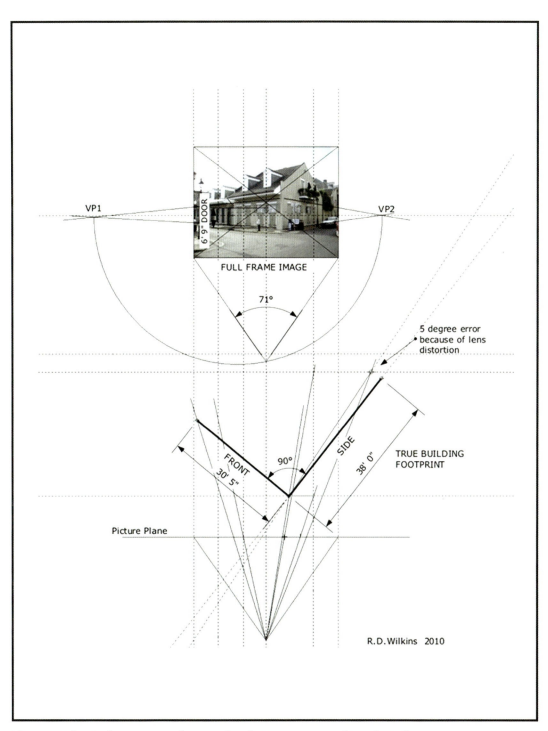

Figure 4.15b Back Projection done in Sketch-Up. Courtesy of Randy Wilkins.

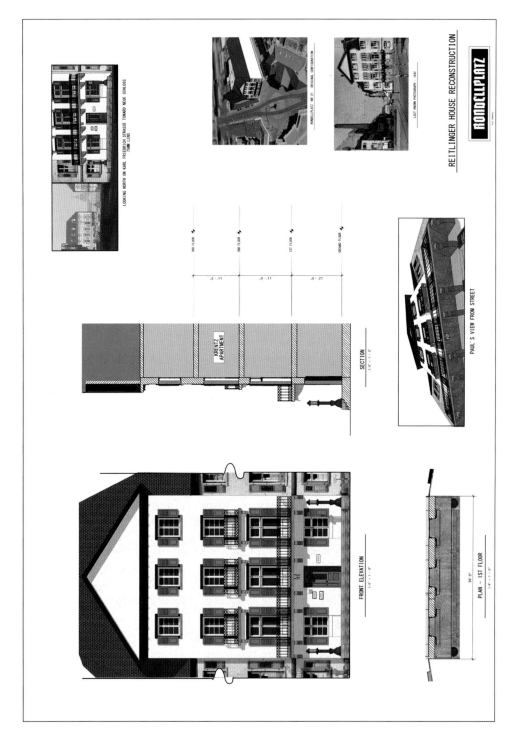

Figure 4.16   Layout drawing of the reconstructed Reitlinger building. Courtesy of Randy Wilkins.

● *Is there a specific time you can recall when SketchUp was particularly important/helpful?*
There were several times while I was working on the television show *Heroes* that I really began to see the potential of the program. The show was very ambitious; it was like making a feature film every eight days. For one episode, we had to create an internment camp similar to Manzanar. We had three days to do the design and drawings and eight days to build it. After it was shot, the construction crew and painters had 14 hours to add 45 years of age. The production designer Ruth Ammon gave me sketches of what she wanted as she was leaving for the location scout of the build site. I asked her to send me the GPS coordinates of the center of the camp and a photo showing the orientation. By the time they got back from the scout I had downloaded the site with the topography from Google Earth, dropped the camp model onto it and laid in the new road. It saved me at least two days.

● *How are you using the Advanced Camera Tools plugin in your work?*
I can now say that SketchUp really is the perfect software for film design. There is very little I can think of that I can't do with it. When you have a digital model up on the screen, the first thing a production designer or director will ask is, "What focal length is that?" The most important thing we must consider is what the camera is going to see; everything else for us is secondary. If it can't be shot it won't work. So regarding this, I had a work-around process for using camera angles that I've been using but it's cumbersome. The new Advanced Camera Tools plugin is fantastic. I can change the focal length while in the camera mode and not have the camera move its current position, or I can change the aspect ratio or the tilt or the height without having to reposition anything. And having the data right on the screen is a big help.

This means SketchUp is now very useful for the major three visualization areas: d-vis or design visualization, pre-vis and post-vis. Design visualization is the new version of the traditional pre-production design phase where the sets and environments are created and SketchUp is already the standard modeling program for that task. Pre- and post-visualization are more concerned with exactly what is seen through the camera and the combining of real and computer-generated elements. With the Advanced Camera Tools (ACT), you can now view a model and be very specific as to camera position, aspect ratio and lens focal length. That for me was the missing piece of the software, and now, one of the strengths of the program.

● *What advantages does it give you over other similar programs?*
To get data and camera control comparable to the new ACT, I would have had to bring the model into Maya or Rhino, much more expensive programs. Now I don't need to go to that trouble and expense. ACT suddenly becomes a more useful tool for storyboarding. There are a number of programs such as Frame Forger that are popular 3D storyboarding programs because they provide specific camera and lens data. You now have all those capabilities with SketchUp. And when you create those boards in LayOut, they are automatically updated when there are changes to the model. That's a huge advantage.[10]

HAND DRAFTING

Set designers, or draftsmen, are the unsung heroes of the art department. They are responsible for the actual design of the film because they are the most intimate with the drawn details. The adage "God is in the details" can be conveniently modified to suit our needs by realizing that "The details are in the set design." And those details are most typically found in one-quarter scale (3″ = 1′) or in full-scale (1′ = 1′) as architecturally drawn detail for all scenery, although other scales are used as required. What the full-scale detail (see Figure 5.9 or 5.10) does is to act as an interpreter of specific information when a set designer or art director cannot be present in the woodshop as construction questions arise. Details also insure the preferred but sometimes counterintuitive look of how scenery is built. A good example of this is obvious in any of the *Star Trek* films—in the pneumatically driven double sliding doors of the *Enterprise* spacecraft—they are not typical doors so they need to be articulated by drafted, full-scale details.

In more general terms, a draftsperson is actually designing within the strict parameters of the Production Designer's conception of the film's visual requirements. These limitations are not as confining as one might think; a set designer is well paid to have the time to work out the details of how the scenery will physically be constructed. Consequently, set designing provides the necessary nuts-and-bolts pragmatism in the overall design process. The draft person's drawing table is a place where the realities of the physical world meet the vagaries of the realm of concept and ideas. Barbara Mesney, a senior level, union Set Designer, shared thoughts and facts about her work as a film design professional.

Interview with Barbara Mesney

● *Is draftsperson the politically correct term for your title?*
Draftsperson is a valid title. I prefer the term set designer. Interestingly, the nomenclature was a great part of the negotiations when the Hollywood set designers' union was started. Basically, what a set designer is doing all day *is* designing; we are not just drafting someone else's scenery.

● *That's certainly true from my perspective as an art director. Barbara, your passion for drawing is obvious in your drafting. It's beautifully rendered, has just enough detail, and shows significant info for the carpenters. How would you rate yourself as a set designer?*
Thank you. Well, I know what I want to be. I currently work at selling myself as a first-rate set designer. My goal is to become the Reginald Bream (most sought-after English draftsman) of Hollywood. The point of this is not to price myself out of the market, but rather to make myself so indispensable and invaluable that I'll always be employed. Basically, no one wants to do this job. It requires intense focus and a lot of mental concentration. It requires sitting in one room for the sole purpose of doing math and art all day long. Most people don't want that much focus, you know, especially in a world like theater or film where it's more social. I emerge from my cocoon, make a cup of tea, say some friendly words in the art department bullpen, and then disappear back into the drafting vortex. It's exactly what I did as a child in my basement studio by focusing creatively in solitude. This suits me perfectly.

Comparatively, most people in this business need more social interaction than I do. It's understandable why there are more art directors than set designers; it's not that it's particularly an easier job. From my point of view, as an art director you're on call 24-7, you're married to the project, and your butt is constantly on the line. Too many drawbacks to consider for the trade-off of better pay for the personal toll it demands. That's much too extreme. Because producers don't like paying overtime, the set designer's hourly contract is much more manageable. You put your pencil down, and you are off for the day. I go home and have a life. In film terms, having a life is golden. My art director friends never sleep.

● *Aside from speed, how much about being a set designer is about patience?*
[Chuckles] Patience, first, and lack of noticeable ego, second. Because you're designing all day long, you know a particular set more than anyone else in terms of what it can or can't be, and what it can or can't do. Any number of people will come into my cocoon and ask me to change any and every aspect of what I'm drafting. This happens all day long. Every day. You simply say, "OK" and make the changes knowing full well that everything you've just done for hours becomes obsolete and all that info goes into the delete file. So there can't be any ego involvement. Also, the ultimate end of the project is not yours despite the fact that you've invested time and creative effort.

What I've found to be the most fascinating aspect of this dance is the fact that in my experience, at least 50% of the time we always come full circle. There's a moral here that cautions to never toss away the first drawings in a series of changes. So, I have to qualify that delete file I just mentioned—it's actually a *faux* delete file that might be filled, but never gets emptied. Putting it aside for future reference is always the best recourse.

● *Resigned or not, this caprice must take a toll. How do you balance yourself?*
My own art—the fine art painting I do on a regular basis—is what saves me. In that world, I have the final say-so; all the decisions are mine alone. My painting is totally gratifying.

● *When is a set design finished? There are instances when even after the drawings are signed and built, change is still in play, isn't it?*
The nature of the business dictates this. Everything moves at lightning speed with little time to do anything properly, right? People on the front end, namely the production designer and art director with the director and cinematographer, are doing their damnedest to think things through, but inevitably something will slip between the cracks and changes will have to happen. This doesn't happen through any direct fault of theirs, especially when some of the most important decisions are made in the scouting van in-between looking at locations for the film with little reflection. Given all this, where mistakes and subsequent changes can be made, it's my job as a methodical set designer to check the details and communicate any discrepancies to the AD and construction coordinator.

● *Given the trend toward technology, are you now pressured to be adept at CAD programs?*
I'm not using CAD because it's more suited to architecture where many revisions and overlays are required; CAD hasn't adapted as well to our uses for it in Hollywood. VectorWorks, formerly known as MiniCAD, has been adopted by television designing more in Hollywood as the drafting software of choice. It's a highly intuitive and remarkable program, and yes, I am studying it to stay competitive.

I was talking recently with my current art director about how ill-suited VectorWorks can be for film. Film is so variable compared to TV, which deals more with stock flattage, more like theater. In terms of organic drawing, it's also less effective. Several months ago I was drawing an African spirit hut. Even though it's possible, it's not practical to do it effectively in any form of CAD, including VectorWorks. The truth is a great deal of what I do is to make organically designed scenery forms work. Contrary to popular belief, there are fewer straight lines and a lot more freehand drawing in film than you can imagine.[11]

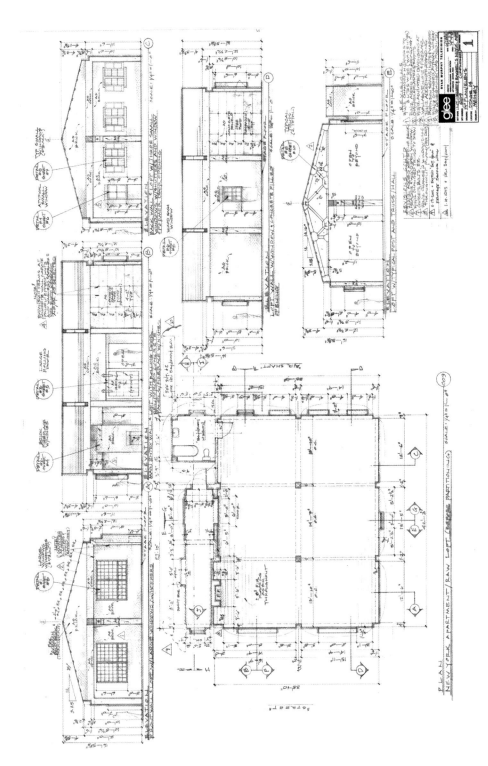

Figure 4.17 Hand-drafted N.Y. Loft plan and elevations for *Glee*. Season 5. All rights reserved. Courtesy of Barbara Mesney.

Injecting the visual concept into the design of the physical scenery is an involved task. The Art Director, via his/her activity and communication skills, performs the injection for the Production Designer. And, it requires Job-like patience on the part of the Set Designer, who interprets that information and then designs, draws and redraws it numerous times. According to digital set designer J. André Chaintreuil (*The Amazing Spider-Man, X-Men: First Class, Minority Report*):

> *From a digital set designer's point of view, the idea of timing and pacing is slightly different than an ordinary set designer. I find it's easiest to model even the simplest set in 3D because of the way I can analyze and troubleshoot in 3D. I ultimately learn, for example, two planar surfaces might collide in a specific corner and will not work. These decisions can be discovered faster and influence a design. Some other advantages of digital set design are when a set has a complex shape or a lot of repetition such as a bank of lights or a colonnade. Revisions also go quickly in a digital format. Once a 3D model has reached a satisfactory level of design, it can be translated into drawings very quickly, and the model can be easily shared with other departments.[12]*

This technology in current digital designing has become a necessity and the working knowledge of how to manipulate the software, a prerequisite for any aspiring digital concept modeler, draftsperson, or art director. A final question remains: is there a valid reason for scenery to be drafted with an adjustable triangle and mechanical pencil? Archaic or not, it's really important to know how to do this, especially in case of the obvious: a grid freeze and/or loss of power. When fast changes need to happen, no production designer or director in the world has the patience to wait for the power to resume before seeing new pages of drafted scenery. Knowing how to draft traditionally as a set designer or art director is the surest way to cover all your bases and make sure you are that more marketable.

At this point in this chapter, we have only discussed how the various players in the art department would ideally interact and join the art director's forward movement. In order to better understand the working process of real-time filmmaking creation, let's catch some glimpses of the challenges of solving daily issues on *GI Joe: The Rise of Cobra* (2009).

REAL-TIME SCENARIO

An initial "issue" for the *GI Joe* art department team to solve was the massive construction scheduling challenge commanding all of their experience, talent and stamina. Viewable as Figure 4.18 a–d on these two pages as a strong graphic vector, it can also be seen in much greater detail online.

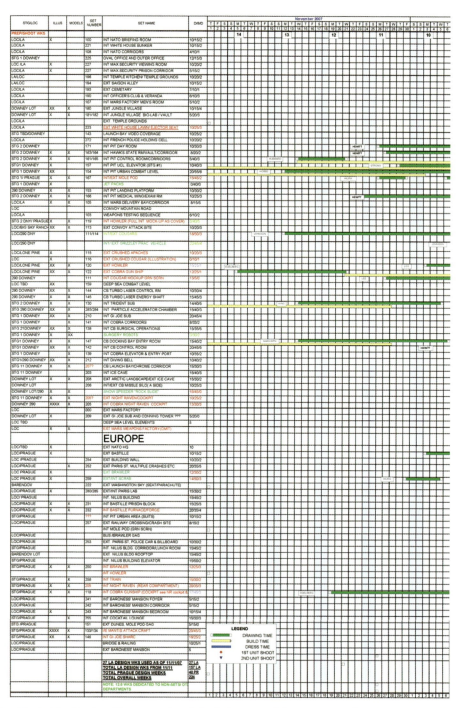

Figure 4.18a   Dark Sky Design/Construction Schedule created by Greg Papalia, Supervising Art Director, *G I Joe: Rise of Cobra* (2009). Courtesy of Greg Papalia.

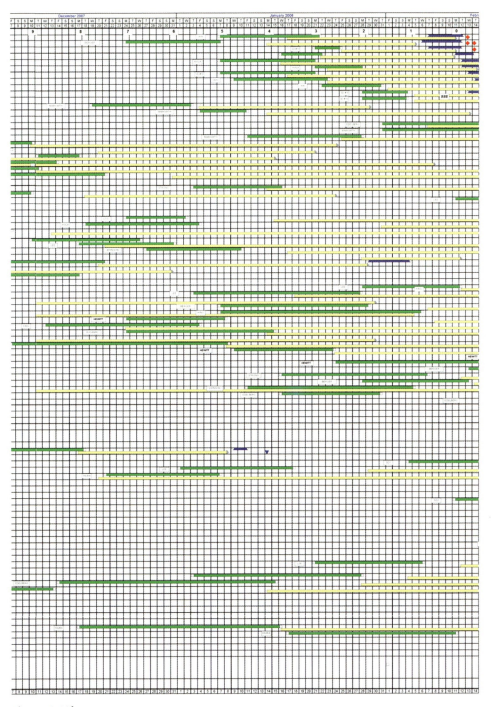

Figure 4.18b

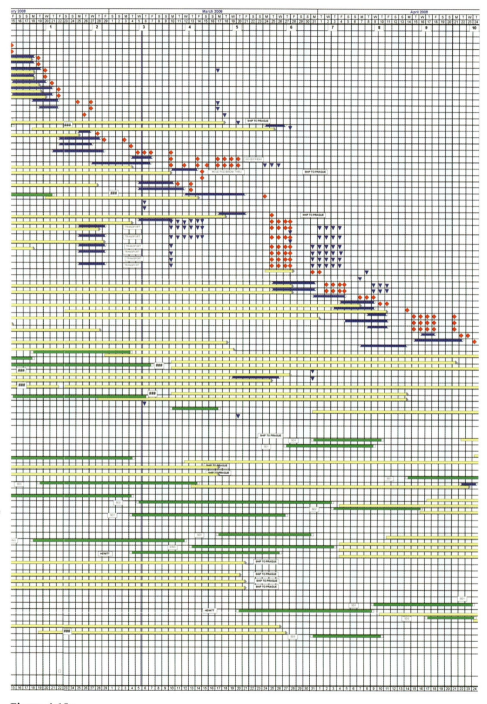

Figure 4.18c

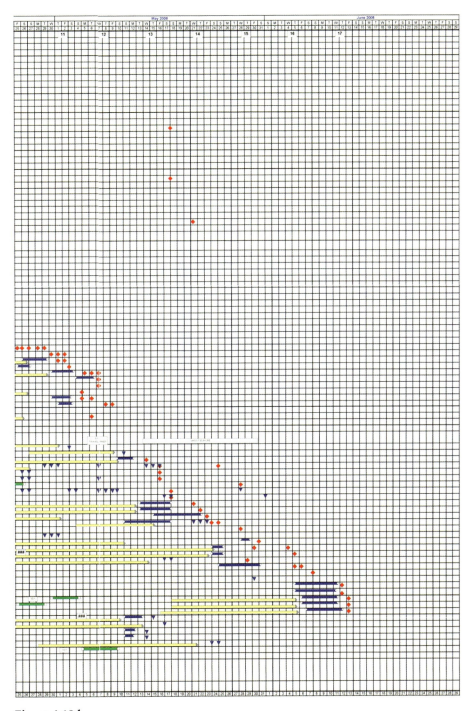

Figure 4.18d

Compared to other $200–300 million-plus international film projects, no other schedule compares with the scale and hubris of the intent evident in this schedule—as an exceptional example, this blockbuster piqued my interest enough to include it in this book. Art department began work with the initial script in August-September 2007. The director/writer provided an initial 30 script pages and outline with the caveat that it all would change. Construction schedule was created with US and European shooting commencing with first unit shooting, beginning February 2008 in these locations:

- Arctic (second unit shots only)
- Barrandov Studios, Prague, Czech Republic
- Bishop, California, USA
- Downey Studios, Downey, California, USA (four stages and exteriors)
- Dumont Dunes, California, USA
- Fort Irwin, California, USA
- Huntington Library, Pasadena, California, USA—Japanese Gardens
- Lone Pine, California, USA
- Los Angeles, California, USA (downtown locations and warehouse, fifth Stage)
- Los Angeles National Cemetery, Los Angeles, California, USA
- Old Town, Prague, Czech Republic—Kozi Square, Castle Kost, Kolodeje Mansion
- Paris, France
- Prague, Czech Republic
- Simi Valley, California, USA
- Tokyo, Japan—Tokyo was matted into Chung King Alley, downtown Los Angeles

Then the writer's strike happened and lasted through January 2008. Regardless, the art department team was mandated to pressed on despite all this, and never having a revised full script again. By the time they had wrapped in Prague, the script had cycled into quadruple white pages—translation: revised portions of the script cycled through the normal paper colors of white, yellow, green, buff, goldenrod, cherry and blue, four times *after* the writer's strike had ended. This scenario sounds a lot like a typical episodic TV scenario; there no longer are scheduling/timing contrasts between the two media, both running on little time and money. Remarkably, Ed Verreaux and Greg Papalia successfully delivered this film on schedule.

Interview with Greg Papalia

- *How did you not only keep track of all the items on this behemoth schedule, but stay current with shooting schedule changes, actor availability, new script pages and rewrites?*
  At the time I first arrived in the art department, there was a writer's strike going on, with an actor's strike imminent. Everything had to land by June 30, meaning we had to have everything completed despite the fact they started late. All departments had the shared burden of having to address so much material in so little time. Ed Verreaux, the Production Designer, and I were given

the first 30 pages of the script. I had never seen scriptwriting so dense (one to three sets or vehicles required per page) and remarked that if this is an indication of the rest of the script, then we're dead (when you view the film, you will quickly be aware of a different set on screen every minute to 90 seconds). Production also clearly understood that this was a shared problem, where no schedule changes were possible without touching off a serious domino effect. One important factor I had in my favor was that we had enjoyed previous working relationships with both the line producer and UPM—so there existed more than the normal cooperation and trust one would hope for when tackling a shared challenge.

Strategically, I remained in close communication with the first AD of each shooting unit. I also had to be vigilant in order to make adjustments along the way although there was little wiggle room. This gave me the up-to-the-minute info I needed to finesse the schedule where I could. The other half of my strategy was an idea suggested by Chad Frey, which was to divide the scope of this huge schedule into pieces. So, using the format of a comprehensive and detailed flow chart, I broke the larger schedule into five week increments to establish an overall of the workload in terms of how long it would take to design, built and rig each set piece. This method helped me explain and visually illustrate to everyone, the enormous task at hand. After segmenting my first scheduling pass, I called Ed into my office for his input. It took a few minutes of explanation to overcome his sense of disbelief.

■ *Yes, I'd think denial would be most people's reactions to the enormity of what you were proposing.*
[A hearty chuckle] A horrified look played on the faces of most folks who saw this chart. To this day, it turns my stomach to look at it. [Laughs again] A singular saving grace was that Ed is a gifted and remarkable artist. He can stand next to you and draw very rapidly what is in his head. This particular gift got us through the thickest parts of the film. Many production designers in a similar situation will hire an army and divide them into strategic positions to come up with the design/solutions. That's not Ed. He's much more involved and hands-on in guiding the design process. I knew I had to organize things in a pipeline so I didn't overwhelm him with too large an army but with a select enough group of people to get the job done.

My next task was to inform our producers of the monumental challenge at hand. Time, not money, would be the biggest challenge for all of us.

My philosophy as a supervising art director is you never bring your problem to the producer—you always bring their problem to them, with solutions. The schedule you refer to in your question was more than just a marching list for the construction and art departments; it represented to the producers and UPM that they would be faced with multiple and simultaneous work crews, trucks, equipment, rigging, etc., in addition to the needs of the art department and construction crews. The size of just the construction crew held more than 300 craftsmen. I next explained what would happen in each subsequent five week period, starting with 16 simultaneous set builds including vehicles; then increasing to 41 set builds in the next five weeks; then 54 sets mid-schedule in two countries, at the height of the schedule. It didn't stop there: as the pace slowed in the US down to 34 being constructed at one time, there would still be 23 sets under construction in the Czech Republic. [Another chuckle] The producer's short response was to ask if it was possible. My response: what I am showing you on the wall is the scenario that makes it possible. The only caveat was that no one on this film can approach the schedule in a "business-as-usual" mode. For example, waiting for producer's set approval was not possible. In this case, with director's approval, we began the build according to this schedule. Everyone who left the conversation did so with the understanding that our collective behavior necessary to accomplish the task at hand would have to be as unique as the situation we faced together.

● *Was the Director in agreement with all of this?*
He was in agreement, though he had an elaborate third act battle sequence in mind. If he could save shooting time in terms of days or weeks, then he could pad the VFX budget for the finale. So, in doing a camera set-up eight times out of ten, instead of doing static camera shots with dialogue pick-ups, he would set up an appropriate size crane for a sequence shot and do a "move" instead of a "cut," subsequently saving time and getting ahead of schedule. We had an 85-day schedule and we shot it in 82 days. Understand that every set was completed the day before or, worst case, on the day of shooting. Every department was forced to adjust to this unexpected piece of news. To maintain the integrity of my schedule, the tight relationship I had cultivated with the first ADs and the VFX coordinator, proved to be essential. Before an adjusted schedule was circulated, they would consult me about the ramifications. That way, the director got his shots and the schedule for all related departments stayed relatively intact.

● *How did you distribute the work to your art directors?*
Each art director had the equivalent of a full film on their hands. LA sets and locations were headed by Chad Frey and Randy Moore, and assisted by Eric Huganin; vehicles and mockups handled by Kevin Ishioka, assisted by Kevin Loo and Brad Ricker; Prague and Paris locations supervised by Anne Seibel, assisted by Jean-Eves Rabier. We were fortunate to have been able to talk Anne Seibel into taking on the Prague portion of the film—she is French and happens to live and work in Paris—as we were shooting Prague for Paris, this was a good fit and proved to be critical to our overall success. In December, just prior to commencement of principal photography, the full company scouted the elaborate car chase scene in Prague and left behind the second unit to lock down the streets and break out portions of the sequence along a mile of real estate. Several weeks later, upon second unit's return to Los Angeles, I asked the first AD about the pre-vis shot list. At that moment I learned that a specific breakdown of the sequence in regard to what piece of action would be shot, where one had not been accomplished. I also learned that there was a zero possibility of them returning to Prague to hash things out prior to shooting. Understand that the final chase sequence in the film involved heavy SFX coupled with equally heavy and specific VFX. The decisions made during the previous tech scout specified that the chase, spread over four separate sections of the city, were locked without any chance of deviation. For example, explosions were allowed in certain areas, while flipping cars were allowed in other areas, as well as chase action and gunfire. I was fielding calls from the Prague producer, concerned about what we were planning to do. In Prague, the locations procedure works very differently than in the US or Canada. Everything must be determined at least two months ahead of schedule to give local locations people time to work their way through the neighborhoods in the city. The laying out specific parameters are paramount to success and

getting what you want. For example, if you specify a camera position and determine that you will need a lock off of 350 yards down a road to run a car to cover action on a specific intersection, storefront and street corner, that's exactly what you get–no more, no less. By the time you're ready to shoot, deals have been made and the *exact* amount of real estate has been reserved. Without specific information to relay to our producers in Prague, all of our forward movement and planning would come to a complete standstill. With the blessing of our producers, VFX, SFX, and stunt coordinators, and production designer, it was agreed that I would return to Prague to lock down all the specifics of the chase. Whatever I picked, they would live with and ultimately shoot.

So, I returned to Prague. I mapped and photographed every street, every shooting direction and how/where cars were going to fly on streets that doubled for other streets. I broke it down to match the pre-vis, shot by shot, and published this shooting manual and reviewed it with my colleagues, including both first ADs. When we all returned, I explained to both directors and cinematographers what the shots were and how they would be accomplished. The city of Prague and our producers were happy with our plan, but accomplishing it nearly killed me.[13]

Concept Illustrations

Let's begin with concept illustrations to provide an overview of the visual tone Ed Verreaux, Production Designer, envisioned with the help of David Negron. The Pit, a subterranean installation is the terrestrial base of the GI operations; good guy operations were conceived of as earth-based as opposed to MARS (Military Armaments Research Syndicate), Destro's underwater base, represented by more curvilinear, somewhat serpentine imagery. David Negron envisioned the "Pit concept" by incorporating three simultaneous views of upper, middle, and lower levels in a slender vertical format; it's frugal and effective and it indicates the full range of a camera tilt and the literal depth of the GI installation. In a more typical horizontal format, the "GI training area" evokes a clear sense of the halogen-lit, subterranean world of the Joes—more clearly seen in a digital version of the image. Negron's concept images and the finished sets are not exact replicas; digital set designs intervened, finessing the broader strokes which translated globally as recognizable visual detail in scenery, weaponry, and vehicles.

Conceptual 3D renderings depicted as the Cobra Base Surface Entry, shown as the top image in Figure 4.23a, or the SketchUp concepts for the interconnected Cobra corridors, in Figure 4.23b, supported the development process of the scenic design.

Ed Verreaux is a production designer who has the facile ability to sketch as he is explaining his concept for a set, shooting sequence or vehicle shape. A developed a concept drawing of the layout of the Cobra Complex, Figure 4.22a, is a typical example of Ed's skill; from this seminal image all others emerged, i.e., Figure 4.22b. The subterranean world of the Joes was not visited as much during the course of the film as the MARS sets in the sub-Arctic Ocean refuge of Destros' world. Here is where the bulk of the activity tells the story and where the money was spent (Figure 4.23a and b). These images express different aspects of the visual concept of "glacial evil" in the Arctic Surface

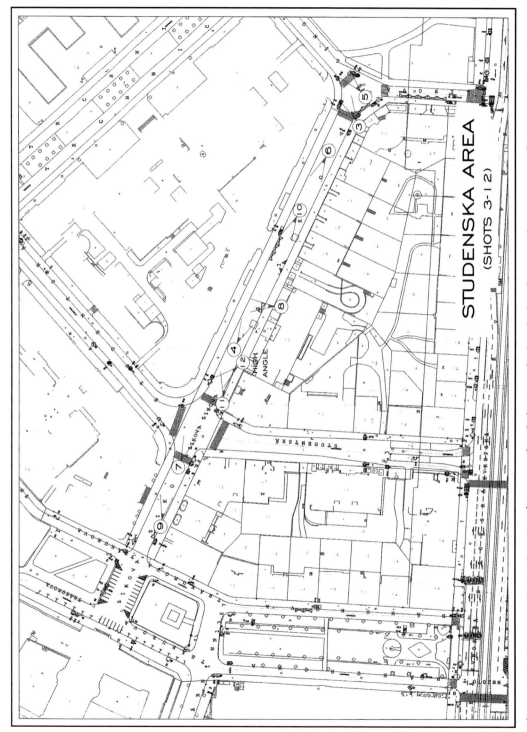

Figure 4.19 Prague as Paris: Greg Papalia mapped and photographed each shot for a car chase sequence for *G I Joe: Rise of Cobra*. Courtesy of Greg Papalia.

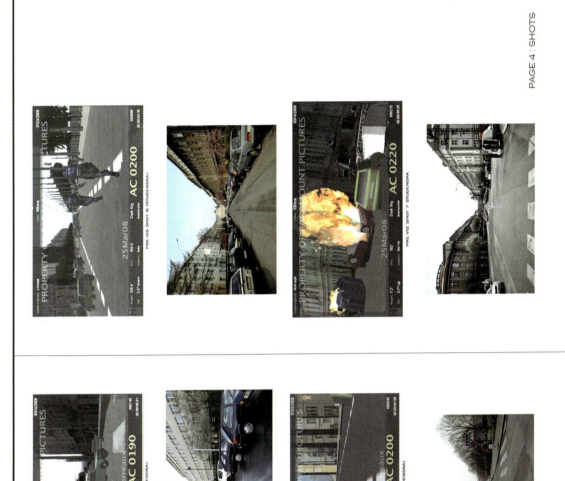

Figure 4.20   A section of Greg Papalia's Prague shooting manual for G.I. Joe: Rise of Cobra—Pages 3 & 4. Courtesy of Greg Papalia.

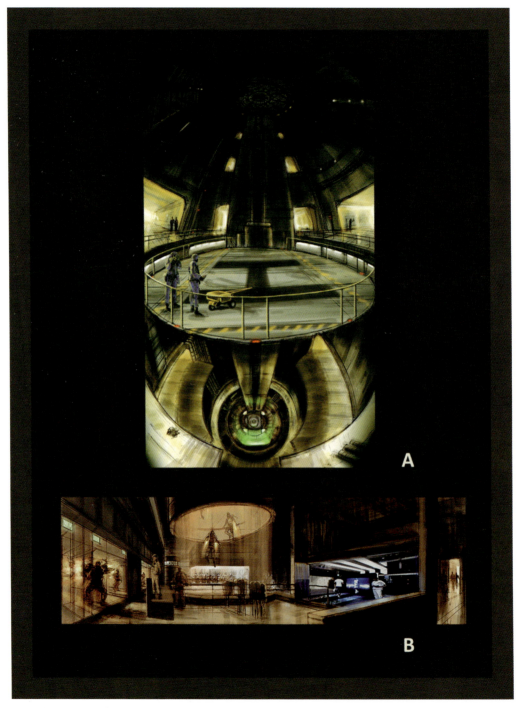

Figure 4.21 A) G-I Pit and B) G-I Training Area for *G I Joe: Rise of Cobra*. Both concept illustrations were created by David J. Negron, Jr. Courtesy of by David J. Negron, Jr.

entrance to Destros' world, the MARS Entry Corridor, Interior Corridors, and Surgical Operations Room.

Interview with Ed Verreaux

● *You've worked on a handful of projects as a production illustrator. As a production designer, is this where your design process begins?*

My design process begins in a number of places but usually starts with a script or some narrative of the story and the world being created. As I read, images bubble up and those are my first impressions of what the film might look like. After that it's an ongoing discovery process aided by research, illustrations, a lot of thumbnail sketches, doodles, many meetings with the director, producers and others . . . and a lot of coffee.

● *So is pre-vis more of a design tool or a pragmatic indicator?*

Pre-vis for me is a design tool in that it doesn't so much tell me what the environment will look like as much as how much of the environment will be seen and how we will see it. It's become a vital part of visual effects shot planning. In that sense it's helpful in determining how much set to build, but it only works if you're working with a director who pays attention and sticks to what's been planned, otherwise you're aiming at a moving target.

● *What is your philosophy about the digital art department?*

With so much digital interfacing between everyone on the planet, the digital art department has become ubiquitous and unavoidable. Geography is also unimportant: two of my last five projects have been done via the Internet between myself and illustrators working at home in LA, as well as the director, art director, producers, and construction working first in Philadelphia, then in New York. I guess it enables us to get the work done regardless of the circumstances.

The mythologist Joseph Campbell said that there are basically seven stories that get told and retold every generation in the light of that generation's perspective, so in that sense, we're doing Greek tragedy. Film is storytelling, so digital or otherwise, it won't change. What will change is how the story is told.

● *How did* Looper *differ from any movie you've done thus far?*

Looper was different from other projects I've worked on in that it had a script that was really tight from day one. There were very few changes, which is helpful when trying to create a big-looking picture on a small budget, especially when that picture is about a dystopian future. Director and screenwriter Rian Johnson had thoroughly prepared so there was very little wasted energy revisualizing and re-creating things at the last minute. It was a tremendously complex movie and the preparation made all the difference in the world. I wish all film projects could be run so well.

● *What do you expect from an art director?*

I expect an art director to be thoroughly versed in the craft of filmmaking from set design and construction to budgeting, scheduling, and planning, as well as dealing with last-minute changes that have become more and more a part of the filmmaking process. They should be able to work

Figure 4.22a   The Revised Art Department. Courtesy of Alex McDowell (C) 2002.

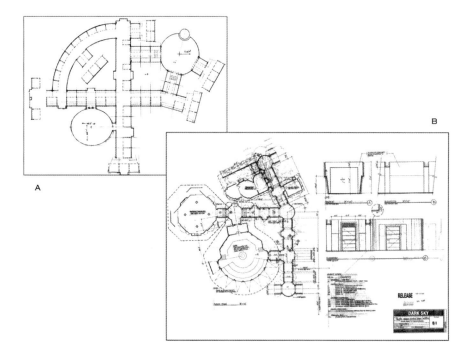

Figure 4.22b   A) Several preliminary ground plans developed like this example drawn by an Art Director from E. Verreaux's conceptual sketch. B) More well-resolved final floor plans like "The Pit" General Floor Plan Layout, was drawn by Jim Hewitt for *G I Joe: Rise of Cobra*. Courtesy of Chad Frey.

Figure 4.23a   A) Ext. Cobra Base Surface Entry—Preliminary Conceptual Rendering, version 3—Greg Papalia. B) Cobra Corridors: Surgical Operation Room—Set photograph. C) Cobra Docking Bay Entry—Set photograph. Courtesy of Chad Frey.

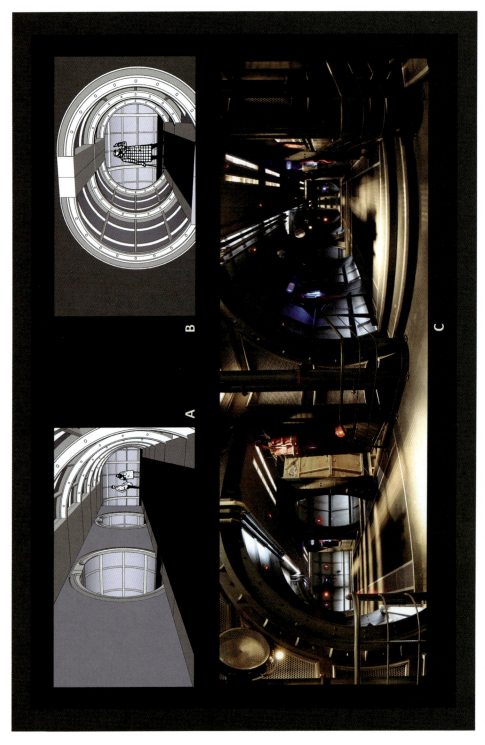

Figure 4.23b Inter-connecting Cobra Corridors: A&B) Sketch-Up Concepts, and C) Set Photograph. Courtesy of Chad Frey.

well with people and be able to bounce back when things change at the last minute. It's a business of change.

- *How will the art department look in a decade?*
  I can't say how the art department will look in a decade. Certainly there won't be very many pencil sharpeners around.

- *What's more important, a server or digital modeler?*
  A server, or dropbox, or something like that is always important for information sharing among departments, a digital modeler less so. That is unless you're making a futuristic film with a lot of soft edges. I'm joking here just a little bit. I think it changes with every project and there isn't a hard and fast answer. With the advent of 3D modeling programs the illustration function has expanded beyond the 2D picture plane.[14]

Docking Bay Entry Room

The finished set photograph of the Cobra docking bay entry (Figure 4.24d) lit with a heavily-saturated, comic book chic illuminates a high level of subtle, textural details designed into the walls of this entry space to the Cobra complex. Ribbed sections of curved wall and upper soffits, perforated metal mesh of various sizes, and multiple areas of metallic surface treatment from medium to fine grade all provide a subconscious texture of smooth, sinuous snake skin. Jeff Markwith, the set designer who drafted the pages shown here in Figure 4.24a–c, indicates all detail clearly and accurately, but also goes a step further—as a hand-draftsperson, he treats each drawing as a piece of artwork—flooring detailing, particularly, is not random but well-considered and aesthetically rendered. Of course, this kind of finishing detailing on a page is achievable with CAD drafting, but the "feeling" of the scenery is more accessible in drawing plates like this. Early on, a production designer and art director will discuss which drawing platform or styles are appropriate for the entire project or different aspects of the project.

Missile Silo

The warhead in the missile silo set was designed by the property master, Brad Einhorn. It was modeled by Christopher Ross in Rhino—this hero prop, like all other models he created for the show, was sent directly to a fabricating sub-contractor to ensure accuracy and believability in the final hand props. With the Rhino model and manufactured pieces of the warhead in hand (Figure 4.25d), Jim Hewitt, set designer, drew a series of assembly pages (See Figure 4.25c for a drafted detail) to facilitate blocking direction and acting business for on-camera scenes shot on the set—Note: all gantry movement worked on camera. The **reach envelope** from the end of the 32-foot long gantry leading to the warhead at the top of the missile was a practical bit of business that would reset quickly for several takes. Jim's assembly pages addressed the details that would ensure the mechanical functionality of the pistons driving the cradle that would open/close onto the warhead placed into position by an actor.

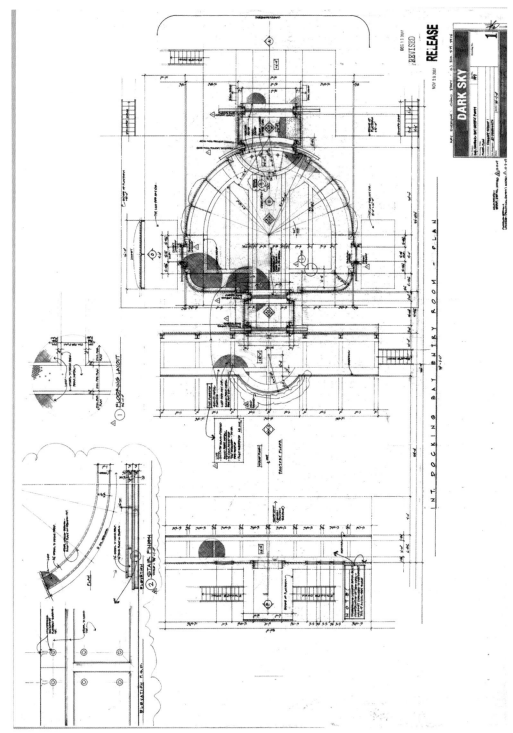

Figure 4.24a   Docking Bay Entry Room: Ground Plan, drawn by Jeff Markwith. Courtesy of Jeff Markwith.

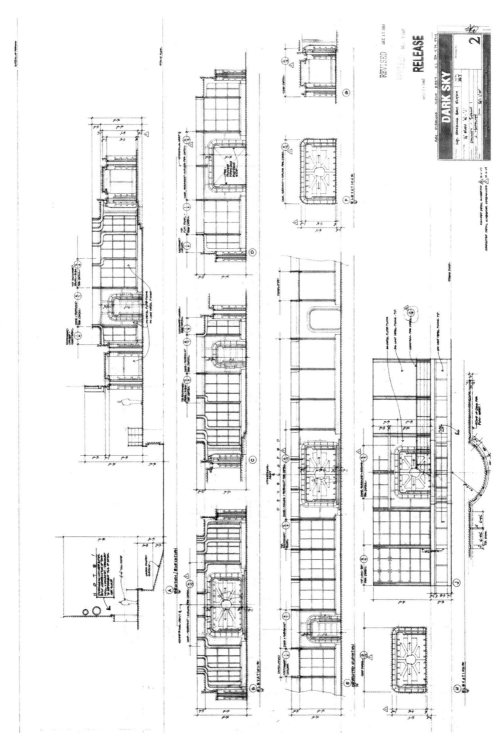

Figure 4.24b   Docking Bay Entry Room: Sections, drawn by Jeff Markwith. Courtesy of Jeff Markwith.

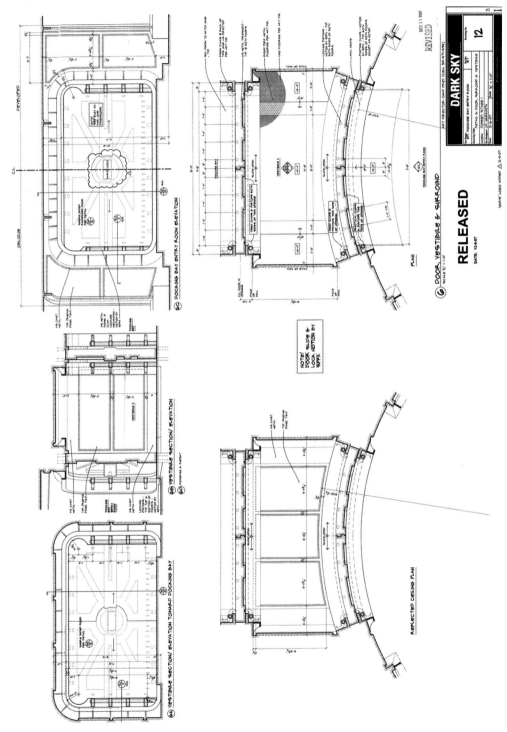

Figure 4.24c Docking Bay Entry Room: Elevations, drawn by Jeff Markwith. Courtesy of Jeff Markwith.

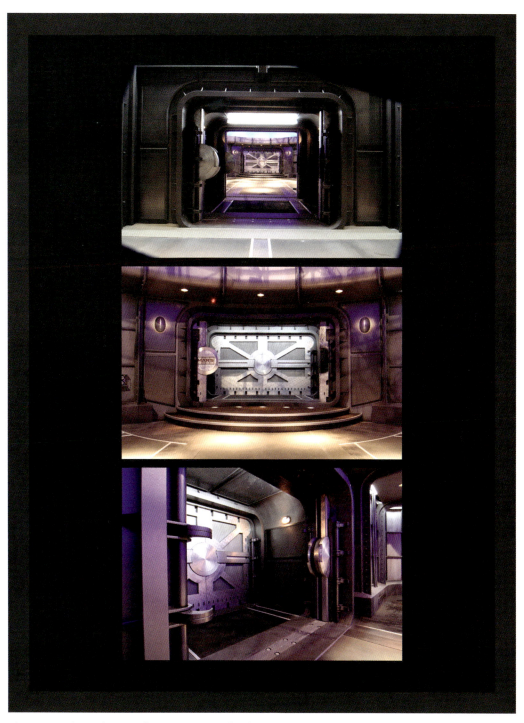

Figure 4.24d   Cobra Docking Bay Entry final set photograph. Courtesy of Chad Frey.

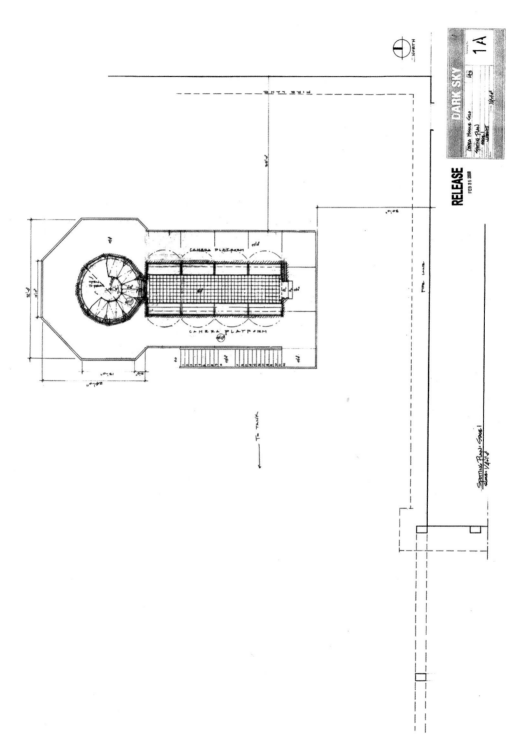

Figure 4.25a   Missile Silo: Ground Plan, drawn by Jim Hewitt. Courtesy of Jim Hewitt.

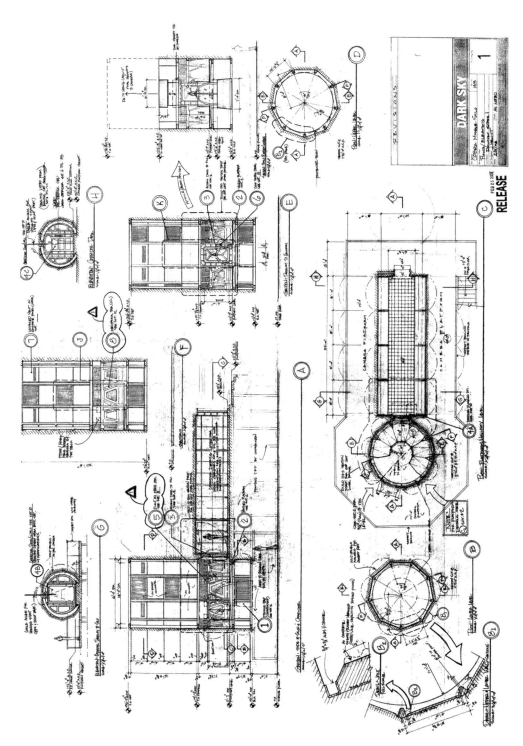

Figure 4.25b   Missile Silo: Section showing vertical tube and gantry, drawn by Jim Hewitt. Courtesy of Jim Hewitt.

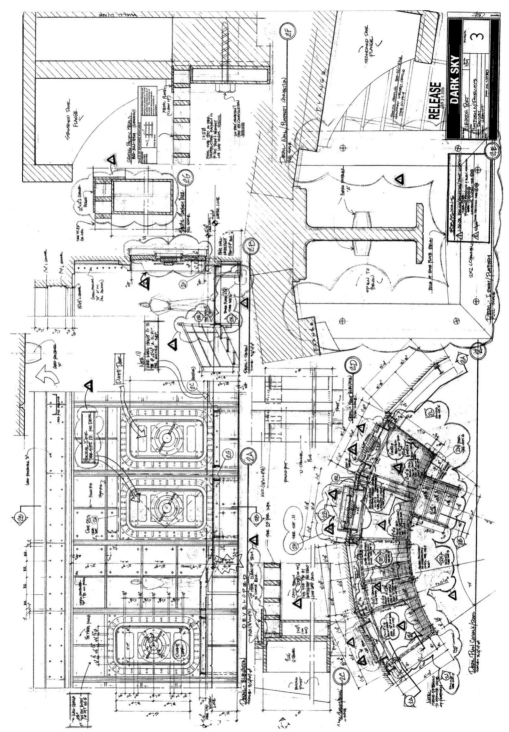

Figure 4.25c Detail: Assembly Page 1, drawn by Jim Hewitt. Courtesy of Jim Hewitt.

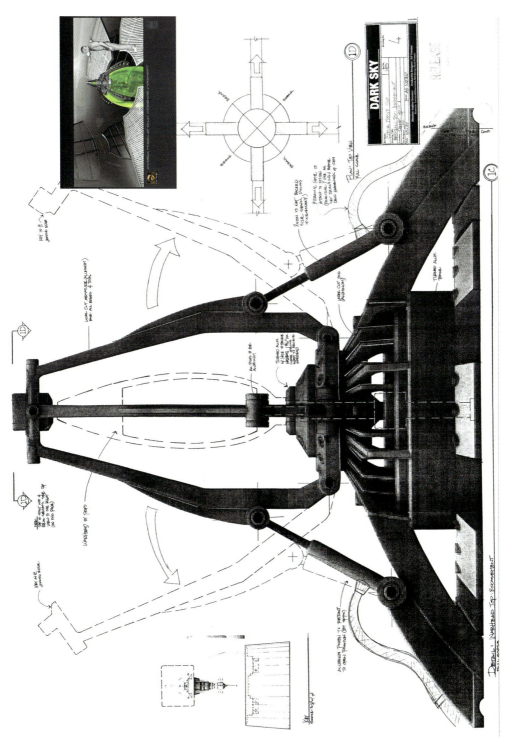

Figure 4.25d War head Rhino model, designed by Prop Master, Brad Einhorn. Concept illustration drawn by Christopher Ross. Courtesy of Jim Hewitt.

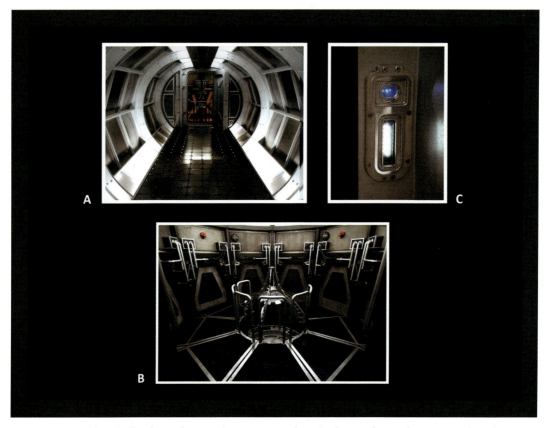

Figure 4.25e   Missile Silo final set photo. A) Gantry to Silo, B) Silo, medium close-up, and C) door hardware detail. Courtesy of Jim Hewitt.

The silo tube that connected to the gantry walkway was 36 feet high and 16 feet wide, and did not touch the floor of the stage. The reason for this was simple: the floor below the silo tube was a blue screen—the wall starting at six feet off the deck and rising to its maximum height—this limited blue screen reflected spill onto the bottom of the silo walls and the top of the missile shaft, ensuring a cleaner digital extension of the missile shaft "below" the built set pieces. Of course, the railing was removable for production value and for close-up camera work.

Cobra Control Center

This set was designed to withstand a flood of water so it was situated by Art Director, Chad Frey into a spotting plan configuration within the footprint of an existing swimming pool at Downey Studios in Downey, CA (Figure 4.26a–c). The uppermost of three levels of this elliptical set contains a large, oval window that explodes with the planned torrent of seawater.

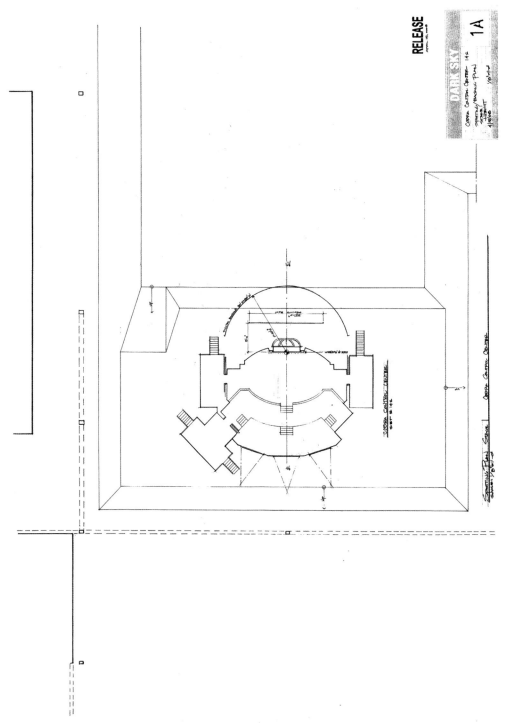

Figure 4.26a   Cobra Control Center: Ground Plan, drawn by Jim Hewitt. Courtesy of Jim Hewitt.

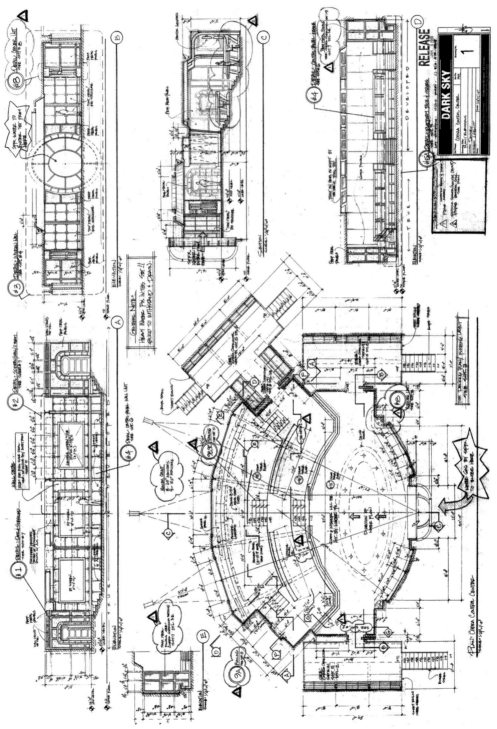

Figure 4.26b Cobra Control Center: Wall Elevations, drawn by Jim Hewitt. Courtesy of Jim Hewitt.

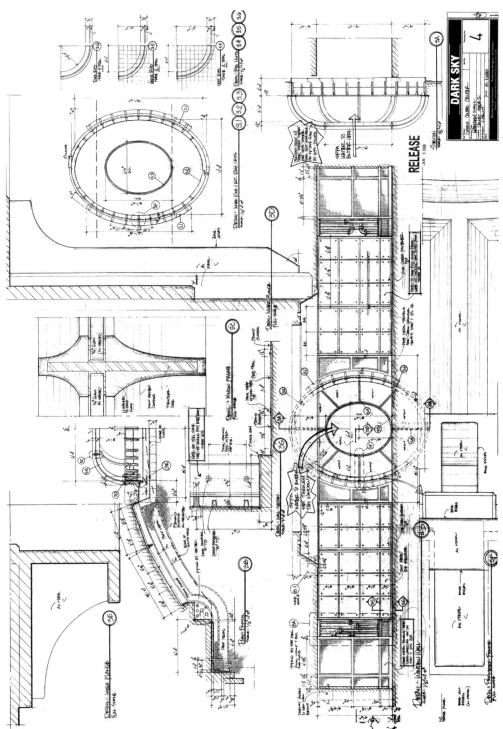

Figure 4.26c Cobra Control Center: Section, drawn by Jim Hewitt. Courtesy of Jim Hewitt.

Figure 4.26d A) Upper breakaway window wall. B) Mid-level breakaway computer bank glass wall. Both walls were constructed to be rigged for multiple takes to replace breakaway glass panels. This entire set was designed with water-drainage and water-tightness in mind. Courtesy of Jim Hewitt.

After the window had been breached, the water flooded down through a mid-set, plate glass wall—also designed for multiple takes of breakaway glass, into the two lower levels, drained by strategically placed floor grating and weep holes. As you might imagine, this was a particularly large shared project between the SFX department and the art director, as the elliptical set spanned a 52′ × 84′ area.

Diving Bell and Entry Chamber

The SFX department was also busy in this water effects set. Basically this was a 32′ diameter circular set with a diving bell chamber at the 12 o'clock position on the floor plan—this was the entry point for the water into the set. Conceptually, divers would enter the bell chamber through a sliding portal at the back, move to center as the water would drain out of it, allowing them to emerge from the front of the bell into a dry entry chamber. The only indication of the water level in the bell was by viewing the change in water level of two groups of three acrylic columns flanking the solid metal chamber's entry door. A semi-circular fan of grated steps helped drain the huge flood of breaking water; other areas of the grated lower floor area helped the quick draining. Unlike the control room set, a weir wall was constructed and sufficiently waterproofed to help contain the torrent, take after take. As the design details of this set developed, Jim Hewitt realized that an array of energy pump vents on the lower wall sections of the main chamber would more thoroughly tell the story of the room's functionality; since there was little to no dressing in this set, layers of surface detail would be an excellent visual substitution.

Vehicles and Weapons

Hero weapons and hand props were conceived and illustrated by Christopher Ross and vehicles by Robert Johnson. A military action-thriller like *GI Joe* would be incomplete without heaps of state-of-the-art weaponry and hand props, or an obligatory fleet of iron-plated vehicles. The latter required the attention of a dedicated art director, Kevin Ishioka, and assistants, Brad Ricker and Kevin Loo, to babysit the entire design process from concept, approval, mockup, redesign, approval, and fabrication, tracked like everything else produced by the art department. I've combined weaponry and vehicles in this section because they are both props of different sizes and uses, and because both require training and mastery to operate believably.

DESIGNING FOR THE LENS

Nothing we do can happen without light; it enables the entire operation of the motion picture process. Insufficient light compels the **gaffers** to make it adequate and operable for the cinematographer. Sufficient light showcases the scenery, the costumes, and the actors wearing them. Light is also the critical element driving movie cameras, theater projectors, and computer monitors. The entire movie industry is built around light as a stimulus,

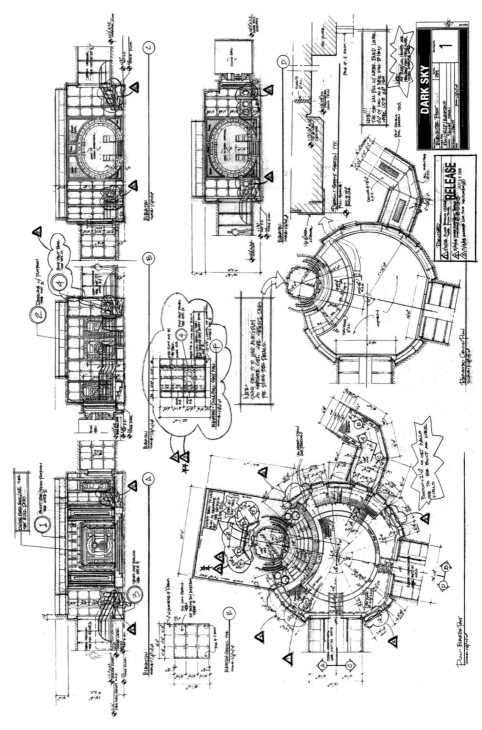

Figure 4.27a Diving Bell and Entry Chamber: Plan—RCP— Elevations drawn by Jim Hewitt. Courtesy of Jim Hewitt.

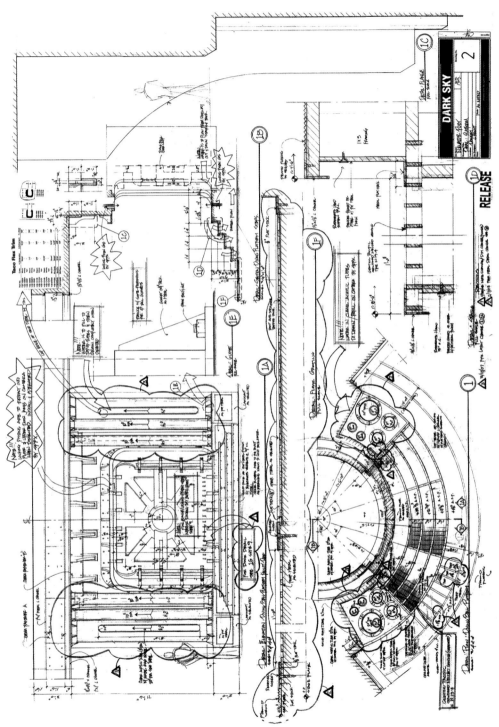

Figure 4.27b Diving Bell and Entry Chamber: Platform and Elevations, drawn by Jim Hewitt. Courtesy of Jim Hewitt.

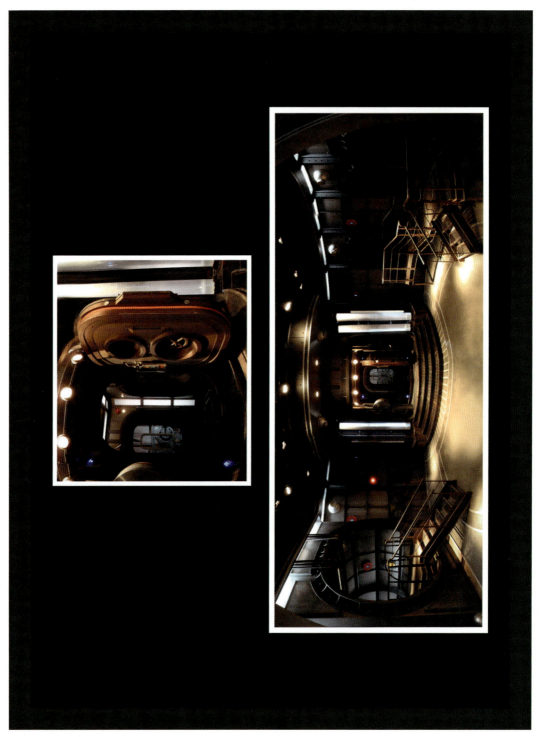

Figure 4.27c Finished set photograph: A) Diving Bell AtriumChamber door. B) Diving Bell Atrium. Courtesy of Jim Hewitt.

Figure 4.28 Hero hand props and weapons for *G I Joe: Rise of Cobra* designed by Christopher Ross, Concept Illustrator. Courtesy of Christopher Ross.

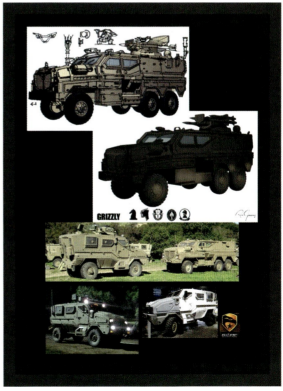

Figure 4.29a Vehicles for *G I Joe: Rise of Cobra* designed by Robert Johnson. Courtesy of Robert Johnson.

the manipulation of light, and light as the delivery system for our well-crafted images. In the art department, we design for the audience through the camera lens. As cinematography is basically a photographic medium, those same principles apply for our purposes as designers. Table 4.1 introduces the basic effect of light on lens systems.

LENSES 101

An aperture is the hole through which light passes into a human eyeball or camera. Light is focused through a lens and is captured and fixed on film emulsion creating an image. Cine lenses are made of glass elements and are grouped into three commonly used types of wide (10–35mm), medium (35–100mm), and narrow (100–1,000mm) fields of view. Lenses have two names, e.g., 50mm f1.4: the first name tells us the focal length of the lens in millimeters, and the second name indicates the maximum aperture opening of that lens. The focal length is

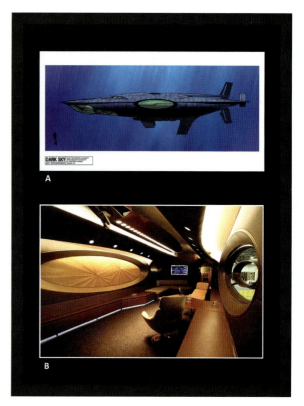

Figure 4.29b Water Craft conceived and designed by Darren Gilford for *G I Joe: Rise of Cobra.* Courtesy of Chad Frey.

the measurable distance from the optical center of a lens, focused at infinity, to the film emulsion surface where an image is recorded. The depth of field is the area between the nearest point and infinity that an object in front of a lens will be in acceptable focus.

In cinematic terms, the area in front of the lens system is referred to as the *object space*; the area behind the lens system, the *image space.* Similarly, the object space is described in terms of depth of field, and the image space in terms of focal length. The light that passes through a lens system is captured or stored on an area of a given size called the *film format* in the back of the image space—or camera's "retina," if you will. A film format is based on the physical size of the film stock being used to capture an image through the lens system attached to the camera. The aperture is adjustable within fixed intervals for a specific lens and is given prescribed numeric values of 1.4, 2, 2.8, 4, 5.6, 8, 11, 16, and 22—largest opening to smallest. F-stops are mathematical ratios between the size of the hole and the focal length of the lens. To go a step further, if the amount of light allowed to pass through the lens is measured, a T-stop value has been recorded. Both F- and T-stops are used interchangeably in cinematography to describe the change of the amount of light from one stop to the next. Depending on the direction you are going, each stop either

Table 4.1 Linking the camera obscura, the human eye, photography, and cinematography.

MODERN APPLICATIONS OF THE CAMERA OBSCURA

OUTSIDE—IN	*Concept*: An exterior light source passes through an adjustable opening and falls on a receiving surface, inverted and reversed. Inside the human eyeball, the brain flips and reverses the image so we can make sense of the world around us. This process reproduces a smaller image from the original, real image on the retina but retains the integrity of the original image in our mind's eye.	
	Light Source	*Lens*
	Adjustment * *Pupil* **	*Shutter*
	Iris **	*Emulsion*
	Image Capture *Retina*	
INSIDE—OUT	*Concept*: A powerful interior light source, e.g., xenon bulb or carbon arc, passes through the film strip at the gate of the projector and translates the moving image through the lens system, to a size a hundred times larger on a movie screen. This reverse process magnifies the original image, presenting what exists in the collective imaginations of all involved.	
	Light Source	*Film Strip*
	Imaging Device	*Projector Lens*
	Image Capture	*Movie Screen*

* Adjustment refers to the lens as a collecting or imaging device. ** Pupil and iris are elements of the human lens system

halves or doubles the amount of light with relation to the next stop. These numbers are so reliable that they have been etched onto the focus rings of all cine lenses.

ASPECT RATIO

Three elements—depth of field, aperture, and aspect ratio—must be considered when referring to cinematic images. The first two, depth of field and aperture, have been briefly discussed. The third, aspect ratio, is synonymous with image format or the frame through which a film is viewed. What a lens "sees" is the angle of view, referring to both the horizontal angle of sight and the vertical angle of sight—together they create an aspect ratio, the numerical relationship of the width and height, respectively, of image formats used in film and television. There are several standard image formats used internationally, such as:

- 16mm
- Super 16mm
- 1.33:1 [TV] 35mm
- 1.85:1 35mm or Normal Academy aperture
- 2.40:1 [anamorphic] 35mm
- 8-perforation VistaVision® 35mm, 65mm
- 15-perforation IMAX 65mm

The most common aspect ratio found through the 1950s was called Academy Aperture, at a ratio of 1.33:1—the same as 4:3 on a TV screen. New widescreen formats and aspect ratios were introduced in the 1950s, from 1.66:1 and higher. CinemaScope® was a widescreen movie format used in the US from 1953 to 1967, and other anamorphic systems such as Panavision® or Technovision® have a 2.40:1 AR, while 70mm formats have an AR of 2.2:1. Cinerama® had a 2.77:1 AR; letterboxed videos for widescreen TVs are frequently in 16:9 or 1.77:1 AR. The cinematographer determines which type of lens and format (AR) to use based on script indications, technical considerations, and creative collaboration of the director-design team.

The *American Cinematographer Manual* not only contains an "All Format Depth of Field Table," but more importantly, a "Field of View Table" for 8mm to 400mm lenses.

How does all of this relate to scenery? The latter table, especially, is helpful during the initial stages of scenery design. If an art director knows that the cinematographer will be shooting an interior set with a 35mm lens in 1.85:1 format, normal Academy Aperture, then Table 4.2 provides valuable design parameters. The "field of view table" for a 35mm lens displays a black horizontal row named "angle of view." For each format listed in the row below, it assigns a horizontal (H) and vertical (V) angle of vision for each dimension of the aspect ratio: 33.3° and 18.4°, respectively. If an art director also knows that the camera will be placed 18 feet from a dining table sitting in the middle of the set, then the vertical angle of the frame can be checked to know how much ceiling above the shot might be seen. Why is ceiling a consideration? Ceilings are more prone to being photographed because of the greater height of the 1.85:1 aspect ratio, see Figure 4.31. In order to properly check this,

Figure 4.30a Aspect Ratio: Flat Widescreen for 35mm Camera Aperture. In 1931, the American motion picture studios adopted a new standard image size for 35mm sound films. The aspect ratio was 1.37:1, only slightly different than the larger 1.33:1 silent ratio frame that had been used for almost three decades. The camera aperture was standardized at .864" wide by .630" high. Projector apertures must be slightly smaller, and the standardized dimension was .825" wide by .602" high.

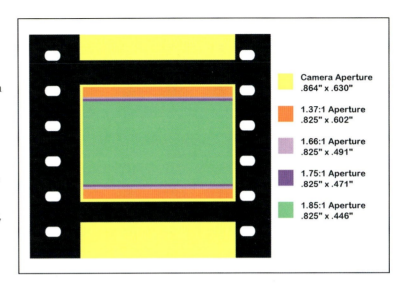

Camera Aperture
.864" x .630"

1.37:1 Aperture
.825" x .602"

1.66:1 Aperture
.825" x .491"

1.75:1 Aperture
.825" x .471"

1.85:1 Aperture
.825" x .446"

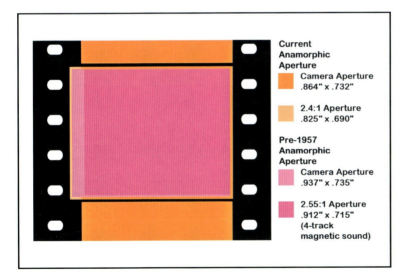

Current Anamorphic Aperture

Camera Aperture
.864" x .732"

2.4:1 Aperture
.825" x .690"

Pre-1957 Anamorphic Aperture

Camera Aperture
.937" x .735"

2.55:1 Aperture
.912" x .715"
(4-track magnetic sound)

Figure 4.30b Aspect Ratio: Anamorphic Widescreen— Current and Pre-1957. From 1957 through today, there have been a number of small changes to the anamorphic projector aperture recommended standards. Today the vast majority of non-anamorphic films are composed for exhibition at 1.85:1 with consideration for the 1.78:1 (16 × 9) ratio adopted for HD Television.

a quick section view of the set should be drawn including the position of the camera, and most importantly, the height of the center of the lens at 4'-6" from the floor. Using the 18.4° vertical angle of vision found in the "field of view table," we know that a portion of the ceiling will not be seen, see Table 4.2. Set pieces like ceilings restrict the lighting crew; partial and removable ceiling pieces should be considered whenever possible. The "field of view table" is indispensable in resolving these questions, and it should be referred to continuously throughout the designing process.

Table 4.2   35mm Field of View Hummel, R. (Ed.). (2002). American Cinematographer Manual, 8th Edition. Used by permission of the American Society of Cinematographers.

35mm FIELD OF VIEW

SETUPS (Approximate Distance)	Full Aperture	Academy 1.33:1	Academy 1.66:1	Academy 1.85:1	Anamorphic 2.40:1	Super 35 1.85:1	Super 35 2.40:1	VistaVision	VistaVision 1.85:1	VistaVision 2.40:1	65mm
Ext Close Up	1' 5"	1' 8"	2' 0"	2' 2"	1' 5"	2' 0"	2' 7"	1' 1"	1' 3"	1' 8"	1' 2"
Close Up	2' 2"	2' 7"	3' 1"	3' 5"	2' 2"	3' 2"	4' 1"	1' 8"	2' 0"	2' 7"	1' 9"
Medium Shot	4' 1"	4' 9"	5' 9"	6' 5"	4' 1"	5' 10"	7' 7"	3' 1"	3' 9"	4' 10"	3' 4"
Full Figure	11' 3"	13' 1"	15' 10"	17' 8"	11' 4"	16' 2"	21' 0"	8' 5"	10' 4"	13' 4"	9' 2"
Angle of View	H 39.2° V 29.9°	H 33.3° V 24.6°	H 33.3° V 20.4°	H 33.3° V 18.4°	H 62.7° V 28.5°	H 37.9° V 21.0°	H 37.9° V 16.3°	H 56.6° V 39.6°	H 56.6° V 32.5°	H 56.6° V 25.4°	H 73.9° V 36.4°
2	1' 1" / 1' 5"	0' 11" / 1' 3"	0' 9" / 1' 3"	0' 8" / 1' 3"	1' 1" / 2' 6"	0' 9" / 1' 4"	0' 7" / 1' 4"	1' 5" / 2' 2"	1' 2" / 2' 2"	0' 11" / 2' 2"	1' 4" / 3' 0"
2½	1' 4" / 1' 9"	1' 2" / 1' 7"	0' 11" / 1' 7"	0' 10" / 1' 7"	1' 4" / 3' 2"	0' 11" / 1' 9"	0' 9" / 1' 9"	1' 9" / 2' 8"	1' 5" / 2' 8"	1' 2" / 2' 8"	1' 8" / 3' 9"
3	1' 7" / 2' 2"	1' 4" / 1' 11"	1' 2" / 1' 11"	1' 0" / 1' 11"	1' 7" / 3' 9"	1' 1" / 2' 1"	0' 10" / 2' 1"	2' 2" / 3' 3"	1' 9" / 3' 3"	1' 4" / 3' 3"	2' 0" / 4' 6"
3½	1' 10" / 2' 6"	1' 7" / 2' 2"	1' 4" / 2' 2"	1' 2" / 2' 2"	1' 10" / 4' 5"	1' 4" / 2' 5"	1' 0" / 2' 5"	2' 6" / 3' 9"	2' 0" / 3' 9"	1' 7" / 3' 9"	2' 4" / 5' 3"
4	2' 2" / 2' 10"	1' 10" / 2' 6"	1' 6" / 2' 6"	1' 4" / 2' 6"	2' 1" / 5' 0"	1' 6" / 2' 9"	1' 2" / 2' 9"	2' 10" / 4' 4"	2' 4" / 4' 4"	1' 10" / 4' 4"	2' 8" / 6' 0"
4½	2' 5" / 3' 2"	2' 1" / 2' 10"	1' 8" / 2' 10"	1' 6" / 2' 10"	2' 5" / 5' 8"	1' 8" / 3' 1"	1' 3" / 3' 1"	3' 2" / 4' 10"	2' 7" / 4' 10"	2' 0" / 4' 10"	3' 0" / 6' 9"
5	2' 8" / 3' 7"	2' 3" / 3' 2"	1' 11" / 3' 2"	1' 8" / 3' 2"	2' 8" / 6' 3"	1' 10" / 3' 5"	1' 5" / 3' 5"	3' 7" / 5' 5"	2' 11" / 5' 5"	2' 3" / 5' 5"	3' 3" / 7' 6"
5½	2' 11" / 3' 11"	2' 6" / 3' 5"	2' 1" / 3' 5"	1' 10" / 3' 5"	2' 11" / 6' 11"	2' 0" / 3' 9"	1' 7" / 3' 9"	3' 11" / 5' 11"	3' 2" / 5' 11"	2' 6" / 5' 11"	3' 7" / 8' 3"
6	3' 2" / 4' 3"	2' 9" / 3' 9"	2' 3" / 3' 9"	2' 0" / 3' 9"	3' 2" / 7' 6"	2' 3" / 4' 1"	1' 9" / 4' 1"	4' 3" / 6' 6"	3' 6" / 6' 6"	2' 8" / 6' 6"	3' 11" / 9' 0"
6½	3' 6" / 4' 8"	3' 0" / 4' 1"	2' 6" / 4' 1"	2' 2" / 4' 1"	3' 5" / 8' 2"	2' 5" / 4' 5"	1' 10" / 4' 5"	4' 8" / 7' 0"	3' 9" / 7' 0"	2' 11" / 7' 0"	4' 3" / 9' 9"
7	3' 9" / 5' 0"	3' 2" / 4' 5"	2' 8" / 4' 5"	2' 5" / 4' 5"	3' 9" / 8' 10"	2' 7" / 4' 10"	2' 0" / 4' 10"	5' 0" / 7' 7"	4' 1" / 7' 7"	3' 2" / 7' 7"	4' 7" / 10' 6"
8	4' 3" / 5' 8"	3' 8" / 5' 0"	3' 0" / 5' 0"	2' 9" / 5' 0"	4' 3" / 10' 1"	3' 0" / 5' 6"	2' 3" / 5' 6"	5' 8" / 8' 7"	4' 8" / 8' 7"	3' 7" / 8' 7"	5' 3" / 12' 0"
9	4' 10" / 6' 5"	4' 1" / 5' 8"	3' 5" / 5' 8"	3' 1" / 5' 8"	4' 9" / 11' 4"	3' 4" / 6' 2"	2' 7" / 6' 2"	6' 5" / 9' 8"	5' 3" / 9' 8"	4' 1" / 9' 8"	5' 11" / 13' 6"
10	5' 4" / 7' 1"	4' 7" / 6' 3"	3' 9" / 6' 3"	3' 5" / 6' 3"	5' 4" / 12' 7"	3' 9" / 6' 10"	2' 10" / 6' 10"	7' 1" / 10' 9"	5' 10" / 10' 9"	4' 6" / 10' 9"	6' 7" / 15' 0"
12	6' 5" / 8' 7"	5' 6" / 7' 6"	4' 7" / 7' 6"	4' 1" / 7' 6"	6' 4" / 15' 1"	4' 5" / 8' 3"	3' 5" / 8' 3"	8' 7" / 12' 11"	7' 0" / 12' 11"	5' 5" / 12' 11"	7' 11" / 18' 1"
14	7' 6" / 10' 0"	6' 5" / 8' 10"	5' 4" / 8' 10"	4' 9" / 8' 10"	7' 5" / 17' 7"	5' 2" / 9' 7"	4' 0" / 9' 7"	10' 0" / 15' 1"	8' 2" / 15' 1"	6' 4" / 15' 1"	9' 2" / 21' 1"
16	8' 6" / 11' 5"	7' 4" / 10' 1"	6' 1" / 10' 1"	5' 5" / 10' 1"	8' 6" / 20' 1"	5' 11" / 11' 0"	4' 7" / 11' 0"	11' 5" / 17' 3"	9' 4" / 17' 3"	7' 3" / 17' 3"	10' 6" / 24' 1"
18	9' 7" / 12' 10"	8' 3" / 11' 4"	6' 10" / 11' 4"	6' 1" / 11' 4"	9' 7" / 22' 7"	6' 8" / 12' 4"	5' 2" / 12' 4"	12' 10" / 19' 5"	10' 6" / 19' 5"	8' 1" / 19' 5"	11' 10" / 27' 1"
20	10' 8" / 14' 3"	9' 2" / 12' 7"	7' 7" / 12' 7"	6' 10" / 12' 7"	10' 7" / 25' 2"	7' 5" / 13' 9"	5' 9" / 13' 9"	14' 3" / 21' 7"	11' 8" / 21' 7"	9' 0" / 21' 7"	13' 2" / 30' 1"
25	13' 4" / 17' 10"	11' 5" / 15' 9"	9' 6" / 15' 9"	8' 6" / 15' 9"	13' 3" / 31' 5"	9' 3" / 17' 2"	7' 2" / 17' 2"	17' 10" / 26' 11"	14' 7" / 26' 11"	11' 3" / 26' 11"	16' 5" / 37' 7"
50	26' 8" / 35' 7"	22' 11" / 31' 5"	18' 11" / 31' 5"	17' 0" / 31' 5"	26' 7" / 62' 10"	18' 7" / 34' 3"	14' 4" / 34' 3"	35' 7" / 53' 11"	29' 2" / 53' 11"	22' 6" / 53' 11"	32' 10" / 75' 2"

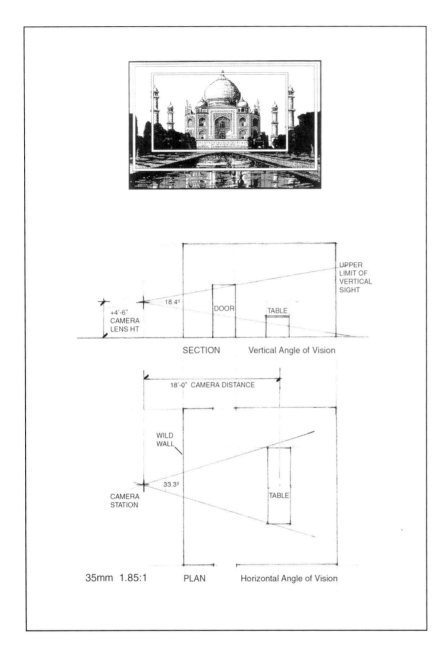

SECTION   Vertical Angle of Vision

35mm 1.85:1   PLAN   Horizontal Angle of Vision

Figure 4.31   A) Aspect Ratio 185:1. The larger and smaller rectangles shown here refer to the width and height, respectively, of the 1.85:1 AR as equal to the 2.40:1 AR. Depending on framing, the Normal Academy aperture will always show the same width but considerably more height than its 2.40:1 counterpart. For this reason, some cinematographers see it as a preferable lens choice in some situations. B) Vertical Field of View for a 35mm lens showing the plan and corresponding section. Using both horizontal and vertical angle of view shown in the Field of View Table contained in the ASC Manual is always helpful in determining wall heights, ceiling coverage, and height of translates and green screens. Hummel, R. (Ed.). (2002). *American Cinematographer Manual*, 8th Edition. Used by permission of the American Society of Cinematographers.

LENS TEST

Figure 4.32 displays a series of lens tests taken to determine the best establishing shot for the scenery elevation photographed in the example. A previously drawn landscape plan was used to reference general distances from the 1865 White House front porch overhang for the TV movie *The Day Lincoln Was Shot* (1998). Subsequent lens tests were taken at 18mm at 120′, 25mm at 130′, 35mm at 190′, and 50mm at 284′. Close inspection of the photo samples reveal more foreground detail with the widest lens shown, although there is greater background detail and texture in the photo shot with the 50mm lens. The director-camera-design team made an appropriate decision based on this information and what would best forward the storytelling.

An art director should also be aware of the opinion that sets can be less wide if a 1.85:1 format is used instead of 2.40:1. Is this fact or myth? Figure 4.32, clearly shows two very important aspects of a 1.85:1 AR: 1) the vertical value is greater than its 2.40:1 counterpart, but 2) it shares the same horizontal value as the 2.40:1 AR. Obviously, format doesn't necessarily dictate the width of a set—a normal Academy Aperture might require as wide a set, depending on the design and composition required by the Cinematographer and Director.

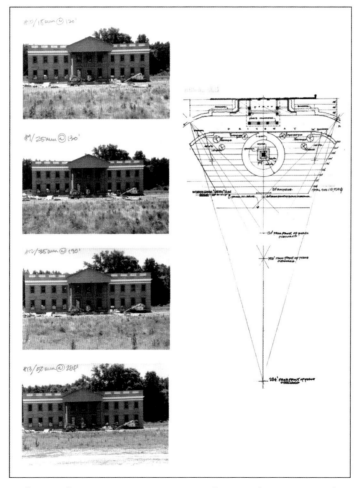

Figure 4.32   Lens test taken with 18mm, 25mm, 35mm and 50mm lenses at 120 feet, 130 feet, 190 feet and 284 feet, respectively. © Michael Rizzo.

CAMERA ANGLE PROJECTION: A PERSPECTIVE MASTER CLASS

This final application of depth of field, aperture, and aspect ratio can now be explained in graphic terms. A working knowledge of basic two-point perspective and projection techniques are invaluable for an art director to determine what the camera, fitted with a particular lens, will see in any given shot. Art Director, Harold Michelson, cleverly devised the **Camera Angle Projection** method as a foolproof technique for previewing set plans and camera placement. The method is a step-by-step process of using plan and elevation information to plot a simple perspective drawing, according to the rules of linear perspective. At first glance, this process seems complicated but once the fundamental concept of the system is understood, it is logical, methodical, and accurate. A working knowledge of drafting and a basic understanding of cinematography—briefly presented here—will support anyone's skill at this kind of informative perspective drawing.

One-point perspective tells us that all outlines of object surfaces in the picture plane meet at the same vanishing point on the horizon—this is called **convergence**. From this we can draw a parallel in terms of how the focal length of a lens determines the degree of convergence in a photographic image. An art director can use the angle of view for a lens to determine graphically the degree of convergence in a perspective set drawing. Any perspective drawing can be made to represent what any given lens would see in terms of its focal length and its degree of convergence.

Harold Michelson, the storyboard artist represented in Figure 4.9a–b, clearly understood this relationship and devised a system of perspective drawing for cinematography. This method he created informed all of his work as an illustrator, production designer, and art director as well as his prolific storyboarding ability. Since Harold devised this system, its concept has been translated into the 3D modeling programs we use in the art department today, e.g., 3D Studio Max, Maya, SoftImage, etc.—animatic programs use the concept of this system as well, as shown in Figure 4.10a–d.

This seminal technique of projecting a plan into a third dimension perspective drawing has been well-explained and interpreted by Stephen D. Katz, author of *Film Directing Shot by Shot*, and by the master/originator of this projection method, Harold Michelson. I am not interested, here, in reinventing the wheel. What might be far more interesting for you, the reader, is to examine the text of several of Michelson's original notes and see copies of his original drawings and a pamphlet he created, specifically to share his perceptions and efforts with his colleagues. Harold applied for a patent on July 26, 1950 (See Figure 4.33) and he continued to revise and improve the presentation of his invention at every lecture he gave for other art directors, storyboard artists or illustrators (See Figure 4.34a–c). Remember: his brilliant mind compensated for the lack of computer technology in the mid-twentieth century—although he referred to the "Perspective Plotter" implement, Figure 4.35, he invented to draw a camera angle projection as his "computor."

Imagine not having computer software and a super-fast processor at your disposal, but only having a ground plan and aspect ratio information of your camera lens to work with. What do you do? You must figure a methodical way to transform all key points on your set's ground plan into the lines of the vertical picture plane of your set rendering.

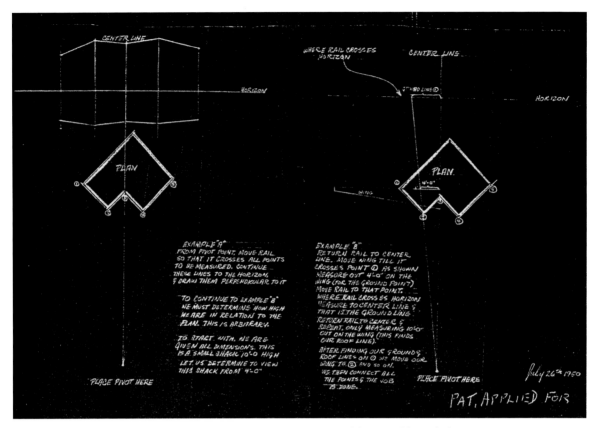

Figure 4.33   A blueprint drawing submitted for patent approval by Harold Michelson, Art Director. Courtesy of Harold Michelson.

Guessing at it is not an option; the rendering must indicate exactly what a camera's shooting lens will see when placed a specific distance from the scenery. Michelson created a surprisingly simple method to solve this problem with his Perspective Plotter. The plotter consisted of a "rail" and a "wing": the former being a long, flat length of metal like a ruler with a drilled hole at one end; the latter being a variation of a scale ruler split at center with quarter inch scale (typical ground plan scale) on the left and three-quarter inch scale (typical elevation scale) on the right. Other tools he used were a pair of architect's drafting dividers for transferring measurements, a ¼" scale ground plan, some pushpins, a mounting board, tracing paper, and camera lens aspect ratio angles printed on clear acetate—samples shown in Figure 4.36a–b. With his "computor and peripherals," he determined manually what technology software does automatically today.

The Perspective Plotter pamphlet provides a simple and quick method of projecting a floor plan into a 3D perspective drawing. As a shorthand review of main bullet points in

Figure 4.34a Various samples of Camera Angle Projection used by H. Michelson used at many Art Director Guild functions. Harold was always acutely aware of camera angle/placement and composition as a prolific storyboard artist, illustrator and art director. Courtesy of Harold Michelson.

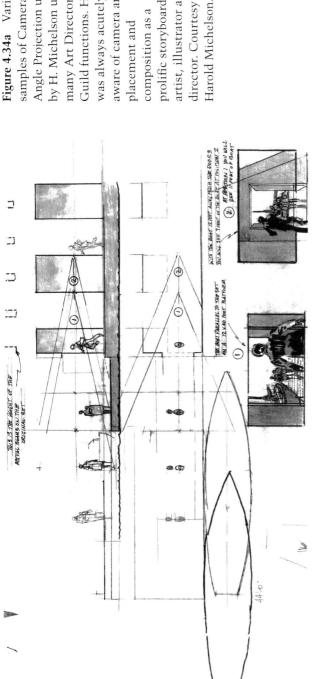

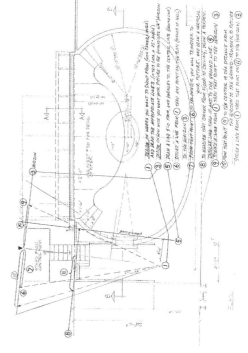

Figure 4.34c

Figure 4.34b

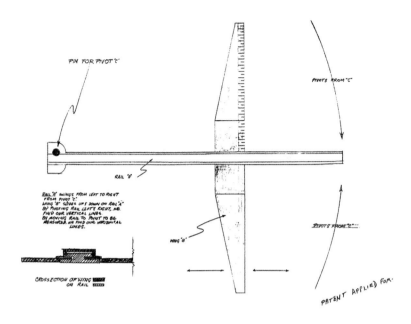

Figure 4.35 A drawing of his invention: a Perspective Plotter, submitted for patent approval by Harold Michelson, Art Director. Courtesy of Harold Michelson.

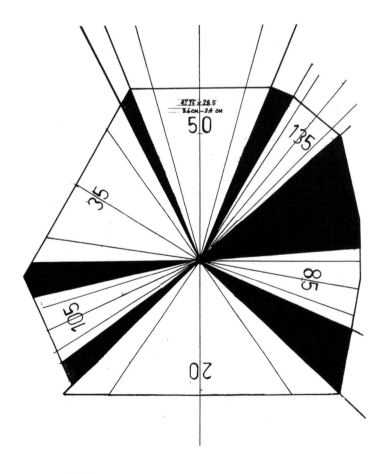

Figure 4.36a Camera Lenses: 20°, 35°, 50°, 85°, 105°, and 135° degrees for a 1:1.85 Aspect Ratio. Each lens indicates two camera angles: the height of the frame (dotted) and the width of the frame (solid). This sectioned chart is an earlier version of two that Harold Michelson used as he developed his Camera Angle Projection method.

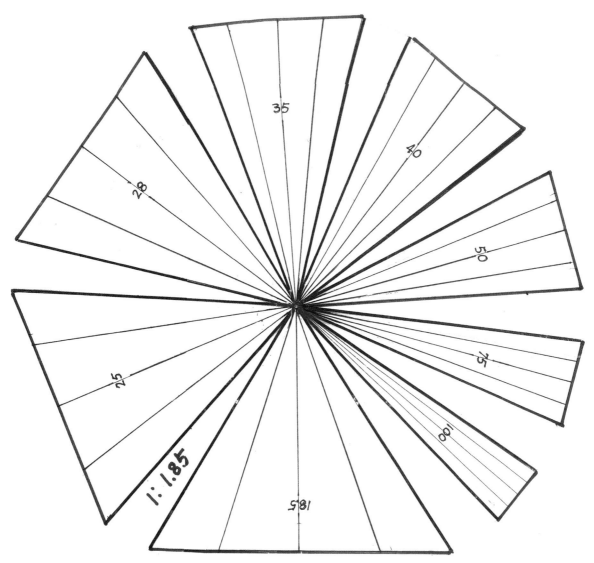

Figure 4.36b   Camera Lenses: 18.5°, 25°, 28°, 35°, 40°, 50°, 75°, and 100° degrees for a 1:1.85 Aspect Ratio. Each lens indicates two camera angles: the height of the frame (dotted) and the width of the frame (solid). This later chart indicates the remaining available lenses for cinematography. You'll notice that the two most used lenses: the 35mm and 50mm appear on both sectioned charts. This chart more easily lends itself to being cut into pieces and printed onto clear acetate pages for easy C. A. P. method use. Courtesy of Harold Michelson.

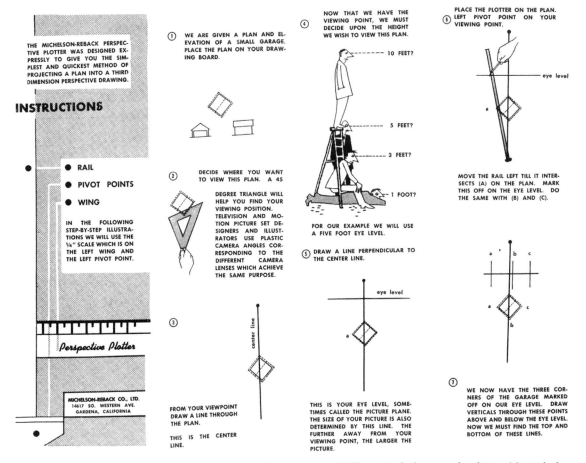

THE MICHELSON-REBACK PERSPECTIVE PLOTTER WAS DESIGNED EXPRESSLY TO GIVE YOU THE SIMPLEST AND QUICKEST METHOD OF PROJECTING A PLAN INTO A THIRD DIMENSION PERSPECTIVE DRAWING.

INSTRUCTIONS

● RAIL

● PIVOT POINTS

● WING

IN THE FOLLOWING STEP-BY-STEP ILLUSTRATIONS WE WILL USE THE ¼" SCALE WHICH IS ON THE LEFT WING AND THE LEFT PIVOT POINT.

Perspective Plotter

MICHELSON-REBACK CO., LTD.
14617 SO. WESTERN AVE.
GARDENA, CALIFORNIA

① WE ARE GIVEN A PLAN AND ELEVATION OF A SMALL GARAGE. PLACE THE PLAN ON YOUR DRAWING BOARD.

② DECIDE WHERE YOU WANT TO VIEW THIS PLAN. A 45 DEGREE TRIANGLE WILL HELP YOU FIND YOUR VIEWING POSITION. TELEVISION AND MOTION PICTURE SET DESIGNERS AND ILLUSTRATORS USE PLASTIC CAMERA ANGLES CORRESPONDING TO THE DIFFERENT CAMERA LENSES WHICH ACHIEVE THE SAME PURPOSE.

③ FROM YOUR VIEWPOINT DRAW A LINE THROUGH THE PLAN.

THIS IS THE CENTER LINE.

④ NOW THAT WE HAVE THE VIEWING POINT, WE MUST DECIDE UPON THE HEIGHT WE WISH TO VIEW THIS PLAN.

10 FEET?

5 FEET?

3 FEET?

1 FOOT?

FOR OUR EXAMPLE WE WILL USE A FIVE FOOT EYE LEVEL.

⑤ DRAW A LINE PERPENDICULAR TO THE CENTER LINE.

THIS IS YOUR EYE LEVEL, SOMETIMES CALLED THE PICTURE PLANE. THE SIZE OF YOUR PICTURE IS ALSO DETERMINED BY THIS LINE. THE FURTHER AWAY FROM YOUR VIEWING POINT, THE LARGER THE PICTURE.

⑥ PLACE THE PLOTTER ON THE PLAN. LEFT PIVOT POINT ON YOUR VIEWING POINT.

eye level

MOVE THE RAIL LEFT TILL IT INTERSECTS (A) ON THE PLAN. MARK THIS OFF ON THE EYE LEVEL. DO THE SAME WITH (B) AND (C).

⑦ WE NOW HAVE THE THREE CORNERS OF THE GARAGE MARKED OFF ON OUR EYE LEVEL. DRAW VERTICALS THROUGH THESE POINTS ABOVE AND BELOW THE EYE LEVEL. NOW WE MUST FIND THE TOP AND BOTTOM OF THESE LINES.

Figure 4.37a   Camera Angle Projection: Steps 1–7, courtesy of Lillian Michelson, wife of Harold Michelson; Camille Abbott, Production Illustrator; and Daniel Raim, Videographer. Courtesy of Harold Michelson.

this step-by-step guide, the pamphlet, shown here in Figure 4.37a and b, only really serves as a quick outline of what Michelson might have explained in a more in-depth lecture. A modern interpretation of one of Michelson's lectures is Stephen Katz's more simplified translation of the Camera Angle Projection method in the appendix of his book. In it, he substitutes the rail and wing with a 90° and a scale ruler. His comprehensive explanation is accompanied by simple diagrams that clearly and brilliantly reflect the text—he transforms what can be initially complicated into something obvious and effortlessly understandable. To be honest, it takes a few passes at reading Katz's material to fully grasp the concept and several experiments on your own to test your comprehension. Practice and patience will reveal the elegance of Harold Michelson's blend of pragmatism, aesthetics and functionality.

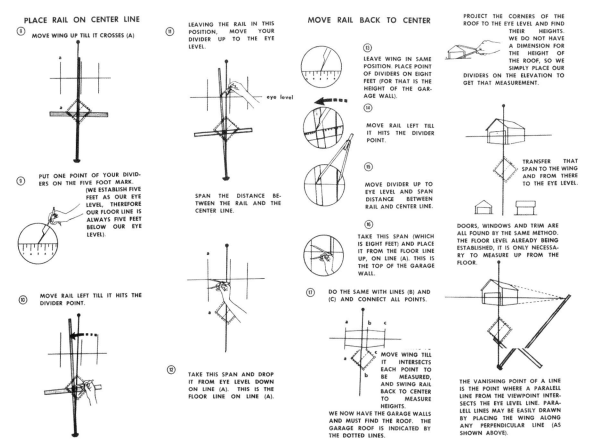

Figure 4.37b Camera Angle Projection: Steps 8–16, courtesy of Lillian Michelson, wife of Harold Michelson; Camille Abbott, Production Illustrator; Daniel Raim, Videographer. Courtesy of Harold Michelson.

Applying the process of Camera Angle Projection in reverse is a foolproof method of breaking down location photographs into usable ground plans. Michelson realized this early on and devised an early, graphic example in Figure 4.38—Katz also explains the reverse process clearly and simply at the end of the appendix section of his book. You may recall that this concept has also been previously introduced earlier in this chapter by Randy Wilkins in Figure 4.15a and b. He offers the example because he regularly uses it as a set designer, consequently, it is a process that you will likely use regularly. It too is worth taking the time to master—regardless of the current ease of technology, this is an excellent skill to develop.

With some basic camera lens and respective aspect ratio theory in place, let's make it real by putting some practical questions to cinematographer, and respected colleague on *Glee*, Joaquin Sedillo (*Glee, Veronica Mars, The Italian Job, Memento*). At the onset of

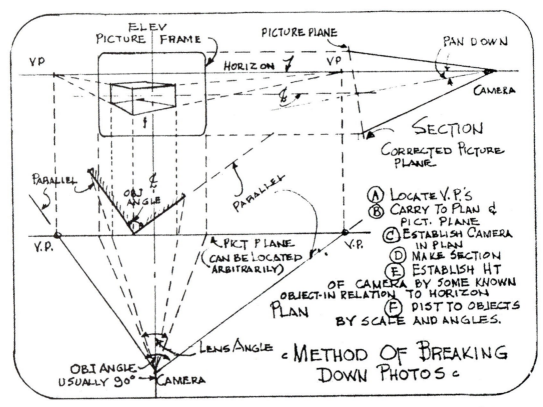

Figure 4.38   Harold Michelson realized early on that the reverse process of his Camera Angle Projection, or back projection, would be another useful method of breaking down photographs of location buildings, for instance, into workable ground plans. Courtesy of Harold Michelson.

Glee Season 5, he made a change from shooting film stock to digital video. He gets general and specific as we talk, migrating from film to HD, and what defines a great art director in terms of effective storytelling.

Interview with Joaquin Sedillo

● *On* Glee *Season 5, why the shift from film to HD? Do you anticipate more/less work and/or an economy in time, materials and crew costs?*
  It was strictly an economic choice. I suspect there will be some savings but not the vast savings we might anticipate. Otherwise, we have spent a substantial amount of money shooting film these past few years, so some savings will be welcomed.

● *Film has been a beautiful look for the show.*
  Film provides a great texture, no doubt, and it's something I love doing. Some less confident cinematographers might not think they can achieve a film-quality look in HD but it is very

possible. When I first interviewed with executive producer, I was asked if I had adequate experience shooting on film—a legitimate question considering I had previously done a lot of TV—but the truth is I had shot a lot of film for years. Just then, his assistant passed the open door and the producer exclaimed, "Joaquin has shot film!" It was as if I had ridden to the interview on a dinosaur and presented the Ark of the Covenant. [Hearty laugh] To get back to your question: It's not necessarily an issue of older film versus newer digital approaches, but how a cinematographer uses whatever option he/she chooses in new and provocative ways while interpreting the script. After the results of the camera tests we recently shot came back to us, I'm now very confident that we can achieve a film-quality look with an HD camera.

● *Is the RED camera the obvious choice?*
No. The Alexa. I recently shot a pilot on the RED but I'm personally not a fan. On the other hand, the Alexa possesses similar characteristics as many of the film cameras, and the depth of field is much shallower for me in this instance. *Glee* tends to bounce back and forth creatively between long lens pieces and very wide, in-your-face close-ups. Our camera tests for both circumstances showed the shallowness as much more than we expected. The show's execs were happily surprised but I knew this would be the case. Even our show's lighting designer remarked on how much our color tests, especially, resemble the general look established on the first few season's original film-camera work. So, I think the Arriflex Alexa will work exceedingly well as an option.

● *How is an art director most effective in terms of the camera and lighting departments?*
An effective art director for me is someone who gets the concept of depth, layers, and dimension. This person should also have a clear understanding of how a set is photographed. It's critical to be aware of how the camera will travel through the set and how color, texture, dimension, and shape are layered in to support the richness we are working to translate as an appropriate background to the story being told. In an antique store location, for example, a seasoned art director will insist on moving through the space with me and my viewfinder before layers of stuff are removed before we shoot. Most likely, a lot of the stuff will remain in place once the camera lens reveals the story in terms of the potential of this kind of location. A simple solution to a less attractive, relatively bare location is the addition of a single practical placed in the furthest corner of the space, or in an adjoining room. Simple, real solutions like that define a great art director from a good one. In my experience, knowing how texture, color and shape translate through movement is innate, but it can be learned if the willingness is there.[15]

The Alexa camera has the support of other film professionals for these reasons:

1. Alexa's great dynamic images allow workability as with a 35mm camera producing a staggering cinematic quality.
2. It doesn't feel electronic in the highlights.
3. The ergonomic menu system and functionality of the Alexa are based on film cameras. With little if no cinematic richness lost, Joaquin praises the Arriflex Alexa is an excellent choice.

The creation, refinement, manufacture and management of the physical scenery eventually produced by the Mill, will continue to be the focus of the next few chapters. The creation and refinement aspects of the process will draw on modes of motion picture in-camera production and in-studio production. Scenery construction only, commences once the design is approved and formalized (on paper). It's now time to consider the intermediate and final phases of the growing physical design.

NOTES

1 www.nytimes.com/2013/02/17/opinion/sunday/why-we-love-beautiful-things.html.

2 http://en.wikipedia.org/wiki/Rhinoceros_3D.

3 http://en.wikipedia.org/wiki/Photoshop_cs6.

4 www.sketchup.com/product/features.html.

5 Linda Berger interview, August 16, 2004, North Hollywood, CA.

6 Colin Green interview, September 13, 2004, Burbank, CA.

7 James Clyne interview, May 17, 2004, Santa Monica, CA.

8 Victor Martinez interview, April 21, 2004, North Hollywood, CA

9 Luke Freeborn Interview, May 6, 2004, West Los Angeles, CA.

10 http://sketchupdate.blogspot.com/2011/03/sketchup-pro-case-study-randy-wilkins.html Adapted from "SketchUp Pro Case Study: Randy Wilkins," SketchUp website. Posted March 17, 2011 by Gopal Shah, product marketing manager.

11 Barbara Mesney interview, November 13, 2003, Venice Beach, CA. View Mesney's artwork on her website, www.bmesney.com.

12 J. André Chaintreuil interview, April 28, 2004, North Hollywood, CA.

13 Greg Papalia interview, March 5, 2013, phone interview.

14 Ed Verreaux interview, September 3, 2013, email interview.

15 Joaquin Sedillo interview, July 25, 2013, Hollywood, CA.entrance to Destros' world, the MARS Entry Corridor, Interior Corridors, and Surgical Operations Room.

CHAPTER 5

The Physical Design

THE LOCATIONS DEPARTMENT AND SCOUTING

Cinema design essentially comes from two sources: the creative efforts of the art depart-ment design team and from the well-informed searching of the locations department. Both sources take their direction from the screenplay; both resulting "shopping lists" are com-pared and finally become the first set list for a film project. That's it in a nutshell. The remainder of this chapter will explain and expand on these activities.

Sometimes it's easier and less expensive to retrofit an existing location than to build it onstage. This determination is an ongoing discussion between the locations and design departments—the final decision is made by the latter. Several steps are undertaken in order to distill a set list into locations and onstage scenery to be shot. The first location scout between these two department heads begins this involved process.

FIRST SCOUTS

Within my first hour of my first day in the production office, the Locations Manager is one of the first people I am most likely to meet. He and the Production Designer, among the first arrivals, have already begun the locations search by looking through dozens of images found online or binders prepared by the locations assistants. After culling down the options to a manageable handful of reasonable locations, their first series of scouts take them out of the production offices to check out those locations as set possibilities for initial presentation to the Director. This process must start early and happen quickly because it can be a long, intensive one—typically running the course of pre-production and part of production time if necessary. During this process, many extraneous options are eliminated from the prime choice list and tossed into the seconds pile. Winning a director's confidence and enthusiasm is the first goal. Once decisions about specific locations are decided upon, the final goal of obtaining neighborhood permissions and signing contracts begins.

While I am guiding the art department coordinator through our office setup and initial search for scenery reference material, I am also viewing laminated sequences of interior and exterior locations and corresponding details (see Figure 5.1).

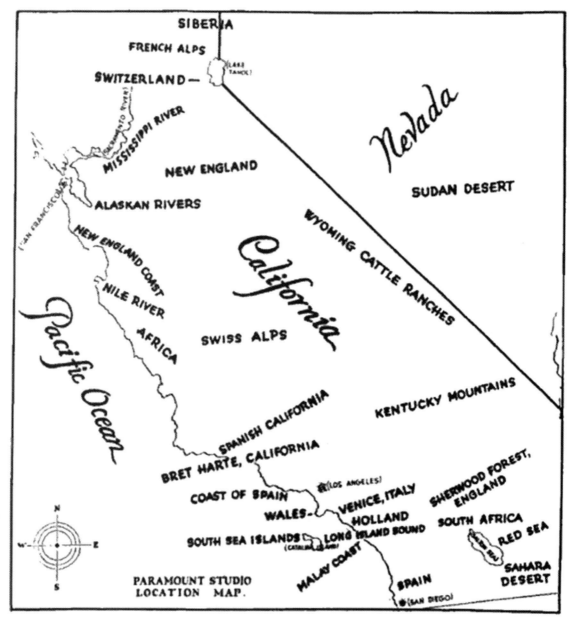

Figure 5.1 This map published in 1927 was used by Hollywood film studios to find nearby locations to film foreign locales, establishing Los Angeles and southern California as the "film capital of the World". Courtesy of *The American Film Industry* written by Tino Balio.

What makes this moment significant is that these montages are the first step in translating the text of the screenplay into tangible shooting realities. Together, the locations manager and designer have seriously begun the visualization process of the art department. Their first efforts are color-copied and slipped into clear page covers collected in a binder and passed among the designer, director, UPM, producer, art director, and locations department. In most cases, I have already seen digital versions of these initial locations' images on the art department Web server if I am working on a film that has provided one. Mine is not the only preview available on the server as it is at the disposal of the digital designers, graphic artists, set designers, and model makers coming aboard, as well as whoever else is working during the early phases of film production. Digital artwork overlaid onto location images is next presented to the Director, alongside research and concept art. Even with our active sharing of digital images, the instinctive process continues to be primarily hand-to-hand in the initial throes of our collective, creative bonding experience.

Once the ongoing process of location finding is underway, logistical concerns like location base camp setup, caravan setup (crew parking and production vehicle parking), getting in and out of locations, and logical placement of the staging of scenery are addressed. As project manager for the art department, my concerns parallel those of the locations manager in terms of practicality and operations management. For example, cover sets, especially those outside of the studio, are insurance that shooting will continue despite the prevailing weather conditions. Successful location manager/art director teams will always include cover sets within the logistics of location scheduling.

SECOND SCOUTS

The initial round of scouting completed, a second series of scouts begins between production designer and art director. Second scouts serve two purposes by allowing the production designer to confirm the quality of choices made with the locations manager and by providing bonding time between both heads of the design team. Physically visiting the locations and sharing their possible shooting potential also transfers creative and managerial responsibility from the designer to the next-in-charge. From this point onward, whatever changes happen will be handled by the Art Director, including interfacing with locations reps and agents outside of the film, retrofitting physical location changes in preparation for shooting, organizing the logistics of getting into the location site, staying and working there, getting out with little difficulty, and, most importantly, the return of the location to its original state after shooting.

In the example shown (Figure 5.2), scout notes can be copious but are always detailed. Location managers would rather have too much detail than too little for the benefit of the agent renting the location to the production. Scout notes are most likely retyped by the art department coordinator from an art director's handwritten notes into a simple, readable

Figure 5.2 Typical locations folder: Left: Bradford Building, L.A., Top panorama: Ford Theatre, D.C., Middle panorama: Farmhouse, Luxembourg, Bottom panorama: Moab, UT.

text document and then distributed initially to the following departments: locations, set decorating, construction, paint, special effects, rigging grips, lighting, and props. Combined with the preliminary script, this list becomes the basis of the preliminary set list, compiled from my notes and distributed by the art coordinator (Figure 5.3).

THIRD SCOUTS

The third series of **rekkies** during pre-production are fact-finding missions. They occur for the benefit of the set designers during a full-day visit to all existing locations. By and large, most locations are retrofitted, temporary sets that must be carefully analyzed. Specific measurements of loading docks, elevators, and similar building entrances or egresses are recorded to determine the size of scenery modules to be designed to load easily in and out of the building. Width, length, and height dimensions of rooms including doors and windows, hallways, stairwells, skylights, and other shootable areas of location spaces are also recorded for retrofitted scenery.

With necessary gear in hand, accuracy for drawing ground plans, elevations, and construction details can easily happen (See Figure 5.4). Planning several trips to a location is a realistic consideration; not everything can be thought of for a single comprehensive trip. If a specific location requires a great deal of time-intensive detailing, then arrangements must be coordinated with the locations department for access and additional measuring time (see "Fifth Scouts," this chapter).

FOURTH SCOUTS

The last formal scout happens before the final production meeting and commencement of principal photography. During this Tech Scout all production and department heads including the director, his/her personal assistant, first and second ADs, producer, UPM, head accountant, production designer, art director, set decorator, leadman, cinematographer, first assistant cameraman, gaffer, key grip, rigging grip, visual effects coordinator, construction coordinator, lead scenic, mechanical effects coordinator, transpo captain, location manager, and assistant location managers are assembled for several daylong rekkies. Scheduling this event is comparable to organizing a mini-production meeting-on-wheels in two production vans with scheduled lunch and dinner stops. Seating in the vans reflects each work-related group, positioned within earshot so that logistical questions that arise can be solved during the course of the day. As problems are solved and other considerations arise, cell phones are in constant use for ordering equipment and supplies, rescheduling dinner, making logistical changes, texting vendors, and updating assistants and department coordinators. All iPads are lit and functioning, organizing timelines, filling in notes, and checking email. The production designer and I are usually found explaining and simultaneously sketching concept ideas or working through foreseeable problems. All in all, this last series of scouts codifies the final onstage and locations set list and the shooting schedule.

"My Fellow Americans" Location Information				last modified: 3/20/96

Script Date: March, 1996			Director: Peter Segal	Production Designer: Jim Bissell
Producer: Warner Brothers			Michael Ewing Jean Higgins	Production number: Page number: 8

Set #:	Loc:	Type:	Set Description:	Location Notes:
435	Asheville	Int	Hollis Horsebarn-night → NOT A DAIRYBARN	~~Biltmore Estate~~ TBD. SAME AS 447
			scenenumbers: 195,196,222	
436	Asheville	Ext	Maryland Road-Day	TBD-Schedule Driven
			scenenumbers: 199	
438	Asheville	Ext	White House Kennedy Garden	Build at Biltmore
			scenenumbers: 237,243	
439	Wash	Ext	White House N.E. Gate	TBD ?
			scenenumbers: 248	
441	Asheville	Int	Witnaur's bedroom	Biltmore Forest GINGER 274/4768. 25 → S. FOREST MALL, JUST PAST BROWNTOWN RD, HT 2ND LEFT, 9 DEERFIELD.
			scenenumbers: 145	
443	L.A. Loc	Ext	Highway/Helicopter duel/culvert	TBD LA
			scenenumbers: 106,107,108,109,110,111,112,113	
444	Asheville	Int	Wayne & Genny's Trailer-night	Cover Set-Find location for Factory Lunchroom and build in space nearby DRAW.
			scenenumbers: 128	
445	Asheville	Ext	White House S.W. lawn	Construct -Biltmore
			scenenumbers: 214-228,232,233	
445	Asheville	Ext	White House Southwest Lawn	White House
			scenenumbers: 238,239,240,241	
446	Asheville	Int	Factory Lunchroom-Cleveland	Asheville Warehouse DRAW.
			scenenumbers: 252	
447	Asheville	Int/Ext	Hollis Kitch/Ext Barn	TBD ? SAME AS 445.
			scenenumbers: 221	
701	2nd Unit	Ext	Sky/Airforce 2	Stock footage?
			scenenumbers: 18	

Figure 5.3a   Scout notes for N. Carolina locations on *My Fellow Americans.*

RED DRAGON ART DEPARTMENT, SET BREAKDOWN, 4TH REVISION - AS OF JANUARY 3, 2002

LA LOCATIONS

1.	INT	Concert Hall	No tie-in. No EXT.	N	sc 2
2.	INT	Lecter's Dining Room, Entry	Ties in to EXT Townhouse Location(MD)	N	sc 3, 5
3.	INT	Lecter's Study, as LA Location	Ties into Lecter Dining Rm. Location	N	sc 5, 6
4.	OMIT				
5.	EXT/INT	Leeds House, incl. Kitchen, Stairs, Den, Hall, Master Bedrm., Bath (video:Kitchen -D-sc 35,136)	Bare-tree look is all Night. Summer look on video is all Day. Ties in to Leeds Bathroom Studio Set Note: Lattice outside Kitchen door.	N	sc 11, 12, 16
6.	EXT/INT	Sherman House video, incl. Backyard, Den	No tie-in. Summer look only. Note Rain outside Den windows.	N	sc 114
7.	INT	Reba's Apartment, incl. Living Rm., Kitchen	Ties in to EXT Reba's Apt.Location (MD) Note Rain outside windows.	N	sc 62, 63
8.	INT	Crawford Bedroom and Den	No tie-in.	N	sc 83, 87
9.	EXT	Omni Hotel, Atlanta, estab.	Tie in to INT Hotel Rm. Studio Set.	N	sc 17
10.	INT	Coffee Shop	No tie-in.	D	sc 24
11.	INT	Bookstore	No tie-in.	D	sc 53, 55
12.	INT	FBI Apartment	Tie in to EXT FBI Apt. DC	D	sc 98
13.	INT	Atlanta Police Squad Rm., incl. Springfield's Office.	Tie in to EXT Atlanta Police Station (MD).	D	sc 21, 22
14.	INT	Asylum, Chilten's Office, Corridor, Staircase	Tie in to EXT Asylum (MD), & tie in to Lecter's Cell	D	sc 26, 27 sc 28
15.	INT	Asylum Exercise Pen	Tie in to EXT Asylum (MD).	D	sc 51
16.	EXT	Chroma-Lux Inc., include. estab., parking lot, loading dock, bus stop	Tie in to INT Chroma-Lux Locations (LA). Note Rain for 1st parking lot night scene.	D N N	sc 56 sc 59, 60 sc 142
17.	INT	Chroma-Lux, incl. machinery maze, Personnel Office, Corridor.	Tie in to EXT Chroma-Lux (LA). Tie in to INT Reba's Darkroom Studio Set	D N	sc 57 sc 141, 144,
18.	INT	Law Office (Birmingham) No tie-in.		D	sc 66
19.	INT	FBI Offices, including Task Force Office sc 65, 69 Interrogation Rm. sc 96, Conference Rm. 122,136,128 Crawford Office -N- 161,162	Tie in to EXT FBI Headquarters Location (DC)	D D	sc 65, 69 sc 107
20.	INT	FBI Labs, including Hair & Fiber Lab sc 72 Latent Fingerprints Lab 74,162 Document Lab sc 76	No tie-in.	D	sc 72, 74, 76
21.	INT	Library Study Carrell	No tie-in.	N	sc 84
22.	INT	Tattler Printing/Bundling Room	No tie-in. Papers loaded onto trucks.	D	sc 82
23.	INT	Tattler Garage	Tie in to EXT Tattler Street (MD).	D	sc 101
24.	INT	Zoo Infirmary	No tie-in.	D	sc 110
25.					
26.					
27.	EXT	St. Louis Newsstand	No tie-in.	N	sc 100
28.	EXT	Rooftop Helipad w/ Helicopter	Tie in to INT FBI Helicopter (DC)	D	sc 71
29.	EXT	Dolarhyde Mansion, include. Garret POV to Garden. (-D- sc 120)	Tie in to EXT Dolarhyde Grounds(MD), & INT Dolarhyde Mansion Studio Set Note Fire.	D N N	sc 45 sc 104 sc 157
30.	EXT	Dolarhyde Roadwork			

(continued)

Figure 5.3b   Preliminary set breakdown for *Red Dragon*. (2002)

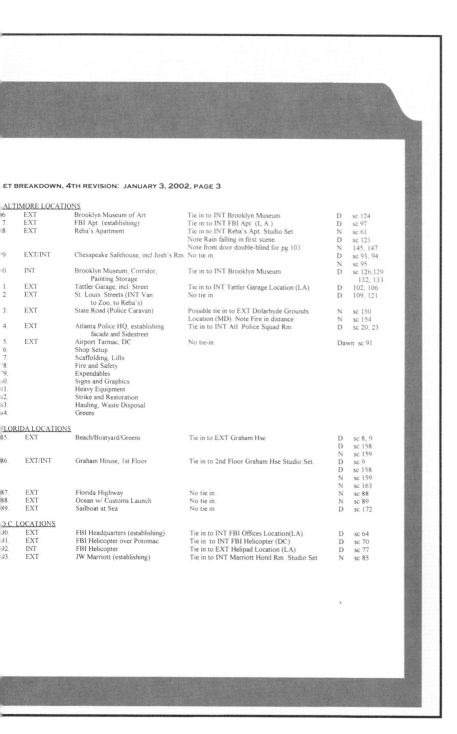

ET BREAKDOWN, 4TH REVISION: JANUARY 3, 2002, PAGE 3

ALTIMORE LOCATIONS

6.	EXT	Brooklyn Museum of Art	Tie in to INT Brooklyn Museum	D	sc 124
7.	EXT	FBI Apt. (establishing)	Tie in to INT FBI Apt. (L.A.)	D	sc 97
8.	EXT	Reba's Apartment	Tie in to INT Reba's Apt. Studio Set	N	sc 61
			Note Rain falling in first scene.	D	sc 121
			Note front door double-blind for pg 103.	N	145, 147
9.	EXT/INT	Chesapeake Safehouse, incl Josh's Rm.	No tie in.	D	sc 93, 94
				N	sc 95
0.	INT	Brooklyn Museum, Corridor, Painting Storage	Tie in to INT Brooklyn Museum	D	sc 126,129 132, 133
1.	EXT	Tattler Garage, incl. Street	Tie in to INT Tattler Garage Location (LA)	D	102, 106
2.	EXT	St. Louis. Streets (INT Van to Zoo, to Reba's)	No tie in.	D	109, 121
3.	EXT	State Road (Police Caravan)	Possible tie in to EXT Dolarhyde Grounds Location (MD). Note Fire in distance	N	sc 150
				N	sc 154
4.	EXT	Atlanta Police HQ, establishing facade and Sidestreet	Tie in to INT Atl. Police Squad Rm.	D	sc 20, 23
5.	EXT	Airport Tarmac, DC	No tie-in.	Dawn	sc 91
6.		Shop Setup			
7.		Scaffolding, Lifts			
8.		Fire and Safety			
9.		Expendables			
0.		Signs and Graphics			
1.		Heavy Equipment			
2.		Strike and Restoration			
3.		Hauling, Waste Disposal			
4.		Greens			

FLORIDA LOCATIONS

5.	EXT	Beach/Boatyard/Greens	Tie in to EXT Graham Hse.	D	sc 8, 9
				D	sc 158
				N	sc 159
6.	EXT/INT	Graham House, 1st Floor	Tie in to 2nd Floor Graham Hse Studio Set.	D	sc 9
				D	sc 158
				N	sc 159
				N	sc 163
7.	EXT	Florida Highway	No tie in.	N	sc 88
8.	EXT	Ocean w/ Customs Launch	No tie in.	N	sc 89
9.	EXT	Sailboat at Sea	No tie in	D	sc 172

D.C. LOCATIONS

0.	EXT	FBI Headquarters (establishing)	Tie in to INT FBI Offices Location(LA)	D	sc 64
1.	EXT	FBI Helicopter over Potomac	Tie in to INT FBI Helicopter (DC)	D	sc 70
2.	INT	FBI Helicopter	Tie in to EXT Helipad Location (LA)	D	sc 77
3.	EXT	JW Marriott (establishing)	Tie in to INT Marriott Hotel Rm. Studio Set.	N	sc 85

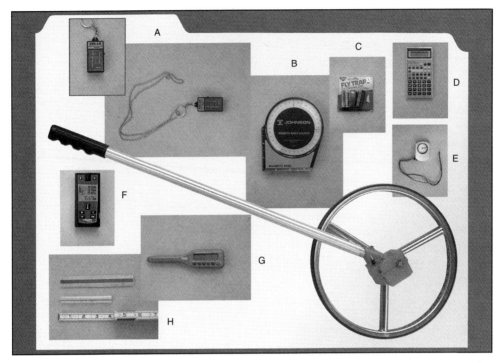

Figure 5.4 A) Solar anti-mosquito guard, B) Magnetic angle locator, C) Fly catcher strip, D) Professional Measure Master II™, E) Suunto inclination device, F) Hilti laser measure, G) Scale Master Classic™ digital plan measure, H) Rulers: flat architectural scale ruler, three-sided architectural scale ruler, and a wooden scissor-extension ruler (diagonal). A 12″-diameter measuring wheelie with an extendable tube makes measuring over terrain easy up to 999′ without the digital exactness of a laser measuring device.

FIFTH SCOUTS

For one reason or another, locations change at the last minute. In terms of scenery, this can pose a problem because much of it is retrofitted for a particular location. Practicality dictates that whatever can be salvaged from scenery already designed and completed is used in the new location; new retrofits are discussed as additional budget items and are always approved by the UPM as overages in golden time man-hours in order to get the new scenery done on time. In addition, directorial changes regarding aspects of locations originally considered alter how locations are re-retrofitted and consequently require another visit. Subsequent scouts to and from contracted locations with a set designer and location construction foreman are arranged through the locations department, as are changes and revisions that occur during the final production meeting.

Within the preceding few pages, we have seen how vital the affiliation of an art director and location manager and his/her department is in terms of how the scout list, master set list, and set construction budget emerge out of the first levels of location scouting. This initial, physical work, i.e., scouting, measuring, and photographing architectural and location detail, provides a counterpoint to the development of the design concept and research explored in Chapter 4.

CONSTRUCTION: IDEA BECOMES REALITY

Once hand-built and digital models are constructed, and drafting is detailed and approved, then blueprints are distributed to all department heads; hard copies as well as a digital distribution are emailed to the same colleagues so that all bases are covered. All revisions must be noted and all drafting redistributed. Although, once the construction department has blueprints in hand, the design is committed to physical form from that point onward. Changes are expensive. It's wiser to wait a day or two for a firm decision from an indecisive production designer than to rush plans into the shop and literally pay for the consequences. This isn't necessarily a rule-of-thumb, but it is worth considering in the midst of the hundreds of trade-offs having to be weighed every day. Each situation will certainly dictate which realistic options to consider and how important timing or spending is at the moment a decision is made. One point can certainly be stressed, and that is, make your decisions as a manager; ultimately, the artistic decisions are finalized by the designer.

At this point in the process, drafting flows from draftsmen's computers or drafting tables to the Mill for the duration of pre-production. What is typically built from the blueprinted page for the camera are rooms from bottom to top: floors, then walls containing openings like doors, fireplaces, arches, windows, staircases, and ceilings fitted with recessed lighting, staircase openings, support beams, trusses, and skylights. Appendix A of this handbook provides current reference and source lists in Los Angeles for most design and construction needs.

What is typically exercised during the building process is total quality management (TQM). This phrase is an American translation from the original Japanese business concept *kaizen,* or continuous improvement. Construction detail management is an ongoing process. To prevent being overwhelmed by every detail that must be built exactly as drawn, it might be advisable to appoint a trustworthy proxy in the shop to sweat the small stuff, while your sights are focused on the hero items that require more intense focus. If your prep work is being done at a studio where, in some rare cases, the art department and the construction shop are close by, then your senior draftsman or assistant art director can be supervised to oversee various smaller sets and corresponding details. Delegating the workload advances the concept of continuous improvement and collaboration. TQM applications in art direction find greatest expression in the work of the set designers. On a draftsman's PC screen or drafting tabletop, a benchmark of consistent improvement and high-level design quality is maintained by detailed, accurate construction drawings. Two general categories of interior and exterior sets are where TQM is exercised and will be examined here.

INTERIOR SETS

Interior scenic design problems were resolved clearly and exactly by Maya Shimoguchi (*Terminator 3: Rise of the Machines, Minority Report, Memoirs of a Geisha, Watchmen*) in her drafting for interior city jail/Henri's cell for *Murder in the First* (1995). The holding cell in Figure 5.5a and b is based on a concept idea created by the

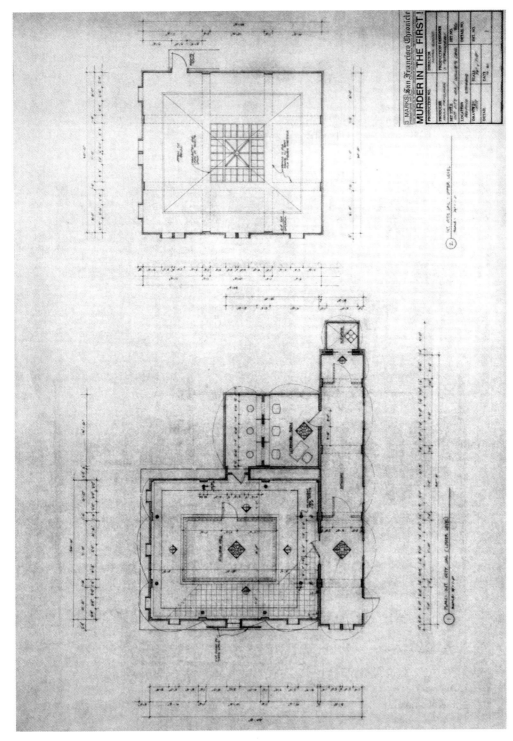

Figure 5.5a Hand-drafted city jail plan—upper and lower levels—by Maya Shimoguchi. MURDER IN THE FIRST © 1994 Warner Bros., a division of Time Warner Entertainment Company, L.P. and Le Studio Canal + (U.S.). All Rights Reserved.

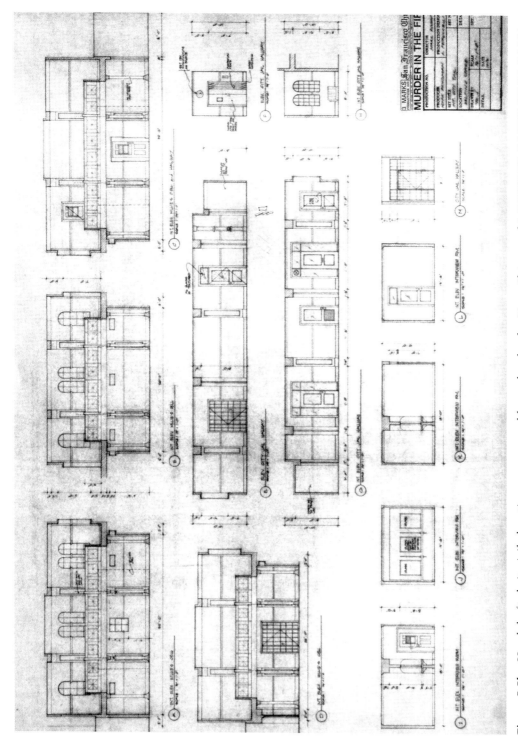

Figure 5.5b　Hand-drafted city jail elevations—upper and lower levels—by Maya Shimoguchi. MURDER IN THE FIRST © 1994 Warner Bros., a division of Time Warner Entertainment Company, L.P. and Le Studio Canal+ (U.S.). Licensed by Warner Bros. Entertainment Inc. All rights reserved.

production designer Kirk Petrucelli (*The Incredible Hulk, Lara Croft: Tomb Raider, The Patriot, Blade*) and director Marc Rocco (*The Jacket, Where the Day Takes You, Dream a Little Dream, Scenes from the Goldmine*) as to what could be shot for greatest production value as opposed to the reality of where a typical prisoner might have been held.

The holding cell was theatrically placed in the center of the stage space as a cage to scrutinize Henri, the main character. It comprises the largest area of the plan, also including an interview room to its right and an access corridor, running along its bottom length and connecting to an elevator at its far right end. The reflected ceiling plan (Figure 5.5a) of the main holding cell room is shown to the right of the floor plan. Figure 5.6 shows the same ceiling, containing a skylight that loomed almost 20 feet above. The center of the skylight, where all structural ribs met at a central circular hub, was also expanded as a full-size detail, calling out molding and mitered angles.

The pieces of the cage—four walls and ceiling—sitting at the center of the main holding set, were as real as any built for a zoo or maximum-security prison with ¾" steel rods woven through a ½" × 1½" steel bar sitting on a heavily reinforced 6" platform scenically painted as concrete. All sections were wild as per the Director's request. Director of Photography, Fred Murphy (*October Sky, Secret Window, The Good Wife, The Mothman Prophecies, Auto Focus*), figured a way to seamlessly pull out of a side of the cage and begin a circling motion around it, without drawing attention to the fact that one of the heavy metal walls had swung open, allowing a Steadicam to continuously shoot without cuts or edits. The execution was astonishing when you think about the heft of all that metal and the sound that it might make during the choreography of the shot.

Two drafting styles are tolerated in Hollywood art departments: the architecturally derived style (Maya Shimoguchi: Figures 5.5a, 5.5b, 5.6, and 5.9) and a theatrical style used for theater and opera (Mine: Figures 5.8 and 5.10). Both are valid and useful, just so long as information on the page is clear and readable, although the former is a preferred convention. The drawings for the interior courtroom set, *Body of Evidence* (1993), were originally drawn by me in theatrical style and later revised as the courtroom set for *Murder in the First* two years later. It was decided that the original *Body of Evidence* set would be purchased as is, and added to or subtracted from in order to satisfy set budget limitations at the time. Retrofitting significant architectural detail on the original set with redesigned windows, judge's bench, and column capitals was an oddly familiar exercise. The twin angels wielding swords (Figure 5.7) were newly designed additions to the original set. This kind of serendipity was atypical of the movie business and provided an unusual continuity of business as usual.

The courtroom and judge's chamber sets were constructed and assembled in Stage 12 at Culver Studios in Culver City, shown in Figure 5.8 as a spotting plan for the sets. A prominent hero set scheduled for several weeks of continuous shooting, the courtroom set's placement and location onstage were important considerations. It was home for the shooting crew during that section of the shooting schedule, making everyone's experience

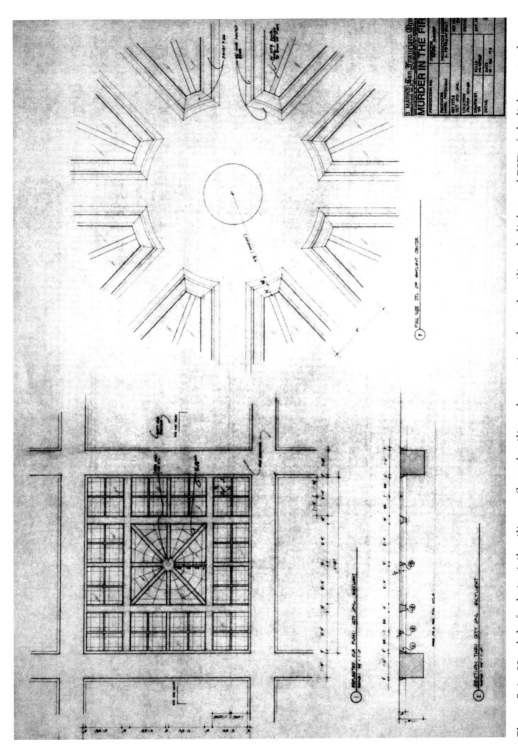

Figure 5.6 Hand-drafted city jail ceiling: reflected ceiling plan, section through ceiling skylight, and FSD of skylight center by Maya Shimoguchi. MURDER IN THE FIRST © 1994 Warner Bros., a division of Time Warner Entertainment Company, L.P. and Le Studio Canal+ (U.S.). Licensed by Warner Bros. Entertainment Inc. All rights reserved.

Figure 5.7   Foam sculpted courtroom angels pictured, with art department crew. MURDER IN THE FIRST © 1994 Warner Bros., a division of Time Warner Entertainment Company, L.P. and Le Studio Canal+ (U.S.). Licensed by Warner Bros. Entertainment Inc. All rights reserved.

more effective and enjoyable. Everything around the judge's bench wall changed between films, as each designer interpreted the contents of their respective scripts into visual terms. For instance, the retrofitted columns were repainted as dark malachite with gilded detailing throughout the set as well as the witness stand, designed as a movable set piece on wheels for the *Murder in the First* set. These changes are obvious in the drafting compared in the plates provided, Figures 5.9 and 5.10.

We have briefly explored some traditional aspects of scenery drafting and design, as well as creative decision-making based on collaboration and script requirements. The advent of CGI—by incorporating technology into the mix, has spawned digital concept drawing and modeling. Many questions arise as a result of this evolutionary step into the twenty-first century. Perhaps it's best to analyze the perceptions of digital set designers regarding

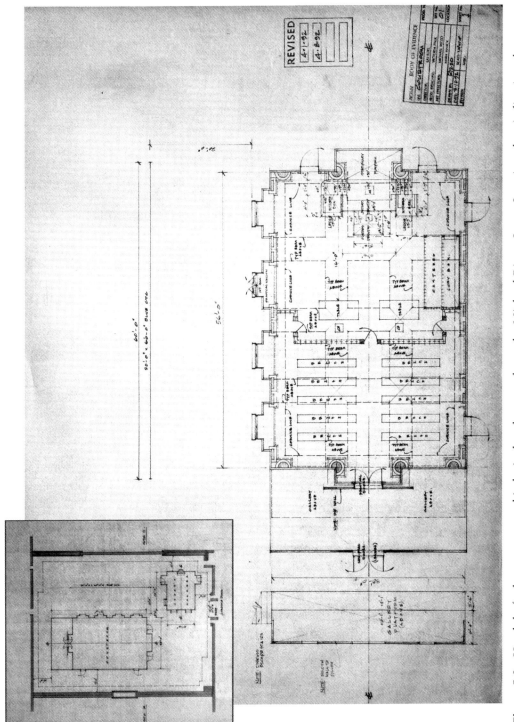

Figure 5.8 Hand-drafted courtroom and judge's chamber sets drawn by Michael Rizzo. Inset: Spotting plan, indicating placement on Stage 12, Culver Studios. From the movie MURDER IN THE FIRST © 1994 Warner Bros., a division of Time Warner Entertainment Company, L.P. and Le Studio Canal+ (U.S.). Licensed by Warner Bros. Entertainment Inc. All rights reserved.

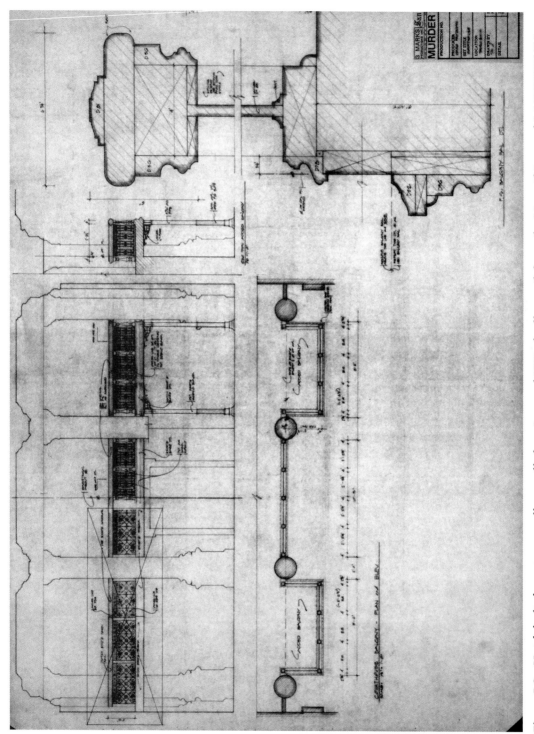

Figure 5.9 Hand-drafted courtroom gallery wall elevations and FSD of gallery rail drawn by Maya Shimoguchi. MURDER IN THE FIRST © 1994 Warner Bros., a division of Time Warner Entertainment Company, L.P. and Le Studio Canal+ (U.S.). Licensed by Warner Bros. Entertainment Inc. All rights reserved.

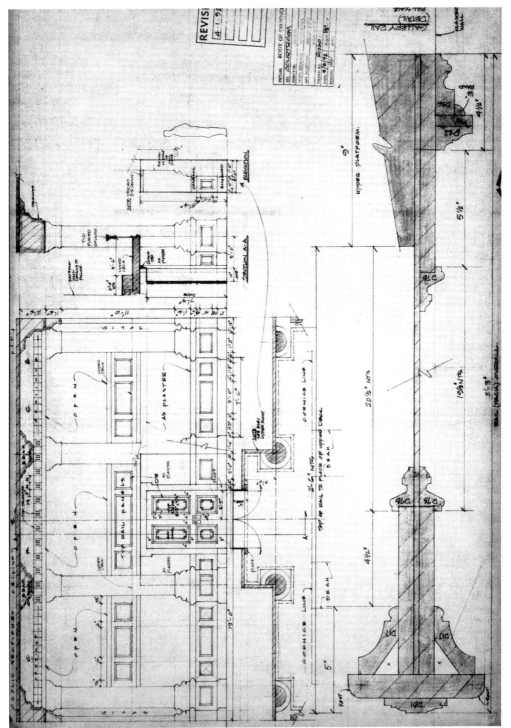

Figure 5.10 Hand-drafted courtroom gallery elevation, plan and section and FSD of gallery rail drawn by M. Rizzo for *Body of Evidence*.

traditional vs. digital filmmaking. From a recent interview, Victor Martinez (*The Terminal, The Cat in the Hat, Minority Report, Valkyrie, Avatar, TRON: Legacy*) had this to say:

> Digital film environments have become the norm, although it will probably be difficult to find just digital art departments; the same goes for films that will be solely hand-drawn. In any art departments I've worked in, there are sets that lend themselves more to being drawn by hand and others being drawn on computer [see Figures 5.12 and 5.13]. On The Cat in the Hat, I worked on a very complex interior set design for the inside of the house that is transformed [Figure 5.11], and it wasn't your typical process of designing a set. There were days when I was just modeling in clay in order to whip out sketch model ideas for the more resolved digital model. I'm not one who's going to close the door on any process. A good digital designer must have training in handcraft as a way to problem solve, otherwise the process of working is robotic and straight out of a manual. My physical art background is very important to this. The people I work with and respect have worked by hand or at least understand that mode of working.[1]

CG modelers and CAD draftspersons in digitized art departments work in tandem with each other and their traditional counterparts. A digital modeler might clearly see a structural problem in a set that an analog draftsperson might otherwise overlook. In this way, all bases are covered. The beauty of CAD is the speed of making changes, regardless of whatever caprice is tossed at the draftsman. To use an example from the *Minority Report* (2002), the rendered Rhino model and resulting AutoCAD drafting for the building of the interior pre-cog chamber evolved through many permutations. From digital set designer, J. André Chaintreuil's perspective:

> A few of us worked together on a piece of the egg interior set, or chamber, where the pre-cogs were kept: Victor Martinez played with the exterior, and David Chow and I worked on the interior. In the end, it became my job to do all the construction documents for the egg interior. On that egg, every single angle was unique so I worked with the 3D model in Rhino and then drafted everything in AutoCAD. I would often section or slice the model by extruding or projecting curves through it at any angle that was appropriate. In the same way, I could take any plane and fold it flat or develop any surface I wanted. The pages you see [as he flips through a wad of CAD drafting] are just a small percentage of a ream's worth of paper for one set of working drawings. [Laughs] It was massive, but it was the best way to communicate with construction about how to cut every angle on every unique piece. The construction crew made the frame of the egg set, which we called "the cookie cutter." While the frame pieces were individually being cut and assembled, we sent the computer files

Figure 5.11 Form Z model of interior house set for *The Cat in the Hat* by Victor Martinez. Courtesy of Universal Studios Licensing LLP.

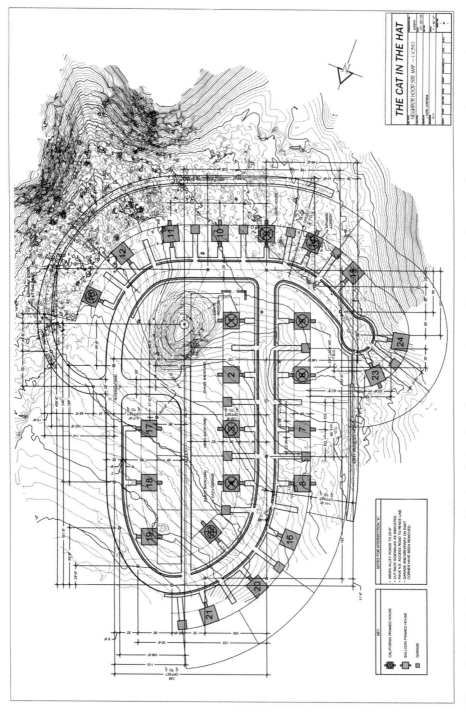

Figure 5.12 LIDAR exterior neighborhood plan for *The Cat in the Hat* by J. Andre Chaintreuil. Courtesy of Universal Studios Licensing LLP.

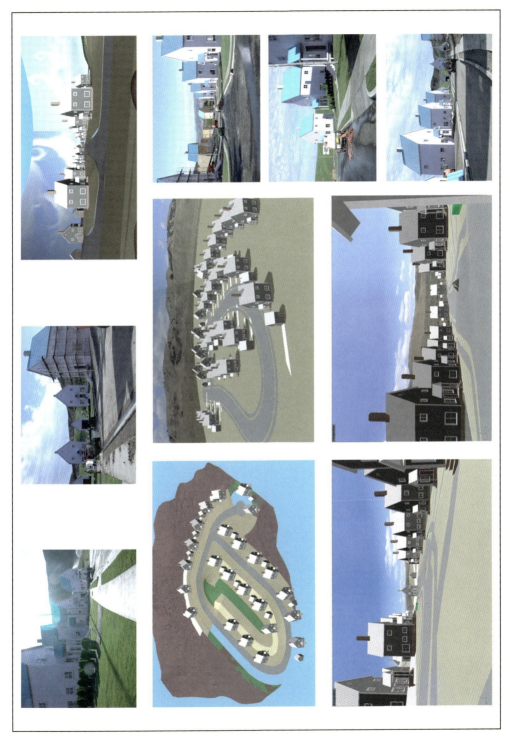

Figure 5.13 CG model of exterior neighborhood for *The Cat in the Hat* by J. Andre Chaintreuil. Courtesy of Universal Studios Licensing LLP.

out to a company in San Francisco called Kreysler & Associates, who used their computer-numerically-controlled, milling machine (CNC) to carve the interior sculptural surface of the egg. These CNC pieces were then fitted into the cookie-cutter frame as the finished interior surface was crafted. It was composed of two overlapping waves moving in opposite directions creating a beautiful, woven texture from Styrofoam blocks.[2]

As you can see, the options for visualizing are limited to the imagination and subsequent needs of the designer. The egg was derived specifically from the aesthetics of working in the computer (Figures 5.14 and 5.15). Alex McDowell, the designer, specifically hired digital designers because he wanted a digital aesthetic for the movie. The same process of concept designing applied to other aspects of this film. J. André Chaintreuil explains:

My main set for Minority Report was called the "Hall of Containment" where the prisoners were confined to vertical sleds that rose out of the ground as a telescoping, horizontal arm swung around to access them. The visual image was like blades of grass in the wind or much like a device called "Pin Art" you've probably seen where you can press your hand onto a frame of blunted pins that mimic the shape of your hand. I collaborated with illustrator James Clyne on this set [Figure 5.16]. In 3D it's so easy for me to create a shape quickly and accurately then share renderings with an illustrator like James. A benefit of sharing files like this is that it saves an illustrator the time to properly set up a perspective view so more time can be spent adding textures, creating mood, and furthering the set design. We already know from the 3D model how much of the set will be built for the camera. The other beautiful thing about these modeling environments is that everything is life-size—my one-quarter, my three-quarter, and my full-size are all the same image, just printed out at different scales.

I really was thrilled in the end and very happy with the world we had created. Alex McDowell, Production Designer, composed some books we eventually called "The Bibles" for Minority Report. They explained the theory of the city so if you ever got stuck and couldn't find an art director, you could pick up one of these reference books and find your answer. It was brilliant. I've never seen it on another show. Also, the research material was overwhelming, and it was everywhere.[3]

EXTERIOR SETS

My Fellow Americans (1996) required the design and construction of the south façade, south portico, and rose garden of the White House on the sycamore grove of the Biltmore Estate, Asheville, North Carolina (see Figure 5.17). Another architecturally

Figure 5.14 Pre-Cog chamber showing concept model of the set. Courtesy of Alex McDowell. *Minority Report*, Pre-cog Chamber (2002). From *Minority Report* © 2002 Twentieth Century Fox. All rights reserved.

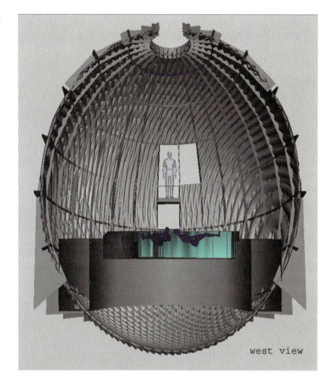

Figure 5.15 Set shot of Pre-Cog chamber. Courtesy of Alex McDowell. MINORITY REPORT © 2002 Twentieth Century Fox. All rights reserved.

Figure 5.16   Concept illustration by James Clyne for the Hall of Containment. Courtesy of Alex McDowell. MINORITY REPORT © 2002 Twentieth Century Fox. All rights reserved.

Figure 5.17   The Biltmore Estate, Asheville, North Carolina.

trained pencil draftsman at the time, Senior Set Designer, Harry Otto (*The Terminal, 8 Mile, Minority Report, Van Helsing, Star Trek*) wrestled with the ⅛" scale elevations provided by the White House PR department and reliable photo book research to achieve a realistic and architectural believability in his larger scale details. Our phone relationship with our contacts at the Oval Office was less encumbered before 9/11 than it is now. One fact hasn't changed—location shooting in and around the White House is not an option. It compelled us to design believable and accurate scenery. We amassed a ton of applicable research and pencil-designed an identical, digital-quality copy of the original in Washington, DC. Harry's drafting shown in Figures 5.18 and 5.19 shows the level of meticulousness to architectural detail necessary for the brief glimpses of believability we see onscreen, even for a high-concept comedy. Harry Otto reminisces:

A contact through the Dave (1993) art department was kind enough to send us some of the blueprints of the south porch with the stairs that radius around and down to the driveway. The problem with these drawings is that the plans were drawn at a reduced scale for two reasons: 1) that part of the White House was shot at a distance; and 2) they wanted to cut costs. Although our timeframe was compressed, those drawings just couldn't be traced off, retitled, and blueprinted for building, especially when you consider the staircase treads were 8" and the risers were 3", making them unusable unless reconfigured to full scale. I remember searching through some terrific reference material from the Wilson period–1913 through 1921–that included aerial shots of the White House and close-ups of the president in the Rose Garden. I remember going over those with a magnifying glass to discern what the profile of the moldings looked like, and what the scale relationships were. Several days later, other well-photographed, contemporary coffee table books showing other excellent details were brought into the office to complete the picture, so to speak. With all of those pieces quickly snapping together, I was able to blast out the drawings for our set. All in all, it was a real challenge and a good learning experience to do it fast and get it right.[4]

The plates of drafting shown here are a small sample of the larger bulk of work Harry turned out over several weeks. All of the plates were drawn in architectural style and most of them held full-scale details of the miles of finishing fiberglass molding eventually air-stapled onto the completed building façades.

As Harry was working out the building details, I had arranged a topographic survey of the sycamore grove where the sections of White House would stand. The survey, Figure 5.20, indicated existing trees, underground water pipes, and most importantly, which areas of the grove were prone to flooding. If you look closely at the back of the West Wing section under construction (Figure 5.21), you will see that the walls are supported by

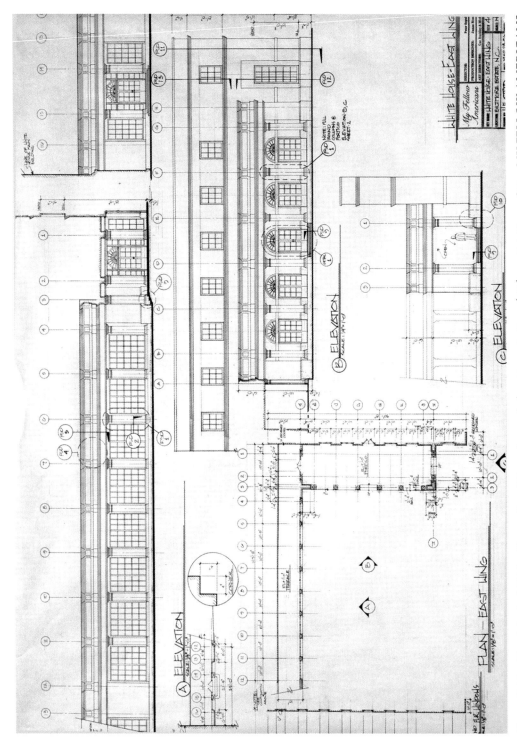

Figure 5.18 Hand-drafted White House East Wing plan and elevations A, B, and C by artist Harry Otto. MY FELLOW AMERICANS © 1996 Warner Bros., a division of Time Warner Entertainment Company, L.P. Licensed by Warner Bros. Entertainment Inc. All rights reserved.

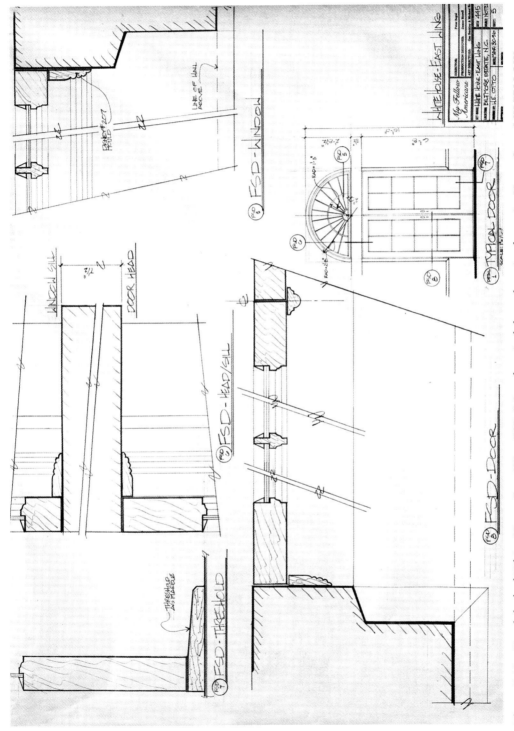

Figure 5.19 Hand-drafted White House East Wing FSD 5-8 and typical door elevation by artist Harry Otto. MY FELLOW AMERICANS © 1996 Warner Bros., a division of Time Warner Entertainment Company, L.P. Licensed by Warner Bros. Entertainment Inc. All rights reserved.

telephone poles securely set into the ground. Knowing exactly where the water main and other vulnerable buried utilities were located allowed us to stabilize the set pieces without worry. Finally, with all of the details of the survey in place, we could determine how the White House building sections should stand relative to the sun's position and the quality of daylight in early spring.[5] Sun declination is a consideration of all cinematographers shooting exterior scenery and acting sequences in a motion picture—ours was not a special case.

During the first stage of White House construction, Production Designer, Jim Bissell was with the main shooting crew in LA. There, the art department crewmembers had built a replica of the White House in ⅛″ scale (Figure 5.22). It was used to plan the shooting sequences of two former presidents galloping on horseback around the building from the north porch to the East Wing rose garden on the North Carolina set. The result of these shot planning meetings was a series of sketches and other visual material developed by the designer. He began with a rough sketch (Figure 5.23, A) as a quick visual outline for several key exterior day shots, scenes 227, 228 pt., 235, 237, 240, and 242A, and later completed a more developed director's plan (Figure 5.23, B). As I was emailing progress shots of our daily work to him, Jim was composing a revised storyboard sequence of shots (Figure 5.24, A) against what we were building in North Carolina by sketching on top of my photos (Figure 5.24, B). Jim's enhanced storyboard sequence provided a clear indication of how he saw the shots in terms of how they would finally play on the exterior set at the Biltmore Estate, Ashville, North Carolina. As these pages provided more fodder for our discussions, the crew continued their work.

Imitating the greenscape of the existing White House exterior was the daunting project of Head Greensman, Henry Dando (*Wrestling Ernest Hemingway, Shutter Island, The Hunger Games, Lincoln*), with the help of Stephanie Girard, landscape architect and set designer. Their collaborative effort required just as much zeal for detail as Harry's, but in the texture and dynamic terms of this large, green exterior set. Thousands of square feet of sod and rows of manicured box hedges and small trees helped anchor the overall look of the landscape. Our greatest challenge was creating the 200-year-old magnolias flanking both sides of the south porch steps. Henry's solution was to build two armatures into which huge magnolia boughs could easily be inserted. Early spring in the western hills of North Carolina could not provide us with usable boughs, so we were forced to investigate sources in the warmer regions of Georgia and then transport truckloads of refrigerated magnolia limbs to our Biltmore location. This specific set was an expensive one (see Figure 5.26). The eight-day shooting timeline on the finished set happened without a schedule change, which would have jeopardized the freshness of the Jeffersonian magnolias and greenscape, requiring continual irrigation and maintenance.

The overall design of this vast exterior set was the brainchild of Stephanie Girard (*Any Given Sunday, Holy Man*). It developed from her patient skill with a magnifying glass and photographic landscape details of the rose garden taken at the existing White House grounds (see Figure 5.25a–d).

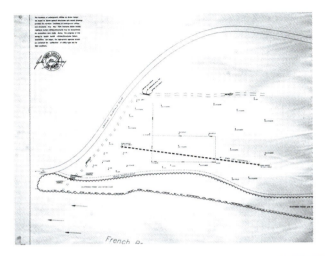

Figure 5.20 Site survey of the typography of a section of field and French Broad River at the Biltmore Estate by Webb A. Morgan and Associates, P.A., Asheville, NC.

Figure 5.21 In-process construction photo of the back of the West Wing scenery. Artist Jim Bissell. MY FELLOW AMERICANS © 1996 Warner Bros., a division of Time Warner Entertainment Company, L.P. Licensed by Warner Bros. Entertainment Inc. All rights reserved.

Figure 5.22 Replica of the White House constructed by L.A. art department model makers. Artist Jim Bissell. MY FELLOW AM ERICANS © 1996 Warner Bros., a division of Time Warner Entertainment Company, L.P. Licensed by Warner Bros. Entertainment Inc. All rights reserved.

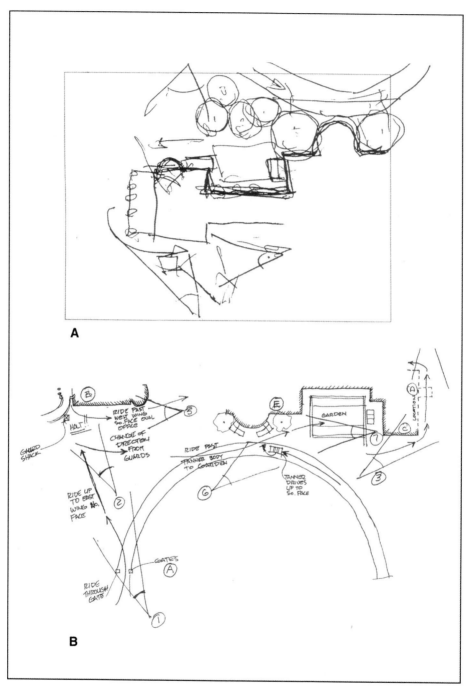

Figure 5.23   A) Rough shot sketch and B) Developed Director's plan drawn by Jim Bissell of the White House South Lawn exterior set. MY FELLOW AMERICANS © 1996 Warner Bros., a division of Time Warner Entertainment Company, L.P. Licensed by Warner Bros. Entertainment Inc. All rights reserved.

Keep in mind the fact that the existing sycamores dotting the Biltmore field had to be located, plotted, and worked into the larger design; the site survey also helped her develop her design. Stephanie's experience as a landscape architect imbued her drawings seen in Figure 5.27 with the authenticity and credibility the set demanded as the greenscape neared its completion (see Figure 5.28). It's interesting to see how precise our efforts were by comparing the research shots of the existing rose garden to the shots of our completed scenery.

The timeline, including my arrival in Asheville, meeting with the locations manager and Biltmore representatives, enrolling the surveyors into the project, completing the survey, orienting the set to the site, overseeing the building, painting, and dressing of the set sections, as well as the design of the landscaping and finishing the set for shooting, took eight weeks. In retrospect, big thanks must be extended to Harry, Henry, and Stephanie for their vision, experience, and collaboration—all visible in the set photos—and for Jim's unerring guidance.

The rhythm from page to scenery outlines an art director's daily preproduction routine. Awake at 5:00 am and in the shop by 6:00 am to begin the day with the folks in the construction shop to answer any related questions, then back to the art department by 8:00 am for check-in with the production director and the art department folks. Participating in various interdepartmental meetings including mechanical effects, set decorating, and production office considerations, fills the early morning hours. The late morning is spent running to locations to view building progress or double-checking details or solving problems, digitally photographing the progress, and helping solve PR issues that might have arisen between the location point-person and the activity of our construction crew. The early afternoon might require a return to the shop periodically throughout the remainder of the workday to check on progress or solve additional problems, then on the drive back to the office check/answer vocal text messages, or email progress images to the designer or other department heads, and talk through changes in scenery design and modification. Any free time in the office demands the completion of current paperwork, the double- and triple-checking of schedules relating to the construction timeline, inserting revised script pages, checking the iPad with updated shooting schedule changes, quickly drafting ¼″ scale plans or elevations on a sheet for the designer's emergency meeting at day's end, and reviewing the next day's agenda. Final check-in with the art department folks happens by early evening. Design changes are noted, approved, or modified, and, if time allows, prints are made in multiple for construction and other departments, as well as a revised digital distro, and setting out whatever is physically necessary to take along to the shop for the 6:00 am visit, including drafting, printed material, color photocopies of research, paperwork, or materials samples. The day ends by around 8:00 pm. Most often, meals are gulped on the fly or missed altogether as the pre-production schedule quickly moves toward our first day of shooting.

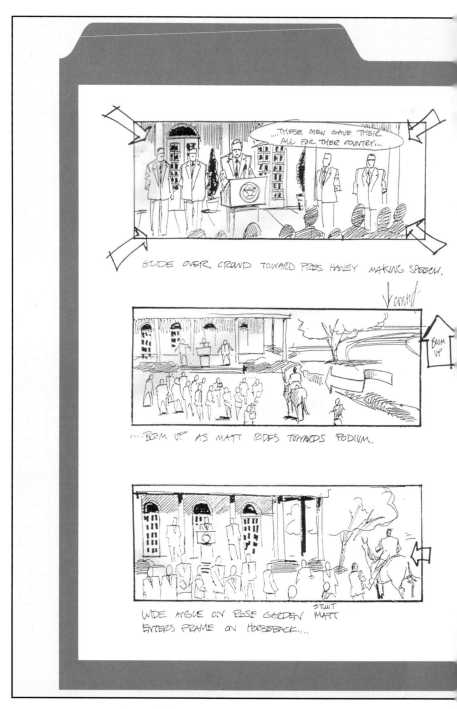

Figure 5.24a Dan Sweetman's storyboards showing White House Rose Garden speech. MY
FELLOW AMERICANS © 1996 Warner Bros., a division of Time Warner Entertainment
Company, L.P. Licensed by Warner Bros. Entertainment Inc. All rights reserved.

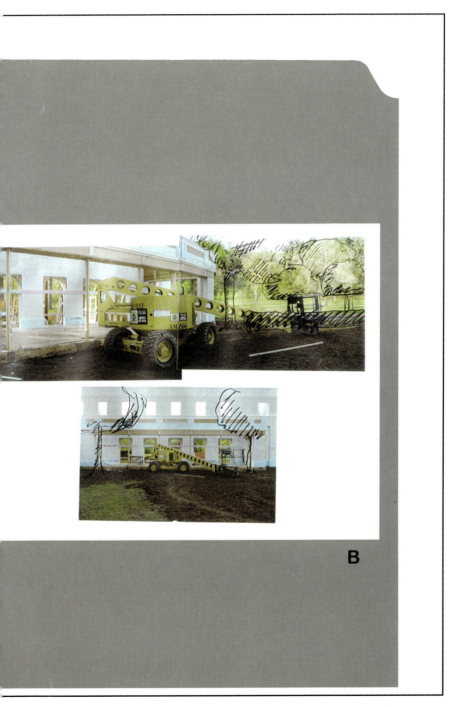

Figure 5.24b   Laminated photo showing construction progress of the White House Rose Garden. MY FELLOW AMERICANS © 1996 Warner Bros., a division of Time Warner Entertainment Company, L.P. Licensed by Warner Bros. Entertainment Inc. All rights reserved.

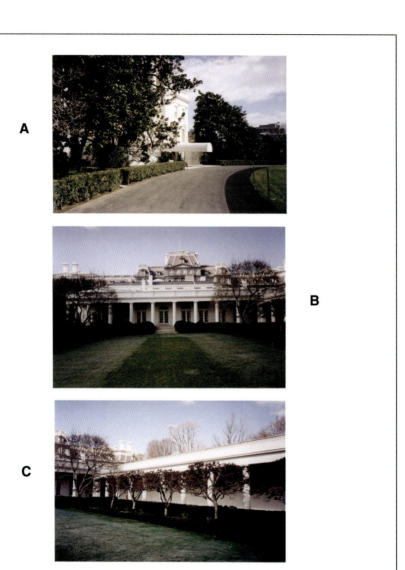

Figure 5.25 White House research photos: A) The driveway flanking the South Portico steps in Washington, D.C., B) White House East Wing colonnade seen from the center of the Rose Garden, C) White House Rose Garden side colonnade, D) White House Rose Garden looking toward the East Wing. MY FELLOW AMERICANS © 1996 Warner Bros., a division of Time Warner Entertainment Company, L.P. Licensed by Warner Bros. Entertainment Inc. All rights reserved.

"My Fellow Americans" Construction Estimate					Last modified	3/16/96	
Script Date: March 8, 1996			Director: Peter Segal		Production Designer: Jim Bissell		
Producer: Warner bros.			Michael Ewing Jean Higgins		Production number:		
					Page number: 7		
Set #:	Loc:	Type:	Set Description:	Const. Estimate	Sign Estimate	Greens Estimate
---	---	---	---	---	---	---
445	Ashevill	Ext	White House gate/N. Lawn	$50,000.00	$0.00	$5,000.00
445	Ashevill	Ext	White House Front entrance	$100,000.00	$1,000.00	$10,000.00
445	Ashevill	Ext	White House Kennedy Garden	$100,000.00	$500.00	$10,000.00
445	Ashevill	Ext	White House Southwest Lawn	$100,000.00	$500.00	$10,000.00
446	Ashevill	Int	Factory Lunchroom-Cleveland	$5,000.00	$2,000.00	$0.00
447	Ashevill	Int/Ext	Hollis Kitch/Ext Barn	$15,000.00	$0.00	$0.00
701	2nd Unit	Ext	Sky/Airforce 2	$0.00	$0.00	$0.00
702	2nd Unit	Ext	Moutainous area	$0.00	$0.00	$0.00
704	2nd Unit	Ext	Train barrels through N.C. Countryside	$0.00	$0.00	$1,000.00
705	2nd Unit	Ext	"Scoggin's" truck barrels down hwy	$0.00	$0.00	$0.00
706	2nd Unit	Ext	Maison Blanc restaurant	$0.00	$0.00	$0.00
			Totals:	$XXX,XXX.XX	$XXX,XXX.XX	$XXX,XXX.XX

Figure 5.26 A Construction Estimate page showing the item cost of the White House South lawn green set budget.

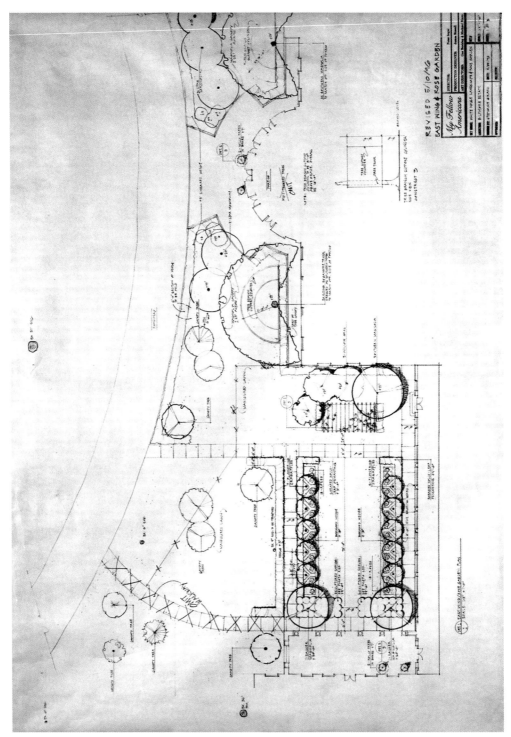

Figure 5.27 Hand-drafted White House East Wing Landscape and Rose Garden by Stephanie Girard. MY FELLOW AMERICANS © 1996 Warner Bros., a division of Time Warner Entertainment Company, L.P. Licensed by Warner Bros. Entertainment Inc. All rights reserved.

Figure 5.28 Finishing up: Set photos of: A) White House southwest lawn and West Wing, B) South Portico and C) Rose Garden Pergola, D) East Wing-façade, E) White House East Wing and Rose Garden. MY FELLOW AMERICANS © 1996 Warner Bros., a division of Time Warner Entertainment Company, L.P. Licensed by Warner Bros. Entertainment Inc.

VENDORS

An enormous industry of support businesses was established both within and outside of the studio system in Hollywood. At this time it exists to service all Indie and studio filmmaking projects. As film and TV production has extended well beyond Hollywood and the U.S., so has the vendor/sub-contractor support industries in those given locations. Everything an art director can imagine or need, can be found in the greater Los Angeles area. The remainder of this chapter will focus on the highlights offered by studio facilities, rental backing companies, and industry support vendors in the Hollywood neighborhood.

Studio Facilities

The major studios in Los Angeles in 2013 are 20th Century Fox, Disney Studios, Paramount Pictures, Sony Pictures, Warner Bros., and Universal Pictures-MCA. A comprehensive list of the major studios helps to determine which offer the following production services: mill and molding shop, painting and sign shop, hardware shop, **staff shop,** metal shop, and scenic backings. Detail items like latches, pulls, knobs, escutcheon plates, special wood or plaster molding for period windows, doors, and walls, or painted and photographic backings used for interior, onstage sets are easily found in any of the studio shops. For the most part, the studio prices for these services and items are as competitive as those of any other vendor. The advantage of using major studio facilities is experience; they have decades of know-how and a vast stockpile of options that work for all production needs.

Warner Bros. staff shop has an 80-year archive and the largest selection of architectural, plaster model detail available as fiberglass capitals, corbels, brackets, rosettes, ropes, and friezes, as well as a large assortment of brick, stone, and rock options, including "Bumstead" and "Murder Your Wife" brick skins, for all production construction needs. A CD version of the catalogue is available to anyone who calls to request one—guild membership affiliation is not a prerequisite. After continuous requests made by architects and landscape designers eager for this data, as well as designers and draftspersons in the movie industry, the website provides a downloadable copy of their *Architectural Ornamentation Catalogue* (see http://studiofacilities.warnerbros.com/design-construction/staff-shoparchitectural-ornamentation/). In addition to the staff objects listed above, their products and services include:

- 90+ fabricated surfaces in Vacuform or Fiberglass.
- Original designs and styles in every era and architectural style.
- Manufacturing in a variety of materials including: plaster, fiberglass, resin, pre-cast concrete and GFRC.
- Custom sculpting and casting from original designs, samples or photos.
- Construction concrete and plastering.
- Set plastering, skim walls, textures and faux finishes.

- Foam and urethanes.
- Thousands of molds in inventory.

WB Hardware Rental department showcases one of the largest selections of contemporary and period hardware including door knobs and plates, hinges, window fixtures, elevator panels, and train and boat accessories.

WB's Design Studio incorporates state-of-the-art technologies for sign production and scenic arts projects with the traditional applications of these disciplines as well. The studio has the capability to create large-format and flatbed digital prints and seaming space, two router rooms, a plotter room, a paint booth, extensive production space, and a scenic loft with 30×100 foot frames.

WB's Digital Services are competitive with Universal's and include:

- New hybrid large-format printing.
- Flatbed printing.
- High-resolution scanning.
- Digital prints up to five meters of seamless printing width.
- Theatrical backings—front and backlit.
- Billboards.
- Murals.
- Banners.
- Vehicle wraps.
- Printed flooring.
- Retouching.
- Commercial building signs.
- Interior identification packages.
- Custom artwork and photography

Universal Staff Shop challenges Warner Bros for first place position regarding the quality and uniqueness of its staff pieces—it creates a variety of custom staff products and more:

- Flex moldings—200 styles available.
- Vacuform options: including rock, bricks, stone and custom patterns.
- Molded ornament options: cast in fiberglass, plaster, and silicone.
- Fiberglass casting and fabrication—50 designs of fiberglass skins.
- Binks Fiberglass Chopper Gun.
- Building ornament options: rosettes, cornice, brackets, and columns.
- Door and lock hardware, antique locks, wall plates, doorknobs, light switches and electrical plates.
- Sculpting services.
- Foam and urethanes.

- Construction concrete and plastering.
- Set plastering, skim walls, textures and faux finishes.

Printed and digital catalogues are available upon request and delivered to your office.

Universal's Property Department houses nearly half a million of items comprising the largest and most diverse selection of props in the industry, housed on three spacious floors filled with complete selections of furniture, household items, fixtures, office and restaurant equipment, and properties. And, the Drapery Department, housed in the same building, contains pillows and bedding, and provides sewing/construction services for everything from slipcovers to awnings.

Uni's Graphic Design and Sign Shop, featuring a team of gifted graphic artists, offer full design services for film and television productions and other industry clients. Their full service operation is state-of-the-art, including:

- Large format printing.
- CNC routing.
- Custom wallpaper.
- Hand lettering.
- Vinyl graphics.
- Prop packaging.
- Standees.
- Mounting and lamination.
- Floor graphics.
- Vehicle graphics.
- Specialty printing (canvas, backlit, art papers, Tyvek, cling)

Shop hours are set at 6:00 am–5:00 pm or as production requires. The digital skills of the well-trained, professional staff create a consistent environment where quality is consistent, service is impeccable, and turn-around is fast. Located just north of the Hollywood Hills, it's the first stop off the freeway on the way to Rick's Hardware on Lankershim Blvd.

Sony, Disney, Paramount, and Fox studios have vacuum form and fiberglass staff shops providing light, paintable, durable capitals, rosettes, and brick skins. To a greater or lesser degree, all studio facilities offer full services for carpet and drapery, state-of-the-art graphics capability for signage, and limited greens. Their products are time-tested and competitively priced.

Unique among the majors is 20th Century Fox Studios because of its library service. The Fox Research Library is the entertainment industry's premiere production research library and service. Created in 1923 specifically to meet the needs of filmmakers, it provides visual and background research exclusively for Fox film and TV projects, and legal and marketing departments. The library's unique and extensive special collections of production materials include: Fox history, Fox location photos, illustrations, books, photographs, DVDs and VHSs, periodicals, and clipping files dating from the mid-nineteenth century to the present day.

Lower-budget film and Indies will likely find prices for rental space at the major studios unaffordable. Begin your search by consulting "LA Soundstages" in Appendix A—the list includes a plethora of smaller spaces at reasonable prices including: Radford Studios, Hollywood Center Studios, LA Center Studios, Quixote Studios, Raleigh Studios, Santa Clarita Studios, and Sunset Gower Studios. These mini-soundstages and warehouse spaces offer a more moderate level of facilities and services than the big guys, but do offer any smaller budget production the luxury of control of image, sound, and scheduling. Any of these lists organized in the Appendix exists to assist young art directors and UPMs in determining the best sound stage for upcoming scenery projects.

A quick solution to a limited construction budget would be to visit the Molding Center in North Hollywood, inventorying a solid selection of standard moldings, stairway items, and pre-mitered door sets. They do not have a website. Another source for non-union, pre-built scenery items such as walls, doors, windows, kitchens, and architectural details like arches, columns, bookcases, cabinets, staircases, and fireplaces can be found at IDF Studio Scenery's website (http://idfstudioscenery.com/index2.html) and its land-based store in North Hollywood.

Rental Backings

This category explains the significant differences between source options for a range of rental or custom **colortrans** and **translite** photographic backdrops, painted backings, digital imaging sources, and rental or custom fabric backings available in Los Angeles.

- **JC Backings:** Celebrating 50 years serving art department needs, Sony Picture Studios is home to JC Backings, owner of more than 4,000 rental backings, including historic stock from MGM, Fox, Universal, and Disney. Its website at http://jcbackings.com/index.php showcases its land-based warehouse containing five paint frames and a state-of-the-art photo lab with digital print machine. Its quality and prices are competitive with those listed in this section.
- **Pacific Studios:** Pacific Studios provides online (www.pacificstudios.net) and hard copy catalogues containing over 1,200 chromatrans photographic backdrops for rental, or custom fabrication, shot on location for film production; it creates translites of all types from their large format image library; and works in all media types, including front and rear lit vinyls, or day/night and UV-curable display film besides more classic work on duratrans. Pacific also has greenscreens. As a prime quality, large-format photographic company, it is well known in the industry and has serviced film production companies since 1928.
- **Rosco Digital Imaging:** According to its website www.roscodigital.com, Rosco Digital Imaging has been servicing the entertainment business since 1909. It is competitive with JC Backings and Pacific Studios not in its inventory of stock, but in its ability to custom photograph quality translites, trademarked as Roscolite™ backdrops. It also offers RoscoJet™, super large format photo for graphics, and lenticular 3D prints available in billboard sizes. RABBIT (Rosco Animated Bluescreen and Backdrop Image

Technology) opens up an entirely new approach to background images, www.roscodig ital.com/rabbit/index.cfm. Rosco's vinyl backdrops are now available with motion plates shot on the Red One camera at full 4K resolution, at no extra cost—you only pay for a RABBIT if you use it. Its extensive portfolio showcasing both TV and film projects is impressive and should be considered as a competitive alternative.

- **24Frame** specializes in HD Projection Car Process Playback and capture process plates for rear-projection playback on set; video and computer playback services; as well as custom stock graphics and set dressing. Take a look at the HD car projection video on their home page, www.24frame.com.

- **Superior Backings, Inc.** is a full service theatrical scenery studio with more than 80 years of experience, specializing in scenic backdrops, hand-painted murals, custom-painted flooring, faux finishing, fine art reproduction, and matte shot painting for movies, television, theater, and concert tours. They also provide soft goods: drapery, curtains, **borders and legs,** scrims, and Kabuki drops at reasonable prices. After 35 years at Warner Bros. Scenic Art department, Ronald Strang assembled a group of Hollywood's finest scenic artists and started Superior Backings. Combined With **Trio Entertainment Group** in the Media Center of Burbank, they are conveniently located near the major motion picture studios and television networks, http://www.superiorbackings.com/.

- Both **Grosh Backdrops and Drapery** (www.grosh.com) and **Schmidli Backdrops** (http://schmidli.com) are painted backdrop companies, differing only in placement on an historic timeline. Grosh rents older, extremely well preserved, thematically painted backdrops where Schmidli, a newcomer, provides exquisitely painted, abstract products for rental. Both are capable of custom work. Specifically tagging them in this sourcing section signifies the high level of the quality of their work.

- **Fore-Peak, Inc.** (http://fore-peak.com), **Rose Brand** (www.rosebrand.com), and **Dazian Theatrical Drapery** (www.theatricaldrapery.com) all rent and custom-sew black velour and duvetyne **drops,** borders and legs, blue/green screens, a range of **sharktooth scrims, bobbinettes,** fabric **cycloramas,** fiber-optic curtains in extra-wide, flame retardant, or theatrical fabrics. They are the mainstays of standard backing products offered at reasonable rental prices.

- Two companies, owned and operated by the same partners, offering diverse support and service to the entertainment industry are **Sky Drops, Inc.** (http://skydrops.com) for rental and custom painted backdrops and photographic translites, and **Really Fake Digital** http://reallyfake.com), state-of-the-art digital production services. The owners complement one another as jacks-of-all-trades, including art directing and designing sets and graphics. They are another viable option for budgetary or subcontracting consideration.

Industry Service Listings

As you might well imagine, the phonebook roster of movie industry service listings is as gigantic as the sprawling landscape of Los Angeles. A practical solution to compiling the definitive source listing for this overwhelming task began more than a decade ago, as the search for resources became a continuous activity. The resulting entries, "Film Pocket Listings," are compiled in Appendix A in the most comprehensive list my successive art departments and I could collectively manage for both editions of this book. I have included only the sections from a larger list that are applicable to art direction. What has been overlooked is included in one of a handful of print directories available, listed below:

- *LA411®* and *Debbie's Book®* continue to vie as "the" premier print and online resource for the industry. As vast databases in either category, each resource has its strengths. *LA411* (as well as *NY411®*) has been a print directory for 24 years. The seminal source for crew-related or a production resource, *LA411* is an indispensable directory in book form, or click on http://variety411.com/us/los-angeles. It includes listings for production companies and ad agencies, financial services, crew listings, sets and stages, location services and equipment, support services, camera and sound equipment, grip and lighting equipment, props and wardrobe, post-production services, and hotel and related services. It is comprehensive and provides an online service for a fee for adding and updating personal and business listings in *Crew411®*. It is a tremendous resource for newcomers. *Debbie's Book*, originally known as *The Prop & Set Yellow Pages*, has been a print directory for 36 years. Where *LA411* is more crew or production service-oriented, *Debbie's Book* is more of a vendor source. Organized primarily by category, you can find most film things and services in this comprehensive, spiral-bound resource. Debbie's Book Online at www.thesourcebookonline.com is a fast and convenient website directory of companies and individuals that supply merchandise and services to the entertainment industry and planners of events, theatrical productions, themed environments, and parties. It is organized into almost 1,000 categories to help you quickly find the exact item you need, and it is constantly updated to provide accurate contact data and new sources.[6]
- The following two source books are excellent supplemental directories in their own right. *Creative Industry Handbook®* is one of six print products for various LA markets including: the *Interior Design Resource Book*, the *Los Angeles Resource Book*, *Advertising and Print Services Resource*, *Medical and Health Industry Handbook*, and *Universal City: North Hollywood and Toluca Lake*, printed by GMM, a marketing company. Its website at www.creativehandbook.com is simple, direct, interactive, and less cumbersome than the *LA411* and *Debbie's Book* websites, easily straddling both land and Web-based distribution options.
- *The Acme Resource Directory®* has the potential to become the most prolific of the print and online entertainment related sources highlighted here. In addition to its comprehensive, spiral-bound print directory for props, costumes, sets, decor, construction, special effects, picture cars, graphics, prop makers, the *Acme* website, www.theacme.com/?art=resource_directory contains links for architecture, art, books, building materials, design centers, design research, design furniture and accessories, libraries and museums, motion picture and television, online reference tools, and world news. The website also provides a list of two dozen American cities from Albuquerque to

Wilmington, each hyperlink providing other links to resources in each city—indispensable for location work. Organized by fellow art director Libby Woolems, *Acme* is on its way to becoming a fully connected and more deeply integrated resource on a level that the dynamic changes in the movie industry currently demands.

- ***Production Yak®*** (http://productionyak.com) is a networking source for entertainment industry professionals—newly created and uploaded by a dynamic group of five production office coordinators: Lisa Becker, Lark Bernini, Susan Dukow, Daren Hicks, and Lois Walker. This extraordinary new site can answer the questions: 1) Why would you need an "O" visa from the US Immigration Service? Or 2) How can I charter a private jet plane tonight? For starters, Production Yak expands *Debbie's Book*'s "Main Category Listings" to include a very practical "Search by State" section, offering database production information for 21 production-friendly US states. Other useful widgets an art director might not find on any of the above listed sites are: currency conversion, sunrise-sunset, weather forecast, and driving directions, concentrated in the "Tools" section. Another reason to check out the site is the interviews and articles shared by industry professionals from all disciplines. Lark Bernini, a Yak site creator adds her thoughts in a brief interview:

Interview with Lark Bernini

- *Why not just go to* Debbie's Book?
  Yak is easier to search. We created Yak to respond to our users' needs as if they had gone to their production coordinator for information. The Production Yak database is in the YAK 411 tab. It is an ever-expanding list of vendors covering a great many categories. Plus, Yak offers a vendor the ability to enhance their listing. A business can add photos, maps, special information about their company; in fact, they control the listing and can constantly update it with fresh information and news. Yak is also a lot of fun: there are interviews and articles related to the work we do in entertainment. Yak wants to help make your working life easier. As career production coordinators, the five of us have long-standing relationships with a long list of entertainment industry vendors. They believed in what we were offering and wanted to be able to reach the people who use their services every day. Throughout the Yak site you will see their beautiful and interesting advertisements. We are so pleased to be putting their names in front of thousands of potential clients. We offer very friendly ad rates and we work with any budget. Yak is about keeping everyone working and productive.

- *Does membership have special privileges?*
  Well, we think you're special as soon as you become a Yak user. Industry professionals who provide credentials are vetted and become Yak Pack Members. This gives you access to all areas of the site, particularly "I need it now!" This is where you go to post requests for information you need fast! We are constantly amazed at how fast users get what they need from fellow users. People are so generous, which is what Yak is all about . . . sharing information.

- *Will there be an app?*
  It is something we have always planned for Yak and it's in development![7]

MECHANICAL EFFECTS: A PRACTICAL GUIDE

Clarification

In Chapter 1, a distinction was drawn between the terms for production designer and art director regarding basic definition, function, and areas of overlap. Within the world of effects, distinctions must also be made. As you might already understand, visual effects are vastly different from special effects. The former is created on a computer screen, the latter happens in the physical world. Still, these terms are used interchangeably in error. Like the term art director, "special effects" has been a term used throughout the twentieth century as a catchall phrase to explain that "Hollywood trick photography," defining the elusive magic of the movies. There is nothing tricky or facile about it; special effects have developed as a craft around and for the film industry. Generations of stuntmen and women, a parallel Guild, http://www.stuntmen.com/ continue to act as stand-ins or body doubles in the danger zone of Hollywood. What's more, the mechanical effects and stunt sub-industries are inextricably linked—the symbiotic relationship of the effects crew and the stunt persons mirrors the designer/art director relationship in terms of concept or strategy versus tactical application in cinematic problem-solving. In simple terms: the stunt people do what directors and stunt coordinators dream up—and, they do it flawlessly, take after take.

Before the advent of digital moviemaking, mechanical effects—formerly called special effects—defined Hollywood worldwide. These technical tricks-of-the-trade continue to be an integral part of the physical filmmaking process: bathroom shower stall sets continue to need running water and steam; exterior street scenes still require controllable rain, fog, or snow supply and wet-downs; and stunt people rely on the expertise of mechanical effects' fire monitoring, as they run from burning buildings. The purpose of this section, then, is to familiarize the reader with some of the fundamental techniques used in mechanical effects production today. Understanding that these techniques are based on common sense and safety considerations provides a good foundation for the untrained visionaries in the art department. Details on how the physical world works and of the science/physics that support mechanical effects solutions should be left to the adept professionals who perform "the effects."

Mechanical effects are designed and built into physical scenery. Squibs or bullet hits, fire, smoke, steam, breakaway and crumbling scenery walls, all types of explosions, water, rigging for tanks or pools for underwater work, rain, snow, wind, electronics, mold-making for retractable weaponry and breakaways, moving set pieces (i.e., centrifuges and gimbals), use of air cannons, rigging for accidents, crashes, near misses, flying rigs, and vehicles are basic items on a mechanical effects to-do list. The coordination of draftsmen, construction foremen, and effects foremen is where an art director's participation can be an asset. More complicated sets requiring involved mechanical effects attention should always be at the top of an art director's scenery-to-design-and-build lists, next to other more involved, challenging Hero scenery demanding a longer timeline for completion.

During the mid-1990s on *RocketMan*, I met one of my most enduring mentors, Mechanical Effects Supervisor, Jeff Jarvis (*Poltergeist*, *Firestarter*, *Year of the Dragon*,

Always, Nowhere to Run, Cast Away, Star Trek). By experience and example, he taught me how to focus and be more logical; how to stay well ahead of the shooting schedule; what "no" really means; and that the simplest solution is oftentimes the most elegant. He challenged me and taught me how to make decisions I would've never considered, but in doing so, tripled my learning curve. What he didn't do was to convince me to become an effects supervisor, but his effect on me must be shared here. As usual, an interview will continue to act as the most accessible way to deliver the goods.

Interview with Jeff Jarvis

● *In the movie* Poltergeist, *there is a superb mechanical effects scene: the swirling cyclone of wind in the young boy's room carrying a spinning bed; the flurry of books; the cowboy riding the rearing horse; the lampshade twisting itself onto the top of a self-lighting lamp and the 45-rpm record played by a drafting compass were extraordinary considering the level of technology then. Were there any big challenges there for the art department?*
For the record, the cowboy and phonograph were optical effects, but the rest was mechanical. Those spinning objects were easy to figure out and pull off–if you think about each one long enough, you can come up with a simple way to make it work. There were other things in there that you probably didn't notice–that was filler–like the thousand Super Balls we tossed into the set from above. They moved so fast and sustained their velocity for such a long time that even if you couldn't focus on them you were still aware of a whoosh that went by every other second. On top of the other stuff listed in our scripts we *had* to give the Tobe, the Director, the extra stuff was what made working on that scene a lot of fun.[8]

Our conversation didn't go into set construction detail beyond this section of interview. I would assume that the set would have to be "effects proof" by fastening wall dressing and anything else in the room needing to be stationary, the bed would have to be reinforced or just built by the effects team from scratch, and the ceiling and walls designed in removable sections for easy access. Substantial mechanical effects performed in this or any other interior set will most likely require custom design and art direction.

Always (1989), a noteworthy fire effects film, provides an example of utmost collaboration between art and mechanical effects departments in creating the best non-digital, realistic, exterior fire set. By continuing this interview, some of the more memorable highlights were recounted by this forest fire master:

Interview with Jeff Jarvis continued . . .

● *Jeff, the forest fire in* Always *was not a controlled burn on a Hollywood back lot or computer-generated as a greenscreen filler. What location allowed you and your crew to burn dozens of 40–100-foot high trees?*
I actually started on *Always* on second unit. At around the same time there was a huge forest fire up in Montana so we took a helicopter with key crew people and a director to the site and shot some footage that could be added to the main picture. Mike Woods, who had coordinated the

show, asked me to supervise all the exterior fire footage up in Montana. So I set up rigs for fire in the scenes where characters were supposedly trapped.

- *How many rigged trees were there?*
  We built 25-30 propane trees. We plumbed the bottom with propane hoses and mixed liquid and vapor propane to fully develop them for film takes. Once that was done, we had each tree redressed by the art department with multiple takes of branches that burned away so quickly under the intensity of the heat. Our burning set was all mounted in the same area where a recent fire was, just outside of Libby, Montana. This location was secured by the Locations and the Designer as a believable, burned-out area as a background for our forest fire. We also got permission to crawl up the back of the real burned-out trees to lace them with propane pipes so that we could create the appearance of a much larger fire. Of course, we had split-second control of the fire for the shooting crew and just had miles and miles and miles and miles of propane hose. To show you how huge this was, the first day we went through 12,000 gallons of propane because they were shooting a lot of master shots. Then we slowed down, but the semis were still lined up off camera waiting to be used—that was still 750-1,000 gallons of propane a day.

- *The bottom line for you is safety. Would you talk about your perspective on safety and control?*
  Fire is one of my specialties. Whether we're using fire pipe, propane hose, truck, or propane bottle with manifolds, it's all carefully laid out. I stand out in front of whatever we're going to burn with a schematic showing a number corresponding to a name of a technician who is operating a specific propane valve. *Firestarter* is where I learned to develop this system, and it works very well for me. Another fire film was a Jean-Claude Van Damme picture *Nowhere to Run* (1993), where there was a big barn fire and a water tank that fell over and a large propane tank that exploded. In the barn set, of course, there were horses that are normally afraid of fire and a lot of actors. In a set like that any of the wood near the fire pipes has to be made out of a fire retardant material like wallboard and painted like wood, or if it is real wood, it has to be soaked in fire retardant. During burn scenes, the whole place needs to be cleared of loose hay and bales and anything flammable. I don't leave anything to chance. If you don't think about a precise schematic for the burn and explosions, someone could get seriously hurt. Afterwards, Jean-Claude came up to me, looked me in the face and said, "You're really good with fire." It's not about better or best—you just can't throw a fire pipe in a corner and call it an effect—you have to plan it out very carefully.

- *Your work on* Always *was an exceptional showcasing of your mastery with fire effects. Can you recall a project with other challenges for your mechanical effects crew?*
  Earlier on, when I did the Michael Cimino picture *Year of the Dragon* (1985), we were asked to create a tremendous amount of shoot 'em up in this Chinese restaurant set they built in North Carolina. I had more than 25,000 bullet hits pre-rigged into the set walls. In a case like this, collaboration with the Art Director and the art department was crucial. Design and color of the place, then, became secondary and the material of the walls became the most important focus—and rightly so. We needed all the time we had for prep alone. That's because the squibs

need to be set properly into the wall structure. I rely on a good art director to understand what physically happens when a squib goes off and how it affects the scenery material. Someone with a good head on his shoulders can make my job a lot easier by getting the practical stuff right and then working on the art. We're there to make the gags in the script work and to serve any director.

● *There are two other examples of collaboration of specially designed rooms that immediately come to mind that specifically used a gimbal: the mom's room in* Poltergeist *and the spaceship vestibule in* RocketMan. *Would you care to elaborate?"*

There are many types of gimbals for different rotation and use. The *RocketMan* scene where the characters danced on the curved walls of the spaceship was really about the placement of the camera. The rotation speed of the room and the fixed camera position had to be equal or it wouldn't have worked. The gimbal for that particular room versus the one we built for *Poltergeist* had a different function and approach. Mike Wood and I called in our foreman, Sam Price, to help us make sure we were thinking right. As our foreman, he was the guy who built that room. In that case, the first thing you do is build the room and balance it. That takes some patience. When you're done, a man could walk the walls of the room and by the sheer force of his weight would cause the room to easily rotate, even before we attached any hydraulics. That particular room was on an A-frame with a center pick at dead center of the set, similar to a Ferris wheel, without a metal exoskeleton. On the other hand, the *RocketMan* room was built with two-channel iron frames in a wheel shape. Instead of using hydraulics, we used two air-winch motors that were cable driven. One was used as an airbrake and the other made it rotate. Even though the effect is similar, each one solves a different, specific problem for each project.

If you remember the *Poltergeist* scene in the mom's bedroom, there was very little dialogue but a lot of screaming and sliding around on the walls. [Laughs] Usually when we get into heavy mechanical stuff, it gets pretty noisy; it didn't matter for *Poltergeist,* but it did for *RocketMan.* The spaceship had no props that could move or fall away because if anything moved, it would give away the illusion of this room rotating in space. Also, when you're building anything mechanical, the simplest way is usually the best way. Many times you can get into out-tricking yourself by not keeping it simple.

I didn't invent these tricks. We've all learned from the guys before us by improving on their mistakes and their successes. Eventually, every improvement makes it better and easier, so nobody gets hurt and nothing unfortunate happens.[9]

RocketMan was a heavier mechanical effects show than most. The script called for a full-scale, working centrifuge. Early in the design process we contacted NASA to begin our research through the Ames Research Center in California. They were compliant with our requests and generously provided more data than we could use. Some of it is presented here (Figures 5.29 and 5.30) to give the reader a more comprehensive idea of how involved research on a scientifically based film can be. Both NASA documentation, government image research, and our own research images allowed us to cover all bases in order to design the best centrifuge for this Disney comedy.

NASA

National Aeronautics and
Space Administration

Ames Research Center
Mountain View, CA 94035-1000

For Release: Immediately

Photo No. AC89-0097-15

20-g Centrifuge

One cab of the Ames Research Center's 20-G centrifuge is shown in this photo. With its 50-foot diameter arm and its two cabs, one at each end, the centrifuge is structurally capable of operating at levels up to 20-Gs, or 20 times normal Earth gravity. It is rated for human-occupied operations at levels up to 12.5 Gs. The 20-G centrifuge is available to conduct equipment checkouts under simulated space launch conditions and for studies of human physiological and behavioral functioning under various simulated gravity loads.

SL Hyper-G Facilities

Facility	Use	Capacity	G-Level	Species	Status
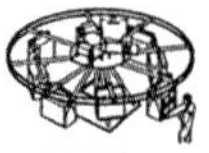 12-Foot Radius	Chronic Weeks Months (Two 1/2-hr stops per week)	20 Cages (~320 rats)	0 - 4.15 G (various radii)	Rodents Sq. Monkey Rhesus*	Operational (In use)
 52-Foot Diameter	Chronic Weeks Months	Flexible Enclosed rotating room (~50 rats)	0 - 3 G (continuous radius)	Humans Rodents Sq. Monkey Rhesus	Operational *This is being rebuild*
 4-Foot Radius	Chronic Days Weeks (Two 1/2-hr stops per week)	10 Cages (~20 rats)	0 - 10 G 4-ft. radius	Rodents Sq. Monkey*	Operational

*Restrained, only

Figure 5.29   Centrifuge research documentation.

Figure 5.30   Some centrifuge research image choices.

Recalling the plan and section for the centrifuge set reminds me of the list of requirements we had to consider:

1. Both the director and cinematographer specifically requested the viewing booth be at a comfortable height so that the window would not be more than five feet above the centrifuge bucket, allowing the actor's face to be clearly visible for a tilt down-shot. Figure 5.31 shows that specific relationship.
2. In addition to the viewing booth, a camera window was cut in the compound-curved wall to catch sight of the bucket as it whizzed past at maximum speed.
3. To address budget constraints, we only designed and built the viewing booth with wild back wall and ceiling pieces, access stairs, and two-thirds of the centrifuge's circular perimeter wall. Aside from saving a few dollars, this was done for easy crew access for operation of the centrifuge or for emergencies that might arise.
4. The viewing booth glass had to be gimbaled, or angled, to avoid reflection and be easily removable.
5. Jeff Jarvis and crew only requested the plan and section you see here and not a fully developed set of drawings for the centrifuge base and arm (Figure 5.31). The rationale was that the mechanism was delicate in terms of weight balance and movement physics; rather than be a design piece, it was to be used as a functional, engineered piece. As a rotating truss system, it would have its own mechanical aesthetic.
6. Finally, in our overall design, we had to be mindful of four shots that would complete the shooting of this scene:
   i. The medium tilt-down from the inside of the booth.
   ii. The medium close-up shot from the camera window.
   iii. A medium-long shot from the removed section of perimeter wall.
   iv. A close-up shot from a remote camera mounted directly in front of our screaming hero in the bucket.
   The final set piece (Figure 5.31, bottom image) shows the rig during dress rehearsal.

The mechanical effects crew did an outstanding job designing the centrifuge arm and base. Not only was it beautiful, but also it worked without a problem at various speeds. Once the unit was assembled in place at our shooting stages in Houston, director, cinematographer, and key shooting crew personnel arrived for a brief show-and-tell session. The arm was rotated with and without a passenger, as lenses and focal distances were double-checked by respective shooting crewmembers. Grips and first AD asked technical questions about the operation of the rig, even though the centrifuge would be solely operated by the mechanical effects foreman who built it on the actual day of shooting. Once the formality was over, several of us took turns in the bucket, celebrating a job well done in our mini-amusement park.

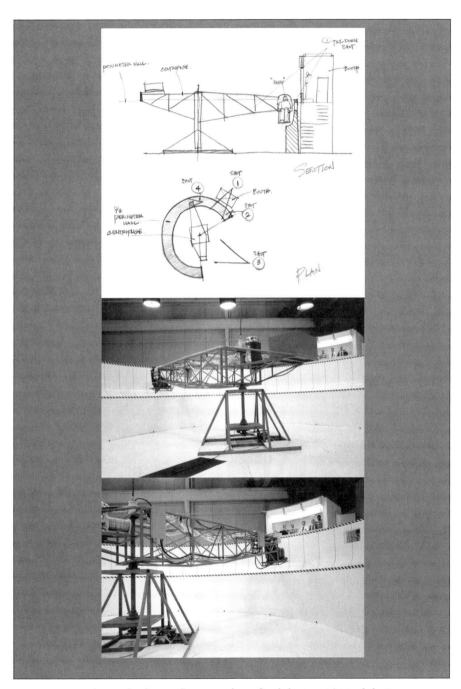

Figure 5.31   A) Rough plan and section for a final design. B) Final design.

Interview with Jeff Jarvis continued. . .

● *Are the* Matrix-*inspired rigging effects more intricate than mechanical effects rigs?*
Not really. It seems that way only because they hyped it. We were doing that stuff years ago. There was a lot of fancy ninja fighting on *RoboCop 3* (1993). After Glen Randall, English effects supervisor, came off *Raiders of the Lost Ark,* he visited Mike and me and showed us pictures taken at a British air force base of "free-fall simulators," used to teach paratroopers how to properly jump out of planes. For us, this technology revolutionized high falls off the tops of buildings. They're now called **descenders.** Basically, a person's weight determines how large an air paddle is used on the device. Originally, we used 3/32″ airplane cable, but now with advanced opticals we can get away with 1/4″ cable. For a long time Glen, Mike, and I were the only people in the United States who had them. A lot of people will tell you that they were the first to use them, but they're lying. British paratroopers were the first, and *we* borrowed from them.[10]

SPECIALTY PROPS AND ANIMATRONICS

Filmmakers will always draw on solutions from proven options because nothing succeeds like success, especially in Hollywood. A state-of-the-art effects solution might not necessarily be the optimal solution in some cases—using a traditional technique, or better yet, improving upon a tried and true technique might provide the ultimate solution. This point of view is typical of a mechanical effects approach to problem-solving. Animatronics is different. Although not scenery, animatronic objects like the half-cockroach, half-type-writers created for a movie like *Naked Lunch* (1991) fall into a specialty props category, likely to be initially designed by a concept illustrator or digital modeler in the art department. It is a specialized subdivision that thrives on innovation and unbounded creativity. Jamie Hyneman and his electronic effects production company, M5 Industries, fit that description. He is a specialty prop supervisor working in the Bay Area for 20 years, who talked at length about his attempts to reconcile the demands between his training in traditional mechanical effects and visual effects components now demanded for TV and film projects. He also appears regularly on the HBO show, *Mythbusters.*

Interview with Jamie Hyneman

● *Jamie, were you the shop supervisor of the 21-man animatronics team for* Naked Lunch *(1991)?*
No, I was not, though I was one of the lead mechanics responsible for a number of the major mechanical effects on that show. I cut my teeth on the animatronics for *Arachnophobia* (1990). I interviewed at Chris Walas Inc., who did *Naked Lunch*. At that time I was told about a film they would be doing about spiders that would be starting up in a couple of months. I went home and overnight made a spider out of wire with steel tips on the ends of its eight legs, and ran it across the bottom of a broiler pan lined with two rows of magnets. The effect made a very creepy, spider crawl as each leg moved across the path of each magnet. I went back the next day and showed them my spider. They were actually impressed and when they crewed up, I got my job. That gag never was used because it was too inflexible, and it would have to run on a track. But I did learn two things: 1) that ingenuity and passion will get you a job and 2) I also learned patience.[11]

It was obvious that M5 Industries warehouse/office space is a place of serious creative business as Jamie gave me a well-rehearsed tour. Neatness prevailed despite the company's relentless activity and the palpable sense of creativity and chaos all around. Larger specialty props were sturdily hung from the truss system above, imposing floor items were pushed carefully aside to allow easy flow around machinery and worktables, and hand-sized objects were carefully strewn across many rows of wall shelving (see Figure 5.32).

Interview with Jamie Hyneman continued . . .

My skill designing more flexible, lifelike spiders improved through using super magnets. We made simple, rubber spiders and embedded very tiny super magnets into the tips of each leg. The idea was to toss them at a metal wall surface and as they neared the metal surface they actually looked like they're reaching forward and grabbing to latch on. It was a wonderful, simple effect they used all the time. Later on, my particular contribution to the show was the leg joint design for the more articulated spider in close-up scenes. I simplified the process by perfecting the mechanics of one-cable-in-one-leg by pulling at the base of it and curling up the whole leg. It worked on the principle of the parallelogramming arms of an architect's lamp. As I refined it, I found a way to have one cable do the work of the equivalent of three cables with a solid linkage not being as sloppy or as jerky as it can when this type of mechanism gets more complicated. My solution made the process more elegant and more bulletproof.

● *Much of the work you've done is object-oriented. Have you done any work within scenery like in the movie* Delicatessen *(1991), for example, in which the physical effects and scenery were combined?*
Since we've been doing *Mythbusters,* people have been asking us to do that a lot more. Anyone can do the traditional effects—pyro, rain, fog, and wind—but I'm the guy you come to when things get problematic. I'm a generalist and a problem-solver. A production company would approach me if there were something that required a solution that went outside of the normal range of physical effects. *The Darwin Awards* required my shop to supervise traditional wind, rain, fire, and explosions—a welcomed change to our show, *Mythbusters,* in which we actually do the real stuff and don't fake anything. By working outside of LA, we have the advantage and disadvantage of being a premier boutique shop for animatronics here in the Bay Area.

● *Jamie, is this machine used for 3D sculpting? [Pointing to a smaller CNC rig in the upstairs prototyping room.]*
Yes, and that's why it intrigued us enough to buy it for the work we do. The fine sculpting ability of this machine rivals what any gifted modeler can do with clay by going beyond human capability. For example, the ½" by ½" relief figure of this tiny prototype you see is at 200%. Its normal size was eventually put on the side of a pen as part of a packet for kids. To sculpt this detail in reality with traditional sculpture methods is impossible. But in this medium, I can fill the monitor with the detail of this animation character's finger and satisfy the needs of a film's marketing department.

● *What is its non-commercial name?*
It's a CNC, computer-numeric-control, digital milling machine (see Figure 5.33a–d). Once it is programmed with a digital design including the scale of the desired object, the machine will run

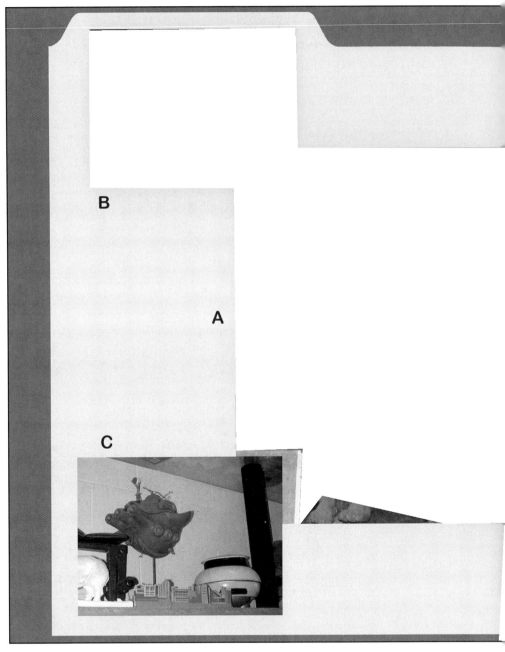

Figure 5.32   M5 Industries ANIMATRONICS: A) Latex creature prototype, B) Mechanical Mogwai head, C) A shelf of recognizable specialty film props. D) Animatronics for an over-scale spider puppet, E) Latex tarantula prototype, F) Radio-controlled puppet developed for a TV commercial—a considerably advanced puppet incorporating miniature radio, servo, and battery technologies not available before 1990. Courtesy of M5 Industries.

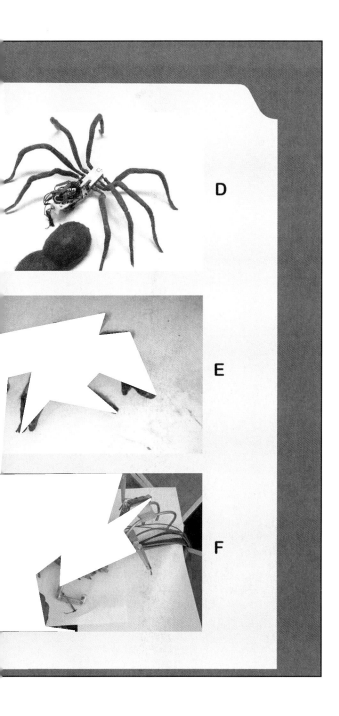

D

E

F

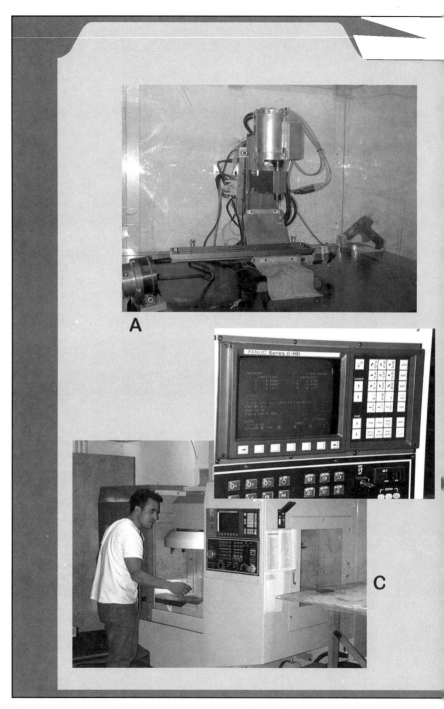

Figure 5.33 M5 Industries MACHINERY: A) Smaller CNC machine, B) Larger CNC machine, C) Insert: CNC readout screen, D) 3D stylus for sculpting tool. Courtesy of M5 Industries.

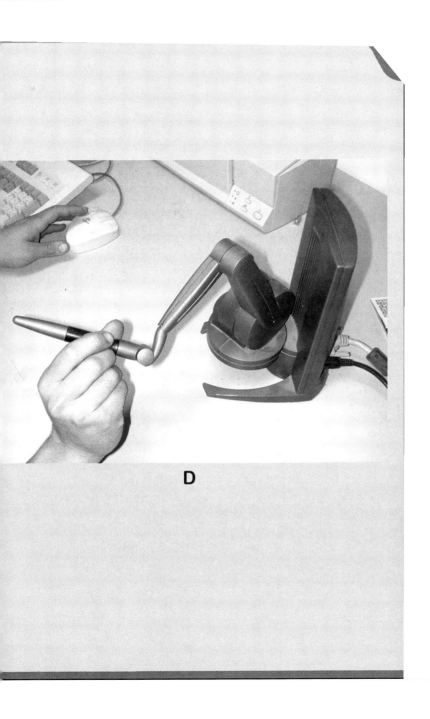

D

all night and produce the high quality detail you see on the surface of this object, or just carve the object itself. FreeForm Plus software works with this Phantom sculpting tool; otherwise, we typically use Rhino software to model polygonal surfaces. It outputs a file that generates a tool path, or series of locations, for the cutting bit to remove material and create the image. The CNC is a versatile machine tool to carve a shape out of plastic or wood in the case of a sculpture, or metal in the case of a mechanical part. We chose this because of the dual purpose and economy of the machine. You can set it so it will take a pass and then move over a thousandth of an inch and take another pass—so you can get an extremely fine resolution to carve things that it would be practically impossible for a human to actually sculpt in clay. For sculpting alone, a printer is easier to use, although not capable of as fine a resolution. Scale and design changes can tip the balance in choosing between CG versus traditional options; if it is anticipated that many, minor changes may be needed in the production of a piece, then the computer is the best choice because it can make the changes more often with ease, and be much more cost-effective.

- *So, this is a prototyping machine.*
  Exactly—the larger machine, the 3D printer, downstairs is the same kind of machine. The difference is that the CNC subtracts surface and the 3D printer adds or builds surface to create a sculptural form.

- *Explain how a 3D printer works.*
  Digital information is fed to the printer, and it reads it and sculpts the object in wax, cornstarch, UV curing resin, or even metal powder that gets centered by impregnating it with another metal that wicks into it and solidifies it. We've limited our CG adventure to designing models for prototypes when either the work is too small for a clay sculptor, or multiples of the same metal parts need to be replicated quickly and efficiently. [Pointing to a desktop PC] This SenseAble Forced-Feedback™ system works optimally for projects with scale issues; otherwise, a traditional human sculptor can handle it. [His assistant pulls up a 3D model of the profile of one of the *Mythbusters* crew on a nearby computer screen.]

- *So your approach to CG is very practical—you're not making art for art's sake.*
  Yes, by being practical we're not biased. We use whatever method, traditional or digital, that gets the job done. Our practicality is about speed and efficiency. An interesting little detail about this SenseAble™ tool is the 3D mouse. The operator simply moves this 3D wand in space and that's where the digital model goes. For speed in determining the screen model, there's nothing like it. The only flaw in doing a prototype as opposed to a purely CG model is actually being able to tell what you've got. The image on the monitor is an educated guess or estimate of what you would really have in actual versus virtual space. This is one of the biggest flaws we found as a reality check for this type of technology in terms of the crossover between the digital and physical models. We find that it's a worthwhile tool to have, although our first inclination is to put a sculptor on the project first.[12]

The 3D modeler, suggested I grasp the wand and "feel" the solidness of the onscreen sculpture (Figure 5.34). Holding the stylus and running it over the surface of the sculpted profile on the PC screen was a remarkable feeling. My fingers actually sensed the tactile

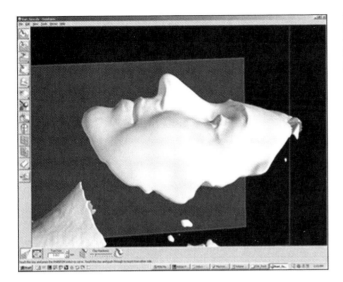

Figure 5.34 Screen capture: Side view of a human profile transferred from a 3D scanner into a FreeForm™ software document. Courtesy of M5 Industries.

sensation of sculpting in 3D, especially when I ran it around the tip of the nose or to the edge of the cheek and behind to the back. This unexpected virtual lesson with a 3D mouse clarified just how powerful this technology really is. It also drove home the concept that experience is the best teacher.

Art directors who have a working knowledge of mechanical effects and how they're integrated into built scenery are at an advantage. Understanding what materials should be used in scenery for multiple retakes of a series of physical effects shots, not only supports the success of the gag, but it prevents compromising of the look of the scenery. To review an important concept in this chapter: achieving believability through our highly developed craft of deception is our continual goal. What we have encountered here should support the fact that mechanical effects continue to be an intrinsic aspect of the filmmaking process. Physical effects and stunts will never disappear.

HAND PROPS

Like SFX, the prop department is not located in the physical art department space. The Prop Master is one of the avatars of the Production Designer on the set, presenting an extreme close-up of the visual images the art department presents to the camera lens, and the On-set Dresser is a set dressing employee, pulling double duty for both the Production Designer and Set Decorator. The Art Director, then, ensures that the quality of graphics on handheld media devices, cereal boxes, or convention badges, remains consistent throughout the shooting process. At the busiest times, it's easier to lose track of smaller details in hand props but it's important to remain vigilant, nevertheless, by relying on the ability and thoroughness of your on-set dresser. The challenge with any of the departments closely related to the actual art department is that they have their own budgets to manage; consequently, controlling the aesthetic of a prop or mechanical effect requires an artful dose of finessing on a regular basis without a heavy-handed bullishness—no one likes being told how to spend their money. It's best to begin developing a relationship with props, especially, while the art department is gearing up; pre-production is an excellent time to enroll the prop master within the visual vocabulary of the art department process by offering a reasonable level of active involvement.

Another factor that plays into the success of an art director–prop master relationship is the input of the Director in pre-production. Almost all prop masters guard their intimate connection to their director with religious fervor. A wise art director will establish a strong bond with his/her director in the presence of a prop master, to make sure that in the thick of the shooting schedule madness, the aesthetic needs of the art department have a better chance of carrying equal weight against the goal of the Prop Master to give the Director what is demanded in the heat of the moment. The immediate needs-of-the-moment on the set trump everything; having laid a solid foundation always helps drive the art department MO.

There are times when the question arises: "What department is responsible for this prop?" Michelle Collier, art department coordinator on *Iron Man 2* recalls:

Interview with Michelle Collier

> This question was asked about Iron Man's suit, which, oddly enough, was considered a hero prop. Creative input from the Prop Master, Art Director, Concept Illustrator and the Director imagined the character Tony Stark opening his suitcase, placing it on the floor and stepping into it as the Iron Man suit began unfolding and snapping into place as it "climbed" up his body, finally covering him toe-to-head. The initial idea was conceptualized in the art department by the Concept Illustrator, Ryan Meinerding. It was engineered in the costume shop as "technological body armor." Finally, the Prop Master took responsibility for it simply because it "grew" out of a suitcase, even though the suit itself was a hero costume.[13]

Again, this example reinforces the reality that certain hero props are the product of many cooks—and, the Art Director's mission is to defuse the bright-burning egos of those involved into a cooler mix of well-intentioned and efficient collaboration.

NOTES

1 Victor Martinez interview, April 21, 2004, North Hollywood, CA.

2 J. André Chaintreuil interview, April 28, 2004, North Hollywood, CA.

3 Ibid.

4 Harry and Suzanne Otto interview, April 25, 2004, Silverlake, CA.

5 Sunlight should not be confused with daylight. Sunlight is the light of the sun only. Daylight is a combination of sunlight and skylight. For consistency, 5500°K is considered to be nominal photographic daylight. Hummel, Rob (ed.), 2001. *American Cinematographer Manual*, 8th Edition. Hollywood: The ASC Press, page 130.

6 Hamela, Deborah A., 2004.*Debbie's Book: The Source Book for Props, Set Dressing and Wardrobe.* Pasadena, CA: Deborah A. Hamela.

7 Lark Bernini interview, August 13, 2013, Internet interview, Los Angeles, CA.

8 Jeff Jarvis interview, September 5, 2002, Saugus, CA.

9 Ibid.

10 Ibid.

11 Jaime Hyneman interview, June 26, 2004, San Francisco, CA.

12 Ibid.

13 Michelle Collier interview, July 12, 2013, Paramount Studios, Hollywood, CA.

CHAPTER 6

A Legacy of Historical Techniques

The mirror represents the objects faithfully but retains them not; our canvas shows them with the same exactness and retains them all.[1]

Tiphaigne de la Roche

Leonardo da Vinci first advocated the use of the camera obscura, or dark room, as an aid to drawing. It wasn't until 1827, a little over 300 years later, that Joseph Nicéphore Niépce in France produced the first successful picture image created from chemical materials that hardened after an eight-hour exposure to light. Just 50 years beyond that time in 1878, *Scientific American* published an article on Eadweard Muybridge's animal and locomotion photographic sequences, and then a few years later when George Eastman introduced flexible, photographic film for his box cameras at the turn of the century, photography become available to the masses. The still image rapidly became a moving image in America as early as 1908 at Black Maria, Thomas Alva Edison's revolving film studio built around the turn of the century in Orange, New Jersey. There he experimented with short films such as *Boxing Cats* or *A Kinetoscope Record of a Sneeze* (both 1894), freeing artists to create moving images "without the aid of a pencil or brush." This new medium was by no means an American invention—it was European: originally developed by the French, then adapted by the early American entrepreneurs in New York City, such as William Fox. Americans saw its value as a product by developing and marketing it as the nickelodeon—a customer paid a nickel to watch a minute-long movie in a box. Soon after that, film production was established in Los Angeles in the early teens of the Twentieth Century by Thomas Ince, Joe Brandt, Jack and Harry Cohn, Carl Laemmle, William Fox, Marcus Loew, the Warner brothers and Adolph Zukor, making the rest film history. We continue to investigate the legacy of both manual and digital modes of cinematic image-making, respectively, within the following two chapters, beginning with the historical techniques used by the art department.

PAINTED GLASS

Filmmaker Norman Dawn—who was either Argentinian or Bolivian, but who spent a number of years in Australia and America—while working as a still photographer c. 1905, used the glass matte process, and later translated its use into filmmaking technique in his films *For the Term of His Natural Life* (1927) and his chef-d'oeuvre *Tundra* (1936). A photograph (Figure 6.1) documenting one such photographic project where he shot footage in Tasmania in 1908 reveals a platform protected by a canvas cover supporting his camera rig. If you look carefully, the painted element is visible on a sheet of glass. It is a replica of the roof of a historically important building partially destroyed, then restored in the accompanying composite below. Later on, the "Dawn process" created a matte box that could be mounted on the camera for steadier glass-shot photography (Figure 6.2). It's interesting to see how these techniques cross-pollinated from Europe to Australia to America in the earliest years of the Twentieth Century and vigorously developed in precision and quality. What is even more remarkable is the fact that simple techniques like the glass shot haven't lost their effectiveness almost a century later.

The glass painting technique is one of the earliest techniques used to combine, or **composite,** additional visual information onto action footage. It is one of several foundations of the compositing process to be explored here. This technique was perfected by the mid-twentieth century and was in use worldwide. Graphic examples of the work of designer John Graysmark (*Courage Under Fire, Blown Away, So I Married an Axe Murderer, White Sands, Robin Hood: Prince of Thieves, Gorillas in the Mist, Duet for One, The Bounty, Ragtime*) will serve to expand the text throughout the rest of this chapter. As my early mentor, his invaluable experience appropriately illustrates examples of traditional moviemaking techniques through his early art directing filmography, including *Anastasia* (1956), *The Inn of the Sixth Happiness* (1958), and *2001: A Space Odyssey* (1968). Note: All drawings and sketches were completed by John Graysmark in 2005 for this publication.

Sometimes an exterior location is perfect for shooting except for a hydroelectric plant looming in the distance. This was a scenario encountered while filming the village of Yang Cheng for *The Inn of the Sixth Happiness*. A present-day solution would simply be to shoot the scene digitally and then erase the unwanted sections. Technology in 1958 provided a solution in glass painting, by using a large piece of glass to act as a mask between the camera and actors. Categories explaining the shot, the scenery, technique involved, and an explanation are as follows:

Shot: The main characters were filmed crossing the mountainside with a locked-off, or stationary camera on a tripod. The shot was **blocked** with actors working behind a large, painted piece of glass to mask out unwanted objects in the distant landscape.

Scenery: A 6′ × 8′ piece of ¼″ tempered glass was used as a transparent canvas between the locked-off camera and actors.

Technique:

1. Several days before the shoot, the camera was set up in exactly the spot where the scene would be shot with exactly the same lens to be used in the action sequence shot.

Figure 6.1   The earliest known photograph of the glass shot setup pioneered by Norman Dawn. Courtesy of Dr. Raymond Fielding.

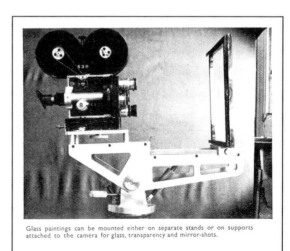

Glass paintings can be mounted either on separate stands or on supports attached to the camera for glass, transparency and mirror-shots.

Figure 6.2   A modern example of the Dawn process camera and glass rig. Courtesy of Dr. Raymond Fielding.

2. The glass was sturdily set on sandbagged **C-stand frames** and surrounded with a large enough black velour box (the American equivalent would be **duvetyne**), eliminating all ambient light and reflection on the glass (Figure 6.3).
3. Ideally, it would be best to have two scenic artists working on this step to expedite the work at hand. One scenic artist would draw with a wax pencil on the glass within the area in the landscape needing to be obscured; the other would check through the same lens to be used in the final shot, to see that the masking drawing was on the correct area of the glass.
4. The landscape was painted to "soft mask" the unwanted objects in the distance—in this case, the hydroelectric plant. The position of the sun, i.e., time of day, was noted to insure that real shadows cast in the distant landscape in the final shot would match the painted shadows on the painted mask.

Explanation:

Once the glass was painted, the shot could then include the masking image on the glass. Care had to be taken that the actors would not move any part of their bodies behind the section of masked painting on the glass for fear of spoiling the shot. For that reason the shot had to be carefully orchestrated.[2]

Again, two points to remember are for the artists to have the exact lens in the camera for reference while working on the matte painting and for the camera operator to shoot at the same time of day the painting was completed in order to achieve a perfect match.

GATE MATTING

According to John, this particular technique of matting footage for compositing was originally a French technique where the matting happened within the camera in the matte box at the gate (Figure 6.4), as opposed to outside of the camera as discussed in the painted glass technique. (Although the schematic in Figure 6.4 features the interior of a projector and not a film camera, the concept is the same.) Apparently, for Stanley Kubrick, Director of *2001: A Space Odyssey* (1968), the use of the gate matting technique was a quality control decision as well as an aesthetic one.

Shot: The monolith embedded in the archeological pit at Clavius was surrounded by the lunar landscape and deep space.
Scenery: The walkway surrounding the perimeter of the dig site at Clavius and all scenery in the foreground were built on the silent stage at Shepperton Studios in Middlesex, UK.
Technique: A grid was drawn to scale over the ground plan (Figure 6.5), suggesting where and how the silent stage set and model piece would be composited. The Clavius set was shot with the matte—an ultra-thin zinc plate—in place in the camera's matte box,

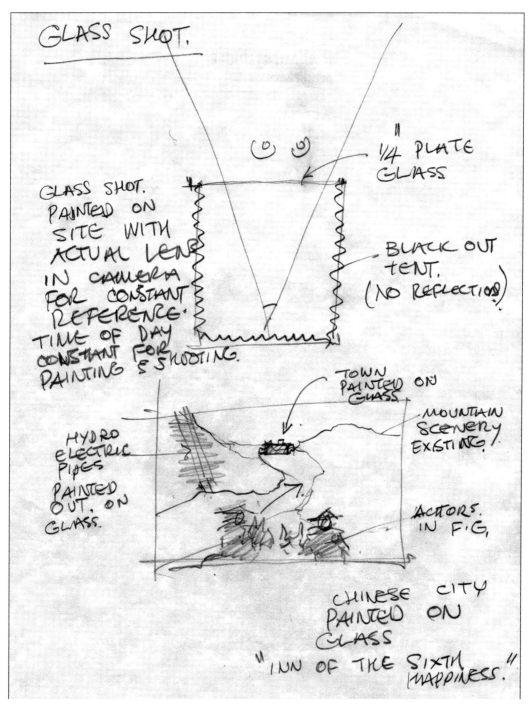

GLASS SHOT.

1/4 PLATE GLASS

GLASS SHOT.
PAINTED ON
SITE WITH
ACTUAL LENS
IN CAMERA
FOR CONSTANT
REFERENCE.
TIME OF DAY
CONSTANT FOR
PAINTING & SHOOTING.

BLACK OUT
TENT.
(NO REFLECTION)

TOWN
PAINTED ON
GLASS.

MOUNTAIN
SCENERY
EXISTING.

HYDRO
ELECTRIC
PIPES
PAINTED
OUT. ON
GLASS.

ACTORS.
IN F.G.

CHINESE CITY
PAINTED ON
GLASS
"INN OF THE SIXTH HAPPINESS."

Figure 6.3   Sketch of painted glass setup in plan and section by John Graysmark for *Inn of the Sixth Happiness*. Courtesy of John Graysmark.

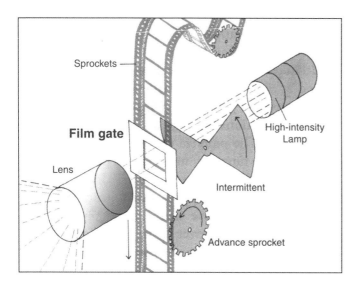

Figure 6.4   Simplified schematic of the interior of a projector showing the location of the "Film Gate."

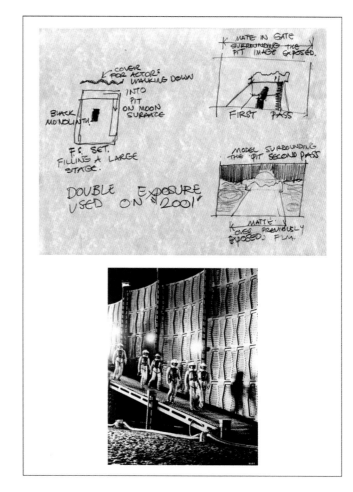

Figure 6.5   A) Sketch of onstage set showing the elevation and plan by John Graysmark of Clavius Lunar Site in *2001: A Space Odyssey*. Courtesy of John Graysmark. B) Descending into Clavius Lunar Site. Courtesy of MGM/The Kobal Collection/Art Resource.

Figure 6.6 Set shot of Clavius Lunar Site in *2001: A Space Odyssey*. Courtesy of MGM/The Kobal Collection/Art Resource.

masking out the top of the frame including the area of the lunar landscape and deep space in the background (Figure 6.6). On the sketch, it is labeled as "first pass." The scene was then shot, exposing that half of the film emulsion on every frame. Then a reverse matte—a precisely cut, opposite puzzle piece of zinc plate—was placed in the matte box masking out the scene previously shot in the set on the bottom half of the frame. (Notice that in the schematic in Figure 4.4, the film emulsion is just behind the film gate as the filmstrip is pulled down through the intermittent movement.) "The background miniature of the lunar landscape and deep space was then exposed, frame per frame, for one plus minutes in the camera gate at very slow exposure, to burn the crisp blacks and whites of space without atmosphere."[3]

It is important to understand that both top and bottom matte halves were carefully manipulated and shot *within* the camera to insure an exact registration of the foreground action in the studio and the miniature in backgrounds of Figures 6.6 and 6.8. This example of precisely planned, double-exposure is typical of the Director's obsession for control.

Explanation: Kubrick's reasoning made perfect sense considering the film was being shot as if it were chronicling events in deep space—in a vacuum of crystal clarity. The exact fit of composited elements had to ensure jigsaw puzzle precision (Figure 6.7). As you watch the film, all model shots consistently display the deepest blacks and high-key luminous whites in this contrasted image technique (Figure 6.8).

Kubrick was interested in controlling every aspect of the shooting and editing process. Consequently, the bulk of in-studio shooting he did on *2001: A Space Odyssey* used many miniatures and models. The **in-camera** techniques he employed also assured the integrity of the 70mm film stock he used. In other words, every time a strip of film was printed, a generation of clarity or resolution was lost—70mm film has four times as many frames as 35mm film, making it four times larger. If a single **dupe,** or duplicate, of the originally shot film had to be made, it would "degrade" to 35mm status and be acceptable for theatrical viewing.

I have intentionally focused on this film because it is a characteristic example of a contemporary film shot entirely **in-studio** using the most state-of-the-art in-camera

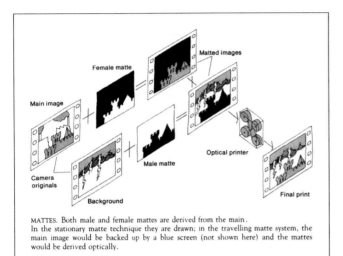

Figure 6.7   Simple schematic showing how a male-female matte works. Fielding, R. (1979). *The Techniques of Special Effects Cinematography*, 8th edition. Focal Press. Courtesy of Raymond Fielding.

Figure 6.8   *2001: A Space Odyssey* miniature shot. MGM/The Kobal Collection/Art Resource

techniques at the time. The Designer's and Art Director's functions were to design the scenery especially for many of the in-camera sequences to comply with how the film was shot and processed. Obviously, the design team was not just making pretty scenery; process was just as important as production value.

THE PROCESS CAMERA

As we've just seen, in-camera **matte shots** required successive re-exposure of the original negative. **Optical printing,** another aspect of adding to or subtracting from original film stock footage, concerns itself primarily with master positives and dupe negatives. Bi-pack

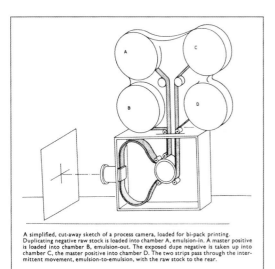

A simplified, cut-away sketch of a process camera, loaded for bi-pack printing. Duplicating negative raw stock is loaded into chamber A, emulsion-in. A master positive is loaded into chamber B, emulsion-out. The exposed dupe negative is taken up into chamber C, the master positive into chamber D. The two strips pass through the intermittent movement, emulsion-to-emulsion, with the raw stock to the rear.

Figure 6.9 The process camera. Courtesy of Dr. Raymond Fielding.

contact matte printing was a transitional technique that replaced older glass and matte techniques. The term "bi-pack" refers to two **magazines** or spools of film; one spool contained a master positive struck from the original negative and one spool contained a roll of fine-grain, negative raw stock (Figure 6.9). Negative raw stock (A), emulsion in, was threaded into a process camera with the master positive stock (B), emulsion out. Both strips of film were placed emulsion-to-emulsion just behind the aperture plate in the **intermittent movement** of the process camera. As the filmstrips were pulled together through the printer, each was re-collected into its own receiving spool (A into C) and (B into D). The goal of this setup was to use this **process camera** as a **step printer.** In photographic terms, a step printer is an apparatus that develops film, whether it is 35mm film from a reflex camera or a 35mm movie camera. (Remember, cinema is fundamentally photography.) Keeping this concept in mind, the master positive was used in the bi-pack process as a "negative," and the raw film stock was used as high quality photographic "paper" to accept a new printed image. Anyone who has spent time in a darkroom is familiar with how film is developed. Early filmmakers realized this and used these fundamental concepts for their new craft. What would the new image be? It would be whatever needed to be added to the master positive to complete the finished image on the filmstrip.

How was a new image added to the master positive? Figure 6.9 also shows a square of matte board that acted as a rigid easel for holding either matte or counter-matte images like those shown in Figure 6.10a and b. As long as the image on the matte board was evenly lit, the light rays bouncing off the board would act as the primary light source in the photographic step printer, etching a new image as it passed through the aperture and the master positive onto the raw film stock behind. The new image would be a combination of the originally shot footage with the image on the matte board. This technique of manipulating film stock and images was prevalent during the years 1965–1980. Although this information

Note: The punched holes at the right of the sheet which allow for peg-bar registration.

See Fig 4-10b for final composite.

Figure 6.10a   Matte/Counter Matte . . .
Courtesy of Dr. Raymond Fielding.

is somewhat technical, the concept is important. Once the range and technique of any of these processes is understood, the concepts can be more confidently applied as the basis for solutions to new problems. Speed and greater precision are what digital techniques add to the foundation of these concepts.

TRAVELING MATTES

Compositing foreground action with actors and a background shot elsewhere onto the same piece of film has been the concern of filmmakers since the beginning years of the commercial film industry. An original solution to this problem was resolved through rear projection. The translucent projection screen was substituted for the glass (as in the painted glass shot) and a projected photographic film image was applied to the back of the screen instead of paint. The rest is self-explanatory. More complicated compositing processes allowed actors to move about within the frame without disappearing behind matted background areas. The Dunning-Pomeroy self-matting process accomplished this by allowing changes in background position, size, and composition from frame to frame, giving an actor and director free movement within the picture frame. This revolutionized moviemaking but had its drawbacks: it was limited to black-and-white cinematography, and was not flexible in the editing or post-production process. Unfortunately, once the final positive was composited then that is how it remained.

First printing for a bi-pack matte shot combining two live-action scenes.

Second printing, adding background detail photographed from the top of a ten-storey building.

Final composite. See Fig 4-10a for mattes used for this shot.

Figure 6.10b   . . . and resulting composite image. Courtesy of Dr. Raymond Fielding.

Early cinema pioneers continued to learn valuable lessons from color photography and applied this knowledge to the filmmaking process. Each of the primary colors of red, blue, and green (also known as **hues** or **chroma**) could be separated and placed on their own film-strips. Combining this fact with the need to solve the flexibility problem mentioned above, the traveling matte process improved dramatically. **Chromakeying,** or separating the primary light colors out of the original color image, and using the black-and-white photographic process in conjunction with the color process utilized a more exacting and successful compositing system.

The key steps in contact printing, a conventional traveling matte in popular use during the last quarter of the last century (Figure 6.11), begin with an actor shot in color negative in front of a bluescreen (Step A in Table 6.1). The entire process as seen in steps A to H shows a flip-flopping between color and black-and-white negatives and positives to arrive at the male and female composite strips to be married onto a single strip of film. Table 6.1 replaces words for images in explaining Figure 6.11. Hopefully, this will simplify your understanding.

Once these challenging concepts are understood, the reader will be able to easily apply the fundamentals of the traveling matte process to the current applications of this relatively simple technique to digital filmmaking.

Figure 6.11
Conventional
bluescreen traveling
matte. Courtesy of
Dr. Raymond Fielding

Table 6.1   A bluescreen traveling matte is achieved through optical printing.

Explanation of the **Bluescreen Traveling Matte** Printing Process		
A An actor is photographed with white light on color negative film stock in front of a bluescreen.		**B** The resulting color negative is step-printed in contact with a black-and-white master positive of the same scene; this records only the blue chroma component of the scene. The result of this step is a hybrid, B/W color separated positive with a clear background.
C Repeating step B, the color negative is printed onto another B/W master positive, but this time separating out the red chroma component. The resulting background is black. This positive is step-printed to a duplicate on high-contrast film, producing its corresponding negative image with another clear background [as in step B].		**D** In this step, the blue chroma positive and the red chroma duplicate are optically printed using the bi-pack method onto additional high-contrast B/W stock. At this point, A TRAVELING MATTE is the result, showing a black background matte and clear area signifying the actor in the foreground action.
E A corresponding male counter-matte is simply printed from the female traveling matte in step D.		**F** This step shows the male traveling matte [E] of the actor combined with the background master positive.
G This step shows the female traveling matte [D] of the background combined with the actor master positive.		**H** Either a color or B/W composite is produced here from bi-packing the composites in steps [F] and [G].

Rotoscoping, borrowed from animation, was a technique of tracing each frame of live action and then hand painting in the silhouette (see Figures 6.7 and 6.10a–b) (see also: Rotoscoping main heading at the beginning of Chapter 7). The silhouetted artwork was either photographed or used directly to composite the foreground or background with the same camera to create the matte. This technique is still used today with imaging programs like Avid Illusion® or Commotion®. Although originally a time-consuming process, modern software programs produce flawless animation and super-fast results.

At one time a phenomenon, digital compositing is now universally accepted as the norm in the pre- and post-production process. The vivid blue or green backing against which the foreground action is shot becomes a criterion for color difference matching. Digital compositing artists working in VFX film departments must do four things with this digital data:

1. Check the backing screen for irregularities and correct for uniformity—this is also known as *screen correction.*
2. Create an alpha channel or silhouette mask, as the original rotoscope artists once did.
3. Check the foreground for screen reflections and suppress them by giving them a value of black—also known as creating a processed foreground.
4. Combine the elements into a believable composite.

All of this is just an updated version of bluescreen traveling matte work done with an optical printer.

Questions about color remain: Why a bluescreen and not red? The answer lies within the skin tones of any given actor. It's simply easier to separate out the blue tones than the red tones of the skin pigment. Even with the precision of getting down to the pixel in digital film production, the bluescreen has been upgraded to a **green-screen** in certain instances but still works exceptionally well. Wardrobe color and exterior location (foliage) also determines the use of either color. One advantage green has over blue is less grain noise in shadows or semi-transparent objects found in foreground action.[4]

MINIATURES

Three types of **miniatures** have been used in traditional moviemaking:

1. The miniature is used as an element inset, backing through an opening in the set.
2. The model is shot as is.
3. The model is used as a component in image replacement for a composite.

By comparison, a miniature is a 3D alternative to a 2D matte image (see "glass shot" discussed previously in this chapter). Where a glass painting incorporates fixed light, shadow, and perspective, these same elements can be varied, making miniatures more versatile. Miniatures can be static as viewed in a long shot, for example, or as moving pieces, increasing the realism and believability of a shot.

Common sense and experience tell us that familiar objects at rest and in motion behave a certain way in the physical world. If they do not or if we perceive the slightest deviation from an expected norm, we become suspicious. We either think about checking our eyesight, or wonder about a psychological aberration. If all else fails, we realize we have been deceived. Deception is what we work at and ultimately do best in the art department. It's our stock-in-trade. Cinematic deception is derived from using the laws of physics to our advantage through a proven formula or by twisting those formulas into desired shapes through trial and error. Insight is an additional ingredient that helps to fill in the gaps.

To be effective, miniatures shot "as is" must be as close to full scale as possible. Remember full scale shows a relationship of 1:1 or 1′ = 1′. The optimal range from the largest to the smallest models should fall between quarter scale: 1:4 or 3″ = 1′ to twelfth scale: 1:12 or 1″ = 1′. Comparatively, it costs less to build a larger miniature than a smaller one in terms of detail and time. Mobile models smaller than the range noted require extremely high-speed camera drives to capture movement, increasing time and labor costs. This information should serve only as a guideline. Different projects will dictate requirements and budgets; these variables will affect how problems are solved and how rules are appropriately broken to serve the solutions to those problems.

Combining miniature use with live action lends itself to unquestioning believability. Why? As detailed and realistic as the model might be, the live action playing in front of it is a diversion by pulling enough focus to enroll the audience. If the miniature and live action sequences are to be shot separately, then it would be best to build the miniature and shoot it first, and then shoot the live action footage to work within its parameters. With this information in mind, let's get to some historic examples.

Hanging Foreground Miniature

As a young draughtsman, John Graysmark encountered this simple technique on *Anastasia* (1956). Wallace Smith's drafting was used for the construction of the miniature. Details of the process follow:

Shot: A transatlantic crane, very high, slowly panned across the nighttime expanse of the city of Paris (c. 1928, during Russian Easter) to the bell tower of the Russian Orthodox Church. The shot was held, faded, and then tilted down below the miniature, hanging piece to the street and church below.

Scenery: An architectural miniature of the bell tower (Figure 6–12) was suspended in the foreground above, with the nighttime city of Paris in miniature in the background. This hanging miniature was in quarter scale, corresponding to the full-scale church and street built on the studio lot below. The miniature was bordered on the bottom with a course line of bricks and finishing molding—this acted as a hard cutting edge for the transition between the miniature bell tower model and full-scale church and tower on the studio lot.

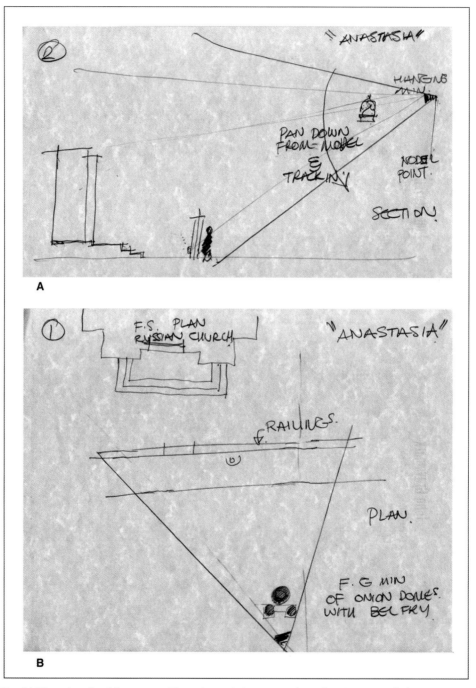

Figure 6.12   A) Plan sketch of foreground hanging miniature set by John Graysmark for *Anastasia*. Courtesy of John Graysmark. B) Elevation sketch of foreground hanging miniature set by John Graysmark for *Anastasia*. Courtesy of John Graysmark.

Technique:

There were two issues to consider: the depth of field and the nodal point of the camera lens. The same camera lens was used for shooting both the model miniature in front of its Parisian background miniature and the full-scale church and street scene. By using the same lens but adjusting for focal distance when shooting the miniature tower and full-scale tower, the transition was smooth from the bottom of the suspended tower miniature to the body of the full-scale church.

According to Graysmark, "Using a tilting pan head would've been incorrect—the camera must have a nodal head because the center of the lens had to be stationary, acting as a fixed fulcrum point for the movement—in this case, by tilting.[5]

Explanation: The reason for transitioning from the miniature to the full-scale church is to create a believable opening shot for the movie (the skyline of Paris looked different in 1956 when the movie was shot, as opposed to when it was scripted to take place in 1928). "The POV, or the focal distance from the camera lens to the miniature, stayed the same. That way the scale of the miniature didn't distort, and it worked beyond depth of field as the camera refocused on other objects."[6]

The reason why John differentiates between the tilting pan head and nodal head is fundamental (see Figure 6.13). A nodal head operates much like a human head as it nods up and down "yes" (tilt), or turns left and right "no" (pan) while the body is seated in a fixed position (fixed fulcrum). The tilting pan head works exactly the same way *except* the camera base (body holding the head) rides an arc, much like being on a playground swing (changing fulcrum point). A change in fulcrum, or position, for the camera lens located in the head, also changes the depth of field and focus as it moves along an arc. If the body were sitting still on the swing with no movement at the valley of the arc, nodding up and down, then the effect of a nodal head is once again at work. The shot in the scene described previously would have obviously looked very different without the use of the nodal tilting head. This illustrates a critical design point. Without an understanding of basic camera movement, lens choice, and employment of various tricks-of-the-trade to successfully make a shot, any design produced in the art department is incomplete and misinformed.

Foreground Miniature

Escape to Athena (1979) provides a quick and simple example of the use of a foreground miniature (see Figure 6.14). Before we analyze this, it's important to note that:

1. A 25mm wide angle lens for best depth of field was used.
2. The F-stop indicated by the cameraman for this lens provided to the art department with the exact depth of field as an exact reference, e.g., 2'-10" to 5'-2".

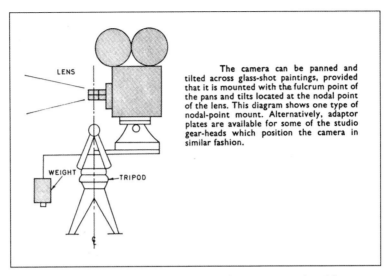

The camera can be panned and tilted across glass-shot paintings, provided that it is mounted with the fulcrum point of the pans and tilts located at the nodal point of the lens. This diagram shows one type of nodal-point mount. Alternatively, adaptor plates are available for some of the studio gear-heads which position the camera in similar fashion.

Figure 6.13   Schematic of a nodal point mount. Courtesy of Dr. Raymond Fielding.

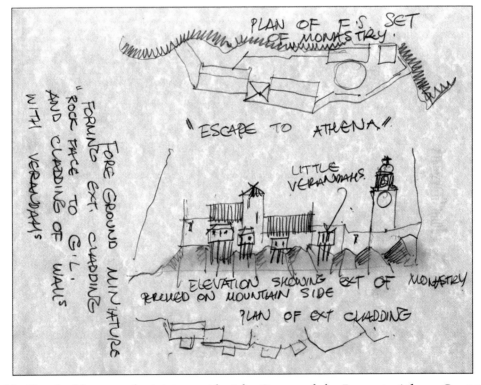

Figure 6.14   Sketch of foreground miniature set by John Graysmark for *Escape to Athena*. Courtesy of John Graysmark.

Shot: Climax scene of actors hiding behind protective rocks at the bottom of the frame as the monastery explodes above them at the top of the frame.

Set: The miniature monastery in question was built in one inch to one foot or 12:1 scale on the ground to imitate the look of a mountainous outcropping along the coastline on the island of Rhodes, matching shots both before and after it.

Technique and explanation: The split matte used for this scene was shot at two different speeds. The miniature, above, was shot at 120 frames per second and slightly beyond proper depth of field at 5'-3" to keep it out of focus and ensure believability. The actors, below, were shot at a normal 24 frames per second. Compositing the images in bi-pack created an acceptable scene of potential danger as a resolution to the movie. Going against logic in terms of keeping the foreground miniature slightly out of proper focus, worked best for the shot and the art department as well as shooting at 120fps adjusted the speed of the fireball.

Cutouts: A Variation on Miniatures

Design work on *White Sands* (1992) filmed in Alamogordo, New Mexico, at the National Monument required miniature building and an explosion. The restrictions of this fragile location were:

1. No vehicles allowed on the pristine, white gypsum sand.
2. Wind gusts were a regular, unexpected occurrence.
3. A limited timeframe was strictly enforced to complete our work and leave without a trace, or face stiff penalties.

Shot: An arms-operative fired a shoulder missile at a tank in the near distance to prove the accuracy of his new product.

Set: Quonset huts and a breakaway tank were among other disused military vehicles on an abandoned army base.

Technique: The first part of our solution was photographic. Our set photographer accumulated a variety of both truck and tank views with a 35mm reflex camera at a nearby military installation. Selected images were mounted to framed lauan and cut cleanly around edges to give us a workable 2D view of the vehicles. The next part of our solution was practical. By combining the front and side views of a typical tank, we created a half-scale model of it that could be easily "destroyed" by the shoulder missile. The mechanical effects department required multiples for three takes. Additional side views or front views were individually mounted on lauan, framed, jacked, and heavily sandbagged into regimented rows in the distance. The mechanical effects department did several tests. The day before the shoot they also cable-rigged the dummy missile just above the actor's shoulder level from the locked-off position to its target at the breakaway tank cutout.

Explanation: The shooting sequence followed this pattern:
1. On cue, the shoulder missile was fired by the effects crew.
2. It "hit" its target by stopping short of the cutout tank model.

3. Cut.
4. A fireball explosion was detonated and filmed.
5. Cut.
6. Explosion debris was prepared by the scenics and scattered by the on-set dressers around the explosion site after the effects crew removed the cutout. We repeated with several takes for assurance.

This scene was filmed at night to accentuate the smoke and fire of the explosion. This technique was easy to pull off and worked, when methodically executed, in a variety of situations (*Tora, Tora, Tora* or *Courage Under Fire*) where it's easier to scenically paint or apply a photograph to a cutout surface than to transport large and expensive pieces of set dressing into a remote and fragile location. It saves money and time, and is very controllable.

Forced Perspective

This is a practical technique for shooting a scene in a studio with less space than might be required. How can that happen? Isn't the size of a studio predetermined by the number of sets scheduled to occupy the space? Initially, it is. Then any number of things could happen: the schedule changes or a critical location is lost or an additional series of shots are added to forward the storytelling. At that point, a forced perspective set might be squeezed into the empty space previously occupied by a set already shot and wrapped.

The 1994 film *Blown Away* provides an example of forced perspective (Figure 6.15). During the movie's **exposition,** this technique remains onscreen for two seconds before the shot changes. Here is the analysis:

Shot: The hero emerges from an upper floor stair landing as he runs into a hallway junction, pauses a moment to decide where to go, then exits through the door, camera right. The stationary camera pans from right to left, pauses, and pans briefly back to the right.

Scenery: The top section of a stair landing with window and translucent backing beyond leads up into an MIT hallway wall with a practical door leading into an office.

Technique and explanation: In the scene previously described, we are looking through the **picture plane,** noted as "PP" in the plan drawing, to several pair of pilasters and headers diminished in scale toward a back wall that included a door with a translucent glass panel and a translucent transom. This picture plane was physically created by the closest set of pilasters and header to the camera. The floor of the hallway was purposely set on a steep slope, forcing the perspective through exaggeration. The "camera POV" noted in the section sketch below the plan sketch was fixed except for the minimal panning it did—watching this shot several times, one could estimate the fixed height of the camera lens at the same height as the translucent, glass paneled door at the far end of the forced perspective hallway. Lasting just a couple of seconds, this shot forwards the storytelling successfully via this highly believable and compelling technique.

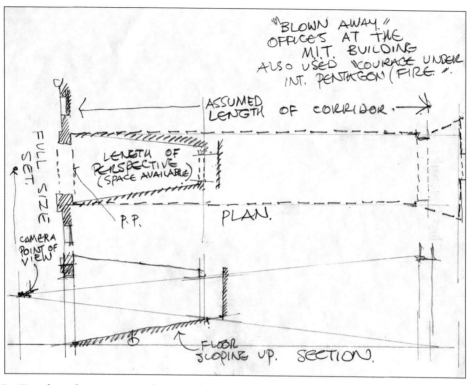

Figure 6.15 Two forced-perspective sketches drawn by John Graysmark for *Blown Away* (2005). Courtesy of John Graysmark.

This technique clearly uses forced perspective scenery as a 3D miniature glass painting. Seven decades earlier on a production of *Monte Cristo* (1922), a similar use of this technique extended the believability of a hallway that would otherwise be too costly to build. By forcing the linear perspective, the physical reality of scenery closest to the camera was distorted; the distortion continued rapidly as the distance was compressed. It is important to note from a design point of view that perspective detail on the built scenery tended to fall away as the eye of the viewer moved gradually down the forced perspective hallway (Figure 6.16). To push the illusion even further, an art director could insert a pale gray bobbinette into the width of the hallway somewhere just beyond the first third of the distance of the corridor. Backlighting a bit more intensely in the remainder of the corridor beyond the fine scrim forces the bobbinette to "go transparent" and creates a visual sense of atmospheric perspective. This technique is borrowed from the theater. Given this example, it is easy to use the phrase "trick-of-the-trade" to explain this and other techniques, but it is a misnomer. There is no trick involved, only careful, collaborative planning—calculated deception based on experience, yes, but no trickery.

A hanging miniature is a partially-constructed model which is interposed between a full-scale set and the camera.

The finished composite. Note the false perspective which is produced by continuously varying the scale of the hanging miniature.

Figure 6.16 Hanging miniature built in forced perspective also acts as a 3D glass painting. Courtesy of Dr. Raymond Fielding.

Mobile Miniatures

Mobile miniatures demand that attention be paid to time-scale relationships, i.e., the laws of physics, namely gravity, buoyancy, velocity, and friction. *Speed* (1994), a high-concept action-adventure designed by Jackson De Govia, showcased the most excellent use of miniatures as it addressed the three laws of inertia, velocity, and friction. This is expressed in two prominent miniature sets: an LA skyscraper elevator shaft and a section of the LA Metro subway train. Once research and fundamental design decisions had been completed and built for onstage shooting, the development and supervision of each miniature set was subcontracted to Grant McCune Design (GMD) for the elevator/shaft and Sessums Engineering for the LA Metro work. Not only is this commonplace in the movie industry but also necessary. GMD is a mini-film studio offering the following in-house services: art department, dark room, machine shop, metal fabrication, woodshop, milling, model shop, paint shop, mold shop, production offices, production lot (12,000 sq ft), and production motion control/smoke stage (5,000 sq ft). GMD offers any level of miniature photographic supervision from storyboarding to prop design and graphic production, as well as providing any three-dimensional object needs: set pieces, sculptures, miniatures, table top props, mechanical props and rigging, theme park models, promotional items, prototypes, replicas, and rentals.[7] Professional studios like this become a temporary arm of the art department by thoroughly assisting production design teams while remaining under strict supervision. The superb craft of GMD's elevator shaft and elevator car miniatures were seen during the opening credits of the film, foreshadowing general clues about the plot and the events of the first near-catastrophe we encounter.

Shot: A motion control crane descended along the vertical length of a multiple elevator shaft, displaying the opening credits of the film. The camera was angled in a medium close-up on the respective floor numbers, as well as the adjacent shaft showing the intermittent movement of other elevator cars. A horizontal I-beam at the bottom of each floor station cleverly wiped each credit off the screen and revealed the next as the camera slid down the chute. This POV shot began at the 41st floor, paused at the 32nd floor long enough for the film title, *Speed,* to quickly appear and disappear, progressed to the tenth floor, displaying the production design credit, and continued its descent below the first floor lobby to P4 garage. The shot continued, pulling back from the elevator along a short corridor, and rested about 20 feet from a door. Cut to the full scale set and a close-up of a sign on this door reading "Caution."

Scenery: "The entire first shot was a miniature including the shaft and elevator cars, the corridor, the door, and the sign. The details of the miniature set were taken from the full-size set pieces onstage and shot after most of the full-size sets were struck. The miniature set measured 27½″ × 57″ × 69′ in ⅛″ scale and included 46 floors and eight elevator bays. It was laid on its back on the stage and shot horizontally."[8]

Technique and explanation: A motion control crane shot the opening sequence by simply rolling on a dolly trough to the right side of the miniature set. This counterintuitive approach worked with gravity, making the shots easy and practical.

The LA Metro sequence used inter-cuts of miniatures and full-size, live action footage. Miniatures of subway tunnel, terminus station, and trains were designed and built by Sessums Engineering, another full-service Hollywood production house. This sequence precedes the end of the film and is analyzed below:

Shot sequence: Three main shots make up this sequence: the first car of the runaway train splits from the second car, the lead car slides into a vertical I-beam and splits in two, and then it continues up a ramp out from the underground.

Scenery: In eighth scale or 1½″ to 1′, miles of subway track connecting tunnel sections between stations, unfinished North Hollywood terminus station and subterranean model work filled a newly acquired Sony ImageWorks warehouse at the time. Sessums Engineering, headed by Jack Sessums, undertook another, painstaking quest by detailing its train miniatures for the closing scenes of the movie. The miniature production company used two of the four extruded aluminum cars. The super-detailing of the subway cars was specific down to the rubber window gaskets. Allan McFarland, lighting wizard for Sessums, lit the cars with 9″ fluorescent tubes imitating that of the full-size cars. Sessums' mechanical effects department carefully constructed one of the breakaway cars to split in two on impact.

Technique and explanation: Anyone who has played with a model train set has a basic idea of the intricacies and patience involved in creating a satisfying fantasy. Choreographing the derailment according to the dictates of the **storyboards** was Sessums Engineering's biggest challenge. First, the mobile miniatures had to move quickly from inertia to 11–12mph. A DC motor powered the lead car on its downhill slide. The rest was left to the Sessums' special effects crew and airplane cable working in the sliding car miniature set. The derailment and split of the first and second cars was accomplished by pulling each car onto its own train track by guide cables. Once derailed, the same cable rig guided the main car toward the vertical I-beam that splits it in half, much like flying a kite. The cable and pulley system was attached to a longer cable leading outside the warehouse to Jack Sessums driving a Suzuki ATV. The miniature design team cleverly suspended all vertical posts in this set, several inches above the floor so that the cable/pulley kite system could slide beneath without jamming or tangling. A truckload of peat moss covered the floor to aid sliding and to mask the cable rig. "Once cameras were ready to roll, the room was lightly smoked and two, multi-camera takes for each setup went smoothly. Retake setup took 4–5 hours on average. Most of the shots were one-take shots covered by several cameras; there were no problems with dailies, requiring no further retakes."[9]

FRONT PROJECTION

2001: A Space Odyssey was the first motion picture to perfect the technique of front projection. The process was as simple as it looked.

Shot: A stationary camera shot the famous scene of an ape seated on the savanna pounding a small pile of dried bones with a large femur bone.

Scenery: The foreground savanna set—small, **raked,** and rocky—was placed in front of a **highly directional,** front-projection screen acting as background. The curved screen was equidistant at all points from the center of the locked-off camera lens. This assured that there would be no falloff in picture density, thereby retaining full focal distance and focus on any point of the curve.

Technique: The camera shot directly into the center of the set. It employed a projector at a 90° angle to the camera lens and a plate of surface-silvered mirror on a 45° angle sitting in front of the camera, fully covering the scope of the aperture opening (Figure 6.17). The projection screen, made of 3M material, was highly-directional meaning it reflected most of the light back to the camera with little ambient light loss; the surface-silvered mirror has a 50/50 reflective/see-through capacity and a perfect ability to both reflect and transmit light. The projector transmitted the background image to the glass, reflecting it onto the screen behind the actor and savanna set placed on the same axis of the camera, as the scene was shot. Very little of the reflected light was lost from the screen as it returned to the camera lens through the mirrored glass and struck the film stock, burning the image onto the film emulsion.

Explanation: Why were there no shadows on the screen behind the actors on the set? There are several reasons for this:

1. The camera was on the same axis as the projected image.
2. As long as the camera remained stationary, the shadows were cast, unseen, directly behind the actor on the screen in background.
3. Fill lights, placed on either side of the set, washed across the center of it erasing any ghost shadows playing on the background screen.[10]

All of these factors made the shot perfectly executed.

Another ingenious use of front projection was on the Cannon movie *Lifeforce* (1985), designed by John Graysmark and shot at the *Star Wars* stage at Elstree Studios, London.

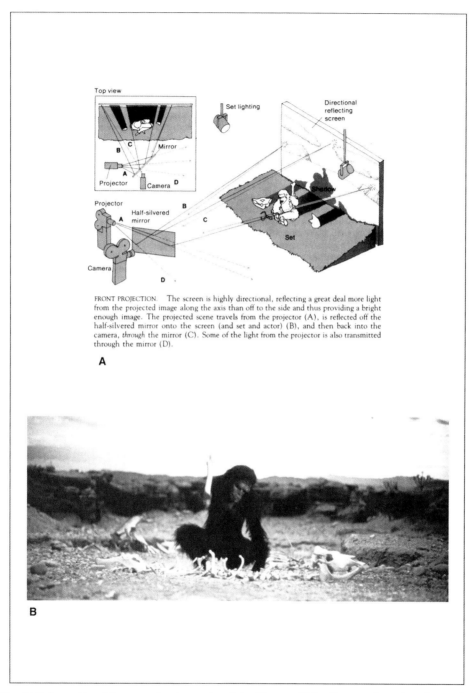

Top view

Set lighting

Directional
reflecting
screen

Mirror

B C

A

Projector

Camera D

Projector

B

Half-silvered
mirror

A

C

Shadow

Set

Camera

D

FRONT PROJECTION. The screen is highly directional, reflecting a great deal more light from the projected image along the axis than off to the side and thus providing a bright enough image. The projected scene travels from the projector (A), is reflected off the half-silvered mirror onto the screen (and set and actor) (B), and then back into the camera, *through* the mirror (C). Some of the light from the projector is also transmitted through the mirror (D).

A

B

Figure 6.17 A) Schematic of front projection using "the Dawn of Man" scene from Stanley Kubrick's *2001: A Space Odyssey*. From *How to Read a Film 4E* by James Monaco (2009) Figure 2.62 from p. 155. Used by permission of Oxford University Press, USA. B) Set shot of "The Dawn of Man" scene from Stanley Kubrick's *2001: A Space Odyssey*. MGM/The Kobal Collection/Art Resource.

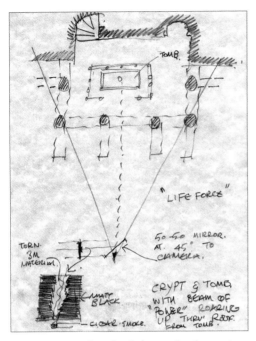

Figure 6.18 Sketch of plan and schematic by John Graysmark for *Lifeforce* Cathedral scene, front projection technique. Courtesy of John Graysmark.

Shot: A stationary camera photographed actors on top of a crypt in a cathedral apse. From there, an energy field was supposed to stream from the body of one of the actors up through the dome to a craft hovering above the church.

Set: A colonnade of six columns, containing a sarcophagus surrounded by a railing, framed the apse. Tony Reading, John's art director, master-minded the geometric projection sequence for the climax scene set in a cathedral crypt with a front projection screen behind the actors on the tomb (Figure 6.18).

Technique and explanation: John conceived a simple solution to the required effect by using two pieces of projection screen material. One smaller, jagged piece of 3M material was mounted against black velvet. A crewmember blew cigar smoke from beneath. The projector just behind the mirror placed on a 45° angle to the camera lens, threw the image of the swirling smoke 20 feet in front of the camera onto a translucent projection screen just beyond the actors on top of the sarcophagus in the crypt area, noted as "tomb" in the sketch. "The effect showed an energy field roaring up to the ceiling and out of the building to a spacecraft above. The visual effect was relatively simple and extremely effective."[11]

A final example of front projection is found in the film *Young Winston* (1972), production designed by Don Ashton, who used front projection technique on a large scale.

Shot: A brief meeting and conversation between two actors takes place in the corridor and is filmed by a stationary camera.

Scenery: The location of the central octagonal lobby of the House of Commons Palace of Westminster was the design base for an interior set that was too unjustifiably large to build onstage (see Figure 6.19).

Technique: The designer took multiple exposures in an 8 × 10 plate camera of the actual lobby, much like tiling a montage of images into Photoshop to create a larger image. According to John, this was an intensive, all-night process. Once developed, these large format images were combined, providing a super-size, perspective image of the rear of the octagonal lobby and into the corridors beyond. This giant, composite photo was versatile enough to work for front-projected screen images. A large backing piece of 3M screen material, the same size as the actual lobby, touched down behind the high end

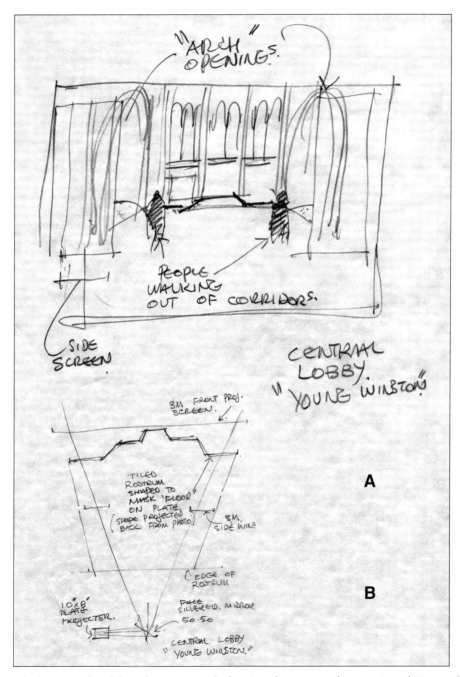

"ARCH"
OPENINGS.

PEOPLE
WALKING
OUT OF CORRIDORS.

SIDE
SCREEN

CENTRAL
LOBBY.
"YOUNG WINSTON"

3M FRONT PROJ.
SCREEN.

TILED
ROSTRUM
SHAPED TO
MASK 'FLOOR'
ON PLATE
(SHAPE PROJECTED
BACK FROM PHOTO)

3M.
SIDE WIRE

A

EDGE OF
ROSTRUM

B

10"x8"
PLATE
PROJECTER.

HALF
SILVERED. MIRROR
50.50

CENTRAL LOBBY
"YOUNG WINSTON."

Figure 6.19   A) Elevation sketch by John Graysmark showing the onstage, front-projected House of Commons Lobby set (2005). Courtesy of John Graysmark. B) Plan sketch by John Graysmark showing the onstage, front-projected House of Commons Lobby set (2005). YOUNG WINSTON © 1972, renewed 2000 Columbia Pictures Industries, Inc. All Rights Reserved—Courtesy of Columbia Pictures. Courtesy of John Graysmark.

of the raked stage floor, exactly matching where the black-and-white tiling of the real set floor would continue back in perspective. Two flats covered with 3M front projection material were also placed each side of the center image closer to the camera, allowing actors to enter the stage floor from behind "the foreground, projected architecture," camera-left and camera-right, and work between the rear backing piece and two front projection panels on the set.

Explanation: This technique, described in each of these three scenarios, was a viable solution to today's greenscreen process by providing a practical alternative to the challenges encountered on this production.

REAR PROJECTION AND MIRRORS

The *2001: A Space Odyssey* art department also employed some good examples of the rear projection technique. All of the graphics displayed in various monitors in the pod bay of the lunar shuttle set, as well as the activity in the windows of the lunar base miniatures, were mini-movies shot in 16mm for those smaller screens. The graphic geometry, animated by Doug Trumbull, Technical Graphic Animator, was shot for the 16mm rear projection monitors in these sets and seen as animations in real time within the larger screen.

> *And often, if we couldn't get the projectors to do a straight throw, we'd use mirrors to halve the distance and make the images work. The problem then was Stanley's consideration about what percentage of light was lost in the mirror reflection—all that photographic stuff was his game. Of course, he would go to the movie theater and read the light output directly from the projection screen. He was a mad perfectionist.*[12]

"Making pictures" as John learned it and refers to it was a total, artistic process from the drafting of Palladian quality plates, to the manipulation and shooting of carefully designed, built scenery. Because every piece of it was an artifact created with sublime effort, the quality of the film as a whole was elevated as an art form. Proper learning of movie craft was essential for the system to operate correctly.

> *The lords of the industry at the time in Hollywood's Golden Age, namely Alfred Junge who ran MGM-England and Cedric Gibbons who ran MGM-Hollywood, earned the right to occupy their places at the top of these studios. Today, the learning of film craft through a comprehensive guild system is sadly lacking. When you boil it all down, you're given the script and must figure how you present the best solution to tell the story cost effectively. The job of a properly trained art director is to use these tools to make the scenery work to interpret the script so the story can properly be told.*[13]

NOTES

1 Tiphaigne de la Roche, 1760. *Giphantie.* Paris (English translation, *Giphantia,* London, 1761). Retrieved from www.holonet.khm.de/Antizipation/Tiphaigne_de_la_Roche.html on October 1, 2004. The full translation of the book's section is as follows:

    That window, that vast horizon, those black clouds, that raging sea are all but a picture. You know that the rays of light, reflected from different bodies, form a picture, and paint the image reflected on all polished surfaces, for instance, on the retina of the eye, on water, and on glass. The elementary spirits have sought to fix these fleeting images; they have composed a subtle matter, very viscous and quick to harden and dry, by means of which a picture is formed in the twinkling of an eye. They coat a piece of glass with this matter and hold it in front of the objects they wish to paint. The first effect of this canvas is similar to that of a mirror; one sees there all objects near and far, the image of which light can transmit. But what a glass cannot do, the canvas by means of its viscous matter, retains the images. The mirror represents the objects faithfully but retains them not; our canvas shows them with the same exactness and retains them all. This impression of the image is instantaneous, and the canvas is immediately carried away into some dark place. An hour later the impression is dry, and you have a picture the more valuable in that it cannot be imitated by art or destroyed by time . . . The correctness of the drawing, the truth of the expression, the stronger or weaker strokes, the gradation of shades, the rules of perspective, all these we leave to nature, who with a sure and never erring hand, draws on our canvasses images which deceive the eye.

2 John Graysmark interview, April 5, 2004, Mar Vista, CA.

3 Ibid.

4 Pages 300–360 of the *American Cinematographer Manual,* 8th edition examine optical printing and traveling mattes in greater detail.

5 John Graysmark interview.

6 Ibid.

7 Retrieved November 10, 2004, from the Grant McCune Design website at www.gmdfx.com.

8 Quoted from conversation with Smokey Stover of Grant McCune Design, November 16, 2004, North Hollywood, CA.

9 Quoted from conversation with Jack Sessums of Sessums Engineering, November 17, 2004, North Hollywood, CA.

10 Note: 3M reflective materials are versatile and ubiquitous, seen on every road sign in any given city. This material was also used on the light-saber blades for the *Star Wars* films. The facets of three-sided, light-saber blades were covered with narrow strips of 3M reflective materials. The blade revolved in its handle at high speed. Once shot on film, the light reflecting off the rotating blades was later enhanced as "glowing" by Frank Van der Veer, rotoscope specialist, optical cinematographer, and photographic effects supervisor, at the ILM Studios for Lucas.

11 John Graysmark interview.

12 Ibid.

13 Ibid.

CHAPTER 7

CGI and Digital Filmmaking

If anything can be certain about the future, it is that the influence of technology, especially digital technology, will continue to grow and to profoundly change how we express ourselves, how we communicate with each other and how we perceive, think about and interact with our world. These "mediating technologies" are only in the first stages of their modern evolution; they are still crude, unwieldy, impersonalized, and poorly matched to the human needs of their users. Their fullest development in those terms is emerging as one of the principal technical and design challenges of the emerging information age.[1]

ROTOSCOPE

Max Fleischer was the inventor of rotoscoping—patented by him in 1917. His *Out of the Inkwell* series (1918–1929) demonstrated the new, simple technique of drawing onto live action footage on a frosted glass panel. His animation materials consisted of a projector, an easel, a glass pane, and an ink pen. His mastery produced Koko the Clown, Betty Boop, and Popeye. *Cartoon Factory* (1924) is a black and white animated short starring Koko the Clown engaging in a playful battle with his creator, Max, using the power of the ink pen. The short animation utilizes cut-out animation, traditional hand-drawn techniques, and live-action in the form of Max himself. The link provided here, http://aidyreviews.net/dave-max-fleischer-cartoon-factory/ exposes Max Fleischer as a genius, brilliantly marrying animation to live action, thereby taking the nascent animated art form to the next level.[2]

Seven decades later, Photoshop provided the next significant advance in the rotoscoping technique for two Richard Linklater films: *A Scanner Darkly* (2006) and *Waking Life* (2001). Film was shot on handheld Sony video cameras, then a team of illustrators washed stylized line and color over each frame, then the footage was uploaded onto Mac workstations. Animation was overseen by Austin artist Bob Sabiston, whose software allowed

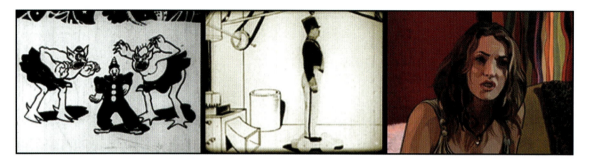

Figure 7.1   Rotoscoped characters: *KoKo the Clown* (1919), *Cartoon Factory* (1924), *A Scanner Darkly* (2006).

animators to use video images as a kind of sketchpad for drawing: a twenty-first-century rotoscope update. Instead of frosted glass plates, artists traced images directly onto live-action QuickTime video using Wacom tablets. One of the features Sabiston built into the application was **interpolation,** which meant that the artists didn't need to draw as many individual frames as they would have using traditional animation techniques. The software automatically **tweens** or fills in the transitions between the images. The paranoid scene from *A Scanner Darkly,* for example (www.youtube.com/watch?v=hhsbXxQ4tOc), demonstrates the fluid movement of the characters in the set. The video found at http://carliihde.deviantart.com/art/Animated-Rotoscope-Reaction-What-352889273 employs a different illustrative technique from an animated blog created by Carli Ihde. These updated rotoscope techniques firmly establish where we are at present. But, we're getting slightly ahead of ourselves chronologically. Let's slide backward three decades to examine a significant early advance in digital moviemaking

TRON

A lover of cinematic history can easily appreciate the efforts of those early visionaries who contributed to the digital moviemaking tradition now over 30 years old. Back in the late 1970s the Internet was referred to as ARPANET, Microsoft was still a fledgling company, and video games were found in experimental form, offered as Atari VCS and Mattel's Intellivision. In 1981, production designer Dean Mitzner (*1941, Nine to Five, Looker, Princess Daisy, The Man with One Red Shoe, Charmed*) had just begun his contribution to the fledgling visual effects revolution. His participation in *TRON* (1982), an animated/live-action Disney experiment, heralded a creative departure for him by its presentation of a bold design concept. In technical terms, it ventured beyond the marriage of traditional animation techniques and live-action in *Mary Poppins* (1964) by also including backlit animation to the mix. It was the first film to use CGI for its vehicles and in its action sequences, and involved the completion of more than 1,000 visual effects shots that required compositing on the average of 12 to 15 layers, or wedges, per frame. Each **wedge** presented a different light intensity: the background being the least intense and the

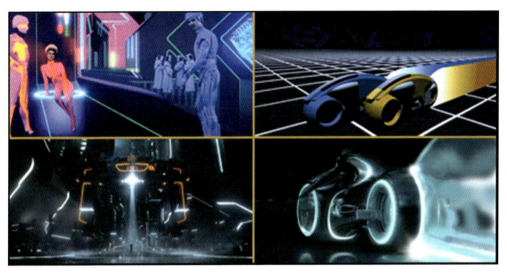

Figure 7.2 Visually compare these classics: *TRON* (1982) top images. *TRON: Legacy* (2012) bottom images.

helmeted faces sitting on the top layer, the most intense. In order to provide the most optimal, physical background for the actors in the live-action sequence shooting, Dean covered every inch of scenery with black-flocked paper, inadvertently giving the film a handmade quality—a cinematic paradox—successfully absorbing all ambient light and providing the perfect, non-reflective palette for Director, Steven Lisberger. *TRON* presented a vividly striking, minimalist beauty of its innovative scenic design. Nevertheless, the Academy of Motion Picture Arts and Sciences disqualified the film from being nominated that year for a deserved visual effects Oscar because it "cheated" by using computers. What an amusing thought!

Dean candidly admits to having felt somewhat in the dark at the time by designing scenery for a high-concept film cutting inroads into such uncharted territory.[3] Nevertheless, he can take full comfort in knowing that without his unshakable faith in the vision of his intrepid director and the solidness of his own talent, the success of this technical milestone and the subsequent trailblazing of other experiments such as *The Matrix*, *Lord of the Rings* trilogy, and even *Toy Story* would have never been possible. *TRON*, a precursor of next-generation, animated, live-action motion pictures, clearly predicted the direction of future—including Oscar wins.

MERGED MEDIA

Merged media converging in the new and improved art department is blurring titles, rewriting job descriptions, and re-establishing it as the crucible of all cinematic imagery. What was once done in optical houses after the fact is now performed as a matter of course

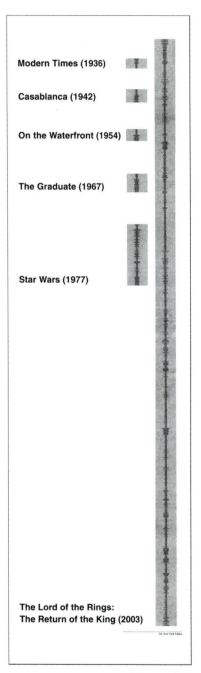

Modern Times (1936)

Casablanca (1942)

On the Waterfront (1954)

The Graduate (1967)

Star Wars (1977)

The Lord of the Rings:
The Return of the King (2003)

Figure 7.3 A comparison of the credit lists of six films from *Modern Times* (1936) to *Lord of the Rings: Return of the King* (2004). Courtesy of the New York Times: Baseline/Filmtracker and New Line Cinema.

by using pre-vis techniques at our work stations. Pre-vis and visual effects, now sub-departments of a greater conceptual dynamic, begin the process of design analysis and proactive certainty much earlier in the pre-production process with the Director and Production Designer. Combining all aspects of the analog and digital tools spectrum, they guarantee a richer visual product. The only downside is the length of the credit crawl at the end of today's digital films (See Figure 7.3). Otherwise, what is old is certainly new again. Many of the techniques of the digital cinema process rely on traditional methods of achieving the same effects within a "modern" context. The preceding chapter was methodical in its analysis of the tried-and-true, nuts-and-bolts techniques discussed. The conceptual ideas in this chapter will be presented in full interview format, either cited by face-to-face interviews when time and space permitted or by Internet interviews where time was short and space nonexistent.

Digital filmmaking has inadvertently done a good thing. By default, it has created a new playing field where designers are embracing the new technology and reclaiming visual control of the moviemaking process. Victor Martinez, conceptual designer, added his response to the question about the merging of traditional and digital techniques at an Art Directors Guild lecture and workshop held in the spring of 2003:

Now, there is no longer the notion of "mixed media," but rather, "cross-media." This implies that there is an active exchange of ideas through the use of different techniques (i.e., hand/analog versus computer/digital) and that this exchange produces work that transcends any original gesture by either hand or computer. It becomes about the design. More importantly, under such a process, the art department can engage more complicated design projects, whether technical, physical, or artistic, and bring more control back into the art department in terms of development of work most often reserved for post-production—and do so more efficiently and critically. That is how an efficient art department should be organized—it should take the best of what is already there and use digital tools to expand upon that foundation, and vice versa, allowing the art department to broaden its capabilities.[4]

Currently, there are a handful of designers who have done just that. Alex McDowell, whose interview follows, has forged a solid career as a digital production designer. Mavericks like McDowell have begun to cut serious inroads into the reorganization and redefinition of what the art department is and how it must operate at the center of the new paradigm. His successful hybrid status offers authority when addressing questions pertaining to his experience as a digital designer.

Formerly, the perception, understanding and language of digital technology for film production came largely from post-production and the visual effects department. That usage was applied only remotely to the new applications of these tools in pre-production. Although we—the design department and visual effects—are currently using many of the same tools, our use of digital technology in the art department has very specific applications and to a large extent a different organizational language. Despite this, a common, ongoing language is developing between departments to expedite the efficiency of the pre-production pipeline—this is where convergence is born and sustained.

CONVERSATIONS ON THE VISIONARY FRONTIER

Alex McDowell, Production Designer

(*Man of Steel, Watchmen, Charlie and the Chocolate Factory, The Cat in the Hat, Minority Report, The Lawnmower Man*)

Film technique is universal and easily applied to its industry operating in any country in the world. The international filmmakers I've had the great pleasure to work with practice their craft just as assiduously as anyone else, and once a film product filters through the Hollywood system in production or distribution, it loses its accent. The expansion of cinema iconography into the digital realm similarly defines no political boundaries. As we continue our discussion, the fact that the following section will focus on another, more recent production designer of English cinema culture, Alex McDowell, is purely coincidental. In this case, my connection to Alex is derived through American art department artists who have worked with him on the projects noted, and it exemplifies the organic process of film networking, and ultimately, of how this handbook was written. An ongoing Internet conversation with Alex has produced a continuous dialogue to be shared here. How fitting that the data explaining the philosophy of twenty-first-century cinema process was exchanged through cyberspace.

Let's begin with the digital art department: what is your philosophy about it?

Digital technology is opening up a growing wealth of new design resources for the film art department. Digital tools are more than just an extension of the design toolkit. Because the most sophisticated software is now available to the individual designer, not only is the art department able to explore the possibility of sets before they are built, but we are also providing accurate visual data to many departments, particularly visual effects. The look of sets that will not be fully realized until post-production can now be under discussion with the director and cinematographer in enough time to affect the development of the content of a film.

A sophisticated understanding of digital technology and a networked team of people using digital tools places the Production Designer back at the center of the flow of information that will determine and control the look of a film. For example, a large amount of the output from the *Minority Report* art department was focused on elements that would be built by the VFX houses, particularly ILM. In the past few years, as the idea of VFX really took hold, the designer took a back seat as VFX houses built up their own art department for CGI sequences. In contrast, not only were matte paintings and set extensions conceptualized within the art department, the designers also built all the key 3D elements and designed all the animations of the Hovership, Maglev vehicles, and traffic system, the Spyders, and the Hall of Containment sequence.

How do you implement the digital art department: the setup, the practical aspects of operation, etc.? What positions have been added/subtracted?

The digital aspects of the art department should be set up at the beginning of production, so that as the department expands each person plugs directly into the network, connected to one another through the server. This means that tech support from the production and within the art department is essential. I have found that on average it takes three to four weeks to set up the server and network, which means motivating production to set this in motion often before the art director is hired.

The digital art department is essentially straightforward to set up. Most office spaces that are offered up as art department space are already set up with an Ethernet network. A studio that is already using a network for accounting, for example, can assign part of that server space to the art department for archive, dropboxes, etc. Or an external hard drive can be plugged into an Ethernet network as a server.

The researcher and archivist scan images and archive them on the server to be accessible to concept artists as they start work. The locations department downloads all files to the same archive, where stitched images are stored by location and accessible to art directors and concept artists. Digital artwork overlaid onto location images is presented to the director, alongside research and concept art. The department starts to release a growing catalogue of images that portray an accurate picture of the director and designer's vision of the film, long before anything physical exists. The 3D set designers work alongside traditional set designers, often in tag teams. The 3D files are sent through dropboxes on the server to the concept artists, who lay lighting, textures, set dressing, and set extensions over an accurate lens view of a potential set. The 3D files are also sent to the pre-vis artists, who combine the set models with storyboard information to create animated sequences within virtual sets that the director can control.

There are some issues with using a PC-based server if the design team is mostly Mac-based, but these problems are regularly overcome. The important thing is to have good IT support within the production, and definitely to have a very savvy computer techie in the art department. Generally, this person is employed as high-tier PA, and will be crucial to the Archivist, setting up the digital art department, maintaining the server, and constantly updating all publication of design data and images to the server. That person will be constantly busy.

On a small film, what's more important—a server or a digital modeler?

The server. Even if your small film is only using a digital locations department, producing graphics digitally, or distributing storyboards, the server will increase the efficiency of the visual communication.

Do you consider power backup for your server in case of an emergency?

Power backup is definitely essential. Also a daily auto backup of the data isn't a bad idea.

Are online servers useful or not customizable enough?

There are a couple of problems with online servers. They are likely not to be large enough to support the equipment and data storage that are generated by a department whose stock-in-trade is high-resolution imagery. And there are often security issues—production offices are very reluctant to allow any kind of system that involves an outside agency, or one that can be accessed externally.

During the Post Digital Workshop hosted by the Art Directors Guild at the Panavision Screening Room in 2003, you used a graphic at the beginning of your PowerPoint presentation depicting the sphere or structure of the digital art department. This image directly corresponds to the paradigm of the "new" art department and how it is being reclaimed through technology.

Yes. But please note that this is a work in progress, and only hints at the complexity of the film production structure. It is a good way to look at the consolidation of the design departments into all aspects of production, and how new technology can and will alter the structure of production itself. It's already true that pre-vis and VFX are starting much earlier, and that the art department is actively involved in post-production planning, as well as driving design through to the end of post.

It is not noticeable at the moment that any positions are being dropped in the art department because of the increase in the use of digital technology. Certainly, there is a trend in both set design and concept design toward embracing these new tools, and I no longer work with any concept artist who does not use 2D or 3D software as well as pencil.

In set design, it's important to note, that although film is far behind architecture in its complete embracing of digital tools, there are good reasons for film design not to commit fully to CAD and 3D. The most successful design teams that I've worked with have been a 50/50 split between digital and analog. The traditional or analog draftpersons have a deep knowledge of film and theater craft that is often not reflected in the younger digital designers who are tending to come into the industry from architecture. But more to the point, film is unique in that it deals with the re-creation of history, and where digital tools might be appropriate across the board for a futuristic film, the pencil will probably always be more relevant for the design of period and decay.

The digital archivist is a position that we created and that developed out of the combination of research and the opportunity that a server provides to both store a huge database of images and make those images, including concept art, animation, location images, graphics, etc., accessible and available to all the departments. Currently, our archivist publishes new images and references to the server on a weekly basis where the whole crew can be updated with new material. The side product of this is that the crew is receiving a common set of images, leading to a much greater consistency on the look of the film.

What's the greatest argument an art director can make about the position of archivist as a vital member of the art department?

The argument is quite simple. Scanning and inputting research, concept, or location images onto a server that everyone can access saves equipment rental costs and printing costs, provided the server is properly administered by an archivist. Similarly, the digital storage of design imagery, plus data and images from many other departments, gives the producers a readily accessible archive in the post-production and marketing phases of a film. This is a completely new resource that in the past would not have been available, but is only possible if the data is constantly maintained and packaged into an accessible database by the archivist. This position is necessarily one that requires both a good visual background and an excellent knowledge of digital tools and a wide range of software.

Cite specific instances—with images—where this was clearly the case: The Lawnmower Man, Fight Club, Minority Report, *or* Charlie and the Chocolate Factory?

I have had the digital archive in place since 1998 when we set up the *Minority Report* art department. At that time I had a computer specialist and a researcher working hand in hand to provide a research/archive/tech support department that worked well. Since then I have tended to separate research from IT, which works equally well and allows me to use researchers who do not necessarily have extensive computer skills. For *Charlie and the Chocolate Factory* (2005), I had a good system with: 1) a researcher inputting to and updating the research archive; 2) all designers networked and constantly downloading new design work to the server where the research processes, prints, and archives; and 3) a locations department with their own digital unit for downloading, stitching, creating presentations, and archiving to the server. These days I show fewer and fewer images to the Director, because I can view the selection onscreen before any prints are made, and digitally we can create more easily a few shots at a high resolution that give a clear idea of a location.

It is important to note that, for each show, the art department has to set up and impose a clear file-naming protocol that each designer/user is responsible for maintaining with his/her own work. Otherwise the network will fall apart. This is as important as correctly labeling and distributing blueprints—an area that could be vastly improved through a digital system.

Your primary focus, then, is on hiring people adept at solving problems both traditionally and digitally?

The most effective crew I have found is one that balances the traditional skills with those adept at using state-of-the-art technology and tools. The individual draftsperson tends to specialize at one end of the spectrum or the other so the ideal for me is to tag team the pencil designer with the digital designer. The same applies to the combination of 2D and 3D—the 3D designer can be working in a complex, and therefore slower environment, while outputting 2D views that a 2D artist can take to a much higher resolution.

Are storyboard artists valuable to you?

I do a great deal of my design work with concept artists. They can render design ideas to a greater degree of accuracy and at a photo-real level. That makes discussion with director and crew much more informative than a rough sketch. Increasingly, the concept artists are either using a combination of 2D and 3D tools themselves, or they are working on top of specific views that are selected by the designer from 3D set design images or 3D files from pre-vis. These views represent a specific camera lens and position and give a director the most accurate view possible of a set not yet built, complete with atmosphere, lighting, color, and set dressing.

Storyboard artists are valuable because they are connected straight into the Director's back brain. Storyboards are a very effective way to interpret and break down a script. They tell us a great deal about the reality of shooting any complex sequence. But they are increasingly becoming a vital step toward a pre-vis model that can incorporate a narrative sequence into a 3D environment. Many 3D animation artists are as adept at the storytelling eye that a storyboard artist has traditionally provided. Both *The Terminal* and *Charlie and the Chocolate Factory* were driven by directors who felt constrained by storyboards; pre-vis was able in many sequences to replace a frame-by-frame approach with an environment that reflected the needs of the sequence without pinning the director down to specific action within the space.

Colin Green, of Pixel Liberation Front, shared the story of the "big shot" seen early on in the movie Panic Room *where, through the use of animatics, David Fincher and colleagues determined that the Gazelle crane would be the most expedient piece of equipment to navigate every aspect of that complicated shot. Is this what you're referring to? Can you cite a similar personal experience?*

There are a number of instances where we have used pre-vis to drive the production and design approach. In *Minority Report*, the scene where the Tom Cruise character is hiding from the Spyders in a seedy hotel was conceived as a single overhead shot from a crane. However, this required a large scope of travel—more than a conventional crane could feasibly handle. By building the imagined environment accurately in pre-vis—including crane, track, and camera body with specific lenses—we found that the shot was feasible using a Super Technocrane. The physical track was laid according to the pre-vis data, the shot rehearsed manually with grips following the pre-vis on a playback screen, and the highly complex sequence was achieved on the shoot day in four takes. This was not a VFX problem, but a physical one solved in camera by using a powerful digital tool.

On *Charlie and the Chocolate Factory*, pre-vis has been used in coordination with director, choreographer, and composer to lay out a complex dance sequence performed by CG characters in a physical set.

The Terminal set was built in pre-vis to allow the Director to test the limits of a space that was on camera for 80% of the film. The same data was taken to a higher and higher resolution as it was first used as the visual basis of a traditional painted backing, and then for the 3D animated environment as a composited background element.

Along these more technical lines, would you cite specific projects that clearly translate a historical technique like traveling or working matte processes with a digital solution? Perspective registration? Plate photography? Multi-camera moves?

I've used a couple of glass mattes and foreground (in-camera) miniatures in the past and enjoyed it. These days it's just not economical to have a camera set up for a couple of days in a setting while these traditional techniques are enacted. Historic theatrical techniques are being updated constantly. Glass mattes developed into rear projection that transitioned into 2D paintings as composites that are now 2½D and 3D miniatures; rather than disappearing, they are becoming fundamental elements tracked into camera moves or as composites. Still, whenever possible I would use old-fashioned theatrical tricks because the in-camera solution is almost always the most economical.

The most effective VFX work is always that which uses several techniques to solve the inherent problems. Mixing methodologies between sophisticated VFX and in-camera sleight-of-hand within a sequence is the best way to support the gag and impact the audience. The films I've worked on in the past few years are so strewn with effects solutions of every description that it's hard to pick out specific examples. The plane crash sequence in *Fight Club* (1999) is a classic use of combined live action and post effects, with motion-controlled camera, digital actors, live actors, physical set, set extension, and digital matte all combined in one sequence and planned to the millisecond and millimeter in previs. *Charlie and the Chocolate Factory* used every resource—traditional and state-of-the-art digital—in combination to solve a highly complex set of problems involving reduced scale Oompa Loompa characters in a live environment.

What do you expect from a digital art director?

I expect from any art director that they be open-minded, hardworking, creative, intelligent, and questioning. I do not use an art director specifically for digital elements, because I see it as a disadvantage to make a separation between digital and analog. We use the tools at our disposal, and at any time one tool may be more appropriate than another, even within the same set.

How can traditional art directors make a successful leap into digital filmmaking?

There is no such thing as a traditional art director. It is the particular job of an art director to stay current with filmmaking processes. Other designers in the art department can specialize in traditional film craft and the Production Designer can be a curmudgeonly Luddite, but the Art Director's job is to coordinate all aspects of the filmmaking design process with full peripheral vision. If an art director chooses to stay "traditional," then he or she is in denial of one of the basic truths of filmmaking: that it is an art that is constantly reinventing itself. Film as a young medium does not possess a traditional label at all.

To answer your question more specifically, I think an art director can usefully know the principles of digital technology without needing to use all available software, just as he can direct a construction department without having all the skills of a finish carpenter. By this I mean knowing what 2D and 3D design tools are capable of, and knowing enough of the language of these tools to be able to push their limits. One should always question the self-imposed limits of any technology, traditional or digital.

It is interesting to notice that as the digital tools become more ubiquitous, more universally based in 3D, there is a democratizing of the process that breaks down the artificial divisions between skillsets. When the lit and texture-mapped output from a set designer's 3D model looks just like the output of a concept artist's 3D rendering based on the same data (as was true of the images that we outputted for Steven Spielberg for *The Terminal*), it may be time to start hiring individuals for their specific skills rather than because they are labeled with a certain skill set. My approach now is rather to create interlocking design teams, comprised of a pencil designer, a 3D set designer, and a CAD designer, with a satellite 3D modeler and a 2D or 3D concept artist. This is a structural model closer to VFX than an art department but more appropriate to the tools available.

So, do you use pre-vis as a design tool or a pragmatic indicator?

I am the primary interface from my department with pre-vis. It is a design environment that I use more and more frequently to hammer out spatial problems. I'm increasingly comfortable working in a 3D space where the issues of that space are much more clearly defined. It is not only the 3D, but also the added elements of animation and space meeting time that I find liberating as a designer. This is the appropriate testing ground for film language. I often use pre-vis as a forum for discussion of lighting, visual effects, or special sequences with the appropriate keys. The place where narrative meets environment is a good place to chat with the director. Outside the design process once the pre-vis data is fairly fixed, it becomes an excellent tool to indicate production strategies, and is becoming the tool of choice for several departments.

How has your process as a designer been changed by comparing The Lawnmower Man *and* Minority Report, *e.g., a significant difference in approach or use of more developed technology to solve similar design problems?*

Basically, the more we experience, the wider the range of tools we stumble across and learn. Of course, the dramatic difference between *The Lawnmower Man* and *Minority Report,* other than budget, was the access to affordable digital tools that could be brought into the art department or accessed through outside vendors even in other industries. Seeing CNC tools produce a set like the pre-cog chamber cheaper than it could have been constructed by hand would have been a technology that we would likely have employed on *The Lawnmower Man,* had it been available.[5]

Colin Green: Pre-visualization Supervisor

(I, Robot, Van Helsing, Elf, The Matrix Revisited, Fight Club)

After you finished training at MIT, wasn't your early work based on the East Coast?

Starship Troopers (1997) was the contract that brought us out to Los Angeles, while we maintained a base office in New York City. During the course of that project, we realized that computer visualization service was something we could market and sell. A lot of people didn't even know what it was, thinking it was referring to storyboards. They didn't realize that it was three-dimensional, offering specific benefits to the process and saving money. Now we don't have to explain ourselves.

We have to build a digital version of everything you see in the movie in terms of the detail level and what the quality threshold will be. Part of the skillset in being a specialist in pre-visualization is figuring out what the important details are and then portraying them accurately. Often a director will be right there with us, but he expects what we're doing to be accurate enough for him to focus on other things. In terms of checking the accuracy of what we're showing people, we can usually do that with the art department, specifically the art director. The physical reality also needs to be checked so we will do a site survey and base the detail of our pre-vis on that.

As an art director, I would insist on providing you with both raw and specific site survey measurements previously taken by the set designers responsible for drawing up the physical scenery. Is that level of participation helpful or a hindrance?

Integrating set drawings in an efficient and accurate manner is one of the more difficult things to do. It is not a necessarily fast process. In addition, if drawings are coming from a CAD-based art department, the expectation is that the data will be used. The fact is the CAD files are not terribly user-friendly or compatible in our Softimage 3D environment, mainly because the way you might depict things in a CAD file is different from how you structure it in a 3D scene. So there's a good amount of boring legwork that goes into taking that information and turning it into a set. Keeping on top of the most current set of drawings generated in a given art department is slow, time-consuming, and definitely a challenge. We usually require one person from our staff to be focused just on keeping track of the up-to-the-minute changes. Sometimes, our process is generating the revisions. We'll be sitting with a director who is having a sightline problem through a doorway. He requests it to be widened, and we do it instantly. We then note the change and communicate it to the art director who follows through with the physical changes to the set. But once the request is made through our contact with the director, then it is our responsibility to track the change and keep on it until it's completed.

What do you require from an art director?

We require ground plans at ¼″ scale. After that we give our corresponding sets a simplified color scheme just to give our models a simple aesthetic.

Can you use photographic references provided by the art department as texture maps?

It is possible to take location stills and use them as texture maps for our pre-vis set, but often they are not necessary. A good amount of time goes into applying the map and making it work. Usually, it's problematic.

How are you budgeted?

On *Panic Room* (2002) there was a very long and elaborate pre-visualization phase that overlapped with the photography. We didn't stay on until the wrap of principal photography, but we did manage to finish sequences we were contracted to complete. After the design was built, we were busy doing what we called "rapid response" to explore requests from the Director, such as the removal of a wall and how it affected the sequencing. This impacted the cost, but unlike most departments, we didn't have a fixed budget. Usually these are discretionary costs requested by the Director, making the budget line we fit under a struggle for the accounting department. Similarly, a production designer might request the pre-vis process to happen, but there is often no money in the art department budget allocated to cover the cost for our services.

Is the transfer of data from computer hard drive to camera similar to the path from, say, a PC to a printer?

If only it were that easy. Yes, the digital aspect is flawless; then there are the physical aspects. The lens has to be nodalized. Then, once calibrated, the same kind of head has to be used every time. All working parts of the camera have to be physically adjusted to exactly match the digital data fed to the camera. If you think about when, in the early 1990s, we first started to explore the idea of doing camera moves on computer, then exporting them was, in a way, revolutionary. No one fully believed it could be possible.

It is interesting to see how the goal of pre-vis has changed over the years. Early on, the goal was to save money and be more efficient with shooting resources. And certainly, we did help with a lot of those things. Now, primarily we gave a director like David Fincher a tool to direct a better film. It was much more in the seminary of the cinematic process where we were able to make a contribution, rather than saving money on stage days, for example. The movie became a much higher expression of the level of directing David wanted from the process. He was able to make decisions with far better knowledge of what the limitations were. He had tried four different versions of it, knew how it fit and cut, and overall, had a total lock on what he was trying to do. We enhanced his ability to do that.

Panic Room was definitely an extreme case of a director being very focused on specific details and wanting to get things exactly right. Usually there is a car crash or similar stunt problem that needs to be solved; they bring us in to help figure out answers for those questions. It was also an extreme of how much we overlapped into shots that had no technical reason to be pre-visualized.

Who are you most likely to hire into your company, Pixel Liberation Front?

The basic things are solid, fundamental computer skills. A newcomer doesn't necessarily have to know the exact packages we are using. We would expect a person to know what QuickTime movies are, what Premiere does, what Photoshop is, and of course, have a thorough knowledge of the 3D modeling environment. On top of that, knowledge of filmmaking is important: composition and framing, camera moves, etc., that don't look like computer graphics skills but instead look like filmmaking skills. A lot of computer animating has a very marked aesthetic, but our focus is to simulate as closely as possible the filmmaking vernacular. Communication skills as far as understanding what someone is saying when they are describing a shot sequence are important, as well as being a high level communicator about creative things. Architecture school is good training as it encourages people to talk about the design process, which is vague, unfinished, and evolving. This can be translated into later conversations with a production designer or director. By restating in different words what has just been said, confidence is created about your understanding and ability as a communicator. If you can establish that trust through communication, then you're in good shape.[6]

Doug Chiang: Director of Concept Design, Visual Effects Art Director, Production Designer

(Star Wars: Episode I—The Phantom Menace and *Episode II—Attack of the Clones, Forrest Gump, Death Becomes Her, Ghost, The Polar Express)*

This Internet interview reveals the experience and thoughts of a real groundbreaking collaborator. Doug's work with Rick Carter, the "other" production designer of *The Polar Express,* brings the art of digitally captured live-action motion movies full circle, as it also explores their successful experimentation with 2½D. Animation links the beginnings of moving picture creation to its most current explorations in the illusion of moviemaking. The work of Doug and Rick signals a new synergy between a director and designer. It will be examined in the dialogue and analysis to follow:

Do you use pre-vis as a design tool or a pragmatic indicator?

Both. It's a powerful design tool mainly because of the speed in which you can see, in rough form, what the sets and action will be. It's also a great reality check to make sure that the designs can really work as planned—or not—or in some cases pointing out where we have to cheat to get the set design and shots the director wants. Pre-vis allows us to get this information as early as possible in the design process.

Have the pre-vis folks been absorbed within your larger art department as a sub-department?

The pre-vis artists are integrated into the rest of the art department—at least in the ones I've set up. I think it's important to have lots of crossover so people have multiple jobs and responsibilities. This is essential to make the art department more flexible and efficient. For example, on *The Polar Express* (2004), many of the pre-vis modelers were also very good designers so it really helped to have them build models while designing them at the same time. And likewise, the 2D designers could take the rough work from the pre-vis team and design right on top of that work. The design process went back and forth, and the lines between 2D and 3D were often blurred. That was the biggest difference between the *Polar* art department versus previous art departments that I've worked with. We were able to merge 2D and 3D design into one streamlined process.

Could you define the term "director of concept design?"

Basically, it's a variation on the production design credit. *Star Wars* was unique in that two distinct art departments were created to design the film. My primary role was to be in charge of the designs for the film including sets, characters, vehicles, environments, storyboards, etc., essentially everything a typical production designer would do with the exception of actually building the sets. My work started long before the production designer came on board and ended long after he left. It was just the nature of that *Star Wars* film, the design work started very early before there was a script and ended just weeks before the film's release.

How does The Polar Express *differ from any movie you've done thus far?*

The main difference for me was primarily in the art department. It was the first film where Rick Carter and I tried to merge 2D and 3D design, in essence making the 3D design process as efficient as 2D. This really simplified and sped up the overall design process, enabling us to integrate set designs with lighting design at a very early stage so Robert Zemeckis could see how his film could look even before he finished writing.

Would you go into some detail about working with another production designer, Rick Carter, i.e., benefits or downsides?

There were no downsides, only benefits. On a film like *The Polar Express*, it was necessary to divide up the work and attack it from our two diverse design backgrounds. *Polar* was also unique in that going into it we weren't really sure how we were going to do the film, both in terms of design and execution. It really challenged both of us, and I don't think it could've been designed any other way. We were a great team. We were able to combine our strengths to achieve something that had never been done before. You can look at *The Art of The Polar Express* to get more info if you like. The book was released November 2004 from Chronicle books.

What is your philosophy about the digital art department?

I believe it's the next step. Digital makes sense because filmmaking is changing and art departments need to be on the leading edge of that change. We are often the first people to visualize the written idea, and any tools that make that process more efficient are good. But this doesn't mean that the old tried-and-true methods will go away. On the contrary, I sincerely hope we never lose that real-world component to design. Nothing can replace a real, physical model. What will change is the process of how that model is made. I like to think that traditional model-building will always be an integral part of the art department just as quick sketches on napkins will never disappear. Digital art departments will be hybrids, combining the best of both worlds.

How will the art department look in a decade?

That's a tough question since it's hard to anticipate what technology and tools will be available by then. One thing that is certain is that the new tools will definitely make us more efficient. New tools have always allowed us to try different ideas quickly and modify things more efficiently. For example, with 3D prototype machines, future art departments will be able to quickly create 3D models in the computer and make "hard copies" of designs as quickly and as easily as it is now to make photocopies. That technology during our work on *Polar Express* was very expensive, but in ten years I'm sure it'll be commonplace.

Technology will always be very liberating and allow us to try more ideas. This will be the biggest difference—more ideas in a shorter amount of time. But the bottom line is that it'll still be up to the talent of each individual artist. They can never be replaced by technology. The positions will remain the same; only the tools will be different. Even in the past two years, I've noticed a radical shift from designers doing most of their work on the computer instead of with pencil and paper. However, what still matters are the ideas. Future art departments will have the ability to create and implement more, which will result in a higher level of work. It's always about the ideas and how we can get them from our mind's eye to the paper in front of us.

Thinking way out there, wouldn't it be wonderful if someday a tool could be invented that could take our mental image and put it out there for everyone else to see? Now that would be the future, since often it's too hard to depict what we see in our minds. But that's too much sci-fi, of course!

What positions have been added/subtracted?

From my perspective, it's more adding instead of subtracting positions. We still need solid set designers and model builders, only now we augment that with artists who are skilled at 3D modeling in the computer.

How does the digital art department directly borrow from traditional filmmaking?

The process is similar. The only difference is the tools. Instead of perhaps a traditional modeler, I use a CG Maya modeler to model the sets in the computer. However, I should note that even though we are a digital art department, I still think it's crucial to have practical card models made. Nothing can really replace a physical model that everyone can hold and study. The other advantage of building CG models is that often these sets are being produced digitally in post-production so the various post-production houses can use our models directly without having to completely rebuild them. This is obviously a big time- and cost-saver in addition to ensuring that what is finally built remains true to the original vision of the Director.

On a small film what's more important: a server or a digital modeler?

Digital modeler. I prefer good talent to equipment.

Do you consider power backup for your server in case of an emergency?

Not yet. We routinely back up daily. Someday, as demands force us to grow, a power backup would make ultimate sense. We don't use online servers since there are still problems with networking and security. All of which can be overcome, but to keep things simple and efficient, we don't. But that also could change very soon.[7]

CHROMAKEY: THE BASICS

What You Thought You Knew

There is some debate over which materials are acceptable for use as a greenscreen. Keeping this in mind, the first things to consider are size and use; the script will provide initial information but a good art director will apply fundamental greenscreen knowledge to specific requirements in all new situations. Use the spotting plan of where your set *must* be sitting on a designated stage to optimize the space. Understand that if your set includes a balcony, for instance, you will need 15–20 feet beyond the balcony perimeter to adequately light your balcony area and chromakey backing—the distance indicated allows little if no light spill between these two designated areas—no light spill is ideal for cinematography and keeping your relationship with the camera department intact and viable. Perform a quick check on site lines using the Camera Angle Projection technique discussed at the end of Chapter 4; then, you can operate with certainty. The practical truth is: an experienced lighting designer can "live with" less distance but this consideration should *only* be made if there is no other possible alternative to your existing studio space. Rule of thumb: keep the backing *at least* 20 feet from the perimeter of scenery at all costs. Also, having the conversation about chromakey issues with your lighting designer/cinematographer is smart and inclusive; no one likes surprises especially when everyone is running and gunning to get in and out of sets with little drama and finger-pointing. Furthermore, it's your job as art director to be practical about spotting plans for shooting multiple sets on the same large soundstage.

If your construction budget includes a backings line item, then pay the appropriate rental fees and have it delivered to stage for installation by the rigging grips. Many professionals will tell you that the color must be just the right shade of green, or that the screen must be made of certain material.

- *Don't assume that all chromakey backings are the same.* Again, a conversation with the visual effects or camera department will provide exactly the information needed to avoid misunderstanding and enable you to provide a specific backing product for a specific shot.
- *Do assume that fetching the greenscreen is your responsibility* (unless otherwise instructed).
- Make it your business to know what cameras/film stock will be used and to understand how the folks in pre-vis and camera expect to be working. Proactive designing and informed, practical action are good habits to develop early in one's career in order to achieve a total quality management style of working.

Fabric

There are some vital facts you should be aware of regarding chromakey material:

- For best results, this smooth plane of stretched material must be lit consistently—material too reflective creates lighter "hotspots" and is undesirable.
- A lighter, brighter green is better than dark green.
- Material which is crease-resistant is very desirable; wrinkles are the enemy. The chromakey material will likely be reused several times so it is important that it can be rolled to be transported without destroying the smoothness.
- Heavy material that is consistent in texture and color is preferred; however, it can be prone to more creasing.

Creases and wrinkles can be removed once the fabric is frame-stretched and in place by having the scenic artists Hudson spray the back of the chromakey with very hot water, or by using a professional quality fabric steamer, traditionally a set dressing kit item. In some rare cases, you might find yourself on an older soundstage containing a hard cyclorama, that is, a built chromakey wall that connects to the deck with a smooth curving cove, allowing chromakey paint to run from the top of the hard cyclorama wall down onto the floor. If the size is appropriate for your needs, then you've struck gold. Before painting, have the scenics fill/sand any blemishes to ensure the smoothest surface possible. Then, several coats of chromakey green paint will finish the task. Note: be sure that the set is placed at that magic 20 feet and you are ready to shoot a scene or two without having to ask other departments for assistance.

Alpha Channel: Using Chroma Key Footage

Having a basic grasp on the concept of what happens beyond the set up and shooting of a green screen provides a level of credibility to an art director who participates in digital filming discussions. The basic process of transforming a chroma key background to an alpha channel used in graphics and video editing/compositing is about transparency and substitution. An alpha channel can be thought of as a mask, matte or stencil, but it primarily defines the areas of an image which are transparent, acting as a placeholder for another image. The Adobe Creative Suite products are 32-bit graphics systems containing four 8-bit channels: one each for red, green, and blue, plus one alpha channel. Some applications use a 16-bit alpha channel. Once you have recorded your greenscreen footage you will obviously need to remove the green area of the image and replace it with your own background. Chromakeying is the name of this process which means selecting a chroma key color (green, in this example) and removing every instance of that color in the image. Any image placed "behind" this chroma key image then becomes visible. Exactly how you do a chroma key will depend on the editing software you use but the general process used by most applications goes like this:

1. Place the green screen footage on a layer in the timeline.
2. Place the footage or image to be used as the background on a layer below the green screen footage.
3. Add a greenscreen or chroma key effect to the top layer.
4. Select green as the color to use in the key.
5. After selecting the color, parts of the image will become transparent and you should see the background appear in these parts.

Low-Budget Films

Be aware that professional greenscreen material can be quite expensive, especially if you require a screen in excess of 70' wide by 18' high—typical dimensions are 100' wide by 20' high in most cases. For much smaller projects, corners can be cut *only* if you can provide all of the above parameters by using less expensive materials like rolls of photographic seamless paper. This material can easily be rigged with a few C-stands and crossbar piping, which the grips can provide, but this only works on a small scale. Otherwise, do a Web search for greenscreen material; numerous websites sell specialist material and with a little research you can find something to suit the needs of your specific project. This link might be helpful, www.mediacollege.com/video/special-effects/green-screen.

If you need to pack up the material for storage or moving, roll it rather than fold it—this helps reduce wrinkling. It's a good idea to use a cylindrical object with a diameter of at least 4–6″ to roll the material onto, like the heavy cardboard tubes used as the center of rolls for carpeting. Remember: your cleverness and practicality score high points if you can satisfy the basic needs of your VFX or camera colleagues.

Final Notes

- *Do not* use green objects in front of a greenscreen, or blue in front of a bluescreen; this includes graphics, props, vehicles, set dressing or wardrobe.
- As well as avoiding green or blue, you will probably notice that some colors and shades work better than others. For example, dark-colored clothes may create more of a green rim around foreground objects than light colors.
- In most studios there will be some variation in the screen color, no matter how hard you try to make it consistent. When selecting the key color, choose a part of the screen that best represents the overall color.
- Key parameters to adjust include *similarity* and *blending.* Experiment with these to see how they work. You will almost always have to adjust these to get a suitable effect.
- Note: Some software packages provide dedicated green- and bluescreen effects that may require the screen to be a very specific color.

MOCAP: THE CUTTING EDGE THRESHOLD

Motion capture—**mocap**—is a way to digitally record human movements. Mocap cameras record only the movement, not an image of an actor playing a scene for a feature film, animated film, television show, or video game. A physical, performance recording can be accomplished accordingly: an actor wears a spandex suit along with head cap for full body capture. These digital camera readings are fed into linked computers, where the data is recorded and interpreted into motion sequences. From there the recorded sequences can be imported into 3D animation programs such as 3D Studio Max, and then applied to character models by mapping recorded motion data onto key points defined on those 3D models. Think of this as digital rotoscoping or applying an image mesh onto the structure of a 3D armature. All recorded data can be monitored and played back in real-time. Captured data can be exported to various file formats. The system should be flexible and able to be configured to capture many kinds of objects and movements—perfect for computer games, film, and TV.

Goal of Motion Capture

The technical goal of motion capture is to collect the motion data of certain key points on the body of a subject, so that some parameters of the motion, e.g., speed, angle, distance, etc., can be calculated or the data can be used to control or drive something else. If parameters of the motion are calculated, the application may be motion analysis, sports analysis, biomechanics, biodynamics—Eadweard Muybridge would have appreciated the mechanical/

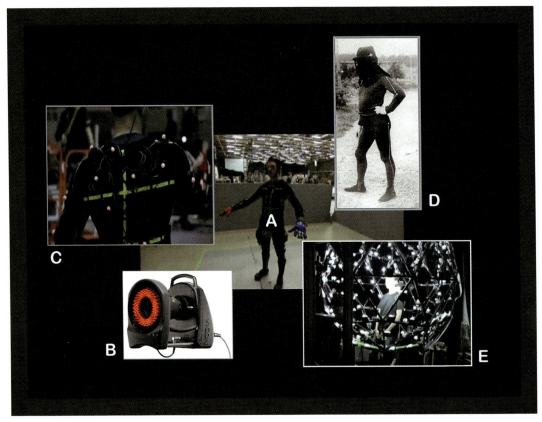

Figure 7.4   MOCAP Gear: (Center) A) Full body performance capture suit. (Lower left going clockwise), B) a Virtual Camera, C) Body suit back detail, D) Bodysuit photographed in motion studies by Etienne Marey over a century ago, E) Performance capture sphere.

scientific applications of human movement analyzed in this organizing application. If the data is used to control a machine, then the application may be tele-surgery, tele-robotics, or motion feedback control. If the data is used to control some displays or something else, then the application may be virtual reality, interactive games, virtual training, virtual rehabilitation, or motion directed music. If the data is used to drive a computer-generated character or scenery to mimic motion, then it is referred to as animation or VFX.

The Polar Express

What is particularly interesting regarding *The Polar Express* (2004) is the fact that there were no prohibitively expensive sets to build, no time-consuming lighting rigs to consider, or bulky heaps of camera equipment to grip to location. Most importantly, there was no film. There was only the story, the actor, and the director. Does this concept totally threaten the jobs of the traditional filmmaking population, reducing the size of film crews to a fraction of their current size? In this world of "no cinematography" per se, how do we see the unseen?

Mocap is the "threat" and solution. Yes, film crews will be impacted, but not particularly in size. Mocapographers are replacing on-set wardrobe assistants and camera crew, as they will outfit actors in form-fitted body suits and head caps, much like scuba gear, studded with tiny reflectors. They are also replacing on-set carpenters and set dressers by preparing and maintaining the "volume," or 10′ × 10′ × 10′ performance space, with a network of infrared sensors mounted to the interior surface of its structural, capture dome. This was certainly the case on *The Polar Express* set. The job titles may have changed, but it still takes a small army to create the product.

All movements of an actor within the parameter of *The Polar Express* performance space were reflected off the mocap suit and grid of 150-facial reflectors, and digitally recorded as points of light floating in a black volume of 3D virtual space. The performance capture infused the digital action with the believability of humanness. It then became the task of an army of digital artists to preserve the individuality of the actor, embedded within the cloud of the actor's motion, as they painstakingly connected the dots into the fabric of the storyline. *The Polar Express* laid an early foundation for the development of facial performance capture to this new paradigm.

The film pays homage to the book of the same name, written and illustrated by Chris Van Allsburg. The fundamental premise of the design collaborators, Doug Chiang and Rick Carter, was to keep visually true to the book by establishing a template based on the author's pastel and oil painted palette. Their solution was not about what the PC could do, nor about the best technique to overlay, but it was about seeing the visual template from the inside out. In other words, could the PC make the story true to itself? Interestingly, the original presentation of what was possible was grounded more in a tangible, emotional reality than an actual, visual metaphor as the larger picture of this experiment held "belief" as the nucleus of the story.

Technically, the process was quite simple. It happened in three general strokes:

1. The performance capture was saved in the computer hard drive.
2. Deconstruction.
3. Presentation of a theater-in-the-round type of experience.

In more specific terms, steps 2 and 3 were derived in Maya, where the 3D environment was comprised of three distinctly different scales: the adultscale, childscale, and elfscale. The 3D volume was quickly modeled from storyboards in lo-res, structural form and corresponding global lighting, as an underlay for the final painting. Lens choice, focal distance, and camera angles were determined next. Then set dressing and lighting based on the camera angles and nighttime light were specified. The final painting was applied to line up with the 3D image, completing the process all within a week's time, defining the 2½D landscape. (In essence, the final painting describes the basic process of rotoscoping.) Of course, this was the working template for the imagery in every scene; the final, overall working process totaled two and a half years. This 2½D journey deconstructed the illusion of space and the suspension of disbelief. It forced the participants to reconsider the question, "What is live action?" The answer was found somewhere between mocap and the PC's interpretation of our physical reality.

The greatest difficulties in the creation of *The Polar Express* were not in the technical challenges but "overcoming fear by having fun with doubt," honestly spoken by Rick Carter. In a 2004 tribute to Carter and Chiang sponsored by the Art Directors' Film Society, Rick also pointed out, "The production designer gets to be the first believer."[8] In his interpretation of his relationship with Robert Zemeckis, he asserted that the Director was the primary medium of the story being written. As Rick interacted with Robert Zemeckis, he realized he could not get in the way of the vision, but rather be a secondary medium for the story to express itself, unencumbered. In this way, the story pre-exists everything and before we can successfully perform our work, we must believe the reality of that world. The only way to do that is to trust in the truth of creativity and collaboration.

Avatar

In less than the span of a decade, the technology employed to create Pandora, the world inhabited by the Na'vi, far surpassed the digital work on *The Polar Express.* As a matter of fact, the necessary technology was not yet available to achieve James Cameron's vision of his film in 1994 upon completion of the treatment; Cameron began developing the screenplay and fictional universe of his game-changing film in early 2006. Production design for the film took several years. The film had two production designers, Rick Carter and Robert Stromberg, and two separate art departments, one of which focused on the flora and fauna of Pandora, and another that created human machines and conditions in the human world. The size and parameters of the performance/shooting space multiplied to a warehouse space large enough to contain a rainforest; the server farm required several **petabytes** of digital storage; and the crew expanded from hundreds to thousands. What followed was unprecedented.

Avatar is not an animated film. This is very clear—every nuance of the physical and emotional performance was created by the actors and recorded by performance capture devices. Mocap does not just capture motion but most importantly, the intent of the actor. Actors in this seminal film wore suits with markers and worked on the sound stage known as "The Volume" with hundreds of virtual cameras on the ceiling to record their performances. From this, the computer-captured, data-generated characters could be devised. Many of the creatures were roughed out on the performance capture stage. Puppeteering was a way to work out creature movements by manipulating the work of stunt people. Aerial craft and flying creatures were made as wireframe toys that a stunt person could carry and "fly" by manipulating with both hands, like children playing with toy planes, face-to-face in real time, as cameras recorded their movements.

In essence, *Avatar* took mocap and made it **performance capture.** The tight close-up is where the movie lives and breathes; dozens of handheld digital cameras captured the facial performances to ensure the careful recording of every muscular/emotional nuance—formally referred to as facial image-based performance capture technology. The main performance recording device—a small boom containing a camera, like a helmet mike—was created to image the face while the actor performed. This was the first time that real time performance capture was employed in a direct filmmaking sense. To help with this, the virtual camera was built to see in real-time what was being shot on the performance capture stage. On *Avatar*, it was used in three important stages:

1. Initially it was used to just look around in the scene; it's where the movie was art directed.
2. Next with the actors it was used to block the scene the same way a director would use his/her viewfinder—what is seen is the CGI character and the world it inhabits. It allows more flexibility on the virtual production stage than in a live-production shoot on a traditional soundstage.
3. Working with all the cameras for all the scenes. The virtual camera doesn't have a lens in the traditional sense; the performance captured is translated as 3D animation in the computer. It's as close to live action as one can get in a CG world.[9]

Where it Lands

Photography did not replace painting as some predicted. It has found its own place in the visual arts. We believe that motion capture is finding its own place in motion picture and interactive arts. Granted, mocap is a very fast and accurate way to bring human e-motion into a 3D computer animation, but it is not always the best way. Mocap technology exhibits its remarkable strengths for some projects while other methods, such as key-framing, work much better for some other projects. We all need to make sure that whichever the method we decide to use, that's the most effective method for the project.[10]

As provocative as Cameron's process of imagining-while-working seems, this same fundamental concept, takes us back to older theater days where there is one chair on a black box stage and everything that happens around the chair and the character is fully imagined by the actor and the audience—as evidenced in the eight-and-a-half-hour adaptation of Charles Dickens' novel *Nicholas Nickleby* (1981)—a world where everyone participates.

We can now view the art of motion pictures, examined in these last three chapters, as it progresses toward a future that is firmly rooted in and clearly defined by the past. Catapulting from the earliest visual effects attempts in Georges Méliès' *Voyage Dans La Lune* (1902) to the advanced motion-capture techniques of James Cameron's *Avatar* (2009), moviemaking continues to be the layering of dream upon dream, culminating in our current legacy of technology's digital presence.

NOTES

1 MIT: Media Lab Web site. Online source: *Program in Media Arts and Sciences, Massachusetts Institute of Technology—General Information for Applicants.* Retrieved from www.media.mit.edu/mas/index.html on April 10, 2004.

2 Check out the original article at Dave and Max Fleischer, "Cartoon Factory" Review, AIDY Reviews . . . , http://aidyreviews.net/dave-max-fleischer-cartoon-factory/#ixzz2d8WIeoqT.

3 Art Directors' Film Society tribute to Dean Mitzner: *"TRON:* Production Design and the Next Generation of Animated, Live/Action" presented June 6, 2004 at the Directors' Guild, Los Angeles, CA.

4 Art Directors Guild workshop, "Post Digital: The Redesign of Pre-Production Through the Digital Art Department" held on Saturday, April 5, 2003 at Panavision, Woodland Hills, CA. Victor Martinez, one of six panel participants is quoted here.

5 Alex McDowell Internet interview, October 19, 2004, from his location at Pinewood Studios, UK.

6 Colin Green interview, September 13, 2004, Burbank, CA.

7 Doug Chiang interview, retrieved from the World Wide Web on October 15, 2004.

8 Art Directors' Film Society tribute to Rick Carter and Doug Chang: *"The Polar Express:* The Production Designer Comes Full Circle" presented December 5, 2004 at the Directors' Guild, Los Angeles, CA.

9 Retrieved from YouTube: *"Avatar* Featurette: Performance Capture", August 18, 2013, www.youtube.com/watch?v=OJ1JzYPjcj0.

10 "MoCap for Artists: Workflow and Techniques for Motion Capture," Midori Kitagawa and Brian Windsor. Amsterdam: Focal Press, 2008, p. xiii.

Production and Post-Production Processes

CHAPTER 8

Navigating Paperwork and Daily Shooting-Process Tasks

PRODUCTION OFFICE "PAPER"

Film production companies generate stacks of paper during the activity of delivering a film product to the Studio. Script revisions run the gamut of white, blue, pink, yellow, green, goldenrod, buff, salmon, cherry, tan, gray, and ivory. The remainder takes the shape of contracts, forms, lists, and memos. The good news is most production companies provide large recycling bins for the waste. Technology has, for some unexplained reason, increased the volume of paper, not lessened it. I've recently managed to reduce the number of one-inch binders I fill to one; I rely on the laptop, iPhone, and iPad to hold the bulk of the data for easy retrieval, with a fraction of the weight or guilt. If you are serious about doing this work, you might want to consider this or develop a similar system of data entry and rapid retrieval. It will save time—and ultimately, forests.

THE ONSET OF PRINCIPAL PHOTOGRAPHY ON A FEATURE FILM

Production Meeting

The final production meeting is a formal, well-structured event held at the end of the pre-production phase—a day or two before the onset of principal photography. The First Assistant Director 1st A.D. presides over the meeting. It is well publicized and requires the mandatory presence of all department heads and their assistants. The meeting opens with brief, round table introductions; then it proceeds directly to an item-by-item review of the **one-liner schedule** and **shooting schedule,** highlighted in Figures 8.5 and 8.6. The bulk of this three- to four-hour meeting is focused on:

1. Giving general clarification and commentary on the shooting schedule and providing detailed answers to the items specified on it.
2. Updates from various departments.
3. Production office news and information pertaining to subsequent first day of principal photography.

Additional in-depth conversations are inevitable and become sidebar, or post-meeting discussions, extending the time away from all participant's daily routines well into the afternoon. As a result, everyone is asked to make his or her questions, comments, and information as brief as possible. The tone and efficiency of the final production meeting is a good indication of the swift and efficient working style of the 1st AD. During this meeting, she/he assumes responsibility for the organization of the shooting schedule, the shooting crew, and commits to the timeline of delivering the film on time.

THE SCHEDULES AND LISTS

The following schedules and lists seem repetitive but have different purposes and will be discussed in more detail in the following pages. They are created by the assistant directing staff (first AD, second AD, and second second AD), reviewed by the 1st AD and UPM, and distributed by the production office into designated organized cubbies or manila pouches affixed to a production office wall. In addition, this same hard copy information is digitally distributed to everyone on the production crew by the production office staff.

Script Breakdown

The scenes called out in the script are transformed into a list of built and digital sets for shooting. This sequential process of text to sets looks like Figure 8.1. The pivotal item in this sequence is the set or design breakdown (Figure 8.2), generated by the Art Director,

Script Text > *Script Breakdown* > *Set List* > *Budget* > *Sets*

Figure 8.1   Progress from text to sets

"My Fellow Americans" Design breakdown				last modified: 3/20/96	

Script Date: March 8, 1996	Director: Peter Segal		Production Designer: Jim Bissell	
Producer: Warner Bros.	Michael Ewing Jean Higgins		Production number:	
			Page number: 5	

Set #:	Loc:	Type:	Set Description:	To be Designed:
434	Asheville	Ext	Hollis Farmhouse	

A.D.: Michael Rizzo   **Shoot Date:**   6/8/96

Set Des: **Design Completion Date:**

435	Asheville	Int	Hollis Horsebarn-night	

A.D.: Michael Rizzo   **Shoot Date:**   6/8/96

Set Des: **Design Completion Date:**

436	Asheville	Ext	Maryland Road-Day	

A.D.: Gae Buckley   **Shoot Date:**

Set Des: **Design Completion Date:**

438	Asheville	Ext	White House Kennedy Garden	Design and build

A.D.: Michael Rizzo   **Shoot Date:**   5/15/96

Set Des: **Design Completion Date:** 4/1/96

441	Asheville	Int	Witnaur's bedroom	

A.D.: Michael Rizzo   **Shoot Date:**   6/2/96

Set Des: **Design Completion Date:**

444	Asheville	Int	Wayne & Genny's Trailer-night	Int. Trailer Set

A.D.: Michael Rizzo   **Shoot Date:**   5/22/96

Set Des: **Design Completion Date:** 4/5/96

445	Asheville	Ext	White House S.W. lawn	White House Facade

A.D.:   **Shoot Date:**   5/17/96

Set Des: **Design Completion Date:** 4/1/96

445	Asheville	Ext	White House Southwest Lawn	

A.D.:   **Shoot Date:**   5/15/96

Set Des: **Design Completion Date:** 4/1/96

Figure 8.2   Typical Set Breakdown page organized by Jim Bissell, Production Designer, *My Fellow Americans.*

providing essential data for each set, derived from every scene in the script. From this small, encapsulated version of vital information, the set list and corresponding construction budgets are developed. Of course, the format for any of these lists is dependent upon which text-generating software is used; this is not as important as what information is included. Every art director has his/her own organizing quirks. Christa Munro explains hers:

Interview with Christa Munro

After having made the first pass through the script, the creative process begins in your imagination. At this point, how do you begin to translate the text into imagery? I have a little trick I learned from Gene Rudolf, visual consultant and art director (*Raging Bull, The Right Stuff, Diner*). I repunch the holes of my script so that the backs of the script pages are on the left side of my binder when the book is open. When I read through the script on my first pass, I can scribble my first impressions on the clean backside of the next page. That way, the script, my initial ideas, and my notes are all in the same binder. The first pass is just my "dreaming." I realize the production designer might have something completely different in mind, but this will contribute somewhere down the line and also helps me know if I'm on the right track. After that, I do my set breakdown, and then I keep distilling it. That completes the first set breakdown. I add other elements later on. This is the best way I know to organize my thoughts.[1]

Personally, I prefer to use both the list and per page items in order to comprehensively cross-reference and double-check the data. These lists are only effective if they are updated on a daily basis. You can design set breakdown item pages in Microsoft Word, however, in preparing the set list for construction estimate or budget breakdown (Figure 8.4), I've found the Microsoft Excel to be indispensable because each page of a typical document is set up as a table by default, allowing automatic subtotals to be generated as item costs are entered. Figure 8.3, shown as "set list," was created in FileMaker Pro—an older, more cumbersome software. Rule of thumb: Choose a software format that is universally compatible but supports your comfort level.

One-Liner Schedule

As you can see, the one-liner Schedule (see Figure 8.5) is very straightforward and self-explanatory, as a shorthand version of the longer, more detailed shooting schedule, by distilling the information down to: shoot day number, date, scene number, single-line scene description, scene time of day (day, night, etc.), scene location type (interior, exterior), location place (stage description or location description), and number of pages to be shot (noted by eighth of a page increments, e.g., 2 5/8 pages).

Set #:	Loc:	Type:	Set Description:	Scene Numbers:

"My Fellow Americans" Set List — last modified: 3/17/96

Script Date: February 19, 1996
Director: Peter Segal
Production Designer: Jim Bissell
Producer: Warner Brothers
Michael Ewing / Jean Higgins
Production number:
Page number: 4

Set #:	Loc:	Type:	Set Description:	Scene Numbers:
301	Wash	Int	Kramer's Limo-day	39,41
302	White House	Ext	White House-establishing shots	21,47,200
303	Wash.	Ext	Wasington Street	39
305	Wash	Ext	Union Station	56
306	Wash	Ext	Street/Union Station	57,58,59,60,61,62
308	Wash	Ext	White House roof	229,330,238,242
309	Wash	Ext	Street-Wal and Talk	46
310	Wash	Int	Reynolds' Outer Office	42
311	Wash	Int	Reynolds' Office	43,45,49
312	Wash	Int	Office building corridor/Elevator bank	44
313	Wash	Ext	The Mall-Washington -Morning	147,148
314	Wash	Ext	Street bordering White House	234
317	Wash	Ext	White House West Wing	234a

Figure 8.3 Typical Design Breakdown page organized by Jim Bissell, Production Designer, *My Fellow Americans*.

"My Fellow Americans" Construction Estimate				Last modified	3/16/96		
Script Date: March 8, 1996			Director: Peter Segal		Production Designer: Jim Bissell		
Producer: Warner bros.			Michael Ewing Jean Higgins	Production number:			
				Page number: 4			
Set #:	Loc:	Type:	Set Description:	Const. Estimate	Sign Estimate	Greens Estimate
309	Wash	Ext	Street-Wal and Talk	$0.00	$0.00	$0.00
310	Wash	Int	Reynolds' Outer Office	$0.00	$0.00	$0.00
311	Wash	Int	Reynolds' Office	$0.00	$1,500.00	$2,000.00
312	Wash	Int	Office building corridor/Elevator bank	$0.00	$0.00	$0.00
313	Wash	Ext	The Mall-Washington -Morning	$0.00	$1,000.00	$1,000.00
314	Wash	Ext	Street bordering White House	$0.00	$1,500.00	$5,000.00
317	Wash	Ext	White House West Wing	$5,000.00	$0.00	$0.00
401	Ashevill	Ext	Private Runway	$0.00	$0.00	$0.00
402	Ashevill	Ext	Funeral/Cemetery-D	$3,000.00	$2,000.00	$3,000.00
403	Ashevill	Ext	Baseball Field	$0.00	$0.00	$5,000.00
404	Ashevill	Ext	Another wooded clearing-explosion	$3,000.00	$0.00	$2,000.00
405	Ashevill	Int	Train Station Restroom	$18,000.00	$2,000.00	$0.00
406	Ashevill	Int	Train Car	$3,000.00	$3,000.00	$0.00
407	Ashevill	Int/Ext	Small town train station-night	$15,000.00	$1,500.00	$1,000.00
408	Ashevill	Ext	Another Train station platform	$30,000.00	$2,000.00	$1,000.00

Figure 8.4   Typical Construction Estimate page organized by Jim Bissell, Production Designer, *My Fellow Americans* .

```
                              "My Fellow Americans"                    Page 13
                                 ONLINE SCHEDULE                   Wed, May 1, 1996
                                                                     10:34 PM
              _____
                         End Day #36 -- Total Pages: 2 4/8
              _____


     Shoot Day #37 -- Wed, May 15, 1996
     _____
     Scs. 6              INT   Century Plaza - Backstage            NIGHT    4/8 pgs.
                               Haney prepares to go on stage for his victory speech
                               ID 3, 4, 5, 81
                               _____
        Biltmore Hotel              Pete's Sequence Name:  Cold Opening

     Scs. 20,22pt         EXT   Arlington Cemetery                  DAY      5/8 pgs.
                               Matt and Kramer continue their discussions; Matthews gives his eulogy
                               ID 1, 2, 5, 18, 19, 35, 36
                               _____
        Biltmore House,             Pete's Sequence Name:  Cemetery
        Asheville,North Carolina
              _____
                         End Day #37 -- Total Pages:  1 1/8
              _____


     Shoot Day #38 -- Thu, May 16, 1996
     _____
     Scs. 214pt           EXT   White House South Lawn              DAY      2/8 pgs.
                               Haney at reception; Tanner gets call
                               ID 3, 7
        Biltmore Estate, North Carolir  Pete's Sequence Name:  Guest Quarters

     Scs. 235             EXT   White House South Lawn              DAY      1/8 pgs.
                               Haney speaking at ceremony
                               ID 3, 26, 27
        Biltmore Estate, North Carolir  Pete's Sequence Name:  Horse Race

     Scs. 243             EXT   White House South Lawn              DAY      3/8 pgs.
                               Matt and Kramer arrive at ceremony; Ask to speak to Haney
                               ID 1, 2, 3, 26, 27, 100, 101, 102
        Biltmore Estate, North Carolir  Pete's Sequence Name:  Horse Race

     Scs. 227             EXT   White House Gate House              DAY      3/8 pgs.
                               Tanner spots the boys riding away; They give chase
                               ID 1, 2, 7, 8, 100, 101, 102, 111
        Biltmore Estate, North Carolir  Pete's Sequence Name:  White House Gate

     Scs. 228pt           EXT   White House Northeast Lawn          DAY      1/8 pgs.
                               Presidents riding across lawn
                               ID 100, 101, 102
        Biltmore Estate, North Carolir  Pete's Sequence Name:  Horse Race
              _____
                         End Day #38 -- Total Pages:  1 2/8
              _____


     Shoot Day #39 -- Fri, May 17, 1996
     _____
     Scs. 248             EXT   White House                         DAY      2 1/8 pgs
                               Matt tells Kramer that he taped the conversation
                               ID 1, 2, 18, 19, 23, 35
        Biltmore Estate, North Carolir  Pete's Sequence Name:  White House Drive
```

Figure 8.5   Typical One-Liner page authored by the Assistant Director's team for *My Fellow Americans.*

Shooting Schedule

This is the master list for the shooting process (Figure 8.6), compiled by the Unit Production Manager and 1st AD, but ultimately the responsibility of the latter. It is generated from the script breakdown of scenes into information items such as day, night, interior, exterior, scene name, scene description, and shooting location. It further distills the script down into workable, daily units of shooting: total number of scenes and corresponding scene numbers, and total number of pages of script to be covered. For example, each day of the shooting schedule has a number, i.e. Shoot Day #15 and on that particular day specific scenes are scheduled to be shot based on script requirements, logical sequencing, and actor availability. Cast required for that day are listed as principles, stand-ins, and atmosphere (atmos) or background/crowd people. Additional data is provided to each department, where necessary, indicating special equipment, special effects, specific hero props, costuming, set dressing, scenery pieces, or even special painting notes, i.e., "light aging on hero car." The shooting schedule is updated when significant changes occur because it acts as everyone's "shooting bible" for the duration of the production phase of filmmaking.

Figure 8.6 shows an additional version of the shooting schedule plotted on a calendar page. This example tracks art director, shooting crew, and actor movement to and from distant locations, as well as set prep and how many days a specific set is scheduled to play. The calendar page version of the shooting schedule can also be found on the walls of the art department. There, large-scale calendar pages are similarly color-coded with Post-It notes to easily track the same items mentioned above. (Sadly, the color coding is not shown here but is presented in black and white.) Again, this data is also repeated on smartphone screen readouts and iPads.

Day Out of Days

The "day out of days" chart almost always pertains to actor working schedules. It is significant for an art director to use as a guide for special equipment—such as boats, vehicles, planes, or other craft—on pictures that specify their continuous use. This is a particularly good tool for refining "hero detailing" in conjunction with the shooting schedule so that no item is forgotten.

Call Sheet

The call sheet is a daily reminder of expectations and activities, planned for the shooting crew and remains the responsibility of the Second AD. It includes scenes to be shot that day, the weather forecast, and shooting location, and also lists by department all crew and actors either needed on set or expected to be on stand-by during various times of the day. It is the final, printed, daily version of the more general shooting schedule previously distributed, and it demands drop-dead, faithful commitment from all crewmembers. The actual signature of the 1st AD on this sheet confirms the data, and it signals to the

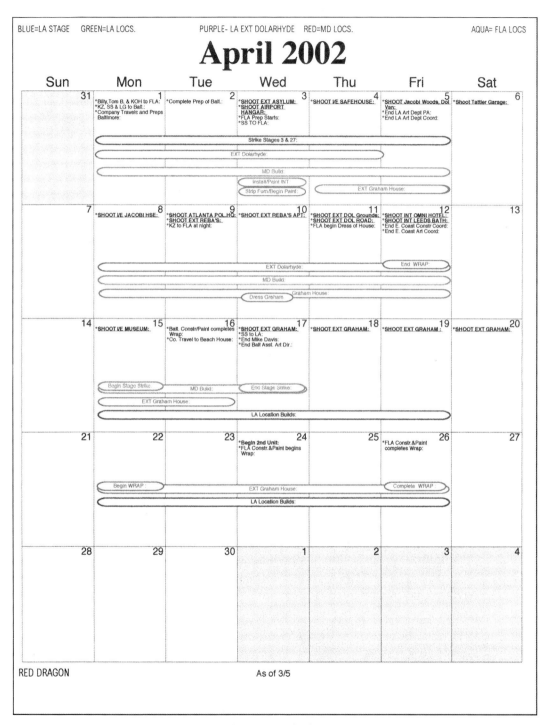

Figure 8.6   Typical Shooting Schedule calendar page 3 of 5 from *Red Dragon*. Courtesy of Steve Saklad, Art Director.

accounting department and the studio the budget expenditure for that particular day of shooting. Now, the process has become serious business.

Crew List

All company and crewmembers' names, addresses, office phone extensions, smartphone numbers and email addresses are compiled on this extensive list and organized by department. The list is arranged hierarchically beginning with department heads and ending with assistant crewmembers; it is the precursor of the final crew list distributed by the production office at wrap.

DIRECTOR'S PLANS

The art department PA photocopies, collates, and delivers every set scheduled to be shot from its original 24″ × 36″ blueprinted format (typical) onto an 11″ × 17″, three-hole paper format. A small booklet of plans is distributed to all key people in the production office, shooting crew, and art department who need access to the footprint of every location and onstage studio set. Final distribution of the director's plans packet happens at the final production meeting. For those who prefer digital files, the art department office PA provides the same data electronically via the server.

Figures 8.7 and 8.8 display how various aspects of a typical director's plans are drawn for use. As shown, several generations of the same location sets are combined in the overall packet to provide more specific information. You can never provide too much detail or too much seemingly insignificant information. The minutiae will always fill in the gaps somewhere for someone.

ART DEPARTMENT PRODUCTION TASKS

The first day of principal photography marks the first day of the production or shooting process, typically ranging from 60 to 70 days, but at times extending to a year or two. It is a time when the camera stops only at scheduled intervals like national holidays and for emergencies. Otherwise, the course of the film is relentlessly driven by the shooting schedule and First Assistant Director.

Clearances and Product Placement

A product placement and clearance coordinator employed in the production office, or the parent film studio, or from an independent company must clear any likeness, individual name, business name, telephone number, license plate number, street addresses, actual product depiction, signage, or item of set dressing or clothing placed in front of the camera displaying a logo, graphic, or icon for use on a particular film project. If this clearance is not sought or if the process is not effective, lawsuits are not unlikely.

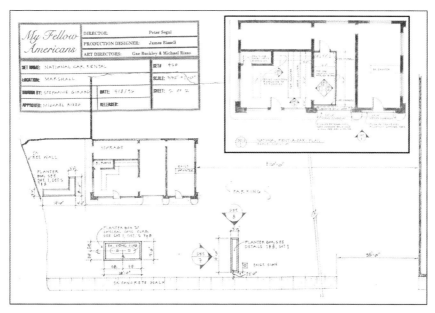

Figure 8.7 Director's plan-A: Site plan of car rental agency drawn by Stephanie Girard with inset: Location set plan. MY FELLOW AMERICANS © 1996 Warner Bros., a division of Time Warner Entertainment Company, L.P. Licensed by Warner Bros. Entertainment Inc. All rights reserved.

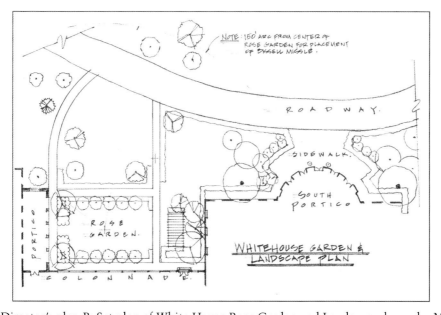

Figure 8.8 Director's plan-B: Set plan of White House Rose Garden and Landscape drawn by Michael Rizzo. MY FELLOW AMERICANS © 1996 Warner Bros., a division of Time Warner Entertainment Company, L.P. All Rights Reserved.

Although placing a can of Coke as set dressing in a kitchen set is actually free advertising, the Coca-Cola company reserves the right to know how the product is displayed. It also needs to be assured that its product is not used in a way that will defame it or show it in a negative way. The Art Director should be actively involved with a product placement/clearance person by supervising important hero items mentioned above, in order to carefully control details in a timely manner before any special content is shot. Wrong information can create a damage control situation that can easily turn into a nightmare if not properly handled.

Keeping Ahead of the Camera

Once the camera begins to roll, it remains faithful to its relentless shooting schedule. During the shoot, focus is on the set. It is the job of the Art Director to remain far ahead of the shooting timeline while supplying the daily needs of the shooting crew in terms of scenery or special props and effects listed on the daily call sheet. The goal is to make the shoot as smooth as possible despite unexpected changes or events that will occur. This goal can only be attained if a solid, pre-production strategy is in place and is continuously monitored and adjusted as needed. Communication is the key to resolving any issue. Here are some helpful suggestions for exercising that skill.

On-Set Presence

During the shoot, an art director's task list becomes longer as the length of the day remains the same. The shorthand communication already established within your working relationships during the pre-production phase becomes an asset in getting the expanding job done. Smartphones as prime communicating devices enhance the speed of receiving and exchanging of information. While art directing on *Vanilla Sky* (2001), we were first introduced to the newest line of Nextel™ cell phone/walkie-talkies—they were everywhere in the 1990s and started our industry's addiction to instantaneous communication. Presently, our incredibly fast, lightweight handheld devices fulfill that need. Speed is expected during the filming process; it counterbalances the weight of the growing list.

An art director is in many places throughout the day. During production, the rhythm of the "daily routine" adjusts to accommodate the needs of the shooting crew—but more importantly, to stay ahead of it. Before anything can be accomplished during the day, the set needs attention. Awake at 5:00 am and on set by 6:00 am, the Art Director begins the day with the art department crew to discuss any last-minute questions for scenic requirements for either later that day or short-range considerations for the rest of that week. Details are constantly in flux and in need of modification and fine-tuning; on-set dresser, greensman, and on-set painter are constantly with the shooting crew with no time to leave the set. Supplying the physical and emotional needs of your on-set people, especially on location, is important. Spending time with the on-set art crew also allows time to get a sense of how they are relating to the rest of the shooting crew and vice versa. Often, misunderstandings between departments result from vague definitions about who will actually deliver what to the camera on smaller productions with less experienced crew. Guidance from an art director can often help resolve the issue at hand. The intensity of the work requires special attention to conflicts and productive relationships by being specific and clarifying on-set responsibilities, resolving issues, and encouraging onset harmony.

Opening a new set with the Production Designer and Director is a welcomed ritual. It signifies the culmination of another job well done by the entire art department. This event happens well before call time the day the new set is scheduled for shooting. Those involved do a **walk-through** to point out pertinent details and scripted features in the set. The Director or First AD delivers last minute notes with the on-set crew in earshot; the Art Director gives further instruction to hasten the process. The trick is to be the first group to receive notes so that tasks can be completed while other departments are receiving their instructions. The experience and skill of your on-set crew helps to make impromptu challenges like this effortless. Once notes are completed, the Art Director is free to visit the catering truck for a quick breakfast. It is time to take a moment to relax and wait for the shooting crew to get the first shot off. Again, "first time" sets need much attention until the first scene is in the can to assure a smooth, continued process for that day.

Walking over to a standing set and physically checking it over is a good idea. Actively looking for discrepancies with working parts of the set—i.e., doors, windows, and built-in special effects sections—might avert potential problems. Scenery suffering the effects of extended use might need minor repairs or touch-up paint overlooked during a demanding shooting schedule. Expensive or irreplaceable set dressing should also be examined or noted as missing in action, as well as other conditions around the set like dangling lighting instruments, poorly hung backings, and other accidents waiting to happen. Nothing is too obvious to be overlooked or triple-checked.

After watching the completion of the first scene during setup for the next shot, quick informational exchanges with other on-set departments enhances thorough communication. There are often details or changes gathered from on-set crewmembers that happen before there is a formal notice on a call sheet. A conversation-in-passing with a director's personal assistant, for example, might provide a significant heads-up and require further investigation. No one's participation is too obvious to be overlooked or used to get a jump on new changes—everyone on the set is a wealth of information.

Talk directly to the directorial staff to get advance reports on any formal, upcoming changes and double-check any on-set rumors. The production office, location department, and the directorial staff monitor weather forecasts throughout the day. Need for cover sets is directly dependent on that incoming data. Finding oneself out of the loop belies sloppy communication and on-set networking skills—entertaining "surprise" is not an acceptable work skill. A daily check-in with the 2nd AD over hot coffee and a breakfast burrito is a habit worth developing. Being a great communicator ensures good PR both on the set and with production.

If there are no pressing issues for an art director in the construction mill, in the art department, or on a location being prepped, remaining on the set throughout the day ensures art department presence and staying fully within the loop. Participation in various interdepartmental meetings including set decorating, mechanical effects, visual effects, and production office considerations can be done on a conferenced Skype or FaceTime call, or on a hot set in a standing set or the **feeding tent,** if necessary. Otherwise, the late morning is spent running to location(s) to view building progress or double-checking details or solving problems, digitally photographing the progress, and helping solve PR problems that might have arisen between the location point-person and the activity of the construction crew. Wi-Fi service, where available, allows easy email access for sending scenery progress images; on location, the production trailer or AD trailer will always have a strong Wi-Fi signal. In addition to emailing set photos, smartphone connectivity enables the completion of current paperwork, the double- and triple-checking of schedules relating to the construction building schedule, reviewing the next day's agenda, and keeping up with vendors and subcontractors' progress and delivery timelines.

Leaving the set in early afternoon might require a return to the mill to check on set construction progress or to solve additional problems in person by talking through changes in scenery design and modification. A quick call to a set designer relays those changes or alerts that draftsman to emergency adjustments to be made to ¼" scale plans or elevations for the designer's new meeting time in the next 20 minutes. If distances aren't too great, then returning to the set is an option. Otherwise, final check-in with the art department folks happens in person by early evening. Additional design changes are noted, approved, or modified, and—if time allows—multiple prints are made for construction crew and other departments. Before leaving the office, setting out whatever is physically necessary to take to the set for next day's call time includes drafting, printed material such as revised director's plans, color photocopies of new research, paperwork for on-set crew, or materials/construction samples, which all goes into the backpack. The day typically ends by around 8:00 pm at the set to gather last minute bits of information or to just hang out as the crew gets the **martini shot.** An important point to remember: an art director is always on call when the crew is shooting.

Cover Sets

Weather conditions can be one of the few things altering or stopping the shooting schedule altogether, and this must be avoided at all costs. The art department is directly responsible for keeping the shoot on schedule by providing cover sets. An art director does not accomplish this alone. Assistance from locations, production, and the directorial staff help forecast and communicate changes in weather and scheduling tactics. Ideally, cover sets are established early during pre-production and are fully dressed and ready to be utilized. The location of the film and time of year will determine the number of cover sets. For instance, if you are shooting the bulk of a film in Ireland, chances are that every interior set will be considered a cover set. During the shoot for *White Sands* (1992) in New Mexico, daily summer thunderstorms in the late afternoon were forecast—so they were factored into the weekly shooting schedule plan. The ability to be fast and flexible arms a vigilant art director.

Communication with the Trinity

Diligent service to the Director, Cinematographer, and UPM are expected (see "Hierarchy of Responsibilities" in Chapter 2). Both direct and indirect communication with these key players supports the efficiency of the production. Presenting new research or new data not previously considered enhances the continuation of the collaborative creative process. Some changes to scenery, dressing, or visual and mechanical effects, for instance, are also reasonable suggestions to entertain, but, sometimes it's also important to say "no."

The creative filmmaking process is an organic one. Most changes a director or cinematographer make mid-stream are acceptable. How do you determine which are unacceptable? Additions or changes that affect the scenery budget in a big way demand immediate attention and analysis. Having a strategy already in place regarding the inevitability of these requests helps the speed of decision-making. Experience helps determine early on which sets will most likely receive additional work: Hero sets will probably require this kind of attention, some sets are important for storytelling but not critical—and other sets are "dispensable"—in budgetary terms. As a result, the original set list is continuously modified throughout production, as well as corresponding budget items. Your job as budget watchdog requires your active participation. Input from the construction coordinator or mechanical effects supervisor is helpful, but the final decision is in the hands of the Designer or UPM once your financial caveat is delivered. This is not to suggest stubbornness or unreasonableness on the part of the Art Director. Rolling with the changes is a big part of the job description. But it is important to remain firm in your judgment of what changes will be acceptable or not. Shooting from the hip is necessary, but not at the expense of your budget, your crew, or yourself.

Telling the Truth

Stress is a given while principal photography progresses: demands are great, tension is high, time is metered, and personalities are volatile. Having knowledge of up-to-the-minute changes, ability to quote budget numbers on the spot, and having critical data at hand are several ways to offset the stress an art director experiences. A practical art director is well-prepared to negotiate every situation that arises. Understanding the facts and telling the truth matter the most. Those involved in on-set disputes look for the level-headed, logical, and factual input of an art director. Although sometimes difficult to hear, the truth will dispel fear and resolve a conflict. Combining diplomacy with truth-telling makes all the difference.

ART DEPARTMENT TACTICAL STRATEGY

Handling Changes

Moviemaking is a volatile creative process. Developing an operational plan flexible enough to withstand small and large scale shifts is practical. Most of the changes are likely to occur within the building and finishing stages of scenery production, once the designing process on the page is done. For instance, repainting an interior set is an inconvenient task that disrupts the timeline. Because the construction crewmembers have already been assigned to complete a given number of sets, additional crew would have to be hired as well as additional materials to complete the job. Annoying at best, it is achievable mainly because each budgetary item on the set list is figured with a 10–15% contingency cushion, allowing for these kinds of budget and time disruptions. While this same, small emergency crew of painters is still on payroll, they might also be utilized on other sets where crew is getting into a jam—this is another justification for hiring additional crew in the first place. A major addition to the timeline schedule, such as building a duplicate of a set, demands special attention. Most likely, it will require an emergency meeting with the producer or UPM, construction coordinator, mechanical and visual effects supervisors, the head accountant, and art director to decide on the best tactical solution (details will be discussed later in this section).

The art department Coordinator handles the bulk of paperwork generated in the art department for production and studio files. This includes the filling out of art department crew time cards, keeping track of check request forms, organizing petty cash disbursement and receipt envelopes for the design team, personal phones distribution lists, accident coverage and worker's compensation forms, distribution of car cards and similar ID tags for admittance to a hot set, securing certificate of insurance forms required by certain vendors, and tracking of most clearance materials and information for product and name usage. Free from these smaller, vital operational tasks, an art director can more fully concentrate on onstage scenery production and finishing touches, set dressing, hero props, completion of location sets, and cover sets. From time to time personality or stress-induced conflicts in the art department will erupt but end quickly, simply because there is little time to sustain an argument. Any lingering discord needs to be immediately resolved by an intruding art director to keep morale high and productivity on schedule.

Vendors

Vendors are a vital part of the support structure of the film industry; as subcontractors, they provide solutions to a demanding workload. Graphics and signage, billboards, or site surveys for location sets are examples of many jobs outsourced to other companies. The progress of those projects requires daily management scrutiny. Dealing with vendors in Los Angeles is simpler, in many ways, because they understand how urgent the time factor is in the overall process; most businesses are multigenerational and understand the whys and hows of last minute, emergency requests. In some cases, you will receive outsourced work before a deadline, and this is good. When working out of town, most art directors are subcontracting to vendors who are highly motivated to participate but lack the ability to move quickly. If the options are narrow, then an art director must impress on the vendor the fact that their participation requires them to make sure the needs of the film take precedence over anything else. This is an arrogant request, but it must be made up front and verbally agreed to, otherwise not having established that basic understanding will surely cause setbacks in production schedules. Be clear, firm, and thorough to prevent any misunderstandings. An excellent idea worth noting is to set a precedent by being highly organized and providing exactly what the vendor will need to fulfill the demand—a sloppy art director can't expect much more. Another point to consider is properly reading your audience. Depending on where you are located, cultural rules are better followed than not. If you are in an area where politeness and a certain amount of small talk precede business, it might be worthwhile to follow suit. Enrolling other people's help and enthusiasm by respecting their cultural expectations will most likely satisfy your time constraints and produce a better product.

Minding the Budget

Adjustment prompts the dynamic nature of a set budget. Set overages will occur as a result of second thoughts, **acts of God,** or actor availability, but usually happen as a result of a director modifying a creative decision. Consider the following scenario: The original decision to digitally film sections of a hero house in flames changes ten days before shooting. Having watched several films as reference during late pre-production phase, the Director and Cinematographer decide that technology hasn't perfected digital flame and smoke well enough to satisfy the visual and emotional aspects of the storytelling. Instead, the Director opts to have a duplicate of the house built as an exterior shell on location for the burning sequence. It is felt that real flames will inspire more compelling performances and dispel any reservations that the director might have about digital flame and smoke.

The emergency meeting that ensues among producer, or UPM, location manager, construction coordinator, mechanical and visual effects supervisors, the head accountant, and art director might offer the following tactical decisions for discussion:

- The original two-story house set budgeted at $187,000 primarily as an onstage cover set; per the Director's current request, it will now cost twice as much. For starters, the art director might suggest building a quarter-scale miniature of the house constructed in high detail as an exterior model, and burning it in real time with mechanical effects flame and smoke.
- Or, a simple, duplicate façade of the miniature house could be burned on a greenscreen stage. Shot digitally, the real flames could then be used in miniature as a composite plate.
- Any foreground action could also be composited with mid-ground flames and background exterior shots of the house.

With some quick figuring by all participants present, the addition cost by combining construction, visual effects and mechanical effects' budgets is $85,000, or $272,000 proposed total cost. The producer will most likely be satisfied with a $102,000 savings over the $374,000 total cost of building a duplicate full-scale set on location. If agreed upon, this solution would minimally compromise all budgets involved, would give the Director what she wants, and aesthetically enhance the final product. It is questionable whether this scenario might ever happen, or resolve itself in this way but it is an example of what an art director is likely to encounter on a daily basis. Quick thinking and collaboration are key points to consider regarding this issue. In order to more fully convince the Director, photographic and film examples of proven successes with miniatures, fire, and digital compositing work of all departmental participants will help sell the idea. Although the idea works for those at the tactical meeting, the Director might remain unconvinced. Preliminary tests of variations of the solution should exist as options. One of the options will prevail, at which point, all department heads will speed the respective changes, along within the scope of the new budget item and the blessing of the producers.

Scenarios like this are creative shell games an art director and other department heads manipulate to adequately shift the weight of impromptu decisions to balance their respective and collective budgets. It happens on every show. Experience is the determining factor in making the right solutions happen.

Keeping a Chronicle

Entering daily agenda data into a digital device is a foolproof way to chronicle art department events. Now that iPhones are designed with voice activation, this daily activity is effortless. Even if blessed with a photographic memory, digital or written documentation of a phone conversation with a vendor or crewmember will help jog a memory working on overtime, recalling data items like budget figures and shooting schedule details. You can't remember everything, so carefully organize your data and revise calendars and schedules accordingly.

I've found that keeping a personal diary and a separate production notebook are helpful. The pages are dated and provide an informational base for a vendor forms, check requests, etc. Idea sketches, design development, and graphic explanations accompanying conversations link the note-taking between the pages. At the end of each week, it's a good idea to print the pages as a backup when the iPad is inadvertently sitting at home or lost. A database of vendors, contacts, and networking information will be created from the notebook or its copy. Your art coordinator can assist by creating a data file. Whether on location or not, the information is easily uploaded or downloaded from iPad to Cloud to laptop. By the end of the show, this database list and other printed material collected in a 4″ binder becomes the Art Director's wrap binder. This tome of visual and written data becomes your bible in post-production phase or for reshoots of various sections of that movie.

Protecting the Crew

In general terms, the well-being of the art department crew, including that of the Production Designer, must be ensured. Optimal physical and psychological conditions enhance optimal performance. Obstacles need to be constantly removed, even to the point of providing comic relief to cut the level of stress and promote a positive working vibe. Creatives seem to work best in this type of minimal stress, maximal inspiration environment. On more reasonably scheduled shows, I insist on the art crew leaving the premises for lunch and organizing regular group lunches or dinners whenever possible. Also, enforcing regular morning and afternoon breaks are refreshing segues to all the intense work and stress it generates, and reinforces union mandates. Personally, getting regular exercise and eating well have proven beneficial to managing continuing physical, mental, and emotional health. Bottom line is that consistent communication and cheerleading make a difference in people's productivity.

POST-PRODUCTION

Finishing Up

A typical show will have an art director and art department operating at top speed through the last day of principal photography—slow, steady easing off of workload is rare and should be enjoyed. Take advantage of being in production mode during the last week of shooting by reconnecting with your network and announcing your imminent availability for a new project. In the meantime, there is still much work to do.

Archiving

An art director's principal activity after the last formal day of shooting is archiving; this process should have been an ongoing one since your first weeks in the art department. It concludes with the organizing of final documents and images into both the art department production manual and its digital counterpart in database format. With the continued help of the art coordinator and archivist, this final task can be swift and comprehensive.

Wrapping the Art Department

Unless the art department is located in a furnished office suite found in any of the LA studio complexes, the physical activities of returning rental furniture, office machinery, and the boxing physical models, prototype props, document and drafting duplicates all fall within the jurisdiction of the art coordinator and PA staff. For anyone in the department who has generated creative documents, files, or prints, it is a time to collect copies for personal website and portfolio use in the ensuing job hunt. Legally, all artwork created for the show is the property of the studio or producing entity, and it must be packaged for storage.

Reshoots

The shooting schedule for a film is prescribed at roughly two months. When a UPM figures the length of the shooting schedule, a fairly accurate, educated guess determines that decision. So many factors are considered that any one of them has the potential to shift and consequently affect the others. "Making the schedule" is the positive attitude everyone adopts throughout the shooting process and it is rarely compromised. In cases of mechanical failure, accident, or natural disaster, days are lost and must be retrieved.

Reshoots typically happen at the end of principal photography and might also include problematic scenes needing to be reworked for physical, timing, or aesthetic reasons. Depending on how extensive the list of scenes, one can figure on an additional two to three weeks of work. This process should not interfere with post-production editing and must happen as quickly as possible. It requires a greatly reduced number of crew and equipment. The most logical head of the reshoot crew is the Second Unit Director accompanied by key shooting crew personnel and key department representatives required by the new shooting schedule. Reshoots are mini-productions and should not be confused with "pick-ups" or close-up shots never gotten during the production schedule.

With new shooting schedule and one-liners in hand, a short production meeting is held to discuss the scope of the next few weeks. If not already standing and in storage, interior sets marked for reshooting are spotted onto the ground plan of a warehouse or available stage floor; sets are then erected, rigged, retouched with paint, and redressed. Exterior locations are prepped according to the specs of the new shooting schedule, and the process continues with daily call sheets until final day of wrap. After a month of down time, the Director returns to begin the post-production process, editing in the additional material with the rest of the footage already in the can.

Sequels

Having worked on the first film of several headed for **sequel** status doesn't guarantee steady employment. Interviewing for the next job and getting it is the only sure guarantee of employment. One might expect the original production designer to be hired back to design a sequel in order to maintain an outstanding visual look for the next film in the series, but this also is not guaranteed. The phrase, "You're only as good as your last job," certainly comes to play in this situation. In general terms, the only thing that *will* guarantee that you work at all is a steady track record with your designer, director, and producers. An art director is in an enviable position to be all things to all people. Attend to your position, perform outstandingly, and leave without any regrets—it's all you can do.

Tossing your name in the hat and being called back to art direct a sequel is a turn of great luck and an advantage to you. Your last efforts on the previous film have left you with the art department production book, a larger database, and a research-rich digital image file. Even if the new Production Designer or Director will not be following the same visual path, this is certainly a good place to begin. Main hero sets in storage will certainly be considered for use—and that includes the built props and dressing that furnishes them. No doubt some of your past images and ideas might also be considered, and your experience will be respected. At this point in time, you can pat yourself on the back for a job well done.

Landing the Next Job or Taking a Vacation

The instability of keeping actively employed in the movie industry compels most lifers to accept whatever projects are offered in order to remain solvent. The mixture of a slight bit of workaholic ethic and superstition prevents the enjoyment of our time off between jobs—there are few people who actually know how to relax and catch a breath. For some, working on location is vacation enough; for others, the buzz of just doing what they love day in and out, precludes the thought of some time off. Art Director, Phil Dagort has this to say:

Interview with Phil Dagort

● *At the end of your process, when do you begin your search for the next job?*
  I'm not especially good at that kind of multitasking. I've always been a one-job-at-a-time kind of person. Maybe by the time the job is winding down, I just want time off–plus, a lot of my daily phone time is devoted to multitasking on the current work. I usually don't have time to make calls about another job. If I did, I wouldn't be doing the current job very well.

  Lately, on smaller to medium projects we are working like crazy up to our last day. A week or two after the project has wrapped is when I begin my phone calling, after enough down time to just change gears. If I plan anything first it's a vacation after a job ends, and that's the first week after wrap. The next job usually waits until after that. But once I've returned, there's going to be at least a month of job-hunting for the next project, sometimes more.[2]

Playtime is just as critical as making a living. Taking time to recharge by doing nothing, catching up on reading, taking a short class, or jumping into a favorite hobby needs some serious consideration. This has to be said because there are people who overlook the opportunity. The truth is that there will always be a new show to jump onto, most often when you least want it or expect it.

EPISODIC TELEVISION

Episodic TV demands speed. *Glee,* a one-hour television musical format, demands even more. The demands on the *Glee* design team goes beyond the search for the best visual image for an episode or individual song performance. Any given script contains references to pop music culture in the forms of music video and musical film homages. In some cases, strict adherence to the iconic visuals for a particular song reference, are required—so **screen-grabs** from film/video sources or past episodes of *Glee* are cut-and-pasted onto concept boards for subsequent creative meetings and referral throughout the design process. At the beginning of Season 5, we were asked to design a New York City "performance diner" as a permanent set on the Paramount Studios lot. Our preliminary research and SketchUp concept sketches of the exterior and interior of the "Spotlight Diner" are shown in Figure 8.9a–c.

Most often, Internet research is practical and expedient, where searching for a physical reference book is time consuming. Thinkstock, Corbis, and Getty Images are fast, indispensable online sources not only for reference material but for graphics as well. What's important about these subscription and image pack option sources is the significant fact that they are royalty-free photos. In a world where clearance permissions carry legal ramifications, these Web-based options are perfect, providing serious bang for your buck.

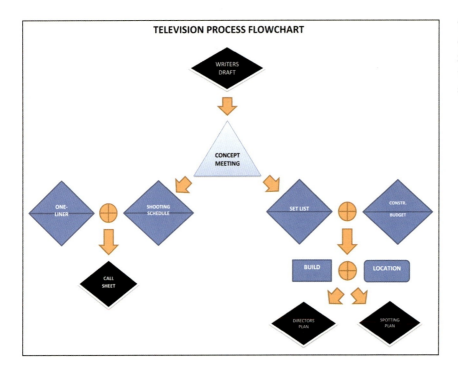

Table 8.1 Flowchart depicting the process from initial script pages to call sheets and shooting plans.

Figure 8.9a *Glee*_Episode 501_Int. Spotlight Diner: Research and Material samples. SketchUp concept sketch by David Utley.

Figure 8.9b
*Glee*_Episode 501_Ext. Spotlight Diner: Research samples. SketchUp concept sketch by David Utley.

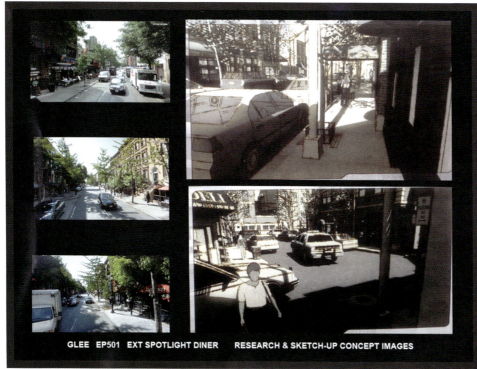

GLEE EP501 EXT SPOTLIGHT DINER   RESEARCH & SKETCH-UP CONCEPT IMAGES

Figure 8.9c
*Glee*_Episode 501_Ext. Spotlight Diner: Research samples. SketchUp concept sketch by David Utley.

Concept Meeting

Episode scripts are seldom distributed intact; what's more likely is to receive the first three acts of a six-act writer's script. With that in hand, all department heads are invited to a concept/production meeting, run by the First AD. A micro-synopsis of each scene is noted as the 1st AD moves through the script fielding questions and encouraging responses from the Director and creative network producers. This first *and only* group meeting is likely to produce a preliminary one-liner, revealing a best-guess scene shooting sequence for the upcoming eight-day shooting period for that episode.

Sidebar meetings are arranged post-meeting to insure that all detailed answers to all questions that are raised during the meeting are answered. For example, one scene might describe a character as having created dry macaroni and bean portraits of pop culture icons. The question will invariably arise: what department is responsible for manufacturing these hero items? After a few minutes of volleying, a list of reasons of why neither the art department PAs nor the Set Decorator nor the Prop Master claim ownership until it is decided that the property department will source people online with this specific skill to make six of these portraits over a long holiday weekend.

Following the meeting and subsequent side-board meetings, the concept notes (Figure 8.10a and b) are emailed from the design team to colleagues in the following departments: prop, set dressing, construction, paint, rigging grip, and lighting. The notes determine what recurring sets will be spotted on which **swing stages** and what new sets will be built. The notes also spawn the set list (see Figure 8.11) and the first pass at the construction budget, backings list, the graphics list, and product placement/clearance list (see Figures 8.12–8.15). At the same time, a preliminary one-liner is emailed to department heads. Now the ball is in motion.

Construction Budget

With the one-liner, partial script and concept meeting notes as a guide, the Art Director and Construction Coordinator combine their efforts to organize the construction budget for the episode at hand. Note: The list of sets for each episode is created from the script by the Art Director and art department Coordinator. Episodic TV divides a fully programmed season into 22 episodes, each to conform to a prescribed budget "**pattern**" for a one-hour musical dramedy like *Glee*. The budget for a more musical and performance-heavy episode will land beyond the pattern target; a **bottle show** might very well settle at, or just below pattern. As you can see, the construction budget indicates labor, materials, and fringe. Each of these items is carefully discussed to insure that a particular episode will not be overspent. After a concept meeting, the producers will indicate where the financial-pattern-numbers for an episode per department will land. For example, elaborate breakaway costumes for a specific dance number (wardrobe), a slip 'n' slide sequence in a dorm hallway (mechanical effects), or the aftermath of a plane crash (art department)

```
EPISODE 501_CONCEPT MEETING NOTES


GENERAL CONCEPT:
Rich looking and big
Spring: space, atmosphere, sky.

Sc2 Broadway Theatre
General: Old, dark burgundy curtain, "old school", dark atmosphere.
Must be a location
Wings/Black Legs
"Yesterday"

Sc3 Backstage Hallway
General: Nostalgic, old.
Brick wall covered with Autographs of former performers
Show posters, cast photos

Sc5&6 Central Park
General: air, space, water, spring.
Benches

Sc7 Subway Car
(Media Graphics) Rachel looks at pix of her friends

Sc10 Hallway
"Drive My Car"

Sc12 Ext Bumper Cars
(Media Graphics) Kitty's Phone: Several photos and animated gifs of Kitty&Artie
"Drive My Car"

Sc13, 27 Spotlight Diner
General: Iconic, Technicolor, popping reds.
Exterior: spring look.
Bwy and 49ᵗʰ Street
Awnings
Sandwich board
Main Sign
Door sign, misc. signage
Int: Looks like an upgraded Ferrel's Donuts
Jukebox guts visible
Embedded counter footlights
Hop-scotch from table to table
"Hard Day's Night"
```

Figure 8.10a *GLEE* Episode 501—Concept Meeting Notes, page 1.

```
Sc14 WMHS Courtyard
General: Heightened Realism: Sgt. Pepper
Art directed picnic
Marching brass band
"Got to Get You Into My Life"

Sc19 Hallway
"You've Got to Hide Your Love Away"

Sc24 Carmel High School
General:  Use one of our classrooms.
Sign: "Vocal Adrenaline Private Rehearsal—Keep Out!"
Background scenery is rehearsal mode.

Sc25 Haverbrook School for the Deaf
Choir risers in front of windows

Sc29 Dalton Academy
English telephone booth

Sc30 Auditorium
General: Gypsy—Mama Rose
Burgundy curtain, black scrim reveal

Sc31 Figgins' Office
"Principal Sylvester" nameplate

Sc32 Home EC Class
(Graphics) "Home-Ec Class! Assignment: Gay wedding cakes!"

Sc34 Choir Room
No Entenmanns

Sc39 Auditorium
Ed Sullivan CBS Beatles set for American Debut
 [Check color 'values' for B&W shift mid-song]
Uncovered pit
"I Saw Her Standing There"

Sc41 Dalton Academy
General: Cirque du Soleil: hula hoops, streamers, big fun.
Huge finale
Troupe of horns
"All You Need is Love"
```

Figure 8.10b *GLEE* Episode 501—Concept Meeting Notes, page 2.

would each increase the overall size of a budget, needing specific approval from the UPM. In most cases, the construction budget is surrendered to the UPM the day after the production meeting.

Backings List and Budget

A photographic translite is an expensive piece of full-scale background artwork. This is because it is a high-resolution image that must be flawlessly photographed by industry professionals to meet industry standards. In most cases, a translite is rented from one of many companies for a weekly or production (season) rental fee; it is noted as a line item on the construction budget. A script will designate whether a photographic or painted backdrop is required. Or a limbo space is created with a day-gray or night-blue, devoid of an image. Frequently, soft goods are used as a fabric texture instead of a background image;

Set #	Set Name	STAGE/LOC
	glee EPISODE 501- "LOVE, LOVE, LOVE"	
01	NEW YORK DINER	BACKLOT
02	AUDITORIUM	STAGE 16
03	CHOIR ROOM	STAGE 15
04	CLASSROOM-LG-HOME EC	STAGE 15
05	CLASSROOM-SM-HISTORY	STAGE 15
08	FIGGIN'S OFFICE	STAGE 15
11	SCHOOL-HALLWAYS	STAGE 15
12	NEW YORK LOFT	STAGE 14
18	CLASSROOM-MISC.	STAGE 15
19	COURTYARD	BERNSTEIN
20	DALTON	RED CROSS
21	CARMEL HS STAGE	STAGE 16
22	HAVERBROOK/DEAF SCHOOL CLASSROOM	STAGE 14
23	CAR (BURT'S)	LOCATION
24	CARNIVAL	PARKING LOT
25	INT. BROADWAY THEATRE	LOCATION
26	EXT. BROADWAY THEATRE	LOCATION
27	EXT. NEW YORK CITY	LOCATION
28	AUDITORIUM- "Getting Better"	STAGE 16
29	AUDITORIUM- "I Saw Her Standing There"	STAGE 16

Figure 8.11   *GLEE* Episode 501 Set List

the cost for a weekly or production rental of crimson velour borders and legs, for instance, would be found as a line item on the set dressing budget, also organized by the art department Coordinator.

Graphics List and Budget

A graphics list is generated from the script but can also be requested from the Director, Production Designer or Set Decorator. *Glee* has a designated Graphic Designer; although, the union now recognizes Assistant ADs as Graphic Designers. Logos and signage are conveniently produced by a studio sign shop at competitive prices. Sometimes the trick to getting the price of graphics to fit the budget is to get cost comparisons from several studio sign shops and allow competition to drive in the best bid. The graphic demands for a show like *Glee* can threaten an established budget—it is wise to inform the UPM when a particular episode will be unusually heavy on graphics so allowances can be made to the graphics pattern budget. Graphics and product placement/clearances are intimately related. A book jacket about Scientology, for instance, must strictly comply with **standards and practices** to avoid any legal trouble.

Glee
Season 5 Amort
Construction Budget

			Labor	Material	Greens	Total
1	Int	New York Diner	$ 107,250.00	$ 57,750.00	$ -	$ 165,000.00
2	Ext	New York Diner	$ 32,500.00	$ 17,500.00	$ -	$ 50,000.00
3	Ext	Base Camp				
		Paint Planter Boxes	$ 1,320.00	$ 330.00	$ -	$ 1,650.00
		Metal Frames	$ 450.00	$ 4,050.00	$ -	$ 4,500.00
4	Int	Auditorium				
		Stage Floor - Repair Tiles	$ 825.00	$ 825.00	$ -	$ 1,650.00
		Stage Floor - Epoxy Floor	$ -	$ 6,500.00	$ -	$ 6,500.00
		Wash Orange Walls	$ 760.00	$ 190.00	$ -	$ 950.00
		Paint	$ 3,850.00	$ 1,650.00	$ -	$ 5,500.00
5	Int	WMHS - Main Hallway				
		Paint	$ 3,850.00	$ 1,650.00	$ -	$ 5,500.00
6	Int	WMHS - Choir Room				
		Paint	$ 3,150.00	$ 1,350.00	$ -	$ 4,500.00
		Add 5 Foot Soffit around 3 walls	$ 5,250.00	$ 2,250.00	$ -	$ 7,500.00
		Add new facing to existing Risers	$ 1,750.00	$ 750.00	$ -	$ 2,500.00
		Clean Tops of existing Risers	$ 595.00	$ 255.00	$ -	$ 850.00
		Rebuild existing book shelf in 3 sections	$ 8,750.00	$ 3,750.00	$ -	$ 12,500.00
7	Int	WMHS - Large Classroom				
		Paint	$ 1,462.50	$ 787.50	$ -	$ 2,250.00
8	Int	WMHS - Courtyard Area				
		Paint	$ 1,787.50	$ 962.50	$ -	$ 2,750.00
	Int	WMHS - Figgin's Office				
9		Paint	$ 1,397.50	$ 752.50	$ -	$ 2,150.00
		New Carpet & Cove Base	$ 647.50	$ 1,202.50	$ -	$ 1,850.00
10	Int	WMHS - Teachers Lounge				
		Paint	$ 1,202.50	$ 647.50	$ -	$ 1,850.00
11	Int	WMHS - Locker Room				
		Clean, Touch Up, And Seal Floors	$ 1,852.50	$ 997.50	$ -	$ 2,850.00
12	Int	WMHS - Sue's Office & Hallway				
		Paint	$ 2,437.50	$ 812.50	$ -	$ 3,250.00
		New Carpet & Cove Base	$ 577.50	$ 1,072.50	$ -	$ 1,650.00
13	Int	WMHS - Library	$ 8,625.00	$ 2,875.00	$ -	$ 11,500.00
14	Int	Loft	$ 1,800.00	$ 450.00	$ -	$ 2,250.00
15	Int	Dance Studio	$ 15,375.00	$ 5,125.00	$ -	$ 20,500.00
16	Int	Stage 11 Clean Up	$ 3,375.00	$ 1,125.00	$ -	$ 4,500.00
		Greens Labor	$ -			$ -
		Strike Labor	$ -			$ -
		Greens - Purchases & Rentals				$ -
						$ -
		Total	$ 210,840.00	$ 115,610.00		$ 326,450.00
		Fringe				$ 80,119.20
		Total With Fringe				$ 406,569.20

Figure 8.12 *GLEE* Episode 501 Construction Budget

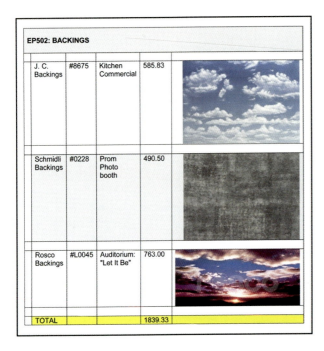

EP502: BACKINGS

J. C. Backings	#8675	Kitchen Commercial	585.83	
Schmidli Backings	#0228	Prom Photo booth	490.50	
Rosco Backings	#L0045	Auditorium: "Let It Be"	763.00	
TOTAL			**1839.33**	

Figure 8.13   *GLEE* Episode 502 Backings List

EPISODE 321: Nationals

SCENE	SET	TYPE	NAME / TEXT	DEL. DATE	SHOOT DATE	COST
7	Ext Chicago Theater	Awning	Cover existing awning text: 8" x 10' [x2]	4/23/2012	4/27/2012	2,066.75
			Cover existing awning text: 8" x 9'-6" [x2]			
		Small vinyl banners	"Nationals": 6'w x 18"h [x2]	4/23/2012	4/27/2012	
		Poster on 1/8" sintra	Free-standing: 61 3/4"w x 33 3/4"h	4/23/2012	4/27/2012	
		Adhes. vinyl letters	"Bertha Honore Palmer Fine Arts Complex": 15'-4"w x 24"h	4/23/2012	4/27/2012	
		NOTES:	Remove [6] existing banners.			
			Lg. Banner on Student Union cannot be removed.			
26	Int Chicago Th. Lobby	Large vinyl banner	"2012 National Show Choir Competition"	4/23/2012	4/27/2012	
			4'-6"h x 13'-6"w [cover area: 48.5" x 13'-3"]			
		Lg banner Plug	[Add: 12" to bottom of the existing banner]	4/23/2012	4/27/2012	190.31
20	Int Chicago Theater	Translucent Vinyl	Upper/Lower Pinball Graphics	4/20/2102	4/25/2012	2,175.00
		Opaque Vinyl	Silhouette Graphics as lite gobos for Translucent Vinyls			
		Ext. Shell Stencils	Side Graphics for [4] Pinball Machines	4/23/2012	4/25/2012	2,417.52
4, 5	Chicago Hotel Hall	Door Hangtags	"Holden Court"	4/18/2012	4/20/2012	1,019.54
	Green-Judges Rm	Door Number Signs	"Holden Court Chicago"			
		Banner	"Congratulations New Directions"			
		Door Number Signs	"Dressing Room", "Green Room"			
	TOTAL					**7,869.12**

EP501 Graphics						
8/16/2013	32	Thinkstock	1 year subscription-split 3 ways	Subscription	796.00	Amort
8/16/2013	30	Corbis	2 images-Season 5 license fee	License Fee	1,200.00	Amort
				Total Amort:	**1,996.00**	
8/16/2013	CR	PHR Industries	Graphics work for awnings	Purchase	1,915.14	501
8/16/2013	28	Paramount Sign Shop	6 invoices	Purchase	1,188.11	501
8/16/2013	33	AAA Flag & Banner	Chevron/McKinley banners	Purchase	553.18	501
9/6/2013	CR	Kevin L. Raper	NY Unit-"Funny Girl" Marquee	Purchase	450.00	501
				Total 501:	**4,106.43**	

Figure 8.14a–b   *GLEE* Episode 501 Graphics List

EP501 CLEARANCE LIST

A-1-Broadway Posters
A-2-List of store names for the backlot
A-3-A Cry of Players graphic
A-4-Theater name
A-5-Spotlight Diner logo graphic
A-6-Beatles logo/stage set up
A-7-Neon Server sign
A-8-"Funny Girl" dialogue/script clearance
A-9-Hardware store signage-Visa/Mastercard, etc.
A-10-Toys at Carnival games
A-11-Greek Food Truck name, address, and website clearance
A-12-Construction company names for backlot
A-13-Sanitary Inspection Grade graphic
A-14-Dalton images from Corbis
A-15-NY Ghost Sign
A-16-Sardi's signage and caricatures

C-1-Ben Sherman shirt

P-1-Acting books
P-2-"Mein Kampf" book, Hitler signature
P-3-Created porn magazines
P-4-Sanders Chocolate "Bumpy Cake"
P-5-Instagram on phone

S-1-Bob Harris name clearance

SD-1-Dave Beckerman photos
SD-2-Sabrett's name/logo
SD-3-Background "Playbills"
SD-4-New York City vintage posters
SD-5-"Stage Door Canteen" and "Broadway Babies" posters
SD-6-H.A. Dunne photographs
SD-7-Metroscape New York photos
SD-8-Jaguar school posters: anti-bullying
SD-9-Synchronized Swimming art
SD-10-PRS Guitars
SD-11-Santa Cruz bikes
SD-12-Daily Racing Form name/logo
SD-13-Existing photos at Million Dollar Theater (location)
SD-14-Classic World Wall Map clearance-Intelligent Direct, Inc.
SD-15-Artwork for School of the Deaf
SD-16-Food and Health Posters
SD-17-Multiple headshots clearances
SD-18-Seeburg juke box usage

Legend: A=Art, C=Costumes, P=Props, S=Script, and SD=Set Dec

Figure 8.15   *GLEE* Episode 501 Clearance List

THREE-DAY SETS

In a perfect world, there would be enough reasonable time to put sets in front of the camera. That is more the exception than the rule—the fact is: there is a scarcity of time and the focus on budget is a relentless reality. The preliminary one-liner and a subsequent shooting schedule for a *Glee* episode are both actor- and music-driven. Most likely, a new swing set could appear within the first or second day of shooting a new episode, rather than be scheduled at the end of the nine-day shooting week. Typically then, we blast forward, translating research into preliminary drawings. My set designer and I review the scripted scene, assess how big the set should be and where it will live on one of our two swing stages. A recording studio scene that is three-eighths of a page in length, for example, will likely cover a smaller footprint than a normal size set written for two and six-eighths pages of work—and, most likely, be spotted inside of a larger set occupying the bulk of one of those two swing stages—this is an exceptional case. The Spotlight Diner set, once designed, required a typical spotting plan and director's plan (see Figure 8.16a and b). Understand that each drawing must be discussed with the construction foreman/buyer so that all pertinent

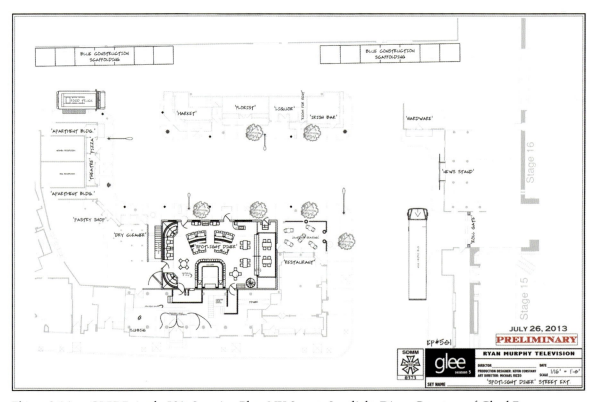

Figure 8.16a   *GLEE* Episode 501: Spotting Plan-NY Street: Spotlight Diner Courtesy of Chad Frey

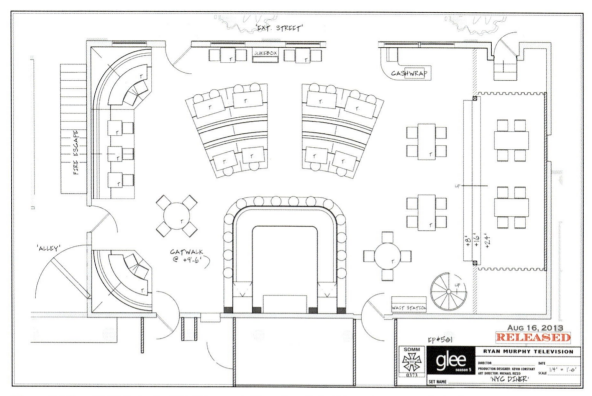

Figure 8.16b   *GLEE* Episode 501: Director's Plan: Spotlight Diner Courtesy of Chad Frey

materials can be sought and be in-hand *within a half-day* so building can commence, with verbal approval from upper management. A similar conversation happens with buyers in the set decorating department for set dressing that will impact the construction process—such as carnival booths, fluorescent fixtures, or large kitchen appliances, for example—each fitting properly into a floor plan and elevation (see "Local 44 Budgeting Guidelines," Appendix A. These guidelines indicate what departments are responsible for certain questionable, crossover items; it resolves more disagreements than it inspires). At the same time, color paint tiles, paint finish samples, and plaster texture samples are provided to match research images that are being designed into the look of the set. The most volatile aspect of the process is for graphic requests from multiple sources, i.e., the Director or any of the creative department heads—most of these requests can be fulfilled on time; a decorator's requests are most common and the costs will be absorbed by the decorating budget.

A department head one-liner might emerge at this time (Figure 8.17). I make it a point to review it with my leadman, lighting gaffer, and rigging grip so they are fully

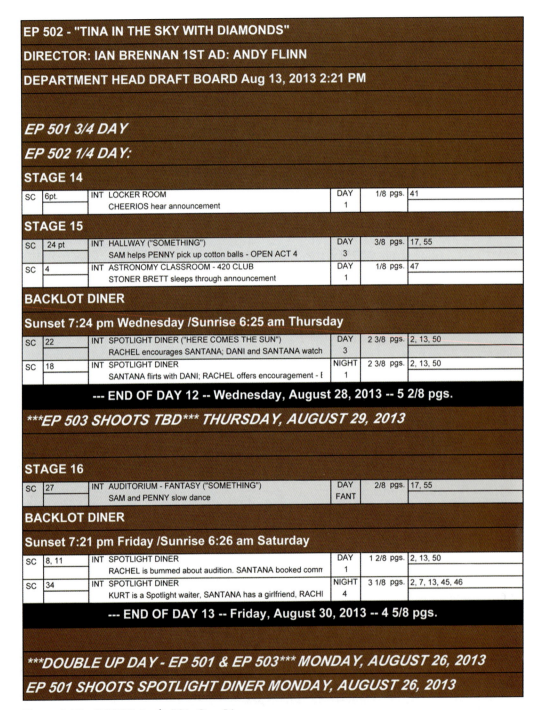

EP 502 - "TINA IN THE SKY WITH DIAMONDS"

DIRECTOR: IAN BRENNAN 1ST AD: ANDY FLINN

DEPARTMENT HEAD DRAFT BOARD Aug 13, 2013 2:21 PM

EP 501 3/4 DAY

EP 502 1/4 DAY:

STAGE 14

SC	6pt.	INT LOCKER ROOM	DAY	1/8 pgs.	41
		CHEERIOS hear announcement	1		

STAGE 15

SC	24 pt	INT HALLWAY ("SOMETHING")	DAY	3/8 pgs.	17, 55
		SAM helps PENNY pick up cotton balls - OPEN ACT 4	3		
SC	4	INT ASTRONOMY CLASSROOM - 420 CLUB	DAY	1/8 pgs.	47
		STONER BRETT sleeps through announcement	1		

BACKLOT DINER

Sunset 7:24 pm Wednesday /Sunrise 6:25 am Thursday

SC	22	INT SPOTLIGHT DINER ("HERE COMES THE SUN")	DAY	2 3/8 pgs.	2, 13, 50
		RACHEL encourages SANTANA; DANI and SANTANA watch	3		
SC	18	INT SPOTLIGHT DINER	NIGHT	2 3/8 pgs.	2, 13, 50
		SANTANA flirts with DANI; RACHEL offers encouragement - E	1		

--- END OF DAY 12 -- Wednesday, August 28, 2013 -- 5 2/8 pgs.

EP 503 SHOOTS TBD THURSDAY, AUGUST 29, 2013

STAGE 16

SC	27	INT AUDITORIUM - FANTASY ("SOMETHING")	DAY	2/8 pgs.	17, 55
		SAM and PENNY slow dance	FANT		

BACKLOT DINER

Sunset 7:21 pm Friday /Sunrise 6:26 am Saturday

SC	8, 11	INT SPOTLIGHT DINER	DAY	1 2/8 pgs.	2, 13, 50
		RACHEL is bummed about audition. SANTANA booked comn	1		
SC	34	INT SPOTLIGHT DINER	NIGHT	3 1/8 pgs.	2, 7, 13, 45, 46
		KURT is a Spotlight waiter, SANTANA has a girlfriend, RACHI	4		

--- END OF DAY 13 -- Friday, August 30, 2013 -- 4 5/8 pgs.

DOUBLE UP DAY - EP 501 & EP 503 MONDAY, AUGUST 26, 2013

EP 501 SHOOTS SPOTLIGHT DINER MONDAY, AUGUST 26, 2013

Figure 8.17 *GLEE* Episode 501: One-Liner

aware of where the schedule is headed—given the lack of time, this is an absolute necessity more than a courtesy. Their working time in constructed sets is inevitably cut short if any part of the building or painting process is lengthened. Revising drafted scenery, while building at mach speed, will frustrate every department, especially if sections of a set require rebuilding—impacting plaster, paint, set dressing, lighting, and rigging crews, and creating a major time setback. A 12:01 am call time for the painting crew, for example, isn't uncommon on *Glee* so that other groups can get in and finish for a 7:00 am call time. Generally, those last departments allowed into a finished set are forced to work around each other; the agreement to do this would have been made a day or so earlier, at a sidebar tech meeting after the initial concept meeting. Because we are forced to build as we draw, final pages are formally stamped "released" during the building process, not before. This seems counterintuitive and illogical, and it is by most standards. But, for episodic television, it is the norm, so the finished drafted page, although redundant once it is built, acts as a reference page stored on an in-house hard drive or in the flat file a year later. Once a drafted page is released, it is uploaded to the online server for access to all art department personnel.

Sometime between beginning the shooting of a new episode in established sets and moving in the latter part of the week to new sets or locations, there is a tech scout to visit those upcoming locations for information gathering on behalf of all departments. A television schedule demands a reasonable proximity of a location to the studio because moving the shooting crew off the lot costs valuable time and money. Ideally, all locations are approved before the scout happens.

Production also operates pretty much the same way. The official (UPM approved) one-liner, shooting schedule (see Figures 8.17 and 8.18) and final script or production draft, often appear a day or so into shooting a new episode as the entire process is volatile and organically evolving. Another helpful document is a **one-sheet,** generated by the second AD (see Figure 8.19)—printed on an 8½ × 14 sheet, it is an even shorter version of a typical one-liner, fitting every scene to be shot in the upcoming schedule on a single, neat page. Remember, the shooting of episodes is either finishing or beginning, so there is always overlap of multiple shooting crews. The daily crew **call sheet** (Figure 8.20) will reflect this: two separate crews shooting their respective episodes simultaneously constitutes a "**double-up day**"; the same shooting crew finishing up one episode, then continuing onto the subsequent episode with a different director defines what is called a "**split day**" schedule. This same concept applies on a film, when a second unit is scheduled the same day the first unit is also shooting. In musical episodic television, it is just a more continuous process. Creating shootable sets for HDTV in three days is remarkable in itself; what's *truly* remarkable is that they are film quality sets. If you've worked in both mediums, you can fully appreciate the impact of this. Adapting an often-used Bette Davis line: "Episodic TV ain't no place for sissies."

"LOVE. LOVE. LOVE"   Page 18
Shooting Schedule
Aug 6, 2013

Scene #27   **INT M**   **SPOTLIGHT DINER ("HARD DAY'S NIGHT")**   **DAY**   3 1/8 Pgs.
RACHEL has some unexpected guests

CAST   **PROPS**   **TRANSPO**
  2. RACHEL   CUP OF COFFEE   1 BUS W/DRIVER
  13. SANTANA   DINER FOOD AND DRINK   1 MFT
  48. PAOLO SAN PABLO   MILKSHAKES   1 NYCPD CAR
  49. RUPERT CAMPION   PLATES   6 NYC TAXIS
  220.6 DANCING WAITERS   QUARTER
  221.6 DANCING WATRESSES   RACHEL'S PHONE   **WARDROBE**
ATMOS   TOWELS TO WIPE COUNTERS   1 COP UNIFORM
  1 CASHIER   TRAYS   6 TAXI DRIVERS
  1 POLICE OFFICER   **SPECIAL EFFX**   APRONS
  10 - 35-45   ATMO SMOKE   BUSBOYS
  10 45-60   WAITER UNIFORMS
  15 ND BG   **MUSIC**   WAITRESS UNIFORM
  15 ND WITH CARS (7 HIGH   HARD DAY'S NIGHT   **SOUND**
  PROFILE VEHICLES)   VOCAL COACH   PLAYBACK "HARD DAY'S
  2 SODA JERKS   NIGHT"
  20 TOURISTS
  4 BUSBOYS   **CAMERA/GRIP/ELECTRIC**
  6 TAXI DRIVERS   20ft. TECHNO
                                                                         3RD CAMERA & CREW
                                                                         HEAD
DANCE   **ART DEPT/SET DEC.**
  CHOREOGRAPHER   JUKEBOX

                                                      DOUBLE UP WITH EP 502

END OF DAY #10 - 5 1/8 Total Pages

                                                                                      NYC

Scene #1   **EXT**   **BROADWAY THEATRE**   **DAY**   1/8 Pgs.
RACHEL arriving at theatre

CAST
  2. RACHEL
ATMOS   **WARDROBE**
  CONSTRUCTION WORKERS   RACHEL'S JACKET

                                                       ART DEPT/SET DEC.
                                                         MARQUEE GOING UP

Figure 8.18   *GLEE* Episode 501: Shooting Schedule

WHITE ONE-SHEET   10-8-13 530P

SET/SCENE DESCRIPTION	SCENES	CAST	DAY	PAGES	LOCATION / NOTES
ADVANCE SCHEDULE					
Thursday, October 10, 2013 **DBL UP 505/506**	******DOUBLE UP	*****DOUBLE UP	****DOUBLE UP	*****DOUBLE UP	*****DOUBLE UP
EP 505					
INT BOYS BATHROOM-MONTAGE	10	23, 41, 47	D1	2/8	STAGE 11
Bree kisses Jake, Stoner Brett sees it					
INT HALLWAY/BOYS ROOM	26	20	D5	1/8	
Unique cautiously enters Boys Room					
INT BOYS BATHROOM ("IF I WERE A BOY")	27	20, 52, 54, 56	D5	1 4/8	
The jocks hassle Unique, she wets herself					
INT BOYS BATHROOM-MONTAGE	13, 13A	BG	MONT 3	tbd	
BG Kids coming and going from bathrooms					
INT KURT & RACHEL'S LOFT	17	2, 7	D4	2	STAGE 14
Rachel tells Kurt they need to dive head first into life-ACT 2					
INT CHOIR ROOM ("IF I WERE A BOY")	28	1, 8, 9, 16, 17, 20, 22, 23, 24, 25	D5	1 1/8	STAGE 15
Unique performs, boys know something is wrong					
				Total Pgs	**5**
EP 506					
INT KURT & RACHEL'S LOFT ("JUST THE WAY YOU ARE")	39	2, 7, 13, 16, 17	N	2 5/8	STAGE 14
Kurt, Rachel, Santana, Blaine & Sam discuss NY					
INT HALLWAY	41	22, 23, 25	D	1 4/8	STAGE 15
Ryder wants to go out w/ Marley again, Jake offers congrats					
INT EVANS' HOUSE (flashback)	18	17k	D FB	1/8	STAGE 11
Young Sam emulates male models					
INT ANDERSON HOUSE (flashback)	32	16k	D FB	1/8	
8 yr old Blaine practices with "Operation"					
				Total Pgs	**4 3/8**
Friday, October 11, 2013 **DBL UP 505/506**	******DOUBLE UP	*****DOUBLE UP	****DOUBLE UP	*****DOUBLE UP	*****DOUBLE UP
EP 505					
INT FUNNY GIRL REH ("YOU ARE WOMAN, I AM MAN")	5	2, 48, 49	D1	2 7/8	STAGE 12
Rupert loves Rachel's performance and haircut					
INT HALLWAY	33	22, 41	D6	1 4/8	STAGE 15
Cheerios giggling at Marley's "twerking" on Bree's phone					
INT HALLWAY	36	22, 23	D7	1 1/8	
Marley wants to see Jake's male					
INT BATHROOM-MONTAGE	13, 13A	BG, 41	MONT 3	tbd	
Bree coming and going from bathroom					
INT GIRLS BATHROOM	8	20, 41	D2	7/8	STAGE 11
Unique tells Bree she is not comfortable using Boys bathroom					
INT GIRLS BATHROOM	12	BG	MONT 3	1/8	
Girls ditch line to use Boys Room					
				Total Pgs	**6 4/8**
EP 506					
INT HALLWAY ("AN INNOCENT MAN")	28	22, 25	D	7/8	STAGE 15
Ryder asks Marley out and sings					
INT CHOIR ROOM ("AN INNOCENT MAN")	29	1, 8, 9, 20, 22, 23, 24, 25	D	1 3/8	
Ryder continues to sing to Marley as NDs watch, Jake storms out					
EXT NY STREET-SUBWAY ("MOVING OUT")	4	16, 17	D	4/8	BACKLOT
Sam and Blaine take the city					
INT DINER ("PIANO MAN")	8	2, 7, 13, 16, 17, 45, 200	N	3 3/8	
Sam and Blaine visit Spotlight Diner, Blaine performs					
				Total Pgs	**6 1/8**
Monday, October 14, 2013 **DBL UP 505/506**	******DOUBLE UP	*****DOUBLE UP	****DOUBLE UP	*****DOUBLE UP	*****DOUBLE UP
EP 505					
INT WOHN	16	5, 60, 61	N3	1 5/8	STAGE 11
Sue says we are at war with "twerking"-END ACT 1					
INT GIRLS BATHROOM-RAVE	14	20, 47, 200-203, 204-208, X	MONT 4	3/8	
It's a RAVE!!!!!					
INT FIGGINS OFFICE	30	1, 5	D6	5/8	STAGE 15
Sue tells Will she got Unique his own bathroom					
INT FIGGINS OFFICE	40	1, 5, 58	D7	1 6/8	
Will throws tantrum, Becky joins in-ACT 6					
INT HISTORY CLASSROOM	6	1, 20	D2	3/8	
Unique needs to be excused					
IN HALLWAY/GIRLS ROOM	7	20	D2	1/8	
Unique looks, then goes in					
INT BOYS BATHROOM-MONTAGE	13, 13A	BG	MONT 3	tbd	
BG Kids coming and going from bathrooms					
				Total Pgs	**4 7/8**
EP 506					
INT KURT & RACHEL'S LOFT	30, 33, 35	7, 16	D	2	STAGE 14
Blaine tells Kurt he doesn't want to got to NYADA					
INT KURT & RACHEL'S LOFT ("MOVING OUT")	5	2, 7, 13, 16, 17	D	4/8	
Blaine & Sam arrive at Kurt & Rachel's					
INT KURT & RACHEL'S LOFT	17, 19, 21	2, 17	N	2	
Sam tells Rachel he doesn't want to go to college					
INT KURT & RACHEL'S LOFT	24	2, 17, 66	D	7/8	
Rachel archestrates Sam's photoshoot w Barbara Brownfield					
Photoshoot-Sam's bus shot					
				Total Pgs	**5 3/8**
Tuesday, October 15, 2013 **DBL UP 505/506**	******DOUBLE UP	*****DOUBLE UP	****DOUBLE UP	*****DOUBLE UP	*****DOUBLE UP
EP 505					
INT TBD SET-("WRECKING BALL")	37	22, X	D7	7/8	STAGE 16
Marley performs "Wrecking Ball"					
INT DINER	43	2, 7	D4	2/8	BACKLOT
Kurt shows off his tattoo					
INT TATTOO PARLOR	32	7, 62	D3	2 2/8	
Louis offers to fix Kurt's tattoo					
INT TATTOO PARLOR	24	2, 7, 62	N1	1 1/8	
Rachel & Kurt waiting to get tattoo-END ACT 2					
INT SALON	4	2	NY-D1	2/8	STAGE 11
Rachel needs a transformation					
				Total Pgs	**4 4/8**
EP 506					
EXT OSU-QUAD	36	8, 58, 67	D	2/8	PASEO NEAR PARAMOUNT THEATER
Artie and Becky are lead through the quad by Monica Perez					
INT OSU-CLASSROOM	37	8, 58, 67, 68, 69	D	1 1/8	STAGE 12
Artie & Becky visit an independent living class					
INT SCIENCE CLASSROOM	26	8	D	2/8	STAGE 15
Artie reacts to Sue's call					
INT FIGGINS OFFICE	27	5, 8	D	1 4/8	
Sue admonishes Artie, then softens					
INT FIGGINS OFFICE	25	5	D	2/8	
Sue summons Artie					
INT CAFETERIA-KITCHEN	23	22, 34	D	1	STAGE 12
Marley talks to her mom about Jake					
				Total Pgs	**4 3/8**
Wednesday, October 16, 2013					
EP 506					
Thursday, October 17, 2013					
EP 507					
Friday, October 18, 2013					
EP 507					
Monday, October 21, 2013					
EP 506					
Tuesday, October 22, 2013					
EP 506					
Wednesday, October 23, 2013					
POSS DBL UP 506/507					
Thursday, October 24, 2013					
POSS DBL UP 506/507					

Figure 8.19 *GLEE* Episode 501: One-Sheet

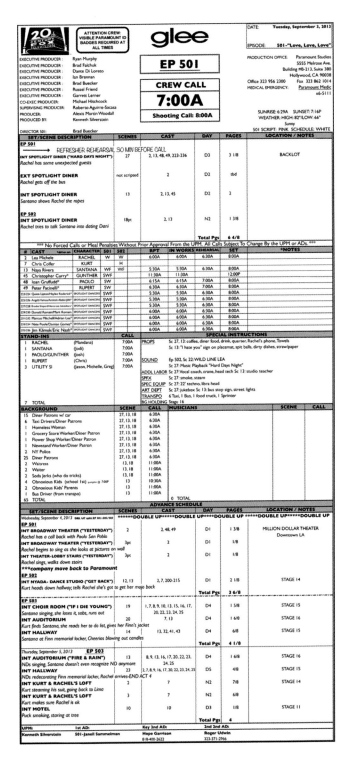

Figure 8.20 *GLEE* Episode 501: Call Sheet

ALL ABOUT PLANS

Outside of their practical use by the construction department, floor plans are communication devices between the art department and everyone else. Understanding how to use a scale rule is the only way to properly read a plan; the scale of the drawing is always found in the lower right-hand corner or **title block** of the page. In the United States, all drawing scales are based on fractions of an inch, and are typical to TV and film; the rest of the world uses metric scales.

- Spotting plans (⅛″ or ¼″ scale): The most basic tool that emerges from a set design. At a glance, it indicates how many sets will comfortably fit on a swing stage or where rigging grips will hang a soft backing. It also determines floor lamp placement and overhead electrical pipe position for electricians, or reveals the best area to set up video village. All *Glee* spotting plans show a bar scale in 1′, 5′, and 10′ increments to indicate relative sizes on the drawing, as well as the noted scale below the drawing.
- Directors plans (⅛″ or ¼″ scale): Originally designed to assist directors in blocking scenes, it is now used as a page for jotting tech scout notes or for 2nd AD to determine number of extras to fill a set, for example.
- Instrument plans (⅛″ or ¼″ scale): These plans are specific to a show like *Glee* or *Smash*; based on a typical orchestral instrument arrangement, this plan locates musician positions within any given set where a sung performance is to be filmed.

Table 8.2 Typical drawing scales and paper sizes.

DRAWING NAME	DRAWING SCALE	PAPER SIZE	SET PLACEMENT
SPOTTING PLAN	1/4″and 1/8″	11″ x 17″ paper	Soundstage
DIRECTORS PLAN	1/4″ and 1/8″	11″ x 17″ paper	Soundstage or Location
INSTRUMENT PLAN	1/4″and 1/8″	11″ x 17″ paper	Soundstage
LOCATION PLAN	1/8″ and 3/16″	11″ x 17″ paper or 24″ x 36″ sheet	Location

- Concept sketches: Often, these sketches drawn by an illustrator, production designer, or art director. They can be loose and quick or very developed and will accompany an instrument plan to indicate to the Lighting Designer the intent of the production design team. Our assistant art director draws SketchUp concept sketches.
- Location plans (3/16″ or ⅛″ scale): Most filming venues outside the studios are private homes or apartments, municipal buildings or large outdoor areas like parks. These smaller scales allow us to fit the plan to the size of the page, e.g. 11″ × 17″, also a typical non-construction page size.

All sets noted on the shooting schedule and one-liner are emailed to all department heads by an art department production assistant. Hard copies printed on 11″ × 17″ paper are also distributed by the same PA for note-taking and notebook reference. The same size hard copy is stored in the office flat files; paper copies of both 11″ × 17″ and 24″ × 36″ sizes reflect digital copies stored online. Organization is the only way to survive a 22-episode season. Do it, flawlessly.

A TYPICAL DAY

Crew Call Tasks

In all honesty, it is not possible to work less than a 12-hour day. The crew is usually called at 7:00 am on Monday, having had crew breakfast at the centralized craft service area by 6:30 am. Just before rehearsal is a good time to update several people about new scenery and the day's work: Leadman and On-set Dresser about changing or adding set dressing requested by the director; the Key Grip regarding wild walls; reminding the Greensman about the onset of spring and not overdoing the tiny chartreuse leaves on stock treetops; and minor touch-up notes for the On-set Painter. Checking in with the UPM isn't a bad idea—shifts in actor availability or music clearance are issues that drive the schedule—as the scenery fabrication schedule would adjust accordingly to comply with a current shift in production schedule, meaning the budget might need to be augmented. In adjacent stages, I also revisit the sets being shot later in the day or ones still being prepped for subsequent days, with a checklist on the iPad to prevent any embarrassing mishaps.

Rehearsal happens with principal characters for **blocking and marking.** When completed, the principals leave for hair and make-up and **stand-ins** step onto their respective principal's marks for lighting and camera positioning. Once principals return to set, I wait until we've gotten our first shot; before heading for the mill, I'll check in with the ADs for schedule changes or revisions.

Supervising Scenery Construction

Consistent communication and supervision ensure the visual consistency of the drafted scenery as it is interpreted and fabricated by the carpenters and surfaces are finished and aged by the painters. Larger or more complicated sets require more continuous interaction as construction groups move through each progressive phase of set building and finishing. Consequently I'm in the mill several times a day for updates. With the General Foreman's help, materials called out in the drawings are not only reviewed but discussed in realistic terms of availability with an eye on the insistent shooting schedule; very often substitutes for flooring, hardware or window glass are chosen as rapidly as possible so the schedule isn't compromised.

Please note, there are two things the construction crew is not responsible for:

1. Backings: Although this is a line item on the construction budget, the department only pays for the rental cost, but rigging grips hang them.
2. Signage: Most pre-made, rental signage—such as neon—is installed on a set by the set dressing swing gang, although most signage fabricated by the studio sign shop is hung by carpenters both on location and on studio set walls (see "Local 44 Budgeting Guidelines," Appendix A).

A check-in with the Construction Coordinator is most likely necessary, perhaps about a budget item questioned at breakfast by the UPM, or to clarify the preferred use of one building material over another, or to talk about the probability of weekend work. Painting finishes are less forgiving in terms of design expectation. We work diligently to keep as many finishing processes intact to preserve HD video quality, for obvious reasons. There are times when it's necessary to be with the painters at 4:00 am to look at step three of a four-step paint process before a final finishing coat is applied to a scenic surface. The payoff happens during a lunchtime crew screening, as the Lead Painter and I silently nod a shared approval in the dark theater. Going the extra distance always makes a difference.

Art Department Check-In

Questions and answers take place in the wood shop and continue in the art department. The set designer begins the day early and leaves early. If drafted pages are not completed by the end of a ten-hour day, then those drawings are promised at morning coffee break, when several copies are provided for construction breakdown. Stray questions regarding details and upcoming sets are addressed before "preliminary" stamped drawings are finally stamped "released" on the sheets to be printed for construction. The same drawings are uploaded to the server and the design process is complete. Generally, I handle the translation of the printed stuff that emerges from the art department. This includes support renderings or packets of research material—anything that will enhance a carpenter's understanding of how to build our scenery. If questions arise and I'm not available, the set designer is qualified to clarify a drawing's intent, especially for full-scale detail drawings. The Graphic Designer, servant to several masters, can suddenly become inundated so I check in twice daily to know who has requested what, and ask for digital copies for my records.

In rare quiet times, like riding the elevator to our offices, I'll check the phone for messages, or simply do it at my laptop. This particular ritual happens easily a dozen times a day; there are many people to account to during the course of 12 fast hours, but this is just mid-morning.

Before the Production Designer lands at the office, I'll text images of scenery in process and any other information as "a most current update." In the same text, I also include a list of issues that need our combined attention over research materials and a cup of coffee. In preparation for our conversation, I gather paint samples, drawn sketches or SketchUp models, drafting in process and spotting plans for review. My goal is to gather missing information for anyone working in the mill *before* lunch break so my afternoon time can be spent focused on reading new script pages and the rapid shift of onstage scenery for upcoming episodic script demands. Lunch happens in the art department, courtesy of the production office, around our conference table. Afterwards, wallpaper swatch books, as well as paint, carpet, and other material samples and research photos replace the lunch spread. There, the art department coordinator and PA assist by compiling a list of tasks to accomplish immediately:

- Using the square footage figured per set, call for wall and floor covering materials.
- Print additional research images, if necessary, and large graphics on our color plotter.
- Organize new drafting into flat files to reflect what the Draftsman has uploaded to the server.
- Pick up adhesive vinyl and hard graphic signage from the sign shop and deliver to our paint department for installation.
- Double-check orders and pick up from/arrange delivery dates with other vendors.
- Arrange for rental backings to be put on hold for picking up.

The reason for completing this list immediately is because it can seriously impact the production of finished scenery; all material samples chosen by the designer should include first, second, and third choices. Swift and accurate action ensures scenery load-in either on or before schedule—a very good thing indeed.

After lunch, many of the crew I met with seven hours earlier begin to randomly filter through the art department on the way to the production office to do paperwork or argue about potential overtime hours. So, those conversations continue in my office in detail. Our lighting designer, Andrew Glover, always greets you with an engaging, "What's going on?" Well, that's the point, isn't it? "As scheduling changes, let me know," is what he's really saying. Advance schedule notice is powerful information, sought after by everyone. My back pocket sources are on the shooting crew: script supervisor, on-set dresser, or cameramen are the first to overhear conversations between the Director and upper management; this information is the most reliable. Regardless, one needs to check other sources especially if there are no official announcements being made. This is precisely why Andrew double-checks with me or whoever else is close to schedule revision info. A final source of reliability is the UPM or the Production Supervisor; either will dispel inaccurate rumors or provide bankable information if they have it.

The last hour of my 12-hour daily schedule is spent quickly organizing the digital and hard copy distribution of Director's and instrument spotting plans for upcoming scenes containing musical numbers. The goal is for colleagues to have these pages in-hand at least two days before shooting the scenes noted on these plans.

Season Schedule

A typical one-hour episodic television program begins its new season the last week of June or the first week of July, when the art department reconvenes by slamming into designing the first permanent sets for the new season. First day of photography begins toward the last half of August, a month later and the first episode airs within the first weeks of September. Major holidays provide three- or four-day weekends for the crew, except for the two-week Christmas hiatus. Once back to work in the New Year, the fast-paced episodic schedule crashes to a halt by the second week in May—then a four- to six-week hiatus, completing the dizzying ten-month production schedule.

Renewal and Wrap

Working on a show that is renewed from season to season provides more than another year's salary for the crew; five running seasons or 100 episodes provide syndication status for the producers. Syndication is where a lot of revenue is accrued in reruns, especially for super-successful shows like *Cheers, Friends,* or *Glee.* It is the reason why producers and crews hang in year after year: a steady cash flow and reliable bankability. Obviously, working on a continuously renewed television series provides "steady" employment unlike film work which is intermittent at best. An episodic show—like *Breaking Bad, Dexter,* or *Glee,* for example—is structured to span over several seasons with a plotline or story arc arriving at a logical conclusion in the season finale. At the end of such a long run, it is once again time to take advantage of your network to secure your next project, either television or film, and extend your personal career arc.

NOTES

1 Christa Munro interview, September 11, 2004, Flintridge, CA.
2 Phil Dagort interview, June 6, 2004, Toluca Lake, CA.

CHAPTER 9

Networking and Self-Promotion

This category is a purely selfish one. Networking is how we create careers. It incorporates every aspect of our managing skills and our personalities into what an interviewer sees and how this person is convinced to hire us. Self-promotion is a place where *you* get to be the product or service. If you were going to market yourself, how would you begin? Probably the best way is to define your target audience. The production designer is your obvious target market, but you will also be interviewing with the UPM to negotiate your deal memo. Each prospect in your target market will be receptive to different metaphors and some will overlap.

INTERVIEWING

Production designers expect loyalty, amenability, creative thinking, leadership, follow-through, and attention to detail. Unit production managers expect attention to detail, follow-through, leadership, budget focus, frugality, and flexibility. Notice the overlaps and the outliers. Tweaking the outlier attributes addresses the niche market you happen to be playing to at the moment; the middle range or overlapping attributes cover the normal range. These guidelines are worth thinking about before interviewing with a Designer or the UPM. Lack of experience is a blatant non-attribute. Projecting the qualities you do have is sometimes more convincing than a range of experience. Think about your personal qualities and prepare your "pitch" that will indicate who you are, what your accomplishments are, skills you have, where your passions lie, and what job you are seeking. The point is to be honest and sincere. Although you are playing to a particular audience during an interview, your focus isn't artifice—the greatest actors come from a place of sincerity and honesty in order to create believability. Reading your audience at the time of an interview, or understanding who you are playing to at the moment is the key: you are a mirror for the Production Designer or UPM as you sell yourself, playing back to that person an eager romantic who once sat where you are sitting. Project a positive, likeable memory, and you most likely will be hired. The fascinating thing is that we tend to surround ourselves with likenesses of ourselves as it provides a good comfort zone. Using these parameters for an interview and landing the job are the payoff of a good networking strategy.

THE NETWORKING PROCESS

The networking process that unfolds before getting a job interview provides the foundation for a solid career. Networking style varies among people. Those strategies used by highly successful people in any given industry are worth analyzing for obvious reasons.

Catherine Hardwicke

Director: *Lords of Dogtown, Thirteen, Twilight*. Production Designer: *Laurel Canyon, Vanilla Sky, Three Kings, 2 Days in the Valley, Tank Girl*. She recalls her early years working on films like *Thrashin'* (1986), *Mr. Destiny* (1990), and *Tombstone* (1993), and provides insight as a designer, screenwriter, and director.

As I remember you telling the story, you were too creative for architecture and encouraged not to be an architect. How did you react to that news—was it difficult to hear?

[Soft laugh] Exactly. Yes, it was because I had worked for five years in college, and I had busted my butt and I loved it. Then at the end of it, my instructors said that my creativity would be so stifled doing just architecture that I'd probably be disappointed. They predicted I would be put in a box and just be asked to do the graphics for the firm. Needless to say, it didn't sound too good, but I did immediately go and make my own project as an architect: a 20-acre subdivision containing 120 townhouses. That was really fun, but people wanted me to recreate the same look again and again. Since I had created this successful design, new clients only wanted that, but I didn't want to repeat myself—at that point I had already thought that design was kind of boring. I wanted to do something wilder. That's why I *thought* film would give me the opportunity to do more creative stuff. It's just not always the case. [Big laugh] On most projects you're asked to re-create reality. Unfortunately, there aren't that many *Cat in the Hat* projects around.

Having had some solid architectural training, did you also take courses on directing?

I finished a five-year professional degree in architecture, then I worked as an architect and contractor for three years, then I went to UCLA grad school for film for one year and studied animation and live-action. I made a small animation/live-action film that won a Focus Award. An agent at the awards festival for the film noticed me and signed me because I had also written a screenplay with Michael Werb (*Lara Croft: Tomb Raider*), while we were at UCLA. After the film was greenlit and budgeted, the head of the studio changed, and it never happened. Not soon after, I met a producer dancing in a club here in LA, who was working on a skateboard movie. Knowing I was an architect, he suggested I production design his movie called *Thrashin'*. I didn't know or understand the names of the categories of production designer or art director at the time but it was a non-union film, so I did everything on a creative level. I also hired three people on my staff who stayed at my house or lived in the art department truck. It was a $1 million movie, but I learned a lot and met all these famous skateboarders who I worked with again on my 2005 movie *Lords of Dogtown*, which I directed. [Giggle] Full circle. It's all come full circle. So, I accidentally, randomly wandered into art direction and loved it. After that I got offered many other movies.

When I first moved here I didn't know anybody in LA or the film business. After I got that first job by dancing like a crazy person, I continued going to the clubs. People would meet me, dance with me, and hire me [Raucous laugh].

So, for anyone who is coming up in the ranks, is studying architecture essential for designing?

It's really fantastic. I've had mostly architecturally trained people work for me. By the way, Carnegie Mellon has a theater design program that's just as hardcore and radical as UCLA. I think anything can work, but the architecture is clearly helpful. If I were advising somebody, I would suggest that and also photography. AFI has a great production design program, as well as UCLA. Any well-known film school program will do. And, of course, there's no substitute for just working in the business.

In your early career, then, did you do any art directing?

After designing several movies in the $3–4 million range, I decided to do bigger movies at the higher end of the independent film range. I found an agent who suggested I art direct for a designer one time for a studio feature. That's why I took *Mr. Destiny* (1990) as an art director. The experience taught me what I needed to know about the studio system. It's the only art direction job I had.

Would you give us your thoughts on three aspects of designing low budget films by addressing these questions: 1) What is a good deal versus a bad deal? 2) Is screen credit enough or should you ask for more? 3) How do you resolve creative vision versus budget?

In 2003 I made *Thirteen* as a director, a $1.5 million film. Carol Strober, my production designer, had to work under the same constraints I had about 13 years before. In retrospect, it was fascinating to see how you can pull it off with no money and lots of passion and inspiration. To answer all of your questions, my best advice is, if you think the Director is prepared and talented, and the script has integrity, then commit yourself. With those two things in place, it's a good indication that the project could get released and might see the light of day, and then it doesn't matter if you get paid. The goal is to work on a good movie. Always try to work with the best people you can. This could jump-start a career faster than anything else. Then if you have an opportunity to contribute to a project headed by a talented director, writer, and producer—well—anything could happen. Once you're in, you need to put your heart and soul into it every minute of every day and do whatever it takes to be the best you can possibly be.

One year at Sundance, there were 900 entries. That means 900 art directors and production designers worked on 900 movies probably for free or little money on Indie movies. Twelve made it above the competition to finally be screened at the festival. Our little movie was one of those. The people who worked with me were paid a box of dirt, almost nothing, but they busted their butts, and the movie was not only good but also recognized. For them, having *Thirteen* on a resume as an Oscar-nominated movie has to help a hell of a lot more than getting paid a decent wage.

So, you've got to find a way to get to the good people. Join IFP West, volunteer at the film schools in LA, find out who has something special that's going to make a good Indie film. Then do anything to work on it. On *Thirteen,* even though I was the Director, the set-decorating five-ton truck backed up to my house and took half of my stuff to the set. *Lords of Dogtown* was a $30 million picture for Sony, but still we took stuff out of my house. Having an attitude of entitlement isn't going to do anybody any good. You're only going to succeed if you work real hard and your work is great.

Thank you. You nailed it. What did you enjoy or not enjoy about art directing?

I like the whole process: coming up with an idea and seeing it built five minutes later, making it look good, and having to solve unseen problems. I like all those challenges. I like to have to come in on a budget. In some ways I think it makes your job better. You have to be more creative.

I don't like the politics: figuring out which producer to get on your side to release more money for a set or pay people to stay on an extra day. There's always the psychological game-playing. If the Director doesn't have as much vision as you have, then it's your challenge to convince them that your idea is their idea. The trick with that is to get him or her excited or inspired but not overwhelmed by you. As an art director, your biggest challenge is how you manage your crew. Most of those people are artists and that can make it more stressful for an art director to make the experience a creative one for everyone in the art department. It's hard to have your crew understand that they are significant and are making a substantial contribution. It's just hard to do your job and to keep all those artistic temperaments happy—that's the biggest challenge for an art director. Most of us never went to business school; most of us were never trained in management styles. I'm sure that hundreds of decisions I have had to make in my career could have been solved more easily if I had had a couple of management courses under my belt. When I finally started catching on, I realized that when I was talking to the line producer/production manager they only care about one thing—that I'm doing something smart for them. I'd come up with an idea that saves money. I'd recycle this set into that set or reconfigure scenery in other ways. I'd have to tell them about my ideas in terms that they'd understand. When I go to interviews, I not only take drawings and photographs, but I take budgets, just in case a line producer is sitting in on the interview.

What qualities do you expect and prefer in an art director?

Super-organization. Someone who is so organized that, even if they're out on a job site, I can go to their desk and look at a copy of their notebook or a PC file to get the information I need. Now more than ever, I need someone who is multitalented and can jump on the computer and do great stuff. Also, I always consider someone who's creative and provides good ideas and contributes to the process. You know, I just want the best person on the planet—someone that blows me away.

Describe your designing process. How do you pre-visualize?

Different projects require different processes. Some projects are historical and require research. What does Iraq look like now? On *Three Kings* (1999) that was all just research for me at first, and then I started getting excited about it through the process. We called the Kuwaiti Embassy, found lots more research, and investigated newspaper footage. And then sometimes it's more imagination where you do just, "Ah—I'm going to design the coolest set." And, I then just start sketching out something crazy. So, it really depends on the project.

Have new technologies made your relationships with the director easier or more challenging?

Easier. It helps you to see how things might look a lot faster. It's a plus.

Generally, how do you create a healthy relationship with your visual effects coordinator?

The projects I've done have not been as visual effects intensive as Alex McDowell's have. On my former projects somehow, instantly, because visual effects people are all great artists, we just end up sharing fun ideas and inspiring one another. It's more inclusive and about being a fun, creative process. I've really just had super-positive experiences. In my post-work for *Dogtown*, I had a great relationship with Gray Marshall of Gray Matter, who did our visual effects. I stopped at his office on the way to do post at Sony to work out ideas and do sketches. It was fun and I loved it. I worked at a visual effects company when I first got here while at UCLA so I have some understanding of what's currently being done.

How can the art department operate more smoothly?

Every member of the staff is vital. From the art coordinator to the PA, everyone can potentially make a vital contribution. On *Tombstone* (1993), a non-union film, my art department PA became an art director by the end of the movie. Chris Gorak is now a big production designer. On the same movie, there were seven people with master's degrees in architecture on my staff, so everybody was brilliant. Everybody was able to leap to the challenge with more or less experience in film. It made the project a success.

So, do you think the visual effects and art departments are beginning to merge with all the sharing and overlapping that's going on at this time?

Yes and no. Finishing *Dogtown*, the art department production people were gone when a lot of the heavy visual effects started. That's an interesting question that needs to get figured out over time. How much does a production designer stay actively involved in post? When do the overlaps occur and how can they be positive, especially with new advancements coming into play? On past movies when I was off payroll, I was involved with the visual effects people because I wanted to be. There's always more to know.[1]

Other art directors' job finding experiences are worth considering. Excerpts from longer interviews with Gae Buckley, Phil Dagort, Steve Saklad, Christa Munro, and Linda Berger provide equally valuable examples of networking strategy.

Gae Buckley

(The Book of Eli, He's Just Not That Into You, The Sisterhood of the Traveling Pants, Open Range, Coyote Ugly, What Women Want)

> *Gae, how did you begin to create your career network in Los Angeles?*

As a child I studied painting and drawing with my mother, an artist. I also worked as an architect in NYC and wondered about continuing when I got an offer to work on a music video. The next year I worked in music videos in many different aspects of production, but still decided to try architecture again. Another friend called to lure me into scenic painting and art directing music videos, commercials, and small TV shows. Beyond that, my goal was to be in Los Angeles working on features. I moved there from New York in 1988.

When I arrived in LA, I knew no one. I was first hired in a set-building shop as a sculptor on a commercial. The next commercial they hired me as a scenic painter, and the next as a set designer. Soon after, Penny Hadfield (aka Veronica Hadfield), the queen of the movie of the week and mini-series, called to ask me to be a set designer. A few weeks later Cynthia Charette, the Art Director, left to design a Wes Craven movie so I moved into her position. Penny and I worked together for a couple of years and when I left her I began my career as a feature art director.

> *The process is different for everyone. And, if we dig a little deeper, the network lines will emerge.*

Well, the reason I got the job with Penny was because Cynthia Charette had just come off a show in Boston, and I had worked with some Boston crew in New York. She had heard my name so when I arrived in LA she recognized it, and I was hired. So, yes, it was that direct and that simple.[2]

Phil Dagort

(Huff, Six Feel Under, X-Files, Crazy Stupid Love, The Hunted, Hard Target)

> *After graduating architecture school, how did you begin your film career?*

The irony is that soon after I graduated with an architectural degree in the late 1970s there was a recession. There were not as many jobs as before I started and with a shrunken architectural market, the film business was the perfect place to look for a job. Of course, I had planned to do this all along. My parents just wanted me to have a degree. Little did I know I was way ahead of my time—after I got into the industry, people I went to school with were calling looking for work.

When I first started in the business, like most people, I knew no one. I began by getting designers' names and setting up interviews, and I suppose I did this by six degrees of separation. I asked everyone I knew and finally had a list. Only one designer I met actually had an opening for an assistant, but during my interview he was dwelling on my lack of experience and familiarity in knowing where to shop for set dressing. At another interview the same day I met Debbie Hemela. She was selling this guide for set dressing that she had just completed. So I bought one and turned around and went back to the interview I had just left, placed the book on his desk, and said "Now I know where to find stuff." The designer then hired me on the spot. So, I guess landing a first job is about a bit of chutzpah and a bit of luck. (That book has now become *Debbie's Book*.) I went right to work and learned on the job, mistakes and all. In the beginning, I came up into the business as an assistant in videotape where we all crossed over job positions. We drafted the set first, supervised set going into the shop for building and finishes, and then went out and shopped the set dressing. Videotape at the time wasn't governed by the film agreements, so the benefit was that it was excellent overall training ground to learn all the pieces of the puzzle.

Now my process for finding work or hiring people is based on whom I like to work with because of their taste and how well we get on. I look at the *Hollywood Reporter* to get a sense of what's going on and that might springboard me into a possible job contact, but I tend to refer to my list of every person I met and have worked. The list just builds on itself. It might take 20 years, but an original contact might eventually land me a new work situation.[3]

Steve Saklad

(Spider-Man 2, Red Dragon, Message in a Bottle, The Mambo Kings)
Explain your networking process going from Yale Drama School to film.

Out of Yale, I first assisted Broadway set designers David Mitchell and later Tony Walton on a series of Broadway plays and musicals. During the 1980s in New York City, I was typically involved in segueing between assistant art directing/drafting on movies and working as assistant designer on Broadway shows. I first met art director, W. Steven Graham, when he hired me to draft on *Radio Days* in 1985, and later hired me to work as a set designer for Stuart Wurtzel on *Old Gringo* in 1988. Stuart and I hit it off, and eventually it was Stuart who gave me my first shot at art directing for him when we made *Mermaids* (1990). I attribute the rest of my film career to Steve and Stuart, as these two connected me with a solid networking base in film. In the early 1990s, there was a lockout by the West Coast studios against the New York unions' demands for better pay scales. Most movie work dried up, signaling a large exodus for many of us to the West coast. Knowing no one in LA at first and waiting for East Coast designers coming west with projects-in-hand, I began designing commercials for TV. My early career has bounced back and forth between designing commercials and art directing on features.

I never seem to know what my next project will be while I'm still working on the current one. That's where designing commercials for the same director/producer team since 1994 has been a godsend for me. By 2000, I'd chosen an agent at ICM to represent me for commercial design on the proviso that he would make his percentage from all projects other than this particular commercial company I had already secured. One great dividend from my connection with ICM has been a growing relationship with their team of agents devoted to feature films. It was one of those who secured my first feature film design job, *Shadowboxer* (2005). Now the question presents itself: do I want to art direct a $50 million movie or wait around for the next low-budget script I can design? Even the small Indie project to design can be more satisfying in a way that the biggest summer blockbuster to art direct may not. Ultimately, as a creative person, I get to try it all as a production designer in a way that you don't as an art director.

Any advice for working on Indies?

You only get to be a virgin once. The idea of throwing away that status on a Santa Claus-gore-fest-horror-thriller shot in Canada is something to think hard about, considering you might become known as The Designer of Gore Movies. The important things to consider are the script, a credible director, and notable actors. Then you have something; you have credibility, a calling card.[4]

Christa Munro

(Jack Reacher, Mission Impossible: Ghost Protocol, Priest, The Spiderwick Chronicles, Good Night and Good Luck, Erin Brockovich)

Did the beginnings of your networking experience grow out of the theater, art school, or something else?

While working in a local art store connected with the Art Center here in LA, I was aware of this guy who graduated from Art Center who I would bug for freelance work. One afternoon he came into the store and offered me a job. He needed drawings for large-scale models he was working on at his studio for the ancient library of Alexandria, Egypt, for Carl Sagan's show *Cosmos*. We went over to Paramount Studios to check in on how the shooting crew was getting on with the models and *wham!* That was the beginning of it. It was like giant doors had been thrown open by a cool gust of wind on a hot day. I continued on that project until it wrapped. Through the contacts I made there, I was introduced to some LA companies that did commercials, a couple of the feature contacts, and it just took off from there. Eventually, the networking lines crisscrossed back to my college acquaintances at Art Center who had continued into filmmaking. We reconnected, started working together doing *Playboy* projects, and having a ball. Needless to say, this was a classic networking experience. Combined with your technical skills, it's the people skills that make a career—and for that matter, what moves the whole industry.

How do you handle the stress?

As you know, the 14-hour days, five days a week, in addition to any weekend work make it overwhelming. Playing polo is really the only activity I do that totally overrides the effects of the work schedule because you have to be extremely focused on the game at hand. I guess the intensity of one has to equally balance the other.[5]

Linda Berger

(Almost A Woman, Forrest Gump, Death Becomes Her)

Linda, what's your networking story?

It's pretty brilliant—not my brilliance—but I essentially did it twice: once in 1985 in videotape and then in 1990 with film.

Let me quickly backtrack. From the age of 11, I knew I wanted to design films after seeing a double billing rerelease of *The Man Who Shot Liberty Valance* (1962) and *Forbidden Planet* (1956). Watching two films of totally diverse genres told me that the sky was the limit. Creatively, it was possible to design a black-and-white historical western, or a

Technicolor, cinemascope sci-fi drama based on Shakespeare's *Tempest*. Another film that deeply impressed me even earlier was *Helen of Troy* (1956)—it was one of the first films I ever saw. I was very young and my dad took me—he loved historical epics and he wanted me to see this one. I still remember how I felt when I first saw the giant horse onscreen. When I met Ken Adam—to be able to ask him about working on that film as an assistant art director was a high point in my life.

Determined to creatively be in both worlds, I went to the Goodman Theater and Art Institute of Chicago as a theatrical designer and fine artist in a magnificent reciprocity program that no longer exists. Soon after graduating, I lost track of a fellow lighting designer classmate, Edgar Swift, who was one of my very best friends all through school. The CBS affiliate television studio in Seattle hired me as an art director. I did everything from news graphics, *TV Guide* ads, public service announcements, sets for special programs, and a Sunday <u>60 Minutes</u>-style news show called *KIRO Newsline*. I also did hundreds of commercials for a related in-house commercial production company. I did JC Penney's regional/national commercials there. This all tested my creativity and earned me several Emmy nominations and an Emmy Award. Photographs of some of my work were published in a book put out by the Broadcast Designers Association. The head of the art department of ABC in Los Angeles at the time saw my work and got in touch. He extended the invitation to see him at ABC when I came down next. Once there during my interview, he gave me my first networking list of television contacts, including the head of operations and supervising head of the art department at NBC, Ed Swift. I did not make the connection. I was escorted into his office, and there was Edgar, my art school friend. He took my portfolio, put it in a corner, and took me out to lunch. I couldn't believe my eyes. We were both flabbergasted. It was outrageous. But it was wonderful. That was the beginning of my five years at NBC.

It's never been easy, but it's always astonishing. I feel like I'm riding on a train watching the ever-changing scenery and stepping off along the way to explore—then stepping back on to enjoy the ride—not having a clue about where I'm headed, but I know it's somewhere wonderful.

In 1990 came a second serendipitous and lucky opportunity via a connection at Paramount Studios. I was aware that Herman Zimmerman (*Star Trek: Nemesis, First Contact*, and *Generations*), whose work I admired, was on the Paramount lot so I took a chance and knocked on the door of his office. I thought that perhaps he might give me an appointment for an interview later, but instead he invited me in right then to speak with him. What a wonderful thing! (Little did I know then that literally one brave chance would change everything for me and send me off into a new direction—one I had actually been striving toward since I was a young girl of about 11—to design motion pictures.) Anyway, I always had my portfolio with me so Herman Zimmerman looked through every page. I asked lots of questions, and he gave me really helpful direction and advice and real encouragement about my potential and design skills. I described working at NBC among many other assignments, as an assistant to the late John Shrum, creator of the *Johnny Carson Show* settings and many of the now classic television shows. John had spoken with great pride about one of his earlier assistants, Herman Zimmerman, and I related John's story and my pleasure at having had the opportunity to work with this great early television designer, for he had been so wonderful to me. Toward the end of our talk, Zimmerman graciously offered to call J. Michael Riva (*Charlie's Angels, Iron Man, The Color Purple*) on my behalf, and as a result I was able to get an appointment to see him the following week. I went to the Columbia Pictures lot, now Sony Pictures, and J. Michael Riva and I sat and talked for at least an hour. He gave me excellent advice, a lot of encouragement, and thought enough of my work to give me a list of the names and phone numbers of 15 people to see, including Patrizia von Brandenstein, Albert Brenner, Dick Sylbert, and Rick Carter. The final person on this list I saw was Rick Carter (*Polar Express, Forrest Gump, Avatar*), who was working in a trailer at Universal Studios filled with drawings and concept models as he prepared the initial ideas for the future *Jurassic Park* (1993). There were the most amazing drawings and illustrations on every wall—models of the future buildings of the island—and dinosaurs everywhere. Like the others, he was so very generous with his time and willingness to offer great advice and direction. Several weeks later I invited him to lunch to talk again. I asked lots of questions, and his advice and insights were of great value to me. To my great surprise and excitement, several months later he called and invited *me* to lunch with him and his art director, Jim Teegarden; it was then that they offered me the chance to work with them as an assistant art director on *Death Becomes Her* (1992).

Earlier in the process of enjoying the gift of this wonderful list J. Michael Riva had given me, I had the great opportunity to interview with Richard Sylbert (*The Bonfire of the Vanities, Dick Tracy, Splendor in the Grass*). Talking with Dick Sylbert was really a lesson in designing film scenery when the conversation moved to the film *A Face in the Crowd* (1957) he designed with his twin brother, Paul, for Elia Kazan, and starring Andy Griffith. I asked him about designing this film because I felt the settings were so powerfully evocative of the story, and I wanted to understand why. One of the last images in the film had stayed with me since I first saw the film: Griffith's character's penthouse apartment with the bridge-like path in front of huge windows leading from a tall winding staircase. He explained how the scenery clearly defined how the main character keeps going up in life, but really goes nowhere after all. Through my discussion with Dick, I learned how images could be symbolic for storytelling and character analysis; this clearly showed how he designed character development into his films. I was later thrilled to be asked to join his art department on *The Witching Hour*, a project that had a couple of false starts and then never happened. Sylbert was a mentor to Rick Carter so I was doubly fortunate.

When I was hired by Rick Carter on *Death Becomes Her* as assistant art director, Rick went to Gene Allen, the head of the Art Directors Guild, on my behalf to plead my case because I had only worked in "tape" in LA. After a long process of filling out forms, petitioning the Guild with my record of working hours at NBC, and submitting the full body of my work, I was given the status I needed. I owe it all to Rick Carter—and of course, Herman Zimmerman.

We had to shoot several endings for *Death Becomes Her*, and I was asked to art direct the reshoots while Rick and Jim Teegarden, art director, were in Hawaii beginning pre-production for *Jurassic Park*. I ran everything I needed to do by Rick and then shepherded the last part of the movie for him. I later joined them on *Jurassic Park* and later again on *Forrest Gump*.

Rick had such tremendous trust and respect for those of us who worked closely with him. What I learned most from Rick was that the art department must be a place of pleasure and respect where it was our job to simply create the movie. Rick ran political interference for us so we could do just that. That was a particularly wonderful experience for me.[6]

PAYING DUES

Your film relationships are your most vital resource. The maxim, "You're only as good as your last job" must have originated in Hollywood. From what I've seen, people are hired primarily for attitude, especially newcomers whose skill level is questionable. So, be prepared to do whatever it takes, even if it means erasing your personal life for the duration of a project. Eve Light Honthaner, author of *The Complete Film Production Handbook*, reinforces this point:

> *The trick is to be the very best production assistant, runner, apprentice, or secretary that ever existed. Short of being totally abused and terribly exploited, don't whine or groan when asked to do something you don't want to do. Accept tasks willingly. No one is asking you to do anything just to make your life miserable. If it has to be done and falls within your sphere of responsibility, you don't have much choice. Do not complain. Everyone is busy, and no one wants to hear it. Be a pleasure to have around; be a team player and if you have any extra time, volunteer to help others with their work. Everyone will agree that you are wonderful, and they will all want you to work on their next picture and the next one after that.[7]*

As harsh as it sounds, the people who hire you want to see total commitment. The harsher fact is the line around the building is long, and we are all replaceable. The positive side is that the rewards of going the distance are reaped by eager recommendations at the end of a film project. Sublimating your will and life to the project proves that you "are one of us" and that you have the stamina for the process. When the baptism of fire is over, requests will begin to fill up your voicemail and email.

FAQS

I am constantly asked a handful of questions that might be of help here:

Do I need a degree to work in the art department?
No, a degree for art department work is not necessary. Solid training in a reputable film school or university or college film program or art school is preferred—the degree is secondary to the school attended and academic training experience.

Which are the best education choices?

With film design in mind, a school choice should complement your personality and needs. A film school per se will stress technique, theory, and hands-on experience, university or college education might be more general in scope but might offer excellent computer graphics courses, art schools will focus on hand skills and computer skills that directly refer to art department creative work. In addition to these suggestions, you must do a good deal of research in order to tailor your training to your temperament.

What should I study?

With film design in mind, you should study architectural drafting, art history, cinematography, and **CAD** or computer-assisted drawing and drafting software.

Which computer programs are most important to know?

You must have a solid working skill level with Adobe Photoshop and Illustrator, Macromedia Director, AutoCAD or VectorWorks. A good, basic understanding of Maya or 3D Studio Max will help navigate the modeling environments. Microsoft Office Suite—especially Word, Excel, and Access—is an important software package to know extremely well because it will help you correctly interface with other film departments and keep yourself organized.

What other skills are necessary?

Communicating ideas through drawing and sketching are paramount skills. Well-developed interpersonal and social skills are the basis of the collaborative nature of the film business. The rest is found in Section II of this book.

Should I work as a production assistant first?

If it is the only job available in the art department, it is an excellent place to begin hands-on education. Experience on one non-union film from the first days of pre-production to the last days of art department wrap provides a good basis for all you will need to know for the rest of your career as an art director or designer.

Are there sources for lists of art department jobs?

Trade papers including *The Hollywood Reporter, Daily Variety,* and *Below the Line* magazine should be checked regularly for shows in development or various stages of prep with pertinent information on resume submission. **Motion Picture Space** at http://www.motionpicturespace.com connects union and non-union entertainment industry people on a highly interconnected database. Also industry related websites such as http://LA411.com, http://productionyak.com/, and http://TheAcme.com are all indispensable for posting a resume through modest membership fees. Spiral, printed versions of these sites are also available, as well as other helpful industry site links found on these websites.

Appendix A of this book contains "Film Pocket Listings," covering movie industry categories and accompanying Web addresses, as well as other resources for additional information.

Do I have to live in Los Angeles?
The film industry is now global. Presently, international hot spots are located in Canada, Mexico, Australia, New Zealand, Czech Republic, England, France, and Germany. In the US, filmmaking centers are currently located in New Mexico, Georgia, Florida, and North Carolina. What's been outlined above are major centers of film activity; in addition to being global, moviemaking is done locally at every level.

Doing your research homework for filmmaking in the area you are going to school or living is practical and most often overlooked. For example, you will not only get your feet wet working on an Indie in Buffalo, New York, you also will have invaluable experience and a final crew list of references for your next gig. Using the information outlined above will transport you directly to where you are headed, and might present some unimagined possibility. Organizing the unplanned situations that might randomly appear into opportunities you *can* choose to be helpful stepping stones on your career path is a vital skill that deserves deliberate, creative thought. Call it sorting the chaos or learning to roll with the punches, but developing the ability to make any situation work to your benefit is priceless. Don't dismiss anything or reject an offer because it doesn't perfectly fit the parameters of your goal. Regardless of how you might have planned your career path, the most unlikely surprises along the way might prove to be the most beneficial in the long run. Taking that temporary job as an assistant editor for two weeks might open another door to designing you hadn't considered or ultimately introduce you to your real niche, revealing that you have been misguiding yourself with thoughts of production designing. If anything, a career in movie work can provide a template for life lessons as well as nourish creativity and career success.

NOTES

1 Catherine Hardwicke interview, June 22, 2004, Venice Beach, CA.

2 Gae Buckley interview, September 4, 2011, Studio City, CA.

3 Phil Dagort interview, June 6, 2004, Toluca Lake, CA.

4 Steve Saklad interview, August 17, 2004, Silverlake, CA.

5 Christa Munro interview, September 11, 2004, Flintridge, CA.

6 Linda Berger interview, August 16, 2004, Studio City, CA.

7 Honthaner, Eve L. *The Complete Film Production Handbook.* Boston: Focal Press, 2001, page 345.

CHAPTER 10

Non-Union vs. Union Status

MAKING THE GRADE OR NOT

A majority of the readers of this book will begin working in the industry with a non-union status. There is great freedom at this level of filmmaking. Not bound by union restrictions, crewmembers are free to double-up on job responsibilities—an especially good thing if you are learning the ropes and need to experience all aspects of your chosen job description. A young art director will work in the art department with an assistant or two, and will most likely be doing research and graphics, designing and drafting scenery, shopping for dressing and hero props, acting as art department coordinator, construction foreman, and lead scenic artist. In the process, an enterprising art director will see to it that both assistants are quickly trained to act as art department coordinators and help with the graphic design, drafting, and set dressing search. Salary and fringe benefits, hovering between 15–20% are lower than union wages and fringe set at 33%, but the potential for training in a chosen department and gaining experience, not to mention screen credit, is invaluable.

Many non-union films are shot in **right-to-work** states because film companies are not required to hire crew with union status if they choose not to. Seeking out films on these locations has its drawbacks: neither housing nor per diem will be provided and, as is the case with all non-union films, overtime and penalties associated with union film work will rarely happen. Payment of proper wages is negotiable but not guaranteed. At times these conditions are harsh, but it's important to remember that *everyone* working with you, including the producers, is experiencing the same learning curve. To compensate for the range of advantage and disadvantage, the morale is generally high and the quality of the overall experience reflects the freedom from the non-union situation.

DESIGNING INDIE FILMS

In some ways Indie movie production is a smaller-scale version of its commercial Hollywood counterpart; otherwise, it operates as its own animal. Financial constraints force low-budget production to be infinitely more creative in format and style, compelling those involved to adopt a more realistic attitude. A smaller, leaner, optimal crew inspires greater creative intimacy and multitasking. Creative restrictions force all participants to make decisions out of practicality. Overall, it is an excellent training ground for economy and pragmatism not found elsewhere.

Before we begin, here is a big word of advice: if the financing for the prospective film of your interest has *not been completed,* then walk away. Courteously ask that the director and producer keep you in mind when financing is complete. But don't stay on a promise; whether they do phone you back or not, they will respect you for your decision. It's disappointing to work passionately on something that may or may not happen. What I'm also suggesting here is to do as much homework before your interview as you possibly can. Use the Internet Movie Database (www.imdb.com) to properly investigate prior work of Indie producers and directors—the subcategory of "Independent Film" on the title bar of the website will link you to pages of very helpful data. Remember that you are interviewing them as much as they are interviewing you.

Production Value = Budgeting + Scheduling

A designer is hired to develop the visual aesthetic of a film. S/he also gets to be art director, set designer/draftsperson, prop person, mechanical effects supervisor, set decorator, and shopper. Multitasking creates long lists, but it affords the eager designer near total visual control. Insist on as many bodies to inhabit the art department as possible and be organized enough to use everyone's energy to get the job done.

In the commercial film arena, an art director is required to think like a director; in the realm of the Indie, an art director is required to think like a producer. More than aesthetics, budget is the most important obsession. On any given day, a coin toss will resolve this argument, as learning to blend both considerations into an effective solution provides a win-win for all involved. How? The following discussion on budget types based on film size and scheduling based on budget type will answer this question.

Indie Budget

Gone With the Wind (1939) was considered a blockbuster in its time. *Cleopatra* (1963), adjusted for current inflation rates, was the most expensive movie ever made at the end of the twentieth century—its budget of $44 million is equivalent to $270 million in 1999 dollars. Current blockbuster budgets range from $180 million to $280 million. Typical Hollywood studios consider making 18–30 films per year for budgets ranging from $40 million to $80 million. Inflated actor salaries and the high cost of marketing are reasons for these figures in the upper and middle range movies. Up-and-coming actors and directors, as well as creative teams, make a mark on smaller budget films made by subdivisions of the studios, comprising the lower end of the Hollywood studio range from $20 million to $40 million. In general terms, anything falling below $10 million to $20 million is considered an independent film—this fact will be argued by anyone you might encounter. Regardless, an excellent script supported by passionate, talented artists can attract the attention of or even change the cultural zeitgeist.

Table 10.1 features reasonable costs on a film budgeted at less than $1 million dollars. It was composed to demonstrate how all aspects of a basic film budget are allotted

Table 10.1   Sample budget for a less-than-$1-million film.

Production Costs for a Less-than-a-Million-Dollar Film

Accounting code	Description	Amount
	Above-the-Line Costs:	
100	Script	5,570
200	Producer	13,000
300	Director	13,000
400	Talent	36,750
500	Fringes	3,675
	Total: Above-the-Line	**71,995**
	Pre-Production & Production Costs:	
600	Production staff	18,615
700	Camera staff	11,510
800	Art department staff	17,270
900	Visual effects staff	4,800
1000	Locations department staff	5,015
1100	Electrical department staff	6,315
1200	Grip department staff	3,620
1300	Sound department/equipment	3,100
1400	Stunts/SFX	12,470
1500	Camera rental	11,140
1600	VFX equipment costs	16,900
1700	Raw stock/developing	46,365
1800	Sets/prop rental	20,980
1900	Locations fees	19,200
2000	Grip-electrical package	28,485
2100	Wardrobe/Makeup	16,000
2200	Transportation	14,760
2300	Picture vehicles	835
2400	General office	18,350
2500	Craft service/catering	17,150
2600	Police/Fire/Safety	465
2700	Accommodation	5,570
2800	Insurance	13,925
2900	Legal	13,200
	Sub-total: Below-the-line	**326,040**
	Post-Production Costs:	
3000	Editing	20,000
3100	Music	3,175
3200	Post-production Sound	35,235
3300	Answer print	9,140
3400	Titles and Opticals	10,575
	Sub-total: Below-the-line	**78,125**
3500	Miscellaneous	41,700
3600	Total: Above-the-line	71,995
3700	Total: Below-the-line	404,165
3800	3,600 + 3,700	476,160
3900	Applicable taxes	39,283
4000	Contingency	47,616
	TOTAL [US Dollars]	**604,759**

Table 10.2   Sample rental schedule for a one-week film shoot.

< < < O N E W E E K > > > >							L O N G W E E K E N D			
Friday	Saturday	Sunday	Monday	Tuesday	Wednesday	Thursday	Friday	Saturday	Sunday	Monday
Pickup rentals end of day.	< < < < T H E S H O O T I N G S C H E D U L E > > > >									Return rentals early morning.

and where the art department monies stand in contrast to the remaining budget items. Efficient scheduling of rental items keep limited budget lines in balance. Most low budget shooting schedules are three weeks long, but consider the advantage of a one-week shooting schedule regarding rentals and apply it to three-week schedules (see Table 10.2).

A three-week shoot is common, but a one-week shoot is smart. You might find yourself shooting ten pages a day (double the normal five to six pages a day), but cast members, especially, will be more eager to commit to it than for three weeks, which translates into a month when all is said and done. With some persuasive coercion, an extended one-week rental can work to the benefit of your limited budget. Your ability to convince a vendor demands that you keep your end of the bargain by returning goods on time with no excuses. Vendors renting props and set dressing to small film companies have heard every story imagined about why a rental item cannot be returned on time. Either return items on time or be prepared to pay another week's rental fee. In the big picture, you are cultivating a customer base here; respect the rules and the intelligence of your vendors, and you will have their loyalty for the duration of your career.

Indie Schedule

Timing is of the absolute essence. Get your hands on the most current copy of the script revisions and the preliminary one-liner or **strips** as soon as you can, to get an idea of how the shooting schedule will be organized. On a three-week shooting schedule, the strips (Table 10.3) will indicate, for example, that the antique domino set might play intermittently throughout the first few weeks of shooting, affecting length of rental time and cost. A location set can also triple its production value if it is located on an intersection with usable front, side, and back view both painted and dressed differently to suggest different locales, if possible. Don't wait for the UPM or First AD to tell you the schedule, but work out the logistics of when a specific piece of set dressing, or a hero prop should play based on its availability, and present it to the makers of the production shooting board. You'll be seen as a valuable team player, and

Table 10.3 Typical Production Board. Courtesy of Nancy Weems, screenwriter of *Citizen Darmont*.

TITLE: FLESH & BONE
DIRECTOR: NANCY WEEYMS
PRODUCER: PIEBALD PROD.

SHOOTING DAY	DAY 1				DAY 2			DAY 3		
DAY/NIGHT	D	D	D	D	D	D	D	D	D	D
INT/EXT	Ext	INT	INT	E/I	EXT	EXT	INT	INT	INT	INT
LOCATION/STUDIO	S	S	S	L	L	L	S	L	L	L
PAGE COUNT	5/8	3/8	11/8	3/8	6/8	5/8	14/8	10/8	9/8	7/8
SCENE NUMBER	12A	12C	38D	14	1	4	8	44	22	41
CAST:										
ACTOR 1 ROBERT	1		1	1	1	1	1	1	1	1
ACTOR 2 ANTOINETTE		2	2	2	2	2		2		2
ACTOR 3 CHARLOTTE		3	3	3	3	3				
PROPS:										
1 DOMINOES (DO)			DO					DO		
2 QUILL PEN & LEDGER (PL)			PL					PL		
CAMERA EQUIPMENT:										
1 DOLLY (DO)	DO	DO	DO	DO				DO	DO	DO
2 CRANE (CR)	CR			CR	CR	CR				CR
3 GRIP (GR)	GR	GR	GR	GR	GR	GR	GR	GR	GR	GR
SPECIAL EFFECTS:										
1 FIREPLACE FIRE (FP)			FF					FF		
2 FOG (FG)				FG						FG
3 BLOOD (BL)				BL			BL			BL
ANIMALS:										
1 DOGS (D)	D			D			D	D	D	D

you will also safeguard your budget. Remember that you have three options to always consider, you can be:

1. On time, but over-budget;
2. Overtime but on budget.
3. On time and on budget.

Always strive for the latter.

Four and a half months into indie film prep, the crew is hired. Four weeks later, casting will be completed, as well as locations secured, equipment, dressing and props rented, and scenery in finishing stages. Two weeks later, at six months into prep, the shooting begins. The one-line schedule enables an art director to use tools discussed in Chapter 8, namely the script breakdown, set list, and day out of days. Efficient use of time and money will establish your reputation with producers and directors—the people who count. Your aesthetic skills and delivering on time will ensure your being rehired.

Image and Format

The smaller films you encounter will first be shot in digital video (DV) and left in that format for distribution, which is the current trend. Why? It is cheaper in the long run, and the quality is excellent. A working understanding of digital video format is another important aspect of an art director's learning curve. As a sculptor chooses a particular medium to optimally express an idea in 3D volume, a cinema artist must choose the proper digital medium to translate the "tone" of the screenplay. Truth in choosing a medium is just as important as how a story is told.

Even the finest grain film stock has a texture. This subtle surface attribute adds resonance to the literary and emotional context of a script. Consequently, it will also superimpose an additional layer of visual varnish on the design of a movie. You will never be asked to choose a film stock, but knowledge about DV camera features reinforces design concept choices.

The next few paragraphs will take us back to thinking like a director by literally examining the shooting technologies at your disposal. Budget will once again determine which camera pack is chosen, with the interpretation of the script highlighted as a secondary motive. The market offers cheap, medium, and expensively priced cameras; advantages and disadvantages define each. The signal recorded on a cheap model or an expensive professional model is the same; the difference lies in the quality of the lenses and the camera's format capabilities: 4:3 is conventional TV ratio and 16:9 is HDTV quality. HD, or high definition, has four times the resolution as the standard definition format of a medium range Digital Betacam camera. Resolution or clarity of image captured on a less expensive camera is lost when an image is enlarged to theatrical proportion from a PC (or TV) screen. Less expensive cameras work fine for medium shots and close-ups but blur out in wide shots and rapid pans, although a few lower-priced cameras can still deliver broadcast quality images. Medium range DigiBeta cameras are typically used for SDTV digital formats (at 4:3 ratio), but for eventual 35mm blow-up, it just squeaks by as the minimum quality. The resolution of either camera's quality range is an important consideration before rental or purchase. Of course, HD cameras promise enhanced picture quality and crystal clear resolution. Although this quality camera is somewhat untouchable in purchase price, it is a money-saver on the back end; the high costs of transfer to film are counterbalanced in some cases by significant savings. This is a final decision made by the producer, director, and cinematographer. In the final analysis, practical hands-on experience with any of these DV tools gives an art director a huge advantage over those who remain unfamiliar with the technology.

Securing CG Talent

Having already secured the hardware and software package from your producer, you can staff a small but impressive visual effects/art department core. The crew should consist of at least three animators: a character animator, a background animator, and a supervisor. This key person should be somewhat skilled in art and commerce. Creative strengths in working knowledge of pre-vis and visual effects, plus someone who can jump in whenever necessary to carry the load, will take care of the technical art requirements—you can take care of the creative remainder. Control of the budget and the willingness to make judgment calls based on experience with tools and process allow you, the art director, to supervise expenditures and the work to be accomplished on the financial end.

A prime place to look for a visual effects crew is at a local digital studio. There, salaried assistant animators would be most likely to trade their time-off hours for film credit. Non-payment is a sensitive issue that must be handled correctly. An agreement to work for credit or very little salary implies several things to you as the art department employer. Trading for credit means that:

1. All necessary equipment will be there for the artists without question and is the very least that can be expected. This should be guaranteed through the producers before you sign your contract to work on a digitally driven film project, otherwise you are fighting a losing battle.
2. You and your animation supervisor will develop a carefully devised work schedule, based on shooting schedule that might be available from the UPM. It should include reasonable work hours and time for meals, subsidized by the production.
3. However this shakes out, you should be absolutely clear about what you expect and what you are offering. Without good organization and honesty, you will lose your support team. If they are well-informed and treated reasonably, they will stay through the rough spots. You must champion their best welfare—it is not only good policy but also good management—it will come back to you one hundredfold.

Other options for talent are film schools, architectural schools, and university/college film programs. Doing thorough crew research in these areas is just as important as visual research for your design concept. Not all Indie films will require VFX support, although films shot in DV will require digital supervision by the head of the art department to insure the truth of the visual storytelling. The Art Director and Producers will make this judgment call where necessary.

Cinematography in the DV medium enhances the speed of a project, and also invites the creative participation of all key players. With heightened creativity and likelihood for iconoclastic moviemaking, there also exists the possibility of the breaking of rules in the working environment. Safeguarding this and other principal aspects of the filmmaking process is the function of the Unions.

THE ART DIRECTORS GUILD, USA

There are many unions and guilds that comprise the motion picture industry (see "IATSE Membership Guilds," Appendix A). Each organization has its own set of requirements for entry. The Art Directors and Scenic, Title and Graphic Artists Local 800, at www.adg.org, requires proof of a specified number of hours and days worked on a particular non-union job and proof of expertise in art directing. While working in the non-union arena, document your progress as you go. Save original deal memos, paycheck stubs, crew lists, call sheets, one-liner and shooting schedules, calendar agenda archives, photocopied petty cash envelope information, timecards, and mileage reports. Before leaving a non-union gig, ask the producer for a written statement on production letterhead of your job responsibilities and dates worked. Be sure to photograph the sets on shooting stages of your film work: every set designed, drawn, built, painted and dressed, shooting crew setups, and locations photos. Leave no stone unturned. The more documentation you have organized, the easier your entry into the Union will be (see "Motion Picture Industry Experience Roster," this chapter). The Art Directors Guild presents a packet of information to newly inducted art director members. With the permission of the Guild, I would like to share some of the basic information with anyone aspiring for membership:

The Union exists to serve and protect your economic and creative interests. The IATSE (IA) oversees hundreds of local unions, including Local 800. Part of every member's dues is remitted to the IA to fund its various activities on behalf of all the locals, including negotiating collective bargaining agreements and organizing new productions. Your dues enable the Local's staff to work on your behalf and assure you at least the following benefits of membership:

- Minimum wage scale (based on the current contract).
- Grievance procedure.
- Training and education (seminars, training facilities, discounts).
- Access to employment information—availability list.
- Future and present production listing (JIM and Local 44).

- Weekly e-newsletter (*News You Can Use*).
- Website (with member area, forums, archives, "Find an Artist," showcase of Local 800 to the public).
- Scholarship fund.
- *Perspective* (bi-monthly ADG magazine).
- Film Society.
- Gallery 800.
- Figure-drawing workshop.
- Credit union.
- Actors fund.[1]

Membership

Classes of Membership

There are three principal classes of membership in the Art Director's Guild:

- Art director, whose duties are defined in our basic collective bargaining agreement as "an employee who directs the preparation and/or prepares sketches and designs of motion picture sets and/or backgrounds and generally supervises the execution of such designs and the decorating of sets and/or backgrounds."
- Assistant art director generally "aids the production designer and art director in the performance of their respective duties including research and helping to coordinate the work of set designers and others in the art department." Visual consultant "must possesses special and unique visual skills and talents of a nature that will assist the art director or production designer in performing his or her function with ideas relative to mood, visual concepts, appearance, etc. of the motion picture sets and/or backgrounds. Such an individual shall work under the supervision of the art director or production designer."
- Production designers develop the look of a motion picture or television production through the conception and creation of stage sets and the selection and alteration of practical locations. The titles "art director" and "art direction" are often used interchangeably with "production designer" or "production design." The screen credit of "production designer" may not automatically be given to an art director on a motion picture; permission to grant this credit comes from the Local.[2]

The following appears in Art Directors Basic Agreement 2012, Article VII, at Paragraph 95 of the Basic Agreement under "Duties and Division of Work":

- "Art director" shall be deemed to mean an employee who directs the preparation and/or prepares sketches and designs of motion picture sets and/or backgrounds and generally supervises the execution of such designs and the decorating of sets and/or backgrounds.
- "Assistant art director" shall be deemed to mean a person employed as such to assist an art director in the performance of his/her duties.[3]

Individuals who perform covered work as an art director or assistant art director under a Local 800 or IATSE collective bargaining agreement may apply for membership 30 days following commencement of employment. The individual is obligated to submit an application and the required fees in accordance with the agreement under which he/she is employed as the necessary pre-condition to continued employment under a union agreement. Many of the Local 800 agreements require that preference of employment be given to those individuals having previous work experience in the motion picture industry (see "Motion Picture Industry Experience Roster," this chapter). Eligibility for application and admission into Local 800 as an art director or assistant art director is typically triggered by working for a **signatory** company in a Local 800 covered classification. Thirty calendar days from the start date, the employee is required to join Local 800. And there are four typical scenarios:

a) When a project starts out non-union then signs an IA agreement; that is, it's organized. Employees working in a Local 800 covered classification when the project is organized are "grandfathered" into the union.
b) Employees also become eligible when they work on signatory commercials and music videos.
c) If a signatory company not covered by b) above (say one doing a television show or feature film), wants to hire an art director or assistant art director, and the individual is not on the Industry Experience Roster, the company may petition the Local to do so under the applicable Off-Roster side letter to the Local 800 Basic Agreement. If the petition is granted by the Off-Roster Hiring Review Committee, the individual may be hired and is eligible for admission into the Union.
d) If the individual in c), above, is already on the Roster at the time he/she is hired by the signatory company (see below), the company doesn't require the Guild's permission for that hire, and the individual is eligible for admission into the Union and is required to join after 30 calendar days.[4]

The Guild does not maintain a hiring hall. Prospective employees or members should contact employers by letter and resume and express an interest in employment. A portfolio clearly demonstrating skills and abilities generally will be required at all employer interviews. A resume may be forwarded to the Union office where it will be maintained on file for six months.

Health and welfare, retirement benefits, and minimum wage scales and working conditions are negotiated by the Union in the majority of its collective bargaining agreements, and the employers make contributions on behalf of covered employees, in accordance with those agreements. Employee/members are notified when they've qualified for benefits.

Breaking into the business depends on timing and patience. Somewhere in-between the non-union and union worlds exists a professional limbo that few people survive—one such person is Andrew Leitch. Andrew, currently assistant art director for *Glee*, reflects back on the good fortune of gaining some initial television experience and being in the right place at the right time:

Interview with Andrew Leitch

- *Did your graduate school theater training provide an adequate foundation for the work you are currently doing in episodic television?*

  My undergrad school work at Carnegie Mellon University was focused on basic storytelling through the processes of theatrical design: set, lighting, and costumes. The academic conversations about design existed in the abstract; in a working scenario, the everyday design process is informed by those abstract training values. I think theater training was an excellent foundation.

- *Would you have been able to get your first job in LA without academic training?*

  A newcomer might be fortunate enough to get a foot in the art department door but I'm not sure just how effective you would be without formal training. It's apparent that most people who currently work in the industry are well-trained, so in order to be competitive it's wise to do the same. For me, more than the nuts-and-bolts training was the solid alumni network my grad school had already established here on the west coast. Before I finished the grad program, I had already made my first connection in LA; that's how I got my first job.

- *And your first job in LA was as production assistant on* Dexter?

  Yes. I contacted the designer, a Carnegie alumnus, took the interview and was hired. I'm not sure just how unique that situation was, but I admit I was uniquely fortunate. My advice to anyone without previous connections is: meet as many people as you can to show your portfolio in person. I sense that most people who are established in the business are open to helping newcomers get a foothold. I guess it's because we're not yet a direct competitive threat.

- *How do you describe your duties as a PA?*

  It's basically on-the-job training. You're also a facilitator: doing tasks to help make the art department run smoothly and also interfacing between departments. The learning curve is sharp so you're required to quickly understand how the process works without prior experience–to just jump in and make it happen. It's a great position to be in because you don't have any significant creative responsibility; you can take it all in as you're swiftly helping facilitate daily operations of the art department, i.e., photocopying drawings, researching, answering phones, etc. The PA position gives you the part of the design equation you didn't take away from school–that is, the office social skills and day-to-day shorthand. That's very valuable stuff to personally take away to the next level.

- *Currently, after having worked as a PA on both* Dexter *and* Glee, *you have been offered a position as assistant art director.*

  Because I had former PA experience on *Dexter*, I was hired onto *Glee* in the same position. Several months into the season, the assistant art director was called away to design another TV program and I was lucky enough to be promoted. Right now I'm not on the Roster because I still need my 30 days of work in the assistant AD category, although I'm in the union and pay my dues. As soon as I complete the obligatory 30 days, I'll have full Guild status.

● *So, what is beyond* Glee *Season 6 for you?*

Now that I am working with a title in the art department, my main focus is to sharpen my skills. The most practical thing for me to do is develop my CAD skills. I'd like to be able to go back and forth between art directing and drawing to ensure a steady work flow for myself and address my creative desires. The bigger career challenge now that I'm in the union is to stay gainfully employed. So, I think remaining open, refreshing my software skills, honing my art directing skills and growing the social network might be the best way to accomplish my current ambitions.[4]

Motion Picture Industry Experience Roster

Entrance onto the Industry Experience Roster assures the individual preference of employment over all others not on the Roster; placement on the Roster is a necessary pre-condition for art directors and assistant art directors wishing to work on most film and television projects. To get onto the Industry Experience Roster, one must apply to Contract Services and have worked a total of no less than 30 days for one or more signatory companies, within a period of 365 consecutive calendar days immediately preceding the time the person makes application for Roster placement. Another way to qualify for Roster placement would be to have worked 175 days as an art director/assistant art director, union or non-union, in the three year period preceding application for Roster placement. There is also a Commercial Industry Experience Roster; 30 days working for a commercial signatory is required, and an additional 60 days of commercial work qualifies the person for placement on the Motion Picture Industry Experience Roster. Once on the Motion Picture Industry Experience Roster, individuals are eligible to work on signatory projects without having to get the Guild's permission. And when the individual begins work on the signatory project in a Local 800 covered classification, he/she must join the Local on or after the 30th calendar day from that date.

Taft–Hartley

Taft and Hartley were two US Senators who, in 1947, birthed the general, anti-labor legislation bearing their names. Among the legacies of Taft–Hartley in "grandfathering": persons who work for companies that are "organized" automatically qualify for admission into the union and must become members in good standing of the union not later than a specified 30-day period. In addition to entry through organizing, the other principal way persons join Local 800 is when they meet the experience requirements of an assistant art director or art director side letter to the basic collective bargaining agreement. Check with the Guild for further details.

Basic Collective Bargaining Agreement Selected Provisions

- All members hired by signatory employers must be and remain members in good standing of the union on and after the 30th day following their first day of employment.

- Employees are free to negotiate terms and conditions from their employers better than those provided in the Basic Agreement.
- Any disputes with employers concerning wages, hours, working conditions, or the interpretation of the Basic Agreement concerning these matters, may be grieved and arbitrated at no cost to the employee.
- The following studio minimum wage scale is effective for the period commencing August 1 to July 31 of every calendar year.
- Art directors are considered weekly "on call" employees: they work no prescribed number of hours in a day or week, and are paid a guaranteed weekly wage.
- Payment for art directors employed on features or TV begins on the earlier of the date of script delivery to the art director or on the first conference of the script.
- Employees are entitled to no less than five working days' notice of lay-offs (by "lay-off" we refer not only to instances of dismissal for lack of work but also dismissal because the regularly scheduled production work has concluded).
- Rules with respect to payment for sixth and seventh days on distant location:
    1. For each sixth day worked in an employee's workweek during a full six day work-week, the employee receives one and one-half times one-fifth (1/5) of the "on call" weekly rate in effect, the addition to the "on call" salary in effect.
    2. For each sixth day *not* worked in an employee's workweek during a full six day workweek, the employee receives an allowance of one-twelfth of the scheduled minimum "on call" weekly rate, plus pension and health contributions for seven hours.
    3. For each seventh day *not* worked in an employee's workweek, the employee receives an allowance of one-twelfth of the scheduled minimum "on call" weekly rate, plus eight reportable hours for the seventh day not worked.
    4. For each seventh day worked in an employee's workweek, if the employee actually performs work at the direction of the Producer, the employee is paid an additional amount equal to one-third of the "on call" weekly rate in effect.
- The amount of over-scale pay employees have bargained for may *not* be applied against any other payments due under the Basic Agreement, except with respect to allowances for airplane flights.
- You may be removed from the Industry Experience Roster for failing to pay required dues and/or initiation fee.
- Employees are entitled to screen credit in a "prominent place" on and long-for TV such as **MOW**s. "Prominent place" means single card credit whether in the main or end titles, and the only "technical" credit that may be placed more prominently is that of director of photography, and on short-form productions the only technical credit that can be placed more prominently, again is that of cinematographer.
- Producers must come to the union and get its approval if they wish to provide the credit "production designer" or "production design by" instead of the art director credit.

Table10.4 Local 800 Code of Professional Conduct. Courtesy of Local 800. The ADG is comprised of Art Directors, Graphic Artists, Illustrators, Matte Artists, Model Makers, Scenic Artists, Set Designers and Title Artists—and protects the rights of all crafts within its jurisdiction.

<u>LOCAL 800 CODE OF PROFESSIONAL CONDUCT</u>

The Basics

* Hire union members; engage only union facilities.
* Always work within, and not outside, your craft's jurisdiction.

* Do not accept less than scale pay for the work you do.
* Notify the Guild of each employment you obtain.

Workplace Jurisdiction

Art Directors

• Direct preparation and/or prepare sketches and designs of sets and backgrounds (and may do rough set lay-outs, and make sketches and occasional working drawings).

• Supervise execution of designs and decoration of sets and backgrounds.

[CANNOT do rough lay-outs or sketches or occasional working drawings if done to displace Set Designer (s) and/or Illustrator (s). CANNOT perform work reserved to other crafts.]

Set Designers and Model Makers

• **Senior Set Designers:** Prepare lay-outs and working drawings for motion picture sets, set models and backgrounds.

• **Specialist Set Designers:** Design/draw boats, trains, airplanes or other agreed upon specialties.

• **Senior Set Model Builders:** Design/construct set models for study/presentation, not for photographic purposes.

[CANNOT create models for photographic purposes. CANNOT perform work reserved to other crafts.]

Illustrators and Matte Artists

• **Illustrators:** Create three-dimensional illustrations, continuity illustrations, and/or sketches or designs for prep/production of motion pictures.

• **Matte Artists:** Sketch, draw, paint photographic-like paintings or composites to be combined with live action to create illusion of reality

[CANNOT perform work reserved to other crafts.]

Scenic, Title and Graphic Artists

• **Scenic Artists:** Prepare for, and draw and paint on, scenic backings, freehand decorations and fine art work on motion picture sets, and draw/paint all portraits and figures.

• **Title Artists:** Lay out, draw and paint main titles, inserts, trailers, narrative titles and screen advertising.

• **Graphic Designers:** Prepare designs for graphic elements (signage, logos, printed props, vehicle graphics, etc.); prepare designs for wallpaper, carpet and other textiles.

[CANNOT perform work reserved to other crafts.]

<u>Geographical Jurisdiction</u>
For Art Directors: U.S. outside of New York City and vicinity
For Set Designers, Illustrators and Scenic/Graphic Artists: LA County, and outside LA County if hired within LA County and transported outside

----

ADG MISSION STATEMENT: PROTECT, PRESERVE AND ENHANCE THE ECONOMIC AND PROFESSIONAL INTERESTS OF ITS MEMBERS.

Training

Each year for the last four years Local 800 has received grants of several hundred thousand dollars from CSATF to enable members to attend craft-specific training courses in cutting-edge and traditional technologies. Providers of such courses are Gnomon School of Visual Effects, and Studio Arts. For the first time in several years, such funds were not forthcoming from Contract Services in calendar year 2004; the Guild is currently exploring alternative funding and training options.[5]

PA Training Program

An additional job classification in the art department, the art department production assistant or PA, is being redefined in the basic division of labor. Technology has forced us to rethink non-union classifications like this, frankly because producers have taken advantage of the position by defining a PA as an assistant art director, a flagrant violation of the Basic Agreement. According to the Local 800 website stipulations, an art department PA may not be used as alternative low-cost employee or displace Guild members essential covered work on the production. Any art department guilty of doing otherwise can be **grieved.** In an attempt to resolve this legitimacy issue, the Guild has created the ADG Production Apprentice Training Program, which briefly stipulates the following:

This is an ADG-Art Directors Branch administered and funded program. It has been designed for the purpose of providing mentorship, supervision and on-the-job training to future Production Designers/Art Directors. The ultimate goal is to provide Production Apprentice (PA) Trainee participants with a clear and direct path towards obtaining real-time workplace training, and, on completion of their term of training and a satisfactory mentorship review, membership within the ADG Art Directors Branch as Assistant Art Directors.

- The goal of the PA Training Program is to expose PA trainees to a full range of workplace experiences (feature, episodic, commercials, reality shows, live events, and theme parks).
- Once admitted, the PA trainee's name will be placed on an availability list managed by the program's staff supervisor.
- The program requires 260 days of consecutive or non-consecutive participation by those accepted.
- Announcements will go out to all Guild production designer/art director members that PA trainees are available for immediate placement on film, TV, or commercial projects. (Note that placement is not guaranteed and will depend on the schedules and requirements of the production designer/art director members and the projects on which they are employed.)
- PA trainees would be hired, compensated, and insured in the same manner as all other production assistants by the producers of the particular production.
- PA trainees will be supervised by the show's production designer and art directors. These members will serve as the PA trainee's primary mentors and networking agents for their further placement and advancement during their training period.
- Guidelines governing the assignment, supervision and periodic assessment of the PA trainee's progress will be issued by the PA Training Program to the participating production designer/art directors.
- PA trainees may not displace Guild members or other IATSE represented crafts. Only productions that have fully satisfied their required staffing for all positions may partic-

ipate in the program. PA trainees may not be used as alternative low-cost employees for the creation of essential covered work on the production.

• PA trainees are responsible for their own housing, transportation and living expenses.[6]

Additional information is provided in Appendix A or at www.adg.org/?art=about-adg-apprenticeship.

The PA Apprenticeship Program is currently in its infancy with some of the initial candidates still complying with the training, and others continuing beyond the program.

The information provided in this chapter is based on the ADG website, a more comprehensive source of detailed facts and answers to any questions an aspiring art director might have, it is also a great support to a working art director. It provides clearly drawn guidelines for hiring of art department crew, resolving confusing issues, defining changes in annual wage rates so a proper deal memo can be signed with a UPM, as well as benefits, legal support, and connection to related industry organizations and events. A working art director relies on the union to maintain the status quo as s/he attends to the business of filmmaking. To further clarify these points and to shed additional information about the workings of the Art Directors Guild, Chad Frey, a former ADG officer, answers a few questions by sharing his experience as a seasoned art director.

Interview with Chad Frey

● *As vice-president (Emeritus) would you give a brief history of Local 800?*
Union representation for production employees actually started in the late 1800s with stage hands and creative professionals working in live theater on the East Coast. As these creative individuals were hired in the early film business the unions—there were several at the time—adapted to the new media and expanded west as the studios moved their production focus from New York to Los Angeles. In the early half of the 1900s the IATSE became the primary representative body for the "below-the-line" employees. When the art directors, set designers, and illustrators organized, all into separate Locals, they each joined **IATSE.** IATSE and the studios negotiated a set of contracts known collectively as the Basic Agreement wherein each craft worked under contracts specific to its individual discipline. Fast-forward to 2009 and you find the art directors, set designers, illustrators, and scenic title and graphic artists have all been merged into the same Local (IATSE Local 800) but each craft is still basically under the same contracts that were negotiated in the 1930s.

The union exists to protect its members from any and all professional abuse through these Basic Contract Agreements. When the core art department crafts were first organized, the art directors, set designers, and illustrators were separated; there also existed a management level and a blue-collar level, each at separate pay scales. Each studio had a system in place whereby a set designer or illustrator could gain experience in a studio art department and advance from the basic blue-collar level up into the art direction or management level. That training disappeared during the 1960s through the 1970s as the studios dissolved their in-house production facilities. The onset of digital tool use over the past 20 years has inspired a current transitional period; it has signified the passing of many of our traditionally trained designers, many of whom trained me and my contemporaries, as well as general political upheaval within the Art Directors Guild itself. During the 1990s the film industry as a whole was going through dramatic changes, informally related to **runaway production** and the Art Directors Guild (still a separate Local at this time) was able to negotiate national jurisdiction over their work. The 1990s also saw the Art Directors Guild transitioning from a small selective group (some might say a "good ol' boy" society) to an organization that welcomed almost anyone with talent and a modicum of experience. Unfortunately, with this transition, the mantle of training and holding new members to a high standard, as they would have been by the studio system, was ignored. This has led to a deterioration of the general level of skills, respect and payment for today's union art director. This is an ongoing issue for the Union.

- *During your three-year term as vice-president, what issues did you tackle?*
Historically, the Art Directors Guild has always thought of itself as a social club much more interested in the upper echelon of production designers, and not so much the issues of art directors or assistant art directors. When the International decided to force the set designers and illustrators to merge with the art directors in 2009 they compounded a whole series of problems and failures within the Art Directors Guild. I've been a member of both set designers and art directors for more than 17 years. I and many of my "dual card" colleagues watched as Set Designers Local 847, the Local that supported and protected us, become swallowed by the Local that failed us, Art Directors Local 876. The merger did not address the shortcomings, nor the underlying problems or failures of Guild leadership—and this was frustrating, at the very least. Indeed, for the last decade, the Guild leadership has chosen to actively ignore the demands of an industry that is changing and evolving at an amazingly rapid pace. As working professionals we are dealing with cutting edge technologies and job expectations that change almost weekly and contracts that are basically 70 years old. We have a large membership spread across the country with nowhere to turn for comprehensive training as our jobs become ever more complex, nor do we have competent support or protection against ever more aggressive employers. The issues I was interested in when I ran for office, and am still pressing today, are simple: the protection and support of members in the workplace; member education; jurisdiction issues; contract understanding and enforcement; studio/producer/UPM education; greater transparency; and opportunities for member participation in Guild decisions. I was successful with some of it; I failed with some of it. This is what the recently elected officers in 2013 are inheriting.

    At present there is not much of a unified, cohesive body within our union. So, there are a number of things we can and must change with incoming art directors and how they look at, embrace and deal with an acceptable level of skill in the art department in general.

- *Do you feel that the Master Classes are a good basis for guild training?*
Yes, because Master Class training starts to address some of these issues: most importantly, that there are a lot of people out there who don't know what they're doing and making life difficult for those who do know what they are doing—and devaluing all of us in the process. How do we go about adequately training these people? The Master Class concept was a direct, postured response to that question.

● *How do you overcome membership inertia? We can't reinstitute a full studio-type training system that existed in Hollywood's Golden Age but as new people come into the union, there needs to be a more active enrollment/teaching program to get them engaged in an easy way via new media. Also, a re-enactment of a certification system would also be a benefit to everyone.*

A system for internal Guild training and certification was proposed a few years ago but it was quickly squashed by the entrenched leadership. The set designers used to have a series of written tests and portfolio reviews when newbies entered the union but that was replaced by 24 hours of classroom training years ago. There are no aptitude tests for assistant art directors, art directors or production designers. We can only hope that the idea will be taken up again by the new board of directors because it is both desperately needed by the membership and seen as a value by the employer. It's important that producers know that they're getting trained, qualified people when they hire Local 800 members and this type of training would mirror what is done by the DGA, which a great many producers and UPMs expect as they went through the DGA program. In lieu of an actual training and certification program, the Master Classes are an attempt to catalogue and pass on vital knowledge.

As for overcoming "member inertia" . . . that's a tough one. Today's art director has an average work week that is longer than 60 hours—often much longer. If you add family and other responsibilities outside of that, you see that there is very little time to attend seminars and classes. For those working out of town, it's practically impossible. Streaming these events on-line, inviting member participation through the internet and archiving these events for later access are all ways of helping our members get connected and involved. Ultimately, I think the best way to overcome the "inertia" is to institute a voluntary training and certification program that can help art directors raise their negotiated rate. If members can gain a tangible, financial benefit for their efforts it would probably go a long way to motivating them to take time out of their already too busy lives.

● *In making a deal with a producer, would you say reading and understanding the contract for the project at hand is the key to creating a successful agreement, highlighted by an acceptable rate?*

Most definitely. In addition to the Basic Agreement created for each guild there are now currently 53 other agreements that exist. The International's main concern is that people in the industry who are working are receiving benefits; consequently, a greater number of agreements have been negotiated as different types of production entities have been created. If you are a working art director you need to be familiar with any contract you are working under for two reasons: 1) it is going to directly affect your personal working conditions and compensation, and 2) it is going to directly affect how you organize and staff your department. It was once almost impossible to find these contracts but, in a nod to the new leadership of Local 800, all of the current contracts are now available for the membership to access via the member's area of the Guild website.

When preparing for an interview or going into negotiations with a producer or UPM, find out what contract you will be working under, get a copy of that contract form the union or from the union website, read it completely, and make sure you understand it. It will dictate what your rate should be and what benefits you can expect. It will also affect the deals others you hire will make under your supervision. (For set designers and illustrators it's a little easier because they don't have all the side letters to consider.) Rest assured the producer and UPM will know that contract inside and out and they will push a contract's limits and boundaries, but if you are familiar enough with the contract your success rate in getting what you contractually deserve—and possibly negotiating for more—will be much more assured.

Most of us consider ourselves "artists" and as such are hesitant or ill prepared when it comes to business negotiations. It's not to our advantage individually or collectively to negotiate in an amorphous way. For a UPM or producer who does nothing all day long but sit and read over contracts, our behavior of fumbling through a phone call deal is very frustrating. Here's how I personally approach my negotiations: at the onset of my phone introduction, I ask to send a written proposal of what I'd like to discuss. This does two things: 1) it provides the producer or UPM with a familiar document to mull over, and 2) it provides a conversation piece for subsequent detailed negotiating: rate in town, rate out of town, vehicle provided, cellphone provided, equipment rental, bonded equipment shipping in both directions, travel, etc. Hitting every bullet point that would appear in a final contract, increases your odds substantially. These are things in the Basic Agreement they are required to provide and additional items which I am negotiating for above and beyond. Whether or not they will grant the extras doesn't matter, I will ask for them anyway at the outset. Usually, my punch list will be rejected at our initial meeting, at which point I will use my revised notes to adjust our talking points into a new contract proposal which I email back saying: "This is how I understand our recent conversation and how I expect to read the details of our final agreement." Take note here: be sure to save all email and written or faxed correspondences for future recall of responsibilities on both sides.[7]

THE INTERNATIONAL FILMMAKING COMMUNITY

The film community is multinational, extending far beyond the borders of the United States to all continents and the countries within them. Familiarity with other design guilds is practical and necessary but has consistently been overlooked or flatly dismissed in the past by the American filmmaking community. Americans will deny it; everyone else will agree with the charge. This attitude ends here, now.

Europe supports a thriving, interconnected film industry, including Britain, as do Australia and Canada. The British Film Designers Guild serves as a model for guilds outside the US. A fundamental model for any design guild is tailored to the needs and requirements of a particular country or region. Make it your business to develop a healthy understanding of other guilds and seize the opportunity to be an international participant.

British Film Designers Guild

Pinewood Studios
Pinewood Road
Iver Heath

Bucks SL0 0NH
info@filmdesigners.co.uk
www.filmdesigners.co.uk
office: 44 (0)1753 509 013
cell: 44 (0)7768 573 450

The British Film Designers Guild (BFDG) has members in every grade of the art department, from draftspersons to costume designers, set decorators to production designers, and was formed with the aim of raising the standards and the profile of the art department and protecting the interest of its members. The BFDG answers queries as to the availability of all members and holds a complete list of their work. A 24-hour answering service helps producers and production designers to crew up from the BFDG membership list as quickly as possible. This information is regularly updated with the aim to make the BFDG the first stop for art department recruitment both nationally and internationally. Applicants seeking membership eligibility are asked to have at least five credits attained at the level of interest. These applications are agreed to by peer review as well as with Internet Movie Database validity, occasionally used to quantify film or television programming value. The BFDG also publishes a monthly newsletter which is open to contribution from any member and aims to keep all members up-to-date with the latest information on production and employment prospects. In addition the BFDG publishes a brochure of all its members with a list of their latest credits, which is sent to production companies and producers all over the world.

The official website, www.filmdesigners.co.uk, gives the latest credits of all members. A PDF download of "How to Find Work in the UK Business Art Department", is available at www.filmdesigners.co.uk/sites/default/files/files/BFDG%20%27How%20to%20get%20 work%20in%20the%20Film%20UK%20%26%20TV%20Business.%27.pdf.

European and Asian Guilds

Most European design websites offer German, French, or sometimes English versions of their sites on the homepage. Whether or not you are multilingual, the visual nature of our work allows relatively easy navigation. The Austrian Film Designers Association (AFDA) offers German and English, for example, and appears to be most inclusive in linking to colleagues in other European countries' design pools. The list of additional European film design guilds, below, is generated from the AFDA website:

- Austrian Film Designers Association, www.filmdesigners.at/index.php?spr=5&ctrl=link&mid=25
- German Association of Production and Costume Designers, www.sfk-verband.de
- Swiss Syndicate Film and Video, http://ssfv.ch/
- The French Production Designers Association, www.adcine.com
- Italian Association of Production and Costume Designers, www.aesseci.it
- Association of Production Designers in Japan, www.apdj.or.jp

China's film industry is still emerging as a well-organized, international filmmaking participant. Although it doesn't yet have an official design guild, it does participate in a robust film festival community:

- Beijing College Student Film Festival, www.isfvf.cn/en
- Changchun Film Festival, www.cnfilmfest.com
- Golden Rooster Awards, http://wn.com/golden_rooster_awards
- Hong Kong Asian Film Festival, http://bc.cinema.com.hk/adhoc/hkaff_2007/about/index.html
- Hong Kong International Film Festival, http://hkiff.org.hk/en/index.php
- Hundred Flowers Awards, http://wn.com/hundred_flowers_award
- Macau International Movie Festival, www.macaodigitalcinema.com/en/festival/home
- Shanghai International Film Festival, www.siff.com/InformationEn/Index.aspx

Motion pictures were introduced to China in 1896; its first film, the recording of a Peking opera, was filmed in 1905; Americans trained the first Chinese filmmakers, as the industry blossomed in the 1920s and 1930s. Since the 1980s, China has enjoyed considerable commercial success with its films abroad. Whether or not China develops reciprocal design guilds to rival the more established European film industries is more a question of politics than culture.

Australian Production Design Guild

PO BOX 60
Broadway NSW 2007
www.apdg.org.au/contact
George Liddle: 0414887946
Charlie Revai: 0407929053
Victoria: Simon McCutcheon—simon.mccutcheon@apdg.org.au
Queensland: Michael Rumpf—michael.rumpf@apdg.org.au
Western Australia: Herbert Pinter APDG—herbert@apdg.org.au
New South Wales: George Liddle APDG—george@apdg.org.au

As in other countries physically separated from both America and European filmmaking culture, Australian film consciousness awakened in 1896 when the first public screening of a Lumière brothers film was shown in Melbourne. It wasn't soon after, in 1906, that *The Story of the Kelly Gang* became the earliest feature film made Down Under. Today, Australia's filmmaking productivity is undisputedly some of the best in the world.

The Australian Production Design Guild (APDG) was established in 2009 as a non-profit organization committed to raising the profile of stage and screen design by highlighting the creative contribution made by the *mise en scène* of its members. By drawing attention to professional standards, the APDG recognizes excellence and outstanding achievement through annual awards. It strives to encourage young designers and associated professionals to participate in the industry by granting APDG accreditation to outstanding, emerging Australian designers.

Design professionals in the Australian film, television, theatre, interactive media and event industries have been without a voice for many years. The APDG has redressed this and is now striving to establish fairer and more productive working relationships in production design and its related industries.[8]

THE NEW PARADIGM IN EXPERIMENTAL FILM

Since its beginnings nearly 120 years ago, filmmaking has always been a self-evolving, experimental medium. Computer technology has modified that on many levels. Merged media encourages Post-It snippets of everyday iconography captured on smart media devices to filter into shared video blogs on the Web or into art house theaters. Virtual intelligence peering back at us through the inside of our monitor screens demands a reflective and continued dialogue from us. Digital and smartphone advancements in videography captures a highly personal experience as it also enlarges the promise of improvements to everyday technology. We do not live in a static age. The paradigm shift in our culture prompted by technological advances is embraced as a necessity for survival in the capturing of the moving picture, as well as in many other facets of our rapidly changing lives.

Grad students, returning alumni, and faculty at MIT's Media Lab™ work at developing cross-media user applications. Many are Web-based and designed for easy access, and interface with all workable video formats. Much of the data presented on the website www. media.mit.edu is inspired by how popular technology impacts our lifestyles. The Media Lab, through its blurring of the traditional boundaries between the disciplines, and by nurturing relationships between academia and industry, is at the forefront of the new technologies that will, sooner rather than later, be a part of our daily lives.[9]

Cell phones, in particular, are the focus of a great deal of attention; the development of synergies between cell phone capability and other media is found in the existence of Cinemaware™, Emonic™ environment, and Shareable Media™. An example of the Digital Intuition Group's contribution to the laboratory's Object-Based Media Group's paradigm supports the merging of storytelling/creative play and projecting an environment to support the verbal process. This simple concept has far-reaching implications for all entertainment modalities:

Remember telling scary stories in the dark with flashlights? Narratarium is a 360-degree context aware projector, creating an immersive environment to augment stories and creative play. We are using natural language processing to listen to and understand stories being told and thematically augment the environment using images and sound. Other activities such as reading an E-book or playing with sensor-equipped toys likewise can create an appropriate projected environment, and a traveling parent can tell a story to a child at home and fill the room with images, sounds, and presence.[10]

An implacable, creative mind can find uses for these interfaces in cinematography and elsewhere. The Media Lab at MIT encourages exploration. Symposia and proposals for new media apps are provocative; shared insight stimulates re-experience of familiar media and situations. Challenging ourselves to keep our creative institutions flexible is the ongoing goal. Living our lives creatively, through the expanse of media and technology available to us and by fully interacting with it, fortifies us as art directors to be the true action figures we truly are.

NOTES

1 Information retrieved from the ADG website, "Union Benefits: Local 800 IATSE," www.adg.org/?store= art&setTheme=OFF&art=guild-landing&SHOW=union_benefits.

2 Information retrieved from a PDF document link on the ADG website: "The Union—What You Should Know," a document provided by the Art Directors Guild and Scenic, Title and Graphic Artists Local 800 office, www.adg.org/sites/art/pdf/the_union_what.pdf.

3 Information retrieved from the ADG website, "Contract and Rates: Basic Agreements," www.adg.org/ sites/art/information/Contracts/ART_Directors_Agree_2012.pdf.

4 Andrew Leitch interview, November 2, 2013, North Hollywood, CA.

5 Information retrieved from the ADG website, "Membership," www.adg.org/?store=art&setTheme=OFF& art=guild-landing&SHOW=about_adg.

6 Information retrieved from the ADG website, "Art Directors Guild (ADG) Production Apprentice (PA) Training Program," www.adg.org/?art=adg-apprenticeship.

7 Chad Frey interview, March 18, 2013, Paramount Studios, Hollywood, CA.

8 Information retrieved from the APDG website, www.apdg.org.au/about-2.

9 Information retrieved from the MIT Media Lab: Research: Groups+Projects on November 2, 2004, at www. media.mit.edu/about/mission-history.

10 Retrieved from the MIT Object-Based Media Group index page, http://obm.media.mit.edu.

SECTION III

Appendices

Section III is divided into several subcategories, called Appendices A–D, as listed in the Table of Contents.

The subcategories are by no means exhaustive but give the reader a solid foundation of references, Web addresses, and documentation in order to make informed decisions. It is natural that lists will cross-reference and overlap.

Reference and Source Lists

ANTHROPOMETRY

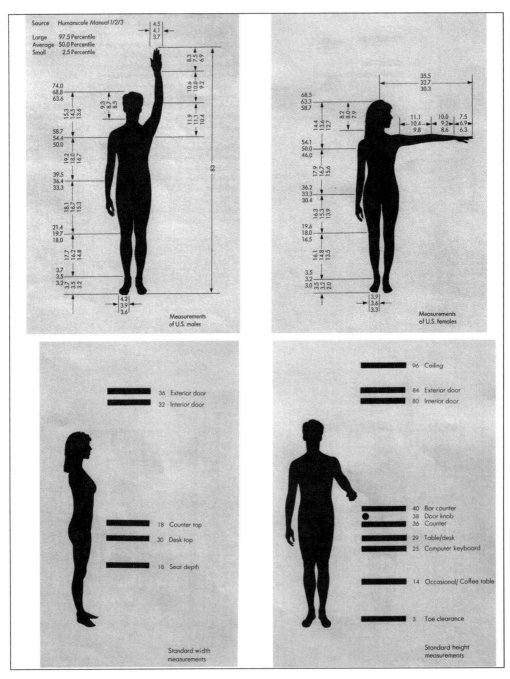

Figure A1.1a *Anthropometry: Conference Space (Read left to right, top then bottom) Measurements of US Males & Females. Standard width and height measurements of humans. Courtesy of Pentagram Design.*

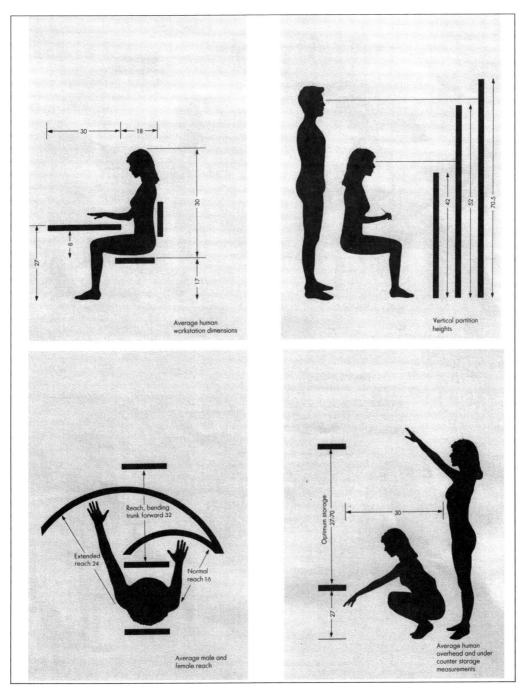

Figure A1.1b *Anthropometry: Average Corridor (Read left to right, top then bottom) Average human workstation dimensions. Vertical partition heights. Average male & female reach. Average human overhead and under counter storage measurements. Courtesy of Pentagram Design.*

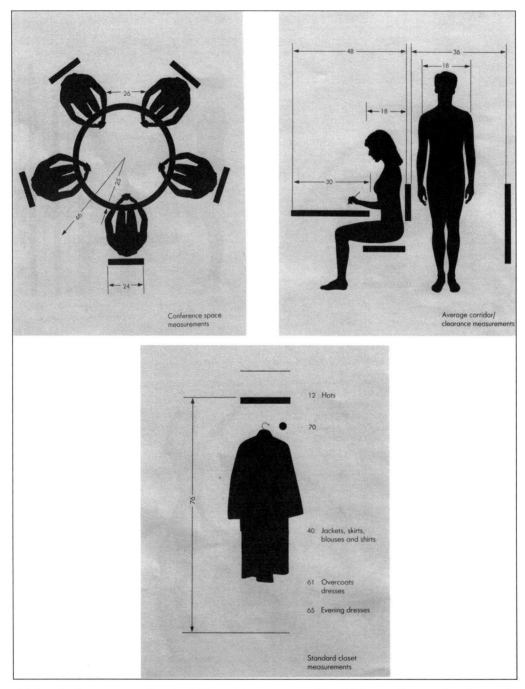

Figure A1.1c   Anthropometry: Standard Closet Measurements (Read left to right, top then bottom) Average human workstation dimensions. Vertical partition heights. Average male & female reach. Average human overhead and under counter storage measurements. Courtesy of Pentagram Design.

TABLE OF FRAMING HEIGHTS

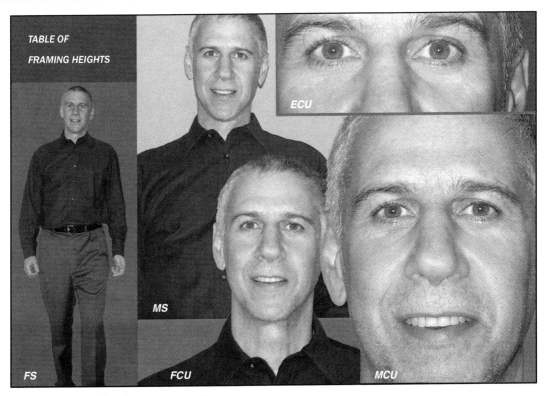

Figure A1.2   Table of Framing Heights.

ASPECT RATIOS

ASPECT RATIOS

FORMAT	RATIO *	
35MM 'ACADEMY'	1.37 : 1	
35MM WIDESCREEN (EUROPE)	1.66 : 1	
35MM WIDESCREEN (USA)	1.85 : 1	
35MM ANAMORPHIC	2.35 : 1	(ALTHOUGH REFERRED TO AS 2.35 THE ACTUAL RATIO OF THIS FORMATS S 1 : 2.4)
65 / 70MM	2.2 : 1	(IN THIS FORMAT THE ORIGINAL NEGATIVE IS 65MM FILMSTOCK WHICH IS PRINTED ON 70MM STOCK FOR EXHIBITION)
HDTV	1.78 : 1	(THIS FORMAT IS SOMETIMES REFERRED TO AS 16:9)

* IMAGE WIDTH : IMAGE HEIGHT

ASPECT RATIOS FOR 35MM FILM

1.33 : 1

THIS WAS THE RATIO FOR STANDARD TV TRANSMISSION. A SMALL PART OF THE ORIGINAL NEGATIVE AREA AROUND THE EDGE IS LOST IN THE PROJECTION PROCESS.

1.85 : 1 WIDESCREEN (USA)

THE RATIO THAT MOST THEATRES IN N. AMERICA ARE SET UP FOR. TYPICALLY THE ENTIRE FRAME AREA OF THE FILM IS EXPOSED BUT ONLY THE OUTLINED AREA IS PRINTED FOR PROJECTION. (...SHOT 'FULL FRAME' FOR LATER TRANSMISSION ON TV...)

2.35 : 1 ANAMORPHIC

FOR THIS RATIO THE FILM IS SHOT USING ANAMORPHIC LENSES WHICH SQUEESE THE FRAME HORIZONTALLY TO 50% OF ITS ACTULA SIZE (ALSO CALLED 2:1). RELEASE PRINTS ARE PRINTED DIRECTLY FROM AN INTERNEGATIVE AND MUST BE PROJECTED THROUGH AN ANAMORPHIC LENSE TO 'UNSQUEESE' THE IMAGE TO ITS CORRECT PROPORTIONS.

© 2013 - C.S.FREY

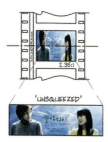

'UNSQUEEZED'

Figure A1.3a   Aspect Ratios—A concise reference page. Courtesy of Chad Frey.

CAMERA ANGLES

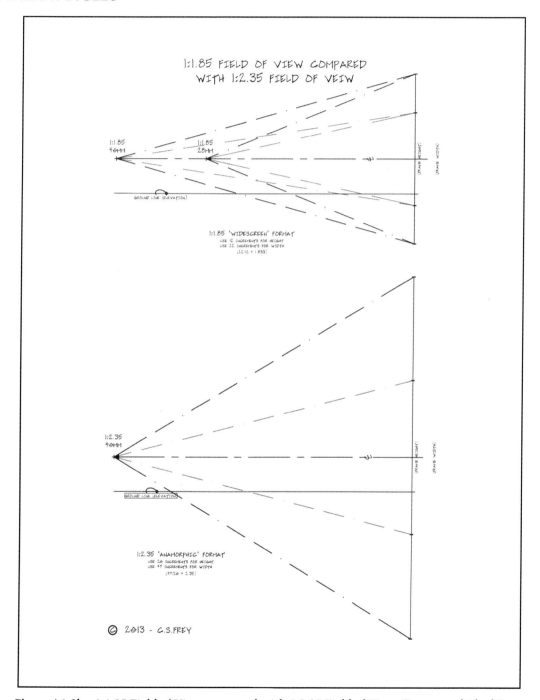

Figure A1.3b 1:1.85 Field of View compared with 1:2.35 Field of View. Courtesy of Chad Frey.

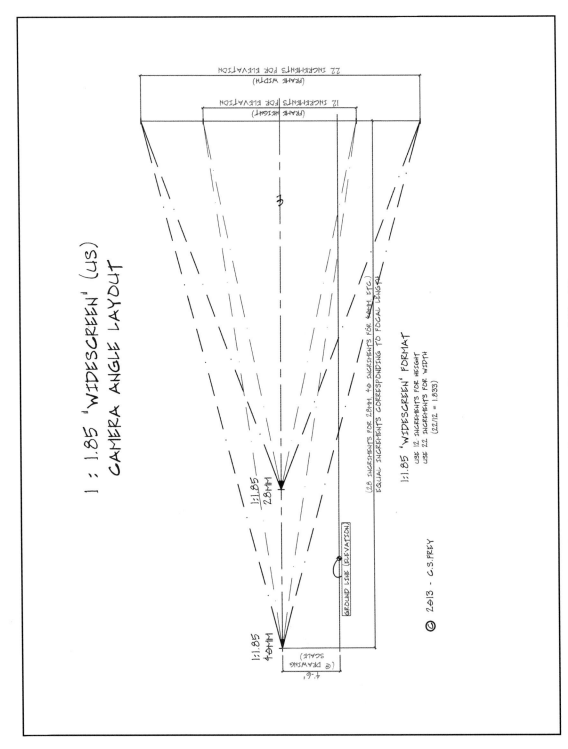

Figure A1.3c   1:1.85 'Widescreen' (US) Camera Angle Layout. Courtesy of Chad Frey.

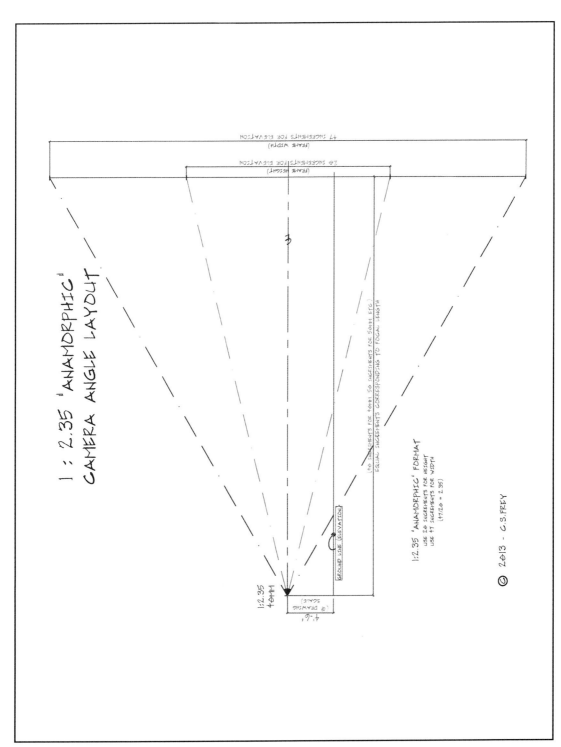

Figure A1.3d 1:2.35 'Anamorphic' Camera Angle Layout. Courtesy of Chad Frey.

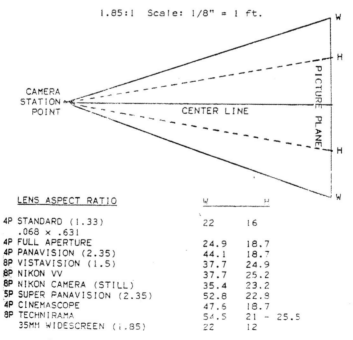

CAMERA ANGLES

    The screen format (aspect ratio, proportion of frame and screen, i.e. width and height) <u>stays the same for each format</u>.
    The lens size indicates the focal length for the center line, so:

        35 mm = 35 ft., 50 mm = 50 ft., 75 mm = 75 ft., etc.

<u>DIRECTIONS</u>: Example for a 35 mm widescreen lens, 1.85:1 format (aspect ratio, proportion of frame & screen).
From Camera Station Point 0, measure 35 feet. At that point, draw a perpendicular line, with the horizontal line at its center. The perpendicular line is 22 feet long. Starting from where the two lines cross, mark points on the vertical line 6 feet in each direction from the center. Draw lines from the Camera Station Point to the ends of the vertical line and to each of the other 2 points (4 lines in all). The larger (outer) angle represents the WIDTH of the picture plane (frame format size), and the smaller (inner) angle represents the HEIGHT. You can use any scale you choose, as long as you remain consistent. 1/4" = 1 foot is the most commonly used scale.

For lenses other than 35 mm, use the width and height measurements listed below:

1.85:1 Scale: 1/8" = 1 ft.

LENS ASPECT RATIO	W	H
4P STANDARD (1.33) .068 × .631	22	16
4P FULL APERTURE	24.9	18.7
4P PANAVISION (2.35)	44.1	18.7
8P VISTAVISION (1.5)	37.7	24.9
8P NIKON VV	37.7	25.2
8P NIKON CAMERA (STILL)	35.4	23.2
5P SUPER PANAVISION (2.35)	52.8	22.9
4P CINEMASCOPE	47.6	18.7
8P TECHNIRAMA	54.5	21 - 25.5
35MM WIDESCREEN (1.85)	22	12

Figure A1.4 Camera Angles—Cheat Sheet. Courtesy of Camille Abbott and Harold Michelson.

THE ULTIMATE TABLE OF FORMATS

The Ultimate Table of Formats—Aspect Ratios

Name	Originator	Year Introduced	Year Abandoned	Format	AR	Frame Area
Kinetoscope	Edison/W. K. L. Dickson	1894	1896	4-35	1.33:1	1.000x0.750
Vitascope	C. F. Jenkins/T. Armat	1895	N/A	4-35	1.33:1	1.000x0.750
Ciné	Lumi&232re Brothers	1895	N/A	4-35	1.33:1	1.000x0.750
Eidoloscope	Woodville Latham & Sons	1895	1897	4-51	N/A	N/A
Demeny-Gaumont/Prestwich	Georges Demeny	1896	N/A	4-60	1.4:1	1.750x1.250
Viventoscope	Blair	1897	N/A	1-48	1.5:1	1.500x1.000
Veriscope	Enoch Rector	1897	N/A	5-63	1.66:1	1.875x1.125
Biograph	American Biograph Co.	1897	N/A	0-68	1.35:1	2.625x1.938
		1900	N/A	4-35	N/A	N/A
Lumiè Wide Film	Lumiè Brothers	1900	N/A	8-75	N/A	N/A
Ciné (a.k.a. Ciné)	Raoul Grimoin-Sanson	1900	1900	10x4-70	360°	N/A
Pathé KOK/Pathescope	Pathé	1912	N/A	4-28	1.33:1	N/A
Panoramica	Filoteo Alberini	1914	N/A	5-70	2.52:1	N/A
		1924	N/A	10-35H	2.52:1	N/A
Widescope	J. D. Elms	1921	1925	2x4-35	N/A	N/A

Figure A1.5a   The Ultimate Table of Formats—An Historical Guide: 1894–1921.

Pathé Baby	Pathé	1923	-	1-9.5	1.33:1	N/A
16mm	Kodak	1923	-	1-16	1.34:1	0.380x0.284
Pathé Rural	Pathé	1926	N/A	1-17.5	1.33:1	N/A
Natural Vision	Radio-Keith-Orpheum	1926	1930	6-63.5	1.85:1	N/A
Magnascope	Paramount	1926	1953	4-35	N/A	N/A
Hypergonar	Henri Chré	1927	1937	4-35A2.0	2.66:1	1.000x0.750
Polyvision	Abel Gance	1927	1927	3x4-35	N/A	N/A
Grandeur	20th Century Fox	1929	1931	4-70	2:1	N/A
Magnafilm	Paramount/L. de Riccio	N/A	1930	4-56	2:1	N/A
Realife	Metro-Goldwyn-Mayer	1930	1931	4-70	2:1	N/A
Vitascope	Warner Brothers	1930	1930	5-65	2:1	N/A
Academy	Academy of Motion Picture Arts & Sciences	1932	-	4-35	1.37:1	0.825x0.602
Double-8	Kodak	1932	-	1-8	1.36:1	0.182x0.134
Cinerama	Cinerama Inc./Fred Waller	1952	1972	3x6-35	2.72:1	3x0.985x1.088
CinemaScope	20th Century Fox	1953	1957	4-35A2.0	2.55:1	0.912x0.715
					2.35:1	0.898x0.715
Glamorama	N/A	1953	1953	10-35H	N/A	N/A
VistaVision	Paramount	1954	1961	8-35H	1.5:1	1.485x0.991
Todd-AO	Michael Todd/American Optical Co.	1955	-	5-70	2.2:1	2.072x0.906
Circarama	Walt Disney	1955	1961	9/11x1-16	360°	N/A
CinemaScope-55	20th Century Fox	1956	1958	8-55.625A2.0	2.35:1	1.430x1.824
				4-35A2.0	2.55:1	0.912x0.715

Figure A1.5b   The Ultimate Table of Formats—An Historical Guide: 1923–1956.

				4-35A2.0	**2.35:1**	0.839x0.715
Technirama	Technicolor	1956	1967	4-35A2.0	**2.55:1**	0.912x0.715
					2.35:1	0.839x0.715
Cinestage	N/A	1956	N/A	4-35A1.56	**2.2:1**	0.912x0.685
Kinopanorama	Russia	1957	-	3x6-35	**2.77:1**	N/A
M-G-M Camera-65	Metro-Goldwyn-Mayer	1957	1966	5-70A1.25	**2.76:1**	2.072x0.906
				5-65A1.25	**2.76:1**	2.072x0.906
				4-35A2.0	**2.55:1**	0.912x0.715
				4-35A2.0	**2.35:1**	0.839x0.715
CineMiracle	Louis de Rochemont	1958	1961	3x6-35	**2.55:1**	N/A
Smith & Carney 180°	Smith & Carney	1958	N/A	4-35	**N/A**	N/A
Circlorama	N/A	1958	1964	11x4-35	**360°**	N/A
Super Technirama 70	Technicolor	1958	N/A	5-70	**2.2:1**	N/A
				4-35A2.0	**2.35:1**	0.839x0.715
Panavision	Panavision	1959	-	4-35A2.0	**2.35:1**	0.839x0.715
Super Panavision	Panavision	1959	N/A	5-70	**2.2:1**	N/A
				4-35A2.0	**2.35:1**	0.839x0.715
Wonderama Arc 120	Technicolor	1960	N/A	4-35	**2.64:1**	N/A
Cine-System 3	U.S.A.F.	1960	N/A	1-3	**1.33:1**	N/A
Techniscope	Technicolor	1963	N/A	4-35A2.0	**2.35:1**	0.839x0.715
Ultra Panavision	Panavision/M-G-M	1963	1968	5-70A1.25	**2.7:1**	N/A
				4-35A2.0	**2.35:1**	0.839x0.715
Dimension 150	Todd-AO/20th Century Fox	1963	1970	5-70	**150°**	N/A
				4-35A2.0	**2.35:1**	0.839x0.715

Figure A1.5c   The Ultimate Table of Formats—An Historical Guide: 1956–1963.

Super 8	Kodak	1965	-	1-8	1.36:1	0.215x0.158
Super 16	Kodak	1970	-	1-16	1.66:1	0.464x0.280[6]
					1.85:1	0.464x0.251[6]
Todd-AO 35	Todd-AO	1971	N/A	4-35A2.0	2.35:1	0.839x0.715
IMAX	IMAX Corporation	1970	-	15-70H	1.43:1	2.740x1.910
OMNIMAX	IMAX Corporation	1973	-	15-70H	Ovoid	2.740x1.980
Circlevision	Walt Disney	N/A	-	5x4-35	200°	N/A
Cinema 180	Omni Films	N/A	-	5-70	180°	N/A
Showscan	Douglas Trumbull	1984	-	5-70	N/A	N/A
Iwerks 870	Iwerks Entertainment	N/A	-	8-70	N/A	N/A
Ultra Toruscope	Torus Films	N/A	-	3x5-70	360°	N/A
Courtesy of en.wikipedia.org © 2013						

Footnotes:

1. N/A signifies that verified information for this category is not currently available.
2. AR is an abbreviation for Aspect Ratio: A ratio of the width of the image to its height, expressed in the form x:1.
3. A dash in the year abandoned column indicates the format is still in use.
4. The frame area is expressed in inches.
5. The film format is expressed using the following notation: *nxp-mmAc.c*
   - Where *nx*, if present, is the number of film strips, e.g. 3x for Cinerama
   - *p* is the number of perforations in one film margin per frame (except centre perf. formats), e.g. 5 for Todd-AO
   - *mm* is the width of the film in millimetres, e.g. 55.625 for CinemaScope-55;
   - *Ac.c*, if present, indicates that the image is anamorphically expanded from the film by expansion factor *c.c*, e.g. A2.0 for CinemaScope
   - and H, if present, denotes a horizontally-running format, e.g. 8-35H for VistaVision

6. Super 16 prints are rarely made. Dimensions given refer to extraction areas for blowing up to 35mm release prints.

Figure A1.5d   The Ultimate Table of Formats—An Historical Guide: 1965–1973.

MOTION PICTURE FILM FORMATS

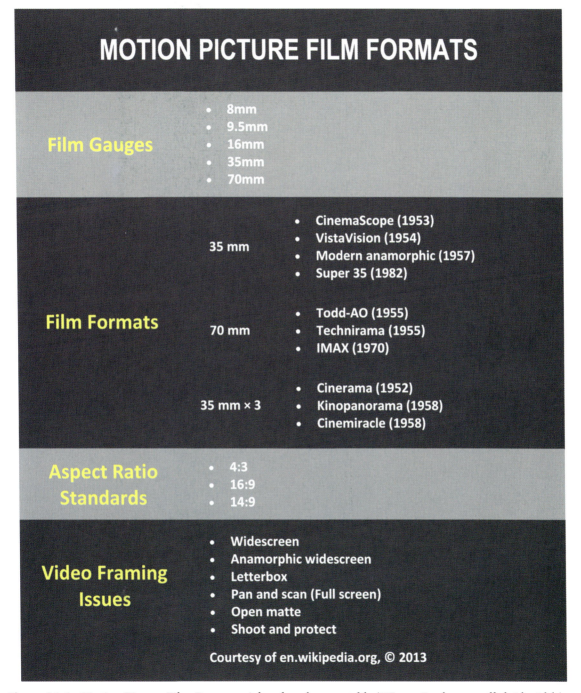

Figure A1.6 Motion Picture Film Formats: A handy reference table ("Gauge" refers to celluloid width).

IEC PREFIXES

PREFIXES FOR MULTIPLES OF BITS [b] OR BYTES [B]

Decimal			Binary				
Value	Metric		Value	JEDEC		IEC	
1000^1	k	**kilo**	1024^1	K	kilo	Ki	**kibi**
1000^2	M	**mega**	1024^2	M	mega	Mi	**mebi**
1000^3	G	**giga**	1024^3	G	giga	Gi	**gibi**
1000^4	T	**tera**	1024^4			Ti	**tebi**
1000^5	P	**peta**	1024^5			Pi	**pebi**
1000^6	E	**exa**	1024^6			Ei	**exbi**
1000^7	Z	**zetta**	1024^7			Zi	**zebi**
1000^8	Y	**yotta**	1024^8			Yi	**yobi**

IEC Prefix		Representations				Customary Prefix	
Name	Symbol	Base 2	Base 1024	Value	Base 10	Name	Symbol
kibi	Ki	2^{10}	1024^1	1024	$\approx 1.02 \times 10^3$	**kilo**	k, K
mebi	Mi	2^{20}	1024^2	1048576	$\approx 1.05 \times 10^6$	**mega**	M
gibi	Gi	2^{30}	1024^3	1073741824	$\approx 1.07 \times 10^9$	**giga**	G
tebi	Ti	2^{40}	1024^4	1099511627776	$\approx 1.10 \times 10^{12}$	**tera**	T
pebi	Pi	2^{50}	1024^5	1125899906842624	$\approx 1.13 \times 10^{15}$	**peta**	P
exbi	Ei	2^{60}	1024^6	1152921504606846976	$\approx 1.15 \times 10^{18}$	**exa**	E
zebi	Zi	2^{70}	1024^7	1180591620717411303424	$\approx 1.18 \times 10^{21}$	**zetta**	Z
yobi	Yi	2^{80}	1024^8	1208925819614629174706176	$\approx 1.21 \times 10^{24}$	**yotta**	Y

Courtesy of en.wikipedia.org © 2013

Figure A1.7   IEC Prefixes. As file storage sizes have expanded with advancing technology, the International Electro-Technical Commission has coined new names to define them.

BUCKLAND FILMOGRAPHY

Wilfred Buckland's filmography lists him as art director, production designer, art department, second unit director or assistant director, and miscellaneous crew.

This list was compiled from the Internet Movie Database (www.imdb.com) and AFI Catalog of Silent Films (www.afi.com).

These films are worth watching.

Table A1.1   Buckland filmography.

Almost Human	1927
Always Audacious	1920
Amarilly of Clothes-Line Alley	1918
American Consul, The	1917
Anton the Terrible	1916
Blackbirds	1915
Call of the East, The	1917
Call of the North, The	1914
Captive, The	1915
Carmen	1915
Cheat, The	1915
Chimmie Fadden	1915
City of Dim Faces, The	1918
City of Masks, The	1920
City Sparrow, A	1920
Clown, The	1916
Conrad in Quest of His Youth	1920
Crooked Streets	1920
Cruise of the Make-Believes, The	1918
Crystal Gazer, The	1917
Cumberland Romance, A	1920
Dancin' Fool, The	1920
Deuce of Spades, The	1922
Devil Stone, The	1917
Don't Change Your Husband	1919

(Continued)

Table A1.1   (Continued)

Excuse My Dust	1920
Eyes of the Heart	1920
Forbidden Woman, The	1927
Fourteenth Man, The	1920
Furnace, The	1920
Girl of the Golden West, The	1915
Girl Who Came Back, The	1918
Goat, The	1918
Hawthorne of the U.S.A.	1919
Held by the Enemy	1920
Her Country First	1918
Joan the Woman	1916
Johanna Enlists	1918
Lady in Love, A	1920
Less Than Kin	1918
Little American, The	1917
Little Princess, The	1917
Male and Female	1919
Masquerader, The	1922
M'liss	1918
Mrs. Temple's Telegram	1920
Old Wives for New	1918
Omar the Tentmaker	1922
One More American	1918
Plow Girl, The	1916
Public Opinion	1916
Pudd'nhead Wilson	1916
Ragamuffin, The	1916
Reaching for the Moon	1917
Roaring Road, The	1919
Robin Hood	1923
Romance of the Redwoods, A	1917
Secret Sin, The	1915
Selfish Woman, The	1916
Something to Do	1919

Soul of Kura-San, The	1916
Source, The	1918
Squaw Man, The	1918
Stella Maris	1918
Such a Little Pirate	1918
Sweet Kitty Bellairs	1916
Thou Art the Man	1920
Trail of the Lonesome Pine, The	1916
Victoria Cross, The	1916
We Can't Have Everything	1918
Whispering Chorus, The	1918
Widow's Might, The	1918
Wild and Woolly	1917
Woman God Forgot, The	1917
Woman Next Door, The	1919
You Never Can Tell	1920
Young Romance	1915
You're Fired	1919

DAILY GEAR LIST

DAILY GEAR LIST

What do you put in your bag?
This practical list will keep you effective and wired through every phase of the process.
The additional lists below it suggests items you might need in-office and on location.

CARRYBAG	NOTES
iPAD or Tablet	Larger screen allows for better show-and-tell.
Smartphone	Just as long as it connects to the Cloud.
Digital Camera	Smartphone image quality sometimes isn't resolved enough.
DVCAM or MiniCAM	Betacam SP quality & at a fraction of the price
Pocket scale rule	The question of dimensions always comes up.
Laser Range Meter	Quick and accurate
Pocket Ref book	Shirt pocket size: 3.2" x 5.4" x 0.9"
Shooting Schedule	Hard copies are always good.
One-Liner	Hard copies are always good.
11" x 17" Plans	Even though they are on the Cloud, have hard copies in your bag.
OFFICE	NOTES
Laptop	Largest capacity available.
External hard drive	Fingertip back-up.
Printer: Epson Stylus series	For excellent color work.
Scanner: Canon series	For dependable 1200 dpi scans.
LOCATION	NOTES
Rubbermaid Canisters	Durable. Filled with bubble wrap and styro p-nuts as a cushion and you're good to go.
Padlocks	For canisters. Keep multiple key sets.
12" Wheelie	Quick walking location scouting.
Fly strips	Your office is likely to be a trailer. You will thank me for this.
Solar Anti-Mosquito Guard	It hangs from a chain around your neck It really works.

Figure A1.8   Daily Gear List.

FILM POCKET LISTINGS

My invention, "Film Pocket Listings," developed over several decades of keeping lists both online and offline. The listing contains a handful of helpful categories to jumpstart searches. Originally, it filled one page and folded neatly into a back pocket before I bought a smartphone and iPad. But it's still handy. For the most part, it's abbreviated to be quick without extra information: just a name and a website address. Additional data, i.e., other contact information would, of course, exist on each website.

As of May 2014, all listings were current and functioning.

Table A1.2   Film pocket listings.

ORGANIZATION RESOURCE	WEBSITE
BOOKS	
CMP BOOKS	www.cmpbooks.com
FOCAL PRESS	www.focalpress.com
HENNESSEY & INGALLS ART	www.hennesseyingalls.com
LARRY EDMUNDS BOOKSHOP	www.larryedmunds.com
MICHAEL WIESE PRODUCTIONS	www.mwp.com
ONLINE DIRECTORIES: L.A.	www.411publishing.com
SAMUEL FRENCH BOOKSTORE	www.samuelfrench.com
VISUAL REFERENCE PUBLICATIONS, INC	www.retailreporting.com
DATABASES	
ACADEMY OF MOTION PICTURE ARTS & SCIENCES	www.oscars.org
ASSOCIATION OF FILM COMMISSIONERS INTERNATIONAL	www.afci.org
CALIFORNIA ARTS COUNCIL	www.cac.ca.gov
CALIFORNIA FILM COMMISSION	www.film.ca.gov
CURRENCY CONVERTER	www.xe.com
DEBBIES BOOK—INDUSTRY RESOURCE	www.debbiesbook.com
FILM L.A. INC	www.filmla.com
FILM & TV ACTION COMMITTEE—RUNAWAY PRODUCTION	www.ftac.net
FILM HISTORY ON THE INTERNET	www.filmsite.org
FILM INDUSTRY NETWORK	www.filmindustrynetwork.biz
FILMMAKING NETWORK	www.indieclub.com
INDUSTRY PORTAL AND WORLDWIDE DATABASE	www.moviemaker.com

(*Continued*)

Table A1.2   (Continued)

INDUSTRY SEARCH ENGINE	www.showbiz.com
INDUSTRY-RELATED WEB DATABASE	www.industrycentral.net
INTERNET MOVIE DATA BASE	www.imdb.com
LOS ANGELES FILM FESTIVAL	www.lafilmfest.com
ONLINE BUSINESS2BUSINESS DIRECTORY	www.la411.com
PLASA ENTERTAINMENT SERVICES & TECHNOLOGY ASSOCIATION	www.plasa.org
THOMAS REGIONAL INDUSTRIAL PRODUCTS & SUPPLIERS	www.thomasregional.com
UNITED STATES INSTITUTE OF THEATRE TECHNOLOGY	www.usitt.org
US NAVY DATABASE	www.aa.usno.navy.mil/data
US WEATHER DATABASE	www.weathermatrix.net
WEB GUIDE FOR MOVIEMAKERS	www.webmovie.com
DESIGN	
AMERICAN SOCIETY OF INTERIOR DESIGNERS	www.asid.org
THE COSTUME WEG RING	www.marquise.de
EVENT PLANNING WEBRING	www.expoworld.net
INTERNATIONAL INTERIOR DESIGN ASSOCIATION	www.iida.com
LIBRARY OF CONGRESS	www.lcweb.loc.gov
UNIVERSITY RESIDENT THEATRE ASSOCIATION	www.urta.com
FILM SCHOOLS	
AMERICAN FILM INSTITUTE	www.afi.com
THE LOS ANGELES FILM SCHOOL	www.lafilm.edu
NEW YORK FILM ACADEMY	www.nyfa.edu
NYU FILM & TELEVISION	www.filmtv.tisch.nyu.edu
SCHOOL OF VISUAL ARTS	www.sva.edu
UCLA SCHOOL OF THEATRE, FILM & TELEVISION	www.tft.ucla.edu
USC SCHOOL OF CINEMA	www.cinema.usc.edu
GUILDS AND UNIONS	
AMERICAN SOCIETY OF CINEMATOGRAPHERS	www.theasc.com
ART DIRECTORS GUILD	www.artdirectors.org
DIRECTORS GUILD OF AMERICA	www.dga.org
INTERNATIONAL ALLIANCE OF THEATRICAL STAGE EMPLOYEES	www.iatse-intl.org
INTERNATIONAL BROTHERHOOD OF TEAMSTERS	www.teamster.org

LOCATION MANAGERS GUILD OF AMERICA	www.locationmanagers.org
PRODUCERS GUILD OF AMERICA	www.producersguild.org
SET DECORATORS SOCIETY OF AMERICA	www.setdecorators.org
SET DESIGNERS & MODEL MAKERS	www.theacme.com
SOCIETY OF MOTION PICTURE & TV ENGINEERS	www.smpte.org
INDIE ORGS	
AMERICAN FILM INSTITUTE	www.afionline.org
ASSOCIATION OF INDEPENDENT FEATURE FILM PRODUCERS	www.aiffp.org
ASSOCIATION OF INDEPENDENT VIDEO & FILMMAKERS	www.aivf.org
INDEPENDENT FEATURE PROJECT	www.ifp.org
FILM ARTS FOUNDATION—INDIE RESOURCE	www.filmart.org
JOBS	
INDUSTRY RESOURCE	www.filmmaker.com
WORLDWIDE DATABASE	www.craigslist.org
WRITERS STORE	www.writersstore.com
INDUSTRY-RELATED WEB DATABASE	www.entertainmentcareers.net
WORLDWIDE INDUSTRY DATABASE	www.mandy.com
WORLDWIDE JOB & RELOCATION DATABASE	www.monster.com
LIBRARIES & MUSEUMS	
AMERICAN MUSEUM OF MOVING IMAGE	www.movingimage.us
LOS ANGELES PUBLIC LIBRARY	www.lapl.org
THE PALEY CENTER FOR MEDIA	www.paleycenter.org
NEW YORK PUBLIC LIBRARY	www.nypl.org
THE INTERNET PUBLIC LIBRARY	www.ipl.org
THE LIBRARY OF MOVING IMAGES	www.moving-images.us
VIRTUAL LIBRARY MUSEUM—	www.archives.icom.museum/vlmp
WORLDWIDE MUSEUMS	http://archives.icom.museum.html
WORLDWIDE ARTS RESOURCES	http://wwar.com
LOS ANGELES MOVIE STUDIOS	
20TH CENTURY FOX STUDIOS	www.foxstudios.com
COLUMBIA-TRISTAR [SONY STUDIOS PICTURES]	www.sonypicturesstudios.com/
DISNEY STUDIOS	www.thewaltdisneycompany.com
MIRAMAX FILM CORPORATION	www.miramax.com
PARAMOUNT STUDIOS	www.paramount.com
UNIVERSAL PICTURES	www.universalstudios.com
WARNER BROS.	http://warnerbros.com/home.html

FILMMAKER'S CODE OF ETHICS

Table A1.3   Filmmaker's code of ethics.

FILMMAKER'S CODE OF ETHICS	
This document, generated by the Locations Department, outlines the appropriate conduct of crew members at any given interior or exterior location. Following these guidelines secures an invitation to return to a hero location; this is especially significant in episodic television.	
1	When filming in a neighborhood or business district, proper notification is to be provided to each merchant or neighbor who is directly affected by the company (this includes parking, base camps, and meal areas). Information includes: • Name of Project. • Type of production, e.g., feature film, movie of the week, TV pilot, etc. • Company contacts, i.e., first assistant director, unit production manager, location manager.
2	Production vehicles arriving on location in or near a residential neighborhood shall not enter the area before the time stipulated in the permit, and they shall park one by one, turning off engines as soon as possible. Cast and crew shall observe designated parking areas.
3	Every member of the crew shall wear a production pass (badge) when issued.
4	Moving or towing of the public's vehicles is prohibited without the express permission of the municipal jurisdiction or the owner of the vehicle.
5	Do not park production vehicles in or block driveways without the express permission of the municipal jurisdiction or driveway owner.
6	Cast and crew meals shall be confined to the area designated in the location agreement or permit. Individuals shall eat within their designated meal area, during scheduled crew meals. All trash must be disposed of properly upon completion of the meal.
7	Removing, trimming, and/or cutting of vegetation or trees is prohibited unless approved by the permit authority or property owner.
8	Remember to use the proper receptacles for disposal of all napkins, plates, and coffee cups that you may use in the course of the working day.
9	All signs erected or removed for filming purposes will be removed or replaced upon completion of the use of that location unless otherwise stipulated by the location agreement or permit. Also remember to remove all signs posted to direct the company to the location.
10	Every member of the cast and crew shall keep noise levels as low as possible.
11	Do not wear clothing that lacks common sense and good taste. Shoes and shirts must be worn at all times, unless otherwise directed.
12	Crew members shall not display signs, posters, or pictures on vehicles that do not reflect common sense or good taste, i.e., pinup posters.
13	Do not trespass onto other neighbors' or merchants' property. Remain within the boundaries of the property that have been permitted for filming.

14	The cast and crew shall not bring guests or pets to the location, unless expressly authorized in advance by the company.
15	All catering, crafts service, construction, strike, and personal trash must be removed from location.
16	Observe designated smoking areas and always extinguish cigarettes in butt cans.
17	Cast and crew will refrain from the use of lewd or improper language within earshot of the general public.
18	The company will comply with the provisions of the parking permit.

LA BACKINGS

This is a short list but a comprehensive one.

Once you've investigated the websites and understand the range of possibilities, this list won't look so small. All of these companies provide painted, photographic, or digital backings for rental or custom translate services—all excellent, all competitively priced.

Please note that while the following list is current, there is no guarantee as to how long any individual website will remain valid. Also note that providing you with this list does not constitute an endorsement of any of the websites nor the services, claims, competitions, or courses they offer.

Table A1.4   LA backings.

ORGANIZATION	WEB SITE
Grosh Scenic Studio 4114 Sunset Boulevard Hollywood, CA 90029 Toll.Free: 877-363-7998 Phone: *323-662-1134* Fax: *323-664-7526* Warehouse/Shipping Locations: California Grosh Scenic Rentals 4114 Sunset Boulevard Los Angeles, CA 90029	www.grosh.com

(Continued)

Table A1.4   (Continued)

JC Backings J.C. Backings Corporation 10202 West Washington Blvd. Culver City, CA 90232 *Contact:* Lynne Coakley, Jim Spadoni or Pierre Steele Office: *310-244-5830* Fax: *310-244-7949* Rental Backings and Image Request Contacts: Lynne M. Coakley or Jim Spadoni Phone: *310-244-5830* Fax: *310-244-7949* Custom Work Quotes: Painted Backing Quotes Lynne M. Coakley or Jim Spadoni Phone: *310-244-5830* Photo Backing Quotes Pierre Steele Phone: *310-841-0123* Digital Print Backing Quotes Pierre Steele Phone: *310-841-0123*	www.jcbackings.com/home.html
Pacific Studios 8315 Melrose Avenue Los Angeles, CA 90069 www.pacificstudios.net Phone: *323-653-3093*	www.pacstudios@gmail.com
Rosco Digital Imaging Rosco Laboratories Inc. 52 Harbor View Ave Stamford, CT 06902 *Contact:* Diane Ricci Email: diane@rosco.com Toll-Free: *1-800-522-1180* Phone: (203) 708-8900 x229 Fax: *(203) 708-8919*	www.roscodigital.com

Rosco Toronto Rosco Laboratories Ltd 1241 Denison Street #44 Markham, Ontario Canada L3R 4B4 *Contact:* Tom Swartz Email: tswartz@roscocanada.com Toll-Free: *1-888-767-2686* Phone: *(905) 475-1400* Fax: *(905) 475-3351*	www.roscodigital.com
Rosco Holland Claus Slutterweg 125/1b 2012 WS Haarlem The Netherlands *Contact:* Lex Verstraaten Email: verstraatenl@rosco-europe.com Phone: *31 (0) 23 5288 257* Fax: *31 (0) 23 5286 754*	www.roscodigital.com
Rosco Sydney Rosco Australia Pty Ltd 42 Sawyer Lane Artarmon, NSW 2064 Australia *Contact:* Adam P. Smith Email: roscoaus@rosco.com.au Phone: *(02) 9906 6262* Fax: *(02) 9906 3430*	www.roscodigital.com
Schmidli Backdrops Los Angeles Schmidli Backdrops 5830 W. Adams Blvd. Culver City, CA 90232 Phone: *323-938-2098* Fax: *323-938-2486* Email: backdrops@schmidli.com	www.schmidli.com
Schmidli Amsterdam 711Rent Amsterdam Sarphatistraat 159 1018 GD Amsterdam Netherlands Phone: *+31-6-349 46 900* Email: amsterdam@711rent.com www.711rent.com	

(Continued)

Table A1.4   (Continued)

Schmidli Hamburg 711Rent Eimsbütteler Chaussee 66 20259 Hamburg Germany Phone: *+49 40 6360669-0* Fax: *+49 40 6360669-99* Email info@711rent.com www.711rent.com	
Schmidli London SNAP Studios 151-155 New North Road London N1 6TA Phone: *+44 (0) 207684 7555* Email info@Snap-Studios.co.uk	

LA SOUNDSTAGES

This list is credited to the Entertainment Industry Development Corporation, http://www.filmla.com/.

Please note that while the following list is current, there is no guarantee as to how long any individual website will remain valid. Also note that providing you with this list does not constitute an endorsement of any of the websites nor the services or claims they offer.

Table A1.5   LA soundstages.

STAGE NAME	CITY	WEB SITE/PHONE #
ABC Prospect Studio	Los Angeles	310-557-7777
ACME Stage	North Hollywood	www.acmestage.com
Arroyo Studios	Sylmar	818-837-9837
Avalon Studios	North Hollywood	818-508-5050
Axel Stages	Burbank	818-556-6182
Action Space	Los Angeles	www.actionspace.com
Barker Hangar	Santa Monica	www.barkerhangar.com
Barwick Studios, LLC	Los Angeles	www.barwickstudios.com
Ben Kitay Studios, LLC	Hollywood	www.benkitay.com
Boyington Film Productions	Los Angeles	323-933-7500
Bruce Austin Productions (BAP)	Burbank	818-842-0820

CBS-MTM Studios (Radford Studios)	Los Angeles	818-760-5000
CBS Television City	Los Angeles	323-463-1600
Carthay Studios	Los Angeles	213-938-2101
Century Studio Corporation	Culver City	www.centurystudio.com
Chandler Toluca Lake Studios	North Hollywood	818-763-3650
Chandler Valley Center Studios	Van Nuys	www.valleystudios.com
Chaplin Stages	Los Angeles	323-856-2682
Cole Avenue Studios	Hollywood	www.colestages.com
Complex Studios	Los Angeles	www.thecomplexstudios.com
Culver Studios	Culver City	310-202-1234
Delfino Stages	Sylmar	www.delfinostudios.com
Disney Studios	Burbank	818-560-5151
Dreamworks SKG	Burbank	www.dreamworks.com
Edgewood Stages	Los Angeles	323-938-4762
Empire Burbank Studios	Burbank	818-840-1400
GMT Studios	Culver City	www.gmtstudios.com
Glendale Studios	Glendale	www.glendalestudios.com
Grosch Productions	North Hollywood	www.gosch.net
Hangar 9 Studios	Santa Monica	310-392-5084
Hayvenhurst Studios	Van Nuys	818-909-6999
Hollywood Center Studios	Hollywood	www.hollywoodcenter.com
Hollywood National Studios	Hollywood	323-467-6272
Hollywood Stage	Hollywood	323-466-4393
Hyperion Stage	Los Angeles	323-665-9983
ICN Productions	West Los Angeles	310-826-4777
KCET Studios	Los Angeles	323-953-5258
Keith Harrier Production Service	Hollywood	323-930-2720
LA Center Studios	Los Angeles	www.lacenterstudios.com
Lacy Street Production Center	Los Angeles	323-222-8872
Lindsey Studios/Warren Entertainment Center	Valencia	661-257-9292
Metro Goldwyn Mayer	Santa Monica	310-449-3000
Mack Sennett Stage	Los Angeles	323-660-8466
Media City Tele-production Center	Burbank	www.mediacitystudios.com
Miramax Film Corporation	New York	212-941-3800
NBC-Burbank	Burbank	www.nbc.com

(Continued)

Table A1.5   (Continued)

NBC Hollywood, Sunset & Gower	Hollywood	323-617-0153
Nickelodeon	Glendale	www.nick.com
North Field Properties/Hangar 8	Santa Monica	310-392-9000
Norwood Stage	Culver City	310-204-3323
Occidental Studios	Hollywood	www.occidentalstudios.com
Oceanside Studios	Santa Monica	310-399-7704
P.K.E. Studio	Culver City	310-838-7000
Paladin Stages	West Hollywood	323-851-8222
Panavision Stages	Woodland Hills	818-316-1000
Pasadena Production Studios 39	Pasadena	818-584-4090
Production Group	Hollywood	www.production-group.com
Quixote Studios	West Hollywood	www.quixote.net
Raleigh Studios	Hollywood	323-466-3111
Raleigh Studios	Manhattan Beach	www.raleighstudios.com
Ray-Art Studios	Canoga Park	www.rayartstudios.com
Ren-Mar Studios	Hollywood	323-463-0808
Riverfront Stages	Sylmar	www.riverfrontstages.com
San Mar Studios	Hollywood	323-465-8110
Santa Clarita Studios	Santa Clarita	www.sc-studios.com
Screenland Studios I	Burbank	818-843-2262
Shrine Auditorium	Los Angeles	members.aol.com/shrineaud
Shutter Studio	Hollywood	323-957-1672
SmashBox Studios	Culver City	www.smashboxstudio.com
Solar Studios	Glendale	818-240-1893
Sony Pictures Studios	Culver City	www.spe.sony.com/studio
South Bay Studios	Long Beach	310-762-1360
South Lake Stage	Burbank	818-953-8400
Studio 57	North Hollywood	818-985-1908
Sunset Gower Studios	Hollywood	323-467-1001
Sunset Stage	Hollywood	323-461-0282
Ten9Fifty Studios	Culver City	310-202-2330
The Lot	West Hollywood	www.thelotstudios.com
Turner Broadcasting System	Atlanta	404-827-1700
Twentieth Century Fox	Beverly Hills	310-369-0900

Universal Studios	Universal City	http://universalstudios.com/studio/hollywood
VPS Studios	Hollywood	323-469-7244
Valencia Entertainment	Valencia	www.valenciaentertainment.com
Walt Disney Studios	Burbank	www.stu-ops.disney.com
Warner Bros.	Burbank	www.wbsf.com
West Valley Studios	Chatsworth	818-998-2222
World Television Productions	Hollywood	323-469-5638

IATSE MEMBERSHIP GUILDS

Table A1.6   IATSE membership guilds

IATSE Membership Guilds
Local 44 Affiliated Property Craftspersons www.local44.org 12021 Riverside Drive North Hollywood, CA 91607 T (818) 769 2500 F (818) 769 1739
Local 600 International Cinematographers Guild www.cameraguild.com 7755 Sunset Boulevard Los Angeles, CA 90046 T (323) 876 0160 F (323) 876 6383
Local 695 International Sound/Cinetechnicians www.695.com 5439 Cahuenga Boulevard North Hollywood, CA 91601 T (818) 985-9204 F (818) 760-4681
Local 80 Motion Picture Grips www.iatselocal80.org 2520 West Olive Avenue Burbank, CA 91505 T (818) 526 0700 F (818) 526 0719

(Continued)

Table A1.6   (Continued)

Local 700 Motion Picture Editors Guild www.editorsguild.com 7715 Sunset Boulevard Suite 220 Hollywood, CA 90046 T 323-876-4770 F 323-876-0861 Ron Kutak, Executive Director Kathy Repola, Assistant Executive Director
Local 705 Motion Picture Costumers www.motionpicturecostumers.org/local705 4731 Laurel Canyon Boulevard Suite 201 Valley Village, CA 91607 T 818-487-5655 F 818-487-5663 Buffy Snyder, Business Agent
Local 706 Make-up Artists & Hair Stylists www.local706.org 828 North Hollywood Way Burbank, CA 91505 T 818-295-3933 F 818-295-3930 Tommy Cole, Business Agent Susan Cabral/Ebert, Assistant Business Agent Butch Belo, Assistant Business Agent
Local 728 Studio Electrical Technicians www.iatse728.org 14629 Nordhoff Street Panorama City, CA 91402 T 818-891-0728 F 818-891-5288 Patrick Abaravich, Business Agent
Local 729 Motion Picture Set Painters & Sign Writers www.ialocal729.com 1811 West Burbank Boulevard Burbank, CA 91506-1314 T 818-842-7729 F 818-846-3729 George Palazzo, Business Agent

Local 767 Motion Picture Studio First Aid
www.iatse767.org
14530 Denker Avenue
Gardena, CA 90247-2323
T 310-352-4485
F 310-352-4485
Rana Platz-Petersen, RN, Business Agent

Local 768 Theatrical Wardrobe
13245 Riverside Drive, 3rd Floor
Sherman Oaks, CA 91423
T 818-789-8735
F 818-905-6297
William N. Damron, Jr., Business Agent

Local 80 Motion Picture Studio Grips
www.iatselocal80.org
2520 West Olive Avenue
Burbank, CA 91505-4523
T 818-526-0700
F 800-994-1080
F 818-526-0719
Thom Davis, Business Agent

Local 800 Art Directors
ADG.org
11969 Ventura Boulevard
Suite 200
Studio City, CA 91604
T 818-762-9995
F 818-762-9997
Scott Roth, Executive Director
John Moffitt, Associate Executive Director

Local 829 United Scenic Artists
www.usa829.org
29 West 38th Street
New York, NY 10018
T 212-581-0300
F 212-977-2011
Michael McBride, Business Agent
 5225 Wilshire Boulevard
Los Angeles, CA 90036
T 323-965-0957
F 323-965-0958
Charles Berliner, West Coast Representative

(*Continued*)

Table A1.6   (Continued)

Local 839 The Animation Guild www.animationguild.org 4729 Lankershim Boulevard North Hollywood, CA 91602-1864 T 818-766-7151 F 818-506-4805 Steve Hulett, Business Agent
Local 871 Script Supervisors/Continuity, Coordinators, Accountants & **Allied Production Specialists Guild** www.ialocal871.org 11519 Chandler Boulevard North Hollywood, CA 91601 T 818-509-7871 F 818-506-1555 Missy Humphrey, Business Agent
Local 884 Studio Teachers www.studioteachers.com P.O. Box 461467 Los Angeles, CA 90046 310-652-5330 Polly Businger, Business Agent
Local 892 Costume Designers Guild (CDG) costumedesignersguild.com 11969 Ventura Boulevard Studio City, CA 91604 T (818) 752 2400 F (818) 752-2402
Local B-192 Amusement Area Employees 10999 Riverside Drive, #301 North Hollywood, CA 91602 T 818-509-9192 F 818-509-9873 Donna Marie Covert, Business Agent

LOCAL 44 BUDGETING GUIDELINES

Local 44
Budgeting
Guidelines

Figure A1.9   Local 44 Budgeting Guide.

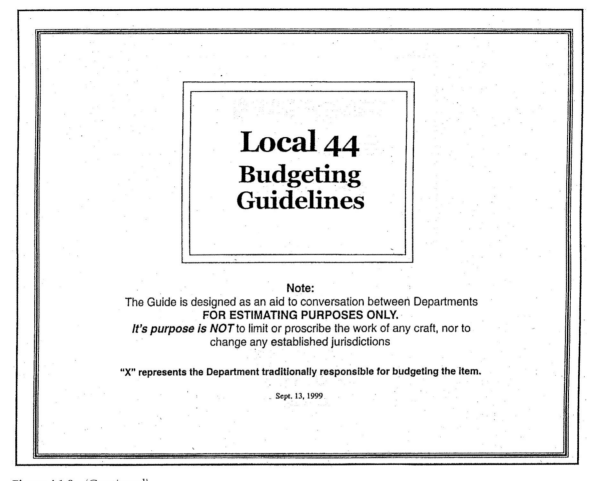

Figure A1.9 (Continued)

UNION DEPARTMENT HEAD RESPONSIBILITIES / BUDGET CATEGORIES

"X" represents the Department traditionally responsible for **budgeting** the item.

DESCRIPTION	Set Decorator Local 44	Prop Master Local 44	Construction Local 44	Special Effects Local 44	Transpo. Local 399	Gaffer/ Set Lting Local 728	40 Shop IBEW Local 40	Grips Local 80	Production -	Craft Service Local 727
Appliances (Domestic/Commercial)										
Cooler Boxes	X									
Counter Top Appliances	X									
Dishwashers	X									
Freezers	X									
Microwaves	X									
Ovens/Wall Ovens	X									
Installation of Wall Ovens			X							
Pizza Ovens	X									
Appliances as Scripted Action Props		X								
Stove Tops/Hoods	X									
Installation of stove tops/hoods			X							
Stoves	X									
Make Practical				X						
Refrigerators:										
Walk-In Refrigerators			X							
Built-In Refrigerators (fronts)	X									
Installation of backing flats			X							
Free-standing Refrigerators	X									
Lighting Hookup/bulb seen				X						
Lighting Hookup/bulb not seen						X				
Rigged to turn off on bell							X			

8/1/97

Page 1

Figure A1.9   (Continued)

DESCRIPTION (continued)	Set Decorator	Prop Master	Construct.	Special Effects	Transpo.	Gaffer/ Set Lting	40 Shop	Grips	Production	Craft Service
Artwork and Sculpture										
Clearances									X	
Decorative and Period Artwork	X									
Paintings,Posters & Sculpture										
Amateur/Children's Artwork	X									
Artist's Works in Progress		X								
*(*Note once again: This X denotes only which Department is budgeting the item. Prop Master and Production Designer should meet regarding creative input.)*										
Murals/Murals in Progress			X							
Poster as Action Prop		X								
Photographs Generic	X									
Photograph as Action Prop		X								
Photographs Scripted W/Actors		X								
Backings										
Plain Color (i.e. Blue)			X							
Scenic			X							
Blackboards/Bulletin Boards										
Schoolroom Blackboards attached to Wall			X							
Bulletin Boards	X									
Display Boards	X									
Bleachers			X							
Boxing Rings										
Wooden Platform			X							
Canvas Pad on top: Installation by Drapery			X							
Pipe Platform: Installation by Grips			X							
Breakaways										
Windows/Doors/Architectural				X						
Dishes/Glassware/Chairs		X								

Figure A1.9 (Continued)

DESCRIPTION (continued)	Set Decorator	Prop Master	Construct.	Special Effects	Transpo.	Gaffer/ Set Lting	40 Shop	Grips	Production	Craft Service
Carnivals										
Games/Background	X									
Games/Hero,Action,Scripted		X								
Carnival Booths, Foodstands, Rides:										
Built/Designed			X							
Rented	X									
Casino Dressing										
Gaming Equipment	X									
Specially Rigged Action Props		X								
Rigging				X						
Classroom/Off Camera Set-Up									X	X
Clean-Up										
Initial Constructon Cleanup at Finish of Build (Construction Labor - Local 724)			X							
Subsequent Clean up										X
Conduit/Pipe/Tubing										
As attached to set dressing items	X									
As part of original architecture			X							
Conduit boxes	X									
Electrical Boxes	X									
Surface Mounted Wiring	X									
Air Conditioning Ducting			X							
Conventions										
Pipe&Drape Booth Dividers/skirting	X									
Counters										
*As Built-in Counters			X							

(*Built-in refers to all counters that in real life would be attached and immovable)

Figure A1.9 (Continued)

DESCRIPTION (continued)	Set Decorator	Prop Master	Construct.	Special Effects	Transpo.	Gaffer/Set Lting	40 Shop	Grips	Production	Craft Service
Bars/Backbars:										
As Built-in			X							
Freestanding backbar			X							
All Scene Dock rentals			X							
Candy Counters	X									
Grocery Gondolas	X									
Portable Display	X									
Jewelry Cases	X									
Portable Steam Table	X									
Doorways & Arches										
Bi-fold Doors/Accordion Doors			X							
Interior/ExteriorDoors			X							
Dumpsters (Seen on Camera as Dressing)	X									
Electronics										
*Built-In: *Refers to all electronics that in real life would be attached and immovable.*										
Cabinet/Console			X							
Lights/Switches			X							
*Free-standing: *Refers to all electronics that are not designed into the set.*										
Cabinet/Console	X									
Lights/Switches	X									
Hookup/Connect				X						
Elevators										
Doors (Rental or Purchase, Scene Dock or Prop House)			X							
Elevator Hardware			X							
Installation			X							
Operation of Switches & Call Lights				X						

Figure A1.9 (Continued)

DESCRIPTION (continued)	Set Decorator	Prop Master	Construct.	Special Effects	Transpo.	Gaffer/ Set Lting	40 Shop	Grips	Production	Craft Service
Decorative Elevator Lights	X									
Emerg Elevator Phone if separate unit	X									
Elevator Operated By				X						
Exterior Dressing										
Bicycle Stands	X									
Billboards larger than a one-sheet			X							
Bus Benches	X									
Bus Stop Signs	X									
Bus Stop Shelters (designed)			X							
Designed Items			X							
Fire Hydrants	X									
Fire Extinguishers	X									
Kiosk:										
Built/Designed			X							
Rented	X									
Kiosk Dressing	X									
Mailboxes	X									
Installation of post			X							
Newspaper Stands:										
Built/Designed			X							
Rented	X									
Newsstand Dressing	X									
Parking/No Parking Signs	X									
Parking Meters	X									
Scripted Signs			X							
Street Signs			X							
Subway Signs			X							

UNION DEPARTMENT HEAD RESPONSIBILITIES

8/1/97

Figure A1.9 (Continued)

DESCRIPTION (continued)	Set Decorator	Prop Master	Construct.	Special Effects	Transpo.	Gaffer/ Set Lting	40 Shop	Grips	Production	Craft Service
Telephone Booths	X									
Vending Carts w/Action		X								
Vending Carts w/o Action	X									
Fire Alarm Box										
Make practical				X						
Fireplaces										
Fire Screens	X									
Tools & Accessories	X									
Firewall			X							
Make Practical				X						
Gas Logs	X									
Rigging of Gas Logs				X						
Mantles/Hearths/Fireboxes			X							
Flags/Banners/Pennants										
Decorative Banners/Rented or Mfg.	X									
Pennants/Flags	X									
Printed Banners as Signage			X							
Flooring										
Area Rugs and Runners	X									
Dance Floor			X							
Tile/Marble/Metal and Stone			X							
Vinyl Wall-to-wall (sheet or tile)			X							
Vinyl Unattached	X									
Wall-to-Wall Carpet			X							
Hardwood or Plank			X							
Cleaning and Maintenance										X

Figure A1.9 (Continued)

DESCRIPTION (continued)	Set Decorator	Prop Master	Construct.	Special Effects	Transpo.	Gaffer/ Set Lting	40 Shop	Grips	Production	Craft Service
Furnaces/Heaters										
Designed/Built			X							
Free-standing Heater	X									
Space heaters	X									
Radiators/Radiator Covers	X									
Covers Designed/Built into Set			X							
Water Heaters	X									
Furniture										
Free-standing - Rental or Purchase	X									
Built-in Furniture			X							
Custom Designed Free-standing	X									
Graveyards										
Tombstones			X							
Flowers/easels/mementos	X									
Caskets/Coffins:										
Standing	X									
Carried or Action		X								
Greens										
Outside Greens tied into Backings			X							
Bouquets/Boutonnieres		X								
Built-In Planters			X							
Trees In Ground			X							
*Trees In Decor Pots	X									
*Not to exceed a 50 gallon container or require special equipment										
Trees/Plants in Jungles/Swamps/Landscapes			X							
Flowers in Vases	X									
Camo Netting			X							

Figure A1.9 (Continued)

DESCRIPTION (continued)	Set Decorator	Prop Master	Construct.	Special Effects	Transpo.	Gaffer/ Set Lting	40 Shop	Grips	Production	Craft Service
Interior Plants	X									
In-Ground Plants			X							
Lawns			X							
Leaves (Blowing, Placing on Trees)			X							
Freestanding/Hanging Potted Plants	X									
Built-in Window Boxes			X							
Flowers/ Plants for Window Boxes	X									
Vegetable Gardens			X							
Hardware										
on Built-In Cabinets			X							
on Doors/Windows			X							
on Free-standing Furniture (pulls, knobs etc.)	X									
Marine Hardware (portholes, etc.)			X							
Electrical Outlets and Plates	X									
Outlet and Plate Hookup (110 V)						X				
Vents			X							
Wall Hooks/Brackets	X									
Helicopter Wind Sock (for landing)	X									
Hospital Rooms										
Wall Electronics Unit	X									
Installation of Wall Unit			X							
Rigging of Wall Unit				X	(*Note: Some rigging may require a medical Technician.)					
Hospital Drape and Ceiling Track	X									
Installation by Drapery	X									
Built-In Counters and Cabinets			X							
Medical Sinks	X									
Install Medical Sinks			X							

UNION DEPARTMENT HEAD RESPONSIBLITIES

8/1/97

Page 8

Figure A1.9   (Continued)

DESCRIPTION (continued)	Set Decorator	Prop Master	Construct.	Special Effects	Transpo.	Gaffer/ Set Lting	40 Shop	Grips	Production	Craft Service
Scripted Equipment (ie: EKG)		X								X
Layout Board										
Lighting and Electrical										
Alarm Systems:										
With Scripted Action		X								
As Background	X									
make Practical/Lights				X						
Christmas/Holiday Lighting & Decorations	X									
Circuit Boxes (as dressing)	X									
Decorative Lighting	X									
Portable Lighting	X									
Dimmer Boxes						X				
Electrical Outlets & Plates	X									
Theatrical Footlights	X									
Runway Lights/Theatrical Ground Row/Apron			X							
Runway Lights - Airport	X									
Stagelights Seen by Camera	X									
Stagelights Off Camera for Set Lighting Purposes						X				
Stagelights Off Camera/Other crew needs							X			
Dressing Room Lights/Power							X			
Work Lights							X			
Lights/power for permanent structures, ie. Offices							X			
Neon:										
Interior/Decorative	X									
Dimmers for set dressing neon		.		X *(May be Local 728 at some studios. Be sure to discuss in prep.)*						
Exterior neon			X							
Scripted neon			X							

UNION DEPARTMENT HEAD RESPONSIBILITIES

8/1/97

Figure A1.9 (Continued)

DESCRIPTION (continued)	Set Decorator	Prop Master	Construct.	Special Effects	Transpo.	Gaffer/ Set Lting	40 Shop	Grips	Production	Craft Service
Period Lighting	X									
Picture Lights	X									
Recessed Ceiling Can *(As part of the architecture and drawn on the plan.)*										
Installation			X							
Speedrail:										
Installation								X		
Connection/Hookup						X				
Attach lights to pipe	X									
Fluorescents:										
Recessed fluorescents *(As part of the architecture and drawn on the plan)*										
Installation			X							
Diffuser Grids for recessed fluorescents			X							
Surface Mount/Hanging Fluorescents	X									
Installation	X									
(For surface mount/hanging fluorescents on a soft ceiling - off-camera battens are provided by Construction.)										
Fluorescents-Bulbs/Pan Not Seen						X				
Tubes						X				
Plastic Strip Lights	X									
Installation			X							
Signal (Traffic)	X									
Installation			X							
Hookup				X						
Street Lamp Fixtures	X									
Special Install. Equip			X							
Installation			X							
Electrical Rigging						X				

Figure A1.9 (Continued)

DESCRIPTION (continued)	Set Decorator	Prop Master	Construct.	Special Effects	Transpo.	Gaffer/ Set Lting	40 Shop	Grips	Production	Craft Service
Switchboxes	X									
Lightbulbs						X				
Male Connectors ("Hubbells")						X				
Hookup						X				
Zipcord/Length:										
*(*Note: 2-wire Zipcord is legal only up to 6' for tablelamps and small appliances.)*										
3' Tail	X									
Additional zip and 3-wire grounded outside of set wall						X				
*(**Note: Local 44 may re-wire table lamps, sconces and flourescents - not including the plug.)*										
Lockers										
Built-In Lockers	X									
Installation			X							
Freestanding Lockers	X									
Mailboxes/P.O. Boxes/ Safety Deposit Boxes/"Pigeon Holes"										
Free-standing	X									
Built into Wall			X							
Mirrors										
Closet/ Clip Attachment	X									
Decorative Mirrors	X									
Gimballing Mirrors			X							
Mirrors as Walls			X							
Medicine Cabinets	X									
Rehearsal Mirrors								X		
Valet/Chevall Mirrors	X									
Morgue										
Body Drawers with Roll-Out Platform			X							
Special Latch Drawers			X							

Figure A1.9 (Continued)

DESCRIPTION (continued)	Set Decorator	Prop Master	Construct.	Special Effects	Transpo.	Gaffer/ Set Lting	40 Shop	Grips	Production	Craft Service
Musical Instruments										
Carried or Played		X								
Decorative or Backgrd/Not Handled	X									
Music Stands and Chairs	X									
Painting										
Furniture Refinishing/Painting	X									
Painting of Greenery			X							
Painting of Hardware			X							
Painting of Marine, Trains, Planes			X							
Painting of Motor Vehicles					X					
Motor Vehicles/Custom Paint		X								
Platforms/Ramps			X							
*Plumbing (*Also See Conduit/Piping)*										
Sinks:										
Free-standing Sinks	X									
Wall mount Sinks	X									
Built in Sinks	X									
Install built-in sink			X							
Make practical				X						
Tubs:										
Free-standing Tubs	X									
Character Tubs	X									
Built-In Tubs			X							
Make practical				X						
Shower Stalls:										
Portable	X									
Built-In			X							
Make practical				X						

UNION DEPARTMENT HEAD RESPONSIBILITIES

8/1/97

Page 12

Figure A1.9 (Continued)

DESCRIPTION (continued)	Set Decorator	Prop Master	Construct.	Special Effects	Transpo.	Gaffer/Set Lting	40 Shop	Grips	Production	Craft Service
Toilets/Bidets										
Make practical	X									
Glass Shower Doors			X	X						
Raingutters			X							
Restaurants/Bars										
Appliances	X									
Bar Sinks	X									
Installation of Bar Sinks			X							
Make Bar Sinks practical				X						
Booths/Banquettes:										
As Built-In: designed OR rented			X							
Beer Pulls	X									
Counter			X							
Back Counter			X							
Food/Background Dressing	X									
Food/Action Props		X								
Menus		X								
Menu Boards	X									
Lg/Designed Menu Bds.			X							
Jukeboxes	X									
Decorative Lighting	X									
Linen	X									
Tables/Chairs/Stools	X									
Vent Hoods			X							
Wait Stations	X									
Rubble										
Dirt			X							
Gravel			X							

UNION DEPARTMENT HEAD RESPONSIBILITIES   8/1/97   Page 13

Figure A1.9 (Continued)

DESCRIPTION (continued)	Set Decorator	Prop Master	Construct.	Special Effects	Transpo.	Gaffer/ Set Lting	40 Shop	Grips	Production	Craft Service
Junk	X									
*Rocks										
*Rocks assembled from stock shall be placed and fastened by Local 80 (Grips). All other including new construction, repair or fitting requiring cutting or addition are by construction.										
Sandbags			X							
Scripted Printed Material		X								
Security Cameras	X									
Shelving										
Closet Shelf & Pole			X							
Built-in Shelves			X							
Wire or Purchased Shelving	X									
Signage										
Banners As Scripted			X							
Billboard (larger than a one-sheet)			X							
Graffiti			X							
Flags	X									
Desk Plaques	X									
Door Signs			X							
Lobby Directory Boards	X									
Logos			X							
Posters	X									
Street Signs			X							
Vehicle Skins		X									
Snow (Falling or Blowing)				X						
Telephones										
Cellular Phones/Car Phones		X								
Pay Phones/Wall phones	X									
Desk Phones	X									
Make practical				X						

Figure A1.9 (Continued)

DESCRIPTION (continued)	Set Decorator	Prop Master	Construct.	Special Effects	Transpo.	Gaffer/ Set Lting	40 Shop	Grips	Production	Craft Service
Telephone Poles										
Boxes/Connectors/Insulators	X									
Poles			X							
Installation			X							
Utility Pole Wires/Pole Cleats			X							
Tents										
Manufactured by 44, Erected, Stored, Maintained by Drapery										
Small (12'x12' & Under)	X									
Larger			X							
Manufactured by Others, Erected, Stored, Maintained by Grips										
Small (12'x12' & Under)	X									
Larger			X							
Tee-Pees:										
Coverings/Skins	X									
Tee-Pee Installation by Drapery	X									
Structure			X							
Camping Tents:										
Action tent		X								
Background camping/Pup Tents	X									
Theater/Stage										
Drapery:										
Drapery used as walls			X							
Backdrops			X							
Doorway Draperies/Portieres	X									
Proscenium Arch, including Legs, Teasers, Tormentors			X							
Installation by Drapery			X							

UNION DEPARTMENT HEAD RESPONSIBILITIES

8/1/97

Page 15

Figure A1.9 (Continued)

DESCRIPTION (continued)	Set Decorator	Prop Master	Construct.	Special Effects	Transpo.	Gaffer/ Set Lting	40 Shop	Grips	Production	Craft Service
Battens/Traveller Track			X							
Installation by Grips			X							
Festoons for Boxes	X									
Festoon Installation by Drapery	X									
Turnstiles	X									
Walls										
Moldings:										
Wood or Plaster Base/Door/Window/Cornice			X							
Rosettes/Pilasters/Filigree			X							
Raised Letters or Numbers			X							
Ext. Storefront Window Backup Walls			X							
Wallcoverings										
Fabric			X							
Installation by Drapery			X							
Wallpaper			X							
Installation			X							
Windows			X							
Architectural Plant-Ons			X							
Window Coverings										
Awning Structure			X							
Awning Covering (Canvas,Fabric, Plastic or Metal)			X							
Blinds: Wood/Metal (Vertical or Horizontal)	X									
Draperies	X									
Draperies Used as Walls			X							
Portieres	X									

UNION DEPARTMENT HEAD RESPONSIBILITIES   8/1/97   Page 16

Figure A1.9 (Continued)

DESCRIPTION (continued)	Set Decorator	Prop Master	Construct.	Special Effects	Transpo.	Gaffer/ Set Lting	40 Shop	Grips	Production	Craft Service
Draperies on Battens			X							
Roller Shades	X		X							
Shutters			X							
Stained/Leaded Glass			X							
Vehicles										
Ambulances (Dressed)		X								
Boats:										
Action (Small)	X	X								
Background Boats (Small)	X									
Yachts					X					
Interior Yacht Dressing	X									
Dock Lines as Dressing	X									
Practical ship docking lines on actual boat/tied off to pier								X		
Trains/Planes/Subways:										
Seating	X									
Mockups:										
Lighting (except recessed)	X		X							
Recessed Lighting			X							
Gauges/Instruments			X							
Upholstery	X									
Signage			X							
Trucks, Cars, Etc.:										
Abandoned					X					
Transportation to set/location					X					
Action					X					
Burned Out					X					
Special scripted burns				X						
Special Dash Instruments				X						

UNION DEPARTMENT HEAD RESPONSIBILITIES

8/1/97

Page 17

Figure A1.9 (Continued)

DESCRIPTION (continued)	Set Decorator	Prop Master	Construct.	Special Effects	Transpo.	Gaffer/ Set Lting	40 Shop	Grips	Production	Craft Service
Electronics Controls					X					
Hookup/Connect					X					
Skins		X								
Interior/ Exterior Painting					X					
Interior Upholstery					X					
Interior Character Dressing	X									
Interior Hero/Scripted Dressing/Props		X								
Horse Drawn:										
Action		X								
Background	X									
Video Playback, Video Equipment, CGI										
(* NOTE: Computer Graphics/CGI is a discussion/budget between the Production Designer/Art Director/Producer/Visual Effects. It does not fall into any of the budget categories here.)										
TV Sets/Monitors w/o playback	X									
Cable/Keyboards/Mice	X									
TV Sets/Monitors w/ playback *(equipment as included in a package deal with playback)*									X	
Cable/Keyboards/Mice *(equipment as included in a package deal with playback)*									X	
(* Note: May be affected by production's deals for playback/equipment and size of particular show/set. Set Decorator should discuss this with UPM/Producer early in prep.)										
Rear View Projection Screens									X	
Playback Rigging									X	
Technician with Equipment									X	
Weapons										
Action Props		X								
Background Dummy Guns/Not handled	X									
(* Note: For safety reasons, ALL guns must be the responsibility of the Prop Master. The Set Decorator and the Prop Master must discuss this in detail during Prep.)										
Decorative Cannon	X									
Decorative antique weapons	X									

UNION DEPARTMENT HEAD RESPONSIBILITIES   8/1/97

Figure A1.9 (Continued)

Page 19

For budgeting of Special Effects the following additions will be included in the next publication of this Guide:

1. Snow sets and dressing, buildings, window frosting, icicles, cars, etc.

2. Rain, waterfalls, creeks, dumptanks, wetdowns, fountains, water agitation (movement)

3. Wind, breeze, gusts, blowing leaves, blowing curtains

4. Fog, haze, dust, smoke, smoke from chimneys, steam, ambient diffusion, bar-b-q's, cars

5. Modification of vehicles, roll cages, cannons, items falling apart, smoking, bouncing (Labamba hydraulics)

6. Hydraulics, rams, motors, pumps, etc.

7. Machining of parts, specialty items, guns, spray heads, turntables, fabrication of aluminum and steel, welding of sets/set pieces, steel framework

8. Fire, burning barrels, houses on fire, torches (making of), fireplace, bar-b-que's, cars, body burns, stoves, etc.

9. Breakaways, balsawood, doors, windows, sets, pulling apart of sets, collapsing buildings

10. Pyrotechnics, explosions, bullet hits, pyrotechnic fires, etc.

Figure A1.9 (Continued)

DESIGN REFERENCE BOOKS

Table A1.7   Design reference books.

DESIGN REFERENCE BOOKS
This is a basic list of design reference books. Some of them are first edition copies; newer editions exist for many of them. I offer these as a starter library for first-time art directors and film designers. After more than two decades of art directing, and steady purchase of reference materials for a handful of films, the library has grown to just under five hundred books. Let this serve as a warning.
Man and His Symbols Carl G. Jung Doubleday & Co. Inc. New York: 1964 ISBN: 0-385-05221-9
Seeing with the Mind's Eye: The History, Techniques and Uses of Visualization Mike Samuels, M.D. & Nancy Samuels Random House, Inc. New York: 1975 ISBN: 0-394-73113-1
The Power of Myth Joseph Campbell Doubleday & Co. Inc. New York: 1988 ISBN: 0-385-24773-7

ARCHITECTURE
A Field Guide to American Houses Virginia & Lee McAlester Alfred A. Knopf New York: 1988 ISBN: 0-394-51032-1
Architectural Graphic Standards, 6th Edition Ramsey & Sleeper John Wiley & Sons New York: 1970 ISBN: 0-471-70780-5
Sir Banister Fletcher's A History of Architecture, 18th Edition J.C. Palmes Charles Scribner's Sons. New York: 1975 ISBN: 684-14207-4

ART HISTORY
A Basic History of Art, 2nd Edition H. W. Janson Harry Abrams, Inc. New York: 1971 ISBN: 0-13-062356-3
Art & Ideas, 3rd Edition William Fleming Holt, Rinehart & Winston, Inc. ISBN-10: 0534613713
Gardiner's Art Through the Ages, 5th Edition Horst De La Croix & Richard G. Tansey Harcourt, Brace & World, Inc. New York: 1970 ISBN-10: 0155011413

FILM HISTORY
Film Directing Shot by Shot: Visualizing from Concept to Screen Steven Katz Michael Weise Productions ISBN: 0-941188-10-8
Grammar of the Film Language Daniel Arijon Silman-James Press Los Angeles: 1976 ISBN: 1-879505-07-X
How to Read a Film: The Art, Technology, Language, History and Theory of Film and Media, Revised Edition James Monaco Oxford University Press New York: 1981 ISBN: 0-19-502802-3

(Continued)

Table A1.7   (Continued)

INFORMATION & SOURCE BOOKS
American Cinematographer Manual, 8th Edition Rob Hummel The ASC Press Hollywood: 2001 ISBN: 0-935578-15-3 **Art Directors Guild Membership Directory** Christa Munro, Ed. Art Directors Guild Los Angeles: 2005 Phone #: 818.762.9995
Backstage Handbook: An Illustrated Almanac of Technical Information, 3rd Edition Paul Carter Broadway Press Louisville: 2000 ISBN: 0-911747-39-7
Handbook of Ornament Franz Sales Meyer Dover Publications, Inc. New York: 1957 ISBN: 0-486-23480-0
Pocket Reference, 3rd Edition Thomas J. Glover Sequoia Publishing ISBN: 1-885071-33-7 (soft cover) ISBN: 1-885071-45-0 (hard cover) Library of Congress Catalog Card Number: 20002091021
Surfaces: Visual Research for Artists, Architects, and Designers Judith Juraacek W. W. Norton & Co. New York: 1996 ISBN: 0-393-73007-7
The Elements of Style: A Practical Encyclopedia of Interior Architectural Details Stephen Calloway, Ed & Elizabeth Cromley, Ed. Simon & Schuster New York: 1991 ISBN: 0-671-73981-6

The MacMillan Visual Dictionary
Natalie Chapman, Ed.
MacMillan Publishing Co.
New York: 1992
ISBN: 0-02-528160-7

The Styles of Ornament
Alexander Speltz
Dover Publications, Inc.
New York: 1959
ISBN: 486-20557-6

Thomas Guide 2013: Los Angeles County (digital edition available)
Thomas Bros.
Rand McNally Co.
Irvine: 2013
ISBN: 0-528-95514-4
ISBN: 0-528-85447-X (digital edition)

STUDIO MOULDING & STAFF SHOPS

Fox Staff Catalog
20th Century Fox Studios
Staff Shop/Vacuumform
Phone #: 310.203.2712 (Shop)
Email: www.foxstudios.com/production_services_depts/staff_shop__vacuumform.html

Fox Molding Catalog
20th Century Fox Studios
Wood Molding Shop
Phone: 310.369.2528
email: www.foxstudios.com/production_services_depts/wood_moulding.html

Sony Pictures Studio Staff Shop Catalogue
Sony Pictures Studios
Production Services
Phone #: 310.244.5541
Email: http://sonypicturesstudios.com/servicessection/staffshop/staff.html

Wood Moulding Catalog
Paramount Pictures
Wood Moulding Dept.
Phone #: 323.956.4242
Email: www.paramountstudios.com/art-services/wood-moulding-and-mill-work.html

(Continued)

Table A1.7   (Continued)

SUPPLIES, HARDWARE, DECORATIVE ARCHITECTURE
Architectural Sheet Metal Ornaments W. F. Norman Corp. Nevada, MO: W. F. Norman Corp: 1990's Phone #: 800.641.4038
Illustrated Catalogue 124 of Period Ornaments for Woodwork and Furniture The Decorators supply Corp. Chicago: 1990 Phone #: 312.847.6300
McMaster-Carr Supply Company: Catalog 101 McMaster-Carr N/A Phone #: 213.956.8488
Moes Enterprises Catalog of Authentic Pre-1939 Builders Hardware Lionel D. Moes Manchester Sash and Door Company Los Angeles: 1994, reissued Phone #: 213.759.0344
The Historical Supply Catalogue Alan Welikoff Rough Hewn Books Baltimore: 1984 ISBN: 0-9648245-0-7

Start Paperwork

START FORM

S 6113385

☐ NEW EMPLOYEE   ☐ RE-HIRE   ☐ CHANGE

PRODUCING CO.	PICTURE TITLE			ACCOUNT CODING

EMPLOYEE NAME	SOCIAL SECURITY NUMBER	UNION	OCC CODE	JOB CLASS

EMPLOYEE ADDRESS	CITY	STATE	ZIP	SEX M F	TELEPHONE ( )

ETHNIC CODE ☐   1 = WHITE   2 = BLACK   3 = HISPANIC   4 = ASIAN   5 = NATIVE AMER   6 = OTHER

EMAIL ADDRESS

CITIZEN STATUS   ☐ US   ☐ RES ALIEN   ☐ OTHER   (MUST HAVE VISA ATTACHED)

CANADIAN INDIVIDUAL TAX NUMBER

NOTE: **This statement must be filled out prior to payment being made.**
UNDER THE PENALTIES OF PERJURY, I CERTIFY THAT I AM A RESIDENT OF THE STATE OF _____
(Employees working more than 6 months in one state should indicate that state as their resident state.)

WORK STATE/CITY/COUNTY

MINOR: IS EMPLOYEE A MINOR?   ☐ YES   ☐ NO

PAYMENT AUTHORIZATION ATTACHED?   ☐ YES   ☐ NO

START DATE

TERMS OF EMPLOYMENT   DO NOT USE SHADED AREAS - FOR OFFICE USE ONLY

HOURLY EMPLOYEE	STUDIO RATE	GUAR HOURS	LOCATION RATE	GUAR HOURS	PAY SCALE
HOURLY RATE*	_____	_____	_____	_____	☐ PAY AT SCALE AND AUTO UPDATE WHEN NEW RATES GO INTO EFFECT.
6TH DAY	_____	_____	_____	_____	
7TH DAY	_____	_____	_____	_____	
IDLE 6TH					
IDLE 7TH			_____	_____	

TERMS OF EMPLOYMENT   DO NOT USE SHADED AREAS - FOR OFFICE USE ONLY

WEEKLY EMPLOYEE	STUDIO RATE	GUAR HOURS	LOCATION RATE	GUAR HOURS	PAY SCALE
WEEKLY RATE*	_____	_____	_____	_____	☐ PAY AT SCALE AND AUTO UPDATE WHEN NEW RATES GO INTO EFFECT.
HOURLY RATE*	_____	_____	_____	_____	*NOTE GUAR HOURS MUST BE SUPPLIED.
6TH DAY	_____	_____	_____	_____	
7TH DAY			_____	_____	
IDLE 6TH			_____	_____	
IDLE 7TH			_____	_____	

*NOTE: **Overtime of not less than 1.5x paid for hours worked in excess of 8 per day or 40 per week as required by law or contract.**

MISCELLANEOUS	STUDIO	LOCATION	SEPARATE	
BOX RENTAL	_____	_____	Y N	_____
CAR ALLOW	_____	_____	Y N	_____
MEAL ALLOW	_____	_____	Y N	_____

By signing this form, I agree that EP may take deductions from my earnings to adjust previous overpayments if and when said overpayments may occur. I acknowledge receipt of "Time Of Hire" and "Medical Provider Network Implementation Notice" (CA ONLY).

FORM W4 EMPLOYEE'S WITHHOLDING ALLOWANCE CERTIFICATE

MARITAL STATUS   ☐ SINGLE   ☐ MARRIED   ☐ Married, but withhold at higher Single rate
Note: If married, but legally separated, or spouse is a nonresident alien, check the single box.

TOTAL NUMBER OF ALLOWANCES YOU ARE CLAIMING.

Additional amount, if any, you want withheld from each paycheck.

$ _____

3. I claim exemption from withholding, and I certify that I meet **both** of the following conditions for exemption:
   • Last year I had a right to a refund of **all** Federal income tax because I had **no** tax liability **and**
   • This year I expect a refund of **all** Federal income tax withheld because I expect to have **no** tax liability.

   If you meet both conditions, write "Exempt" here ....

Under the penalties of perjury, I certify that I am entitled to the number of withholding allowances claimed on this certificate, or I am entitled to claim exempt status.

AGREED-EMPLOYEE SIGNATURE	DATE	AUTHORIZED SIGNATURE	DATE

EMPLOYER

EF-1001 (4/13)

Employment Eligibility Verification

Department of Homeland Security
U.S. Citizenship and Immigration Services

USCIS
Form I-9
OMB No. 1615-0047
Expires 03/31/2016

▶**START HERE.** Read instructions carefully before completing this form. **The instructions must be available during completion of this form.**
ANTI-DISCRIMINATION NOTICE: It is illegal to discriminate against work-authorized individuals. Employers **CANNOT** specify which document(s) they will accept from an employee. The refusal to hire an individual because the documentation presented has a future expiration date may also constitute illegal discrimination.

Section 1. Employee Information and Attestation *(Employees must complete and sign Section 1 of Form I-9 no later than the **first day of employment**, but not before accepting a job offer.)*

Last Name *(Family Name)*	First Name *(Given Name)*	Middle Initial	Other Names Used *(if any)*

Address *(Street Number and Name)*	Apt. Number	City or Town	State	Zip Code

Date of Birth *(mm/dd/yyyy)*	U.S. Social Security Number	E-mail Address	Telephone Number

I am aware that federal law provides for imprisonment and/or fines for false statements or use of false documents in connection with the completion of this form.

I attest, under penalty of perjury, that I am (check one of the following):

☐ A citizen of the United States

☐ A noncitizen national of the United States *(See instructions)*

☐ A lawful permanent resident (Alien Registration Number/USCIS Number): _____

☐ An alien authorized to work until (expiration date, if applicable, mm/dd/yyyy) _____ . Some aliens may write "N/A" in this field.
(See instructions)

*For aliens authorized to work, provide your Alien Registration Number/USCIS Number **OR** Form I-94 Admission Number:*

1. Alien Registration Number/USCIS Number:_____

OR

2. Form I-94 Admission Number: _____

    If you obtained your admission number from CBP in connection with your arrival in the United States, include the following:

    Foreign Passport Number: _____

    Country of Issuance: _____

    Some aliens may write "N/A" on the Foreign Passport Number and Country of Issuance fields. *(See instructions)*

> **3-D Barcode**
> **Do Not Write in This Space**

Signature of Employee:	Date *(mm/dd/yyyy)*:

Preparer and/or Translator Certification *(To be completed and signed if Section 1 is prepared by a person other than the employee.)*

I attest, under penalty of perjury, that I have assisted in the completion of this form and that to the best of my knowledge the information is true and correct.

Signature of Preparer or Translator:	Date *(mm/dd/yyyy)*:

Last Name *(Family Name)*	First Name *(Given Name)*

Address *(Street Number and Name)*	City or Town	State	Zip Code

🛑 *Employer Completes Next Page* 🛑

Form I-9 03/08/13 N

Section 2. Employer or Authorized Representative Review and Verification

(Employers or their authorized representative must complete and sign Section 2 within 3 business days of the employee's first day of employment. You must physically examine one document from List A OR examine a combination of one document from List B and one document from List C as listed on the "Lists of Acceptable Documents" on the next page of this form. For each document you review, record the following information: document title, issuing authority, document number, and expiration date, if any.)

Employee Last Name, First Name and Middle Initial from Section 1:

List A	OR	List B	AND	List C
Identity and Employment Authorization		**Identity**		**Employment Authorization**

Document Title:	Document Title:	Document Title:
Issuing Authority:	Issuing Authority:	Issuing Authority:
Document Number:	Document Number:	Document Number:
Expiration Date *(if any)(mm/dd/yyyy)*:	Expiration Date *(if any)(mm/dd/yyyy)*:	Expiration Date *(if any)(mm/dd/yyyy)*:
Document Title:		
Issuing Authority:		
Document Number:		
Expiration Date *(if any)(mm/dd/yyyy)*:		
Document Title:		**3-D Barcode** **Do Not Write in This Space**
Issuing Authority:		
Document Number:		
Expiration Date *(if any)(mm/dd/yyyy)*:		

Certification

I attest, under penalty of perjury, that (1) I have examined the document(s) presented by the above-named employee, (2) the above-listed document(s) appear to be genuine and to relate to the employee named, and (3) to the best of my knowledge the employee is authorized to work in the United States.

The employee's first day of employment *(mm/dd/yyyy)*: _____ (*See instructions for exemptions.*)

Signature of Employer or Authorized Representative	Date *(mm/dd/yyyy)*	Title of Employer or Authorized Representative	
Last Name *(Family Name)*	First Name *(Given Name)*	Employer's Business or Organization Name	
Employer's Business or Organization Address *(Street Number and Name)*	City or Town	State	Zip Code

Section 3. Reverification and Rehires *(To be completed and signed by employer or authorized representative.)*

A. New Name *(if applicable)* Last Name *(Family Name)* First Name *(Given Name)*	Middle Initial	B. Date of Rehire *(if applicable)* *(mm/dd/yyyy)*:

C. If employee's previous grant of employment authorization has expired, provide the information for the document from List A or List C the employee presented that establishes current employment authorization in the space provided below.

Document Title:	Document Number:	Expiration Date *(if any)(mm/dd/yyyy)*:

I attest, under penalty of perjury, that to the best of my knowledge, this employee is authorized to work in the United States, and if the employee presented document(s), the document(s) I have examined appear to be genuine and to relate to the individual.

Signature of Employer or Authorized Representative:	Date *(mm/dd/yyyy)*:	Print Name of Employer or Authorized Representative:

LISTS OF ACCEPTABLE DOCUMENTS
All documents must be UNEXPIRED

Employees may present one selection from List A
or a combination of one selection from List B and one selection from List C.

LIST A Documents that Establish Both Identity and Employment Authorization	LIST B Documents that Establish Identity	LIST C Documents that Establish Employment Authorization
OR	AND	
1. U.S. Passport or U.S. Passport Card	1. Driver's license or ID card issued by a State or outlying possession of the United States provided it contains a photograph or information such as name, date of birth, gender, height, eye color, and address	1. A Social Security Account Number card, unless the card includes one of the following restrictions: (1) NOT VALID FOR EMPLOYMENT (2) VALID FOR WORK ONLY WITH INS AUTHORIZATION (3) VALID FOR WORK ONLY WITH DHS AUTHORIZATION
2. Permanent Resident Card or Alien Registration Receipt Card (Form I-551)		
3. Foreign passport that contains a temporary I-551 stamp or temporary I-551 printed notation on a machine-readable immigrant visa	2. ID card issued by federal, state or local government agencies or entities, provided it contains a photograph or information such as name, date of birth, gender, height, eye color, and address	2. Certification of Birth Abroad issued by the Department of State (Form FS-545)
4. Employment Authorization Document that contains a photograph (Form I-766)	3. School ID card with a photograph	3. Certification of Report of Birth issued by the Department of State (Form DS-1350)
5. For a nonimmigrant alien authorized to work for a specific employer because of his or her status: a. Foreign passport; and b. Form I-94 or Form I-94A that has the following: (1) The same name as the passport; and (2) An endorsement of the alien's nonimmigrant status as long as that period of endorsement has not yet expired and the proposed employment is not in conflict with any restrictions or limitations identified on the form.	4. Voter's registration card	4. Original or certified copy of birth certificate issued by a State, county, municipal authority, or territory of the United States bearing an official seal
	5. U.S. Military card or draft record	
	6. Military dependent's ID card	5. Native American tribal document
	7. U.S. Coast Guard Merchant Mariner Card	6. U.S. Citizen ID Card (Form I-197)
	8. Native American tribal document	7. Identification Card for Use of Resident Citizen in the United States (Form I-179)
	9. Driver's license issued by a Canadian government authority	8. Employment authorization document issued by the Department of Homeland Security
6. Passport from the Federated States of Micronesia (FSM) or the Republic of the Marshall Islands (RMI) with Form I-94 or Form I-94A indicating nonimmigrant admission under the Compact of Free Association Between the United States and the FSM or RMI	**For persons under age 18 who are unable to present a document listed above:** 10. School record or report card 11. Clinic, doctor, or hospital record 12. Day-care or nursery school record	

Illustrations of many of these documents appear in Part 8 of the Handbook for Employers (M-274).

Refer to Section 2 of the instructions, titled "Employer or Authorized Representative Review and Verification," for more information about acceptable receipts.

EMPLOYEE DEAL MEMO

Production Title:_____ ("Production") Prod. Number:_____

EMPLOYEE: _____ LOCAL #:_____

ADDRESS: _____ CITY: _____ STATE:_____ ZIP:_____

SOCIAL SECURITY NUMBER: XXX - XX - _____ TELEPHONE: _____

DEPT:_____POSITION:_____OCC. CODE: _____ACCT/SUF:_____

LOS ANGELES ONLY: ROSTER / SAFETY TRAINING STATUS CLEARED ☐ CHECKED BY: _____

DGA ONLY: QUALIFICATION LIST STATUS CLEARED ☐   CHECKED BY:_____

ANTICIPATED START DATE:_____EMERGENCY CONTACT & PHONE:_____

Employment to be governed by the applicable collective bargaining agreement, if any.

■TV/FEATURE   ☐PILOT/1ST YR SERIES   ☐2ND YR SERIES   ☐ BASIC CABLE

DIGITAL PRIME TIME (HALF HOUR): SINGLE CAM☐ MULTI-CAM☐ PILOT☐   BASIC CABLE☐

OTHER (PLEASE SPECIFY): _____

COMPENSATION:	DAILY EMPLOYEES		WEEKLY EMPLOYEES	
STUDIO:	$_____ /HR	_____ HR GUAR	$_____ /HR	_____ HR GUAR
	Or $_____	/DAY	Or $_____	/WEEK
DISTANT LOCATION:	$_____ /HR	_____ HR GUAR	$_____ /HR	_____ HR GUAR
			Or $_____	/WEEK

CAR ALLOWANCE: $_____

ADDITIONAL PROVISIONS (NOT for box rental. For box rental, use separate Box Rental Agreement):

STANDARD TERMS:

1. If a Daily rate is indicated, services are for a minimum period of one day. If a Weekly rate is indicated, services are for a minimum period of one week and the weekly guarantee is for the cumulative number of hours specified. There is no other guarantee of the period of services. No expenditures above the budget approved by Producer will be made or authorized by the individual notified hereunder without the approval of the Producer/UPM. If applicable, all provisions of this Deal Memo are subject to and must provide no less than the terms and conditions of the collective bargaining agreement which governs the services rendered by the Employee. If Employee is paid overscale either in wages or hours, Employee acknowledges that any increase to the minimum wage schedules in the Agreements mentioned above may not be automatically applied to his/her already overscale rate or hours.
2. Employee's services are subject to the terms of the applicable collective bargaining agreement, if any.
3. All purchases and rentals must be authorized by approved Purchase Orders prior to transaction. Before any business (excluding Box / Car Rentals) is conducted with a company in which Employee or a relative controls more than 5%, Producer must be advised and a *Related Party Transaction form* must be completed and approved by a Production Executive (except Transportation Rentals). Producer's standard competitive bidding process must also be utilized. Before any equipment or materials (excluding Box/Car Rentals) Employee or a relative owns, or that Employee has a financial interest in, is rented, leased or purchased through any individual or business, Producer must be advised and a *Related Party Transaction form* must be completed and approved by a Production Executive (except Transportation Rentals). Producer's standard competitive bidding process must also be utilized.
4. Petty cash expenses not accompanied by proper receipts in accordance with Producer's policy will not be reimbursed.
5. Employee is responsible for all recoverable items purchased, which must be reconciled with the Accounting Department. All recoverable purchases will be collected at wrap. This shall not be construed as a guarantee of employment beyond one day or one week.
6. No forced calls, overtime, sixth or seventh days or holidays may be worked unless authorized in advance by the Unit Production Manager/Production Management. Time cards must reflect hours worked, not hours guaranteed, meal periods taken, and be submitted before the time designated by the Production Accountant. Employee must be authorized by production management to make offers of employment to potential crew members before making any such offers.
7. All compensation to Employee will be paid on payroll checks and subject to applicable payroll taxes.
8. Car allowances will be prorated for any partial workweek. Any vehicle used by Employee must be fully insured (including but not limited to minimum statutory requirements), and Employee must provide documentation to such effect to Producer. In the event the Employee does not secure the above referenced insurance policy, Employee shall defend, indemnify and hold Producer harmless up to an amount equal to the minimum statutory policy limits from any damages, loss, liability, etc. (including reasonable attorneys' fees) arising out of any claim involving the Employee and/or his/her vehicle. With respect to property damages only, Producer shall have no liability to Employee, Employee's heirs, successors, insurers and/or assigns, or any third party with respect to any loss, theft and/or damage of any kind to said vehicle. Producer shall not provide any coverage for any vehicle or the contents thereof. Employee shall exercise good judgment and caution in bringing any personal effects or personal property to a location and should arrange to have adequate insurance for his/her property. Employee represents and warrants that that any personal vehicle used by Employee has been and will be properly maintained, and that it shall be kept in good workable and safe operating condition.
    PLEASE INITIAL: ▐▬▬▬▬▐ ◄▬▬▬
9. Employee understands that prior to driving, he/she is required to have a valid driver's license and carry at least the state required limit of Automobile Liability Insurance. PLEASE INITIAL: ▐▬▬▬▬▐ ◄▬▬▬
10. No production tie-ins or product placement are to be made without written permission from Producer.

TV\103823 v1 CW 06-25-13
Deal Memo

11. Employee agrees not to give any interviews or authorize any publicity relating to Employee's services, the production, or Producer without Producer's express prior written permission. Employee irrevocably grants Producer, its successors, assigns, and licensees, the right to photograph and make motion pictures, sound recordings and non-photographic likeness of Employee's physical likeness and voice for "behind the scenes" promotional films, and to reproduce the same in any media now known or hereafter devised in perpetuity throughout the universe, without further compensation of any kind. If so-called "behind-the-scenes", "gallery" and DVD shoots routinely take place during the production of Producer programs, Producer may require services in connection with the creation of this material for the production and no additional compensation will be paid for such services, regardless of when other production personnel are called or dismissed. If such services are rendered on other than a regular production day, the applicable minimum call in the controlling Agreement will apply.

12. Any unauthorized travel to distant location is at Employee's risk and liability.

13. Screen Credit is at the sole discretion of Producer unless subject to any applicable collective bargaining agreement. If granted, to read as follows:

14. **PROD. DESIGNER ONLY:** Notwithstanding the above, the words "Production Designer" or "Production Design(ed) by" shall not be used for screen credit except upon written approval of the Local Union. If such approval has not been given by the Local Union the screen credit shall read "Art Director" or "Art Directors". **Please initial:** ◄▬▬

15. **DIRECTOR OF PHOTOGRAPHY ONLY:** D.P. shall be granted access to "Master" to pull selected clips (up to 15 mins. per episode) at artist's expense which shall be used solely for artist's show reel / portfolio. Upon request, D.P. may be provided with a watermarked DVD only (Beta SP, digi-beta, DVCam or any HD format are not permitted). **Please initial:** ◄▬▬

16. Producer has instituted, and each Employee is obligated to comply with, the Injury and Illness Prevention Program, which is contained in the Production Employee Work Rules.

17. In addition to those provisions contained in #1 above, Producer shall have the customary rights of suspension and termination by reason of any event beyond Producer's control which materially hampers production of the project, including but not limited to force majeure, incapacity of key executive production staff, the Director, Director of Photography, or any principal cast member.

18. This Deal Memo shall constitute Producer's and Employee's complete agreement regarding the terms described herein. This Deal Memo may be modified only by written agreement of Employee and an authorized representative of Producer.

19. OWNERSHIP OF PRODUCER'S PROPERTY/CONFIDENTIALITY/UNAUTHORIZED USE: Producer is the sole and exclusive owner of all rights in and to all of Producer's television productions and all other creative works and all elements thereof, including without limitation the development, production and exploitation of the Production, and all elements thereof – including without limitation artwork, call sheets, cast & crew member likeness and information (including their names, personal information and/or business information), creative elements, dailies, locations, one lines, props, scripts, storyboards, the screenplay, edited episodes, screeners, underlying literary material, the business or affairs of the Production or of Producer, or audio, photographic or audiovisual recordings of any aspect of the production (collectively, **"Confidential Information and Materials"**). Should Employee be privy to and/or handle any Confidential Information and Materials or should any Confidential Information and Materials become known to Employee, Employee shall not at any time, directly or indirectly, disseminate, duplicate, dispose of, distribute or, in any other manner, disclose any materials, elements and/or information of any kind dealing with or in any way relating to the Confidential Information and Materials. The disposal of any Confidential Information and Materials does not waive any of Producer's rights therein. It is material to this agreement that Employee shall not make any unauthorized use, reproduction, sale and/or distribution of any production materials (including providing such items free on the Internet), and Employee further agrees to hold confidential, and not disclose at any time to the public, the media or to any person or entity, any Confidential Information and Materials. Employee acknowledges and agrees that the Confidential Information and Materials derive independent economic value from not being generally known to the public or to other persons who can obtain economic value from their disclosure, distribution or use. Employee acknowledges that any breach by Employee with respect to the Confidential Information and Materials will cause irreparable injury to Producer, not readily measurable in monetary damages, and for which Producer, without waiving any other rights or remedies, shall be entitled to injunctive relief. Employee agrees to abide by Producer's policy regarding film, tape, disk or file duplication. Producer has strict policies with respect to the disposal, distribution and/or dissemination of the Confidential Information and Materials. Failure to comply with those policies may, at Producer's election, result in: (i) the immediate termination of Employee's employment ; (ii) the revocation of Employee's privilege of viewing or handling any Confidential Information and Materials; and (iii) the revocation of Employee's privilege of visiting the production, including without limitation the production office, Art Department, set, etc., and Producer may prosecute any such failure to comply to the full extent allowable under law (with both criminal and civil liability). Producer reserves all of its other rights and remedies in the event that Producer's policies with regard to Confidential Information and Materials are not complied with. The Provisions of this paragraph shall survive termination or expiration of this Deal Memo. **PLEASE INITIAL:** ▬▬ ↑

20. OWNERSHIP OF WORK PRODUCTS: Employee agrees that all of the results and product of Employee's services (including any physical materials created by Employee) (collectively, "Work Products") are within the scope of employment and are considered a "work made for hire" and Producer is the sole author and owner of (and, to the extent any such Work Products may ever be determined not to be such a work made for hire, Employee hereby grants to Producer sole ownership of) such Work Products and all rights therein in all media (whether now or hereafter known or created) in perpetuity and for all purposes throughout the universe, including without limitation the right to make any changes. Employee hereby acknowledges that none of the Work Products constitute works of fine art, and hereby waive any and all so called "moral rights", including any prohibitions of intentional defacement, mutilation, alteration or destruction under state or federal law.

21. Before engaging in outside employment/services while employed by Producer, Employees must disclose the outside employment/services and obtain prior written approval from the Production Executive or the Head of Production for Producer. Outside employment/services that conflict with Employees' work assignments, interferes with their work performance or otherwise creates a conflict of interest with their duties and responsibilities for Producer is prohibited.

22. Employee agrees to execute and/or deliver such further instruments as may be reasonably required to carry out or effectuate the purposes and intent of this agreement.

23. In the event of any claim by Employee against Producer, and to the extent permitted by law, Employee shall be limited to Employee's remedy at law for damages, if any, and Employee shall not be entitled to enjoin, restrain or interfere with the filming, broadcast, exhibition, distribution or other exploitation of any of Producer's audio-visual works, other creative works or any of Producer's rights hereunder.

Employee acknowledges by signing below the receipt of the *Production Employee Work Rules* and agrees to read them and to be bound by the standards set forth therein for the term of Employee's employment with Producer. Please be advised that the company has designated the office of the V.P. of Payroll to assist in addressing any concerns from employees that they have not received timely payment of their wages. The office can be contacted at 310-369-2595.

THIS DEAL MEMO IS EFFECTIVE ONLY UPON SIGNATURE OF THE APPLICABLE SVP PRODUCTION, OR ASSOCIATE DIRECTOR OF PRODUCTION.

ACKNOWLEDGED BY: APPROVED BY:

_____   _____
             EMPLOYEE   UNIT PRODUCTION MANAGER

                                                            _____
                                                            SVP PRODUCTION / ASSOC. DIRECTOR, PRODUCTION

TV\103823 v1 CW 06-25-13
Deal Memo

FOR NON-UNION EMPLOYEES ONLY

RIDER TO DEAL MEMO FOR

CALIFORNIA NON-UNION EMPLOYEES

Weekly Employees:

You are guaranteed to be scheduled for _____ hours per week, which means you will be compensated as follows:

$_____ per hour for 40 hours of regular time, plus

$_____ per hour for _____ hours of overtime per week (i.e., $_____ weekly guarantee).

If you work more than your scheduled _____ hours per week, you will be paid at the applicable overtime and/or double-time rates.

Daily Employees:

You are guaranteed to be scheduled for _____ per day, which means you will be compensated as follows:

$_____ per hour for 8 hours of regular time

$_____ per hour for _____ hours of overtime per day (i.e., $_____ daily guarantee).

If you work more than your scheduled _____ hours per day, you will be paid at the applicable overtime and/or double-time rates.

Acknowledged by:

_____   _____

Employee signature   Date

START PAPERWORK ACKNOWLEDGMENT FORM

Production Title:_____

I, (print name)_____ , hereby acknowledge that I have received the complete start work packet / timecard for the above stated TV production on this day of _____ (date).

By signing this letter, I understand and agree to abide by all rules and regulations set forth in the start work packet / timecard and agree that I will complete the start paperwork and timecard and return them to the production office in a timely manner.

_____
Signature

BOX RENTAL WEEKLY INVOICE

PRODUCTION COMPANY: _____

EMPLOYEE: _____ S.S.#: _____

LOAN OUT COMPANY: _____

FEDERAL ID#: _____

RENTAL RATE: $_____ PER WEEK/DAY

(Must be recorded on employee time card each week)

WEEK ENDING DATE: _____

INVENTORY: (Attach additional pages if necessary):

_____

_____

_____

_____

_____

_____

INVENTORY: (Check One)

☐ ON FILE   ☐ ATTACHED

Employee/Loanout agree that the equipment listed herein is rented to Production Company for use under Employee/Loanout's direction and control. Employee/Loanout are solely responsible for any damage to or loss of such equipment and hereby waive any claims against Entertainment Partners for any loss or damage of any kind. Entertainment Partners shall have no obligation to indemnify Employee/Loanout against any losses or damage, or to provide any insurance coverage for the benefit of Employee/Loanout covering the equipment herein described. Further, the Production Company and Employee certify that the equipment listed herein is being rented at competitive rates.

I attest that the above-described equipment represents a valid rental for this production.

_____   _____
EMPLOYEE SIGNATURE   DATE

_____   _____
APPROVAL SIGNATURE   DATE

Staff & Crew Information Sheet

NAME: _____

CELL PHONE: _____

HOME PHONE: _____

EMAIL: _____

DEPARTMENT & TITLE: _____

ARE YOU A DAY PLAYER?   YES   OR   NO

*** *This information is for our staff & crew list only* ***

Figure and Table Lists

FIGURES

3.14b   St. Anthony, a Woman and a Skull (1900) William Dickson.

3.15   TOP IMAGE: Edison's Black Maria Studio. Look closely to see the edge of the turntable on which it rotates. BOTTOM STRIPS: These three images were taken (c. 1894–1899) at the Studio by William Dickerson: A Tough Dance, Sandow the Strongman, Cake Walk. Turn-of-the-20th Century copyright law provided protection for photographs but not for early motion pictures. Edison, among a number of clever early film producers protected their work by copyrighting paper contact prints of the film's individual frames.

3.16   Cinématographe (1895) The Lumière Brothers patented a machine combining camera with printer and projector—a major improvement on Edison's kinetograph and kinetoscope.

3.17a   Motion-capture photos of a heron and a pelican in flight (c. 1894) Étienne-Jules Marey. The image also shows a profile shot of his chronophotograhic rifle and an insert (bottom left) of Marey holding his camera-rifle.

3.17b   Interior mechanism of Marey's chronophotographic box camera (upper left); and various motion capture images. Note: Marey often attached light-reflective strips to the clothes of his subjects to accentuate the movement.

3.18a   Some motion-capture images by Eadweard Muybridge included in a massive portfolio, with 781 plates comprising 20,000 of the photographs, in a groundbreaking collection titled "Animal Locomotion: an Electro-Photographic Investigation of Connective Phases of Animal Movements".

3.18b   Although Marcel Duchamps' Nude Descending a Staircase (1912) combines elements of Cubist and Futuristic movements, he recognized the influence of Muybridge's stop-motion photography. A good example showing art imitating art.

3.20   The whimsical, theatrical genius of Georges Méliès, an inspirational pioneer of the early 20th Century.

3.21   This still from The Tartans of Scotland (1902) remains as an early experiment with a three-color additive color process.

3.22   Screen-grab from Toll of the Sea (1922-MGM) starring Anna May Wong.

3.23   Screen-grab from Becky Sharp (1934-RKO), a break-through success for Technicolor Inc. and a new industry standard for Hollywood. Note: Despite what most people think, The Wizard of Oz was not the first movie shot in Technicolor.

3.24   The Adventures of Robin Hood. Licensed by Warner Bros. Entertainment Inc. All rights reserved.

3.25   Screen grab from The Wizard of Oz (1939-MGM).

3.26   Technicolor Camera

4.1a   Minority Report, Pre-cog Chamber (2002). From Minority Report © 2002 Twentieth Century Fox. All rights reserved.

4.1b   Screen grab of the War Room model from Dr. Strangelove 1964

4.1c   Screen grab at the gambling table from Barry Lyndon 1975

Merrick Morton for the motion picture The Terminal™ © 2004 DW Studios, LLC. All Rights Reserved

4.13 A) CG model of the exterior of the terminal set for The Terminal. B) Aerial view of JFK Airport showing CG addition (circled) for The Terminal. Photograph by Merrick Morton for the motion picture The Terminal™ © 2004 DW Studios, LLC. All Rights Reserved

4.14 A) White model of The Terminal set. B) Finished CG model of the exterior detail of The Terminal set. Photograph by Merrick Morton for the motion picture The Terminal™ © 2004 DW Studios, LLC. All Rights Reserved

4.15a An example of Back Projection calculations in pencil. Courtesy of Randy Wilkins

4.15b Back Projection done in Sketch-Up. Courtesy of Randy Wilkins

4.16 LayOut drawing of the reconstructed Reitlinger building. Courtesy of Randy Wilkins.

4.17 Hand-drafted N.Y. Loft plan and elevations by Barbara Mesney. GLEE. All rights reserved. Courtesy of Barbara Mesney.

4.18a–d Dark Sky Design/Construction Schedule created by Greg Papalia, Supervising Art Director, G-I-Joe: Rise Of Cobra (2009). Courtesy of Greg Papalia.

4.19 Prague as Paris: Greg Papalia mapped and photographed each shot for a car chase sequence for G.I. Joe: Rise of Cobra. Courtesy of Greg Papalia

4.20 A section of Greg Papalia's Prague shooting manual for G.I. Joe: Rise of Cobra—Pages 3 & 4. Courtesy of Greg Papalia

4.21 A) G-I Pit and B) G-I Training Area for G-I-Joe: The Rise of Cobra. Both concept illustrations were created by David J. Negron, Jr. Courtesy of by David J. Negron, Jr.

4.22a Production Designer, Ed Verreaux's concept drawing of the Cobra Complex. Courtesy of Ed Verreaux

4.22b A) Several preliminary ground plans developed like this example drawn by an Art Director from E. Verreaux's conceptual sketch. B) More well-resolved final floor plans like "The Pit" General Floor Plan Layout, was drawn by Jim Hewitt for G.I. Joe: Rise of Cobra. Courtesy of Chad Frey

4.23a A) Ext. Cobra Base Surface Entry—Preliminary Conceptual Rendering, version 3—Greg Papalia. B) Cobra Corridors: Surgical Operation Room—Set photograph. C) Cobra Docking Bay Entry—Set photograph.

4.23b Inter-connecting Cobra Corridors: A&B) Sketch-Up Concepts, and C) Set Photograph. Courtesy of Chad Frey

4.24a Docking Bay Entry Room: Ground Plan, drawn by Jeff Markwith. Courtesy of Jeff Markwith

4.24b Docking Bay Entry Room: Sections, drawn by Jeff Markwith. Courtesy of Jeff Markwith

4.24c Docking Bay Entry Room: Elevations, drawn by Jeff Markwith. Courtesy of Chad Frey

4.24d Cobra Docking Bay Entry final set photograph. Courtesy of Jeff Markwith

width but considerably more height than its 2.40:1 counterpart. For this reason, some cinematographers see it as a preferable lens choice in some situations. Hummel, R. (Ed.). (2002). American Cinematographer Manual, 8th Edition. Used by permission of the American Society of Cinematographers. B) Vertical Field of View for a 35mm lens showing the plan and corresponding section. Using both horizontal and vertical angle of view shown in the Field of View Table contained in the ASC Manual is always helpful in determining wall heights, ceiling coverage, and height of translates and green screens. Hummel, R. (Ed.). (2002). American Cinematographer Manual, 8th Edition. Used by permission of the American Society of Cinematographers

4.32 Lens test taken with 18mm, 25mm, 35mm and 50mm lenses at 120 feet, 130 feet, 190 feet and 284 feet, respectively. © Michael Rizzo

4.33 A blueprint drawing submitted for patent approval by Harold Michelson, Art Director. Courtesy of Harold Michelson.

4.34a–c Various samples of Camera Angle Projection used by H. Michelson used at many Art Director Guild functions. Harold was always acutely aware of camera angle/placement and composition as a prolific storyboard artist, illustrator and art director. Courtesy of Harold Michelson.

4.35 A drawing of his invention: a Perspective Plotter, submitted for patent approval by Harold Michelson, Art Director. Courtesy of Harold Michelson.

4.36a Camera Lenses: 20°, 35°, 50°, 85°, 105°, and 135° degrees for a 1:1.85 Aspect Ratio. Each lens indicates two camera angles: the height of the frame (dotted) and the width of the frame (solid). This sectioned chart is an earlier version of two that Harold Michelson used as he developed his Camera Angle Projection method.

4.36b Camera Lenses: 18.5°, 25°, 28°, 35°, 40°, 50°, 75° and 100° degrees for a 1:1.85 Aspect Ratio. Each lens indicates two camera angles: the height of the frame (dotted) and the width of the frame (solid). This later chart indicates the remaining available lenses for cinematography. You'll notice that the two most used lenses: the 35mm and 50mm appear on both sectioned charts. This chart more easily lends itself to being cut into pieces and printed onto clear acetate pages for easy C. A. P. method use. Courtesy of Harold Michelson.

4.37a Camera Angle Projection: Steps 1–7, courtesy of Lillian Michelson, wife of Harold Michelson; Camille Abbott, Production Illustrator; and Daniel Raim, Videographer. Courtesy of Harold Michelson.

4.37b Camera Angle Projection: Steps 8–16, courtesy of Lillian Michelson, wife of Harold Michelson; Camille Abbott, Production Illustrator; Daniel Raim, Videographer. Courtesy of Harold Michelson.

4.38 Harold Michelson realized early on that the reverse process of his Camera Angle Projection, or Back Projection, would be another useful method of breaking down photographs of location buildings, for instance, into workable ground plans. Courtesy of Harold Michelson.

TABLES

APPENDIX D

Glossary

2:3 pulldown
A technique used to convert film to tape, respectively, from 24 frames/second to 29.97 frames/second, also called a telecine pulldown. See **Telecine.**

Act of God
A natural phenomenon, not man-made—such as extreme weather, earthquake, tsunami, hurricane, tornado, sinkhole, swarm of locusts or bees, fire, or flood—that might shut down film production for a length of time.

Active Listening
A communication technique that requires the listener to feed back what they hear to the speaker, by restating or paraphrasing what they have heard in their own words, to confirm what they have heard and, moreover, to confirm the understanding of both parties.

Aspect ratio
The numerical relationship of the height and width of the image frame used in film and television. There are several standard aspect ratios used internationally: The Academy Aperture is 1.33:1; European standard wide screen is 1.66:1; American standard wide screen is 1.85:1; the 70mm frame is 2.2:1; and the anamorphic ratio is 2.35:1. The most common aspect ratio found through the 1950s was called *Academy Aperture*, at a ratio of 1.33:1—the same as 4:3 on a TV screen. Normal 35mm films are shot at a ratio of 1.85:1. New wide-screen formats and aspect ratios were introduced in the 1950s, from 1.65:1 and higher. Cinemascope™ was a wide-screen movie format used in the US from 1953 to 1967. Other anamorphic systems such as Panavision™ have a 2.35:1 AR, while 70mm formats have an AR of 2.2:1. Cinerama™ had a 2.77:1 aspect ratio. Letterboxed videos for widescreen TVs are frequently in 16:9 or 1.77:1 AR.

Back projection
A photographic technique whereby live action is filmed in front of a transparent screen onto which background action is projected. Back projection was often used to provide the special effect of motion in vehicles during dialogue scenes, but has become outmoded and replaced by bluescreen processing and traveling mattes. Back projection is also known as rear projection, process photography, or process shot as opposed to matte shot. Example: Any film with a moving vehicle and back-projected street scenes viewed through the back or side windows, such as in *To Catch a Thief* (1955).

Below-the-line
Both above- and below-the-line are accounting categories describing the divisions of salary level and perks existing in the film business. Above-the-line includes producers, directors, actors, cinematographers, and some production designers. Below-the-line includes everyone else.

Billing
Name and title placed within the credits listed on a movie or any other media 'delivery' screen, movie poster, or any other advertising of a motion picture.

Biograph
Herman Casler perfected a camera with a mirror device for the Mutoscope in 1894, creating a rudimentary motion picture camera.

Blocked (also **blocking**)
Refers to how a director positions actors on a set in order to properly deliver lines as they play a scene.

Blocking and marking
Given to an actor by a director, blocking describes where to physically be on a set during a scene while performing. Marking is done with a different color of tape for each actor; a piece of tape is torn from a roll and place on a stage floor to indicate where an actor is to land in order to deliver the lines for a particular scene.

Bluescreen
A process in which actors perform in front of an evenly lit, monochromatic, usually blue or green, background. During post-production background is then replaced by **chromakeying,** or allowing other footage or computer-generated images to form the background imagery, around the actor in the foreground footage. Since 1992, most films use a greenscreen. See also, **greenscreen.**

Bobbinette
A loosely woven theatrical fabric, much like a fine fishnet, used for its invisible quality for onstage scenery. See also, **sharktooth scrim.**

Borders and legs
Originally a theatrical term for lengths of black velour material, generally called "blacks," tailored to hang in specific arrangements "to frame" the look of onstage scenery. "Masking stage curtains" is a good way to describe blacks. A border is a horizontal black typically 4–10' high, and in widths varying from 30' to 50'. A leg is a vertical black typically 8–12' wide, and in lengths varying from 12' to 30'. A border and a pair of legs are used in groups. They are attached to suspended pipes or battens by grommeted ties, or small pieces of rope. On film stages, blacks have the same function in terms of scenery—to frame what the camera sees or doesn't see.

Bottle show
The episode of a television series that is extremely confined, either shooting predominantly in permanent sets, or using lots of clips or flashbacks from previous episodes. The intent here is to produce the episode in question at a greatly reduced cost; the cost of leaving the studio and shooting at a location is typically $100,000. Committing to a bottle show will offset the cost of expensively produced episodes.

Breakaway
Refers primarily to glass objects either as plate glass in windows or handheld glasses, cups, plates, etc., used for stunt/mechanical effects gags in a scene. It also refers to

destroyable scenery, e.g., explosions. Or costumes that can be "torn away" to reveal another.

CAD/CADD

A quick difference between CADD (computer-assisted drawing and drafting) and CAD (computer-assisted drawing), must be made here. CADD specifically refers to drafting either architecture or scenery, whereas CAD is a generic term encompassing all computer-assisted drawing software.

CAD/CAM

Acronym for computer-aided design/computer-aided manufacturing. Computer systems used to design and manufacture products. The term CAD/CAM implies that an artist/ engineer can use the system both for designing a product and for controlling manufacturing processes. For example, once a design has been produced with the CAD component, the design itself can control the machines that construct the part.

Call sheet

A page composed by the assistant directorial staff while organizing the daily shooting schedule. It contains all information pertinent to a day of shooting. See also **call time.**

Call time

The specific time each individual is expected to begin work on a film set. This information is indicated on a call sheet, a page composed by the assistant directorial staff while organizing the daily shooting schedule. Traditionally, call times are day scheduled; nighttime shooting schedules require reporting times at night. See also, **wrap time.**

CAM

see **CAD/CAM.**

Camera Angle Projection

A system of perspective drawing for cinematography whereby the dimensions on a plan and elevation can be processed according to the camera angles of a given lens and aspect ratio, i.e., degree of convergence. Using these elements of this system, one can draw an accurate elevation sketch of any set. Harold Michelson—storyboard artist, concept illustrator, and art director—invented this perspective drawing system. (see end of Chapter 4.)

Camera obscura

Literally, "dark room" (Latin). A basic principal of optics. In a darkened room, create a pinhole in a window cover—an inverted image of the scene outside the darkened room will "magically" appear on the opposite wall. This also happens within the human eyeball. Mo-Ti, a fifth-century Chinese philosopher, first recorded this phenomenon—he called this darkened room a "collecting place" or the "locked treasure room" (http://brightbytes.com/cosite/what.html).

CGI

Computer-generated imagery.

Chroma
An attribute of a color derived from splitting a beam of light with a prism producing red, orange, yellow, green, blue, indigo, violet. The light primaries are red, blue, and green; the pigment primaries are red, blue, and yellow.

Chromakey (also **chromakeying**)
An electronic/computerized technique that allows for specific color elements (**chroma**) to be replaced with different picture elements. In simple terms, this is done by separating out the three, primary light colors (chroma) of red, blue, and green onto separate channels and using them to manipulate different aspects of the captured image during the development process.

Chronophotography
Étienne-Jules Marey designed a photographic rifle (1878) to be used for capturing a series of images taken at set time intervals. His chronophotography rifle contained a rotating wheel with slits. When light passed through one of the slits, that portion of the photographic plate was exposed; it was capable of taking 12 consecutive frames a second on its circular, rotating photographic glass plate and disk shutter.

Cinema
A term originally ascribed to a theater that presents films as entertainment. It was coined by the Lumière brothers in 1896 as they established film houses in Western Europe.

Cinématographe
Patented by the Lumière brothers in 1895, it is a machine combining camera with printer and projector. The device was a major improvement on Thomas Alva Edison's **kinetoscope** as it was lighter, smaller, hand-cranked, and used smaller celluloid and an intermittent movement.

Colortrans
A large-scale color photograph printed on a flexible, translucent material. It is the name of a category of photographic backdrop lit from both back and front surfaces, as opposed to painted backdrop, lit just on its front side. See also **translite.**

Composite
The process and product of combining of two images onto a single piece of 35mm film. One component of the composite image is typically foreground action and the other component is background imagery shot elsewhere. The process involves the use of matting or replacing imagery.

Convergence
One-point perspective tells us that all outlines of object surfaces in the picture plane meet at the same vanishing point on the horizon; this implied perception is called convergence.

C-stand
A piece of grip equipment combining the use of an adjustable C-clamp on the neck of a sturdy, metal, three-legged stand.

Cyclorama
A continuous length of fabric at least 20 feet high or a built scenery wall the same height (with variable width), used as a fixed backdrop to suggest sky or similar volumes of space on a stage.

Dailies
A previous day's work shot by principal and second unit shooting crews shown at the end of the next day's shooting. Dailies or rushes are always viewed after the fact.

Descenders
A British term used by paratroopers in free-fall simulator training. Adopted by the American film industry, free-fall simulators revolutionized high-fall stunts.

Digital asset manager or archivist, or DAM
A designated art department position; one who organizes, labels, stores and retrieves digital information and images.

Double-up day schedule
Two separate crews shooting their respective episodes simultaneously on the same day.

Drop
Shorthand for backdrop.

Dupe
Shortened version of duplicate, it refers to the copy of a photographic image.

Duvetyne
A felt-like, black fabric in extra-wide widths used as backing pieces for theater, TV, and film sets.

Economies of scale
A basic financial concept stating: the average unit cost of a good or service can be reduced by increasing its output rate.

Electrostachyscope
From the Greek: "quick view." An early form of animated-picture machine, devised in 1889 by Berliner, Otto Anschutz, in which the chronophotographs were mounted around the periphery of a rotating wheel.

EMI
Electric and Musical Industries Ltd. was formed in March 1931 by the merger of the Columbia Graphophone Company and the Gramophone Company. It was a British multinational music recording and publishing company headquartered in London, United Kingdom.

Exposition
The initial plot layout of a film revealed within the first ten minutes as a psychological or emotional "hook" to dramatically enroll the attention of the audience.

Feeding tent
A large, rented tent set up on location with tables and chairs as a place for the crew to eat.

Flat (also **flattage**)
A scenery wall.

Frames per second (also **fps**)
Present-day films are usually run through a camera or projector at a frame rate, that is, running speed or camera speed of 24 fps. Older films, made at 18 fps, appear jerky and sped-up when played back at 24 fps—this technique is referred to as under-cranking. Over-cranking refers to changing the frame rate, i.e., shooting at 48 or 96 fps, thereby producing slow-motion action when viewed at 24 fps. Example: The William Tell Overture sequence in *A Clockwork Orange* (1971) is an example of under-cranking. Action films often use over-cranking for film explosions so that the action is prolonged.

French New Wave
An informally organized movement of spirited, youthful iconoclasm: using social and political issues of the era and making radical experiments with editing, visual style, and narrative as a formal break with the conservative filmmaking of the 1950s and 1960s.

Fringing
An adverse artifact of **kinemacolor** camera/projectors first used in the 1900s. The process suffered from non-registration or haloing of film images—an insoluble problem as long as kinemacolor remained a successive frame process.

FSD
Shortened version of full size detail. A drawing in actual size indicating up-close detail for exact building purposes.

Fuller's earth
An older name for "**movie dirt.**"

Gaffer
A film electrician. English electricians are called "sparks."

Gimbal (also **gimbaled**)
Traditionally, this cinematic term refers to the mechanism responsible for the spinning of a room or similar interior scenery piece. In contrast, the common use of the term refers to the mechanism that keeps an object, like a compass, horizontal regardless of outside movement—it is related to the working principles of a gyroscope.

Grand Rights
This is a legal and business term that refers to the permissions necessary to stage an opera, play with music, or a work of musical theater. Grand rights must be negotiated between the producer of a production and the publishers and owners of the copyright of the work. Typically a royalty will be paid to the publishers and owners of a work in

exchange for the permission and right to stage the work in its entirety—failure to do so violates the agreement.

Green light
The formal OK given by a film studio to the producer or UPM of film production office to begin pre-production activity.

Greenscreen
A newer technique similar to **bluescreen,** using a chromakey green background in place of an evenly lit blue background. Research has shown that substantially better results could be gained by filming on green instead of blue, as the sensitivity of modern film stock was more sensitive to separating key green light from other foreground colors. See also **chromakeying.**

Grieve
Any member in good standing of an IATSE guild is required by union by-law to report any breach of contract observed in the workplace. Once grieved, a producer or film/television production will be visited by a Union representative to arbitrate the situation. Guilty parties are usually fined according to previous union stipulation.

Gripology
A term most people in the industry use to explain how a physical solution is developed and executed by the onset grip department to solve how a shot for a scene will work per the decisions of a director and cinematographer.

Hero
A term referring to any set, set piece, item of set dressing, prop, or vehicle relating to a main character—male or female. It is used as an adjective and can refer to a hero or villain, i.e., the hero getaway car, or the hero honeymoon suite.

High concept
As in "high concept film." The idea of a sound bite used in pitching or advertising the concept of a film, simply stated and easily understood by everyone, i.e., a pathetic nerd is secretly an invincible superhero.

Highly directional
Refers to the reflective quality of a front projection screen. 3M-screen material reflects most stage light back to the camera with little ambient light loss; the surface-silvered mirror has a 50/50 reflective/see-through capacity and a perfect ability to both reflect and transmit light.

Hot set
A set or location being actively shot on or used by the shooting crew of a film.

Hue
An attribute of a color derived from splitting a beam of light with a prism producing red, orange, yellow, green, blue, indigo, violet. The light primaries are red, blue, and green; the pigment primaries are red, blue, and yellow.

Icon, iconic
Greek: *eikono-, eikon,* image. A simile or symbol, an icon is an image that is what it *is.* Human emotions captured on the screen are icons that can be read in any language—they are universal. When we watch Roberto Benigni (*Life Is Beautiful*) win the 1999 Academy Award for best actor, we understood joy. In the "language of film," which includes semiology, or the study of systems of signs, there is a signifier and the signified. An icon is a sign in which the signifier (image) represents the signified (meaning) through its likeness or close similarity to it.

IATSE
The International Alliance of Theatrical Stage Employees was founded in 1893 when representatives of stagehands working in 11 cities met in New York and pledged to support each other's efforts to establish fair wages and working conditions for their members. Our union has evolved over the succeeding 119 years to embrace the development of new entertainment mediums, craft expansion, technological innovation and geographic growth.

In-camera
This term refers to any processing or optical work done primarily with mattes within the body of the camera, in order to composite companion pieces of film shot for the same scene.

Index
One of three "signs" or metaphorical imagery used in film language. As an image, a sign presumes a sign(ifier) and that which is sign(ified) within the visual syntax of a film. A sign or visual image can be: 1) an **icon** or an image that *is* what it is: a screaming face is horror; 2) an index, an image that suggests an inherent relationship: a wad of bills given to a prostitute; or 3) a **symbol**, an image representing a meaning through convention: a flag symbolizes patriotism. Semantics, you say? Yes, film being a visual language is full of denotative and connotative images.

Indie (also, **independents or independent films**)
Small, low-budget companies, mini-majors, or entities for financing, producing, and distributing films, i.e., Miramax, New Line Cinema, Polygram, working outside of the system or a major Hollywood studio. California-based Miramax, although the leader in the independent film movement in the early 1990s, has become so powerful and successful that it has lost most of its independent studio status. Indie refers to a movie, director, distributor, or producer not associated with a major Hollywood film studio, often with groundbreaking subject matter designed for sophisticated audiences, and not necessarily produced with commercial success as the goal (like mainstream films). Examples of indie films include Jim Jarmusch's *Stranger Than Paradise* (1984) and Kevin Smith's *Clerks* (1994). The cable TV Independent Film Channel showcases Indie films.

Insert shot
Usually a close-up shot of a prop or an actor shot at a later time, out of sequence to the scene it was originally part of. This requires organizing set dressing and wall sections of the related scenery to be set up for shooting on the revised shooting day.

In-studio
The shooting of a motion picture in a proper film studio as opposed to on location.

Intermittent movement
The heart, or essential component, of any motion picture camera comprised of an assembly located just behind the camera lens and aperture, or light opening within the lens mount. The intermittent movement has a double function: it physically pulls the film down by the sprocket holes on either side of the filmstrip, and it alternately exposes the film by "intermittently" blocking the light with a rotating shutter frame by frame.

Interpolation
The process of in-betweening (see **tweening**), or filling in frames between the key frames, in animation. Originally done by hand in the Disney Studios, for example, this process has become computerized and is achieved algorithmically.

Key frame
A single shot image of a digital sketch or model, used in pre-visualization as a visual template.

Kinemacolor
The first successful motion picture color process. It was a two-color additive color process, photographing and projecting a black-and-white film behind alternating red and green filters.

Kinetograph
From the Greek: "writer of motion." An American version of the Lumière brothers' invention, the **cinématographe**, developed by Thomas Alva Edison and William Dickson. Kinetograph was an innovative motion picture camera with rapid intermittent, or stop-and-go film movement (at 46 images per second) to record the movement of images for in-house experiments and, eventually, commercial **kinetoscope** presentations.

Kinetoscope
From the Greek: "to view movement." Developed by Thomas Alva Edison as a peephole device for penny arcades which invited viewers to look into a hole in the top of a large wooden cabinet and experience the illusion of pictures moving. Edison made a fortune with this entertainment device.

LCD
Liquid-crystal display: A monitor screen that use liquid-crystal technology to produce images.

Limbo
A non-descript volume of space used to evoke timelessness or no particular place.

Locked-off
A stationary camera supported by a tripod or camera pedestal base.

Magazine
A spool of film.

Martini shot
The last shot of the last scene of the day—just before wrap time.

Matte shot
The optical process of combining (or compositing) separately photographed shots—usually actors in the foreground and the setting in the background—onto one print through a double exposure that does not meld two images on top of each other, but masks off, or makes opaque, part of the frame area for one exposure and the opposite area for another exposure. It is a photographic technique whereby a painting or artwork from a matte artist—usually painted on glass—is combined with live action footage to provide a convincing setting for the action; also sometimes known as split-screen.

Meme
An idea, behavior, or style that spreads from person to person within a culture. A yawn is an involuntary meme that unconsciously transfers through social contact. Cultural memes are more subtle and more pervasive.

Metaphor
A filmic device in which a scene, character, object, or action may be associated, identified, or interpreted as an implied representation of something else. See also, **symbol** and **trope**.

Miniature (also **miniature shot or model**)
Small-scale models photographed to give the illusion that they are full-scale objects. Example: The spacecraft in *2001: A Space Odyssey* (1968).

Mise en scène
A French phrase literally meaning "putting in the scene" in physical or spatial terms within the frame. In film theory, it refers to staging action that covers or records an entire scene within the frame of the film, and the arrangement, composition, and content of the visual elements before the camera, usually in a long-shot, including settings, decor, props, actors, costumes, lighting, performances, and character movements and positioning. It includes both technical and non-technical elements that make up a scene's look and feel—in general terms, the "on set" responsibility of the Art Director. Its opposite, montage or "putting together," refers to the time element of filmmaking. These twin elements of cinematic space and time fuel the engine of the process. *Mise en scène* is what an art director does.

Mocap
Motion capture describes the process of tracking the movement of an actor with tiny sensors fitted in regular patterns over the surface of a form-fitting suit and head cap. This information is fed to the hard drive of a computer and digitally manipulated for storytelling.

Movie dirt
Name for a taupe colored, powdery substance used primarily to age set dressing or reduce glare on reflective surfaces that the camera sees when shooting.

MOW
Shortened version of "Movie of the Week."

Mutoscope
An early animation device that contained a sequence of photographs arranged around the perimeter of a drum. A simple turn of a handle flipped the image cards on the drum rapidly, creating perceived movement.

Neo-Realism
The era following WW2 leveled Italian film studios; the Italian film industry resurrected itself by focusing on stories of the poor and disenfranchised in this new wave of Italian cinema.

NTSC
National Television System Committee: the older analog television system established in 1941 and used internationally; now we are switching to newer digital television standards, ATSC being one of them.

One-liner (also **one-line schedule**)
A shortened version of the shooting schedule composed by the Unit Production Manager UPM and First Assistant Director (1st AD). See also, **shooting schedule.**

One-sheet
Printed on an 8½" × 14" sheet, it is an even shorter version of a typical one-liner, fitting every scene to be shot in the upcoming schedule on a single, neat page. It is usually produced by a Second Assistant Director (2nd AD).

Onionskin
A term used to describe pieces of yellow tracing paper torn from rolls of various lengths, used to quickly sketch ideas in the designing/drafting process. It is commonly known as tracing paper.

Optical printing
In photographic terms, there are two ways of printing an image: contact printing by placing a negative transparency against a piece of photographic paper, and optical printing or taking a picture of a picture. This is done by placing a transparency in front of a light

box, composing and focusing the positive image on the viewfinder, balancing light intensity with regard to lens aperture and shutter speed, and making a negative from the exposed film. Contact printing two strips of film, emulsion to emulsion, in an optical or process camera accomplishes optical printing in moviemaking. Optical printing is another aspect of adding to or subtracting from original film stock footage, concerning itself primarily with master positives and dupe negatives.

Pattern
A predetermined amount of money a Studio is willing to spend per episode on a television show. For example, a typical police drama might have its construction pattern set at $78,000 whereas a musical dramedy like *Glee* would have its construction pattern set at $111,000 per episode and the set dressing budget patterned at $38,500 (2014 figures). The Studio expects episodic expenses to fall within that pre-established range.

Performance capture
The groundbreaking filmmaking process of the film *Avatar* redefined the word "mocap" by refining the motion capture process.

Persistence of vision
The phenomenon that takes place within the eye by which an afterimage is thought to persist for approximately 1/25 of a second on the retina.

Petabyte
A multiple of the unit byte for digital information. One petabyte is one quadrillion (short scale) bytes, or one billiard (long scale) bytes. The unit symbol for the petabyte is PB. So 1PB = 1,000,000,000,000,000 bytes = 10^{15} bytes = 1000 terabytes.

Phenakistoscope
From the Greek: "a sighting device that deceives or cheats." Invented by Joseph Plateau in 1827.

Photoplay
During the time of WWI, legitimate stage actors on the east coast were lured to Los Angeles to do a "photoplay" or stage play altered for the movie camera.

Picture plane
The imaginary plane of sight through which an audience views a scene. In the theater, the proscenium arch is a physical picture plane or frame through which the audience views the drama of the play it is watching; in film, whatever scenery the camera is shooting can act as a similar, viewing frame of the drama. It is composed either intentionally or subliminally, but is there nonetheless.

Picture vehicle
This term is synonymous with Hero vehicle and refers to the car, motorcycle, bus, truck, etc. of the main character in a movie.

Post-production
The time in film production when the editing of all previously shot footage, sound editing, foley, and optical/visual effects compositing takes place.

Praxinoscope
From the Greek: "an action viewer". An early animation device invented by Charles Reynaud in 1877.

Pre-production
The planning stage in a film's production *before* principal photography commences, involving script treatment and editing, scheduling, pre-visualization, set design and construction, casting, budgeting and financial planning, and scouting/selection of locations; in contrast to post-production. See also, **production** and **post-production.**

Process camera
Optical printing is accomplished in a process or optical camera. See also, **optical printing.**

Production
"The production" refers to the film project itself. "Production" refers to the production office staff and its activity.

Production design
Refers to a film's overall design, continuity, visual look, and composition, i.e., color palette, graphics, pre-visualization, set design and construction, costumes, set dressing, graphics, props, locations, etc., that are the responsibility of the production designer. The art department refers to the people in various roles, e.g., digital concept artists, set designers and draft persons, set decorator and staff, concept illustrators, graphic designers, and storyboard artists, who work under the production designer's supervision. The Art Director is responsible for the film's physical settings, budget, and the combined efforts of all art department crew.

Raked
A surface like a set floor angled up and away from the camera.

Ratings point
A single national ratings point measures the viewership of a particular television program. It is used extensively in the Nielsen media rating system.

Reach envelope
The easy, physical distance from an actor's body to a prop, item of set dressing or scenery to enable comfortable, executable blocking for a scene.

Rekkie (also **recce**)
A New Zealand term for scout or drive.

Reshoot
Additional photography on specific scenes previously shot. This typically happens after the end of principal photography.

Retrofit
Making specific physical changes to a location site to insure that the design concept is seamless and believable.

Right-to-work
As in "a right to work state." In the US, some states comply with **IATSE** in terms of maintaining union-organized shows and some do not. Right-to-work states are the latter, and have more relaxed policies regarding who is hired and how filmmaking can operate. Right-to-work states are the opposite of signatoried states. (See also, **signatory**)

Rotoscoping
A technique of tracing each frame of live action and then hand-painting in the silhouette, invented by Max Fleischer, the pioneer cartoonist who created Betty Boop and Popeye. The time-sensitive technique was regularly used in filmmaking in the Twentieth century until digital editing software was developed based on its principles, to do the work more efficiently.

Runaway production
In the 1990s, the Art Directors Guild was unable to negotiate national jurisdiction over their work. American producers took advantage of this and moved filmmaking to Canada, Eastern Europe, and Australia/New Zealand, and hired local crews. This seriously impacted the credibility and strength of the Local; to this day, this term "runaway production" carries a negative connotation.

Scout
The activity of looking for an appropriate location for a film shoot. Scouts or **rekkies** are organized and conducted by the locations department.

Scouting
Looking for shootable locations.

Screen-grab
Using a computer's copy/paste function to capture an image from a tv show or film. Once downloaded, the image is typically used for reference or concept boards.

Screenplay
The written form of a movie that also includes instructions on how it is to be acted and filmed; in simple terms, a screenplay is the script for a movie.

Second unit
A smaller shooting crew assigned to shoot matching pieces of a scene, to later be edited into the larger scene(s) of a film.

Second Unit Director
The first unit is the main shooting crew of a movie. Second unit crews are appointed by the Director to shoot additional footage. Traditionally, the Stunt Coordinator heads the

second unit on action films. Shooting simultaneously on the regular shooting schedule saves time and money.

Sequel
A cinematic work that presents the continuation of characters, settings, or events of a story in a preceding movie. A sequel is also known as a follow-up, serial, series, or spin-off. Example: *The Maltese Falcon* (1941) followed by *The Black Bird* (1975); *National Velvet* (1944) followed by *International Velvet* (1978). Sequels generally tend to be inferior products—with some exceptions—such as *The Godfather, Part II* (1974), *Toy Story 2* (1999), *The Empire Strikes Back* (1980).

SFX
See **special effects.**

Share
Share is the percentage of television sets in use tuned to a program. It is used extensively in the Nielsen media rating system.

Sharktooth scrim
A tightly woven theatrical fabric, much like a fine burlap, used for its transparency qualities for onstage scenery work. See also, **bobbinette.**

Shooting schedule
This is the master list for the shooting process, painstakingly compiled by the Unit Production Manager and 1st AD, but ultimately the responsibility of the latter. It distills the script breakdown into workable, daily units of the total number of scenes to be shot, item-by-item needs of the shooting crew requested per department for that particular day, and general notes or reminders for everyone connected to the shooting crew.

Signatory
A film company, film studio, or any other filmmaking entity that has signed a basic agreement with the Union to provide adequate working conditions, benefits, and appropriate salaries to members of **IATSE.** Companies making films in "right to work" states in America are most likely not signatory companies. See also **right-to-work.**

Skin
A fiberglass or vacuum formed sheet of fake architectural texture like brick, stone, rock, shingle, slate, Spanish roofing tile, wall tile, lincresta, logs, sandbags, soundproof panels, fluted columns, and cornice molding.

Special effects (also, **F/X, SFX, SPFX,** or **EFX**)
A broad term used by the film industry but specifically referring to mechanical or physical effects such as wind, rain, fog, fire, pyrotechnics as squibs and miniature explosions, i.e., a gunshot, animatronics, or use of electronic puppets in both interior and exterior sets.

Split day schedule
The same shooting crew finishing up one television episode, then continuing onto the subsequent episode with a different director, defines a split day schedule.

Spotting plan
A ground plan for a set indicating placement on a soundstage or warehouse space in relationship with loading doors and distance from existing walls and other sets sharing the space.

Staff shop
That department of a film studio complex housing an inventory of carved plaster molds used as relief or 3D templates for fiberglass copies. From these molds vacuum formed copies are also made, although "staff molding" traditionally refers to horizontal bands of ornately carved, classically derived molding in varying widths and motifs.

Stand-in
There are actors who are hired because they fit the body type, sex, and skin/hair color of a principal actor, whose main purpose is to stand, sit, or lie in place of their principal for lighting and blocking purposes.

Standards and Practices
The name traditionally given to the department at a television network that is responsible for the moral, ethical, and legal implications of the program that network airs.

Step printer
An apparatus that develops film, whether it is 35mm film from a reflex camera or a 35mm movie camera. Photographic printing page or fine grain film stock is exposed to light and holds the reverse image of negative placed between it and the light source.

Stop-motion animation
A visual-effects animation technique where objects, such as solid 3D puppets, figures, or models are shot one frame at a time and moved or repositioned slightly between each frame, giving the illusion of lifelike motion. Stop-motion was one of the earliest visual-effects techniques for science fiction films, now replaced by CGI and animatronics; also known as stop-frame motion. Example: The stop-motion animation in the first great monster movie, *King Kong* (1933).

Storyboard
A sequential series of illustrations, stills, rough sketches, or captions, sometimes resembling a comic or cartoon strip of events, as seen through the camera lens, that outline the various shots or provide a visual synopsis for a proposed film story or for a complex scene. The storyboards are displayed in sequence for the purpose of mapping out and crafting the various shot divisions and camera movements in an animated or live-action film. A blank storyboard is a piece of paper with rectangles drawn on it to

represent the camera frame for each successive shot; a sophisticated type of preview-storyboard, often shot and edited on video, with a soundtrack.

Strips
A quick term for the production boards formerly used in determining the shooting schedule for a movie. Literally, they were narrow, stiff pieces of colored cardboard slipped into predesigned frames, indicating various aspects of scenes to be shot. This is an old-tech way of creating shooting schedules and one-line schedules.

Swing set or swing stage
An intermittently recurring set is spotted, or placed, on a swing stage, which acts as a placeholder for these non-permanent sets. This is an episodic television concept and term.

Symbol
An object in a film that stands for an idea, representing a second level of meaning, e.g., an open window or flying bird for freedom, a dew-laden rose for beauty, etc. The more a symbol is repeated, the greater its significance in a film. See also, **icon, metaphor,** and **trope.**

Tabloid format
A typical paper size (11″ × 7″), used for director's plan and spotting plan distribution.

Telecine
Telecine enables the images of a motion picture, captured originally on film stock, to be viewed with standard video equipment.

Telephonoscope
A fantasy device conjured from the imagination of Albert Robida, visionary artist and novelist in the 1880s. It gives us television, video, video-conferencing, and email all rolled into one, including the cable news channels. A remarkable vision.

Thaumatrope
From the Greek: "wonder-turn." A card with different pictures on opposite sides, appearing as if combined when the card is twirled rapidly, illustrating the **persistence of vision.**

Title block
Traditionally placed at the lower right corner of a page of drafting, indicating the name of the drawing, draftsperson, director, production designer, art director, scale and date.

Translite
A large-scale photograph printed on a flexible, translucent material. It is the general term of a category of photographic backdrop lit from both back and front surfaces, as opposed to painted backdrop, lit just on its front side. Translites are black/white or color. See also **colortrans.**

Transpo
The transportation department comprised of members of the Teamster's Union; the wheels of filmmaking.

Trope
In literary terms, "a rose is a rose is a rose" is what it is: a rose. In film semiology, "a rose is love is death" is a trope—a more complex image. So, a trope is a universally identified image imbued with several layers of contextual meaning creating a new visual metaphor. See also, **metaphor** or **symbol**.

Tween or **tweening**
Tweening or in-betweens are the drawings between the key frames that help to create the illusion of motion in the animation process.

UPM
Shorthand version of unit production manager. A production office crewmember supervising the finances of a film project.

VFX
Shorthand version of visual effects as opposed to SFX, special effects.

Visual concept
Shorthand for a longer explanation; it abbreviates words into symbols or indexes; it is an image that defines the central idea of a movie.

Visual effects (also **VFX**)
Visual and audio fantasy illusions that cannot be accomplished normally, i.e., travel into outer or inner space. Many photographic or optical and filmic techniques are used to produce digital effects, bluescreen or greenscreen chromakeying, motion capture, in-camera effects, and the use of miniatures/models, mattes, or stop-motion animation. Considered a subcategory of special effects; it refers to anything added to the final picture that was not in the original shot. The Visual Effects Supervisor coordinates visual effects.

Vodcast
Shortened version of a "video podcast" downloaded through Web syndication or streamed online.

Walk-through
Touring a set in-progress or a new set to be shot with the Director, Cinematographer, and any required department heads for comments or last looks. Ideally, this is done several days before shooting to have time for revisions.

Wedge
A term coined during the shooting of the original *TRON*. This groundbreaking film was the first film to use CGI for its vehicles and in its action sequences, and involved the completion of more than 1,000 visual effects shots that required compositing on the average of 12 to 15 layers, or wedges, per frame. Each wedge presented a different light intensity: the background being the least intense and the helmeted faces sitting on the top layer, the most intense.

Wild or **wild wall**
A partial or full wall in an interior set designed to be removed to allow shooting crew and camera access for easier shooting ability.

Wrap
The formal end of shooting a film.

Wrap time
The actual time the company stops shooting on any given day on the shooting schedule, or at the end of principal photography. With call time, and breaks during the day, wrap time is noted by the assistant directing staff and script supervisor, recorded, and reported to the studio. See also, **call time**.

Zoetrope
The earliest documented zoetrope was created by ancient Chinese inventor Ting Huan around 180 AD. Later, called the "daedalum" or "the wheel of the Devil." Zoetrope literally translates from the Greek for "live turning" or "animation." This device like the **phenakistoscope** produces the illusion of movement.

Zoopraxiscope
Invented by Eadweard Muybridge, this is a device for projecting motion pictures that pre-dated the flexible perforated film strip used in cinematography.

Index